FRONTIERS OF ANTHROPOLOGY

With Best Wishes.
from Ashley Montagu

FRONTIERS OF ANTHROPOLOGY

EDITED, WITH AN INTRODUCTION AND NOTES,
by Ashley Montagu

CAPRICORN BOOKS
G. P. Putnam's Sons, New York

DEDICATED TO THE MEMORY

OF

CHARLES SPEARMAN

Grote Professor of Psychology at
University College, University of London

Contents

Foreword   xi

Introduction and Acknowledgments   xv

1. Columbus "Discovers" America and Is Enthusiastic About the American Indian   1

2. The Ancient Greeks Do Not Recognize "Race," and, Indeed, Deny It   7

3. Herodotus: The "Father" of Anthropology   19

4. Benjamin Franklin on the American Indian, 1784   46

5. Samuel Stanhope Smith, the First American Anthropologist on the Causes of the Variety of the Human Species   52

6. Charles Darwin on the Origin of Species   91

7. Darwin Carefully Explains What He Means by the Phrase "The Struggle For Existence"   93

8. Paul Du Chaillu and the Rediscovery of the ("Ferocious") Gorilla   98

9. Charles Darwin on the Descent of Man   119

10. Charles Darwin on the Expression of the Emotions   145

11. The Great Debate Between Science and Religion as to Man's Place in Nature   157

12. Thomas Henry Huxley's *Evidence as to Man's Place in Nature*, 1863   160

13. James Hunt and the Negro's Place in Nature   202

14. Bishop Codrington on *Mana*   255

15. Ignorance of Physiological Paternity   260

16. Lewis Henry Morgan and Charles Martin on the American Indian   272

17. Anthropology into Literature, Sir James Frazer   278

18. Arnold van Gennep on the Rites of Passage   315

19. Franz Boas Demonstrates the Plasticity of Human Traits   320

20. Alfred Kroeber on the Superorganic   344

21. What Informed Speculation Can Do. Carveth Read   381

22. W. H. R. Rivers on "The Giving-Up" Syndrome   390

23. Karl Pearson on the Alien Jewish Population of London   409

24. Karl Pearson Soliloquizes as Scientist and Socialist on the Fate of "Superannuated Races"   411

25. The Idea that War Is Natural Anatomized and Decently Interred   421

26. William Ernest Castle on Race and Half-Castes   425

27. The Racists, Eugenists, and Hereditarians Anatomized   436

28. The Solution of the Problem of the Infertility of the Unmarried in Nonliterate Societies   463

29. Malinowski on Method and Functionalism   467

30. Ruth Benedict on the Individual and Culture   486

31. Cashiering the Idea of Race   504

32. The Concept of "Race" Is Challenged   511

33. A Physiologist Explains the Mechanism of "Voodoo" Death   519

34. Why the Mental Capacities of the Various Ethnic Groups of Mankind Are Probably Pretty Much of a Muchness   532

35. Leslie White on the Concept of Culture   539

36. The New Physical Anthropology   566

For Further Reading   597

FOREWORD

WHAT is anthropology? The best and briefest description of that discipline is the one that is customarily given: Anthropology is the science of man, the science devoted to the comparative study of man as an organism and a cultural being. Spelled out, what this means is that anthropology is interested in the study of the origin and evolution of man in all his forms and varieties, prehistoric and present, both physically and in all his particular ways of life. Physical anthropology is the name of the special branch of anthropology which is concerned with man's physical evolution. This involves studies of bones, teeth, blood, genes, anatomy, physiology, growth, development, dating methods, and so on.

Insofar as the study of the evolution of man's ways of life is concerned, the study of prehistoric man clearly must be devoted to the examination and analysis of his cultural remains. This is the branch of anthropology known as prehistoric archeology. Archeology, which has been defined as the science of rubbish, is the science of historical reconstruction and description of cultures which no longer exist, at least precisely in the same form, based on the study of, and inferences from, cultural products and subsistence remains recovered by excavation and similar means. Culture is the way of life of a people, the learned part, the man-made part, of the environment, or that class of things and events, dependent on the symbolic process, considered in an extrabodily context. Cultural anthropology is that branch of anthropology which is concerned with the comparative study of the ways of life of different peoples.

Not many years ago physical and cultural anthropology were pursued by their practitioners as if they were quite independent disciplines. Indeed, physical and cultural anthropologists usually performed their duties in totally different departments of the university, the physical anthropologists usually in the department of anatomy, the cultural anthropologists in the department of anthropology or sociology and anthropology, as if each had no relation to the other. This was a great mistake, for we now know that undoubtedly the most important factors in the physical evolution of man were cultural. For example, there can be little question that the adoption of a hunting way of life by man's early ancestors led to the most significant major changes, resulting in the assumption of the upright posture, the freeing of the hands for toolmaking, the expansion of the brain, not to mention the development of such functional traits as problem-solving ability (intelligence), the loss of sexual periodicity, the permanent attachment of the male to a female, cooperation, and so on. Something of the complexity of this interaction between man's physical and cultural evolution is brought out in one of the major contributions included in the present volume, namely, that by Livingstone. Darwin, as we shall see in the contributions included in this volume, gave the lead many years ago in showing how important behavioral traits were in the evolution of man, but that lead was not taken up for many years afterwards. In the early twenties of this century Carveth Read, the English logician and philosopher, again pointed to the close interconnection of culture and man's physical evolution, but again anthropologists appeared not to be ready for such bold ideas, ideas which have become the commonplaces of the contemporary anthropologists' thinking.

In the present volume I have attempted to communicate something of the gradualness of the changes which anthropology underwent to achieve its contemporary high estate. It is the story of a fascinating and remarkable development.

When I was a student of anthropology, in the early twenties in England, there were only three universities in which the subject was taught, Oxford, Cambridge, and London. In the whole land there were scarcely more than a dozen anthropologists. In the United States the position was somewhat better, for with the establishment of the Bureau of American Ethnology, as a part of the Smithsonian Institution, in 1879, anthropology was officially recognized, and anthropologists were enlisted in the government service. Even so, there were hardly more than a dozen universities in which anthropology was taught, and it was really only after the Second World War that there was an increase in the number of students interested in studying the subject, and a gradual increase in the number of institutions offering courses in anthropology. It was not, however, until the late forties or early fifties that increasing numbers of colleges and universities began to offer anthropology as a part of the liberal arts curriculum, to offer degrees in the subject which would enable the student to go on to graduate studies in anthropology.

In the early thirties, when I attended anthropological meetings of the official American anthropological societies, there would be about thirty members present at the annual meeting of the American Association of Physical Anthropologists and about one hundred at the annual meeting of the American Anthropological Association. Today there are several hundred attending the physical anthropology meetings, and almost four thousand are present at the American Anthropological Association meetings. Anthropologists are today employed in every kind of field, in industry, government, think tanks, and so on.[1] The influence of anthropological findings has been widespread and will continue in ever-widening circles. This is very much to the good. For anthropology, virtually the last of the sciences to be developed in the twentieth century, should form the core part of all education, for what can be more important than knowing ourselves and understanding our neighbors?

Anthropology is able not only to show us the routes by which we have come, but also to indicate those routes we should avoid and those we ought to take in order that every individual may have the opportunity to fulfill himself, in all lands and in all climes, so that, without becoming uniform, all humanity may become a harmonic unity.

The Greek word for man, *anthropos*, is said to be derived from roots meaning "He who looks upward." Whatever the ancient coiner of the word may have had in mind, he could hardly have been more apposite in his invention, for man is, indeed, the creature who looks upward both physically and spiritually. Something of the manner in which this kind of thinking developed through the agency of anthropology is suggested in the following pages.

Anthropology is at once both a humanistic and a biological discipline, with its central referent always man, but not man as an abstraction, as something to classify and put in a museum case or in a textbook, but man as a living, breathing, striving brother, whether a Neanderthal, Australopithecine, or an Australian aborigine. In brief, the ultimate purpose of anthropology is not merely knowledge and understanding, important as they are, but active application of that knowledge and understanding to the welfare of men and women everywhere. In this connection I always think of the beautiful words of May Sarton:

> Never forget this when the talk is clever:
> Wisdom must be born in the flesh or wither,
> And sacred order has been always won
> From chaos by some faithful one
> Whose human bones have ached as if with fever
> To bring you to these high triumphant places,
> Forget the formulas, remember men.[2]

I hope that this book may help us to remember.

---

[1]For a good elementary survey of contemporary anthropology and its various fields see Charles Frantz, *The Student Anthropologist's Handbook* (Cambridge, Mass., Schenkman Publishing Co., Inc., 1972).

[2]From the poem "The Sacred Order," by permission of the author and Rinehart & Co., from May Sarton's *The Lion and the Rose*, New York, 1948.

INTRODUCTION AND ACKNOWLEDGMENTS

IN this book I have endeavored to bring together some of the significant contributions that have been made to the development of anthropology during the last two hundred years, and to add something of the background against which that development occurred. Toward this end I have included several odd pieces. The Columbus Letter is included as a sort of epigraph.

In planning the book I have been guided by several principles. The first has been that each selection shall represent a contribution that has had some influence upon the thinking of men and women who read it. The second principle has been to avoid, insofar as that is possible, reprinting material that is readily available in other sources. The third principle has been to offer material reflecting the thinking current during the last two centuries about the nature of men and their beliefs, as well as of their own place in nature and society. The fourth principle has been to include a selection of works which, though they have not always been recognized as such, constitute major contributions to the development of anthropology—our understanding of the nature of man and his works.

One could have made a very different sort of book with a very similar conception of its structure and function, had the period covered been two thousand rather than two hundred years. But in that event, the book would have run to many volumes and would have defeated the purpose I had in view.

I have desired to give the reader an insight into the development of thinking concerning his origin and evolution, during the last two centuries. The problem has been to maintain a proper balance where there was so much from which to choose. More progress has been made in the study of man during the last fifty years than in all the millennia preceding. I have, therefore, only been able to include a small sample of those contributions in the modern period which have had a major impact on the development of our understanding of man.

A selection of contributions of this kind must finally represent a personal choice. A number of the contributions in these pages have been rescued from an undeserved oblivion, wholly due to the accident of their having been published in obscure places. Every one of them has meant a great deal to me in my development as an anthropologist. I hope each of these pieces will afford the reader as much interest and pleasure as they have the editor of this volume.

Princeton,
New Jersey   A. M.
1973

CONTRIBUTORS

Benedict, Ruth Fulton (1887-1948)
Boas, Franz (1858-1942)
Cannon, Walter Bradford (1871-1945)
Castle, William Ernest (1867-1962)
Codrington, Robert Henry (1830-1922)
Darwin, Charles (1809-1882)
Dobzhansky, Theodosius (1900-   )
Dorsey, George A. (1868-1931)
Du Chaillu, Paul (1831-1903)
Franklin, Benjamin (1706-1790)
Frazer, Sir James (1854-1941)
Gennep, Arnold van (1873-1957)
Gillen, Frank James (1855-1912)
Haddon, Alfred Cort (1855-1940)
Hartman, Carl G. (1879-1968)
Hunt, James (1833-1869)
Huxley, Julian Sorell (1887-   )
Huxley, Thomas Henry (1825-1895)
Kroeber, Alfred Louis (1876-1960)
Livingstone, Frank B. (1928-   )
Malinowski, Bronislaw (1884-1942)
Montagu, Ashley (1905-   )
Morgan, Lewis Henry (1818-1881)
Myres, John Linton (1869-1954)
Paton, John G. (1824-1907)
Pearson, Karl (1857-1936)
Pollard, Albert Frederick (1869-1948)
Read, Carveth (1848-1931)
Rivers, William Halse (1864-1922)
Sikes, Edward Ernest (1867-1940)
Smith, Samuel Stanhope (1751-1819)
Spencer, Walter Baldwin (1860-1929)
White, Leslie A. (1900-   )

COLUMBUS "DISCOVERS" AMERICA
AND IS ENTHUSIASTIC ABOUT THE
AMERICAN INDIAN

THE first letter Columbus wrote to Europe accompanied his account to Ferdinand and Isabella of the discovery of America. The letter, it is generally agreed among scholars, was written 15 February 1493. It was from this letter that Europe first learned of the "discovery." (I put "discovery" in quotes because it was the American Indian who discovered America, *not* Columbus).

Columbus' letter is reprinted here because it gives the first account of American Indians on first contact with them by the white man. "They show greater love for all others than for themselves." Columbus found them to be of "excellent and acute understanding," and whatever new people he encountered offered him and his men "great love and extraordinary goodwill." Again and again, Columbus comments on the amiability and friendliness of the Indians, from "chieftain to child. Columbus was impressed by their gentleness in spite of himself, for his motivation in finding this short passage to the "Indies" was entirely that of an exploiter, in the service of commerce and the Church.[1] Columbus' comments on the good nature of the Indians is, therefore, all the more striking. These are the gentle creatures who were later seen as "wild savages" and destroyed in countless number by those who brought the "benefits" of Christianity and commerce to them. Virtually everywhere where the white man has come into contact with the native peoples the story has been the same, culminating in the sentiment, so succinctly expressed by General Philip Henry Sheridan in 1869, "The only good Indian is a dead Indian." Indeed, "the merciless Indian savages" of The Declaration of Independence. "—and the truth shall make ye free."

[1]See S. de Madariaga, *Christopher Columbus* (New York, Macmillan, 1940).

THE COLUMBUS LETTER

Because my undertakings have attained success, I know that it will be pleasing to you: these I have determined to relate, so that you may be made acquainted with everything done and discovered in this our voyage. On the thirty-third day after I departed from Cadiz [Presumably a mistake of the translator, Columbus sailed from Palos; landfall occurred thirty-three days after departure from the Canaries.], I came to the Indian sea, where I found many islands inhabited by men without number, of all which I took possession for our most fortunate king, with proclaiming heralds and flying standards, no one objecting. To the first of these I gave the name of the blessed Saviour, on whose aid relying I had reached this as well as the other islands. But the Indians call it Guanahany. I also called each one of the others by a new name. For I ordered one island to be called Santa Maria of the Conception, another Fernandina, another Isabella, another Juana, and so on with the rest. As soon as we had arrived at that island which I have just now said was called Juana, I proceeded along its coast towards the west for some distance; I found it so large and without perceptible end, that I believed it to be not an island, but the continental country of Cathay; seeing, however, no towns or cities situated on the sea-coast, but only some villages and rude farms, with whose inhabitants I was unable to converse, because as soon as they saw us they took flight. I proceeded farther, thinking that I would discover some city or large residences. At length, perceiving that we had gone far enough, that nothing new appeared, and that this way was leading us to the north, which I wished to avoid, because it was winter on the land, and it was my intention to go to the south, and the winds were favorable to these plans, I therefore determined that no others were practicable, and so, going back, I returned to a certain bay that I had noticed, from which I sent two of our men to the land, that they might find out whether there was a king in this country, or any cities. These men traveled for three days, and they found people and houses without number, but they were small and without any government, therefore they returned. Now in the meantime I had learned from certain Indians, whom I had seized there, that this country was indeed an island, and therefore I proceeded towards the east, keeping all the time near the coast, for 322 miles, to the extreme ends of this island. From this place I saw another island to the east, distant from this Juana 54 miles, which I called forthwith Hispana; and I sailed to it; and I steered along the northern coast, as at Juana, towards the east 564 miles. And the said Juana and the other islands there appear very fertile. This island is surrounded by many very safe and wide harbors, not excelled by any others that I have ever seen. Many great and salubrious rivers flow through it. There are also many very high mountains there. All these islands are very beautiful, and distinguished by various qualities; they are accessible, and full of a great variety of trees stretching up to the stars; the leaves of which I believe are never shed, for I saw them as green and flourishing as they are usually in Spain in the month of May; some of them were blossoming, some were bearing fruit, some were in other conditions; each one was thriving in its own way. The nightingale and various other birds without number were singing, in the month of November, when I was exploring them. There are besides in the said island Juana seven or eight kinds of palm trees, which far excel ours in height and beauty, just as all the other trees, herbs, and fruits do. There are also excellent pine trees, vast plains and meadows, a variety of birds, a variety of honey, and a variety of metals, excepting iron. In the one which was called Hispana, as we said above, there are great and beautiful mountains, vast fields, groves, fertile plains, very suitable for planting and cultivating, and for the building of houses. The convenience of the harbors in this island, and the remarkable number of rivers contributing to the healthfulness of man, exceed belief, unless one has seen them. The trees, pasturage, and fruits of this island differ greatly from those of Juana. This Hispana, moreover, abounds in different kinds of spices, in gold, and in metals. On this island, indeed, and on all the others which I have seen, and of which I have knowledge, the inhabitants of both sexes go always naked, just as they came into the world, except some women, who use a covering of a leaf or some foliage, or a cotton cloth, which they make themselves for that purpose. All these people lack, as I said above, every kind of iron; they are also without weapons, which indeed are unknown; nor are they competent to use them, not on account of deformity of body, for they are well formed, but because they are timid and full of fear. They carry for weapons, however, reeds baked in the sun, on the lower ends of which they fasten some shafts of dried wood rubbed down to a point; and indeed they do not venture to use these always; for it frequently happened when I sent two or three of my men to some of the villages, that they might speak with the natives, a compact troop of Indians would march out, and as soon as they saw our men approaching, they would quickly take flight, children being pushed aside by their fathers, and fathers by their children. And this was not because any hurt or injury had been inflicted on any one of them, for to every one whom I visited and with whom I was able to converse, I distributed whatever I had, cloth and many other things, no return being made to me; but they are by nature fearful and timid. Yet when they perceive that they are safe, putting aside all fear, they are of simple manners and trustworthy, and very liberal with everything they have, refusing no one who asks for anything they may possess, and even themselves inviting us to ask for things. They show greater love for all others than for themselves; they give valuable things for trifles, being satisfied even with a very small return, or with nothing; however, I forbade that things so small and of no value should be given to them, such as pieces of plates, dishes and glass, likewise keys and shoe-straps; although if they were able to obtain these, it seemed to them like getting the most beautiful jewels in the world. It happened, indeed, that a certain sailor obtained in exchange for a shoe-strap as much worth of gold as would equal three golden coins; and likewise other things for articles of very little value, especially for new silver coins, and for some gold coins, to obtain which they gave whatever the seller desired, as for instance an ounce and a half and two ounces of gold, or thirty and forty pounds of cotton, with which they were already acquainted. They also traded cotton and gold for pieces of bows, bottles, jugs, and jars, like persons without reason, which I forbade because it was very wrong; and I gave to them many beautiful and pleasing things that I had brought with me, no value being taken in exchange, in order that I might the more easily make them friendly to me, that they might be made worshippers of Christ, and that they might be full of love towards our king, queen, and prince, and the whole Spanish nation; also that they might be zealous to search out and collect, and deliver to us those things of which they had plenty, and which we greatly needed. These people practice no kind of idolatry; on the contrary they firmly believe that all strength and power, and in fact all good things are in heaven, and that I had come down from thence with these ships and sailors; and in this belief I was received there after they had put aside fear. Nor are they slow or unskilled, but of excellent and acute understanding; and the men who have navigated that sea give an account of everything in an admirable manner; but they never saw people clothed, nor these kind of ships. As soon as I reached that sea, I seized by force several Indians on the first island, in order that they might learn from us, and in like manner tell us about those things in these lands of which they themselves had knowledge; and the plan succeeded, for in a short time we understood them and they us, sometimes by gestures and signs, sometimes by words; and it was a great advantage to us. They are coming with me now, yet always believing that I descended from heaven, although they have been living with us for a long time, and are living with us to-day. And these men were the first who announced it wherever we landed, continually proclaiming to the others in a loud voice, "Come, come, and you will see the celestial people." Whereupon both women and men, both children and adults, both young men and old men, laying aside the fear caused a little before, visited us eagerly, filling the road with a great crowd, some bringing food, and some drink, with great love and extraordinary goodwill. On every island there are many canoes of a single piece of wood; and though narrow, yet in length and shape similar to our rowboats, but swifter in movement. They steer only by oars. Some of these boats are large, some small, some of medium size. Yet they row many of the larger row-boats with eighteen cross-benches, with which they cross to all those islands, which are innumerable, and with these boats they perform their trading, and carry on commerce among them. I saw some of these row-boats or canoes which were carrying seventy and eighty rowers. In all these islands there is no difference in the appearance of the people, nor in the manners and language, but all understand each other mutually; a fact that is very important for the end which I suppose to be earnestly desired by our most illustrious king, that is, their conversion to the holy religion of Christ, to which in truth, as far as I can perceive, they are very ready and favorably inclined. I said before how I proceeded along the island Juana in a straight line from west to east 322 miles, according to which course and the length of the way, I am able to say that this Juana is larger than England and Scotland together; for besides the said 322 thousand paces, there are two more provinces in that part which lies towards the west, which I did not visit; one of these the Indians call Anan, whose inhabitants are born with tails. They extend to 180 miles in length, as I have learned from those Indians I have with me, who are all acquainted with these islands. But the circumference of Hispana is greater than all Spain from Colonia to Fontarabia. This is easily proved, because its fourth side, which I myself passed along in a straight line from west to east, extends 540 miles. This island is to be desired and is very desirable, and not to be despised; in which, although as I have said, I solemnly took possession of all the others for our most invincible king, and their government is entirely committed to the said king, yet I especially took possession of a certain large town, in a very convenient location, and adapted to all kinds of gain and commerce, to which we gave the name of our Lord of the Nativity. And I commanded a fort to be built there forthwith, which must be completed by this time; in which I left as many men as seemed necessary, with all kinds of arms, and plenty of food for more than a year. Likewise one caravel, and for the construction of others men skilled in this trade and in other professions; and also the extraordinary good will and friendship of the king of this island toward us. For those people are very amiable and kind, to such a degree that the said king gloried in calling me his brother. And if they should change their minds, and should wish to hurt those who remained in the fort, they would not be able, because they lack weapons, they go naked, and are too cowardly. For that reason those who hold the said fort are at least able to resist easily this whole island, without any imminent danger to themselves, so long as they do not transgress the regulations and command which we gave. In all these islands as I have understood, each man is content with only one wife, except the princes or kings, who are permitted to have twenty. The women appear to work more than the men. I was not able to find out surely whether they have individual property, for I saw that one man had the duty of distributing to the others, especially refreshments, food, and things of that kind. I found no monstrosities among them, as very many supposed, but men of great reverence, and friendly. Nor are they black like the Ethiopians. They have straight hair, hanging down. They do not remain where the solar rays send out the heat, for the strength of the sun is very great here, because it is distant from the equinoctial line, as it seems, only twenty-six degrees. On the tops of the mountains too the cold is severe, but the Indians, however, moderate it, partly by being accustomed to the place, and partly by the help of very hot victuals, of which they eat frequently and immoderately. And so I did not see any monstrosity, nor did I have knowledge of them anywhere, excepting a certain island named Charis, which is the second in passing from Hispana to India. This island is inhabited by a certain people who are considered very warlike by their neighbors. These eat human flesh. The said people have many kinds of row-boats, in which they cross over to all the other Indian islands, and seize and carry away everything that they can. They differ in no way from the others, only that they wear long hair like women. They use bows and darts made of reeds, with sharpened shafts fastened to the larger end, as we have described. On this account they are considered warlike, wherefore the other Indians are afflicted with continual fear, but I regard them as of no more account than the others. These are the people who visit certain women, who alone inhabit the island Mateunin, which is the first in passing from Hispana to India. These women, moreover, perform no kind of work of their sex, for they use bows and darts, like those I have described of their husbands; they protect themselves with sheets of copper, of which there is great abundance among them. They tell me of another island greater than the aforesaid Hispana, whose inhabitants are without hair, and which abounds in gold above all the others. I am bringing with me men of this island and of the others that I have seen, who give proof of the things that I have described. Finally, that I may compress in few words the brief account of our departure and quick return, and the gain, I promise this, that if I am supported by our most invincible sovereigns with a little of their help, as much gold can be supplied as they will need, indeed as much of spices, of cotton, of chewing gum (which is only found in Chios), also as much of aloes wood, and as many slaves for the navy, as their majesties will wish to demand. Likewise rhubarb and other kinds of spices, which I suppose these men whom I left in the said fort have already found, and will continue to find; since I remained in no place longer than the winds forced me, except in the town of the Nativity, while I provided for the building of the fort, and for the safety of all. Which things, although they are very great and remarkable, yet they would have been much greater, if I had been aided by as many ships as the occasion required. Truly great and wonderful is this, and not corresponding to our merits, but to the holy Christian religion, and to the piety and religion of our sovereigns, because what the human understanding could not attain, that the divine will has granted to human efforts. For God is wont to listen to his servants who love his precepts, even in impossibilities, as has happened to us on the present occasion, who have attained that which hitherto mortal men have never reached. For if any one has written or said anything about these islands, it was all with obscurities and conjectures; no one claims that he had seen them; from which they seemed like fables. Therefore let the king and queen, the princes and their most fortunate kingdoms, and all other countries of Christendom give thanks to our Lord and Saviour Jesus Christ, who has bestowed upon us so great a victory and gift. Let religious processions be solemnized; let sacred festivals be given; let the churches be covered with festive garlands. Let Christ rejoice on earth, as he rejoices in heaven, when he foresees coming to salvation so many souls of people hitherto lost. Let us be glad also, as well on account of the exaltation of our faith as on account of the increase of our temporal affairs, of which not only Spain, but universal Christendom will be partaker. These things that have been done are thus briefly related. Farewell. Lisbon, the day before the ides of March.

Christopher Columbus, Admiral of the Ocean Fleet.

THE ANCIENT GREEKS DO NOT RECOGNIZE "RACE" AND, INDEED, DENY IT

EDWARD ERNEST SIKES (1867-1940) was Fellow and Tutor and later President of St. John's College, Cambridge University. In his charming, scholarly, and little-known book, *The Anthropology of the Greeks* (London, David Nutt, 1914), Sikes examined the views that the Greeks held of themselves and of the rest of mankind. Sikes points out that "the ultimate criterion," that is, physique, upon which "the modern ethnologist" bases his conception of "race" was wholly neglected by the Greeks. Not alone this, but also mental traits were, according to the Greeks, wholly due to environment.

The modern vulgar idea that there exists an indissoluble association, which is biologically determined, between physical appearance, individual behavior, and cultural achievement, is quite erroneous, and was quite properly denied by the Greeks. The Greeks, as Isocrates (436-338 B.C.) put it, thought of Hellenism as a thing of the spirit rather than of "race." "So far," he wrote, "has Athens outdistanced the rest of mankind in thought and in speech that her pupils have become the teachers of the rest of the world; and she has brought it about that the name of 'Hellenes' is applied rather to those who share our culture than to those who share a common blood." (*Panegyricus,* 4, 50).

The Greeks and the Romans were, indeed, singularly free of anything resembling race prejudice. Indeed, the biological conception of "race" and "race prejudice" is an invention of the early nineteenth century

when, in reaction to the abolitionist movement both in America and
in Europe, the myth of "race" was invented and elaborated by the
pro-slavers.[1]

The Greeks and the Romans were devoted to the institution of slavery, but it was a very different kind of slavery from that which was
institutionalized in the New World, in that it was very much more
humane and even benevolent.[2] The rare occasions on which an attempt
was made to biologize the differences between masters and slaves had
no effect whatever upon the thought of either Greek or Roman.

THE PROBLEM OF RACE*

It has been observed that the Greeks had a natural tendency to
dichotomise—to 'think in pairs,' and to view each object by contrast with its
antithesis. Hence, at any early stage—although, as Thucydides noted, this stage
was not Homeric—the Hellenes distinguished themselves from the other
peoples whom they called collectively and indiscriminately 'barbarians.' They
did not claim to be a Chosen Race, in the Hebrew sense; but they were none
the less conscious of being a peculiar people, differentiated from all others
by superior characteristics.

Possibly we are apt to attach excessive importance to the contrast between
"Ελληνες [Greeks] and βάρβαροι [foreigners (literally barbarians)] owing to
the secondary and regular meaning of the modern word 'barbarian'; but a
general term, which included the wildest savage as well as the most civilised
Asiatic, was bound to have an invidious connotation to the Greeks themselves.
And there is no doubt that Greek exclusiveness was a marked feature in every
period of the national history, until the barriers were finally broken by Roman
conquerors, who were quite free from racial intolerance. Politically, of course,
the Greeks could then no longer afford to be more exclusive than their masters;
but they could still console their wounded pride by insisting on the intellectual
and artistic superiority of their own race, and the Romans were always ready
to abet this claim. As a result, the old antithesis between Greek and barbarian

[1]For a discussion of this see Ashley Montagu, *The Idea of Race* (Lincoln, University of Nebraska
Press, 1965); Ashley Montagu, *Man's Most Dangerous Myth: The Fallacy of Race*, 5th ed. (New
York, Oxford University Press, 1974).

[2]W. L. Westermann, "The Slave Systems of Greek and Roman Antiquity," *Memoirs of the
American Philosophical Society* (Vol. 40, 1955), pp. xi-180.

*Reprinted from E. E. Sikes, *The Anthropology of the Greeks* (London, David Nutt, 1914),
pp. 69-89.

was not destroyed, but readjusted to the new conditions, and the glory of having 'introduced the arts to rustic Latium' remained as a compensation for the loss of political prestige.

It is hardly needful to quote examples of this mental attitude. Any Greek would have thanked God that he was born a Greek, not a barbarian, and we are not surprised to find this rather Pharisaic thanksgiving attributed to various distinguished philosophers. Sometimes the feeling against barbarians is definitely national, and aggravated by growing danger from external enemies. Aeschylus, at least, is generous enough to a beaten foe—the Persian defeat is due to the overweening pride of Xerxes rather than to the degeneracy of his people—but, in the later phases of the long struggle, the tone becomes more bitter: Isocrates alternates between hatred and contempt of the Persians, 'natural enemies' of Greece, and Demosthenes reviles the Macedonians—(who were scarcely outside the Hellenic pale)—as barbarians, and 'not even decent barbarians.' The line in the *Telephus* of Euripides—

> Ἕλληνες ὄντες βαρβάροις δουλεύσομεν;'
> Shall we, being Greeks, be slaves of barbarians?

whether we call it arrogance or proper pride, is characteristic of all Greek political thought.

Apart from politics, there was a powerful motive for despising, or affecting to despise, the barbarian: the vast majority of slaves in Greece were foreigners —Phrygians, Syrians, and the like—and, when enlightened opinion began to doubt the 'justice' of slavery, a belief that the institution was 'natural' must have been a salve to the conscience of the respectable slave-owner. From Euripides to the latest Cynics and Stoics, there were many who doubted or denied the right of one man to enslave another. But the average Greek must always have agreed with Aristotle that the Greeks were naturally free, the barbarians servile.[1] The great philosopher has been blamed for lagging behind the more advanced opinion of his own day; and it must be confessed that his ostensible defence of slavery is weak enough. He emphasises the difference between τὸ ἄρχον and τὸ ἀρχόμενον—the states of ruling and being ruled—and remarks that a man rules over wife, child, and slave in different degrees; but he fails to prove that all these degrees are equally natural—the fallacy slips in with the ambiguous term 'ruling.' But although Aristotle does not make the best of a bad case, he need not be accused of simply reflecting common opinion, fond as he is of deferring to accepted views. His own anthropological system really encouraged, if it did not demand, a belief in the natural slave. All nature is continuous, with imperceptible steps rising from the inanimate to the plant, from the plant to the lowest animal, and from this again to man. But between even the most intelligent animal and the Hellene

(1) *Pol.* i. 3. 1253 *b* 20, 1255 *a* 3, Eur. *Melanippe* (fr. 514, 515 Dindorf).

10   FRONTIERS OF ANTHROPOLOGY

there was an obvious gap, an apparent break in the continuity. This gulf could
only be bridged by the assumption of human varieties whose intellectual equipment was but slightly higher than mere animal intelligence. Nature would like
to distinguish between the bodies of the free and the slaves; failing this, she
has formed a bridge in the human mind, so that the slave has no deliberative
faculty, and differs only from the animals in the power of listening to reason.

A further point must be noticed: Aristotle had not only to describe his nicely-
graduated scale; he had also to explain its significance, to co-ordinate its parts,
and to show their interdependence. The relation of organisms is not temporal,
and so it must be teleological. Aristotle was not acquainted with biological
analogies for human slavery—such as the 'slaves' of ants—but he was content
with the broad principle that Nature means the lower to serve the higher: plants
exist for the sake of animals; both plants and animals for the sake of man.[2]
But, if man himself is unequal, what could be more 'natural' than that the
lower man should exist for the higher—especially as the advantage is
mutual—or, in plain Greek, that the barbarian should be a slave of the Hellene?

But there was another side of the question. If Aristotle found it necessary
to stigmatise the barbarians as a whole class, he was (at least among educated
thinkers) the exception rather than the rule. His advice to Alexander—to treat
the Greeks as a leader and the barbarians as a master—was condemned by
the broad-minded Eratosthenes, who said that men should only be distinguished
by their moral qualities, without regard to race.[3] And, long before Aristotle,
at a time when the Greeks had far more reason for racial pride, we find an
astonishing fairness in their outlook on foreign nations. No writer is more free
from prejudice than the first Greek historian, whose aim, as he avows in his
opening sentence, is to preserve from oblivion the great and wonderful deeds
of the Greeks and barbarians. It is interesting to notice how Lucian perverted
this plain statement by paraphrasing it as 'Greek victories and barbarian
defeats.' But Lucian wrote in days when decadent Greece was forced to draw
freely on the capital of past glory, just as the impartiality of Herodotus surprised and annoyed Plutarch; who calls him φιλοβάρβαρος [lover of for-
eigners], and even grudges his tribute to the Persian bravery at Plataea.[4]
Herodotus was not alone in admiring the quality of the Persians, who taught
their sons to ride and shoot and speak the truth. In the next generation,
Xenophon took Cyrus as his ideal monarch and eulogised the system which
had made Persia an imperial power, while he does not forget to point out
that the Persians of his own day had declined from their former excellence.
Ancient Persia, it is plain, was 'romantic' to an Athenian—for Xenophon, in
spite of his Spartan tendencies, is a typical Athenian—and the choice of Cyrus
as the hero of romance is a deserved compliment to a race whose virtues

(2) II.A. ii. 1. 500 b 33.
(3) Plut. de Alex. fort. 6, Strabo 66.
(4) Lucian, quom. scr. sit hist. 54, Plut. de mal. Herod. 12 and 53; cf. Herod. vii. 238.

Xenophon had learned to appreciate in his short service with the younger namesake of the great King. Antisthenes was not less flattering to foreign virtue in his comparison of Heracles and Cyrus as equal patterns of the strenuous life, although the value of this testimony may be weakened by the cosmopolitan views of the Cynic school.[5] But this Cynic attitude is, of course, in itself a proof that the stronghold of Hellenic pride was never impregnable.

Towards Egypt, again, the earlier Greek feeling was almost entirely respectful. Greece owed a real debt to the ancient Egyptian civilisation, and the debt, so far from being discounted, was often exaggerated, so that Greek religion, philosophy, law and culture were all attributed to the wisdom of the Egyptians. The fascination of Egypt is apparent in Herodotus. But that impartial traveller did not confine his attention to the great centres of ancient civilisation. In the course of his wanderings Herodotus had gained that 'enlightening of man's judgment from the commerce of men' which Montaigne attributes to 'frequenting abroad in the world.' He came into contact with almost every stage of social development, but he records the most savage practice without the slightest tone of superiority. Once or twice he indulges in approval or censure, as in remarking that the marriage-market is the best Babylonian custom, but the prostitution in the temple of Mylitta is 'most disgraceful.'[6] No doubt his usual tolerance may be partly due to the fact that his interest overpowers his moral judgment; as has been said, 'Herodotus is full of intellectual curiosity, but temporarily indifferent to the moral aspects of the story. In that he is a true devotee of θεωρία.' [observation or speculation as opposed to action][7] But this is as much as to say that Herodotus is a true anthropologist—his business is not to moralise, but to observe. Nor is he really careless: his whole outlook shows a deep reverence for custom, which, even if distasteful or horrible, is not lightly to be altered. Only a madman, he thinks, would laugh at the habits of another race. This is not indifference, but respect for the law which—however mysterious in its working—is the unwritten ordinance of the gods. Custom is custom—ἀμφὶ τῷ νόμῳ τούτῳ ἐχέτω ὡς καὶ ἀρχὴν ἐνομίσθη [let custom be held now in the same esteem as it was in the beginning]. So Pausanias, remembering his model Herodotus, passes even the savage practice of human sacrifice—lingering, or believed to linger, in the remote parts of Greece itself as late as the second century of our own era—with the remark 'let it be as it is, and as it was at the beginning.'[8]

It was in this liberal spirit that Herodotus approached the problem of Race. He found human beings traditionally divided into a number of ἔθνεα or 'races,' and although he did not consider the eunow to be an ultimate or original

(5) Diog. L. vi. 2.
(6) Herod. i. 196, 199. See Farnell, *Greece and Babylon*, p. 268, E. S. Hartland in *Anthrop. Essays* to E. B. Tylor, p. 188 f.
(7) Livingstone, *Greek Genius*, p. 153.
(8) Herod. i. 140, Paus. viii. 38, 7.

division of man, he accepted it as the practical unit of classification. Thus, the Greeks themselves were marked off from all other stocks by certain specific differences—the ties of blood, language, religion and culture.[9] Of course this famous definition of Hellenism is not strictly concerned with the criteria of race: it will be noticed that Herodotus *assumes* kinship between Spartans and Athenians (ὅμαιμον) [kinship or blood relationship]; common language, religion and culture are not adduced as evidence of consanguinity, but as facts observable among those whose blood-relationship is otherwise established. At most, such tests offered a good reason why kinsfolk should be friendly; and, failing other evidence, may themselves help to prove community of blood. As we shall see, the predominant Greek criterion of race was tradition; but, before examining the reason for this predominance, we may briefly review the attitude of Herodotus towards other criteria.

With regard to language, Herodotus was at least wiser than our own immediate ancestors; he knew that a nation could acquire a language by contact, and so he never fell into the trap of the linguistic fallacy which caught the modern 'Aryan' philologists. The Aethiopians in Asia and Africa belong to the same race, but they differ in language and hair. At the same time, Herodotus allows philology a reasonable place as an ethnic test, and he admits that the oldest language—if its priority could be proved—would imply the oldest race—a conclusion with which no one presumably would disagree.[10] Similarly, he knew that religions travel. His chief instance of this principle —the derivation of Greek gods from Egypt—was mistaken; but he correctly noted that Greek religion was a compound to which 'Pelasgians,' i.e. the old Mediterranean stock, had contributed their share. In his scale of values, however, a community of cults is superior to the linguistic test: there was a temple of Carian Zeus to which Mysians and Lydians had access by right of blood, and those nations which belonged to a different race, even if they had come to speak the Carian language, were excluded.[11]

Again, to Herodotus the evidence of [culture] (ἤθεα) is important, but, like that of religion, is not in itself a conclusive test of consanguinity. Certain customs may be evolved—or, as Herodotus would have said, may be 'invented' independently. For example, he is struck by the likeness between the Egyptian military caste, who may practise no handicraft, and the warrior-class in Sparta and indeed in all Greek states except Corinth. Here a theory of transmission would have been easy, for the Spartan Kings were believed to have had Egyptian as well as Assyrian ancestors, and Herodotus notes various customs which the Spartans shared with Egypt or Assyria. But he wisely refrains from pushing the hypothesis of borrowing too far, 'since the Thracians, Scythians, Persians, Lydians, and almost all barbarians despise craftsmen in comparison with other

(9) iii. 144.
(10) i. 57, 171; vii. 70; ii. 2, 105.
(11) i. 171; cf. Strabo 659.

citizens and especially with soldiers.' In many cases, however, he believes that culture has been transmitted, and is therefore no evidence in ethnology: Athenian women have borrowed first the Dorian and then the Carian dress; the Persian civilisation is indebted to Media and Egypt, while one at least of the Persian vices is derived from Greece.[12] But, on the whole, the evidence of culture or ritual is admitted as a sound criterion of consanguinity: a difference of ritual observed by Carian inhabitants of Egypt is a proof that they are not Egyptian; and the Colchian practice of circumcision—though Phoenicians and Syrians acknowledged that it was not native to themselves—seems to Herodotus a convincing proof that the Colchians belong to the Egyptian stock.[13] In the latter instance he adds other arguments—a common method of weaving flax and a general similarity in the life and language of the two nations—but these, he thinks, are inconclusive when compared with the striking custom of circumcision; and, in particular, he depreciates the value of physique, which 'comes to nothing, for there are others who have dark skin and curly hair.'

Herodotus may well be pardoned for showing some vacillation in his estimate of culture as a trustworthy criterion of race; the problem is extremely complicated, and could not possibly be solved with the methods and material at his command; and indeed the two theories of independent evolution or transmission divide modern anthropologists into opposite camps. Hitherto the British school have mainly proceeded on evolutionary ideas, holding that similarities of culture in different regions are due to the essential similarity of the human mind, which, in the same conditions, may be expected to produce the same results. On the other hand, an important school is now beginning to attach far less weight to evolution, and explains many resemblances, formerly accepted as independent in origin, by the assumption of contact.[14]

A modern ethnologist, however, will not so readily excuse the Greeks for their serious neglect of physique, which we have learnt to recognise as the ultimate criterion. The chief cause of this neglect was the belief that physical and mental character is entirely due to environment—it is a geographical accident rather than evidence of race.[15] According to Hippocrates, the younger contemporary of Herodotus, 'you will generally find that human physique and character follow the nature of the country.' In particular, the broad distinction between fair and dark races was explained as due to the immediate action of the sun. Aeschylus had already laid stress on the principle: Prometheus,

(12) ii. 167; vi. 53 f.; v. 87, i. 135.

(13) ii. 61, 104.

(14) See F. Ratzel, *History of Mankind* (E.T. 1896) i.; W. H. R. Rivers, *Pres. Address Brit. Assoc.* 1911.

(15) Hippocr. *de aere, aquis, locis* 24, Aesch. *P.V.* 22, 808, *Supp.* 155, 279, 284. See generally Herod. iii. 106, Plat. *Rep.* 435 E, *Tim.* 24 C, *Epin.* 987 D, Arist. *Pol.* vii. 7. 1327 *b* 23, Posidonius in Förster, *Script. phys.* ii. p. 66.

parched by the sun, will change his colour; the Danaids, though originally
of Argive descent, have become like Libyans or Egyptians or Indians, from
the heat of their adopted country; the black Ethiopians dwell by the fountains
of the sun. Even in their own climate the Greeks noted the difference between
the sunburnt men and the 'fairer sex,' whose life was so largely spent indoors,
and the insurgent women of the *Ecclesiazusae*, in their masculine disguise,
pass easily for cobblers, the only 'white men' for whom Athens had any use.[16]
The distinction of colour between the sexes was indicated in certain types of
Greek vases. So, in later times, the curly hair and pigmentation of the black
races was sufficiently explained by the 'neighbouring' sun, and the further differences between Indian and African types could be attributed to the special
influence of local rivers or the atmosphere,[17] for Water and Air, with the Sun,
formed a triad whose action determined physical and moral characters.

In a spirit half mythological, half scientific, Aeschylus pays his tribute to
the river as κουροτόφος, nurturer of the young. To him, as to Herodotus
and many others, Egypt is in a very real sense the gift of the Nile, which
has fixed the type of those who dwell on its banks; and, when Aeschylus
explains the difference between Argives and Egyptians by the remark 'Nile
breeds a race unlike the Inachus', the poet is anticipating the physician Hippocrates, in a work whose very title—περὶ ἀέτων, ὑδάτων, τόπων [concerning
air, water, & land]—shows the influence of air and water in ancient
medicine.

With regard to the third member of the triad, we have already seen the
importance of the Air in philosophy, before Hippocrates made it a matter of
medical study; and, from the fifth century onwards, it was regarded as the
chief, if not the only clue to the variations of human character. Athenians,
'walking delicately through most pellucid air,' gave their climate the credit
for their intelligence. Plato was not so easily satisfied; although far from under-
rating the value of the atmosphere, he knew that a land cannot live on Air
alone—it should have deep soil and good water. Accepting and amplifying
the myths of Athenian greatness in former days, he expected to find a corresponding superiority in Attica over all other lands; for Hephaestus and Athena
had chosen it as suited to the virtue and intelligence of the people whom they
proposed to plant therein.[18] But here a difficulty arose: the Attica of Plato's
day was a 'poor' country, with more than its due share of barren mountain
and stony scrub-land which, like the Corsican *maquis*, can give little sustenance
for man or for his domestic animals, except the goat.[19] Thucydides, in his

(16) *Eccl.* 385, schol. on *Peace* 1310.

(17) Theodectes, fr. 17 (Nauck) *ap.* Strab. 695, where Strabo's own view is given. For Aristotle, cf. *G.A.* v. 3. 782 *b*, *H.A.* iii. 10. 517 *b* 17, [Arist.] *Probl.* xiv. 4.

(18) Eur. *Med.* 825, Plat. *Critias*, 109 B f.

(19) On this feature see J. L. Myres, *Inaug. Lect.* (Oxford 1910), p. 24, who shows that the
encroachment of scrubland is a continuous process, partly justifying Plato's geological theory.

dry way, had suggested that the claim of the Athenians to be autochthonous might be justified διὰ τὸ λεπτόγεων—the thin soil was no temptation to an invader. The inhabitants of Athens were Cranai, 'rock-men'; and, although the title was no doubt confined originally to the primitive settlement on the Acropolis, the ancients thought it appropriate to the whole of Attica. Plato was therefore forced to assume a cataclysmal change in the geological conditions after the mythical age of Athens. Since that prehistoric period—9000 years before Solon—only the 'bones of Attica' had been left, constant deluges having gradually washed away the fertile soil, and denuded the mountains of their finest trees. Attica was no longer the home of 'true farmers with the best land and the most abundant water, as well as the most temperate climate'; and Athenian character had correspondingly degenerated since the old heroic days.[20]

The geographical theory of race reaches its height in Polybius: 'we mortals,' says that historian, 'have an irresistible tendency to yield to climatic influence: and to this cause, and no other, may be traced the great distinctions which prevail amongst us in character, physical formation, and complexion, as well as most of our habits, varying with nationality or wide local separation.' In the introduction to the *Characters* of Theophrastus, the writer expresses surprise that Greek should differ so much from Greek, when all are beneath the same sky and share the same education; and his wonder—although Jebb calls it 'fatuous'—is really quite reasonable on the geographical hypothesis. Strabo seems to stand apart in doubting the effect of environment as the sole cause of variation. The geographer does ample justice to the received theory, emphasising, for example, the natural advantages of Italy, which helped to make Rome mistress of the world; but at the same time he refuses to work a single hypothesis to death. Climate would not account for everything. It would not explain the oratorical talent of the Athenians, which is lacking in their near neighbours the Spartans and Boeotians. The Greeks, in their days of greatness, were not helped, but hindered, by mountains, and the Romans have civilised many tribes in the most unfavourable regions. There is the further objection that, as he notes, the same stage of society—e.g. the Nomadic—is found in different kinds of country.[21]

Habit and training, he concludes, must be taken into account, although he does not explain *why* some nations have acquired better 'habits' than others. A modern upholder of the geographical school might argue that these habits

(20) Thuc. i. 2; cf. Plut. *Solon* 22. Xenophon, however, was enthusiastic over the natural advantages and fertility of Attica (*Vect.* i. 3). On the Cranai see schol. on Aristoph. *Av.* 123, Galen, *Protrept.* 7.

(21) Polyb. iv. 21 (Shuckburgh). For Strabo cf. 286 (122, 376, &c.) in favour of environment; his criticism is in 102 f., 136; cf. 501, 833. The Romans (e.g. Livy xxxviii. 17, Manil. iv. 711 f.) upheld the geographical theory, but laid more stress than the Greeks on heredity. For the modern 'anthropo-geographical' theory see E. C. Semple, *Influences of Geographic Environment.*

do ultimately, though not immediately, depend on the environment—i.e. that Athenian and Spartan characters were differentiated in remote ages when their respective ancestors lived further apart, and under natural conditions more diverse than those of Greece. To Strabo, who believed that both Athenians and Spartans were indigenous, this explanation was not open. But the Greeks in general had an almost pathetic confidence in the efficacy of Law—they had no doubt that a nation could be made sober by Act of Parliament—and Strabo was presumably satisfied with the power of the 'lawgiver' or the philosopher to counteract the effects of environment. Even Hippocrates, with his wholehearted belief in the influence of climate, had attached some weight to government as a factor in moulding national character—Europeans are more warlike than Asiatics, not only because of their climate and country, but because they are not ruled by a despot; and Plato, convinced as he was that 'on winds and temperature and water will depend the virtue or vice of a city's inhabitants,' was as firmly convinced that the final impress of character was stamped by education.[22] Man needs both education and a fortunate nature, if he is not to be the most savage of earthly beings; for breeding and training act and react; 'good nurture and education implant good natures, and these good natures, in their turn, being rooted in good education, improve, and this specially effects the breed in man as in other animals.'[23] Like all the Greeks, Plato had no doubt about the transmission of acquired characters.

By insisting on the paramount importance of training and education, the later Greeks escaped the fatalism of geographic environment—they realised to some extent that, whatever may be the effect of climate and environment on a race in a non-civilised stage, this effect is largely counteracted by civilisation. Race—however it is to be explained—is too rigid to be a mere reflex of locality. It is true that recent investigation rather tends to rehabilitate the Greek geographical theory, as far as physical types are concerned. An American Commission has shown that a change of environment may produce an immediate effect upon immigrants, races with long and short heads conforming equally to the more uniform type of their adopted country.* On the other hand, the persistence of broad racial characters—both physical and moral—under new conditions is a matter of common observation. Both backward and forward races have existed in all quarters of the earth; in Greece itself the Franks and Turks preserved their own physical character, and their own systems of social and political life, with but little conformity to the Hellenic model. A race—like the British—which has already acquired civilisation can migrate to an entirely different climate and retain its institutions with the least possible adaptation to the new environment. Strabo, in particular, stood far in advance of the mod-

---

*This refers to Boas' *Report*. See pp. 320-44 of the present volume.

(22) Hippocr. *de aere* 24; 16, 23. Plat. *Laws* 747 C f.

(23) *Rep.* 424 A, *Laws* 766 A. Plato here agreed with Democritus (ἡ διδαχὴ φρσιοποιέει [the doctrine of remolding] fr. 133 Mullach, p. 186).

ern Hippocrateans, who tried to unlock all ethnological doors with the single key of geography—of all, in fact, from Montesquieu to Buckle, who believed that the different aspects of nature were immediately reflected in the institutions or characters of different races.

To return to Herodotus. As we have just seen, the evidence of language, religion, and culture was important, but not final, while physique was of less value as an ethnical test. What really counted was tradition, even in face of difficulties presented by other criteria. The Sigynnae, a Danubian tribe, claimed to be Medes in origin. Geographically the two peoples were far apart, and Herodotus cannot suggest any proof of the claim, beyond some similarity in dress. But he knew of constant migrations among Greeks and barbarians in the ages preceding his own; and, just as it seemed possible for Aethiopians to be found in Asia and Africa, so Medes might well have migrated to the Danube. Anything, he says, may happen in course of time. So he accepts the bare tradition of the Sigynnae for the same reason that he is satisfied with the authority of Homer for the Aethiopians. As Prof. Myres observes, 'the Greeks themselves held family tradition to be good evidence of common descent; and as a matter of fact the professional genealogist has been beforehand with the anthropologist at nearly all points with the Greek-speaking world.'[24]

In dealing with the Hellenic race, the tests of language, religion, and culture were all favourable; but the final proof was the genealogy of Hellen—an article of faith as unquestioned by Thucydides as by Herodotus. Neither historian grasped the fact that Hellen had been invented to explain the Hellenes.

There was, however, a complication which disturbed the theory of a pure Hellenic stock. Herodotus knew of the 'Pelasgi,' pre-historic inhabitants of Greece, who had not been exterminated or expelled by Greek conquerors. On the contrary, the Arcadians claimed Pelasgian ancestry, and the Athenians were proud of the same descent; indeed, to the Dorian Herodotus only Dorians were originally Hellenic. Aeschylus had reckoned the Pelasgians as old Hellenes, without opening the question how or when the Hellenic race had come into being—the matter did not concern a poet. But the historian felt called upon to account for the relation of the two stocks; and, being obviously puzzled, he took refuge in the vague expression 'the Attic race, which was Pelasgian, learnt the [Greek] language when it changed to the Greeks.'[25] The metamorphosis was gradual, for the Attic Pelasgians had undergone several changes before they became Ionians under the leadership of Ion, grandson of Hellen; and thus contact with the eponymous hero is the last step in Hellenisation.

(24) Herod. v. 9. Myres in *Anthrop. and the Classics*, p. 142, and in *Anthrop. Essays* to E. B. Tylor, p. 255 f.

(25) Herod. i. 56 f., Aesch. *Supp.* 234, 914. See generally Macan on Herod. viii. 44, Myres, *l.c.* p. 152 and in *Journ. Hell. St.* xxvii. p. 170 f., E. Meyer, *Forsch.* i. p. 112 f.

Clearly, then, Herodotus did not regard the Greek race, as a pure stock, fixed from the beginning. His own city Halicarnassus, though a Dorian settlement, contained a large admixture of native Carians; yet the city was 'Greek.' Thucydides is more precise. In his account of Greek origins, Phthiotis appears as the home of the Hellenes, whose name gradually spread, as Pelasgians and other peoples came into contact with the race. Actual consanguinity therefore mattered but little, although no doubt Thucydides believed that long fusion of the original elements justified the later claim of common blood. But he definitely regards Hellenism as a bond of culture established by association, rather than as a racial term. A few years later, Isocrates, the sworn foe of barbarians and the champion of Greek unity, pays little heed to the hall-mark of race: 'our city,' he says, 'has caused the name of Greeks to appear no longer a sign of blood but of mind ($\delta\iota\alpha\nuo\iota\alpha\varsigma$); it is those who share our culture who are called Greeks rather than those who share our blood.'[26]

Plato, too, has visions of a wider horizon, transcending Greek limitations. He is not without political prejudice; for, although he rejects the dichotomy of Greek and barbarian as unscientific—the only ultimate distinction is between male and female—he is none the less emphatic in his practical distinction. The Greek race is one family, separate from all other stocks, and if Athenians are superior to the rest, it is because they are not contaminated by barbarian blood—a commonplace of Attic panegyrists.[27] His objection to slavery goes no further than a protest against Greek enslaving Greek. But there is no room for this prejudice in the dream of his final city, whose pattern is laid up, not in Greece, but heaven. The ideal is for all mankind; 'until philosophers are kings, or kings philosophers, neither the Greek cities *nor the human race* will be free from evil.' Of course, before this consummation can be attained, the world must come into the Hellenic fold. But the fold was open to receive the flock; Hellenism was independent of a single race, a gift to the world.

The Greek had no small pride of birth—we remember the jibes of Aristophanes about barbarians who wriggle into Athenian citizenship—but birth is chiefly valuable as the passport for entrance to the Greek city, with all its advantages of law and order, beauty and culture. Such an attitude had its drawbacks. It ministered to the Greek self-complacency. In Euripides, Jason suggests as an excuse for his faithlessness that he has really done Medea a service by bringing her from a barbarian land to Greece, where she can learn the meaning of justice. With this astonishing argument Euripides (though his own portrait of Medea is a sympathetic study of a foreigner) voices the patronising contempt of Greek for barbarian, which reaches its acme when a slave in comedy is supposed to feel an obligation to his master, 'through whom he learnt Greek laws, was taught letters and was initiated into the mysteries.' Freedom,

(26) Thuc. i. 3, Isocr. *Paneg.* 50.
(27) *Polit.* 262 D, *Rep.* 470 C.

we gather, is less important than philosophy, and we learn—even from Epicurus—that only Greeks can philosophise.[28]

On the other hand, the ancients were apparently quite free from the antipathy of the colour-bar, for reasons political, social, and anthropological. Politically, the later Greeks and the Romans—although they came into contact with various coloured peoples—were never called upon to exercise authority over large masses of dark-skinned races in India or Africa. From a social point of view, men were not classed as white or black, but as free or servile. Black slaves became fashionable (like black pages in England) after Alexander's conquests, and the purchase of an Ethiopian was a mark of 'petty ambition;'[29] but the great majority of slaves were of the same colour as their Greek or Roman masters. There was no occasion for the modern antipathy, whether this has arisen from the fact that slavery has been mainly confined to coloured races, or from the feelings of mistrust and dislike with which the emancipated slave has been regarded in America and elsewhere, or from the conditions of modern imperialism.[30]

Finally, as we have seen, the anthropology of the Greeks discountenanced any special stigma of colour, by regarding it as a mere geographical accident. The Greek was a monogenist: racial types of course exist, but they are not ultimate. To Aristotle man is a single species or εἶδος. He saw nothing abnormal in the Pygmies, 'who are really a small race, with small horses to match,' because such differences of physique, like other variations, could be explained by environment. Strabo, it is true, with his Stoic incredulity, thought the Pygmies to be a fable, and his scepticism was at least praiseworthy—'no credible witness has ever seen them.'[31] But here the Greeks in general agreed with Aristotle, and time has proved him to be right.

HERODOTUS: THE "FATHER"
OF ANTHROPOLOGY

JOHN LINTON MYRES (1869-1954), Wykeham Professor of Ancient History in the University of Oxford, classical scholar, and

---

(28) Eur. *Med.* 536, Theophilus in Bekker *An. Gr.* p. 724. For the monopoly of Greek philosophers see Epic. *ap.* Clem. Alex. *Strom.* i. 15, Diog. L. x. 117.

(29) Theophr. *Char.* vii. (xxi.) with Jebb's note.

(30) See Lord Cromer, *Ancient and Modern Imperialism*, p. 131 f.; Sir C. P. Lucas, *Greater Rome and Greater Britain*, p. 97.

(31) Arist. *H.A.* viii. 11. 597 *a* 6; Strabo, 821.

anthropologist, was a man of great charm and great learning. Myres did much to advance the cause of anthropology at a time, early in this century, when the subject had a difficult time receiving any form of recognition.

"Herodotus and Anthropology" was one of six lectures delivered before the University of Oxford by various authorities in 1907, and published together, edited by R. R. Marett, under the title *Anthropology and the Classics* (Oxford, Clarendon Press, 1908).

Myres' delightful lecture, which was clearly somewhat enlarged for the published version, tells us a great deal, in short compass, about Greek anthropology. Myres' comments on the two kinds of anthropologists is one of the wisest things ever said about those students of man.

Myres makes clear how far in advance Greek anthropology was of anything resembling it for more than two millennia afterward. Except for the Roman Lucretius' *De Rerum Natura*, which was written in the first century B.C., there was nothing in the ages that followed the decline of the ancient world to compare with Herodotus' *History*. Anthropologically the ages were comparatively dark and regressive until the eighteenth century. The evolutionary ideas of some Greek thinkers were so much in advance of anything that followed that we do not encounter their like again until Darwin.

Myres pays a well-deserved tribute to the remarkable anthropological acumen of Herodotus, whose *History* will always remain one of the most excitingly readable works of its kind. Herodotus' dates were 484?-425 B.C. It is around Herodotus and the writings of other fifth century Greek thinkers that Myres so fascinatingly reconstructs the method by which the early history of man and the causes of his variation and of his social condition were being investigated during the fifth century and earlier. It is beautifully done, and remains one of the most informative studies of its kind.

J. L. MYRES

HERODOTUS
AND ANTHROPOLOGY*

Between Homer and Herodotus, Greek Reason has come into the world. After Homer, Greek literature, whether poetry or prose, has its subjective, its reflective side. Man has become the measure of all things; and things are worth observing and recording—they become ἀξιαπήγητα, θέας ἄξια, [worth telling, worth looking at] or the reverse according as they do, or do not, amplify human knowledge already acquired, or prompt or guide human attempts to classify and interpret them. In this high meaning of the word all Greek thought and records are utilitarian, relative to an end in view: and this end is ever anthropocentric, it is nothing less, but it is also nothing more, than the Good Life, the Wellbeing of Mankind. On this broad ground, pre-Socratic and Socratic thought are at one, alike Hellenic in spirit, because alike utilitarian. 'It is not for this that I speculate,' said Thales, when he 'struck oil'. It was precisely for this, to make philosophy useful, that Socrates brought it from heaven down to earth.

So what is proposed, in this lecture, is to attempt an answer to the question, How far was a science of anthropology, in the sense in which we understand it, contemplated as possible in the Great Age of Greece? What were the principles on which it rested? How far had Herodotus and his contemporaries gone in the way of realizing their conceptions of such a science? And what were the causes, external to the study itself, which helped or hindered their realization of it?

It will be clear, I think, from the outset, that this inquiry has nothing to do with the question whether this or that observation on the part of Herodotus was accurately made or not. The only way in which Herodotean error or 'malignity' will concern us at all is if the sources of an error can be so far exposed as to betray what he was thinking about when he made it. For there are two kinds of anthropologists, as there are two kinds of workers in every department of knowledge. But in a science which is still in so infantile a stage as ours, there is more than common distinctness between them.

There is an anthropologist to whom we go for our facts: the painful accurate observer of data, the storehouse of infinite detail; sometimes himself the traveller and explorer, by cunning speech or wiser silence opening the secrets of aboriginal hearts; sometimes the middleman, the broker of traveller's winnings, insatiate after some new thing, unerring by instinct rather than by experience, to detect false coin, to disinter the pearl of great price, βιβλιοθήκη τις ἔμψυχος καὶ περιπατῶν μουσεῖον [living library and walking temple of learning]. To him we go for our facts. His views may matter little;

*Reprinted from R. R. Marett, ed., *Anthropology and the Classics* (Oxford, Clarendon Press, 1908), pp. 120-168.

his great book may be put together upon whatever ephemeral hypothesis he may choose. We learn his doctrine as we master the method of an index; it will guide us, more or less securely, to the data we want; but it is the document in the footnote that we are looking for, and the compiler's voucher (express or implicit) that in his judgement 'this is evidence'.

And there is an anthropologist to whom we look for our light. His learning may be fragmentary, as some men count learning; his memory faulty; his inaccuracy beyond dispute; his inconsistency the one consistent thing about him. But with shattered and rickety instruments he attains results; heedless of epicycles, disrespectful to the equator, he bequeaths his paradoxes to be demonstrated by another generation of men. He may not know, or reason, perhaps; but he has learnt to see; and what he sees he says. For he too is a μουσεῖον [temple of learning]—only in another sense—a Walking Tabernacle of the Nine.[1]

There have been anthropologists, in our own time and before, who have come near to combine both excellences: and in none perhaps are they wholly severed. Least of all do we expect to find both wholly present or wholly absent, in one who has in a sense fallen into anthropology by an accident; and created one science, while he pursued another art. In the Greek compiler who made this 'the plan of his researches, to procure that human acts should not be obliterated by time, and that great deeds, wrought some by the Greeks, some by men of other speech, should not come to lose their fame', we cannot but see a man who *meant*—with good or ill success—to be in the best sense 'a mine of information'. But it is the same Herodotus who put it before him in his title-page 'to discover, besides, the reason why they fought with one another'; and that is why we hail him Father of Anthropology, no less than the Father of History.

Either Herodotus knew himself to be hewing out a new avenue of knowledge, a new vista across the world; or he knew himself to be speaking to an audience of men who themselves were ἀνθρωπολόγοι [anthropologists]. That is the alternative, for those who are moved to deny his originality. If Herodotus was not in advance of his age, then his age was abreast of Herodotus. It becomes, therefore, our first duty to ask what evidence we possess as to the phase in which the fifth century held in mind the problems which for us are anthropological. Now apart from the Tragedians and Pindar, Herodotus, as we know to our discomfiture, is the only pre-Socratic *thinker* whose works have been preserved in bulk: and even his, as we are well assured, are preserved only in *bulk*, not in their entirety. So even the sceptic is driven back upon the alternative, either of arguing from silence and *lacunae*, or of disproving the originality of Herodotus from his very proficiency in the subject.

[1]The Muses were the daughters of Mnemosyne: but who was their Father?

But what can we learn of the state of anthropological knowledge in the days before Herodotus wrote?

The task of the anthropologist is, in its essence, to find an answer to these principal questions:—What is Man? What kinds of Men are there? and how and by what agencies are they formed, and distributed over the lands, as we find them? How is human life propagated under parental sanction, maintained by social institutions, and made tolerable by useful arts? And what part, if any, do either ἀνάγκη or λόγος or τύχη [necessity or reason or luck] play in defining these processes, and the general career of Mankind as an animal species?

Problems such as these were bound to present themselves sooner or later to so reasonable a people as the Greeks. There is no doubt that they were already so familiar, in the fourth century, as to be almost obsolete *as problems*. Otherwise we should find more importance attached to them in the writings of Plato and Aristotle. The question before us now is rather, how early did they present themselves; what methods were applied to deal with them; and how far had Greek thought gone towards a solution, when Socrates stepped down from his Cloud-basket, and substituted psychology as the proper study of Mankind?

To those who are familiar with the early phases of Greek physical inquiry, it is needless to repeat in detail how closely this movement was bound up, in its origin, with that great exploratory movement which littered the shores of the Mediterranean, from Tarsus to Tartessus, and from the Tanais to the Nile, with Greek factories and settlements, and brought all climates, lands, and varieties of men within the scope of one encyclopaedic vision; how the compilers of 'Circuits of the World' had surveyed all shores of 'their own Sea'; how the specialists had treated 'Air, Water, and Places' (if I may antedate the later catch-title) in accordance with the principles of their respective sciences; and how, on the other limit of knowledge, Milesian chronologers and astronomers—the latter with no small glimpses into the storehouse of Babylonian observation—had begun to make just such maps of all time human and geological as Milesian cartographers were making of 'all the sea and all the rivers'. Can we doubt that, in a movement of national inquiry, of this intensity and scope, the question was raised of the origin, the distribution, and the modes of subsistence of Man?

Direct evidence of the existence of an Ionian anthropology has evaded us for the most part. Yet, earlier still, we have the proof that something of the kind was stirring. Hesiod presents us already with a standard scheme of archaeology in which Ages of Gold, Silver, and Bronze succeed each other, classified by their respective artifacts, and succeeded, first by an Age of Heroes—an anomaly, partly of Homeric authority, partly genuine tradition of the Sea Raids and the Minoan *debâcle*—and then by an Age of Iron. More than this, the observation that primitive Man was a forest-dweller, who grew no corn, and subsisted on acorns and beech mast, presumes observation, and inference besides, which were perhaps obvious enough among men of the Balkan fringe, ancient and modern; but at the same time betrays a reasonable interest, and an eye for essentials, which are far beyond the average of archaic or barbarian speculation as to human origins.

Some fragments indeed of this pre-Socratic anthropology have come down to us directly; and, wherever they have done so, they show the same curious combination of folk-lore with mature insight, as do the views about non-human nature which are assigned to the same school. The belief, for example,[1] that human beings originated not by animal procreation, but by the operation of trees and rocks on women passing by, hardly differs in kind from the beliefs imputed to the Arunta; and the Hesiodic belief[2] that the men of Aegina were descended from ants, or men in general from stones dropped by Deucalion and Pyrrha,[3] to totemic beliefs or survivals. But the views ascribed to Anaximander, and later to Archelaus, both of Miletus, show something very far in advance of mere folk-lore. The lower animals were commonly believed to have been produced by spontaneous generation, the effect of the sun's heat on moist earth, slime, or sea water. Anaximander added the descriptive generalization,[1] based on observations on the shores of the sea about Miletus and the Maeander silt, that these lower forms began their cycle of existence 'encysted in prickly integuments, and then at maturity came out upon drier ground and shed their shells; but still went on living for a short while'. The older belief, as we have seen, was that men too originated in this way, either directly or from some invertebrate form, like the ants of Aegina. But Anaximander pointed out an obvious difficulty, and supplied also a solution of it. 'Man,' he said,[2] 'was produced in the first instance from animals of a different sort'; and this he argued 'from the fact that the other animals soon get their food for themselves, and Man alone needs a long period of nursing: for which very reason, a creature of this sort could not possibly have survived'. Here we must note first that a special creation of human beings ready made and mature, as Hebrew thinkers conjectured, and Greek poets had devised in the case of Pandora, was unthinkable to an Ionian naturalist, and merely does not come into question; secondly, that a special creation of human beings in infancy is equally ruled out by the fact of the long helplessness of the human infant; thirdly, that the inevitable alternative is accepted without a hint of hesitation, namely, that Mankind must have developed from some other kind of animal, which, though not human, could and did fend for its young during such an infancy as Man's. Only unacquaintance with the great apes of the tropical world, and very imper-

[1] Schol. *Od.* xix. 163.
[2] *Fr.* 64 (Didot).
[3] *Fr.* 25 (Didot).
[1] Plut. *De Plac. Phil.* v. 19 (Ritter and Preller, 7th ed., 16).
[2] Euseb. *Praep. Ev.* i. 8 (R. P. 16).

fect acquaintance even with imported monkeys, can have prevented Anaximander from assigning to Man his proper place in an evolutionary Order of *Primates*. The other half of our knowledge of Anaximander's anthropology is even more instructive. 'It is clear,' he says,[1] 'that men were first produced within fishes, and nourished like the "mud fish"—τραφέντας ι ὥσπερ οἱ πηλαῖοι; and, when they were competent to fend for themselves, were thereupon cast on shore (or perhaps "hatched out") and took to the land.' Our knowledge of the πηλαῖοι [mudfish] is limited; but the parallel passage throws some light on Anaximander's theory. 'The animals came into existence by a process of evaporation by the sun; but man came into existence in the likeness of another animal, namely, a fish, to begin with.' Here the theory is, clearly, that there was a stage in the evolution of Man when he ceased to conform to the type even of the highest of marine animals; and it was in the guise of some kind of fish that he took to the land. It is not so clear whether we have here merely the conjecture that at some stage marine vertebrates took the crucial step and invaded the dry land; or whether, also, the similitude of the 'mud-fish' is used to report observations which are familiar enough to embryologists now, and in the fifth century were no less familiar to Hippocrates.[2] In any case the views in points of detail which are reported as characteristic of Anaximander presuppose an almost Darwinian outlook on the animal kingdom, and an understanding of comparative anatomy, which hardly becomes possible again before the Renaissance.

No less striking is the testimony of the fragment of Archelaus,[1] one of the immediate teachers of Socrates, to the same evolutionary view. 'Concerning animals he said that when the earth became warm in the beginning in its lower part, where the hot and the cold were mixed, there came to light the rest of the animals, of many dissimilar kinds, but all with the same mode of life, maintained of the slime; and they were short-lived. But, afterwards, interbreeding occurred among these, and men were separated off from the rest, and they constituted leaders and customs and arts and cities and so forth. And, he says, reason is implanted in all animals alike; for each uses it according to his bodily frame, one more tardily, another more promptly.' Here again we have the biological theory of evolution in a most explicit form, with the same distinction as in Anaximander between the short-lived, infusorian, almost amorphous fauna of sun-warmed water or slime, and the higher orders of thinking vertebrates, among whom Man stands merely as an exceptionally rational species.

After this, it is almost needless to note that the physical anthropology of the Greeks was quite unimpeded by those literary misconceptions which so long retarded the study of Man in the modern world. Hecataeus, indeed, had

---

[1] Plut. *Symp. Quaest.* viii. 8. 4 (R. P. 16).

[2] Hippocrates, περὶ φύσιος παιδίον [Concerning the Nature of the Young Child] (ed. Kuhn, Leipzig, 1825, p. 391).

[1] Hippolytus, *Ref. Haer.* i. 9 (R. P. 171).

at one time been misled by the shortness of Greek pedigrees; but his Egyptian researches gave him in good time the larger perspective,[2] as even his critic Herodotus admits. And the first reporter of the fact that Egypt is the 'gift of the Nile' can hardly have failed to see the bearing of this piece of geology upon the question of the antiquity of Man. Herodotus, at all events, has no illusions.[1] Achelous and other rivers are there to show that the Nile is no freak of nature; time future can be postulated to the extent of twenty thousand years; and time past may be measured on the same scale, for the perfecting of the Nile's gift, not to mention the further periods required for the deposit of the shells in the Pyramid limestone.[2] More explicitly still, he is prepared to allow indefinite time for the development and dissemination of human varieties. *How* the Danubian Sigynnae came to be colonists of the Medes, he is not prepared to say; but the thing itself is not in his view impossible. γένοιτο δ' ἂν πᾶν ἐν τῷ μακρῷ χρόνῳ [Anything may happen in the course of time].[3]

It is at this point in our story that we must look at the evidence of Aeschylus. Small as is that portion of his works which has come down to us, it is of high value, both as a record of current knowledge, and as an indication of the contemporary phases of theory. Already we have the elements of the later threefold division of the anthropological horizon corresponding essentially with the tri-continental scheme of the geographers, with which we know from a fragment of *Prometheus Solutus* that Aeschylus was acquainted at a stage of its development, which the quotation fixes for us precisely.[4] Ethnologically, the ἐσχατιαί [most remote of men] are as follows:—Northwards, are found the Hyperboreans.[5] Eastwards, lie the Indians; they are camel-riding nomads, and live next to the Aethiopians.[1] Southward come the Aethiopians proper,[2] with Egypt, the gift of the Nile,[3] and Libya. The black skin of the Aethiopians is sun-tanned.[4] Aethiopia embraces everything from the φοινικόπεδον ἐρυθρᾶς ἱερὸν χεῦμα θαλάσσης to the χαλκοκέραυνον παρ' Ὠκεανῷ λίμναν παντοτρόφον Αἰθιόπων [from the sacred red-bottomed spring of the Erythrean sea to the gleeming all-nourishing threshold of the Ethiopians beside the ocean] where the Sun rests his horses;[5] that is, from the southern margin of Asia (where the Indians live) to the far South-West. In front of the Aethiopians lie the Libyans; in front of the Indians the Empire of Persia (for there are no

[2]Herodotus ii. 143.
[1]Herodotus ii. 10-11.
[2]Herodotus ii. 12.
[3]Herodotus v. 9.
[4]Aeschylus, *Fr.* 177.
[5]*Fr.* 183.
[1]*Suppl.* 286.
[2]*Fr.* 303.
[3]*Fr.* 290.
[4]*P. V.* 808.
[5]*Fr.* 178.

Indians in the *Persae*, and Bactria is the remotest province); in front of the Hyperboreans, the Scythians, the Abioi of Homer, and the Arimaspi; all nomad pastoral peoples.

At the margin of ethnological Man, sometimes merely unisexual, sometimes misanthrope, stand the Amazons: in the *Supplices* they seem to stand for the North,[6] and they lie beyond Caucasus in the *Prometheus*;[7] beyond that margin, there are the one-eyed, breast-eyed, and dog-headed tribes of Hesiod and of common report.

Hesiodic too, in its main outlines, is the sketch of primitive Man in the *Prometheus*, with its hint of spontaneous generation[8] and its fourfold scheme of useful metals.

But for Aeschylus the tribes of men are sundered rather by culture than by race. The two women in Atossa's dream are like sisters in form and figure; it is by their dress that she knows one of them to be Persian, the other Greek.[1] So, too, the king in the *Supplices*[2] knows the Danaid chorus for foreign women by their dress. They might be Amazons, for there are no men with them; but no! they carry no bows.[3] Stay! they *do* carry κλάδοι [entwined olive branches]: that surely is Greek.[4] μόνον τόδ᾽ ἑλλὰς χθὼν συνοίσεται στόχῳ [The Greeks alone of the earth's inhabitants carry these twisted things.] Only in the second place comes language, to decide in a case where dress and accessories are indecisive;[5] and only when the Danaids assure him that they are really Argive, and of his own kin, are new doubts raised by their build and complexion,[6] and he questions again whether they are Libyans (with the Nile and the Κύπριος χαρακτήρ [Cyprian character] thrown in, for the aesthetic types of Egyptian and Graeco-Assyrian art), or Indians, or Amazons; outlanders, that is, of the South, the East, or the North, as we have seen.

These preliminary notes have been designed to give such retrospect over the course of Greek anthropological theory as our fragmentary sources allow: but they have been enough, I hope, to show where matters stood in the lifetime of Herodotus, and also to some degree what the burning questions—or some of them—were. Now we come to Herodotus himself, to take the elements of his anthropology in similar order, and put them into their respective places.

First then, Herodotus gives us for the first time a reasoned scheme of

[6]*Suppl.* 287.

[7]*P. V.* 723.

[8]Compare μύρμηκες [ant hill] in *P. V.* 453 with Hes. *Fr.* 64, about the aborigines of Aegina, and with Lucretius v. 790 ff.

[1]*Persae*, 181 ff.

[2]*Suppl.* 234 ff.

[3]*Suppl.* 287-8.

[4]*Suppl.* 241-3.

[5]*Suppl.* 244-5.

[6]*Suppl.* 279 ff.

ethnological criteria; and it marks at once an advance on that of Aeschylus, and an important modification of it. In the famous passage where the Athenians reject the proposals of Alexander of Macedon, and against immense inducements refuse to desert the Greek cause, they state as their inducement the fourfold bond which holds a nation together. 'Greece,' they reply,[1] 'is of one blood; and of one speech; and has dwelling-places of gods in common, and sacrifices to them; and habits of similar customs': and that is why the Athenians cannot betray their nation. Common descent, common language, common religion, and common culture: these are the four things which make a nation one; and, conversely, the things which, if unconformable, hold nations apart. To this analysis, modern ethnology has little or nothing to add. It might be said, as Professor Flinders Petrie has suggested,[2] that identity of religious beliefs is in the last resort only a peculiarly refined test of conformity of behaviour between man and man; and that community of culture, beyond dumb interchange of artefacts, is inconceivable without community of speech. But the mode of propagation, both of language and of religious observance, differs so greatly in kind from that of the transmission of material culture, that the forcible reduction of the four criteria of Herodotus to the two major criteria of Physique and Culture fails us in practice almost as soon as it is made. So far as Herodotus presents us with an ordered scheme of anthropological thought—with a science of anthropology, in fact—he is little, if at all, behind the best thought of our own day.

It is not, I think, pressing his language too far, if we regard him as stating these four criteria in what he regarded as the order of their relative importance. First, for scientific as for political purposes, comes community of descent; next, community of language; then community of religion; and general community of observance, in daily life, only at the end of all. Contrast with this the method of inquiry in the *Supplices*, where, as we saw, dress and equipment come first, then religious observance, then language; and physique is postponed to all three. That this is not accidental will be seen, I think, from an example of the Herodotean anthropology when applied, so to speak, 'in the field,' to the description of the northern Argippaei where each successive criterion is introduced by a δέ which is adversative to the preceding clause.[1] Here the physical anthropology is given first; then the language, which distinguishes

---

[1]viii. 144 αὖτις δὲ τὸ Ἑλληνικόν, ἐὸν ὅμαιμόν τε καὶ ὁμόγλωσσον, καὶ θεῶν ἰδρύματά τε κοινὰ καὶ θυσίαι ἤθεά τε ὁμότροπα, τῶν προδότας γενέδθαι Ἀθηναίους οὐκ ἂν εὖ ἔχοι.

[2]*Religion and Conscience in Ancient Egypt*, pp. 18-20.

[1]Herodotus iv. 23 ἄνθρωποι λεγόμενοι εἶναι (1) πάντες φαλακροὶ ἐκ γενετῆς γινόμενοι, καὶ ἔρδενες καὶ θήλεαι ὁμοίως καὶ σιμοὶ καὶ γένεια εχοντες μεγάλα, (2) φωνὴν δὲ ἰδίην ἱέντες, (3) ἐσθῆτι δὲ χρεώμενοι Σκυθικῇ, (4) ζῶντες δὲ ἀπὸ δενδρέων. [These men are said to be bald from birth, both men and women alike, and to have snub noses and long chins. They speak a peculiar language, dress like Sythians, and live on the fruits of a tree.] An exactly similar series of adversatives follows in the very next sentence, about the *Pontikon* tree.

these Argippaei from *all* other men, and so forms a cross division athwart the criterion of physique; then, *though* they have a language of their own, yet, till they speak to you, you would not think it, for their dress is Scythian; but after all, Scythians they cannot be, because no Scythian lives on tree-fruit. He is a pastoral nomad, or at best an ἀροτὴρ ἐπὶ πρήσι [ploughman]. Here ἤθεα ὁμότροπα [like habits] hold the last and lowest place; and the cause of this is plain: for their witness agrees not together.

There is a reason for this new emphasis on community of blood and of language in the anthropology of Herodotus. If the Persian War had shown nothing else, it had shown the superior efficiency of an army which was mutually intelligible, over one which might have met, not in Kritalla, but in Shinar; and even more forcibly it had impressed the belief, that what mattered was not equipment, nor language, but breed. It was the Persians who could survey and mark a sea channel like a modern Admiralty,[1] and amazed their captive by those unfamiliar drugs and 'shield-straps made of silky linen' which we call surgical bandages;[2] but it was their prisoner Pytheus who amazed them by the physique and the training which brought him through, when he was literally 'mangled to butcher's meat'.

And there is another reason for this emphasis. Right in sight of Halicarnassus, and hardly two hours' sail, lies the town of Cos, and in its *agora* [market] to-day stands the great plane-tree of Hippocrates; and during the lifetime of Herodotus there was growing up there that latest and fairest flower of pre-Socratic knowledge, the Coan medical school, with an anatomy, a physiology, and an anthropology of its own, superior by far to anything which succeeded it until the seventeenth century.

In what relation the professional science of Hippocrates stood to the penumbral knowledge of Herodotus, and also to the learning and speculations of their predecessors, may be illustrated from their respective treatment of the phenomenon of beardlessness in Man.

All Mediterranean peoples, and all sedentary peoples of the European mainland, agree in this, that their adult males have copious hair upon the face. Herodotus and his contemporaries had no means of foreseeing that this was really the exception rather than the rule among human varieties; that neither the yellow- nor the black-skinned races have this appendage except in a rudimentary degree, and in circumstances which suggest contamination more or less direct with the white men of the north-western quadrant of the Old World. Only the fact that the Australians are hairier in face and person even than the whites saves us from the temptation to adopt into anthropology the popular supersititon that the long beard is correlated with the superior brain. But for Herodotus and the Greek world, beards on men were the rule, and beardlessness an abnormality to be explained.

[1]Herodotus vii. 183.
[2]Herodotus vii. 181.

Now from Homeric times, and before, the Nearer East had been startled
by the raids of a warrior people governed and defended by beardless creatures
of wondrous horsemanship and archery, their bows in particular such as no
mere man could use; inspired, moreover, with a fury like the fury of a woman,
against everything that showed a beard. Beyond the Caucasus they ate their
prisoners; in Tauris they killed all men, at the bidding of beardless leaders;[1]
one band of them penetrated into free Scythia, and were actually taken for
women; among their Sarmatian descendants men and women hunted and fought
side by side. But they were not confined to the trans-Euxine grassland. In
Asia Minor, when King Priam was a lad, they had occupied the plateau, and
were resisting the Thraco-Phrygian invasion. Further to the South-East, another
body of them had harried all Assyria in the seventh century, and at Askalon
their beardless descendants survived. τοῖσι τούτων αἰεὶ ἐκγόνοισι ἐνέσκηψε
ὁ θεὸς θήλεαν νοῦσον [The god sent the female disease to their descendants].
The same defect was observable in one element in the male population of
Scythia in the fifth century.[1] Here we detect three stages of discovery. First,
the beardless people are assumed to be women. Next it is discovered, both
in Scythia and in Palestine, that though beardless (and indeed otherwise hairless) they are really men. Thirdly, the collateral discovery that some mounted
archers were actually women, as in Sarmatia, is held to reaffirm the legends
of Amazons; in spite of the fact that their Sarmatians descendants were known
to belong to a bisexual society, and talked a dialect of Scythian. Thus
Herodotus and his predecessors were put, after all, on a wrong track, in their
inquiry why some Scythians are beardless, and some are not. The test case
is at Askalon; where the Scythians who remained were admittedly beardless;
and the guess was loosely accepted, that all the bearded ones had escaped
the curse and gone away. The outstanding fact is the presence of similar
ἀνδρόγυνοι [hermaphrodites] in Scythia itself; and at this point, candid as ever,
Herodotus throws the outstanding fact into his reader's lap, and passes on to
other things.

At this point we turn to Hippocrates. Here we are at once in the full current
of Ionic rationalism. The theological explanation of the phenomena is rejected
at the outset. 'For my own part, I think these ailments are from God, and
all the other ailments too; and no one of them more divine than another, or
more human either, but all alike from God. Each of such things has a process
of growth, and nothing comes into being without a process of growth.'[1]

The ground thus cleared, Hippocrates notes four points. In the first place

[4]Herodotus iv. 110.
[1]The phrase of Herodotus i. 105, if interpreted strictly, means that the Scythians of Scythia
themselves suffered from this defect, and gave as the reason for it the story which he relates.
[1]Hippocrates, περὶ ἱερῆς νούσου (ed. Kuhn, Leipzig, p. 561), ἐμοὶ δὲ καὶ αὐτέῳ δοκεῖ ταῦτα
τὰ πάθεα θεῖμ Εἶναι καὶ τμλλα πάντα, καὶ οὐδὲν ἕτερον ἑτέρου
θειότερον οὐδὲ ἀνθρωπινώτερον, ἀλλὰ πάντα θεῖα ἕκαστον καὶ ἔχει φύσιν τῶν τοιουτέων,
καὶ οὐδὲν ἄνευ φύσιος γίγνεται.

beardlessness, and its reputed concomitants, were limited to Scythians of wealth, which he explains to be synonymous with hereditary rank; or at least were most common among these. Hippocrates, it is true, puts this down to their equestrian habit, not to a difference of race. Yet it is clear, from Herodotus' account, that the Scythian aristocracy were the result of a quite recent irruption of a purely nomad people from beyond the Tanais, which had displaced, though not wholly, the former population of Scythia. Secondly, he observes that the Scythians in general differ wholly in physique from the rest of the peoples of Europe; but he does not on that ground raise the question of an immigrant origin. The reason for this omission, however, is clear from his third point, that the abnormality in question is such as might be predicted from a consideration of the climate and mode of life of any human inhabitants of Scythia. After this, his fourth point brings him right up to the brink of discovery, though it is not pressed to its logical conclusion by further research; for he is clear both that the beardlessness could exist without further disabilities, and also that, in addition to climate and customs conducive to this bodily habit, the Scythians were naturally inclined to be beardless. But the first of these facts he ascribes, not without professional excuse, to successful preventive treatment; and the latter was clearly regarded by him as the incipient effect of climate and the like upon persons who were congenitally normal. It is curious, meanwhile, that he does not make use of the crucial instance of the beardless Scythians at Askalon, to test his conclusion that beardlessness and the like are the effect of climate; for the climate of Askalon differs from that of Scythia in almost every important particular. It is permissible, however, to suggest that we have here one of the numerous instances in which important statements are recorded by Herodotus, which, whether true or false in themselves, failed for some reason to become assimilated by the learned world of the fourth century.

Herodotus, however, was still anything but satisfied as to the paramount value of the physical criterion of kinship. In the majority of cases it proved either too much or too little. A good instance is his comparison of the Colchians with the Egyptians. Here he bases his argument for their affinity on their common physical characters, dark skin and woolly hair. But this proves too much: there are other peoples with dark skin and woolly hair, who are certainly *not* of Egyptian origin. On the other hand it proves too little; for what he proposes to establish here is not a general community of origin, but direct Egyptian colonization within historic times. For this proof, he prefers to rely on the evidence of a ceremonial custom which he regards as typically African; for it is both Egyptian and Aethiopian; and, as it happens to be a custom involving mutilation of the person, it belongs, as we shall see presently, to a class of observances which were regarded by Greek anthropology as competent to effect real changes of physique in course of time. The merely external evidence of a common industry, such as the linen-weaving which he adduces here, clearly stands for Herodotus on a lower plane, along with their general similarity of culture and language.

Clearly Herodotus was not quite satisfied as to the value of racial types in anthropology. And there were several reasons for this. On the one hand, the Greeks themselves held family tradition to be good evidence of common descent; and as a matter of fact, the professional genealogist had been beforehand with the anthropologist at nearly all points within the Greek-speaking world. Traditions of common descent, in fact, were too deeply fixed already in popular belief, and involved too many practical questions, such as the rights to real property, or to political privilege, to be treated as anything but valid evidence of kinship. Consequently a people's own account of their origin, or whatever story was accepted as such, was held to be evidence of a high order. Such price did Greek science pay for the actual solidarity of Greek phylic institutions.

For example, the Sigynnae of the Middle Danube 'say that they are a colony of Medes. How they have come to be a colony of Medes, I for my part cannot say for certain: yet anything might happen if you give it long enough'.[1] Herodotus is prepared, that is', to allow infinite time to accomplish an almost impossible migration, rather than give up what he accepts as a people's own account of their origin. But obviously this principle of ethnography was likely to lead to great difficulties. The Sigynnae, it is true, wore 'Median dress', presumably trousers of some kind, and perhaps a shaped cap with earguards, no less suitable to a Danubian than to a Median winter. But what of their physique? In this instance Herodotus gives no details; but clearly if conflict were to occur between the evidence for descent and for physique—if, that is, a people claimed descent from another people of a different physical type—it might be the difference of physique which would stand in need of explanation.

There was another reason, besides, why traditions of common descent should seem to deserve tender treatment, even when geographical probability was against them. The whole Eastern Mediterranean was still but imperfectly recovering itself after one of those periods of prolonged and intense ethnic stress to which it is exposed by the permeability of its northern frontier. From Thrace to Crete there were fragmentary patches of Pelasgians; Phrygians from Macedon to Peloponnese, far up the Adriatic, and in Western Sicily; Thracians in Naxos and Attica; and Lydians at Askalon. The Ionian merchant, like the Venetian of a later time, found everywhere before him the tracks of the crusading Achaean. The Dorian Spartan in Cyprus, at Soli and Kerynia, found Kurion already the colony of an earlier Argos; at Tarentum he merely filled a vacant niche in an Achaean, almost a Homeric Italy. If things like these could happen within four or five hundred years, γένοιτο δ ἂν πᾶν ἐν τῷ μακμῷ χρόνῳ [Anything may happen in the course of time]. Outside the Greek world it was

[1]Herodotus v. 9.

the same. Where Sesostris had been, the Scythian and Kimmerian had followed, leaving their trail at Sinope and Askalon, as he in Colchis. Nebuchadnezzar had set the Jews by the waters of Babylon. Darius was but following the rule when he moved Paeonians to Asia Minor, and transplanted Eretrians to Ardericca.

There was another reason also why racial type should be held liable to easy change. The Greeks themselves, and most of their neighbours, were mongrel peoples, for reasons which we have just seen; and there is no doubt that climate and mode of life were actually resulting in ruthless and rapid elimination of intrusive types, wherever these were intolerant of Mediterranean conditions. Now in most of the states of Ionia the blood of the citizens was mixed beyond hope of disentanglement, even by family tradition; for family tradition, as Professor Murray has shown us,[1] was for the most part shattered in the migrations. Yet the external conditions were the same for all; and men saw their blonder kinsmen and townsmen fade and cease out of the land, without fully realizing that what needed explanation was not their failure to survive, but their presence in those latitudes at all. The result, for ethnology, was to encourage a belief that mankind in itself was a pure-bred species, one and indivisible like any other natural kind; and that the marked variations between white and black, straight-haired and woolly-haired peoples, were exclusively the result of climatic, if not human, selection.

Yet another consideration drove men's thoughts inevitably in the same connexion. One of the best inheritances of Greece from the Minoan world was an elaborate apparatus of cultivated plants and animals: our evidence from dogs, and olive-kernels, begins, I think, to justify this view.[1] And in so minutely subdivided a region, special breeds of local origin were bound to result at an early phase of industry; and to be compared and discussed in the markets and on the quays. Every one knew, in fact, that domesticated animals and plants, under human direction, were tolerant of almost infinite and very rapid alteration: and Man himself is the most highly domesticated of all. It is no wonder then that in the fourth century Socrates is represented as arguing habitually as if Man were a domesticated animal, whose breed could be improved at will, and in any direction, physical or psychological. For even psychological breeding had long been reduced to an art, both with horses and with dogs.

Demonstrable migrations of men, therefore, and demonstrable mutations both of men and of animals, offered evidence of a kind which it was difficult to overlook, that natural characters were variable, and also that acquired ones could become hereditary. It was, in fact, not because the Greeks knew so little, but because on certain crucial points they already knew so much, that they formed the views they did as to the instability of human varieties. How far

---

[1] Murray, *The Rise of the Greek Epic*, p. 69.
[1] Egypt, of course, had done great things in this direction under the earliest dynasties.

these views were pressed to their conclusions will be seen best, I think, from a glance at the teaching of Hippocrates, which we may safely take to be near the highwater-mark of fifth-century thought on immediately pre-Socratic lines.

A good example of the doctrine of Hippocrates is contained in his anthropology of the Phasis valley, a region which falls sufficiently within the same limits as the Colchis of Herodotus to be worth comparing with his description of the Colchians. Indeed there is some reason to believe that, for reasons both of geographical theory and of popular ideas of utility, this corner of Hither Asia was attracting a good deal of learned attention from the physicists of Greece. This is what Hippocrates[1] has to say about the Phasis and its people. 'That country is marshy and warm and well watered and thickly clothed with vegetation, and there is heavy and violent rainfall there at all seasons, and the habitat of its men is in the marshes, and their houses are of wood and rushes ingeniously erected in the water, and they do but little walking to and from town and market, but they sail to and fro in dug-out canoes. For there are numerous artificial canals. The waters they drink are warm and stagnant and putrefied by the sun, and replenished by the rains. The Phasis itself too is the most stagnant of all rivers, and of the gentlest current. And the fruits which grow there are all unwholesome, for they are effeminated [he is thinking of the abundance of fleshy pulpy fruit, like the stone fruits—plums, apricots, and nectarines—which were characteristic of this region in antiquity] and flabby by reason of the abundance of water. And that is why they do not ripen fully. And much mist envelops the country as a result of the water. For just these reasons the Phasians have their bodily forms different from those of all other men. For in stature they are tall, in breadth they are excessively broad, and no joint or vein is to be seen upon them. Their complexion is yellow as if they had the jaundice. Their voice is the deepest of all men's, because their atmosphere is not clear but foggy and moist. And for bodily exertion they are naturally somewhat disinclined.'

Here we see an unqualified doctrine of the plasticity of human nature, physical and mental, under the influence of climate and geographical environment, such as his description of the Scythians has led us to suspect already. An adjacent passage adds the further theoretical point, that even acquired variations of wholly artificial character may become hereditary in time. The case is that of the Macrocephali, whose haunts unfortunately are not specified.[1] 'In the beginning it was their custom which was chiefly responsible for the length of their head, but now, their mode of growth too reinforces their custom. For they regard as best bred those who have the longest head.' Then he describes how the heads are remodelled in infancy by massage and bandaging; and proceeds: 'At the beginning the practice itself had the result that their mode of

[1]Hippocrates, περὶ Ἀέρων [Concerning air, water, and land] (ed. Kuhn), p. 551.
[1]Hippocrates, περὶ Ἀέρων [Concerning air, water, and land] (ed. Kuhn), p. 550.

growth was of this kind. But as time went on, it came to be inbred so that their law was no longer compulsory': ἐν φύσει ἐγένετο ὥστε τὸν νόμον μηκέτι ἀναγκάζειν. He then explains that just as baldness and grey eyes and physical deformities are hereditary (for he makes no distinction between natural and acquired varieties), 'now similarly they do not grow at all as they did before: for the practice has no longer any force, through the people's own neglect of it.'

The bearing of this passage, and the doctrine which it expounds, on Herodotus' account of the Colchi, will be obvious at once. Clearly, if the proportions of the head can be affected by artificial pressure, reinforced by social selection of the most successfully deformed—that is to say, of the individuals with the softest skulls; and if, as Hippocrates clearly thought, the colour of the eyes, and presence or absence of hair, were characters of the same order of transmissibility; and if, further, as in the case of the Phasians, skin-colour and bodily proportions resulted from climate and occupation; then clearly it mattered comparatively little to Herodotus whether the Colchians were woolly-haired or not. Woolly hair, like baldness, could be inherited indeed; but it could also be superinduced, like macrocephaly, by assiduous curling, or, as every barber knows, by the subtler influence of atmospheric moisture. It is consequently not only because, as suggested above, there were other woolly-haired people, besides the Egyptians and Colchians who were in question, that Herodotus has recourse to other evidence than that of physique to prove their identity: it is because, for fifth-century anthropology, the evidence of physique itself did not justify conclusions of appreciably higher validity than those which resulted from the comparison of industries or customs.

It will be seen from all this that in questions relating to the evolution of Man, Herodotus exhibits—and shares with the whole thought of his time—precisely the opposite weakness to that of the pioneers of modern anthropology. His mistakes arise, not because he is unable to allow time enough for evolutionary changes, but because he tries to crowd too great an amplitude of change into the liberal allowance of time which he is prepared to grant. Ten thousand years, or even twenty thousand, would be a short allowance, in modern geology, for even so active a river as the Nile to fill up the whole Red Sea; but it is more than double the whole length allotted to 'geological time' within the memory of men still living.

It will also be clear how deep was the impression created on the Greek mind by the minor changes of the seasons and of history. The formula of Heracleitus, πάντα ῥεῖ καὶ οὐδὲν μένει [Everything flows, nothing remains still], had indeed its application to metaphysic; but its origin was in physical science, as a generalization from experience. It had its negative interest as an implement of sceptical destruction. But it had also a high positive value, for it formulated the present as transitional from the past to the future; it emphasized the kinetic and physiological aspect of nature and of science, which has ever been of so far higher value, in research, as in life, than the static and morphological; it substituted an analysis of processes for classification of the qualities of things.

Now it is to this phase of scientific theory that we must assign the first intrusion into scientific terminology of the twin words φύσις [nature or natural processes] and νόμος [law]; in their primitive sense they denote nothing else than precisely such natural processes in themselves, on the one hand, and man's formulation of such processes, on the other.

It is the more important to keep in mind this fundamental conception of Greek physical anthropology when we go on to consider either the treatment of the evidence of language and culture, which we find in Herodotus, or the applications of physical classification to the purposes of logic and metaphysic. To take the latter first: a doctrine of the real existence of natural kinds, corresponding each, as Hippocrates would put it, to a process of growth peculiar to itself, was clearly easier to understand, if not to discover and formulate, when the men who were to discuss it were already brought up to regard the animal world, for example, as consisting of a comparatively small number of fundamental types, and the infinite variety of individual and regional forms as the effect of external forces upon them. Each actual example of horse or dog, for example, was to be regarded on the one hand as the embodiment of a true equine or canine nature, which reason might hope to detect and isolate; but on the other, it lay like the god Glaucus, encrusted with accidental qualities, the effects of its exposure to a particular environment. Seen in the light of their pre-Socratic history, as elements in the terminology of a great school of naturalists, the catch-words φύσις [nature], γένος [race or descent], εἶδος [species], and συμβεβηκὸς [chance or chance event] gain something, I think, in significance. In particular, it becomes clearer why the word εἶδος [species], which continued to be used among the naturalists for the specific outcome of συμβεβηκότα [chance] upon a member or members of a γένος [race], came among the philosophers to supersede the word γένος [race] in proportion as the centre of reflective interest shifted from the objective exponent of a φύσις [nature] to the subjective standpoint of the philosophic observer.

For Herodotus, meanwhile, language and culture can change under stress of circumstances in just the same way as physique; and therefrom follows the possibility of the transmission of culture. Whether any particular custom was to be regarded as innate in the φύσις of those who practised it, or as their response to the stresses of their present environment, or as the result, whether conformable to the environment or not, of intercourse with another variety of Man, was a question to be settled on the merits of each case. It was, in fact, partly the laxness of interest in such matters which resulted from the prevalent theory, and only partly the admitted incompleteness of the observations, that kept ethnographical speculation in so backward a state as we find it in

Herodotus' time. Until the belief in stronger specific characters could be supplemented by some doctrine of cultural momentum, the conception of progress in civilization was hardly attainable at all. This is where the treatment of Hellenic civilization by Herodotus stands in so marked a contrast with his treatment of the civilizations of Egypt and Outland. Egyptian civilization, like Egypt itself, is the gift of the Nile; the φύσις of an Indian attains its τέλος when he has ridden his camels and rescued his gold; the men are black, or tall, or longlived as the effect of natural causes; and as long as these causes persist, so long will there be Indians or Aethiopians with those qualities. Only in Greece is there mastery of man over nature, and that not because nature is less strong, but because Greek man is strong enough to dominate it.

This is how it comes about that barriers of language and of culture, no less than barriers of descent, are powerless in face of a well-defined γένος [race] with a potent φύσις [nature] of its own. Such a γένος [race] can add to the number of individuals which compose it. Pelasgians and Lelegians can *become* Hellenes. For Herodotus, as I have explained more in detail elsewhere, the process of conversion of barbarians to the Hellenic φύσις [nature] is not clear: the verbs which he employs, μετέβαλον, μετέμαθον, [changed, relearned] are intransitive; the general impression which is conveyed is of a kind of spontaneous generation: and the same language is used when τὸ Ἑλληνικόν [the Greek] is described as ἀποσχιοθὲν ἀπὸ τοῦ βαρβάρου [split off from the barbarian] in the earliest phase of all. For Thucydides, on the other hand—as was natural to an Athenian who had seen Atticism triumphant in Hellas—Hellenism is acquired by contact with, and imitation of, the φύσις [nature] of a genuine Hellene. Of course this explanation of Pelasgian conversion only pushes the problem itself one stage further back; but it marks a distinct advance in analysis beyond the point reached by Herodotus; and it is an advance in precisely the opposite direction to that in which naturalists like Hippocrates were being led through their greater insistence on the external factors, which were the main subject of their study. Thucydides in fact stands already on the Socratic side of the line. The explanation of the transmissibility of culture is to be sought for him not in physiology, but in psychology—not in spontaneous or coercive adjustment to inexorable nature, but in intercourse with enlightened minds.

Among the many different classes of information which Herodotus inclines to give about foreign peoples, two kinds of data are more insistently recorded than the others. There are the marriage customs, and the principal source of food. These will be admitted to be obvious points to note; but there was a special motive in the fifth century for collecting each of them; and the history of thought in the century which followed allows us to trace this motive forward into a maturer context.

The problem of the status of the sexes in society was not a new one in fourth-century Greece. As far back, indeed, as we can trace social institutions directly at all, society in Greece had been constituted on patriarchal lines. But patriarchal institutions had far less undisputed acceptance in the Greek world

than they had for example in Italy. It was not merely that Attic rules of inheritance gave a definite, though at all times secondary, status to the mother's
kindred; or that in Sparta, Thebes, and some other states, the women enjoyed
in many respects a social equality with the men which has been explained
in more ways than one. An Ionian Greek had only to travel down his own
coast as far as Lycia to find men reckoning descent through the mother, or
to travel back in imagination to the legendary origins of his own people, to
find that their pedigrees went often up, not to a god, but to a woman. Olympian
society was the same. The consort of Zeus held a very different position from
that of the wife in a patriarchal household; and on the Asiatic shore, at least,
the gods themselves were traced back to a Mother, not to a Father, of them
all.

Hints, too, were not wanting as to the recent arrival, and un-Aegean origin,
of the patriarchal system, which had now prevailed, with its proprietary view
of women; and, no less, of the loose hold which this set of customs had upon
the popular belief and opinion. In the opening chapters of his history,
Herodotus states, and allows his Περσέων λόγιοι [skilled Perisan orator] to
criticize freely, what might be summarized as a *cherchez-la-femme* theory of
the Eastern Question: and the criticism which he records amounts essentially
to the question, 'does the position of women in society, as we know it, justify
the attempts which have been made to explain the great quarrel by incidents
such as those of Io, Medea, and Helen?' Now this criticism is not merely
Persian, nor even Herodotean; the problem whether the Trojan War was really
fought about Helen was at least as old as Stesichorus. No sooner did the waken-
ing mind of Hellas cease merely to believe Homer, and begin to think about
him, than it struck at once upon this very paradox:—'Homer says, and insists
throughout, that all the war was wrought for Helen's sake; but do we Greeks
ever dream of doing anything of the kind? are our women the least worth
fighting about? If they run away with a foreigner, do we not, as a matter
of fact, say "good riddance", and go about our business?' How this paradox
presented itself to Stesichorus and to other literary thinkers of early Greece,
and how Herodotus has chosen to handle their solution of it, is a thricetold
tale. All that I am concerned to suggest, at present, is that, at every point
where we can test it, opinion in Greece was in flux as to the rightful position
of woman in civilized society.

The rapid extension of the field of Greek knowledge of other peoples' customs, which resulted from the voyages and settlements of the seventh century,
no less than the severe strain which the economic evolution in that century
and the next put upon the very framework of society in Greek states, led inevitably, as we know, to very reasonable scepticism as to the naturalness of patriarchal institutions in themselves: and this not only among the Physicists.
We have hints of it in the Lyric, and explicit discussion in the Drama. 'Is

a man nearer akin to his father or to his mother?' that is the point on which for Aeschylus the fate of Orestes turns in the last resort. The Apollo of Aeschylus, Λητοίδης [son of Leto] though he be, is on the side of the angels, but his proof belongs to a phase of observation which, while it conforms precisely to the patriarchal jurisprudence, was obsolete already for Hippocrates. The *Andromache* and the *Medea* of Euripides mark in due course the turn of the tide, even in Drama; and, with the feminist plays of Aristophanes, we are in full course for the *Republic* of Plato, the fine flower, on this side of the subject, of the conviction (which is really pre-Socratic) that social organization, like any other, is at bottom a matter of the adaptation of natural means to ends.

Of this controversy Herodotus is no mere spectator. It can hardly be a chance that every one of the strange marriage customs which he mentions happens to be typical of a widespread type of observance; and that the series of them taken together forms an analysis of such types which is almost complete between the extremes of promiscuous union with classificatory relationship on the one hand, and normal patriarchal monogamy on the other.

Herodotus is of course not writing a history of Human Marriage, or of Woman's Rights; it is only as a current topic of controversy that such matters come into his story at all; but, when they do, I think we can see that his contribution to them is not quite a casual one; that he is not simply emptying an ill-filled notebook on to the margins of his history; but that where he digresses he does so to fill a gap in current knowledge, with materials which, if not new, are at all events well authenticated; and that these materials have partly been elicited by his own interest in specific problems which were burning questions at the moment.

The question of social organization, and provision for orderly descent, was for Herodotus a matter of pure science. But for some of his contemporaries it was different. Archelaus, in particular, the last, and in some respects the most advanced, of the Physicists, has the reputation of having applied physicist methods to politics and morals: καὶ γὰρ περὶ νόμων πεφιλοσόφηκε καὶ καλῶν λαὶ δικαίων [And concerning the laws he applied the method of reason (science) both to the good and the right].[1] Two points in the account given of him by Diogenes have usually been put on one side; that he came from Miletus and had sat at the feet of Anaxagoras, beyond whose physics, however, he failed to advance appreciably;[2] and that Socrates had borrowed from him much of what commonly passed as Socratic. But the two statements go together. An Ionian Physicist, who had passed on to 'philosophize about customs, their goodness and justice', was certainly a pendent portrait to that of the Socrates of the *Clouds* and of the *Memorabilia*, with his earlier interest

[1] Diogenes Laertius ii. 16 (R. P. 169).
[2] Simpl. *in Arist. Phys.* fol. 6 (R. P. 170).

(which his enemies never forgot) in τὰ μετέωρα [abstruse things], and his invincible habit of treating Man as an animal species about which it was permissible to argue by the analogy of other 'rational animals' like horses and dogs. Indeed the predominant interest which the next generation took in the later phases of Socrates the Moralist, have obscured, perhaps unduly, the significance of these glimpses of his immaturer thought.

The same Archelaus is credited—or discredited—with another saying, characteristic of the Milesian way of looking at Mankind:—'Justice and injustice,' he said, 'exist not in nature but in custom.' Here again, the practice of Herodotus is instructive. Repeatedly he notes of distant peoples either that they are the 'justest of Mankind', or that they have this or that 'custom' which is praiseworthy or the reverse; and, even among the highest of civilized beings, 'Custom is King.'

This is not perhaps the place to enter at length on a discussion of the Herodotean usage of νόμος [law], or its relation with its correlative φύσις [nature]. But it can hardly be passed by without the remark that the varying use of the word in Herodotus—and his uses do vary in detail—are all included in that earlier, and characteristically Ionian sense, in which the word is used to denote the formal expression of *what actually happens*, among the people, and in the circumstances, which are in question. This is of course a quite immediate, and very early sense of the word; it connects itself directly with the primary signification of a *pasture* within which a flock may roam unchecked and unharmed, but beyond which it strays at its peril or not at all. Νόμος [Law] has thus exactly the force of the Roman conception of a *provincia*, except that where provincia *prescribed* the limits and the character of appropriate acts, νόμος [law] merely *described* them. In so far then as νόμος [law] answered originally to our word *law*, it answered exclusively to that sense of it in which we speak of a *law of nature*, meaning thereby our more or less accurate formulation, in a descriptive way, of the actual course of events of the given type.

In this sense obviously there is no contrast or antagonism conceivable between νόμος [law] and φύσις [nature]. Let the φύσις [nature] of an oak, for example—the growth-process of that kind of tree—be to put forth branches, leaves, and fruit of a specific sort: this is no less the νόμος [law] of that oak; the way it normally behaves. So, too, with Man. The normal, natural behaviour of the Egyptian is to teach his son a trade, this is one of his νόμος [laws], as seen and described by an observer from outside; but this is also what he and his ancestors have done φύσει [naturally] for generations, till an Egyptian who does otherwise is hardly conceivable. We have already seen in the case of Hippocrates the mode of procedure whereby what began as a νόμος [law] was conceived as modifying the φύσις [nature] by incorporation in it.

What was the outcome of these observations on the family structure of savages, and of the speculations as to their "naturalness" or the reverse? The answer is given, I think, when we look into the fourth century, and find Socrates, the last of the pre-Socratics, propounding in the *Republic*, and justifying by chapter and verse in the *Laws*, the unnaturalness, because the uselessness or inexpediency, of patriarchal society as the Greeks knew it. From Athenian politics patriarchal considerations had been eliminated in theory a century before, by that amazing revolutionary, Cleisthenes; but socially the father still owned and ruled his children; and children paid divided allegiance to their father and to the state. As presented in the *Republic* the Socratic argument has little about it that is anthropological; the appeal is to horses and dogs, not to Sarmatians; but the actual institutions of the Ideal State, the annual mating-festivals, the κομψοὶ κλῆροι [clever lots] by which status is allotted to each infant after inspection by the governors, the whole classificatory system of relationship, are one and all to be found among the curious νόμοι [laws] which we know to have been recorded by the anthropologists of the century before; and recorded, too, with the definite intention of discovering what their causes were, and what were the reasons assigned for those customs by the people who practised and understood them.

It is against such speculations as these, of course, and in particular against the Socratic attempt to make Amazons and Nasamonians rise up in judgement against this generation, that Aristotle was moved to restate in the first section of the *Politics* the orthodox sociology of patriarchal Greece. That in the middle of the fourth it should have been possible for a serious person to maintain the paradox φύσει ἀρχικὸς πατὴρ υἱῶν [father who is a ruler of sons by nature] without instant refutation by the members of his classroom, is a measure of the extent to which the followers of Socrates (though, as we have seen, not Socrates himself) had broken with the fifth-century naturalists, and perhaps even ceased to read them. But it is a measure also of the extent to which an able dialectician could make play with words like φύσις [nature] and νόμος [law], till it almost appeared as if any one who had any νόμοι [laws] to speak of represented a παρέκβασις [deviation] from the φύοει ἄνθρωπος [nature of man]. No amount of *a priori* argument as to the superior strength, or intelligence, or sheer "superiority" of the human male, could obliterate the fact that here women ruled, there they fought, elsewhere they did the work instead of the man, or, bar the reflection, that it was the business of an editor of συνηγμέναι πολιτεῖαι [collected (data) of political institutions] to collect these human institutions too, before generalizing; and, in general, to distinguish τὸ παρὰ φύσιν from τὸ παράδοξον [what is according to nature from paradox].

Alongside of the problem of family organization, lay the other problem of the means of subsistence. Some men live wholly on the fruit of a tree; others eat corn, or milk, or monkeys, or their elderly relatives. And here again the evidence falls into two classes. There are customs in which the eating appears to us as a ritual act designed by those who observed or initiated it to secure some ultimately useful end: they frequently belong to the kind of acts which we class together as Sympathetic Magic. There are also customs in respect of food, which to us appear to have only an economic interest; or if they have wider interest at all, acquire it from another consideration. Current anthropology—French anthropology in particular—and our own economic surroundings combine to bring home to us keenly the thought that the way in which a people gets its daily bread, not to mention the previous question how it is to get anything to eat at all (except, perhaps, its own unemployables), has a direct and profound influence on its social structure. A late stage of Greek thought on this subject is represented by the section in the first book of the *Politics* which classifies the principal βίοι [sorts of lives] which are open to mankind, and hints (though the subject is not pursued) that the Good Life will be pursued with a very different equipment of customs and institutions according as it is pursued by the pastoral nomad "farming his migratory field", or by the miner, or by the merchant seaman. A little earlier in thought as well as in time comes the sketch in the *Republic*, a glimpse of the earlier Socrates who had dabbled in geography and improved the "inventions" of Archelaus. The later Socrates, wise in his own failures, takes his pupils hurriedly past this avenue of inquiry into the structure of society; the disciples, for the credit of the Master's originality, omit all allusion to Archelaus and his work. But the Milesian who began with Physics, and went on to show what nowadays we should call "the applicability of biological laws to Man", cannot have been without weight in the political thought of his time; and it is again to Herodotus that we must turn for indications of the extent to which this inquiry was already being followed in Greece in the generation of Archelaus, and before it.

Already in Homer imagination had been caught by the total distinctness of the mode of life which was followed by the nomads of the North; and a vague connexion had been felt between the purely pastoral existence and a peculiarly orderly habit of life and behaviour. A fragment of Choerilus, whom those who had access to his work felt to stand in some peculiarly close relation to Herodotus, connects these two qualities explicitly;[1] and the same thought recurs twice over in that storehouse of anthropological learning, the *Prometheus*

---

[1]Choerilus is the only early authority for the theory, criticized by Hdt. iii. 115, that the Eridanus is in Germany. Serv. ad Virg. *G.* i. 482 'Thesias (Ctesias) hunc (Eridanum) in Media esse, Choerilus in Germania, in quo flumine Edion (Phaethon) extinctus est.' Fr. 13 (Didot). Choerilus fr. 3 (Didot):

μηλονόμοι δὲ Σάκαι, γενεῇ Σκύθαι, αὐτὰρ ἔναιον
'Ασίδα πυροθόρον, νομάδων γε μὲν ἦσαν ἄποικοι
ανθρώπων νομίμων.

The goat-tending Sacae, Scythians by race, as soon as they inhabited wheat-bearing Asia became settlers, since they were nomads who were law abiding.

Solutus of Aeschylus.[1] In the latter passage it would be forcing the literal sense of the words unduly, to insist that the Gabii are to be pictured as living on wild corn, especially as Greek theory was at all other points unanimous that corn, like the olive and the vine, came to man by special providence as something ἥμερον φύσει [apart from nature]. The Aeschylean picture clearly is that of the virgin soil of the trans-Euxine grass-land, where the spring vegetation will endure comparison with any merely Aegean corn-land.

There is enough in this single example to show that the men of the early fifth century were already aware of the inter-dependence of environment, economy, and institutions. For the generation of Socrates, we have the treatise of Hippocrates already mentioned, "On Air, Water, and Places"; of which the whole burden is, as we have seen, that not only men's social organization, but their very physique, is the result of "acquired variations" initiated by the climate and economic régime.

I hinted, a little earlier, that there is another reason why Herodotus should pay close attention to the peculiar food of strange peoples. That different kinds of food-quest should lead to different manners and institutions was probably, even in the fifth century, a less familiar conception than that the personal qualities of the individual depended directly on the food which he ate. This is of course a matter of elementary knowledge to most savages; it is an explicit principle of the medical doctrine of Hippocrates; it has had the profoundest influence on the vocabulary and ritual of great religions, and it has by no means disappeared from the current thought of mankind; it is still believed, by otherwise intelligent people, that the morals of nations may be mended, by defining the quality of their food and the quantity of their drink. With this conception in mind, we shall cease to be surprised that Herodotus devotes so much time and care to describe the preparation of plum-cake, or kirschwasser, or beer. Man might not live by bread alone; but if you once were certain that a man did live on bread, and not on monkeys, or on lice, you knew already a good deal about the habits and the value of that man.

It was probably the circumstance that this magical interpretation was so commonly attached to food-supply that prevented Greek observers, such as Herodotus and Hippocrates, from pressing home their analysis of the food-quest as an index of the general economic régime. And the same ambiguity envelops

---

[1]Fragment 189 ἀλλ' ἱππάκης βρωτῆρες εὔνομοι Σκύθαι. [But the Sacae who lived under good laws were eaters of cheese made from mare's milk] Fragment 184:

ἔπειτα δ'ἥξει δῆμον ἐνδικώτατον
. . . ἁπάντων καὶ φιλοξενώτατον
Γαβίους, ἵν' οὔτ'ἄροτρον οὔτε γατόμος
τέμνει δίκελλ' ἀρονρατ ἀλλ' αὐτόσποροι

γύαι φέρουοι βίοτον ἄφθονον βρότοις.

Then the most just race will come, a race most just and most hospitable . . . the Gabii so that neither hoe nor plough will cut the ground, but self-sown the lands will bring immortal sustenance (ambrosia?) to mortals.

also, unfortunately, the next recorded attempt at such analysis. It can hardly be accident that, in the sketch of the ἀναγκαιοτάτη πόλις [absolutely necessary city (in the sense of most perfect)] in the *Republic*,[1] the diet of the citizens is wholly vegetarian, and almost wholly cereal. And when Glaucon interrupts, and asks what has happened to the meat, Socrates wilfully misunderstands his question, and prescribes once more only salt, cheese, and *vegetable* relishes—olives, and bulbous roots, and wild herbs, with figs, lentils, and beans, myrtleberries and forest nuts to follow. Glaucon's comment on this is precise and contemptuous: "If you had been planning a city of pigs, Socrates, what other fodder than this would you have given them?" And on being pressed for an alternative, he stipulates expressly for the *customary* food of civilized men, "and meat dishes such as people have nowadays." It is entirely in keeping with all this,[1] that ὄψα [rich food, delicacies] recur further on, along with tables, chairs, and unguents, as signs of a corrupted state; that hunters and cooks appear among the ministers of luxury; and swineherds last of all, for the pig alone among cattle gives neither milk or cheese, but is useful only for meat diet.

Here three distinct lines of argument are inextricably confused. In the first place, we have seen already that it was the regular Greek belief that man began existence as a forest animal, living on the hazel-nuts and acorns characteristic of the Balkan and Anatolian regions; and only acquired the knowledge of corn, wine, and oil by special providence, and at a later time: in this sense, therefore, Socrates is proposing a return to primitive diet. In the second place, the diet which he suggests is the only one possible for people who should try to live a life independent and at the same time inoffensive. But, thirdly, this diet is precisely that which a fourth-century doctor would have been expected to prescribe for a patient τρυφῶντι καὶ φλεγμαίνοντι [worn out with illness and inflammation]. But there is enough of common motive in all three considerations, to make it clear that even one of the least anthropological among his pupils could represent Socrates as starting from a conception of man and his place in the world which is precisely that of a fifth-century physicist.[1]

I conclude with a well-known Herodotean episode, in which much true history has been remodelled clearly in the light of a definite classification of Βίοι [sorts of lives], and a definite theory of their relative values and economic interactions. In the story of the rise of Peisistratus, as told by Herodotus,[2]

---

[1]Plato, *Rep.* 370-2.

[1]Plato, *Rep.* 373.

[1]Far more explicit and detailed is the comparative study of foreign customs which *underlies* Socratic doctrine in the *Laws*. The stock examples of the fifth century, Sarmatians (804 E), Amazons (806 A), Thracians (805 D), and the like, are all there, side by side with the Spartans and the Cretans, the Persians, the Egyptians, and the Phoenicians (750 C). But the anthropological basis of fourth-century thought is a distinct subject, and would require a whole chapter to itself.

[2]Hdt. i. 59.

the *motif* of the action throughout the first phase of his career is that of three contrasted βίοι [sorts of lives]: the life of the shore, of the sea, and of the men from over the hills. In form the division is geographical, but the phrase which is used, τῷ λόγῳ τῶν ὑπερακρίων προστάς [in a word, the highland section], suggests that it is not a district but a region which is in question; and that what differentiated this region from the others was this, that it lay above corn level. Any one who will go in spring-time and look round from the Acropolis upon Attica, will recognize that abrupt change from the emerald green to the purple and brown, which tells where πεδίον [plain] and cornland end, and the goats of the ὑπεράκρια [heights] begin. And I have seen along the base of Taygetus, along the same economic frontier, where a track like a coastguard's path has been worn by the police patrols, in their attempt, not always successful, to prevent στάσις [sedition] from bursting into πόλεμος [war]. We should note in passing that the question whether the pastoral highlanders of Attica exhausted the whole content of the λόγος τῶν ὑπερακρίων [makeup of the highland]—whether, that is, the party of Peisistratus included the mining interests of the district of Laureion, as suggested by Mr. Ure,[1] is totally distinct from the question now before us, which is simply what the word conveyed to the mind of Herodotus the Halicarnassian. And if this distinction be granted, the suggestion, which is after all the conventional one, that the ground of division between the Attic factions was regarded by Herodotus as an economic one, receives much support from the perennial state of Balkan lands, with their oases of corn-growers amid a highland wilderness of Vlachs.

In these circumstances, the fact that Peisistratus, whatever his real character may have been, is described as the leader of the most *backward* section of the population, is entirely in agreement with the rest of the picture. For throughout, in Herodotus' presentation of him, Peisistratus is the man of paradoxes. His father, before his birth, had accepted the omen of the cauldron spontaneously boiling; the son was to kindle a great fire where there was no light—but only plenty of fuel. So again, Peisistratus, unlike the Sibyl, at each rejection offers Athens more. The rejected party-leader becomes Athena's man, the man of an united Attica; and Athena's man, whom Athena's people expelled, rests not till he can offer, of his own, every corner stone of an Athenian Empire in its greatest days. And so here, again, there is *stasis* between rich and poor, between primitive and advanced, between sedentary and nomad—so far as nomadism was practicable in Attica; and it is the λεπτὰ τῶν προβάτων [literally small cattle, in this case sheep and goats], as with Perdiccas and with David, which produce, in due time, the great man. It is a miniature, of course, this sketch of the sixth-century Attica, as befits its modest part in the scheme of the Herodotean drama; but the handling of it is none the less significant, on that account, of the way in which the idea of conflicting νόμοι [laws] is allowed to model and interpret the materials.

I have tried, in brief space, to indicate some ways in which our knowledge of the Greek world, fragmentary as it is, enables us to recover some at least of the broad lines of method by which the early history of Man, and the causes of his variations and of his social states, were being investigated in the fifth century and before: and to interpret some of the results which were reached, in the light of the reasoning which led to them, and the principles by which they were interpreted in antiquity. We have seen that in some points Greek anthropology had gone surprisingly far, in speculation, and in acute observation too; and we have seen it baffled, in other directions, by puzzles and mistakes which seem trivial to us. And we have seen, in the particular instance of one who was at the same time a great historian and an alert observer of anthropological fact, something of the way in which pre-Socratic stages of theory worked out when they were applied to research in the hands of an ordinary man. Above all, I have ventured to suggest—what I hope it may be for others to carry forward—an inquiry into the anthropological basis of the political doctrine of Socrates; and so to link him, on this side of his thought, with that great body of naturalist work, which I would gladly believe that he came not to destroy but to fulfil.

BENJAMIN FRANKLIN ON THE
AMERICAN INDIAN
1784

BENJAMIN FRANKLIN (1706-1790) was a man of so many talents, wit, grace, and so multifaceted in his wisdom, knowledge, and insight, that in almost every sense of the word he was almost globular. Nothing testifies more abundantly to his great wisdom and understanding than his pamphlet,[1] published at London in 1784, *Remarks Concerning the Savages of North America*. This must have been fairly widely read for it went through three English editions and one in Dublin in the year of its publication. It was translated into French by La Rochefoucauld in January 1785. Whether the pamphlet's popularity was

[1]This pamphlet, published under the title *Two Tracts*, contained an additional essay of advice, *Information to Those Who Would Remove to America*.

due to the *Remarks* or to the accompanying tract, *Information to Those Who Would Remove to America*, we do not know. It is characteristic of the kindly Franklin that he should have so clearly appreciated the Indian character. In another place he wrote, "During the course of a long life in which I have made observations of public affairs, it has appeared to me that almost every war between the Indians and whites has been occasioned by some injustice of the latter towards the former."[2]

It is sad to reflect that Franklin's *Remarks* have been so thoroughly forgotten, that except for a few Franklin scholars, hardly anyone today knows of their existence. That is one of the reasons why this sympathetic essay is reprinted here.

REMARKS CONCERNING THE SAVAGES
OF NORTH AMERICA-1784*
BY BENJAMIN FRANKLIN

Savages we call them, because their Manners differ from ours, which we think the Perfection of Civility; they think the same of theirs.

Perhaps, if we could examine the Manners of different Nations with Impartiality, we should find no People so rude, as to be without any Rules of Politeness; nor any so polite, as not to have some Remains of Rudeness.

The Indian Men, when young, are Hunters and Warriors; when old, Counsellors; for all their Government is by Counsel of the Sages; there is no Force, there are no Prisons, no Officers to compel Obedience, or inflict Punishment. Hence they generally study Oratory, the best Speaker having the most Influence. The Indian Women till the Ground, dress the Food, nurse and bring up the Children, and preserve and hand down to Posterity the Memory of public Transactions. These Employments of Men and Women are accounted natural and honourable. Having few artificial Wants, they have abundance of Leisure for Improvement by Conversation. Our laborious Manner of Life, compared with theirs, they esteem slavish and base; and the Learning, on which we value ourselves, they regard as frivolous and useless. An Instance of this occurred at the Treaty of Lancaster, in Pennsylvania, *anno* 1744, between the Government of Virginia and the Six Nations. After the principal Business was settled,

[2]Letter to Samuel Elbert, 16 December 1787, in Albert Henry Smyth, *The Writings of Benjamin Franklin*. New York: The Macmillan Co., 1905-1907 vol. 9, p. 625.

*Reprinted from Albert Henry Smyth, *The Writings of Benjamin Franklin*. New York, The Macmillan Co., 10 vols., 1905-1907, vol. 10, pp. 97-105.

the Commissioners from Virginia acquainted the Indians by a Speech, that there
was at Williamsburg a College, with a Fund for Educating Indian youth; and
that, if the Six Nations would send down half a dozen of their young Lads
to that College, the Government would take care that they should be well provided for, and instructed in all the Learning of the White People. It is one
of the Indian Rules of Politeness not to answer a public Proposition the same
day that it is made; they think it would be treating it as a light matter, and
that they show it Respect by taking time to consider it, as of a Matter important. They therefore deferr'd their Answer till the Day following; when their
Speaker began, by expressing their deep Sense of the kindness of the Virginia
Government, in making them that Offer; "for we know," says he, "that you
highly esteem the kind of Learning taught in those Colleges, and that the
Maintenance of our young Men, while with you, would be very expensive
to you. We are convinc'd, therefore, that you mean to do us Good by your
Proposal; and we thank you heartily. But you, who are wise, must know that
different Nations have different Conceptions of things; and you will therefore
not take it amiss, if our Ideas of this kind of Education happen not to be
the same with yours. We have had some Experience of it; Several of our young
People were formerly brought up at the Colleges of the Northern Provinces;
they were instructed in all your Sciences; but, when they came back to us,
they were bad Runners, ignorant of every means of living in the Woods, unable
to bear either Cold or Hunger, knew neither how to build a Cabin, take a
Deer, or kill an Enemy, spoke our Language imperfectly, were therefore
neither fit for Hunters, Warriors, nor Counsellors; they were totally good for
nothing. We are however not the less oblig'd by your kind Offer, tho' we
decline accepting it; and, to show our grateful Sense of it, if the Gentlemen
of Virginia will send us a Dozen of their Sons, we will take great Care of
their Education, instruct them in all we know, and make *Men* of them."

Having frequent Occasions to hold public Councils, they have acquired great
Order and Decency in conducting them. The old Men sit in the foremost Ranks,
the Warriors in the next, and the Women and Children in the hindmost. The
Business of the Women is to take exact Notice of what passes, imprint it in
their Memories (for they have no Writing), and communicate it to their Children. They are the Records of the Council, and they preserve Traditions of
the Stipulations in Treaties 100 Years back; which, when we compare with
our Writings, we always find exact. He that would speak, rises. The rest
observe a profound Silence. When he has finish'd and sits down, they leave
him 5 or 6 Minutes to recollect, that, if he has omitted any thing he intended
to say, or has any thing to add, he may rise again and deliver it. To interrupt
another, even in common Conversation, is reckon'd highly indecent. How different this is from the conduct of a polite British House of Commons, where
scarce a day passes without some Confusion, that makes the Speaker hoarse
in calling *to Order;* and how different from the Mode of Conversation in many

polite Companies of Europe, where, if you do not deliver your Sentence with great Rapidity, you are cut off in the middle of it by the Impatient Loquacity of those you converse with, and never suffer'd to finish it!

The Politeness of these Savages in Conversation is indeed carried to Excess, since it does not permit them to contradict or deny the Truth of what is asserted in their Presence. By this means they indeed avoid Disputes; but then it becomes difficult to know their Minds, or what Impression you make upon them. The Missionaries who have attempted to convert them to Christianity, all complain of this as one of the great Difficulties of their Mission. The Indians hear with Patience the Truths of the Gospel explain'd to them, and give their usual Tokens of Assent and Approbation; you would think they were convinc'd. No such matter. It is mere Civility.

A Swedish Minister, having assembled the chiefs of the Susquehanah Indians, made a Sermon to them, acquainting them with the principal historical Facts on which our Religion is founded; such as the Fall of our first Parents by eating an Apple, the coming of Christ to repair the Mischief, his Miracles and Suffering, &c. When he had finished, an Indian Orator stood up to thank him. "What you have told us," says he, "is all very good. It is indeed bad to eat Apples. It is better to make them all into Cyder. We are much oblig'd by your kindness in coming so far, to tell us these Things which you have heard from your Mothers. In return, I will tell you some of those we have heard from ours. In the Beginning, our Fathers had only the Flesh of Animals to subsist on; and if their Hunting was unsuccessful, they were starving. Two of our young Hunters, having kill'd a Deer, made a Fire in the Woods to broil some Part of it. When they were about to satisfy their Hunger, they beheld a beautiful young Woman descend from the Clouds, and seat herself on that Hill, which you see yonder among the blue Mountains. They said to each other, it is a Spirit that has smelt our broiling Venison, and wishes to eat of it; let us offer some to her. They presented her with the Tongue; she was pleas'd with the Taste of it, and said, 'Your kindness shall be rewarded; come to this Place after thirteen Moons, and you shall find something that will be of great Benefit in nourishing you and your Children to the latest Generations.' They did so, and, to their Surprise, found Plants they had never seen before; but which, from that ancient time, have been constantly cultivated among us, to our great Advantage. Where her right Hand had touched the Ground, they found Maize; where her left hand had touch'd it, they found Kidney-Beans; and where her Backside had sat on it, they found Tobacco." The good Missionary, disgusted with this idle Tale, said, "What I delivered to you were sacred Truths; but what you tell me is mere Fable, Fiction, and Falshood." The Indian, offended, reply'd, "My brother, it seems your Friends have not done you Justice in your Education; they have not well instructed you in the Rules of common Civility. You saw that we, who understand and practise those Rules, believ'd all your stories; why do you refuse to believe ours?"

When any of them come into our Towns, our People are apt to crowd round them, gaze upon them, and incommode them, where they desire to be private; this they esteem great Rudeness, and the Effect of the Want of Instruction in the Rules of Civility and good Manners. "We have," say they, "as much Curiosity as you, and when you come into our Towns, we wish for Opportunities of looking at you; but for this purpose we hide ourselves behind Bushes, where you are to pass, and never intrude ourselves into your Company."

Their Manner of entring one another's village has likewise its Rules. It is reckon'd uncivil in travelling Strangers to enter a Village abruptly, without giving Notice of their Approach. Therefore, as soon as they arrive within hearing, they stop and hollow, remaining there till invited to enter. Two old Men usually come out to them, and lead them in. There is in every Village a vacant Dwelling, called *the Strangers' House*. Here they are plac'd, while the old Men go round from Hut to Hut, acquainting the Inhabitants, that Strangers are arriv'd, who are probably hungry and weary; and every one sends them what he can spare of Victuals, and Skins to repose on. When the Strangers are refresh'd, Pipes and Tobacco are brought; and then, but not before, Conversation begins, with Enquiries who they are, whither bound, what News, &c.; and it usually ends with offers of Service, if the Strangers have occasion of Guides, or any Necessaries for continuing their Journey; and nothing is exacted for the Entertainment.

The same Hospitality, esteem'd among them as a principal Virtue, is practis'd by private Persons; of which Conrad Weiser, our Interpreter, gave me the following Instance. He had been naturaliz'd among the Six Nations, and spoke well the Mohock Language. In going thro' the Indian Country, to carry a Message from our Governor to the Council at Onondaga, he call'd at the Habitation of Canassatego, an old Acquaintance, who embrac'd him, spread Furs for him to sit on, plac'd before him some boil'd Beans and Venison, and mix'd some Rum and Water for his Drink. When he was well refresh'd, and had lit his Pipe, Canassatego began to converse with him; ask'd how he had far'd the many Years since they had seen each other; whence he then came; what occasion'd the Journey, &c. Conrad answered all his Questions; and when the Discourse began to flag, the Indian, to continue it, said, "Conrad, you have lived long among the white People, and know something of their Customs; I have been sometimes at Albany, and have observed, that once in Seven Days they shut up their Shops, and assemble all in the great House; tell me what it is for? What do they do there?" "They meet there," says Conrad, "to hear and learn *good Things*." "I do not doubt," says the Indian, "that they tell you so; they have told me the same; but I doubt the Truth of what they say, and I will tell you my Reasons. I went lately to Albany to sell my Skins and buy Blankets, Knives, Powder, Rum, &c. You know I us'd generally to deal with Hans Hanson; but I was a little inclin'd this time to try some other Merchant. However, I call'd first upon Hans, and asked him what he would give for Beaver. He said he could not give any more than four Shillings a Pound; 'but,' says he, 'I cannot talk on Business now; this is the Day when we meet together to learn *Good Things*, and I am going to the Meeting.' So I thought to myself, 'Since we cannot do any Business to-day, I may as well go to the meeting too,' and I went with him. There stood up a Man in Black, and began to talk to the People very angrily. I did not understand what he said; but, perceiving that he look'd much at me and at Hanson, I imagin'd he was angry at seeing me there; so I went out, sat down near the House, struck Fire, and lit my Pipe, waiting till the Meeting should break up. I thought too, that the Man had mention'd something of Beaver, and I suspected it might be the Subject of their Meeting. So, when they came out, I accosted my Merchant. 'Well, Hans,' says I, 'I hope you have agreed to give more than four Shillings a Pound.' 'No,' says he, 'I cannot give so much; I cannot give more than three shillings and sixpence.' I then spoke to several other Dealers, but they all sung the same song,—Three and sixpence,—Three and sixpence. This made it clear to me, that my Suspicion was right; and, that whatever they pretended of meeting to learn *good Things*, the real purpose was to consult how to cheat Indians in the Price of Beaver. Consider but a little, Conrad, and you must be of my Opinion. If they met so often to learn *good Things*, they would certainly have learnt some before this time. But they are still ignorant. You know our Practice. If a white Man, in travelling thro' our Country, enters one of our Cabins, we all treat him as I treat you; we dry him if he is wet, we warm him if he is cold, we give him Meat and Drink, that he may allay his Thirst and Hunger; and we spread soft Furs for him to rest and sleep on; we demand nothing in return. But, if I go into a white Man's House at Albany, and ask for Victuals and Drink, they say, 'Where is your Money?' and if I have none, they say, 'Get out, you Indian Dog.' You see they have not yet learned those little *Good Things*, that we need no Meetings to be instructed in, because our Mothers taught them to us when we were Children; and therefore it is impossible their Meetings should be, as they say, for any such purpose, or have any such Effect; they are only to contrive *the Cheating of Indians in the Price of Beaver*.''

NOTE.—It is remarkable that in all Ages and Countries Hospitality has been allow'd as the Virtue of those whom the civiliz'd were pleas'd to call Barbarians. The Greeks celebrated the Scythians for it. The Saracens possess'd it eminently, and it is to this day the reigning Virtue of the wild Arabs. St. Paul, too, in the Relation of his Voyage and Shipwreck on the Island of Melita says the Barbarous People shewed us no little kindness; for they kindled a fire, and received us every one, because of the present Rain, and because of the Cold.—F.

SAMUEL STANHOPE SMITH, THE FIRST AMERICAN ANTHROPOLOGIST, ON THE CAUSES OF THE VARIETY OF THE HUMAN SPECIES

SAMUEL STANHOPE SMITH (1751-1819) published in 1787 the enlarged version of the lecture he had delivered before the American Philosophical Society in Philadelphia. The lecture and the book were entitled *An Essay on the Causes of the Variety of Complexion and Figure in the Human Species*. At the time of publication Smith had been for eight years Professor of Moral Philosophy at the College of New-Jersey (later Princeton University). In 1795 he became President of the College, a troubled eminence from which he was forced to resign in 1812, in part owing to the scientific views he espoused in *An Essay*, especially in the second edition of 1810. The trustees of the College, all of whom were clergymen, did not fail to note the omission of any reference to Divine Cause in the production of the difference in the complexion and figure of the varieties of the human species, which Stanhope Smith sought to explain by environmental influences, the state of society, and habits of living. It is a remarkable, spirited work and quite modern in its scientific outlook. We reprint here the section on the influence of the state of society and the habits of living on the development of the differences characterizing the varieties of man.

The astonishing thing about this book is that it seems to have been wholly forgotten, and has only recently been reprinted, with an excellent introduction by Winthrop D. Jordan by the Harvard University Press, 1965.

Stanhope Smith's notes are full of rich observations which the reader will find highly rewarding.

VARIETY IN THE HUMAN SPECIES*
SAMUEL STANHOPE SMITH

Having, thus far, endeavoured to point out the power of CLIMATE in the production of many of the varieties which distinguish different portions of the human species, I proceed to illustrate the influence of the STATE OF SOCIETY, AND THE HABITS OF LIVING, in creating other varieties, or in aggravating or correcting those which are occasioned by climate.

I join these two causes together in treating of them, because their effects are frequently so blended, that it is difficult, in many cases, precisely to discriminate them, and to assign each to its proper head.

In the first place, climate exerts its full influence, and produces its most deteriorating effects in a savage state of society.

And, in the next place, the peculiar character, and habits of society in which men are educated, and the modes of living to which they are either addicted from choice, or compelled from necessity, tend to create many differences in their complexion, their figure, the form and expression of their countenance, and in their whole aspect.

In the first place, then, climate produces its most deteriorating effects in a savage state of society; and, on the other hand, these effects are, in some degree, corrected by the arts and conveniences of civilization.

A naked savage, seldom enjoying the protection even of a miserable hut, and often compelled to lodge on the bare earth under the open sky, imbibes the influence of the sun, and atmosphere, at every pore of his body. The American indian inhabits an uncultivated forest, abounding with stagnant waters, and covered with a luxuriant growth of vegetables which fall down and corrupt on the spot where they had grown. He generally pitches his wigwam on the side of a river that he may enjoy the convenience of fishing as well as of hunting. The vapor of rivers, therefore, which are often greatly obstructed in their course by the trees fallen, and the leaves collected in their channels, the exhalations of marshes, and the noxious gases evolved from decaying vegetables, impregnate the whole atmosphere, and give a deep bilious tinge to the complexion of the savage.§ And the sun, acting immediately upon the skin in this state, necessarily impressed on it a very dark hue.

---

*Reprinted from *An Essay on the Causes of the Variety of Complexion and Figure of the Human Species*, 2nd ed. (New Brunswick, J. Simpson & Co., 1810), pp. 149-245.

§The forests in uncultivated countries naturally absorb a great portion of the noxious miasmata with which the atmosphere is filled. They do not, however, absorb the whole. Nothing but a skilful agriculture can perfectly purify the air from the insalubrious exhalations created by the causes already mentioned. All uncultivated countries, therefore, tend to produce a bilious habit, and a dark complexion in the savages who range them. It may seem an objection against this observation that, in America we often perceive bilious disorders increase in consequence of extending the plantations. When a few acres only are cleared of their timber and wild vegetables, while

The darkness of the complexion is still further increased by the custom which prevails among them of painting their bodies: a custom to which these savages are often obliged to have recourse in order to protect themselves from the injurious effects of the moist earth, which frequently is their only bed during the night; and of an atmosphere, filled with noxious vapors, to the influence of which they are exposed without covering. Painting taken up at first through necessity, is afterwards employed as an ornament; and an indian is seldom seen without having his skin anointed with some composition that injures the fineness of its texture, and impairs the clearness of its natural colour. If this is the effect of the finest paints and washes which are used for the same purpose in polished society, much more will it be the consequence of those coarse and filthy ungents employed by savages. For if coloured marks or figures inserted by punctures into the skin, are known to be indelible, it is reasonable to believe that the particles of paints, insinuated into its texture by forcible and frequent friction will produce a deep and permanent discolouration.‡

To this may be added the frequent fumigations by which they are obliged to guard against the annoyance of innumerable insects which swarm in undrained and uncultivated countries, and the smoke with which their huts, small and unskilfully built, are constantly filled. Smoke discolours every object long exposed to its action, by insinuating itself into the pores and adhering strongly to the surface. Hence it contributes somewhat to heighten the effect of so many other discolouring causes on the complexion of the American savage.

Lastly, the hardships of their condition, which tend to weaken and exhaust the principle of life;—their scanty, and meagre food, which wants that succulence and nourishment which give freshness to the complexion, and vigor to the constitution; the uncertainty of their provision, being sometimes left to languish with want, and on other occasions furnished with a superfluity, which

---

the marshes around them are not drained, the trees and plants, which formerly absorbed the greater portion of the putrid miasmata, being taken away from the surface of the plantation, these unhealthful vapors consequently fall more copiously on the inhabitants. Besides, the heat of the sun is, in that case, very much augmented. For, while the plantation is scorched by its almost perpendicular rays, the surrounding woods obstruct the free, and refreshing currents of the winds. So that, frequently, excessive heat combined with the unhealthful moisture of the atmosphere will produce, for a time, an increase of those distressing disorders, till the country is laid entirely open to the powerful action of the sun, and the free course of the wind. In clearing a new country of its forests, and preparing it for cultivation, a large grove of trees should be left round the habitation of each planter or farmer. These would detain, and, by their foliage, absorb in a great measure the hurtful vapors which would otherwise fall upon it; at the same time, the fresh and refrigerating perspiration of so many trees would contribute to the salubrity of the air around, and within his dwelling.

‡These paints consist of substances unfit to be taken up by the absorbent vessels of the skin and received into the circulation: they are lodged, therefore, by the force of friction, just beneath the scarf which, being little subject to change, the discolouration is retained with great tenacity.

tempts them to overstrain themselves by a surfeit; and finally, their entire inattention to the cleanliness of their persons, and their huts, all have their influence to heighten the disagreeable duskiness of their colour, and to render the features coarse and deformed. Of the power of these causes in savage life we may frame some conjecture from observing their effects on the poorest classes in society, who are usually as much distinguished by their meagre habit, their uncouth features and their dingy and squalid aspect, as by the meanness of their garb. Nakedness, exposure to the weather, negligence of appearance, want of cleanliness, bad lodging, and poor diet, are always seen to impair the beauty of the human form, and the clearness of the skin. Hence it results, that savages never can be perfectly fair. But when savage habits concur with the influence of an ardent sun, or an unwholesome atmosphere, the complexion of the people will partake of a tinge more or less dark in proportion to the predominance of one, or of both of these causes. Their features will be more coarse and hard, and their persons less robust and athletic than those of men in civilized society who enjoy its advantages with temperance.¶

As a state of savagism increases the injurious influence of climates which are unfriendly to the complexion or fine proportions of the human constitution; civilization, on the other hand, by its innumerable arts and conveniences, contributes to correct that hurtful influence. The comfortable protection of clothing and lodging; the plenty and nutritious qualities of food, and the skilful means of preparing it for use, and rendering it more healthful; a country freed from

¶A few examples, perhaps, may occur among savages of strong and muscular bodies, or of regular and agreeable features; as in civilized society we meet with some rare instances of extraordinary beauty. Yet it is certain that the countenance of savage life is commonly much more uncouth and coarse, more unmeaning and wild, as will afterwards more distinctly appear when I come to point out its causes, than the countenance formed in polished society. And the person is generally more slender, and rather fitted for the activity of the chace, than for great exertions of strength. An American indian is commonly swift, but seldom athletic. And it has been remarked in the many expeditions which have been undertaken against the savages by the people of these States, that the strength of an Anglo-American, in single combat, is usually superior to that of an indian of the same size. The muscles, likewise, on which the fine proportions of the person so much depend, are generally smaller and more lax in them than among a civilized people who are not corrupted by luxury, or debilitated by sedentary occupations. Their limbs, therefore, though straight, are less beautifully turned.

A deception often passes upon the senses in judging of the beauty of savages; and it is often very injudiciously exaggerated in description. We do not expect beauty in savage life. When, therefore, we happen to perceive it, the contrast which it presents to us with the usual condition of men in that state affects the mind with a degree of surprize that very much promotes the deception. And the exalted descriptions of savage beauty which we sometimes read are true only by comparison with savages. There is a difference, in this respect, between man, and the inferior animals which were formed to run wild in the forest. They are always most beautiful when they enjoy their native liberty. They decay and droop when attempted to be confined and domesticated. But man, being designed for society, and civilization, attains, in that state, the greatest beauty of the human form, as well as the highest perfection of his whole nature.

noxious effluvia, and subjected to cultivation; the constant study of elegance, with improved ideas of a standard of beauty for the human form; and the continual effort made to approximate this standard, in ourselves, or to form our children to it by a proper culture, give an immense advantage, in this respect, to cultivated society over savage life.

2. I come now to observe, what is of much more importance on this part of the subject, that all the features of the human countenance are *modified*, and its whole *expression*, in a great measure, formed by the state of society in which men exist.

Every idea, and every emotion which is excited in the mind, affects, in some degree, the features of the countenance, the index of our feelings, and contributes to form its infinitely various lineaments. Paucity of ideas, and of objects to call forth the exercise of the understanding or the passions, marks the countenance with a vacant and unmeaning aspect. Agreeable and cultivated scenes enliven and animate the features, and tend to render them regular and soft. Wild and solitary forests impress on the countenance some image of their own rudeness. Considerable varieties are created even by diet, and the different modes of preparing it for use. A diet composed chiefly of raw and uncooked meats is generally accompanied with ferocity of aspect. And among the various methods of preparing food in civilized nations, some are undoubtedly more favorable to health and vigor, and consequently to personal beauty, than others. Hard fare, and exposure to the injuries of the weather render the features of savages, and the poorer classes of society, coarse and uncouth. The infinitely diversified attentions of men in polished society give great flexibility and variety to the expression of the countenance. The defect of interesting emotions, or of the habits of attention, and thought, leave its muscles lax and unexerted; whence they assume a swoln appearance, and distend themselves to a grosser size.* A general and national standard of beauty, likewise, which is usually aimed at in civilized society, and which, in some respects, is various in different countries, has its effect in forming the features and fashioning the person. Every passion, every emotion, every thought which passes through the mind has its peculiar expression. Each single touch, if I may speak so, may be so fine as to be imperceptible; but frequent repetition will at length, trace on the countenance very distinct lineaments. And these minute causes may again vary their effects according to their respective degrees of strength, according to their combination with other principles, and according to the constitutional peculiarities of individuals, or of nations, that form the ground on which the different impressions are received. And, inasmuch as the advances made in the arts, the prevalent ideas, pursuits, and moral habits of men in different countries, and under different forms of government, are infinitely various, they open a boundless field for variety in the human countenance. It is impossible

---

*Several of these reflections shall be illustrated more in detail hereafter.

to enumerate all these minute varieties.† They are not the same in any two nations, nor in the same nation in any two ages. It would be unnecessary to enumerate them, as my object is, not to enable my readers to become physiognomists, but to suggest a proper mode of reasoning on each new difference among mankind as it occurs to our observation.

For this purpose, I shall endeavour, in the first place, to evince by several facts and illustrations, that the state of society in which men live has a powerful influence in varying the character of the countenance, and even in changing the habit, and appearance of the whole person.

And, in the next place, to shew that some of the most distinguishing features of the savage, and particularly of the American savage, with whom we are best acquainted, naturally result from the rude condition in which he exists.

The influence of the state of society, and of the modes of life which prevail among different nations, or tribes of men, to produce some variety or change in the complexion, and even in the form and proportions of the person, may receive illustration from the variety of aspect exhibited by the higher and lower classes into which the people of almost all nations are divided; and who may be regarded, in some degree, as men in different states of society.

†From various combinations of the causes that have been suggested, and others of a similar nature, we often see different characters of countenance, and habits of body, and even different habitual attitudes, and modes of moving the person, not only in different nations, but in different cities, and districts belonging to the same country. Libavius, a German author, remarked above two centuries ago, this variety in his own nation. "There is one countenance," says he, "belongs to the Thuringians, another to the Saxons, and a different one to the Swedes. Indeed each village almost has something, in this respect, peculiar to itself, so that a person who would accurately attend to this subject might nearly pronounce on the country of a man from his physiognomy." Yet besides these smaller local differences, there is commonly a general cast of countenance, arising from the influence of government, religion, civil occupations, and other causes, which belongs to each nation, and serves to distinguish it from others.

In conformity with the observation of Libavius, and with what I have said above, Camper remarks that it is easy to distinguish at the first view, Jews from Christians, Spaniards from Frenchmen, or Germans, and these again from Englishmen. We can distinguish, says he, the inhabitants of the South of France from those of the North, except where they have been blended by marriage. The cities of Holland, where so many people have been mingled together, no longer present to us distinct features of a national countenance. The inhabitants of the islands only still possess their primitive features entire. In Friesland, for example, the inhabitants of Hindelopen, Molkwerum, and Koudum, still exhibit their thin face and their length of jaw; while those of Bildt, by their short face all crowded together, differ entirely from their nearest neighbors, who inhabit, however, the most ancient portion of the country.

Each people then forms to itself some distinguishing national traits, till at length the mixture of different nations coming in among them effaces this characteristic distinction. Wars, migrations, commercial intercourse, have so confounded nations, anciently posited at the greatest distances from one another, that we can no longer perceive that primitive and specific impression which originally distinguished them. As most neighboring countries, however, form in time pretty intimate connections, they become gradually so blended, that now we do not often perceive very striking and characteristic differences of national countenance but among people whose actual, or present positions are removed from one another at very considerable intervals. Chap. i. p. 13, 14.

The poor and laboring part of the community in every country, are usually more dark in their complexion, more hard in their features, and more coarse and ill formed in their limbs, than persons of better rank, who enjoy greater ease, and more liberal means of subsistence. They want the delicate tints of colour, the pleasing regularity of features, and the elegant and fine proportions of the person so frequently seen in the higher classes. Many particular exceptions undoubtedly there are. Luxury may disfigure the one; a fortunate coincidence of circumstances may give a happy assemblage of features to the other.‡ But these exceptions will not invalidate the general observation. The distinctions which subsist between the several classes of society become more considerable by time, after families have held, for ages, nearly the same stations. But they are more conspicuous in those countries in which the laws or customs of the nation have made the most complete and permanent discrimination of ranks. In Scotland, for example, how wide is the difference between the chiefs of the Highland clans, and the tenants and laborers of the land! A similar distinction takes place between the nobility and peasantry of France, of Spain, of Italy, of Germany, and especially of Poland, because there the vassalage of the peasantry is more oppressive than in any other country in Europe. The noble, or military class in India has been pronounced by some travellers to be composed of a different race of men from the populace who are their traders, and artizans; because, the former, elevated by their rank above them, and devoted only to martial studies and achievements, are distinguished by that manly beauty so frequently found united with the profession of arms; the latter, poor and laborious, exposed to innumerable hardships and privations, and left, by their laws and their religion, without the hope of improving their condition, or the spirit to attempt it, have become timid and servile in the expression of their countenance, diminutive, and often deformed in their persons, and marked by a deeper shade than their superiors in their complexion. In France, says Buffon, you may distinguish by their appearance, not only the nobility from the peasantry, but the superior orders of nobility from the inferior, these from the citizens, and the citizens from the peasants. You may even distinguish the peasants of one part of the country from those of another, according to the fertility of the soil, or the nature of its product. And I have been assured by a most judicious and accurate observer of men and manners, a native of Scotland,§ that there is a sensible and striking difference between the people in the eastern, and those in the western counties of that kingdom. The farmers

‡It should be kept in mind through the whole of the following illustrations, that, when mention is made of the superior beauty of persons in the higher classes of society, the remark is general. It is not intended to deny that there exist many exceptions both of deformity among the great, and of beauty among the poor. And the general remark is intended to be applied only to those who enjoy their fortune with temperance; because luxury and intemperance tend equally with extreme poverty and hardships to disfigure the person.

§The late Rev. Dr. Witherspoon, President of the College of New-Jersey.

who cultivate the fertile lands of the Lothians have generally a fairer complexion, and a better figure, than those who live in the West, and draw a more coarse and scanty subsistence from a thin and ungrateful soil.‡

That respectable naturalist Forster, who accompanied Capt. Cook in his last voyage, in remarking on the inhabitants of the islands of the Great South Sea, observes, with regard to those of the Society-Isles, that the Towtows, or common class of the people, who are the laborers, and, consequently, much exposed to the influence of the sun in fulfilling their tasks, and who, besides, are nourished with a less succulent and abundant provision of food, than the Arees, or dominant class, are also inferior in their stature, not so handsomely formed in their persons, and considerably darker in their complexion. As is

‡It is well known to those who have been accustomed carefully to observe human nature, that coarse and meagre food is commonly unfavorable both to softness and regularity of features, and to the fairness of the complexion. Every change of diet, as I have before remarked, and every variety in the manner of cooking and preparing it for use, is accompanied with some alteration in the system. I have several times witnessed, in my own family, and in those of my friends, the most pleasing changes take place in poor children taken in to service for a term of years, who, in a short period have exchanged their sallow skin, and emaciated appearance, the effect of want and hardship, for a healthful countenance, and clear complexion.

Difference of food, and treatment equally affects the inferior animals. The flesh of many species of game differs both in colour and in flavor according to the nature of the grounds on which they have fed. The flesh of hares, it is remarked by Buffon, that have fed on high lands is much fairer than of those which have fed in vallies, and in damp places. And every keeper of cattle knows how much the firmness and flavor of the meat depends upon the manner of feeding. According to the nature of the food, and the care and treatment bestowed upon them, all domestic animals are infinitely varied in size and shape. The Spaniards inform us that the swine in Cuba grow to nearly double the size of their parent stock in Europe. And according to the testimony of Clavigero, black cattle arrive at a much greater volume of body in the rich forests, and the temperate climate of Paraguay, than the cattle of Spain, from which they have originally sprung. On the other hand, the cattle, in many parts of the United States, and in Canada, being negligently housed, and fed, during our rigorous winters, and often left, through the rest of the year, to gather a scanty subsistence from the pasturage found in our woods, have greatly degenerated from their parent stocks. They are often seen to be diminutive through defect of nourishment, and deformed through weakness, which exposes them to many accidents, and distorts their limbs, by their inability, especially in the spring season, to bear firmly their own weight. Some such facts occurring to the observation of Europeans who had visited this country, gave occasion to the Abbe Raynal to pronounce the American climate unfavorable to the growth and vigor of animal bodies. That rapid philosopher saw the effects, and had not patience to enquire into the proper cause of them; and with characteristic boldness, a boldness, indeed, which we see too often imitated by European travellers and philosophers, pronounced his decision.

Many animals, by the manner in which they are fed and trained may be brought to change, and apparently to lose, the characteristic properties of their nature. Forster remarks of the dogs of Otaheite, which are kept, along with their hogs, and poultry, merely for food, and which are nourished chiefly on fruits and roots, the island furnishing little or no game, have become most inactive and lazy animals. Their heads grow larger than is common to the species; and, in their extreme slugginess, they are hardly ever heard to bark; but utter their languid and uneasy feelings only in a kind of howling.

natural, however, from their habit of carrying heavy burdens, they are, in general, more firmly knit in their joints, and stout in their limbs.

If, in England, as is said, there exists not so great a difference in personal appearance between the higher, and the lower classes of society as in other countries of Europe, it is to be ascribed to the liberty enjoyed under the British constitution, and to the more general diffusion of wealth among the people, which lessens, in some measure, the distance between the ranks of their nobles, and their commons. Science, and military talents open the way to the highest distinctions in that nation. The peculiar institutions, genius, and pursuits of the people favor, in an unusual degree, the acquisition of wealth by the lowest orders of citizens. And these not being prohibited by the laws, or customs of the nation from aspiring to matrimonial connexions with the highest ranks, the different classes are frequently seen to be variously blended together. Often you find in citizens the beautiful figure and complexion of the noblest blood; and in noble houses the coarse features formed in lower life.

In America we have not the distinction of patrician and plebian ranks. And the frequency of migration, in a new and extensive country, has not suffered any peculiar habits of life or local manners, deeply to impress a distinctive character on the people of any state. Great equality of condition in the citizens of the United States, similarity of occupations, and nearly the same degree of cultivation, and social improvement pervading the whole, have produced such uniformity of character, that, as yet, they are not strongly marked by such differences in the expression of the countenance, the composition of their features, or generally in their personal properties, as, in other countries, mark the grades between the superior and inferior orders of the people. And yet there are beginning to be formed certain habits of countenance, the result chiefly of manners, which already serve, to a certain degree, to distinguish the natives of some of the states from those of others.¶ Hereafter, doubtless, they will advance into more considerable, and characteristic distinctions.

If the white population of America affords us less conspicuous instances, than many other nations, of that variety of countenance, and of personal beauty or defect arising from diversity of rank, and refinement in society, the blacks in the southern states afford one that is highly worthy the attention of philosophers.

The field slaves are, in comparison with the domestics, badly fed, clothed, and lodged. They live together in small collections of huts on the plantations on which they labor, remote from the society and example of their superiors.

¶In some of the New England states, for example, we remark, in the body of the people, a certain composed and serious gravity in the expression of the countenance, the result of the sobriety of their domestic education, and of their moral and religious, their industrious and economical habits, which pretty obviously distinguishes them from the natives of most of the states in the southern portion of the Union.

Confined, in this manner, to associate only with themselves, they retain many customs of their African ancestors. And pressed with labor, and dejected by servitude, and the humiliating circumstances in which they find themselves, they have little ambition to improve their personal appearance; and their oppressed condition contributes to continue, in a considerable degree, the deformities of their original climate. The domestic servants, on the other hand, who remain near the persons, and are employed within the families of their masters, are treated with great lenity, their service is light, they are fed and clothed like their superiors; insensibly, they receive the same ideas of elegance and beauty, and discover a great facility in adopting their manners. This class of slaves, therefore, has advanced far before the others in acquiring the regular and agreeable features, and the expressive countenance, which can be formed only in the midst of civilized society. The former are, generally, ill shaped. They preserve, in a great degree, the African lips, nose, and hair. Their genius is dull, and the expression of their countenance sleepy and stupid. The latter frequently exhibit very straight and well proportioned limbs. Their hair is often extended to three and four inches, and, sometimes, to a greater length. The size and form of the mouth is, in many instances, not unhandsome, and sometimes even beautiful; the composition of their features is regular,* their capacity good, and their look animated.

Another example of the power of society in forming the countenance is well known to all those who are acquainted with the savage tribes spread along the frontiers of these states. Among them you frequently meet with persons who have been taken captive in infancy from Anglo-American families, and grown up in the habits of savage life. These descendents of the fairest Europeans universally contract such a resemblance of the natives, in their countenance, and even in their complexion, as not to be easily distinguished from them; and afford a striking proof that the differences in physiognomy, between

---

*The features of the negroes in America, especially of those who reside immediately in the families of their masters, have undergone a great change, while the complexion is not yet sensibly altered. The form and expression of the countenance, and composition of the features being principally affected by the state of society, are constantly receiving some modification from that cause, to improve the negro visage. But the rays of the sun which require, in our climate, the greatest care to prevent them from darkening the fairest skin, may be sufficient, in the exposed condition of the slave, to prevent a skin already black from becoming fair. The countenance of the domestic slaves of the third and fourth race, and, in many instances, even of the second, affords a striking example of the influence of the state of society upon the features. And there is reason to believe that, if these people were perfectly free, and were admitted to all the civil privileges of their masters, they would, in a short period, have few of the distinctive traces of their African ancestors remaining, except their complexion. In the state of New-Jersey, where the hardships of slavery are scarcely felt, we see great numbers of negroes who have the nose as much raised from the face, the forehead as well arched, and the teeth as perpendicularly set in their sockets, as the whites. Some negroes I see daily in Princeton and its vicinity who have the nose turned with a handsome aquiline curve.

the Anglo-American, and the indian depend principally on the *state of society*.†

The College of New-Jersey, a few years ago, furnished a counterpart to this example. A young indian, about the age of fifteen, who had been brought from his nation five or six years before, was studying the latin and greek languages in the institution. And from carefully observing him during the greater portion of that time I received the most perfect conviction that, if the Anglo-American, and the indian were placed from infancy in the same state of society, in this climate which is common to them both, the principal differences which now subsist between the two races, would, in a great measure, be removed when they should arrive at the period of puberty. This young savage had been too far advanced in the habits of his people, before he was introduced into civil society, to render the experiment compleat: for, all impressions received in the tender and pliant state of the human constitution before the age of seven years, or, at the utmost, of nine or ten, are usually more deep and permanent than those made in any future, and equal period of life. A perceptible difference still existed, at the time of his return to his tribe, between him and his fellow students, in the largeness of the mouth and thickness of the lips, in the elevation of the cheek bone, in the darkness of the complexion, and the contour

†The resemblance between these captives and the native savages is so strong as sensibly to strike every observer. Being taken in infancy, before the ideas and habits of civilized society could have made any deep impressions upon them, and spending that tender and forming age in the solitude and rudeness of savage life, they grow up with the same apathy of countenance, the same lugubrious wildness, the same swelling of the features and muscles of the face, the same form and attitude of the limbs, and the same characteristic gait, which is a great elevation of the feet, with the toe somewhat turned in. Exposed without covering, to the constant action of the sun, and of the weather, amidst all the hardships of the savage state, their colour tends to a coppery brown. This example affords another proof of the greater ease with which a dark colour may be stained on a skin originally fair, than effaced from it. The causes of colour are active in their operation, and, entering into the substance of the skin, soon make a durable impression. White is the original ground on which this operation is received. And the whiteness of the skin is to be preserved only by carefully protecting it from the action of these causes. Protection has merely a *negative* influence: applied, therefore, to a skin already discoloured, it will be slow in producing any change towards white as long as the smallest degree of *positive* agency is suffered from the original causes of discolouration. And, as the skin retains with great constancy impressions once received into its substance, all the dark shades of the complexion will be very long retained. That period of time, therefore, which would be sufficient, in a savage state, to change a fair complexion, to the darkest hue which the climate can impress, would hardly remove one shade from a black colour. Unless, then, the climate be such as to operate very great changes on the internal constitution of the body, and to alter the whole state of the secretions, as well as to defend it from the fervid action of the sun, the negro colour may, by the exposure and hardships of a poor and servile condition, be rendered perpetual.

In what page of the essay has a certain annotator in the edition of Rees' Cyclopaedia published by Bradford & Co. in Philadelphia, found it asserted, that the negro complexion has hitherto become sensibly lighter in America? If he has any candor, and possesses, in any degree, the information which ought to distinguish a man who presumes to be an annotator on that work, he will be ashamed of the indiscretion and incorrectness, to give them the softest names they will bear, of some of his remarks under the title, Complexion.

of the face. These differences had sensibly diminished from the period of his coming to the college: and they appeared to be diminishing the faster in proportion as he lost that vacancy, and lugubrious wildness of countenance peculiar to the savage state, and began to acquire the agreeable expression of civil life. The expression of the eye, and the softening of the features in consequence of new ideas and emotions, which had taken birth since he came into society, removed the chief distinction, except that of the complexion, which had been visible originally between him and his companions. Less difference existed at length between his features and those of his fellow students than we often see between persons of the same nation.‡ After careful and minute attention, and comparing each feature with the correspondent feature in many of his companions, the difference was very small, and sometimes hardly perceptible; and yet there was an obvious difference in the whole countenance, created I believe principally by the impression which the complexion, in combination with the other varieties made upon the eye. A few comparisons conducted in this way would result, I am persuaded, in the conviction that the varieties among mankind are much less considerable than, on a slight inspection they appear to be. Each single trait or limb, when examined apart, exhibits no difference from the common properties of the species which may not easily be accounted for. Particular varieties are small. It is the result of the whole, taken in at one impression, which appears difficult to be explained. The combined effect of many minute particulars appears great, and, at the first view, unaccountable. And we have not patience, or skill, it may be, to divide this sum into its least portions, and to perceive, in that state, how easy it is of solution.

Under the head of *the state of society* are comprehended diet, clothing, lodging, manners, government, arts, religion, agricultural improvements, commercial pursuits, habits of thinking, and ideas of all kinds naturally arising out of this state, infinite in number and variety. If each of these causes be admitted to possess, as undoubtedly they do, a small influence in forming the character of the countenance, the different combinations and results of the whole must necessarily seem great, and, united with the effects of climate, which have been already in some degree explained will afford sufficient principles on which to account for all the varieties that exist among mankind.

Another cause of the varieties arising out of the state of society will be found in the power which men possess over themselves, of producing considerable changes in their figure and appearance according to any standard of beauty

‡The complexion of this young lad was not of so dark a copper as that of his native stock, which could be easily discerned by the stain of blushing in his cheek which is never perceived in those dark coloured tribes. The difference of these effects, however, in them and in him, I ascribe rather to the pains used by those savages to increase the darkness of their natural hue by filthy paints, and other means, than to any influence in the change of his manner of living to remove any of the natural shades of the indian colour. But he added nothing to them, while the savages, by their exposure to the injuries of the weather, and the hardships of their state, with other causes which have been mentioned, are continually increasing them.

which they may have framed. Each nation differs from others as much in its ideas of beauty as in personal appearance. A Laplander prefers the flat, round faces of his dark skinned country women to the fairest beauties of England. Whatever be the standard which any people have formed to themselves, there is a general effort to attain it; and it is every where pursued with more or less ardor and success in proportion to the advantages which men possess in society, and to the estimation in which beauty is held.

To this object tend the infinite pains taken in society to compose the features, and to form the attitudes of children. This is the end of a large portion of the arts of polished life. How many drugs are sold, and how many applications are made for the improvement of beauty? How many artists of different kinds live upon this idea of beauty? If children learn to dance it is chiefly in order to improve and to display their beauty. If they acquire skill in the use of the sword, it is more for the purpose of improving personal beauty than for defence. If this general effort for appearance sometimes leads the decripid and deformed into absurdity, and produces fantastic characters among the young, it has, however, a great and national effect in forming the countenance, not less than the attitudes and movements of the person.

Of its effect in creating distinctions among nations in which different ideas of personal beauty prevail, and different means are employed to reach them, we may frame some conception from the differences that take place in the same nation, in which similar ideas exist, and similar means are used to form the person, only in various degrees. What a difference between the soft and elegant tints of complexion generally seen in women who move in the higher circles of society, and the coarse ruddiness of the vulgar!—between the uncouth features, and unpliant limbs of an unpolished rustic, and the complacency of countenance, the graceful figure, and easy air and movement of persons in cultivated life!—between the shaped and meaning face of a well bred lady, and the soft and plump simplicity of a country girl! We now easily account for these varieties which have become familiar to the eye, because we see the operation of their causes. But if we should find an entire nation distinguished by a composition of features resembling the one, and another by the contrary, they would have as fair a title to be ranked under different species by certain philosophers as the German, and the Tartar. The general countenance of Europe was, probably, more various several centuries ago than at present. The differences, which arise out of the state of society as their principal cause are, insensibly wearing away in proportion as, in the progress of refinement, the manners and ideas of the European nations are gradually approximating one standard. But the effect of a common standard of beauty, and the means employed by our own countrymen to form their persons after this ideal model are, through the influence of custom, and general example, often little observed. The means used by other nations, who aim at a different idea, attracting more notice by their novelty, will, therefore, furnish us with more striking examples. Many of the nations beyond the Indus, as well as the Tartars, from whom they have derived their origin,§ universally admire small eyes, and large ears. They are at great pains, therefore, to compress their eye-lids at the corners, and stretch their ears by weights appended to them, or by drawing them frequently with the hand, and by cutting their rims, so that they may hang down to their shoulders, which they consider among the highest ornaments of their persons. For a like reason, they extirpate the hair from their bodies; and, on the face, they leave only a few tufts here and there, which they shave.‡ The Tartars often extract the whole hair of the head, except a long and thick tuft on the crown which they braid and adorn in different forms. Similar ideas of beauty with regard to the eyes, the ears, and the hair, and similar customs among the aboriginal tribes of the greater portion of North-America are no inconsiderable proofs that this division of the continent has been peopled from the north-eastern regions of Asia.¶ In Greece, Arabia, and other parts of the East, large eyes are esteemed beautiful; and in these countries they take extraordinary pains to increase their aperture. In many parts of India they flatten the foreheads of their children in infancy by the application of broad plates of lead. In China they compress the feet of female infants by tight bandages. Among many of the barbarous tribes of Africa, and in the northern regions of Asia they endeavour to assist the influence of the climate by using violence to flatten the nose of every infant in order to mould it after their capricious idea of beauty. The American indians study to render the natural darkness of their complexion deeper by discolouring paints and unguents: and all savages esteem certain kinds of deformity to be perfections; and strive to increase the admiration of their persons by heightening the wildness of their features.

§It is probable that the countries of India and China, considering the pleasantness of those inviting climates, were originally inhabited before the regions of Tartary. But, the frequent conquests to which they have since been subject, particularly, the northern parts of India, from Tartarian tribes, have changed the habits, ideas, and persons of the people even more, perhaps, than Europe was changed by the barbarians who overran it in the fifth and sixth centuries. The present population of Northern India is, in effect, Tartarian, only changed to softer features, and better proportioned persons, by a milder climate, and a more improved state of society.

‡The inhabitants of New Zealand, according to Mr. Forster, although they do not extirpate their beards with tweezers, yet cut their faces, and mark them with such scars, through a preposterous idea of beauty, or manliness, as destroy a great part of the hair.

¶The celebrated Dr. Robertson, in his history of America, deceived by the misinformation of hasty, or ignorant observers, has ventured to assert that the natives of America have no hair on the face, or the body; and, like many other philosophers, has set himself to account for a fact which does not exist. They do not differ in this respect from the rest of the human race. Dr. Blumenbach, through a similar error in his information, supposes that their hair is very thin, and in small quantity. On the other hand, the hair of our native indians, where it is not carefully extirpated by art, is both thick and long. But careless travellers seeing their smooth faces, and bald heads enquired no farther into the cause, but represented the fact as proceeding from a natural debility of constitution and consequent deficiency of this excrescence.

Similarity of customs, of complexion, and countenance between the North-American indians, and north-eastern Asiatics, gives strong indications of a common origin. The South-American con-

I might proceed, in this manner, through every country on the globe, pointing out the many arts which are practised to reach some favorite idea of the
human form. Arts which insensibly, in a long course of time, produce great
and striking consequences,* and which, although commonly supposed to affect
only the person who uses them, are not without their influence on posterity.
The process of nature in this, is as little known, as in all her other works:
but the fact cannot have escaped the observation of those who have paid a
careful attention to her operations. Every considerable change of colour, feature, or figure which has grown into a habit of the body, or indicates any
important alteration in the general action of the system, is liable to be transmitted, along with other constitutional properties, to offspring. The coarse features
of laboring people, created by great hardships, and exposure to the injuries
of the weather, we often see imparted. The broad feet of the rustic, spread
out by often treading the soil barefooted; and the large hand and arm, formed
by constant labor, are often discernible in children. The increase, diminution
or change of any other limbs, or features, resulting from arts, or national habits
which aim at forming the person after any peculiar ideal model may, in like
manner, became hereditary.† The inferior animals afford many examples to
prove the existence of this natural law. The figure, the colour, and many other
properties of the breed of horses are easily changed, by those who have skill
in raising them, according to almost any reigning taste. And they are equally

---

tinent, particularly on the western side, gives no less striking proofs of its having been peopled
from the islands of the Great South Sea; as they were peopled originally from the South of Asia.
The inhabitants of the southern portion of the Farther India are evidently of Malayan origin. And
the same people you trace from that continent through a succession of islands till you approach
the western side of America; whence a population of the same, or very similar character appears
to have spread from Peru and Chili along the Oronoco, and the different tributary streams of
the Maragnon. And here accordingly you meet with various tribes of indians of handsomer form
and features than those of North-America, and not unlike, in their appearance, many of the islanders of the South Sea. Remotely, however, these people have all, probably, the same origin.
The Malays are of Tartar race, improved by the mild climate of Southern Asia. These, passing
through the equally mild climates of the Pacific ocean appear to have reached America in that
direction; while North-America has received her population from Tartary through the rougher
climates of Siberia. Other parts of this continent may have received many accidental emigrants
cast upon its shores, in a long succession of ages, from different portions of the Old World.
The nations from which they parted may have been civilized; but arriving in a new world, without
skill to return, or to hold any intercourse with their ancestral seats, and pressed by their immediate
wants, and the difficulties of procuring subsistence in an uncultivated wilderness, from any source
except from hunting, they would soon lose the knowledge of all other arts, and their posterity
would necessarily become savages.

*National ideas of beauty may often have their source in the tendencies of the climate, and
the natural influences of society; and often in some unaccountable caprice: but, whether derived
from the one source, or the other, they will ever have a powerful effect in forming the attitudes,
the air, the composition of the features, and the whole aspect of the person.

†Is this more difficult to be conceived, or less worthy of credit than that constitutional tendency
to certain diseases which, it is now acknowledged by all physicians, may be rendered hereditary?

susceptible of deterioration by neglect, or by improper treatment. Out of the same original stock, the Germans, who are settled in Pennsylvania, raise large heavy horses for the draught; the Irish in the same state, by a different mode of treatment, raise such only as are much smaller, and lighter in their form. By competent skill, and the application of proper pains, or, on the other hand, by neglect, or ignorance, the races of all our domestic animals may be almost infinitely varied. Human nature being much more pliant than that of most other animals, and being affected by a much greater number of minute causes, according to the state of society in which men are placed, is susceptible, also of a much greater variety of changes from their operation. And among these causes, that which I have mentioned of an imaginary standard of the human form, or of the perfection of social manners, is not the least influential. It is for this reason, perhaps, that in different districts of the United States, in which emigrants from Holland, or Germany, or France, have fixed their residence, in such numbers as, hitherto, to have been able, in a great measure, to preserve their original habits, and manners, and, consequently, their peculiar ideas of personal beauty, grace, or propriety of conduct, they retain also a strong resemblance of the primitive stocks from which they are descended. Whereas those who have not limited their intercourse to the circle of their own countrymen, but have mingled freely with the Anglo-Americans, and have adopted their manners, and habits of thinking, have contracted such similitude to them in their persons, and features that it is now not easy to distinguish from one another, people whose ancestors were discriminated by most obvious national characteristics.

When once any general and standard idea of the beauty of the human person is established in any nation, connexions in marriage will be greatly influenced by it. And these will contribute, in no inconsiderable degree, to perpetuate, or to modify the national countenance.‡ If men, in the union of the sexes, were as much under control as some of the inferior animals, their persons might be moulded, in the course of a few generations, to almost any standard, making due allowance for the influence of climate, and the necessary operation of other causes which may be connected with it. But left as these connexions commonly are, to the momentary passions, the tasteless caprice, or the gross interests of individuals, they are more anomalous in their effects. There is, however, a common idea which men insensibly to themselves, and almost without design pursue. And, in general, they pursue it with more or less success in proportion to the rank and taste of the different classes in society, where accident does not, as too often happens, throw beauty into the arms of defor-

‡Perhaps the power of imagination in pregnant women, which must be always strongly affected by the national character of countenance, may deserve some consideration on this subject. Formerly, the imagination of women was supposed by naturalists to possess a degree of influence in this case which was not justified by the facts relied on to support it. But I am inclined to believe that, at present, opinions have been carried to an extreme on the other hand.

mity, or where, in others, they are governed in forming this connexion by interest ever void of taste. The superior ranks, with few exceptions, will generally excel, in the beauty of their form and complexion, not only because they enjoy, in a higher degree, other advantages which have been already pointed out as contributing to this end, but because they have it more in their power to form connexions in marriage among the most beautiful of the sex. The Persian nobility, who are of Tartarian origin, have, in consequence of their removal into a more favorable climate, and their having adopted the manners of a civilized people, acquired juster ideas of the perfection of the human form than they possessed in their primitive seats. Hence, being led to seek the most beautiful women in marriage, they have exchanged the harsh features, and disproportioned figures of their Tartar ancestors, for a stature tall, and elegant, and a form and expression of countenance noble and commanding. The Turkish families of fortune have, in like manner, improved the physical character of their race. And if we may ascribe any truth to the portraits drawn by the Roman historians of the ancestors of the present nations of Europe, we must acknowledge that the refinement of manners, and the improvements in the state of society, which have been introduced in modern times among their descendants, have contributed also to produce a proportional improvement in their features, and their persons. Nothing can exceed the pictures of barbarism and deformity given us by these writers, of the ancient German and Gothic nations; whereas no nations, perhaps, have ever surpassed the posterity of these rude people in personal beauty. Such examples tend to shew how much national varieties may depend on the state of taste resulting from the condition of society, and the progress, or decline of civilization and the arts. They shew, likewise, how much the human race might be improved in personal, as it is acknowledged it may be in mental qualities, by proper cultivation.

Of all people the ancient Greeks appear to have best understood how much it is in the power of manners to improve the beauty of the human person, and to increase the vigor of the human constitution. To these ends were directed many of their customs, a large portion of their legislative wisdom, and even of the philosophy of their schools, and the whole system of their athletic exercises. And it has been conjectured, not improbably, that the fine living models exhibited in that country to statuaries and painters became a primary cause of the high perfection to which the arts of sculpture and painting arrived in Greece. Hitherto among almost all people, not only matrimonial connexions, but all means of improving the human form, have been abandoned, in a great measure, to accident, and the caprice of individuals. Persons of elevated and noble rank have usually had it more in their power than others to select the beauty of nations in marriage; and thus, while, without system or design, they gratified only their own taste, they have generally distinguished their order as much by elegant proportions of person, by fine features, and a noble expression of countenance, as by their prerogatives in society. And the tales of romance which ascribe superlative beauty to their princesses; and the fictions of poets, which distinguish their kings and princes by the dignity and manly beauty of their persons, are not to be imputed solely to venality, and a base disposition to flatter the great, but have a real foundation in nature.§ And the usual strain of figurative language, which, in order to be just, must be borrowed from nature, strongly supports this remark: a *princely* person, and a *noble* thought, are ordinary figures of speech.

Mental capacity, which is as various as the human physiognomy, is equally susceptible of improvement, or deterioration, from the state of society, and the manners and pursuits, which may form the character of any people. The body and mind have such reciprocal influence upon each other, that we often see certain peculiar powers or tendencies of the rational faculty intimately connected with certain corporeal forms. And whenever the moral, not less than the physical causes, under the influence of which any people exist, have produced any visible effect on the form and expression of the countenance, they will also be found proportionally to affect the operations of the mind. The Boeotian countenance was as dull and phlegmatic as the genius of the people: and though Boeotia and Attica were in the vicinity of each other, and inhabited originally by the same race, the distinction between Boeotian and Attic wit is not to be ascribed solely to national prejudice, but had a real foundation in the different characters of the two people. And the proper source of a distinction so striking and important is to be sought rather in the state of society and manners in those republics, than in the Boeotian air to which it has been sarcastically attributed by ancient writers. By the alteration of a few political and civil institutions, Thebes might have become Athens, and Athens Thebes. Different epochs in society unfold different powers of the human mind. Poetry, eloquence, and philosophy seldom arrive at their highest perfection together;

§The justness of these observations will be less perceived in the United States in which so great an equality prevails among the citizens, and the poorest enjoy comparative ease and plenty, than in Europe where so wide a distinction exists between the highest and the lowest grades of society. They are corroborated, however, by relations formerly referred to in Capt. Cook's observations on the inhabitants of most of the islands which he visited in the South Sea. In remarking on those of the island of Owyhee, he says, "The same superiority which is observable in the *Erees* (or nobles) through all the other islands is found also here. Those whom we saw, are, without exception, perfectly well formed; whereas, the lower sort, besides their general inferiority, are subject to all the variety of make and figure that is seen in the *populace* of other countries." Cook's 3d voyage, book 3d, chap. 6th. These are the remarks of a plain, but most judicious man, who had no theory to support, and was not biased by the opinions of any political party.

Such is the deference paid to beauty, and the sentiment of superiority with which it inspires the beholder, that, to this quality, probably, does the body of princes and nobles collectively taken, in any country, owe great part of their influence over the populace. Riches and magnificence in dress and equipage produce much of their effect in procuring respect, by giving an artificial beauty to the person. How often does history remark that young princes have attached their subjects, and generals their armies by extraordinary beauty of person? And young and beautiful queens have ever been followed and served with uncommon enthusiasm.

not because the mind of man does not at all times possess the same endowments from nature, but because, in the progress of society, new objects arise, and new combinations of ideas are formed which call into exercise different faculties of the soul. If as just and true a picture of the personal as of the mental qualities of men at these different epochs, could be preserved to posterity we should, probably, find as great variety in the one as in the other.‡ The coarsest features, and the harshest expression of countenance, will commonly be found in the rudest states of society. And the mental capacities of men in that condition will ever be proportionally weaker than those of nations who have made any considerable progress in the arts of civilization.¶ They become feeble through want of objects to employ them, and through defect of motives to call forth their exercise. The rudeness of their manners is calculated to quench the first sparks of taste which might be struck out by the grandeur of the objects, and the wild beauty of the scenes which surround them; and even the grossness and filthiness of the food of most savage tribes, and their ignorance of the arts of preparing it so as to render it most nutritious and salutary to the human constitution, tend to blunt their genius. And the Hottentots, the Laplanders, and the people of Tierra del Fuego are the most stupid of mankind for this, among other reasons which have formerly been suggested, that they approach, in these respects, the nearest of any people to the brute creation.*

The effects of savage life upon the human countenance are, in many respects, so peculiar as to merit a more minute illustration. Civilization creates some affinity in the countenances of all polished nations. In proportion to their improvement in the arts, and to the progress of science among them there is a characteristic and common *expression*, which results from the similarity of the operations of the mind, and of the subjects about which these operations are employed. But savages in every region are usually distinguished by a countenance so dull and stupid, when not excited into ferocity by hostile and

‡Of this, the example, which I have before produced of the ancient Germans, and the present nations of Europe, affords a striking proof.

¶The exaggerated representations which we sometimes receive of the superior ingenuity of men in savage life, are usually the result of inconsideration. Savages are the subjects of eulogy for the same reason that we admire a monkey,—that is, a certain resemblance of the actions of men in civilized society which was not expected from the rudeness of their condition. There are doubtless degrees of genius among savages as well as among civilized nations: but the comparison should be made of savages among themselves, and not of the genius of a savage, with that of a polished, people.

*The descendents of the African race in America are, beyond all doubt, more ingenious, and capable of acquiring any new art, than those who have grown up to maturity in the savagism of Africa. Whether they will ever become as susceptible of improvement as the white races, which has been strenuously denied by several writers, and, in particular, by Mr. Jefferson in our own country, will be subject of consideration hereafter.

revengeful passions, as to induce many writers to regard them as an inferior grade in the descent from the human to the brute creation. Civilized nations inhabiting chiefly the temperate latitudes, and savages, except in America, only the extremes of heat and cold, these differences in point of climate, combined with those arising out of their state of society, have produced varieties of aspect so great as to appear unaccountable to those who have only superficially attended to this subject. It is not unworthy of being remarked, however, that the real sum of these varieties, when examined separately, is not so great as the apparent, when taken in at one view. In the latter case, the eye, contemplating at a single glance, not only the variety presented in each feature, but the relations of that feature to every other, and to the whole; and each new relation producing some modification in the appearance of the countenance, the entire sum of these combinations surprizes us by its magnitude.—For example, even a small change in the eye, will produce a striking alteration in the appearance of the whole countenance; because it presents to us, not singly the difference which exists in that feature alone, but all the differences arising from the several combinations of that feature with every other feature in the face. In like manner, a change in the complexion presents, not its own difference alone, but a much greater effect, the result of a similar combination. If both the eyes and the complexion be changed in the same person, each variety affecting the whole system of the features, the union of the two results will be productive of a third incomparably greater than either. If, in the same way, we proceed to the lips, the nose, the cheeks, and to every single feature in the visage, each produces a multiplied effect, by its separate relations to the whole, and the entire result, like the product of a geometrical series, is so much beyond our first expectation that it confounds common observers, in their attempts to explain the cause, and will sometimes embarrass the most discerning philosophers till they turn their attention, in this manner, to divide, and combine effects.

To treat this subject fully it would be necessary, in the first place, to ascertain some general expression of countenance which every where belongs to savage life; and then, as there are degrees of more or less rudeness in the state of savagism, as well as of refinement in civilized society, it would be necessary to distinguish the several modifications which each degree makes in the general aspect; and, in the last place, to consider the varieties, almost innumerable, which arise from combining these general features with the effects of climate and of other causes already mentioned. I shall endeavour merely to draw the general outlines of the human countenance as it is formed by the wildness and solitude which commonly prevails in the savage state. And, in this portrait I shall take my type chiefly from the American savage.

His eye, in his ordinary state of tranquillity, is vacant and unexpressive—the whole composition of his countenance, is fixed and stupid, with little variety of movement in the features—over this unmeaning ground is thrown an air of wildness and melancholy.—The face is somewhat dilated at the sides—its muscles are lax—the mouth and lips large—and the nose, in the same proportion, depressed.

In order to explain this picture, and to point out the causes which concur to create it, let it be observed that the expression of the eye, and of the whole countenance depends, almost entirely upon the objects with which we are surrounded, the impressions which they make upon the mind, and the reflections and emotions they excite. The natural scenery of a country, the occupations, habits, religion, science, government, manners, of a people, all have their separate influences in forming the national character, and expression of face. The justness of this observation is verified by many facts which are daily presented to us in society. How often do we perceive a distinctive character of countenance impressed upon certain religious sects by the peculiar habits and tenets of their profession? Those who practice certain mechanical occupations, and the professors' even of the more liberal arts, are often distinguishable by some peculiarities of aspect, as well as of manners. Every thought that passes through the mind traces its character, in stronger, or weaker lines upon the visage; and total vacuity of thought leaves in it only the expression of stupidity. The infinite variety of ideas and emotions created in civilized society, contribute to give great variety to the lines of the face; at the same time, each class of citizens is liable to be marked by some distinctive expression resulting from their habits and occupations; while each individual will be characterized by some singular, and personal traits according to his genius, education and pursuits. Between savage and civilized society, therefore, there will be all the difference which can arise from thinking, and want of thought. And savages will have all that uniformity among themselves, in the same climate, and country, which naturally arises from vacancy of mind, and the want, especially of all the delicate emotions, which are so varied in society. A vacant eye, and unmeaning countenance, approaching, in some regions, especially under the extremes of heat and cold, almost to a look of idiotism, seem to reduce the savage, in his aspect, many degrees nearer to the brutes, than the civilized man. The solitude in which he lives renders him dull, and gives him an appearance of melancholy. He seldom speaks, or laughs. Society rarely enlivens his features. When not engaged in hunting or in war, having no object to rouse him, he will often sit for hours in one posture, with his eyes fixed to a single point, and his senses lost in sombre, and unmeaning reverie. These solitary feelings, and melancholy emotions, serve to cast over his visage, which other causes render fixed, and unexpressive, a sad and lugubrious air. The wild scenes of nature around him impress some resemblance of themselves on his features; and the passions of war and rage, which are almost the only ones that occupy the mind of a savage, frequently mingle with the whole an aspect of brutal ferocity.†

Paucity of ideas, solitude, and melancholy contribute likewise, in no small degree, to form the remaining features of a savage countenance—a mouth large, and somewhat protruded, a dilatation of the face, and a general laxness and swell of its muscles.

The active exercise of thought, and the intercourse of refined society, induce a tension, and action in the muscles of the face which serve to give it a greater elevation towards the middle. But the vacant mind of the savage leaving these muscles lax and unexerted, they swell into larger dimensions, dilating themselves more towards the sides, than rising towards the center of the face. Hence, perhaps, that plumpness of feature, and roundness of visage, or departure from the oval figure, which we so often find in young persons, and especially young women, who have been bred in the retirement of the country.‡

Grief peculiarly affects the lips by distending them, and giving them a swoln appearance. Solitude, gloom or melancholy, in proportion to the degree in which they prevail are found to be attended with a like effect. Where they naturally arise out of the state of society, therefore, and when they operate from infancy, and are seldom counteracted by the more gay and vivid emotions created in polished life, the effects will, at length, become considerable. The lips of a savage, will, from these causes, generally be large, and in a less or greater degree, thick and protruded.

The nose affects, and is affected by other features of the face. The whole system of the features is so connected, that, if one be remarkably enlarged, it is commonly accompanied with a proportional diminution of some other. A prominent nose is generally joined with a thin visage. On the other hand, a broad face, thick lips, and elevated cheek bones, are no less commonly accompanied with a certain depression of the feature of the nose. It seems as if the extension of the nerves in one direction restrained their growth in another.§ Savages, therefore, have this feature commonly more flat, and sunk

†The inhabitants of most of the small islands in the great Southern and Pacific oceans form an exception to this general character of the savage countenance. Prevented, by their isolated state, from engaging in perpetual hostilities with neighboring and warlike tribes, like the continental savages, and several of those of the larger islands, they are distinguished by an air of mildness and complacency, which is much increased in consequence of their easy and social manner of living. And this is greatly promoted by the mildness of their climate, and the abundance of simple and nutritious food spontaneously supplied by their soil.

‡And may not the superior advances made in society, and the arts, in Europe, with the superior vigor and energy of the human character in that quarter of the world, be one reason of the greater elevation of the European above that of the Asiatic countenance?

§By a small experiment on ourselves, we may render this effect obvious. By a protrusion of the lips, or by drawing down the mouth at the corners, we shall perceive a stricture on the nose,

than civilized nations. This, however, is not to be regarded as the entire cause of that extreme flatness which prevails on part of the coast of Africa, and in Lapland. Climate, probably, enters there for part of the effect; and is aided by an absurd sense of beauty which prompts the natives to depress it by art.‡

The preceeding observations tend to account for some of the most characteristic and distinguishing features which prevail in savage life. To these I might have added another general reason of the peculiar wildness and rudeness which marks them in that state of society. The feelings of savages, when they deviate from their usual apathy at home, are mostly of the uneasy kind; and to them they give an unconstrained expression. Hence will naturally result a habit of the face extremely uncouth; as we see a similar negligence among the vulgar contribute to heighten that disgusting coarseness which so many other causes concur to create.

I have now briefly examined the effects of climate, of various modes of living, and states of society upon the complexion, and figure of the human species. And in this examination we have seen that the pliant nature of man is susceptible of many changes from the action of the minutest causes: and the action of these causes habitually repeated through a sufficient period of time, can create, at length, the most conspicuous distinctions among people originally the same. The effect proceeds, increasing from one generation to another, till it arrives at that point where the constitution can yield no farther to the power of the operating cause. Here it assumes a permanent form, which constitutes the character of the climate, or the nation.

It is frequently asked on this subject, why, unless there be an original difference in the species of men, are not the natives of all climates *born*, at least, with the same figure and complexion? To such enquiries it is sufficient to answer, that it is for the same reason, whatever that may be, that other resemblances of parents are communicated to children. Experience demonstrates that figure, stature, complexion, features, diseases, and even powers of the mind may become hereditary. To those who find no difficulty in acknowledging that these properties may be communicated to offspring according to the established laws of nature, the transmission of the climatical or national differences among men, of which we have treated, can contain nothing which ought to appear supernatural, or incredible.—If it be enquired, why, then, a sun burnt face, or a wounded limb, is not, by the same laws, if they exist, transmitted to posterity? we may justly reply, that these are only partial accidents which pro-

---

that, in an age when all the features are peculiarly soft and pliant, would sensibly tend to depress it. And, continued through the whole of life, would fix it immovably in that habit.

‡Whether the flatness of the African nose be the effect of climate, or of the manner of living, certain it is, that among the posterity of the Africans in America, who are placed in easy and comfortable circumstances, we frequently meet with this feature not only raised like that of the Anglo-American, but beautifully turned.

duce no change on the interior structure and temperament of the constitution. It is the *constitution* which is conveyed by birth. And when any change becomes incorporated, into the system, so as, in any considerable degree, to affect its organization, or the state of its secretions, it then becomes communicable to offspring along with all other constitutional properties?

I proceed, now, to consider the exceptions existing in different regions of the globe which seem to stand in opposition to the principles maintained in this essay.

I begin with recalling an observation which I have formerly made, that these exceptions are neither so numerous, nor so important as they have been represented to be, by inaccurate travellers, and by credulous philosophers. Even Buffon is not altogether free from the charge of credulity, who only doubts concerning the relations of Struys, and other prodigy-mongers, who have filled the histories of their voyages with marvelous tales, the fruit of deliberate falsehood, or of ignorant surprize. Nothing can appear more ridiculous and contemptible than philosophers, like maids and nurses, retailing, with solemn faces, the stories of monsters, and endeavouring to find some cause of their existence in the mysterious operations of nature.¶

In America, perhaps, we receive such tales with more incredulity and contempt than the people of most other nations; because we see, in such a strong light, the falsehood of similar wonders, said to exist in this continent, which, a few years ago, were reported, and believed, and made the subjects of many philosophical disquisitions, in Europe. We hear every day the absurd remarks and false reasonings of foreigners on almost every object which comes under their observation in this new region. They judge of things, of men, and of manners under the influence of habits and ideas, framed in a different climate, and a different state of society. They pronounce concerning all things according to the accompaniments which similar facts would have in their own country: without examining, like true philosophers, the causes of the differences created in the actions of men, and manners of nations, by diversity of situation. They infer general and erroneous conclusions from single and mistaken facts, viewed

¶Buffon who describes the inhabitants of the Ladrone islands as being, in general, of a stature superior to the men of other countries, thinks it not improbable that giants may have been seen there. And the same author admits the story of the existence of a people in New Holland without teeth.

Lord Monbodo, in his treatise of the origin of languages, &c. whimsically enough, supposes that mankind originally had tails; and that they lost this brutal excrescence only in consequence of the progress of civilization. And he believes that there are some nations who yet retain this mark of affinity with the inferior tribes of animals. Sir Walter Raleigh speaks of a people in Guiana without necks, whose eyes, or rather, whose eye, for it is said that they have only one, is in the upper part of the breast. Other writers have described certain hordes of Tartars in a similar stile. The necks of these Tartars are naturally extremely short. And the spirit of travelling prodigy has sometimes undertaken to annihilate them.

through that prejudice which previous habits always form in common minds.*

Since America has become better known, we find no canibals in Florida, —no men in Guiana who have their heads sunk into their breasts,—no martial Amazons. The giants of Patagonia have disappeared. And the same fate should have attended those of the Ladrone islands to whom Buffon, after Gemelli Carreri has been pleased to give an imaginary existence. Tavernier's tales of the smooth and hairless bodies of the Mogul women may be ranked with those which have so long, and so falsely attributed this peculiarity to the natives

*It requires a more minute and accurate attention, and a greater portion of reflection, and the true spirit of philosophy than is possessed, or exercised by ordinary travellers to judge with just discrimination of men and things in foreign countries. Countries are described from a single spot, manners from a single action, and men from the first man that is seen on a foreign shore, and him, perhaps, only half seen and at a distance. Hence America has been represented by different travellers as the most fertile or the most barren region on the globe. Navigators to Africa who have visited only the shores of the Gambia or the Senegal speak of the spreading forests, and the luxuriant herbage of that arid continent. Surprize occasioned by an uncommon complexion, or composition of features, or a stature a little above or below the ordinary standard, has distorted, and increased or diminished the size of the people of different nations beyond all the proportions of nature. Such judgments are similar to those which a Chinese sailor who had accidentally been thrown on Cape May, or Cape Hatteras, would form of the United States; or would form of Great-Britain or of France who had seen only the suburbs of Dover, or of Calais. Besides the limited sphere of observation of such a traveller, he would naturally see every thing with astonishment, or with disgust, which would exaggerate or distort his representation. He would see each action, that might occur to his observation, by itself, without knowing its connexions; or he would give it in his imagination those connexions which it would have in his own country. A similar error led Capt. Cook, in his first voyage to form an unfavorable opinion of the modesty and chastity of the women of Otaheité, which his after experience taught him to correct. Many such false judgments are to be found in almost every writer of voyages or travels. The American savages have often been represented by European writers as frigid towards the sex because they seldom avail themselves of the opportunities almost constantly offered by their state of society, to violate the chastity of their females. And, on the other hand, they are sometimes represented as licentious because they are seen to lie promiscuously in the same wigwam, or round the same fire. Both judgments are false; and result from prepossessions formed in society. Simplicity or rather rudeness of manners, and the hardships of their state, more than constitution, or than climate, create that appearance of indifference, on the one hand, which is esteemed an evidence of frigidity; and give occasion, on the other, to that promiscuous intercourse which is supposed to be united with criminal indulgence. Luxury, restraints, and the manifold arts employed for the purpose, in polished society, contribute to inflame desire, which is allayed by the coarse manners, and the hard fare of savage life, wherein no studied excitements are employed to awaken the passions. And in the midst of this apparently unrestrained freedom, infinitely fewer violations of female honor and safety take place, than are found under the restraints and excitements of our civilized manners. On a like foundation cowardice has been imputed to the aboriginal natives of America, because they prosecute their wars by stratagem,—insensibility because they suffer torture with a patience not to be parallelled in any other country,—and thievishness, because a savage, having hardly any notion of property, except in those things which he has in present occupation, takes, without scruple, what he wants, and sees you do not need.

We see, in innumerable instances, in the narrations of travellers, the act of one man, the figure, or stature of the first vagrant seen upon a distant shore, furnish out the character of a whole nation.

of America. The same judgment may we form of those histories which pretend to describe nations without natural affection, without any sentiments of religion, and without moral principle. In a word, the greater part of those extraordinary deviations from the common laws of climate, and of society which formerly obtained credit in Europe, are found, by more accurate observation, to have no existence. If a few marvelous narrations are still retailed by credulous writers, a short time will explode them all, or shew that the facts have been misunderstood; and, that when placed in a proper light, they are susceptible of an easy explanation, on the known, and common principles of nature.

Leaving such pretended facts, and the inferences to which they have given birth, to deserved contempt, I shall now state a few well ascertained phenomena which appear to imply a deviation from the laws of climate as they have been laid down in this essay; and, by the solution of them, endeavour to confirm those laws.

In tracing the same parallels round the globe we do not discern in every region placed at equal distances from the sun the same features and complexion. In the various kingdoms, and districts of India, and along the northern

---

The false and distorted representations of Europeans who visit the United States are sufficient to make us distrust the narrations of all foreigners who pretend to depict the state and manners of new and distant countries. There is hardly a fact which is not perverted by such men as Weld and Ashe, and the inferences which they draw from what they observe are generally false. They travel without a spark of that philosophic spirit which alone entitles a man to remark on foreign, and especially on new countries. Ashe's distress on the Alleghany mountains on account of wild beasts which never disturb an American: his terrors, his disgusts, and his wonderful descriptions of thunderstorms, fire-flies, and snakes are truly laughable; and almost his whole history equally contemptible and false. The same may be said of a great part of the travels through this country which have been published. Volney who claims to stand in the first ranks of philosophy, writes with little more accuracy or discrimination than these ignorant Englishmen. One of the customs, he says, of the citizens of Philadelphia is universally to indulge themselves in bed for two hours in the afternoon, during which time the streets are absolutely deserted. He may have been acquainted with one or two families in which the ladies gave themselves this indulgence. The rest of the story he must have dreamed. Because he has seen in some houses in Virginia hot buttered rolls served up at breakfast, he says all the Americans eat hot paste perfectly soaked in grease. These are but small samples out of many in which he, and a multitude of others, display their inveterate prejudice, their inexcusable carelessness, or deliberate falsehood.

By such writers, nations have been judged to be without any sentiment of religion, because they have not seen temples, and ceremonies. Others have been pronounced to be without natural affection, because one man has been seen to do an act of seeming barbarity. But the nation which appears to have departed farthest from the ordinary laws of human nature, is that of the Giagas, a people of Africa, mentioned by Lord Kaims in his laudable attempts to disprove the truth of the Mosaic history. This people, he thinks, must be of a distinct race from the rest of mankind, because, unlike all others, they kill their own children as soon as they are born, and supply their places by youth stolen from the neighbouring tribes. One would think that even his lordship's zeal for a good cause might have suffered him to reflect, that they could not have continued a separate race longer than till the stolen children had grown up to manhood.—An excellent specimen of the easy faith of infidelity!—See Ld. Kaims' prelim. disc. to sketches of the hist. of man.

coasts of Africa, nations are mingled together who are distinguished from one another by very conspicuous differences. The torrid zone of Asia is not marked by such a deep colour, nor by such a woolly substance instead of hair, as that of Africa. And the colour of tropical America is, in general, lighter than that of Asia.

The tropical zone of Africa is not uniform. The complexion of the western coast is of a deeper black than that of the eastern. It is deeper on the northern side of the equator, nearly to the tropic, than in the correspondent parallels on the south. The Abyssinians, in the lightness of their complexion, and the length of their hair, form an exception from all the other inhabitants of that zone. And advancing beyond the tropic towards the South, we find the Hottentots who seem to be a race by themselves, less black than the inhabitants of the torrid zone, but in their manners, the most beastly, and in their persons and the faculties of their minds, approaching the nearest to the brute creation of any of the human species.

For the explication of these varieties it is necessary to observe that the same parallel of latitude does not uniformly indicate the same degree of heat, or cold. Vicinity to the sea, the course of winds, the altitude of lands, and even the nature of the soil, create great variety in the temperature of regions posited at the same distance from the equator. The state of society in which any people take possession of a new country, has a powerful effect either in subjecting them to considerable changes in their aspect, from the operation of the various causes which affect the human system, or in enabling them to preserve their original features in opposition to their influences.

Every migration, however, will produce some change, either more or less conspicuous, in their appearance. And the combined effects of many migrations, such as have been made by the greater part of the tribes of the human race, must have contributed greatly to diversify the aspect of mankind in different countries. A nation, for example, which migrates to a different climate, will, in time, be impressed with the characteristics of its new state. If this nation should, in some centuries afterwards, return to its original seats, it would not perfectly recover its primitive features, and complexion; but would receive the impressions of the first climate on *the ground* of those formed in the second. In a new removal, the combined effect of the two climates would become the ground on which would be impressed the characters of the third. We perceive here a new cause of endless variety in the human countenance.

These principles will serve to explain the causes of many of the differences which exist among the inhabitants of those countries which have been the subjects of most frequent conquests, or have most frequently received foreign emigrants into their territories; especially, if religion, manners, policy, or other causes, prevent the old inhabitants from mingling freely, and blending with the new. India, and the northern regions of Africa have been oftener overrun by foreign nations than any other countries on the globe. And many nations who have not attempted conquest, have established colonies among them for the purposes of commerce, invited by the fertility of the soil, or the riches and variety of its productions. We accordingly see in these climates a greater mixture of people than is any where else to be found. These foreign intruders have, all been, in a greater or less degree, civilized. They were able, therefore, to preserve with some success, in their new situations, the resemblance of their original and distinctive properties. The Turks, the Arabs, and the Moors, in the North of Africa,—the Copts, the Mamelukes, the Turks, and the Greeks, in Egypt, will always be distinguishable from one another in their figure, and complexion, as long as their peculiar habits, manners, and religious, or national prejudices are retained, and surround them with those fences which prevent them from amalgamating, and assuming one national character. And India, and the neighboring islands in the Indian Ocean, will ever be filled with a various race of people, while their delicious climate, and its rich productions continue to invite both conquest and commerce. The climate will, doubtless, create a certain change in the aspect of all foreign nations who remove thither; but the difference in the degree of this change according to their different habits, and improvements in the social arts; and the various combinations of the effects of the climate with the original characters of the respective people, will always maintain among them important and conspicuous distinctions.

Along the coasts of the great peninsula of the hither India are scattered the remains of the colonies of many nations who in different ages have held commercial intercourse with those fertile regions. There are found the ruins of ancient and magnificent structures, which demonstrate that this rich, populous but unwarlike country, has, in former periods, suffered the most cruel and desolating ravages by hostile invaders, the remnants of whose armies have, probably, long since been blended with the primitive inhabitants, or formed separate tribes in the midst of them; all which have contributed to multiply the differences of aspect presented to us among that various people. The northern portion of the hither India, and the farther India down to the southern extremity of the peninsula of Malacca, have often been the theatre of Tartar conquests. And in the mass of their population, and particularly in the physiognomy of the *Malays*, we evidently discern the basis of the Tartar countenance now overlaid with the softer feature of the lower Asia: as the countenance of the North American aboriginals is no less evidently the Tartar feature rendered more coarse and harsh by passing through colder climates, and by a more savage state of society.†

†I had not long since a striking proof of the visible resemblance between the figure, countenance, and whole appearance of the Malay, and the American indian. Mr. Van Polanen late minister from the late republic of Holland to the United States, and afterwards holding a high office at the Cape of Good Hope, and in the island of Java, on his return from the East, fixed his residence in Princeton. He brought with him two Malay servants. As they were one day standing in his door, there happened to pass by two or three indians belonging to a small tribe which still holds

Another variety which seems to form an exception from the principles hitherto laid down, but which, when fairly examined, will be found to confirm them, is seen in the torrid zone of Asia which is not marked by so deep a colour as that of Africa; and the inhabitants have universally long, straight hair instead of wool. The African zone is, almost throughout its whole extent, a field of burning sand, which augments the heat of the sun to a degree that can hardly be conceived of by the inhabitants of the temperate latitudes. The Asiatic zone, on the other hand, consists chiefly of water, which, absorbing the rays of the sun, and filling the atmosphere with a refrigerating vapour, renders the winds that fan its numerous islands, and narrow peninsulas comparatively temperate. The principal masses of its lands lie nearer to the northern tropic, than to the equator. In the summer season the chief winds that blow reach them after having deposited their greatest heats in those vast oceans which wash their shores on every side. In the winter, on the other hand, they return in their annual course, from continents which the sun has long deserted.‡

The next apparent exception from our principles we discover in Africa itself. This continent, like Europe and Asia, contains many varieties created by the same causes, vicinity to the sun, elevation of the land, the nature of the soil, the temperature of winds, the manners of the people and the mixture of nations who, at different periods and in a state more or less civilized, have established themselves within it, either by conquest, or for the purposes of trade. But the two principal varieties of complexion which prevail from the northern tropic, or a little higher, to the Cape of Good-Hope, are the negro, and the

---

some lands within the state of New-Jersey. When they approached the door the attention of each party was strongly arrested by the appearance of the other. They contemplated one another with evident marks of surprize. And, by their signs and gestures, discovered their mutual astonishment at seeing such a likeness to themselves. Every person, indeed, who sees these Malays, and is acquainted with the countenance of our native indians, is forcibly struck with the resemblance. The chief difference between them is, that the features of the Malays are more soft, the cheek bone not quite so much raised, and the outline of the face somewhat more circular.

‡The monsoons are found to blow over the whole Asiatic zone, taking their course in the two periods of the year according to the relative position to the sun of the great bodies of land which influence their direction.

In the first edition of this essay, misled by the information of some navigators who had visited many of the larger islands in the Indian seas, I supposed there was a race of negroes inhabiting the interior of the island of Borneo, as well as of some others of those vast insular countries, bearing a considerable resemblance to the negroes of Africa. More accurate information has convinced me that the natives, although black, have more of the Indian than the African feature, and like the former also, their hair is lank and long. The middle regions of those great islands, are very elevated and mountainous; and are, consequently, more temperate than the coasts, which are now almost universally inhabited by descendents of the Malay tribes, who, in some former period, have conquered the level country, and driven the aboriginals, who appear to be of indian descent, into the hills, where they have become savage. That they were not originally savage I conclude from those remains of indian magnificence, and monuments of the Hindoo superstition, which are still discernible in several of the islands, in those parts, from which the aboriginals, now the savage inhabitants of the mountainous tracts, have been expelled.

Caffre. The Caffre prevails chiefly towards the southern angle of the peninsula, and along the southeastern side, distinguished, however, by several varieties of shade, occasioned by the causes which have been already suggested. The negro, which is the blackest colour of the human skin, prevails over the greatest portion of the region between the tropics, but becomes of a more jetty hue as we approach the western coast. The cause of the great difference between the eastern and western sides of Africa will be obvious to those who consider the course of the tropical winds, and the extreme heat they must collect from the immense tract of burning sands which they traverse in passing over that continent, in those latitudes where it spreads itself out to the greatest breadth. The winds under the equator, following the course of the sun, reach the eastern coast after blowing over the Arabian and Indian seas; where the countries of Aian, Zanguebar and Monomotapa, receive their breezes greatly tempered by that vast expanse of waters. But arriving at Guinea, and the neighbouring regions after having traversed three thousand miles of sand heated by a vertical sun, they glow with an ardor unknown in any other portion of the globe. And these countries, lying in that part of the zone where the continent is widest and consequently hottest, the natives are distinguished by complexion of a deeper jet, and by more deformed features than those on the southern side of the equator, on the coasts of Congo, Angola, and Loango. The intense heat which, in this region, produces such a prodigious change on the human constitution, equally affects the whole race of beasts, and of vegetables. All nature bears the marks of a powerful fire. As soon as the traveller leaves the borders of the few rivers which flow through this tract, where he sees a luxuriant vegetation, the effect of moisture combined with heat, he immediately enters on a parched and naked soil which produces little else than a few scrubby bushes, and dry and husky plants. And the whole interior, as far as it has been explored, is represented to be a desert of burning sand which often rolls in waves before the winds.§ The negro therefore, is not changed in a greater degree, from the Caffre, the Moor, or the European, than the laws of climate, and the influence of manners, as they have been already illustrated, might lead us to expect.

In passing above the river Senegal we enter on a lighter shade of the negro colour; after which, as we advance towards the North, and before we arrive at the kingdom of Morocco, we find the darkest copper of the Moorish complexion. But all this tract is filled with various tribes of wandering Moors and Arabs, and often with a mixed breed, the offspring of unions formed between these, and the native blacks, among whom the negro complexion predominates; but their features bear a greater resemblance to those of the Moors, and make

§Buffon speaks of a nation in the center of Africa, the Zuinges, who, the Arabian writers say, are often almost entirely cut off by hot winds that rise out of the surrounding deserts. And in the desert, the ancient Syrtis, the traveller is frequently buried beneath hills of sand raised by hot whirlwinds.

some approach to the European face. When we leave the torrid zone, proceeding to the South, we soon arrive among the Hottentots, and approach the Caffre complexion which prevails near the Cape, and along the south-eastern coast. The Hottentots, however, are of a deeper hue than the Moors in the vicinity of the northern tropic; because the Moors, being more civilized, have been better able to defend themselves against the impressions of the climate. But the Hottentots, being the most savage of mankind, suffer its influence in the extreme. Another circumstance contributes to the difference of the effect. The Moors in the vicinity of the tropic receive the influence of the climate on the basis of a European, or Asiatic, feature and complexion; the Hottentot on a basis formed under the equator. They endeavour, likewise, by every mean in their power, to preserve that primitive countenance with which they must, by habit and education, have associated the idea of beauty. For savage, and almost brutal as they are, they have, as well as the most civilized people, their peculiar notions on this subject. They flatten the nose of every child by pressure; and they endeavour to increase the blackness of their complexion by rubbing the skin with the most filthy unguents, and exposing it, without any protection, to the full force of a scorching sun. Their hair, at the same time, is injured by daubing it, constantly, with the vilest compositions. Yet, against all their efforts, the climate, although it is but a few degrees declined from the torrid zone, visibly prevails. Their hair is thicker and longer than that of the negroes, and their complexion, as they approach the southern point of the peninsula, becomes of the light cast of the Caffre‡.

But the phenomenon which principally merits our attention in the African zone is the Abyssinian person and complexion. We find in this Alpine region, and between the ninth and fifteenth degrees from the equator, a race of men resembling the southern Arabians, only of a darker hue, as they lie nearer to the sun, but extremely dissimilar from the negroes on the West coast. Their hair is long and straight, their features tolerably regular, and their complexion a very dark olive, approaching to black. This deviation from the general law of that zone is explained, according to the principles already laid down, from their position on the continent, in the vicinity of the great Indian or Arabian ocean, and from the elevated and mountainous face of the country, rising at a medium, at least, two miles above the level of the sea,¶ and, at this great elevation, covered with clouds, and drenched by almost incessant deluges of

‡Many peculiarities have been related of these people with regard to their figure and appearance, by careless voyagers, which are either wholly false, or very greatly exaggerated. If we were to trust such narrations, we should suppose them to be hardly distinguishable from certain classes of the brute creation.

¶Philosophers who have visited that country inform us that the mercury in the barometer does not rise there, on an average, more than twenty inches, which corresponds to the altitude of about two miles above the level of the sea.

rain during one half of the year.* This altitude of the general face of the country in Abyssinia raises it to a region of the atmosphere which is equivalent, in its temperature, to several degrees of northern latitude. Thus, the partial civilization of the people, the elevation of the face of the country, the temperature of the tropical winds coming from the Arabian ocean, and the canopy of clouds, and the incessant rains which prevail during that season of the year in which the sun is vertical, afford an adequate cause of that deviation which we find in this region from the ordinary complexion and form of the human person, presented in other parts of the African zone.†

It now remains only to account for that peculiar variety of complexion and countenance exhibited by the savage natives of America. Their complexion is not so fair as that of Europe or of Middle Asia; nor so black as that of Africa. And there is a greater uniformity of countenance throughout this whole continent than is found in any other region of the globe of equal extent.

That the natives of America are not fair results as a natural consequence from the principles already established in this essay. Savages will always be

---

*The periodical rains in Abyssinia are now known to be the cause of the overflowing of the Nile. And as the extent of this deluge demonstrates the prodigious quantities of rain which fall in that mountainous region during five or six months in the year, so the length of the river issuing from those mountains, affords a new proof of their great elevation.

†After these descriptions of the varieties of feature and complexion which exist under the same latitude, and the reasons, I trust satisfactory to the philosophic reader, assigned for them in the essay, it is surprizing to see these very varieties enumerated, by the Critical Reviewers, as objections to the principles of the essay, as if no explanation of them had been given, or attempted. "If we examine the globe," say they, "we shall find a very considerable diversity in countries where the heat and dryness are nearly the same. Let us take the 20th degree of latitude which is within the Tropic of Cancer, and passes directly through the kingdom of the negroes. It cuts Nubia where the inhabitants are not black." I say the inhabitants of Nubia are not so black as those on the western coast between the rivers Gambia and Senegal; but when they say that they are not black, or that Nubia is as hot as the West coast, they have either been badly informed, or are greatly biased by their system. They proceed, "it cuts Arabia almost in its widest part; but the Arabians are only swarthy, and when transported to more temperate climes, are almost fair." On the other hand, the widest part of Arabia lies above the tropic, and there alone we find the swarthy Arab to whom their remarks can apply. And though the southern Arab is not so black as the negro, sufficient reasons, I presume, have been assigned in the essay, for this difference in the comparative temperature of the Arabian peninsula. "It divides," say they, "the Decan where those best defended from the heat are only brown, and the poorer sort are of a darkish hue very different from black." How much the prepossession of system has diluted their colours! But surely after this, they need not complain, as they have done, of the inaccuracy of terms by which the grades of complexion are distinguished in the essay. They have, at least, implicitly acknowledged the great effect upon the human skin which may result from the state of society in which men are placed, combined with the influence of climate. But, if these gentlemen would patiently advert to the comparative mildness of the Indian zone, to the great mixture of northern nations, which time has brought together, especially in upper India, and the vicinity of the twentieth degree of latitude to the temperate climates, they would find little occasion for their remarks. They observe further, "that this parallel passes over the kingdom of Mexico and the south-western end of Cuba." The insinuation implied rather than expressed in this observation will be answered immediately when I come to speak of the climate of tropical America.

discoloured, even in temperate climates, by different shades of the tawny complexion. And if we do not find any tribes resembling some of the nations of Africa in the deep jet of their colour, it proceeds from the mild temperature of the tropical zone in America. Mexico, which forms the northern portion of that zone, consists chiefly of a narrow neck of land dividing the Atlantic from the Pacific ocean, and every where rising into high hills. As you proceed to the South immediately below the isthmus of Darien, Terra Firma, on one side, presents an Alpine bed of lofty mountains. On the other side runs the chain of the Andes, with its elevated summits covered with snow. On the West of these lies the narrow empire of Peru, constantly refreshed by temperate winds from the Pacific ocean, and over-shadowed by a canopy of dense vapour which prevents the rays of the sun penetrating with great force to the earth. On the East is spread out the immense country of Amazonia flooded during a great portion of the year by the waters of the Maragnon, and its tributary rivers, and covered with thick and dark forests, beneath which grows a luxuriant tissue of vines and weeds which can hardly be penetrated by the traveller, and utterly excludes the sun. Here are no arid deserts of sand; and from such a rich vegetable growth arises a refrigerating perspiration which, together with the vapour of so many streams, united with the effluvia of the moist and shaded earth that cannot be wholly absorbed even by the thick vegetation on its surface, produces an uncommon coolness in the atmosphere.‡ This moderate temperature is increased by the East wind which perpetually follows the course of the sun through the equatorial regions. Having deposited in the Atlantic ocean the excessive heats acquired in its passage across the continent of Africa it regains a temperature comparatively mild before it arrives at the American coast; whence it continues its course over thick forests and flooded lands, till it meets the cold ranges of the Andes. The lofty and spreading forests of tropical America are at once a proof of the temperature of the atmosphere, and contribute to promote it. Extreme heat parches the unprotected soil of Africa, and converts it into an arid sand. The luxuriant vegetation which prevails in the tropical latitudes of America is the fruit of a moist earth, and a temperate sky. And the natives, inhabiting perpetual shade, and respiring in the refrigerating and grateful effluvia of a fresh and rich growth of vegetables, enjoy a moderate climate in the midst of the torrid zone.

These facts tend to shew that, as far as heat is concerned in the effect, the complexion of the American, must be much lighter than that of the African,

‡Dr. Robertson quotes two eminent naturalists, Piso and Margrave, who had resided long in Brazil, who represent the climate as being *very temperate and mild compared with that of Africa. The air,* they say, *is not only cool, but chilly through the night, insomuch that the natives kindle fires every evening in their huts.* This is confirmed by different writers concerning various countries within that vast region, viz. Neuhoff concerning Brazil; Gumilla concerning the countries on the Oronoco; Acugna concerning those along the Amazon; and Biet in his voyage de la France Equinox. gives a similar account of Cayenne.—Hist. Amer. Note 5th. vol. 2d.

or even of the Asiatic zone: and the mildness of temperature which prevails over such a vast extent of country contributes, in no inconsiderable degree, to that uniformity of countenance which is thought to be peculiar to the aboriginal tribes of America, but which is the result chiefly of that uniform state of society in which they almost all exist. Except the Peruvians, and Mexicans, and a few smaller tribes in the southern continent, the whole are sunk nearly to the same condition of savagism. Destitute of that variety of ideas and emotions which give variety of expression to the human countenance, the same vacancy of aspect is spread over all; and the same set and composition, nearly, is given to the features. When to this common resemblance, created by their state of society, and similar habits of living, we add that the general complexion of tropical America is but a few shades darker than that which is the natural result of savage life even in temperate climates, we probably perceive the true causes of the apparent *uniformity of the American countenance*. There is, however, a visible increase of the dark hue as we proceed towards the circle of the equator, which is also the widest part of the southern continent. And here, there are many tribes of the natives stained with as deep a colour as the inhabitants of the southern extremity of the Indian peninsula. The Mexicans and Peruvians, and a few small nations in their vicinity, among whom we discern the first imperfect elements of civilized life, although preserving the general outline of the American countenance, have a softness thrown over it which distinguishes it from that of the northern savages. Their features are more regular, and handsomely turned; and they appear to bear a nearer resemblance to the inhabitants of many of the islands of the great South Sea, from whom, it is probable, they derive their origin. The Malays, who were originally Tartars, having, at some remote period, taken possession of the farther India, afterwards spread themselves over the greater part of the islands of that vast ocean, conquering, and driving to the mountains in the interior of some, and in others, reducing to slavery, or extirpating, the primitive inhabitants. Not being addicted to commerce, these insular colonies, have not long maintained any intercourse with the parent country, and have therefore retained the knowledge of only a few of the arts with which their ancestors were acquainted.§ But with these few they have probably advanced from island to island till, at length, they reached the western shore of the American continent. Here they seem to have laid the foundations of those empires which the Europeans, on their

§That either the ancestors of the present inhabitants of many of those islands, or the nations whom they have extirpated, possessed the knowledge of arts which are now lost from among them, is evident from the monuments of architecture and sculpture which still remain. Several monuments of ancient art are found even in the small island of Easter which is so deeply embosomed in the ocean, and approaches so near to the American continent, which are beyond the skill or power of its present inhabitants to effect. The resemblance of the works which are found in Java, and some neighboring islands, to those of Elephanta and Salsette, demonstrate the relation of those ancient people to the nations of India. While the religious worship of the Peruvians bears a strong testimony to their Asiatic origin.

arrival in America, found as yet only in the first stage of civilized society. Their earliest establishments were evidently made in Peru. Afterwards Mexico appears to have been founded about three centuries before the discovery. From this empire a few tribes probably found their way farther up into the continent, to the North of the Mexican gulph.‡ But here they were met by ruder and fiercer tribes whose ancestors had come from Asia by a different route. But whether leaving Asia, and entering America by the North, or by the South, the remote ancestry of both appear to have originated nearly from the same regions. And in all the American indians we discover visible traits of the Tartar countenance.

The last apparent exception to the general principles of the essay which I think it necessary to notice is found in the islands of the Indian and Pacific oceans. In these seas people have been discovered in islands existing in the vicinity of one another, and often in the same island, of various complexions. The chief of them I shall present to the reader as they have been described by some of the most accurate observers, and eminent naturalists who accompanied the celebrated Captain Cook. The inhabitants of Otaheitee are divided into two classes.—The *Towtows*, or servile class, who are occupied in such labors as the simple condition of the people requires: and the *Arees*, who may be regarded as the proprietors of the soil, and who are exempted from every laborious occupation; spending their lives amidst such pleasures and amusements as the climate permits, and their uncultivated state of society affords. The former, besides the burdensome tasks which they are obliged daily to perform, are reduced to a much more scanty provision of food than their masters, and are exposed, without clothing, to the full impression of the sun. These, though not stained with the deep jet of the torrid regions of Africa, are of a much blacker hue, than the superior class of the Arees, who are exposed to no hardships, are always well clothed,¶ and enjoy not only a sufficiency, but abundance of simple, indeed, but nutritious food.* The Arees are represented to be, in general, a people of good stature, fine figure, pleasing features, and proportions of person, and of a complexion so light, in the women especially, as to render the stain of blushing easily perceptible.†

Passing on to the north-east, about the region of the tropic, we come to

---

‡Such were probably the Natchez, several of whose customs resembled those of the Peruvians. And generally, the tribes in that vicinity between the Mississippi and Mexico were of a milder character than the northern indians.

¶In a handsome and light cloth the peculiar fabric of those islands.

*Bread fruit, apples, cocoa-nuts, yams, eddoes, and other excellent fruits and roots which grow in great profusion almost without culture in their mild climate, and fertile soil. Add to these, poultry, and hogs of a very sweet and succulent flesh, and dogs which are there kept only for the purpose of food.

†The principal defects of their countenance are said to be a little bluntness of the nose, a small protuberance of the lips, dilatation of the middle of the face, and a gentle swell or plumpness of its features in general; which, however, in this simple people, appears agreeable.

the Marquesas isles, in which the women, who are clothed like the Otaheiteans, exhibit the same general appearance; but the men, who universally go naked, are of a darker hue. Their food is neither so nutritious, nor so abundant as that of the inhabitants of Otaheitee: and a less fertile soil has imposed upon them a general necessity of labor. Hence, besides the greater discolouration of their skin, they are seldom so corpulent as the Otaheiteans, though commonly of a more muscular form. And these effects are supposed, by the naturalists whom I have before mentioned, to be increased by the position of their habitations, which are never placed like those of the Otaheiteans, on beautiful and fertile plains, but generally on the slopes, and often on the summits of very high hills; so that whenever they move abroad, they are necessarily in a state of strenuous exertion.

From the inhabitants of the Marquesas, the people of the Friendly Isles, who, from choice, or from necessity, are addicted to the same habits of industry and exertion, do not differ much either in complexion or in figure.

But far to the East, and nearly at an equal distance from the Society Isles, and the American continent, we discover the small, and thinly inhabited island of Easter. The natives of this remote and solitary spot are subjected to greater hardships than those of the islands which have just been mentioned; and living in a still ruder state of society, are represented as being more slender in their persons, and more dark and coppery in their complexion, not unlike the Peruvians of the neighboring continent. Several relics of ancient art, however, bearing a striking resemblance to the remaining monuments of ancient indian architecture and superstition, demonstrate that this island has once been possessed by a people who had made greater advances in the progress towards civilization than the present inhabitants.

Within the same latitudes, and not remote from the Society, and Friendly Isles lies the group of the New Hebrides. Of these several are inhabited by a people more savage than the former. Their inhabitants, especially those of Mallicollo, of New Caledonia and Tanna, are distinguished by a sooty complexion. Their hair, though not so short, and closely napped as that of the Africans, is frizzled and woolly. And in their whole appearance, they bear some analogy to the miserable inhabitants of the neighboring region of New Holland; except that their slender persons are better turned, and they possess much greater vivacity of disposition. The natives of Papua, and New Guinea exhibit nearly the same colour of the skin, and the same form of the hair. But in all the large islands near the Indian continent there are very distinctly marked two races of men—one inhabiting the mountainous countries every where occupying the interior of those islands; the other possessing the low and level lands near the sea coast. The former exhibit many points of resemblance with the Hindoo tribes: the latter are evidently of Malayan original.

Thus I have presented to the reader the three principal varieties of men which are found in the Indian and Pacific oceans,—the blacks of New Holland, New

Guinea, the New Hebrides, and Papua; a people of dark olive colour, inhabiting the mountainous interior of the large islands; and those who possess the low and level countries in the same islands, who also occupy the greater part of the groupes of smaller islands scattered through those seas, all of whom exhibit different shades of the tawny complexion. Of these, the first are probably descendents of that original stock who were formed by the climate, while they were yet in their most rude and savage condition. The second have all the appearance of being the remnants of Hindoo colonies who had established themselves in those isles in some remote period when the Indian empire was in a much more flourishing condition than at present. But expelled at length from the sea coast by Malayan conquerors, who form the third race, they have retired to the mountains, and there become savage. These conquerors, in a distant age, issuing from the North of Asia, having subdued the farther India, at length spread themselves over almost all the islands in those extensive seas.‡

If it be asked, why have not these several varieties been long since melted down into one uniform countenance by the operation of the climate which is supposed to possess such a powerful infuence over the human constitution? It is well understood by naturalists that various races capable of propagating their kind, may be formed out of the same original stock of animals, or of plants, and that, by proper culture and care, they may forever be preserved distinct. In forming the different races of men§ other causes are combined

‡This is an inference justified not only by the general resemblance of all these people to one another, but by the evident vestiges of the same language, which those, who are best acquainted with them, discern in the vocabularies of all those islands.

Traces of this language are perceived says Reland, (dissertationes miscilianeae, vol. iii.) not only in the tongues spoken in these numerous isles, but in those used by the continental nations inhabiting the middle of Asia, as the Persic, the Malabaric, and even the Braminic. And the common origin of so many different dialects is most obvious in their vocabularies of names which express the most common, familiar, and useful objects, and such as must have been known, and even necessary, equally to them, and to their ancestors, in every stage of their improvement.

§Blumenbach attempts to throw the different races of men into five principal divisions, viz. the *Caucasian* or handsomest race, the primary seat of which was about the Euxine and Caspian seas, and the countries somewhat to the South, from whom came the Europeans. Second, the *Mongou*, or people inhabiting the North-East of Asia, with their descendents to the East, of that continent. Third, the *African*. Fourth, the *American*. And fifth the *Malayan*, occupying the South-East of Asia, and a great part of the isles in the Indian and great South seas.

Leibnitz, ranks them under four orders—the Laponian, the Ethiopic; the eastern Mongou, comprehending the people of Asia; and the western Mongou, embracing those of Europe.

Linnaeus likewise divides them into four—the red American; the white European; the dark coloured Asiatic; and the black Ethiopian.

Buffon arranges them in six—The Laponian in the North of Europe and Asia; the Tartar in the North-East of Asia; the southern Asiatic; the European; the Ethiopian, and the American.

Various other divisions have been made by different writers; as, the Abbè de la Croix; Kant; Dr. John Hunter; Zimmerman, and others. The conclusion to be drawn from all this variety of opinions is, perhaps, that it is impossible to draw the line precisely between the various races of men, or even to enumerate them with certainty; and that it is in itself a useless labor to attempt it.

not less powerful than climate. Manners, education, habits of living, and all those causes comprehended under the general head of *the state of society*, have a powerful operation in preserving, and augmenting, or in guarding against the impressions of climate, and in modifying the whole appearance of the human person and countenance. And after the characters of a race have once been completely formed, and thoroughly incorporated into the system, they may, by the influence of the same moral causes, and the application of the same arts which contributed to create them, be, in their principal features, perpetuated in the most various climates. Nations, sprung from the same original stock, may be traced, by many points of resemblance, through different climates; and different races may long preserve their peculiar, and most discriminating properties in the same climate; especially if, like the inhabitants of these islands, their customs, their prejudices, or antipathies prevent them from amalgamating, and confounding their stocks. Hence the resemblances and differences which exist among the various people of the numerous islands of the great South Sea, the Indian, and Pacific oceans. And hence that mixture of races extended along the Senegal in Africa, and scattered through the intermediate space between that river and the Gambia, where we meet with negroes, Moors, and Arabs, and often with a race mixed and compounded of all the others.‡

Having now concluded the investigation which I proposed into the causes of the principal varieties in complexion and figure which distinguish the different nations of men from one another, it gives me pleasure to observe on this, as on many other subjects which have been attempted to be formed into objections against the sacred history, that the most extensive and accurate researches into the actual state, and the powers of nature, have ever served, more and more to confirm the facts vouched to us by the authority of holy writ. A just philosophy will always be found coincident with the true theology. But I must repeat here an observation which I made in the beginning of this essay, and

‡This region seems to form the general boundary between the Moorish and Arab, or dusky and yellow population in the northern portion of Africa, and the negro, or black population in the center. It is a broad belt which borders the African zone from the twelfth or thirteenth degree of latitude to the tropic, and extending from the Atlantic ocean, to the mountains of Abyssinia. Mr. Park appears to regard the Foulah tribes, who are lighter in their complexion than other negroes, with softer and longer hair, as related by mixture to the Arabs, whom they resemble in their attachment to a pastoral life. Those wandering and predatory tribes which are called by the general denomination of Moors, who surround and penetrate the great desert, and have dispersed themselves in various hordes as far as the Niger, are, not improbably, the remains of several civilized nations of antiquity, Carthaginians, Phoenicians, Romans who at different periods possessed the North of Africa, blended with the Numidians and Mauritanians, and reduced almost to savagism by being scattered through the inhospitable deserts of that arid and ungenial country.

This is the circle which the Critical Reviewers have dexterously selected for examples of diversity of complexion within the tropical latitudes in order to impugn the principles of this essay while they have not had the candor to notice, as philosophers, the solution which is given of this phenomenon.

which I trust I am now entitled to make with more confidence, that the denial of the unity of the human species tends to impair, if not entirely to destroy, the foundations of duty and morals, and, in a word, of the whole science of human nature. No general principles of conduct, or religion, or even of civil policy, could be derived from natures originally and essentially different from one another, and, afterwards, in the perpetual changes of the world, infinitely mixed and compounded. The principles and rules which a philosopher might derive from the study of his own nature, could not be applied with certainty to regulate the conduct of other men, and other nations, who might be of totally different species; or sprung from a very dissimilar composition of species. The terms which one man would frame to express the ideas and emotions of his own mind must convey to another a meaning as different as the organization of their respective natures. But when the whole human race is known to compose only one species, this confusion and uncertainty is removed, and the science of human nature, in all its relations, becomes susceptible of system. The principles of morals rest on sure and immutable foundations.

Its unity I have endeavoured to confirm by explaining the causes of its variety. Of these, the first I have shewn to be *climate*, by which is meant, not so much the latitude of a country from the equator, as the degree of heat or cold, which often depends on a great variety of other circumstances. The next is *the state of society*, which may augment or correct the influence of climate, and is itself a separate and independent cause of many conspicuous distinctions among mankind. These causes may be infinitely varied in degree; and their effects may likewise be diversified by various combinations. And, in the continual migrations of mankind, these effects may be still further modified, by changes which have antecedently taken place in a prior climate, and a prior state of society. Even where all external circumstances seem to be the same, there may be causes of difference depending on many natural influences with which philosophy is not yet acquainted; as there are varieties among the children of the same family. Frequently we see, in the same country individuals resembling every nation on the globe. Such varieties prove, at least, that the human constitution is susceptible of all the modifications which exist among mankind, without having recourse, in order to account for them, to the unnecessary, and therefore unphilosophical hypothesis of there having existed from the beginning, different original species of men. It is not more astonishing in itself, or out of the order of nature, that nations sprung from the same stock, than that individuals should differ. In the one case we are assured of the fact from observation; in the other, we have reason to conclude, independently on the sacred authority of revelation, that from one pair have descended all the families of the earth.

CHARLES DARWIN ON THE ORIGIN OF SPECIES

CHARLES DARWIN (1809-1882) was a revolutionist, and he is considered to be a most dangerous man, especially by some people in the United States at the present time. For like Copernicus and Newton before him, he challenged existing orthodoxies. Copernicus managed to die on the day his book, in which he set out the evidence for a heliocentric rather than a geocentric world, was published in 1543. Newton managed to be so mathematical that only a few other mathematicians were capable of understanding his system of ordering the events of inorganic nature. But Darwin could be understood by anyone who took the trouble to read his book, *On the Origin of Species By Means of Natural Selection, or the Preservation of Favoured Races in the Struggle for Life*, published on the 24th November 1859 in an edition of 1250 copies, which was sold out on the day of publication. In this revolutionary work Darwin challenged the orthodox view of the separate creation of species and set forth an alternative theory, which he called the principle of natural selection, as the means by which species were modified and new species were brought into being.

The furor to which his book gave rise has not completely died down, but wherever men are capable of examining evidence critically and verifying theory experimentally, the principle of natural selection is accepted as the main agency of evolution.

Here we reprint the opening pages of his epoch-making work from the first edition, in which he gives a brief account of the development of his ideas, and defines the principle of natural selection.

The influence of Darwin's book has affected every aspect of human thought. The explanation he offered for the mechanism of the transmutation of species provided for the first time a workable and verifiable hypothesis by means of which one could begin to think intelligently not only of the mechanism of species formation, but also about the manner in which specific traits came into being.

Unfortunately, physical anthropologists late into the twentieth century, failed to follow Darwin's lead and for the most part misspent their time measuring skulls and bemusing themselves and confusing others by inventing outlandish names by which to describe them. It was not until the advent of Neo-Darwinism, the application of genetics to Darwinian principles, that some young physical anthropologists began to exhibit some interest in joining biologists in a Neo-Darwinian biological approach to the investigation of the evolution of man's physical traits.

Today we know that culture has played a dominant role in the physical evolution of man, a fact first underscored by Darwin in *The Descent of Man*. But, again, there was no one to take up his lead until the nineteen twenties—the lone voice that did so, that of Carveth Read (see pp. 381-89), went unheeded until all his ideas were independently confirmed in the fifties and sixties, by those who had never even heard of him.

ON THE ORIGIN OF SPECIES*

INTRODUCTION

In considering the Origin of Species, it is quite conceivable that a naturalist, reflecting on the mutual affinities of organic beings, on their embryological relations, their geographical distribution, geological succession, and other such facts, might come to the conclusion that species had not been independently created, but had descended, like varieties, from other species. Nevertheless, such a conclusion, even if well founded, would be unsatisfactory, until it could be shown how the innumerable species inhabiting this world have been modified, so as to acquire that perfection of structure and coadaptation which justly excites our admiration. Naturalists continually refer to external conditions, such as climate, food, etc., as the only possible cause of variation. In one limited sense, as we shall hereafter see, this may be true; but it is preposterous to attribute to mere external conditions, the structure, for instance, of the woodpecker, with its feet, tail, beak, and tongue, so admirably adapted to catch insects under the bark of trees. In the case of the mistletoe, which draws its nourishment from certain trees, which has seeds that must be transported by certain birds, and which has flowers with separate sexes absolutely requiring the agency of certain insects to bring pollen from one flower to the other, it is equally preposterous to account for the structure of this parasite, with its relations to several distinct organic beings, by the effects of external conditions, or of habit, or of the volition of the plant itself.

It is, therefore, of the highest importance to gain a clear insight into the means of modification and coadaptation. At the commencement of my observa-

*Reprinted from Charles Darwin, *On the Origin of Species*. London: John Murray, 1859, pp. 2-3.

tions it seemed to me probable that a careful study of domesticated animals and of cultivated plants would offer the best chance of making out this obscure problem. Nor have I been disappointed; in this and in all other perplexing cases I have invariably found that our knowledge, imperfect though it be, of variation under domestication, afforded the best and safest clue. I may venture to express my conviction of the high value of such studies, although they have been very commonly neglected by naturalists.

From these considerations, I shall devote the first chapter of this Abstract to Variation under Domestication. We shall thus see that a large amount of hereditary modification is at least possible; and, what is equally or more important, we shall see how great is the power of man in accumulating by his Selection successive slight variations. I will then pass on to the variability of species in a state of nature; but I shall, unfortunately, be compelled to treat this subject far too briefly, as it can be treated properly only by giving long catalogues of facts. We shall, however, be enabled to discuss what circumstances are most favourable to variation. In the next chapter the Struggle for Existence amongst all organic beings throughout the world, which inevitably follows from their high geometrical powers of increase, will be considered. This is the doctrine of Malthus, applied to the whole animal and vegetable kingdoms. As many more individuals of each species are born than can possibly survive; and as, consequently, there is a frequently recurrent struggle for existence, it follows that any being, if it vary however slightly in any manner profitable to itself, under the complex and sometimes varying conditions of life, will have a better chance of surviving, and thus be *naturally selected*. From the strong principle of inheritance, any selected variety will tend to propagate its new and modified form.

DARWIN CAREFULLY EXPLAINS WHAT HE MEANS BY THE PHRASE "THE STRUGGLE FOR EXISTENCE"

THE phrase "The Struggle for Existence" constitutes yet another cautionary example of the importance of technical terms and phrases, and the care with which they should be thought out before they are ever put into print. Even though Darwin went to great pains to explain in the clearest terms what he meant by the phrase "The

Struggle for Existence"—offered during a period of increasing competition between nations, "races," and classes—it was soon adapted for use by those who saw in it an invaluable shibboleth for their own competitive activities.[1] But Darwin makes it quite clear that he uses neither the term "competition" nor the phrase "The Struggle for Existence" in the kind of belligerent sense to which they were soon put by their misusers. Unfortunately Darwin's efforts to prevent the misuse of these terms did not succeed. Darwin points out that plants may be said to struggle with each other for the privilege of being devoured by birds in order that their seeds may be disseminated, but this is only a metaphoric way of speaking. He had nothing like belligerency or aggression in mind.

The history of the unfortunate phrase gives point to the oft-repeated experience that the meaning of a word is not so much what the user means by it as what the reader chooses to understand by it. As Viola says in *Twelfth Night* (Act III, Sc. 1), "Nay, that's certain; they that dally nicely with words may quickly make them wanton."

THE STRUGGLE FOR EXISTENCE*

I should premise that I use the term Struggle for Existence in a large and metaphorical sense including dependence of one being on another, and including (which is more important) not only the life of the individual, but success in leaving progeny. Two canine animals, in a time of dearth, may be truly said to struggle with each other which shall get food and live. But a plant on the edge of a desert is said to struggle for life against the drought, though more properly it should be said to be dependent on the moisture. A plant which annually produces a thousand seeds, of which only one of an average comes to maturity, may be more truly said to struggle with the plants of the same and other kinds which already clothe the ground. The mistletoe is dependent on the apple and a few other trees, but can only in a far-fetched sense be said to struggle with these trees, for, if too many of these parasites grow on the same tree, it languishes and dies. But several seedling mistletoes, growing close together on the same branch, may more truly be said to struggle with each other. As the mistletoe is disseminated by birds, its existence depends

---

[1]See Ashley Montagu, *Darwin, Competition, and Cooperation* (New York, Henry Schuman, 1952. Reprinted Greenwood Press Publishers, Westport, Conn., 1973).

*Reprinted from Charles Darwin, *On the Origin of Species* (London, John Murray, 1859), pp. 62-68.

on them; and it may metaphorically be said to struggle with other fruit-bearing plants, in tempting the birds to devour and thus disseminate its seeds. In these several senses, which pass into each other, I use for convenience' sake the general term of Struggle for Existence.

A struggle for existence inevitably follows from the high rate at which all organic beings tend to increase. Every being, which during its natural lifetime produces several eggs or seeds, must suffer destruction during some period of its life, and during some season or occasional year, otherwise, on the principle of geometrical increase, its numbers would quickly become so inordinately great that no country could support the product. Hence, as more individuals are produced than can possibly survive, there must in every case be a struggle for existence, either one individual with another of the same species, or with the individuals of distinct species, or with the physical conditions of life. It is the doctrine of Malthus applied with manifold force to the whole animal and vegetable kingdoms; for in this case there can be no artificial increase of food, and no prudential restraint from marriage. Although some species may be now increasing, more or less rapidly, in numbers, all cannot do so, for the world would not hold them.

There is no exception to the rule that every organic being naturally increases at so high a rate, that, if not destroyed, the earth would soon be covered by the progeny of a single pair. Even slow-breeding man has doubled in twenty-five years, and at this rate, in less than a thousand years, there would literally not be standing-room for his progeny. Linnaeus has calculated that if an annual plant produced only two seeds—and there is no plant so unproductive as this—and their seedlings next year produced two, and so on, then in twenty years there would be a million plants. The elephant is reckoned the slowest breeder of all known animals, and I have taken some pains to estimate its probable minimum rate of natural increase; it will be safest to assume that it begins breeding when thirty years old, and goes on breeding till ninety years old, bringing forth six young in the interval, and surviving till one hundred years old; if this be so, after a period of from 740 to 750 years there would be nearly nineteen million elephants alive, descended from the first pair.

But we have better evidence on this subject than mere theoretical calculations, namely, the numerous recorded cases of the astonishingly rapid increase of various animals in a state of nature, when circumstances have been favourable to them during two or three following seasons. Still more striking is the evidence from our domestic animals of many kinds which have run wild in several parts of the world; if the statements of the rate of increase of slow-breeding cattle and horses in South America, and latterly in Australia, had not been well authenticated, they would have been incredible. So it is with plants; cases could be given of introduced plants which have become common throughout whole islands in a period of less than ten years. Several of the plants, such as the cardoon and a tall thistle, which are now the commonest over the wide plains of La Plata, clothing square leagues of surface almost to the exclusion of every other plant, have been introduced from Europe; and there are plants which now range in India, as I hear from Dr. Falconer, from Cape Comorin to the Himalaya, which have been imported from America since its discovery. In such cases, and endless others could be given, no one supposes, that the fertility of the animals or plants has been suddenly and temporarily increased in any sensible degree. The obvious explanation is that the conditions of life have been highly favourable, and that there has consequently been less destruction of the old and young, and that nearly all the young have been enabled to breed. Their geometrical ratio of increase, the result of which never fails to be surprising, simply explains their extraordinarily rapid increase and wide diffusion in their new homes.

In a state of nature almost every full-grown plant annually produces seed, and amongst animals there are very few which do not annually pair. Hence we may confidently assert, that all plants and animals are tending to increase at a geometrical ratio,—that all would rapidly stock every station in which they could anyhow exist,—and that this geometrical tendency to increase must be checked by destruction at some period of life. Our familiarity with the larger domestic animals tends, I think, to mislead us: we see no great destruction falling on them, but we do not keep in mind that thousands are annually slaughtered for food, and that in a state of nature an equal number would have somehow to be disposed of.

The only difference between organisms which annually produce eggs or seeds by the thousand, and those which produce extremely few, is, that the slow-breeders would require a few more years to people, under favourable conditions, a whole district, let it be ever so large. The condor lays a couple of eggs and the ostrich a score, and yet in the same country the condor may be the more numerous of the two; the Fulmar petrel lays but one egg, yet it is believed to be the most numerous bird in the world. One fly deposits hundreds of eggs, and another, like the hippobosca, a single one; but this difference does not determine how many individuals of the two species can be supported in a district. A large number of eggs is of some importance to those species which depend on a fluctuating amount of food, for it allows them rapidly to increase in number. But the real importance of a large number of eggs or seeds is to make up for much destruction at some period of life; and this period in the great majority of cases is an early one. If an animal can in any way protect its own eggs or young, a small number may be produced, and yet the average stock be fully kept up; but if many eggs or young are destroyed, many must be produced, or the species will become extinct. It would suffice to keep up the full number of a tree, which lived on an average for a thousand years, if a single seed were produced once in a thousand years, supposing that this seed were never destroyed, and could be ensured to germinate in a fitting place. So that, in all cases, the average number of any animal or plant depends only indirectly on the number of its eggs or seeds.

In looking at Nature, it is most necessary to keep the foregoing considerations always in mind—never to forget that every single organic being may be said to be striving to the utmost to increase in numbers; that each lives by a struggle at some period of its life; that heavy destruction inevitably falls either on the young or old, during each generation or at recurrent intervals. Lighten any check, mitigate the destruction ever so little, and the number of the species will almost instantaneously increase to any amount.

What checks the natural tendency of each species to increase is most obscure. Look at the most vigorous species; by as much as it swarms in numbers; by as much will its tendency to increase be still further increased. We know not exactly what the checks are even in one single instance. Nor will this surprise any one who reflects how ignorant we are on this head, even in regard to mankind, although so incomparably better known than any other animal. This subject of the checks to increase has been ably treated by several authors, and I hope in a future work to discuss it at considerable length, more especially in regard to the feral animals of South America. Here I will make only a few remarks, just to recall to the reader's mind some of the chief points. Eggs or very young animals seem generally to suffer most, but this is not invariably the case. With plants there is a vast destruction of seeds, but, from some observations which I have made, it appears that the seedlings suffer most from germinating in ground already thickly stocked with other plants. Seedlings, also, are destroyed in vast numbers by various enemies; for instance, on a piece of ground three feet long and two wide, dug and cleared, and where there could be no choking from other plants, I marked all the seedlings of our native weeds as they came up, and out of 357 no less than 295 were destroyed, chiefly by slugs and insects. If turf which has long been mown, and the case would be the same with turf closely browsed by quadrupeds, be let to grow, the more vigorous plants gradually kill the less vigorous, though fully grown plants; thus out of twenty species growing on a little plot of mown turf (three feet by four) nine species perished, from the other species being allowed to grow up freely.

PAUL DU CHAILLU AND THE
REDISCOVERY OF THE
("FEROCIOUS") GORILLA

PAUL DU CHAILLU (1831-1903) is variously said to have been born in Paris, New Orleans, or on the islands of Bourbon or Reunion, of a French father and mulatto mother. The truth is that all these "birthplaces" are in doubt as is the ethnicity of his parents. He was a citizen of the United States, and when he was not abroad, the United States was where he lived most of his life.

Traveler, explorer, writer, and lecturer, Du Chaillu was a remarkably colorful and much-maligned figure. Short of stature, he was a man of great charm, of whom many distinguished friends spoke glowingly, children especially remembering him with enthusiasm. He was the author of, among many other works, several popular children's books. His best known and most influential work was *Explorations in Equatorial Africa*, published at London by John Murray in May, 1861. This dramatic account of his adventures in Central Africa set the world on its ear. It became an overnight sensation and was highly praised by leading scientists and others in the press—but not for long. Soon there appeared a number of criticisms by geographers and zoologists, who almost went so far as to say that much of the work was fiction. Fortunately, Du Chaillu had not long to wait before the critics were shown to be wrong and his work quite dependable. For an account of this period and these events see Michel Vaucaire, *Paul Du Chaillu, Gorilla Hunter*, New York, Harper & Bros., 1930.

Explorations in Equatorial Africa is a highly readable book, and important because, among other things, it gave the first extended account of the living gorilla in its natural habitat.

Arriving in Africa well-seeded with all the myths and prejudices of the white man concerning "Nature red in tooth and claw," and believing all the stories he had heard from the natives of the ferocity of the gorilla, he was prepared to think the worst. Hence, when he finally encountered the animal, he saw it through the distorting glass of his prejudices. He saw the gorilla as a terrifying beast, a monster—a view that prevailed well into the twentieth century. It was a view that was extended to all the apes and even monkeys, and it was an utterly false view, as we now know from the observations of fieldworkers like Schaller, Jane Goodall, and Barbara Harrisson.[1]

Since the apes were considered to be the nearest living relatives of man, and that man was, indeed, descended from them (an erroneous view), and since these apes were so ferocious (also erroneous), the view of man's innate aggressiveness received considerable support from Du Chaillu's book. The book was published just six months after the publication (by the same publisher) of Darwin's *Origin of Species*. "The warfare of Nature" Darwin emphasized in that book received abundant support from Du Chaillu's highly dramatic accounts of his encounters with the "ferocious" gorilla. The truth is that the gorilla is one of the most amiable of creatures, as all apes appear to be.

What a pity it is that instead of shooting them Du Chaillu did not choose to study gorillas, as Schaller did a hundred years later. In influencing the world's thinking about apes and the nature of man, Paul Du Chaillu's honest but erroneous views still exert a baleful influence. Some day mankind may yet come to see how cruelly unjust and destructive of our understanding and relationship with other animals, and especially our nearest relations, the apes, such books as Du Chaillu's have been.

THE "FEROCIOUS" GORILLA*

The next day my men started for a gorilla-hunt. I saw them load their guns, and wondered why the poor cheap "trade" guns do not burst at every discharge. They put in first four or five "fingers" high of coarse powder, and ram down on this four or five pieces of iron-bar or rough broken iron, making the whole charge eight to ten fingers high. But they are not great marksmen, and my skill with the rifle often called out expressions of wonder, and almost of superstitious fear from the best among them.

I killed some birds to-day, but I spent the day chiefly in looking about the town and neighbourhood—really doing nothing. As I walked along a Fan woman gravely asked me why I did not take off my clothes? She felt sure

[1]George B. Schaller, *The Mountain Gorilla* (Chicago, University of Chicago Press, 1963); Jane Van Lawick-Goodall, *In the Shadow of Man* (Boston, Houghton Mifflin Co., 1971); Barbara Harrisson, *Orang-Utan* (New York, Doubleday, 1962).

*Reprinted from Paul Du Chaillu, *Explorations in Equatorial Africa* (London, John Murray, 1861), pp. 68-72; 205-211; 275-277; 296-299; 346-358; 433-435.

they must be a great hindrance to me, and if I would leave off these things I should be able to walk more easily.

The next day we went out all together for a gorilla-hunt. The country hereabouts is very rough, hilly, and densely crowded; consequently, hunting is scarcely to be counted sport. But a couple of days of rest had refreshed me, and I was anxious to be in at the death of a gorilla.

We saw several gorilla-tracks, and about noon divided our party, in the hope of surrounding the resting-place of one whose tracks were very plain. I had scarce got away from my party three hundred yards when I heard a report of a gun, then of three more, going off one after the other. Of course I ran back as fast as I could, and hoped to see a dead animal before me, but was once more disappointed. My Mbondemo fellows had fired at a female, had wounded her, as I saw by the clots of blood which marked her track, but she had made good her escape. We set out at once in pursuit; but these woods are so thick, so almost impenetrable, that pursuit of a wounded animal is not often successful. A man can only creep where the beast would run.

Night came upon us while we were still beating the bush, and it was determined to camp out and try our luck again on the morrow. Of course, I was only too glad. We shot some monkeys and birds, built our camp, and, while the men roasted their monkey-meat over the coals, I held my birds before the blaze on a stick. Fortunately we had food enough, and of a good kind, for next day.

We started early, and pushed for the most dense and impenetrable part of the forest, in hopes to find the very home of the beast I so much wished to shoot. Hour after hour we travelled, and yet no signs of gorilla. Only the everlasting little chattering monkeys—and not many of these—and occasionally birds. In fact, the forests of this part of Africa—as the reader has seen by this time—are not so full of life as in some other parts to the south.

Suddenly Miengai uttered a little *cluck* with his tongue, which is the native's way of showing that something is stirring, and that a sharp look-out is necessary. And presently I noticed, ahead of us seemingly, a noise as of some one breaking down branches or twigs of trees.

This was the gorilla, I knew at once, by the eager and satisfied looks of the men. They looked once more carefully at their guns, to see if by any chance the powder had fallen out of the pans; I also examined mine, to make sure that all was right; and then we marched on cautiously.

The singular noise of the breaking of tree-branches continued. We walked with the greatest care, making no noise at all. The countenances of the men showed that they thought themselves engaged in a very serious undertaking; but we pushed on, until finally we thought we saw through the thick woods the moving of the branches and small trees which the great beast was tearing down, probably to get from them the berries and fruits he lives on.

Suddenly, as we were yet creeping along, in a silence which made a heavy breath seem loud and distinct, the woods were at once filled with the tremendous barking roar of the gorilla.

Then the underbrush swayed rapidly just ahead, and presently before us stood an immense male gorilla. He had gone through the jungle on his all-fours; but when he saw our party he erected himself and looked us boldly in the face. He stood about a dozen yards from us, and was a sight I think I shall never forget. Nearly six feet high (he proved four inches shorter), with immense body, huge chest, and great muscular arms, with fiercely-glaring large deep gray eyes, and a hellish expression of face, which seemed to me like some nightmare vision: thus stood before us this king of the African forest.

He was not afraid of us. He stood there, and beat his breast with his huge fists till it resounded like an immense bass-drum, which is their mode of offering defiance; meantime giving vent to roar after roar.

The roar of the gorilla is the most singular and awful noise heard in these African woods. It begins with a sharp *bark*, like an angry dog, then glides into a deep bass *roll*, which literally and closely resembles the roll of distant thunder along the sky, for which I have sometimes been tempted to take it where I did not see the animal. So deep is it that it seems to proceed less from the mouth and throat than from the deep chest and vast paunch.

His eyes began to flash fiercer fire as we stood motionless on the defensive, and the crest of short hair which stands on his forehead began to twitch rapidly up and down, while his powerful fangs were shown as he again sent forth a thunderous roar. And now truly he reminded me of nothing but some hellish dream creature—a being of that hideous order, half-man half-beast, which we find pictured by old artists in some representations of the infernal regions. He advanced a few steps—then stopped to utter that hideous roar again—advanced again, and finally stopped when at a distance of about six yards from us. And here, just as he began another of his roars, beating his breast in rage, we fired, and killed him.

With a groan which had something terribly human in it, and yet was full of brutishness, he fell forward on his face. The body shook convulsively for a few minutes, the limbs moved about in a struggling way, and then all was quiet—death had done its work, and I had leisure to examine the huge body. It proved to be five feet eight inches high, and the muscular development of the arms and breast showed what immense strength it had possessed.

My men, though rejoicing at our luck, immediately began to quarrel about the apportionment of the meat—for they really eat this creature. I saw that they would come to blows presently if I did not interfere, and therefore said I would myself give each man his share, which satisfied all. As we were too tired to return to our camp of last night, we determined to camp here on the spot, and accordingly soon had some shelters erected and dinner going on. Luckily, one of the fellows shot a deer just as we began to camp, and on its meat I feasted while my men ate gorilla.

I noticed that they very carefully saved the brain, and was told that charms were made of this—charms of two kinds. Prepared in one way, the charm gave the wearer a strong hand for the hunt, and in another it gave him success with women. This evening we had again gorilla stories—but all to the same point already mentioned, that there are gorillas inhabited by human spirits.

On the 4th of May I had one of the greatest pleasures of my whole life. Some hunters who had been out on my account brought in a young gorilla *alive!* I cannot describe the emotions with which I saw the struggling little brute dragged into the village. All the hardships I had endured in Africa were rewarded in that moment.

It was a little fellow of between two and three years old, two feet six inches in length, and as fierce and stubborn as a grown animal could have been.

My hunters, whom I could have hugged to my heart, took him in the country between the Rembo and Cape St. Catherine. By their account, they were going, five in number, to a village near the coast, and walking very silently through the forest, when they heard what they immediately recognized as the cry of a young gorilla for its mother. The forest was silent. It was about noon; and they immediately determined to follow the cry. Presently they heard it again. Guns in hand, the brave fellows crept noiselessly towards a clump of wood, where the baby gorilla evidently was. They knew the mother would be near; and there was a likelihood that the male, the most dreaded of all, might be there too. But they determined to risk all, and, if at all possible, to take the young one alive, knowing what a joy it would be for me.

Presently they perceived the bush moving; and crawling a little further on in dead silence, scarce breathing with excitement, they beheld, what has seldom been seen even by the negroes, a young gorilla, seated on the ground, eating some berries which grew close to the earth. A few feet further on sat the mother also eating of the same fruit.

Instantly they made ready to fire; and none too soon, for the old female saw them as they raised their guns, and they had only to pull triggers without delay. Happily they wounded her mortally.

She fell. The young one, hearing the noise of the guns, ran to his mother and clung to her, hiding his face, and embracing her body. The hunters immediately rushed toward the two, hallooing with joy as they ran on. But this roused the little one, who instantly let go his mother and ran to a small tree, which he climbed with great agility, where he sat and roared at them savagely.

They were now perplexed how to get at him. No one cared to run the chance of being bitten by this savage little beast, and shoot it they would not. At last they cut down the tree, and, as it fell, dexterously threw a cloth over the head of the young monster, and thus gained time to secure it while it was blinded. With all these precautions, one of the men received a severe bite on the hand, and another had a piece taken out of his leg.

As the little brute, though so diminutive, and the merest baby for age, was astonishingly strong and by no means good-tempered, they could not lead him. He constantly rushed at them. So they were obliged to get a forked stick in which his neck was inserted in such a way that he could not escape, and yet could be kept at a safe distance. In this uncomfortable way he was brought into the village.

There the excitement was intense. As the animal was lifted out of the canoe in which he had come a little way down the river, he roared and bellowed, and looked around wildly with his wicked little eyes, giving fair warning that if he could only get at some of us he would take his revenge.

I saw that the stick hurt his neck, and immediately set about to have a cage made for him. In two hours we had built a strong bamboo house, with the slats securely tied at such distances apart that we could see the gorilla and it could see out. Here the thing was immediately deposited; and now, for the first time, I had a fair chance to look at my prize.

It was a young male gorilla, evidently not yet three years old, fully able to walk alone, and possessed, for its age, of most extraordinary strength and muscular development. Its greatest length proved to be, afterwards, two feet six inches. Its face and hands were very black, eyes not so much sunken as in the adult. The hair began just at the eyebrows and rose to the crown, where it was of a reddish-brown. It came down the sides of the face in lines to the lower jaw much as our beards grow. The upper lip was covered with short coarse hair; the lower lip had longer hair. The eyelids very slight and thin. Eyebrows straight, and three-quarters of an inch long.

The whole back was covered with hair of an iron-gray, becoming dark nearer the arms, and quite white about the *anus*. Chest and abdomen covered with hair, which was somewhat thin and short on the breast. On the arms the hair was longer than anywhere on the body, and of a grayish-black colour, caused by the roots of the hair being dark and the ends whitish. On the hands and wrists the hair was black, and came down to the second joints of the fingers, though one could see in the short down the beginning of the long black hair which lines the upper parts of the fingers in the adult. The hair of the legs was grayish-black, becoming blacker as it reached the ankles, the feet being covered with black hair.

When I had the little fellow safely locked in his cage, I ventured to approach to say a few encouraging words to him. He stood in the furthest corner, but, as I approached, bellowed and made a precipitate rush at me; and though I retreated as quickly as I could, succeeded in catching my trouser-legs, which he grasped with one of his feet and tore, retreating immediately to the corner furthest away. This taught me caution for the present, though I had a hope still to be able to tame him.

He sat in his corner looking wickedly out of his gray eyes, and I never saw a more morose or more ill-tempered face than had this little beast.

The first thing was, of course, to attend to the wants of my captive. I sent for some of the forest-berries which these animals are known to prefer, and placed these and a cup of water within his reach. He was exceedingly shy, and would neither eat nor drink till I had removed to a considerable distance.

The second day found Joe, as I had named him, fiercer than the first. He rushed savagely at anyone who stood even for a moment near his cage, and seemed ready to tear us all to pieces. I threw him to-day some pineapple leaves, of which I noticed he ate only the white parts. There seemed no difficulty about his food, though he refused now, and continued during his short life to refuse, all food except such wild leaves and fruits as were gathered from his native woods for him.

The third day he was still morose and savage, bellowing when any person approached, and either retiring to a distant corner or rushing to attack. On the fourth day, while no one was near, the little rascal succeeded in forcing apart two of the bamboo rails which composed his cage, and made his escape. I came up just as his flight was discovered, and immediately got all the negroes together for pursuit, determining to surround the wood and recapture my captive. Running into the house to get one of my guns, I was startled by an angry growl issuing from under my low bedstead. It was Master Joe, who lay there hid, but anxiously watching my movements. I instantly shut the windows, and called to my people to guard the door. When Joe saw the crowd of black faces he became furious, and, with his eyes glaring and every sign of rage in his little face and body, got out from beneath the bed. We shut the door at the same time and left him master of the premises, preferring to devise some plan for his easy capture rather than to expose ourselves to his terrible teeth.

How to take him was now a puzzling question. He had shown such strength and such rage already, that not even I cared to run the chance of being badly bitten in a hand-to-hand struggle. Meantime Joe stood in the middle of the room looking about for his enemies, and examining, with some surprise, the furniture. I watched with fear lest the ticking of my clock should strike his ear, and perhaps lead him to an assault upon that precious article. Indeed, I should have left Joe in possession, but for a fear that he would destroy the many articles of value or curiosity I had hung about the walls.

Finally, seeing him quite quiet, I despatched some fellows for a net, and opening the door quickly, threw this over his head. Fortunately we succeeded at the first throw in fatally entangling the young monster, who roared frightfully, and struck and kicked in every direction under the net. I took hold of the back of his neck, two men seized his arms and another the legs, and thus held by four men this extraordinary little creature still proved most troublesome. We carried him as quickly as we could to the cage, which had been repaired, and there once more locked him in.

I never saw so furious a beast in my life as he was. He darted at everyone who came near, bit the bamboos of the house, glared at us with venomous and sullen eyes, and in every motion showed a temper thoroughly wicked and malicious.

As there was no change in this for two days thereafter, but continual moroseness, I tried what starvation would do towards breaking his spirit; also, it began to be troublesome to procure his food from the woods, and I wanted him to become accustomed to civilized food, which was placed before him. But he would touch nothing of the kind; and as for temper, after starving him twenty-four hours, all I gained was that he came slowly up and took some berries from the forest out of my hand, immediately retreating to his corner to eat them.

Daily attentions from me for a fortnight more did not bring me any further confidence from him than this. He always snarled at me, and only when *very* hungry would he take even his choicest food from my hands. At the end of this fortnight I came one day to feed him, and found that he had gnawed a bamboo to pieces slyly and again made his escape. Luckily he had but just gone; for, as I looked around, I caught sight of Master Joe making off on all fours, and with great speed, across the little prairie for a clump of trees.

I called the men up and we gave chace. He saw us, and before we could head him off made for another clump. This we surrounded. He did not ascend a tree, but stood defiantly at the border of the wood. About one hundred and fifty of us surrounded him. As we moved up he began to yell, and made a sudden dash upon a poor fellow who was in advance, who ran, tumbled down in affright, and, by his fall, escaped, but also detained Joe sufficiently long for the nets to be brought to bear upon him.

Four of us again bore him struggling into the village. This time I would not trust him to the cage, but had a little light chain fastened around his neck. This operation he resisted with all his might, and it took us quite an hour to securely chain the little fellow, whose strength was something marvellous.

Ten days after he was thus chained he died suddenly. He was in good health, and ate plentifully of his natural food, which was brought every day for him; did not seem to sicken until two days before his death, and died in some pain. To the last he continued utterly untameable; and, after his chains were on, added the vice of treachery to his others. He would come sometimes quite readily to eat out of my hand, but while I stood by him would suddenly—looking me all the time in the face to keep my attention—put out his foot and grasp at my leg. Several times he tore my pantaloons in this manner, quick retreat on my part saving my person; till at last I was obliged to be very careful in my approaches. The negroes could not come near him at all without setting him in a rage. He knew me very well, and trusted me, but evidently always cherished a feeling of revenge even towards me.

After he was chained, I filled a half-barrel with hay and set it near him for his bed. He recognized its use at once, and it was pretty to see him shake up the hay and creep into this nest when he was tired. At night he always again shook it up, and then took some hay in his hands, with which he would cover himself when he was snug in his barrel.

On Tuesday, the 20th of April, we set out for one of our great hunts, going up the river a short distance and then striking into the forests. We found many open spots in these woods, where the soil was sandy, and the grass was not very luxuriant, growing not more than two feet high. The sun is very oppressive in these clear spots.

We were troubled, too, on the prairie by two very savage flies, called by the negroes the *boco* and the *nchouna*. These insects attacked us with a terrible persistency which left us no peace. They were very quiet bloodsuckers, and I never knew of their attacks till I felt the itch which follows the bite when the fly has left it. This is again followed by a little painful swelling.

The next day we were out after gorillas, which we knew were to be found hereabouts by the presence of a pulpy pear-shaped fruit growing close to the ground, the *tondo*, of which this animal is very fond. I also am very fond of the subdued and grateful acid of this fruit, which the negroes eat as well as the gorilla. It is curious that that which grows in the sandy soil of the prairie is not fit to eat.

We found everywhere gorilla-marks, and so recent that we began to think the animals must be avoiding us. This was the case, I think, though I am not sure. At any rate we beat the bush for two hours before, at last, we found the game. Suddenly an immense gorilla advanced out of the wood straight towards us, and gave vent as he came up to a terrible howl of rage—as much as to say, "I am tired of being pursued, and will face you."

It was a lone male—the kind who are always most ferocious; and this fellow made the woods ring with his roar, which is really an awful sound, resembling very much the rolling and muttering of distant thunder.

He was about twenty yards off when we first saw him. We at once gathered together, and I was about to take aim and bring him down where he stood, when Malaouen stopped me, saying, in a whisper, "Not time yet."

We stood therefore in silence, guns in hand. The gorilla looked at us for a minute or so out of his evil gray eyes, then beat his breast with his gigantic arms, gave another howl of defiance, and advanced upon us.

Again he stopped, now not more than fifteen yards away. Still Malaouen said, "Not yet."

Then again an advance upon us. Now he was not twelve yards off. I could see plainly the ferocious face of the monstrous ape. It was working with rage; his huge teeth were ground against each other so that we could hear the sound; the skin of the forehead was moving rapidly back and forth, and gave a truly devilish expression to the hideous face: once more he gave out a roar which seemed to shake the woods like thunder, and, looking us in the eyes and beating his breast, advanced again. This time he came within eight yards of us before he stopped. My breath was coming short with excitement as I watched the huge beast. Malaouen said only "Steady!" as he came up.

When he stopped, Malaouen said, "Now." And before he could utter the roar for which he was opening his mouth, three musket-balls were in his body. He fell dead almost without a struggle.

"Don't fire too soon. If you do not kill him he will kill you," said Malaouen to me—a piece of advice which I found afterwards was too literally true.

It was a huge old beast indeed. Its height was 5 feet 6 inches. Its arms had a spread of 7 feet 2 inches. Its huge brawny chest measured 50 inches around. The big toe or thumb of its foot measured 5-3/4 inches in circumference. Its arm seemed only immense bunches of muscle, and its legs and claw-like feet were so well fitted for *grabbing* and holding, that I could see how easy it was for the negroes to believe that this animal conceals itself in trees, and pulls up with its foot any living thing—leopard, ox, or man—that passes beneath. There is no doubt the gorilla *can* do this, but that he *does* it I do not believe. They are ferocious, mischievous, but not carnivorous.

The face of this gorilla was intensely black. The vast chest, which proved his great power, was bare, and covered with a parchment-like skin. Its body was covered with gray hair. Though there are sufficient points of diversity between this animal and man, I never kill one without having a sickening realization of the horrid human likeness of the beast. This was particularly the case to-day, when the animal approached us in its fierce way, walking on its hind legs, and facing us as few animals dare face man.

The next day, 7th [May], we went on a gorilla-hunt. All the olako was busy on the evening of my arrival with preparations; and, as meat was scarce, everybody had joyful anticipations of hunger satisfied and plenty in the camp. Little did we guess what frightful death was to befall one of our number before the next sunset.

I gave powder to the whole party. Six were to go off in one direction for gazelles and whatever luck might send them; and six others, of whom I was one, were to hunt for gorillas. We set off towards a dark valley, where Gambo, Igoumba's son, said we should find our prey. The gorilla chooses the darkest, gloomiest forests for its home, and is found on the edges of the clearings only when in search of plantains, or sugarcane, or pineapple. Often they choose for their peculiar haunt a wood so dark that, even at midday, one can scarce see ten yards. This makes it the more necessary to wait till the monstrous beast approaches near before shooting, in order that the first shot may be fatal. It does not often let the hunter reload.

Our little party separated, as is the custom, to stalk the wood in various directions. Gambo and I kept together. One brave fellow went off alone in a direction where he thought he could find a gorilla. The other three took another course. We had been about an hour separated when Gambo and I heard a gun fired but a little way from us, and presently another. We were already on our way to the spot where we hoped to see a gorilla slain, when the forest began to resound with the most terrific roars. Gambo seized my arms in great agitation, and we hurried on, both filled with a dreadful and sickening alarm. We had not gone far when our worst fears were realised. The poor brave fellow who had gone off alone was lying on the ground in a pool of his own blood, and I thought, at first, quite dead. His bowels were protruding through the lacerated abdomen. Beside him lay his gun. The stock was broken, and the barrel was bent and flattened. It bore plainly the marks of the gorilla's teeth.

We picked him up, and I dressed his wounds as well as I could with rags torn from my clothes. When I had given him a little brandy to drink he came to himself, and was able, but with great difficulty, to speak. He said that he had met the gorilla suddenly and face to face, and that it had not attempted to escape. It was, he said, a huge male, and seemed very savage. It was in a very gloomy part of the wood, and the darkness, I suppose, made him miss. He said he took good aim, and fired when the beast was only about eight yards off. The ball merely wounded it in the side. It at once began beating its breasts, and with the greatest rage advanced upon him.

To run away was impossible. He would have been caught in the jungle before he had gone a dozen steps.

He stood his ground, and as quickly as he could reloaded his gun. Just as he raised it to fire the gorilla dashed it out of his hands, the gun going off in the fall; and then in an instant, and with a terrible roar, the animal gave him a tremendous blow with its immense open paw, frightfully lacerating the abdomen, and with this single blow laying bare part of the intestines. As he sank, bleeding, to the ground, the monster seized the gun, and the poor hunter thought he would have his brains dashed out with it. But the gorilla seemed to have looked upon this also as an enemy, and in his rage almost flattened the barrel between his strong jaws.

When we came upon the ground the gorilla was gone. This is their mode when attacked—to strike one or two blows, and then leave the victims of their rage on the ground and go off into the woods.

We hunted up our companions and carried our poor fellow to the camp, where all was instantly excitement and sorrow. They entreated me to give him medicine, but I had nothing to suit his case. I saw that his days were numbered; and all I could do was to make him easy by giving him a little brandy or wine at intervals. He had to tell the whole story over again; and the people declared at once that this was no true gorilla that had attacked him, but a man—a wicked man turned into a gorilla. Such a being no man could escape, they said; and it could not be killed, even by the bravest hunters. This principle of fatalism and of transmigration of souls is brought in by them in all such cases, I think, chiefly to keep up the courage of their hunters, on whom such a mischance exercises a very depressing influence. The hunters are the most valued men in these negro villages. A brave and fortunate one is admired by all the women; loved—almost worshipped—by his wives; and enjoys many privileges among his fellow-villagers. But his proudest time is when he has killed an elephant or a gorilla and filled the village with meat. Then he may do almost what he pleases. The next day we shot a monster gorilla, which I suppose is the same one that killed my poor hunter, for male gorillas are not very plentiful.

June 11th. Yesterday I had a very severe chill, but was able to check it with quinine, fortunately. The dry season has now definitely set in here, and the days are cloudy and the night somewhat cool. We are no longer obliged to build shelters when sleeping out in the woods; and can hunt all day without being wet through as formerly—all which gives me a good deal of comfort.

The poor fellow who was hurt by the gorilla died on the 9th; and some men went out on the 10th and shot a large gorilla, whose remains were brought into camp with great rejoicings on their parts, but great rage on mine. My hunters had seen me skin gorillas and other animals so often that they thought they could do this for me, and, wanting the meat of this one, they took off the hide. So far so good; but the fellows did not know what a value I placed upon the bones, and, to save themelves time and labour, they broke the bones of the legs and of the pelvis. Thus a fine specimen was spoiled for me, or at least made incomplete. I scolded them so that they ran away into the woods, as they said, to get out of hearing of my tongue.

This gorilla was an adult male, and measured five feet seven inches in height.

Temminck quotes, in his 'Esquisses Zoologiques' upon the coast of Guinea, a passage of Bosman, which seems to refer to the gorilla and chimpanzee. If it is to be counted anything more than a fable, it is a very exaggerated and untrustworthy account. Bosman says: "They [these apes] are in this country by thousands. The first and most common are those which are called by our people *smitten*. They are fawn-coloured, and become very tall. I have seen some with my own eyes who are five feet high, and somewhat smaller than a man. They are very wicked and bold; and what an English merchant told me appears incredible, that there is, behind the fort the English have at Wimba, a great quantity of these monkeys, who are so bold that they attack men."

Bosman continues: "There are negroes who affirm that these monkeys can speak, but that they will not, in order not to work. These monkeys have an ugly face,'' and so on. ''The best thing about these kind of monkeys is, that they can be taught everything their master desires.''

Passing by several other travellers' tales of this kind, we come at last to the first real account of the gorilla. This was given by T. E. Bowditch, in his 'Narrative of a Mission from Cape Coast Castle to Ashantee' published in London, 1819. He, too, is the first to call it by its Mpongwe name. In that part of his work relating his visit to the Gaboon, he says: ''The favourite and most extraordinary subject of our conversation on natural history was the *ingena*, an animal like the orangoutang, but much exceeding it in size, being five feet high and four across the shoulders. Its paw was said to be even more disproportioned than its breadth, and one blow of it to be fatal. It is seen commonly by them when they travel to Kaybe, lurking in the bush to destroy passengers, and feeding principally on wild honey, which abounds. Among other of their actions reported without variation by men, women, and children of the Mpongwe and Sheekaï [Shekiani], is that of building a house in rude imitation of the natives, and sleeping outside on the roof of it.''*

So far all travellers spoke either of the chimpanzee (Troglodytes niger), or related hearsay accounts of the gorilla. It remained for the Rev. Dr. Wilson, an American missionary, to present to the world the first real evidence of the existence of this monstrous animal; and for Dr. Savage and Professor Jeffries Wyman, the celebrated comparative anatomist, of Boston, to give to natural history the first memoir on part of the skeleton and on the cranium. Still, no traveller or resident had succeeded in following the animal to its haunts in the unknown regions of the interior, and such particulars of its habits as came to Europe and America were obtained from the natives, whose dread of the monstrous beast fills their minds with superstitious ideas of its nature, and exaggerated notions of its habits.

My long residence in África gave me superior facilities for intercourse with the natives, and as my curiosity was greatly excited by their reports of this unknown monster, I determined to penetrate to its haunts and see with my own eyes. It has been my fortune to be the first white man who can speak of the gorilla from personal knowledge; and while my experience and observation prove that many of the actions reported of it are false and vain imaginings of ignorant negroes and credulous travellers, I can also vouch that no description can exceed the horror of its appearance, the ferocity of its attack, or the impish malignity of its nature.

I am sorry to be the dispeller of such agreeable delusions; but the gorilla does not lurk in trees by the roadside, and drag up unsuspicious passers-by in its claws, and choke them to death in its vice-like paws; it does not attack the elephant, and beat him to death with sticks; it does not carry off women

*Mission to Ashantee, p. 440.

from the native villages; it does not even build itself a house of leaves and twigs in the forest-trees and sit on the roof, as has been confidently reported of it. It is not gregarious even, and the numerous stories of its attacking in great numbers have not a grain of truth in them.

It lives in the loneliest and darkest portions of the dense African jungle, preferring deep wooded valleys and also rugged heights. The high plains also, whose surface is strewn with immense boulders, seem to be favourite haunts. Water occurs everywhere in this part of Africa, but I have noticed that the gorilla is always found very near to a plentiful supply.

It is a restless and nomadic beast, wandering from place to place, and scarce ever found for two days together in the same neighbourhood. In part this restlessness is caused by the struggle it has to find its favourite food. The gorilla, though it has such immense canines, and though its vast strength doubtless fits it to capture and kill almost every animal which frequents the forests, is a strict vegetarian. I examined the stomachs of all which I was lucky enough to kill, and never found traces there of aught but berries, pineapple leaves, and other vegetable matter. It is a huge feeder, and no doubt soon eats up the scant supply of its natural food which is found in any limited space, and is then forced to wander on in constant battle with famine. Its vast paunch, which protrudes before it when it stands upright, proves it to be a great feeder; and, indeed, its great frame and enormous muscular development could not be supported on little food.

It is not true that it lives much or at all on trees. I found them almost always on the ground, although they often climb the trees to pick berries or nuts, but after eating they return to the ground. By the examination of the stomach of many specimens, I was able to ascertain with tolerable certainty the nature of its food, and I discovered that, for all *I* found, it had no need to ascend trees. It is fond of the wild sugarcane; especially fond of the white ribs of the pineapple leaf; and it eats, besides, certain berries which grow close to the ground; the pith of some trees, and a kind of nut with a very hard shell. This shell is so hard that it requires a strong blow with a heavy hammer to break it; and here is probably one purpose of that enormous strength of jaw which long seemed to me thrown away on a non-carnivorous animal, and which is sufficiently evidenced by the manner in which the barrel of the musket of one of my unfortunate hunters was flattened by an enraged male gorilla.

Only the young gorillas sleep on trees, for protection from wild beasts. I have myself come upon fresh traces of a gorilla's bed on several occasions, and could see that the male had seated himself with his back against a tree-trunk. In fact on the back of the male gorilla there is generally a patch on which the hair is worn thin from this position, while the nest-building *Troglodytes calvus*, or bald-headed *nshiego*, which constantly sleeps under its leafy shelter on a tree-branch, has this bare place at its side, and in quite a different way. I believe, however, that while the male always sleeps at the foot of a tree, or elsewhere on the ground, the female and the young may sometimes ascend to the tree-top, as I have seen marks of such ascension.

Those apes which live much in trees, as the chimpanzee, have fingers on both their fore and hind feet much longer than the gorilla's, which, indeed, approximate much nearer to the construction of the human hand and foot, and are, by reason of this different construction, less fitted for tree-climbing. Here I may state that, though young chimpanzees are often captured by the negroes of the Muni Moonda and Gaboon rivers, which shows that they are somewhat abundant in those regions, I never met with a single shelter, and consequently have come to the conclusion that they make none.

The gorilla is not gregarious. Of adults, I found almost always one male with one female, though sometimes the old male wanders companionless. In such cases, as with the "rogue" elephant, he is particularly morose and malignant, and dangerous to approach. Young gorillas I found sometimes in companies of five; sometimes less, but never more. The young always run off, on all fours, shrieking with fear. They are difficult to approach, as their hearing is acute, and they lose no time in making their escape, while the nature of the ground makes it hard for the hunter to follow after. The adult animal is also shy, and I have hunted all day at times without coming upon my quarry, when I felt sure that they were carefully avoiding me. When, however, at last fortune favours the hunter, and he comes accidentally or by good management upon his prey, he need not fear its running away. In all my hunts and encounters with this animal, I never knew a grown male to run off. When I surprised a pair of gorillas, the male was generally sitting down on a rock or against a tree, in the darkest corner of the jungle, where the brightest sun left its traces only in a dim and gloomy twilight. The female was mostly feeding near by; and it is singular that she almost always gave the alarm by running off with loud and sudden cries or shrieks. Then the male, sitting for a moment with a savage frown on his face, slowly rises to his feet, and, looking with glowing and malign eyes at the intruders, begins to beat his breast, and, lifting up his round head, utters his frightful roar. This begins with several sharp barks, like an enraged or mad dog, whereupon ensues a long, deeply guttural, rolling roar, continued for over a minute, and which, doubled and multiplied by the resounding echoes of the forest, fills the hunter's ears like the deep rolling thunder of an approaching storm. As I have mentioned before, I have reason to believe that I have heard this roar at a distance of three miles. The horror of the animal's appearance at this time is beyond description. At such a sight I could forgive my brave native hunters for being sometimes overcome with superstitious fears, and ceased to wonder at the strange, weird "gorilla-stories" of the negroes.

It is a maxim with the well-trained gorilla-hunters to reserve their fire till the very last moment. Experience has shown them that—whether the enraged beast takes the report of the gun for an answering defiance, or for what other reason unknown—if the hunter fires and misses, the gorilla at once rushes upon him; and this onset no man can withstand. One blow of that huge paw with its nails, and the poor hunter's entrails are torn out, his breast-bone broken, or his skull crushed. It is too late to re-load, and flight is vain. There have been negroes who in such cases, made desperate by their frightful danger, have faced the gorilla, and struck at him with the empty gun. But they had time for only one harmless blow. The next moment the huge arm came down with fatal force, breaking musket and skull with one blow. I imagine no animal is so fatal in its attack on man as this, for the reason that it meets him face to face, and uses its arms as its weapons of offence, just as a man or a prize-fighter would—only that it has longer arms, and vastly greater strength than the strongest boxer the world ever saw.

The gorilla is only met in the most dark and impenetrable jungle, where it is difficult to get a clear aim, unobstructed by vines and tangled bushes, for any distance greater than a few yards. For this reason, the gorilla-hunter wisely stands still and awaits the approach of the infuriated beast. The gorilla advances by short stages, stopping to utter his diabolical roar, and to beat his vast breast with his paws, which produce a dull reverberation as of an immense bass-drum. Sometimes from the standing position he seats himself and beats his chest, looking fiercely at his adversary. His walk is a waddle, from side to side, his hind legs—which are very short—being evidently some-what inadequate to the proper support of the huge superincumbent body. He balances himself by swinging his arms, somewhat as sailors walk on shipboard; and the vast paunch, the round bullet-head, joined awkwardly to the trunk with scarce a vestige of neck, and the great muscular arms, and deep, cavern-ous breast, give to this waddle an ungainly horror, which adds to his ferocity of appearance. At the same time, the deep-set gray eyes sparkle out with gloomy malignity; the features are contorted in hideous wrinkles; and the slight, sharply-cut lips, drawn up, reveal the long fangs and the powerful jaws, in which a human limb would be crushed as a biscuit.

The hunter, looking with fearful care to his priming, stands still, gun in hand, often for five weary minutes, waiting with growing nervousness for the moment when he may relieve his suspense by firing. I have never fired at a male at greater distance than eight yards, and from fourteen to eighteen *feet* is the usual shot. At last the opportunity comes; and now the gun is quickly raised, a moment's anxious aim at the vast breadth of breast, and then pull trigger.

In shooting the hippopotamus at night, and on shore, the negro always scam-pers off directly he has fired his gun. When he has fired at the gorilla he stands still. I asked why they did not run in this case too, and was answered that it was of no use. To run would be fatal. If the hunter has missed he must battle for his life face to face, hoping by some piece of unexpected good fortune to escape a fatal blow, and come off, perhaps, maimed for life, as

I have seen several in the up-river villages. Fortunately, the gorilla dies as easily as man; a shot in the breast, if fairly delivered, is sure to bring him down. He falls forward on his face, his long, muscular arms outstretched, and uttering with his last breath a hideous death-cry, half roar, half shriek, which, while it announces to the hunter his safety, yet tingles his ears with a dreadful note of human agony. It is this lurking reminiscence of humanity, indeed, which makes one of the chief ingredients of the hunter's excitement in his attack of the gorilla.

The common walk of the gorilla is not on his hind legs, but on all-fours. In this posture, the arms are so long that the head and breast are raised considerably, and, as it runs, the hind legs are brought far beneath the body. The leg and arm on the same side move together, which gives the beast a curious waddle. It can run at great speed. The young, parties of which I have often pursued, never took to trees, but ran along the ground; and at a distance, with their bodies half-erect, looked not unlike negroes making off from pursuit: the hind-legs moved between the arms, and those were somewhat bowed outward. I have never found the female to attack, though I have been told by the negroes that a mother with a young one in charge will sometimes make fight. It is a pretty thing to see such a mother with the baby gorilla sporting about it. I have watched them in the woods, till, eager as I was to obtain specimens, I had not the heart to shoot. But in such cases my negro hunters exhibited no tenderheartedness, but killed their quarry without loss of time.

When the mother runs off from the hunter, the young one grasps her about the neck, and hangs beneath her breasts with its little legs about her body.

I think the adult gorilla utterly untamable. In the course of the narrative the reader will find accounts of several young gorillas which my men captured alive, and which remained with me for short periods till their deaths. In no case could any treatment of mine, kind or harsh, subdue these little monsters from their first and lasting ferocity and malignity. The young of the *nshiego mbouvé (T. calvus)*, on the contrary, is very easily tamed, and I had one for some months as a companion. The young orang and chimpanzee have been frequently tamed. Of the new and rare kooloo-kamba I was not so fortunate as to secure a living specimen; but being only a variety of the chimpanzee, the young could be tamed, no doubt. But the gorilla is entirely and constantly an enemy to man—resenting its captivity, young as my specimens were—refusing all food except the berries of its native woods, and attacking with teeth and claws even me, who was in most constant attendance upon them; and finally dying without previous sickness, and without other ascertainable cause than the restless chafing of a spirit which could not suffer captivity nor the presence of man.

The young of the chimpanzee is yellow; that of the nshiego mbouvé is a very pale white; but the young gorilla is coal-black. Even the youngest I got, which was a mere baby in arms and could not walk, was black as jet.

The strength of the gorilla is evidently enormous. A young one of between two and three years of age required four stout men to hold it, and even then, in its struggles, bit one severely. That with its jaws it can dent a musket barrel, and with its arms break trees from four to six inches in diameter, sufficiently proves that its vast bony frame has corresponding muscle. The negroes never attack them with other weapons than guns; and in those parts of the far interior where no European guns had yet reached, as among the Apingi, this great beast roamed unmolested, the monarch of the forest. To kill a gorilla gives a hunter a life-long reputation for courage and enterprise even among the bravest of the negro tribes, who are generally, it may be said, not lacking in this quality of courage.

The gorilla has no cries or utterances that I have heard except those already described, the short, sharp bark, and the roar of the attacking male, and the scream of the female and young when alarmed; except, indeed, a low kind of cluck, with which the watchful mother seems to call her child to her. The young ones have a cry when in distress; but their voice is harsh, and it is more a moan of pain than a child's cry.

It uses no artificial weapon of offence, but attacks always with its arms, though in a struggle no doubt the powerful teeth would play a part. I have several times noticed skulls in which the huge canines were broken off, not *worn* down, as they are in almost all the adult gorillas by gnawing at trees which they wished to break, and which, without being gnawed into, are too strong even for them. The negroes informed me that such teeth were broken in combats between the males for the possession of a female, and I think this quite probable. Such a combat must form a magnificent and awful spectacle. A struggle between two well-matched gorillas would exceed, in that kind of excitement which the Romans took such delight in, anything in that line which they were ever gratified with.

There is no doubt that the gorilla walks in an erect posture with greater ease and for a longer time than either the chimpanzee or nshiego mbouvé. When standing up, his knees are bent at the joints outwards, and his back has a stoop forward. His track, when running on all-fours, is peculiar. The hind feet leave no traces of their toes on the ground. Only the ball of the foot and that thumb which answers to our great toe seem to touch. The fingers of the fore hand are only lightly marked on the ground.

The natives of the interior are very fond of the meat of the gorilla and other apes. Gorilla-meat is dark red and tough. The seashore tribes do not eat it, and are insulted by the offer of it, because they suspect some affinity between the animal and themselves. In the interior some families refuse to eat gorilla-meat from the superstitious belief explained elsewhere, that at some time one of their female ancestors has brought forth a gorilla. The skin is thick and firm as an ox-hide, but, though much thicker than in any other ape, it is very tender; it breaks easily, especially under the arm, near the hip. When the hide is dried, the epidermis comes off very easily, and in this differs much from the skin of the other apes, which, though not so thick, are not so tender.

I do not give here any account of other superstitions of the negroes concerning the gorilla, because they are fully detailed in other parts of the book.

In height adult gorillas vary as much as men. The adult males in my collection range from five feet two inches to five feet eight; and the parts of a skeleton which my friend Professor Jeffries Wyman has, are so much larger than any in my possession, that I am warranted in concluding the animal to which it belonged to have been at least six feet two inches in height. The female is much smaller, less strong, and of lighter frame. One adult female in my collection measured, when shot, four feet six inches.

The colour of the skin in the gorilla, young as well as adult, is intense black. This colour does not appear, however, except in the face, on the breast, and in the palms of the hands. The hair of a grown, but not aged specimen, is in colour iron-gray. The individual hairs are ringed with alternate stripes of black and gray, which produces the iron-gray colour. On the arms the hair is darker and also much longer, being sometimes over two inches long. It grows upwards on the fore-arm and downwards on the main-arm. Aged gorillas, the negroes told me, turn quite gray all over; and I have one huge male in my collection whose worn-out tusks show great age, and whose colour is, in fact, a dirty gray, with the exception of the long black shaggy hair on the arm. The head is covered with reddish-brown hair, short, and extending almost to the neck, or where the neck should be.

In the adult male the chest is bare. In the young males which I had in captivity it was thinly covered with hair. In the female the mammae have but a slight development, and the breast is bare. The colour of the hair in the female is black, with a decided tinge of red, and not ringed as in the male. The hair on the arms is but little longer than that on the body, and is of a like colour. The reddish crown which covers the scalp of the male is not apparent in the female till she is almost grown up.

In both male and female the hair is found worn off the back; but this is only found in very old females. This is occasioned, I suppose, by their resting at night against trees, at whose base they sleep.

The eyes of the gorilla are deeply sunken, the immense overhanging bony frontal ridge giving to the face the expression of a constant savage scowl. The mouth is wide, and the lips are sharply cut, exhibiting no red on the edges, as in the human face. The jaws are of tremendous weight and power. The huge canines of the male, which are fully exhibited when, in his rage, he draws back his lips and shows the red colour of the inside of his mouth, lend additional ferocity to his aspect. In the female these canines are smaller.

The almost total absence of neck, which gives the head the appearance of being set into the shoulders, is due to the backward position of the occipital condyles, by means of which the skull is set upon the trunk. The brain-case is low and compressed, and the lofty ridge of the skull causes the cranial profile to describe an almost straight line from the occiput to the supraorbital ridge. The immense development of the temporal muscles which arise from this ridge, and the corresponding size of the jaw, are evidences of the great strength of the animal.

The eyebrows are thin, but not well defined, and are almost lost in the hair of the scalp. The eyelashes are thin also. The eyes are wide apart; the ears are smaller than those of man, and in form closely resemble the human ear. They are almost on the same parallel with the eyes. In a front view of the face the nose is flat, but somewhat prominent—more so than in any other ape; this is on account of a slightly projecting nosebone. The gorilla is the only ape which shows such a projection, and in this respect it comes nearer to man than any other of the man-like apes.

The profile of the trunk shows a slight convexity. The chest is of great capacity; the shoulders exceedingly broad; the pectoral regions show slightly projecting a pair of nipples, as in the other apes and in the human species. The abdomen is of immense size, very prominent, and rounding at the sides. The arms have prodigious muscular development, and are very long, extending as low as the knees. The fore-arm is nearly of uniform size from the wrist to the elbow. The great length of the arms and the shortness of the legs form one of the chief deviations from man. The arms are not so long when compared with the trunk, but they are so in comparison with the legs. These are short, and decrease in size from below the knee to the ankle, having no calf. The superior length of the arm (humerus) in proportion to the fore-arm, brings the gorilla, in that respect, in closer anthropoid affinities with man than any of the other apes.

The hands of the animal, especially in the male, are of immense size, strong, short, and thick. The fingers are short and of great size, the circumference of the middle finger at the first joint being in some gorillas over six inches. The skin on the back of the fingers, near the middle phalanx, is callous and very thick, which shows that the most usual mode of progression of the animal is on all-fours, and resting on the knuckles. The thumb is shorter than in man, and not half so thick as the forefinger. The hand is hairy as far as the division of the fingers, those, as in man, being covered with short thin hairs. The palm of the hand is naked, callous, and intensely black. The nails are black, and shaped like those of man, but smaller in proportion, and projecting very slightly beyond the ends of the fingers. They are thick and strong, and always seem much worn. The hand of the gorilla is almost as wide as it is long, and in this it approaches nearer to those of man than any of the other apes.

The foot is proportionally wider than in man. The sole is callous and intensely black, and looks somewhat like a giant hand of immense power and grasp. The transverse wrinkles show the frequency and freedom of movement of the two joints of the great toe, proving that they have a power of grasp.

The middle toe, or third, is longer than the second and fourth, the fifth proportionally shorter, as in man.

The toes are divided into three groups, so to speak. Inside the great toe, outside the little toe, and the three others partly united by a web. The two joints of the great toe measured, in one specimen, six and a half inches in circumference. As a whole, the foot of the gorilla presents a great likeness to the foot of man, and by far more so than in any other ape. In no other animal is the foot so well adapted for the maintenance of the erect position. Also, the gorilla is much less of a treeclimber than any other ape. The foot in the gorilla is longer than the hand, as in man, while in the other apes the foot is somewhat shorter than the hand. The hair on the foot comes to the division of the toes. With the exception of the big toe, the others present a great likeness to those of man, being free only above the second phalanx; they are slightly covered with thin hair and free.

Dec. 7th. As we advance the country becomes more rugged and mountainous. On every side brooks and rills and small streams are wending their way down to the Ovigui, or towards the Apingi river, and very frequently we have to march along the bed of a purling brook, the only way which the broken and rocky country affords us. This day was exceedingly trying for our feet. We picked our way through a forest dense and gloomy, every step obstructed by rocks and broken ground. This is evidently the favourite haunt of gorilla. Several times during the day we heard his roar in the distance. We heard also the cry of a nshiego mbouvé at a little distance, and started in pursuit, but the animal made its escape, having probably heard us. At the foot of a tree we found some leafy branches gathered, while in another tree was a shelter completed. No doubt a pair had been at work together. The negroes here told me also that these apes work in pairs, both collecting branches, and the male building the shelter when the material is brought together, while the female carries it up to him.

Judging from his cry, one of the gorillas we heard in the afternoon seemed to be so near that I was tempted to hunt him up. He proved farther off than any of us thought. We wandered nearly three-quarters of an hour through the forest before we reached him. His almost incessant roars, which seemed to denote that he was enraged at something, gave us a good clue to his whereabouts.

I find that I do not get accustomed to the roar of the gorilla. Notwithstanding the numbers I have hunted and shot, it is still an awful sound to me. The long reverberations, coming from his potenteous chest; the vindictive bark with which each roar is begun; the hollow monotone of the first explosion, all are awe-inspiring, and proclaim this beast the monarch of these forests.

When the animal became aware of our approach he at once came towards us, uttering a succession of the short bark-like yells which denote his rage, and which have a peculiarly horrible effect. They remind one only of the inarticulate ravings of a maniac.

Balancing his huge heavy body with his arms the animal came towards us, every few moments stopping to beat his breast, and throwing his head back to utter his tremendous roar. His fierce gloomy eyes glared upon us; the short hair was rapidly agitated, and the wrinkled face seemed contorted with rage. It was like a very devil, and I do not wonder at the superstitious terror with which the natives regard it.

His manner of approach gave me once more an opportunity to see with how much difficulty he supports himself in the erect posture. His short and slender legs are not able firmly to sustain the vast body. They totter beneath the weight, and the walk is a sort of waddle, in which the long arms are used, in a clumsy way, to balance the body and keep up the ill-sustained equilibrium. Twice he sat down to roar, evidently not trusting himself to this exertion while standing.

My gun was fresh loaded, and could be depended upon, so I stood in advance. I waited, as the negro rule is, till the huge beast was within six yards of me; then, as he once more stopped to roar, delivered my fire, and brought him down on his face dead.

It proved to be a male, full grown, but young. His huge canine tusks, his claw-like hands, the immense development of muscle on his arms and breast, his whole appearance, in fact, proclaimed a giant strength. There is enough likeness to humanity in this beast to make a dead one an awful sight, even to accustomed eyes, as mine were by this time. I never quite felt that matter-of-course indifference, or that sensation of triumph which the hunter has when a good shot has brought him a head of his choice game. It was as though I had killed some monstrous creation, which had something of humanity in it. Well as I knew that this was an error, I could not help the feeling.

This animal was five feet eight inches high. In the evening, Monsho brought in a young female he had shot, which measured three feet eight inches.

CHARLES DARWIN ON THE DESCENT OF MAN

THE DESCENT OF MAN was published in two volumes in February, 1871, and immediately encountered a great deal of opposition, even from those who could find Darwin's evolutionary theories acceptable for plants and animals—among them, astonishingly enough, Alfred Russel Wallace, the co-deviser of the theory of natural selection. The London *Times*, April 7-8, said in an unfavorable review that, "Even had it been rendered highly probable, which we doubt, that the animal creation has been developed into its numerous and widely different varieties by mere evolution, it would still require an independent investigation of overwhelming force and completeness to justify the presumption that man is but a term in this self-evolving series." But not all the reviews were unfavorable, and gradually, as Darwin predicted, *The Descent of Man* established itself as the most authoritative book on man's ancestry. However, the principal agency which Darwin argued as the means of producing evolutionary change in man, namely, sexual selection, has not generally been accepted among authorities as sound.* *The Descent of Man* argues that the physical and behavioral evolution of man has come about as a result of the individual choice of mates, chiefly by men—the choice of traits in addition to those of beauty being such as the society has held in high esteem. In this manner those individuals were most likely to contribute, as we would today say, to the gene pool, who were physically most attractive and behaviorally most competent.

The fact, however, is that in prehistoric and in existing food-gathering-hunting communities, in which the total number of members averages about 25 persons, marriage is a matter of availability rather than choice and selection. But altogether apart from sexual selection, Darwin throws so much new light on the processes by which man may have evolved, that his book will always remain the foundation stone and the primary source to which the student of man's evolution will return for inspiration.

In the first of the three excerpts here reprinted Darwin traces the evolution of man's moral faculties. In the second excerpt he discusses the affinities and genealogy of man, and in the third excerpt Darwin presents his views on the development of man's intellectual powers.

ON THE EVOLUTION OF MAN'S MORAL FACULTIES*

Turning now to the social and moral faculties. In order that primeval men,

*Bernard Campbell (editor), *Sexual Selection and The Descent of Man 1871-1971*. Chicago: Aldine Publishing Co., 1972.
*From Charles Darwin, *The Descent of Man* (London, John Murray, 1871), Vol. 1, pp. 161-167.

or the ape-like progenitors of man, should become social, they must have acquired the same instinctive feelings, which impel other animals to live in a body; and they no doubt exhibited the same general disposition. They would have felt uneasy when separated from their comrades, for whom they would have felt some degree of love; they would have warned each other of danger, and have given mutual aid in attack or defence. All this implies some degree of sympathy, fidelity, and courage. Such social qualities, the paramount importance of which to the lower animals is disputed by no one, were no doubt acquired by the progenitors of man in a similar manner, namely, through natural selection, aided by inherited habit. When two tribes of primeval man, living in the same country, came into competition, if (other circumstances being equal) the one tribe included a great number of courageous, sympathetic and faithful members, who were always ready to warn each other of danger, to aid and defend each other, this tribe would succeed better and conquer the other. Let it be borne in mind how all-important in the never-ceasing wars of savages, fidelity and courage must be. The advantage which disciplined soldiers have over undisciplined hordes follows chiefly from the confidence which each man feels in his comrades. Obedience, as Mr. Bagehot has well shewn,[1] is of the highest value, for any form of government is better than none. Selfish and contentious people will not cohere, and without coherence nothing can be effected. A tribe rich in the above qualities would spread and be victorious over other tribes: but in the course of time it would, judging from all past history, be in its turn overcome by some other tribe still more highly endowed. Thus the social and moral qualities would tend slowly to advance and be diffused throughout the world.

But it may be asked, how within the limits of the same tribe did a large number of members first become endowed with these social and moral qualities, and how was the standard of excellence raised? It is extremely doubtful whether the offspring of the more sympathetic and benevolent parents, or of those who were the most faithful to their comrades, would be reared in greater numbers than the children of selfish and treacherous parents belonging to the same tribe. He who was ready to sacrifice his life, as many a savage has been, rather than betray his comrades, would often leave no offspring to inherit his noble nature. The bravest men, who were always willing to come to the front in war, and who freely risked their lives for others, would on an average perish in larger numbers than other men. Therefore it hardly seems probable, that the number of men gifted with such virtues, or that the standard of their excellence, could be increased through natural selection, that is, by the survival of the fittest; for we are not here speaking of one tribe being victorious over another.

---

[1] See a remarkable series of articles on 'Physics and Politics,' in the 'Fortnightly Review,' Nov. 1867; April 1, 1868; July 1, 1869, since separately published.

Although the circumstances, leading to an increase in the number of those thus endowed within the same tribe, are too complex to be clearly followed out, we can trace some of the probable steps. In the first place, as the reasoning powers and foresight of the members became improved, each man would soon learn that if he aided his fellow-men, he would commonly receive aid in return. From this low motive he might acquire the habit of aiding his fellows; and the habit of performing benevolent actions certainly strengthens the feeling of sympathy which gives the first impulse to benevolent actions. Habits, moreover, followed during many generations probably tend to be inherited.

But another and much more powerful stimulus to the development of the social virtues, is afforded by the praise and the blame of our fellow-men. To the instinct of sympathy, as we have already seen, it is primarily due, that we habitually bestow both praise and blame on others, whilst we love the former and dread the latter when applied to ourselves; and this instinct no doubt was originally acquired, like all the other social instincts, through natural selection. At how early a period the progenitors of man in the course of their development, became capable of feeling and being impelled by, the praise or blame of their fellow-creatures, we cannot of course say. But it appears that even dogs appreciate encouragement, praise, and blame. The rudest savages feel the sentiment of glory, as they clearly show by preserving the trophies of their prowess, by their habit of excessive boasting, and even by the extreme care which they take of their personal appearance and decorations; for unless they regarded the opinion of their comrades, such habits would be senseless.

They certainly feel shame at the breach of some of their lesser rules, and apparently remorse, as shewn by the case of the Australian who grew thin and could not rest from having delayed to murder some other woman, so as to propitiate his dead wife's spirit. Though I have not met with any other recorded case, it is scarcely credible that a savage, who will sacrifice his life rather than betray his tribe, or one who will deliver himself up as a prisoner rather than break his parole,[2] would not feel remorse in his inmost soul, if he had failed in a duty, which he held sacred.

We may therefore conclude that primeval man, at a very remote period, was influenced by the praise and blame of his fellows. It is obvious, that the members of the same tribe would approve of conduct which appeared to them to be for the general good, and would reprobate that which appeared evil. To do good unto others—to do unto others as ye would they should do unto you—is the foundation-stone of morality. It is, therefore, hardly possible to exaggerate the importance during rude times of the love of praise and the dread of blame. A man who was not impelled by any deep, instinctive feeling, to sacrifice his life for the good of others, yet was roused to such actions by

[2] Mr. Wallace gives cases in his 'Contributions to the Theory of Natural Selection,' 1870, p. 354.

a sense of glory, would by his example excite the same wish for glory in other men, and would strengthen by exercise the noble feeling of admiration. He might thus do far more good to his tribe than by begetting offspring with a tendency to inherit his own high character.

With increased experience and reason, man perceives the more remote consequences of his actions, and the self-regarding virtues, such as temperance, chastity, &c., which during early times are, as we have before seen, utterly disregarded, come to be highly esteemed or even held sacred. I need not, however, repeat what I have said on this head in the fourth chapter. Ultimately our moral sense or conscience becomes a highly complex sentiment—originating in the social instincts, largely guided by the approbation of our fellow-men, ruled by reason, self-interest, and in later times by deep religious feelings, and confirmed by instruction and habit.

It must not be forgotten that although a high standard of morality gives but a slight or no advantage to each individual man and his children over the other men of the same tribe, yet that an increase in the number of well-endowed men and an advancement in the standard of morality will certainly give an immense advantage to one tribe over another. A tribe including many members who, from possessing in a high degree the spirit of patriotism, fidelity, obedience, courage, and sympathy, were always ready to aid one another, and to sacrifice themselves for the common good, would be victorious over most other tribes; and this would be natural selection. At all times throughout the world tribes have supplanted other tribes; and as morality is one important element in their success, the standard of morality and the number of well-endowed men will thus everywhere tend to rise and increase.

It is, however, very difficult to form any judgment why one particular tribe and not another has been successful and has risen in the scale of civilisation. Many savages are in the same condition as when first discovered several centuries ago. As Mr. Bagehot has remarked, we are apt to look at progress as normal in human society; but history refutes this. The ancients did not even entertain the idea, nor do the Oriental nations at the present day. According to another high authority, Sir Henry Maine,[3] "the greatest part of mankind has never shewn a particle of desire that its civil institutions should be improved." Progress seems to depend on many concurrent favourable conditions, far too complex to be followed out. But it has often been remarked, that a cool climate, from leading to industry and to the various arts, has been highly favourable thereto. The Esquimaux, pressed by hard necessity, have succeeded in many ingenious inventions, but their climate has been too severe for continued progress. Nomadic habits, whether over wide plains, or through the dense forests of the tropics, or along the shores of the sea, have in every

[3]'Ancient Law,' 1861, p. 22. For Mr. Bagehot's remarks, 'Fortnightly Review,' April 1, 1868, p. 452.

case been highly detrimental. Whilst observing the barbarous inhabitants of Tierra del Fuego, it struck me that the possession of some property, a fixed abode, and the union of many families under a chief, were the indispensable requisites for civilisation. Such habits almost necessitate the cultivation of the ground; and the first steps in cultivation would probably result, as I have elsewhere shewn,[4] from some such accident as the seeds of a fruit-tree falling on a heap of refuse, and producing an unusually fine variety. The problem, however, of the first advance of savages towards civilisation is at present much too difficult to be solved.

ON THE AFFINITIES AND GENEALOGY OF MAN*

Even if it be granted that the difference between man and his nearest allies is as great in corporeal structure as some naturalists maintain, and although we must grant that the difference between them is immense in mental power, yet the facts given in the earlier chapters appear to declare, in the plainest manner, that man is descended from some lower form, notwithstanding that connecting-links have not hitherto been discovered.

Man is liable to numerous, slight, and diversified variations, which are induced by the same general causes, are governed and transmitted in accordance with the same general laws, as in the lower animals. Man has multiplied so rapidly, that he has necessarily been exposed to struggle for existence, and consequently to natural selection. He has given rise to many races, some of which differ so much from each other, that they have often been ranked by naturalists as distinct species. His body is constructed on the same homological plan as that of other mammals. He passes through the same phases of embryological development. He retains many rudimentary and useless structures, which no doubt were once serviceable. Characters occasionally make their re-appearance in him, which we have reason to believe were possessed by his early progenitors. If the origin of man had been wholly different from that of all other animals, these various appearances would be mere empty deceptions; but such an admission is incredible. These appearances, on the other hand, are intelligible, at least to a large extent, if man is the co-descendant with other mammals of some unknown and lower form.

Some naturalists, from being deeply impressed with the mental and spiritual

[4]'The Variation of Animals and Plants under Domestication,' vol. i. p. 309.
*From Charles Darwin, *The Descent of Man* (London, John Murray, 1871), Vol., 1, pp. 185-213.

powers of man, have divided the whole organic world into three kingdoms, the Human, the Animal, and the Vegetable, thus giving to man a separate kingdom.[1] Spritual powers cannot be compared or classed by the naturalist: but he may endeavour to shew, as I have done, that the mental faculties of man and the lower animals do not differ in kind, although immensely in degree. A difference in degree, however great, does not justify us in placing man in a distinct kingdom, as will perhaps be best illustrated by comparing the mental powers of two insects, namely, a coccus or scale-insect and an ant, which undoubtedly belong to the same class. The difference is here greater than, though of a somewhat different kind from, that between man and the highest mammal. The female coccus, whilst young, attaches itself by its proboscis to a plant; sucks the sap, but never moves again; is fertilised and lays eggs; and this is its whole history. On the other hand, to describe the habits and mental powers of worker-ants, would require, as Pierre Huber has shewn, a large volume; I may, however, briefly specify a few points. Ants certainly communicate information to each other, and several unite for the same work, or for games of play. They recognise their fellow-ants after months of absence, and feel sympathy for each other. They build great edifices, keep them clean, close the doors in the evening, and post sentries. They make roads as well as tunnels under rivers, and temporary bridges over them, by clinging together. They collect food for the community, and when an object, too large for entrance, is brought to the nest, they enlarge the door, and afterwards build it up again. They store up seeds, of which they prevent the germination, and which, if damp, are brought up to the surface to dry. They keep aphides and other insects as milch-cows. They go out to battle in regular bands, and freely sacrifice their lives for the common weal. They emigrate according to a preconcerted plan. They capture slaves. They move the eggs of their aphides, as well as their own eggs and cocoons, into warm parts of the nest, in order that they may be quickly hatched; and endless similar facts could be given.[2] On the whole, the difference in mental power between an ant and a coccus is immense; yet no one has ever dreamed of placing these insects in distinct classes, much less in distinct kingdoms. No doubt the difference is bridged over by other insects; and this is not the case with man and the higher apes. But we have every reason to believe that the breaks in the series are simply the results of many forms having become extinct.

Professor Owen, relying chiefly on the structure of the brain, has divided the mammalian series into four sub-classes. One of these he devotes to man;

[1] Isidore Geoffroy St.-Hilaire gives a detailed account of the position assigned to man by various naturalists in their classifications: 'Hist. Nat. Gén.' tom ii. 1859, pp. 170-189.

[2] Some of the most interesting facts ever published on the habits of ants are given by Mr. Pelt, in his 'Naturalist in Nicaragua,' 1874. See also Mr. Moggridge's admirable work, 'Harvesting Ants,' &c., 1873, also 'L'Instinct chez les Insectes,' by M. George Pouchet, 'Revue des Deux Mondes,' Feb. 1870, p. 682.

in another he places both the Marsupials and the Monotremata; so that he makes man as distinct from all other mammals as are these two latter groups conjoined. This view has not been accepted, as far as I am aware, by any naturalist capable of forming an independent judgment, and therefore need not here be further considered.

We can understand why a classification founded on any single character or organ—even an organ so wonderfully complex and important as the brain—or on the high development of the mental faculties, is almost sure to prove unsatisfactory. This principle has indeed been tried with hymenopterous insects; but when thus classed by their habits or instincts, the arrangement proved thoroughly artificial.[3] Classifications may, of course, be based on any character whatever, as on size, colour, or the element inhabited; but naturalists have long felt a profound conviction that there is a natural system. This system, it is now generally admitted, must be, as far as possible, genealogical in arrangement,—that is the co-descendants of the same form must be kept together in one group, apart from the co-descendants of any other form; but if the parent-forms are related, so will be their descendants, and the two groups together will form a larger group. The amount of difference between the several groups—that is the amount of modification which each has undergone—is expressed by such terms as genera, families, orders, and classes. As we have no record of the lines of descent, the pedigree can be discovered only by observing the degrees of resemblance between the beings which are to be classed. For this object numerous points of resemblance are of much more importance than the amount of similarity or dissimilarity in a few points. If two languages were found to resemble each other in a multitude of words and points of construction they would be universally recognised as having sprung from a common source, notwithstanding that they differed greatly in some few words or points of construction. But with organic beings the points of resemblance must not consist of adaptations to similar habits of life: two animals may, for instance, have had their whole frames modified for living in the water, and yet they will not be brought any nearer to each other in the natural system. Hence we can see how it is that resemblances in several unimportant structures, in useless and rudimentary organs, or not now functionally active, or in an embryological condition, are by far the most serviceable for classification; for they can hardly be due to adaptations within a late period; and thus they reveal the old lines of descent or of true affinity.

We can further see why a great amount of modification in some one character ought not to lead us to separate widely any two organisms. A part which already differs much from the same part in other allied forms has already, according to the theory of evolution, varied much; consequently it would (as long as the organism remained exposed to the same exciting conditions) be

[3] Westwood, 'Modern Class of Insects,' vol. ii. 1840, p. 87.

liable to further variations of the same kind; and these, if beneficial, would be preserved, and thus be continually augmented. In many cases the continued development of a part, for instance, of the beak of a bird, or of the teeth of a mammal, would not aid the species in gaining its food, or for any other object; but with man we can see no definite limit to the continued development of the brain and mental faculties, as far as advantage is concerned. Therefore in determining the position of man in the natural or genealogical system, the extreme development of his brain ought not to outweigh a multitude of resemblances in other less important or quite unimportant points.

The great number of naturalists who have taken into consideration the whole structure of man, including his mental faculties, have followed Blumenbach and Cuvier, and have placed man in a separate Order, under the title of the Bimana, and therefore on an equality with the orders of the Quadrumana, Carnivora, &c. Recently many of our best naturalists have recurred to the view first propounded by Linnaeus, so remarkable for his sagacity, and have placed man in the same Order with the Quadrumana, under the title of the Primates. The justice of this conclusion will be admitted: for in the first place, we must bear in mind the comparative insignificance for classification of the great development of the brain in man, and that the strongly-marked differences between the skulls of man and the Quadrumana (lately insisted upon by Bischoff, Aeby, and others) apparently follow from their differently developed brains. In the second place, we must remember that nearly all the other and more important differences between man and the Quadrumana are manifestly adaptive in their nature, and relate chiefly to the erect position of man; such as the structure of his hand, foot, and pelvis, the curvature of his spine, and the position of his head. The family of Seals offers a good illustration of the small importance of adaptive characters for classification. These animals differ from all other Carnivora in the form of their bodies and in the structure of their limbs, far more than does man from the higher apes; yet in most systems, from that of Cuvier to the most recent one by Mr. Flower,[4] seals are ranked as a mere family in the Order of the Carnivora. If man had not been his own classifier, he would never have thought of founding a separate order for his own reception.

It would be beyond my limits, and quite beyond my knowledge, even to name the innumerable points of structure in which man agrees with the other Primates. Our great anatomist and philosopher, Prof. Huxley, has fully discussed this subject,[5] and concludes that man in all parts of his organization differs less from the higher apes, than these do from the lower members of the same group. Consequently there ''is no justification for placing man in a distinct order.''

[4]'Proc. Zoolog. Soc.' 1863, p. 4.
[5]'Evidence as to Man's Place in Nature,' 1863, p. 70, *et passim*.

In an early part of this work I brought forward various facts, shewing how closely man agrees in constitution with the higher mammals; and this agreement must depend on our close similarity in minute structure and chemical composition. I gave, as instances, our liability to the same diseases, and to the attacks of allied parasites; our tastes in common for the same stimulants, and the similar effects produced by them, as well as by various drugs, and other such facts.

As small unimportant points of resemblance between man and the Quadrumana are not commonly noticed in systematic works, and as, when numerous, they clearly reveal our relationship, I will specify a few such points. The relative position of our features is manifestly the same; and the various emotions are displayed by nearly similar movements of the muscles and skin, chiefly above the eyebrows and round the mouth. Some few expressions are, indeed, almost the same, as in the weeping of certain kinds of monkeys and in the laughing noise made by others, during which the corners of the mouth are drawn backwards, and the lower eyelids wrinkled. The external ears are curiously alike. In man the nose is much more prominent than in most monkeys; but we may trace the commencement of an aquiline curvature in the nose of the Hoolock Gibbon; and this in the *Semnopithecus nasica* is carried to a ridiculous extreme.

The faces of many monkeys are ornamented with beards, whiskers, or moustaches. The hair on the head grows to a great length in some species of Semnopithecus;[6] and in the Bonnet monkey (*Macacus radiatus*) it radiates from a point on the crown, with a parting down the middle. It is commonly said that the forehead gives to man his noble and intellectual appearance; but the thick hair on the head of the Bonnet monkey terminates downwards abruptly, and is succeeded by hair so short and fine that at a little distance the forehead, with the exception of the eyebrows, appears quite naked. It has been erroneously asserted that eyebrows are not present in any monkey. In the species just named the degree of nakedness of the forehead differs in different individuals; and Eschricht states[7] that in our children the limit between the hairy scalp and the naked forehead is sometimes not well defined; so that here we seem to have a trifling case of reversion to a progenitor, in whom the forehead had not as yet become quite naked.

It is well known that the hair on our arms tends to converge from above and below to a point at the elbow. This curious arrangement, so unlike that in most of the lower mammals, is common to the gorilla, chimpanzee, orang, some species of Hylobates, and even to some few American monkeys. But in *Hylobates agilis* the hair on the fore-arm is directed downwards or towards

[6]Isid. Geoffroy, 'Hist. Nat. Gén.' tom. ii. 1859, p. 217.
[7]'Ueber die Richtung der Haare,' &c., Müller's 'Archiv für Anat. und Phys.' 1837, s. 51.

the wrist in the ordinary manner; and in *H. lar* it is nearly erect, with only a very slight forward inclination; so that in this latter species it is in a transitional state. It can hardly be doubted that with most mammals the thickness of the hair on the back and its direction, is adapted to throw off the rain; even the transverse hairs on the fore-legs of a dog may serve for this end when he is coiled up asleep. Mr. Wallace, who has carefully studied the habits of the orang, remarks that the convergence of the hair towards the elbow on the arms of the orang may be explained as serving to throw off the rain, for this animal during rainy weather sits with its arms bent, and with the hands clasped round a branch or over its head. According to Livingstone, the gorilla also "sits in pelting rain with his hands over his head."[8] If the above explanation is correct, as seems probable, the direction of the hair on our own arms offers a curious record of our former state; for no one supposes that it is now of any use in throwing off the rain; nor, in our present erect condition, is it properly directed for this purpose.

It would, however, be rash to trust too much to the principle of adaptation in regard to the direction of the hair in man or his early progenitors; for it is impossible to study the figures given by Eschricht of the arrangement of the hair on the human foetus (this being the same as in the adult) and not agree with this excellent observer that other and more complex causes have intervened. The points of convergence seem to stand in some relation to those points in the embryo which are last closed in during development. There appears, also, to exist some relation between the arrangement of the hair on the limbs, and the course of the medullary arteries.[9]

It must not be supposed that the resemblances between man and certain apes in the above and in many other points—such as in having a naked forehead, long tresses on the head, &c.—are all necessarily the result of unbroken inheritance from a common progenitor, or of subsequent reversion. Many of these resemblances are more probably due to analogous variation, which follows, as I have elsewhere attempted to shew,[10] from co-descended organisms having a similar constitution, and having been acted on by like causes inducing similar modifications. With respect to the similar direction of the hair on the fore-arms of man and certain monkeys, as this character is common to almost all the anthropomorphous apes, it may probably be attributed to inheritance; but this is not certain, as some very distinct American monkeys are thus characterised.

[8]Quoted by Reade, 'The African Sketch Book,' vol. i., 1873, p. 152.

[9]On the hair in Hylobates, see 'Nat. Hist. of Mammals,' by C. L. Martin, 1841, p. 415. Also, Isid. Geoffroy on the American monkeys and other kinds, 'Hist. Nat. Gén.' vol. ii. 1859, p. 216, 243, Eschricht, ibid. s. 46, 55, 61. Owen, 'Anat. of Vertebrates,' vol. iii. p. 619. Wallace, 'Contributions to the Theory of Natural Selection,' 1870, p. 344.

[10]'Origin of Species,' 5th edit. 1869, p. 194. 'The Variation of Animals and Plants under Domestication,' vol. ii. 1868, p. 348.

Although, as we have now seen, man has no just right to form a separate Order for his own reception, he may perhaps claim a distinct Sub-order or Family. Prof. Huxley, in his last work,[11] divides the Primates into three Sub-orders; namely, the Anthropidae with man alone, the Simiadae including monkeys of all kinds, and the Lemuridae with the diversified genera of lemurs. As far as differences in certain important points of structure are concerned, man may no doubt rightly claim the rank of a Sub-order; and this rank is too low, if we look chiefly to his mental faculties. Nevertheless, from a genealogical point of view it appears that this rank is too high, and that man ought to form merely a Family, or possibly even only a Sub-family. If we imagine three lines of descent proceeding from a common stock, it is quite conceivable that two of them might after the lapse of ages be so slightly changed as still to remain as species of the same genus, whilst the third line might become so greatly modified as to deserve to rank as a distinct Sub-family, Family, or even Order. But in this case it is almost certain that the third line would still retain through inheritance numerous small points of resemblance with the other two. Here, then, would occur the difficulty, at present insoluble, how much weight we ought to assign in our classifications to strongly-marked differences in some few points,—that is, to the amount of modification undergone; and how much to close resemblance in numerous unimportant points, as indicating the lines of descent or genealogy. To attach much weight to the few but strong differences is the most obvious and perhaps the safest course, though it appears more correct to pay great attention to the many small resemblances, as giving a truly natural classification.

In forming a judgment on this head with reference to man, we must glance at the classification of the Simiadae. This family is divided by almost all naturalists into the Catarrhine group, or Old World monkeys, all of which are characterised (as their name expresses) by the peculiar structure of their nostrils, and by having four premolars in each jaw; and into the Platyrrhine group or New World monkeys (including two very distinct sub-groups), all of which are characterised by differently constructed nostrils, and by having six premolars in each jaw. Some other small differences might be mentioned. Now man unquestionably belongs in his dentition, in the structure of his nostrils, and some other respects, to the Catarhine or Old World division; nor does he resemble the Platyrhines more closely than the Catarhines in any characters, excepting in a few of not much importance and apparently of an adaptive nature. It is therefore against all probability that some New World species should have formerly varied and produced a man-like creature, with all the distinctive characters proper to the Old World division; losing at the same time all its own distinctive characters. There can, consequently, hardly be a doubt that man is an off-shoot from the Old World Simian stem; and that under

[11]'An Introduction to the Classification of Animals,' 1869, p. 99.

a genealogical point of view he must be classed with the Catarhine division.[12]

The anthropomorphous apes, namely the gorilla, chimpanzee, orang, and hylobates, are by most naturalists separated from the other Old World monkeys, as a distinct sub-group. I am aware that Gratiolet, relying on the structure of the brain, does not admit the existence of this sub-group, and no doubt it is a broken one. Thus the orang, as Mr. St. G. Mivart remarks,[13] "is one of the most peculiar and aberrant "forms to be found in the Order." The remaining non-anthropomorphous Old World monkeys, are again divided by some naturalists into two or three smaller sub-groups; the genus Semnopithecus, with its peculiar sacculated stomach, being the type of one such sub-group. But it appears from M. Gaudry's wonderful discoveries in Attica, that during the Miocene period a form existed there, which connected Semnopithecus and Macacus; and this probably illustrates the manner in which the other and higher groups were once blended together.

If the anthropomorphous apes be admitted to form a natural sub-group, then as man agrees with them, not only in all those characters which he possesses in common with the whole Catarhine group, but in other peculiar characters, such as the absence of a tail and of callosities, and in general appearance, we may infer that some ancient member of the anthropomorphous sub-group gave birth to man. It is not probable that, through the law of analogous variation, a member of one of the other lower sub-groups should have given rise to a man-like creature, resembling the higher anthropomorphous apes in so many respects. No doubt man, in comparison with most of his allies, has undergone an extraordinary amount of modification, chiefly in consequence of the great development of his brain and his erect position; nevertheless, we should bear in mind that he "is but one of several exceptional forms of Primates."[14]

Every naturalist, who believes in the principle of evolution, will grant that the two main divisions of the Simiadae, namely the Catarhine and Platyrhine monkeys, with their sub-groups, have all proceeded from some one extremely ancient progenitor. The early descendants of this progenitor, before they had diverged to any considerable extent from each other, would still have formed a single natural group; but some of the species or incipient genera would have already begun to indicate by their diverging characters the future distinctive marks of the Catarhine and Platyrhine divisions. Hence the members of this supposed ancient group would not have been so uniform in their dentition,

[12]This is nearly the same classification as that provisionally adopted by Mr. St. George Mivart ('Transact. Philosoph. Soc.' 1867, p. 300), who, after separating the Lemuridae, divides the remainder of the Primates into the Hominidae, the Simiadae which answer to the Catarhines, the Cebidae, and the Hapalidae,—these two latter groups answering to the Platyrhines. Mr. Mivart still abides by the same view; see 'Nature,' 1871, p. 481.

[13]'Transact. Zoolog. Soc.' vol. vi. 1867, p. 214.

[14]Mr. St. G. Mivart, 'Transact. Phil. Soc.' 1867, p. 410.

or in the structure of their nostrils, as are the existing Catarhine monkeys in one way and the Platyrhines in another way but would have resembled in this respect the allied Lemuridae, which differ greatly from each other in the form of their muzzles,[15] and to an extraordinary degree in their dentition.

The Catarhine and Platyrhine monkeys agree in a multitude of characters, as is shewn by their unquestionably belonging to one and the same Order. The many characters which they possess in common can hardly have been independently acquired by so many distinct species; so that these characters must have been inherited. But a naturalist would undoubtedly have ranked as an ape or a monkey, an ancient form which possessed many characters common to the Catarhine and Platyrhine monkeys, other characters in an intermediate condition, and some few, perhaps, distinct from those now found in either group. And as man from a genealogical point of view belongs to the Catarhine or Old World stock, we must conclude, however much the conclusion may revolt our pride, that our early progenitors would have been properly thus designated.[16] But we must not fall into the error of supposing that the early progenitor of the whole Simian stock, including man, was identical with, or even closely resembled, any existing ape or monkey.

On the Birthplace and Antiquity of Man.—We are naturally led to enquire, where was the birthplace of man at that stage of descent when our progenitors diverged from the Catarhine stock? The fact that they belonged to this stock clearly shews that they inhabitated the Old World; but not Australia nor any oceanic island, as we may infer from the laws of geographical distribution. In each great region of the world the living mammals are closely related to the extinct species of the same region. It is therefore probable that Africa was formerly inhabited by extinct apes closely allied to the gorilla and chimpanzee; and as these two species are now man's nearest allies, it is somewhat more probable that our early progenitors lived on the African continent than elsewhere. But it is useless to speculate on this subject; for two or three anthropomorphous apes, one the Dryopithecus[17] of Lartet, nearly as large as a man, and closely allied to Hylobates, existed in Europe during the Miocene age; and since so remote a period the earth has certainly undergone many great revolutions, and there has been ample time for migration on the largest scale.

At the period and place, whenever and wherever it was, when man first

[15]Messrs. Murie and Mivart on the Lemuroidea, 'Transact. Zoolog. Soc.' vol. vii. 1869, p. 5.

[16]Häckel has come to this same conclusion. See 'Ueber die Entstehung des Menschen-geschlechts,' in Virchow's 'Sammlung. gemein. wissen. Vortrage,' 1868, s. 61. Also his 'Natür-liche Schöpfungsgeschichte,' 1868, in which he gives in detail his views on the genealogy of man.

[17]Dr. C. Forsyth Major, 'Sur les Singes Fossiles trouvés en Italie:' 'Soc. Ital. des Sc. Nat.' tom. xv. 1872.

lost his hairy covering, he probably inhabited a hot country; a circumstance favourable for the frugiferous diet on which, judging from analogy, he subsisted. We are far from knowing how long ago it was when man first diverged from the Catarhine stock; but it may have occurred at an epoch as remote as the Eocene period; for that the higher apes had diverged from the lower apes as early as the Upper Miocene period is shewn by the existence of the Dryopithecus. We are also quite ignorant at how rapid a rate organisms, whether high or low in the scale, may be modified under favourable circumstances; we know, however, that some have retained the same form during an enormous lapse of time. From what we see going on under domestication, we learn that some of the co-descendants of the same species may be not at all, some a little, and some greatly changed, all within the same period. Thus it may have been with man, who has undergone a great amount of modification in certain characters in comparison with the higher apes.

The great break in the organic chain between man and his nearest allies, which cannot be bridged over by any extinct or living species, has often been advanced as a grave objection to the belief that man is descended from some lower form; but this objection will not appear of much weight to those who, from general reasons, believe in the general principle of evolution. Breaks often occur in all parts of the series, some being wide, sharp and defined, others less so in various degrees; as between the orang and its nearest allies—between the Tarsius and the other Lemuridae—between the elephant, and in a more striking manner between the Ornithorhynchus or Echidna, and all other mammals. But these breaks depend merely on the number of related forms which have become extinct. At some future period, not very distant as measured by centuries, the civilised races of man will almost certainly exterminate, and replace, the savage races throughout the world. At the same time the anthropomorphous apes, as Professor Schaaffhausen has remarked,[18] will no doubt be exterminated. The break between man and his nearest allies will then be wider, for it will intervene between man in a more civilised state, as we may hope, even than the Caucasian, and some ape as low as a baboon, instead of as now between the negro or Australian and the gorilla.

With respect to the absence of fossil remains, serving to connect man with his ape-like progenitors, no one will lay much stress on this fact who reads Sir C. Lyell's discussion,[19] where he shews that in all the vertebrate classes the discovery of fossil remains has been a very slow and fortuitous process. Nor should it be forgotten that those regions which are the most likely to afford remains connecting man with some extinct ape-like creature, have not as yet been searched by geologists.

Lower Stages in the Genealogy of Man.—We have seen that man appears

[18]Anthropological Review,' April, 1867, p. 236.
[19]'Elements of Geology,' 1865, pp. 583-585. 'Antiquity of Man,' 1863, p. 145.

to have diverged from the Catarhine or Old World division of the Simiadae, after these had diverged from the New World division. We will now endeavour to follow the remote traces of his genealogy, trusting principally to the mutual affinities between the various classes and orders, with some slight reference to the periods, as far as ascertained, of their successive appearance on the earth. The Lemuridae stand below and near to the Simiadae, and constitute a very distinct family of the Primates, or, according to Häckel and others, a distinct Order. This group is diversified and broken to an extraordinary degree, and includes many aberrant forms. It has, therefore, probably suffered much extinction. Most of the remnants survive on islands, such as Madagascar and the Malayan archipelago, where they have not been exposed to so severe a competition as they would have been on well-stocked continents. This group likewise presents many gradations, leading, as Huxley remarks,[20] "insensibly from the crown and summit of the animal creation down to creatures from which there is but a step, as it seems, to the lowest, smallest, and least intelligent of the placental mammalia." From these various considerations it is probable that the Simiadae were originally developed from the progenitors of the existing Lemuridae; and these in their turn from forms standing very low in the mammalian series.

The Marsupials stand in many important characters below the placental mammals. They appeared at an earlier geological period, and their range was formerly much more extensive than at present. Hence the Placentata are generally supposed to have been derived from the Implacentata or Marsupials; not, however, from forms closely resembling the existing Marsupials, but from their early progenitors. The Monotremata are plainly allied to the Marsupials, forming a third and still lower division in the great mammalian series. They are represented at the present day solely by the Ornithorhynchus and Echidna; and these two forms may be safely considered as relics of a much larger group, representatives of which have been preserved in Australia through some favourable concurrence of circumstances. The Monotremata are eminently interesting, as leading in several important points of structure towards the class of reptiles.

In attempting to trace the genealogy of the Mammalia, and therefore of man, lower down in the series, we become involved in greater and greater obscurity; but as a most capable judge, Mr. Parker, has remarked, we have good reason to believe, that no true bird or reptile intervenes in the direct line of descent. He who wishes to see what ingenuity and knowledge can effect, may consult Prof. Häckel's works.[21] I will content myself with a few general remarks.

[20]'Man's Place in Nature,' p. 105.

[21]Elaborate tables are given in his 'Generelle Morphologie' (B. ii. s. cliii. and s. 425); and with more especial reference to man in his 'Natürliche Schöpfungsgeschichte,' 1868. Prof. Huxley, in reviewing this latter work ('The Academy,' 1869, p. 42) says, that he considers the phylum or lines of descent of the Vertebrata to be admirably discussed by Häckel, although he differs on some points. He expresses, also, his high estimate of the general tenor and spirit of the whole work.

Every evolutionist will admit that the five great vertebrate classes, namely, mammals, birds, reptiles, amphibians, and fishes, are descended from some one prototype; for they have much in common, especially during their embryonic state. As the class of fishes is the most lowly organised, and appeared before the others, we may conclude that all the members of the vertebrate kingdom are derived from some fishlike animal. The belief that animals so distinct as a monkey, an elephant, a humming-bird, a snake, a frog, and a fish, &c., could all have sprung from the same parents, will appear monstrous to those who have not attended to the recent progress of natural history. For this belief implies the former existence of links binding closely together all these forms, now so utterly unlike.

Nevertheless, it is certain that groups of animals have existed, or do now exist, which serve to connect several of the great vertebrate classes more or less closely. We have seen that the Ornithorhynchus graduates towards reptiles; and Prof. Huxley has discovered, and is confirmed by Mr. Cope and others, that the Dinosaurians are in many important characters intermediate between certain reptiles and certain birds—the birds referred to being the ostrich-tribe (itself evidently a widely-diffused remnant of a larger group) and the Archeopteryx, that strange Secondary bird, with a long lizard-like tail. Again, according to Prof. Owen,[22] the Ichthyosaurians—great sea-lizards furnished with paddles—present many affinities with fishes, or rather, according to Huxley, with amphibians; a class which, including in its highest division frogs and toads, is plainly allied to the Ganoid fishes. These latter fishes swarmed during the earlier geological periods, and were constructed on what is called a generalised type, that is, they presented diversified affinities with other groups of organisms. The Lepidosiren is also so closely allied to amphibians and fishes, that naturalists long disputed in which of these two classes to rank it; it, and also some few Ganoid fishes, have been preserved from utter extinction by inhabiting rivers, which are harbours of refuge, and are related to the great waters of the ocean in the same way that islands are to continents.

Lastly, one single member of the immense and diversified class of fishes, namely, the lancelet or amphioxus, is so different from all other fishes, that Häckel maintains that it ought to form a distinct class in the vertebrate kingdom. This fish is remarkable for its negative characters; it can hardly be said to possess a brain, vertebral column, or heart, &c.; so that it was classed by the older naturalists amongst the worms. Many years ago Prof. Goodsir perceived that the lancelet presented some affinities with the Ascidians, which are invertebrate, hermaphrodite, marine creatures permanently attached to a support. They hardly appear like animals, and consist of a simple, tough, leathery sack, with two small projecting orifices. They belong to the Mulluscoida of Huxley—a lower division of the great kingdom of the Mollusca; but they

---

[22]‘Palaeontology,’ 1860, p. 199.

have recently been placed by some naturalists amongst the Vermes or worms. Their larvae somewhat resemble tadpoles in shape,[23] and have the power of swimming freely about. M. Kovalevsky[24] has lately observed that the larvae of Ascidians are related to the Vertebrata, in their manner of development, in the relative position of the nervous system, and in possessing a structure closely like the *chorda dorsalis* of vertebrate animals; and in this he has been since confirmed by Prof. Kupffer. M. Kovalevsky writes to me from Naples, that he has now carried these observations yet further, and should his results be well established, the whole will form a discovery of the very greatest value. Thus, if we may rely on embryology, ever the safest guide in classification, it seems that we have at last gained a clue to the source whence the Vertebrata were derived.[25] We should then be justified in believing that at an extremely remote period a group of animals existed, resembling in many respects the larvae of our present Ascidians, which diverged into two great branches—the one retrograding in development and producing the present class of Ascidians, the other rising to the crown and summit of the animal kingdom by giving birth to the Vertebrata.

We have thus far endeavoured rudely to trace the genealogy of the Vertebrata by the aid of their mutual affinities. We will now look to man as he exists; and we shall, I think, be able partially to restore the structure of our early progenitors, during successive periods, but not in due order of time. This can be effected by means of the rudiments which man still retains, by the characters which occasionally make their appearance in him through reversion, and by the aid of the principles of morphology and embryology. The various facts, to which I shall here allude, have been given in the previous chapters.

The early progenitors of man must have been once covered with hair, both sexes having beards; their ears were probably pointed, and capable of movement; and their bodies were provided with a tail, having the proper mus-

---

[23]At the Falkland Islands I had the satisfaction of seeing, in April 1833, and therefore some years before any other naturalist, the locomotive larvae of a compound Ascidian, closely allied to Synoicum, but apparently generically distinct from it. The tail was about five times as long as the oblong head, and terminated in a very fine filament. It was, as sketched by me under a simple microscope, plainly divided by transverse opaque partitions, which I presume represent the great cells figured by Kovalevsky. At an early stage of development the tail was closely coiled round the head of the larva.

[24]'Mémoires de l'Acad. des Sciences de St. Pétersbourg,' tom. x. No. 15, 1866.

[25]But I am bound to add that some competent judges dispute this conclusion; for instance, M. Giard, in a series of papers in the 'Archives de Zoologie Expérimentale,' for 1872. Nevertheless, this naturalist remarks, p. 281, "L'organisation de la larve ascidienne en dehors de toute hypothese et de toute théorie, nous montre comment la nature peut produire la disposition fondamentale du type vertébré (l'existence d'une corde dorsale) chez un invertébré par la seule condition vitale de l'adaptation, et cette simple possibilité du passage supprime l'abime entre les deux sous-regnes, encore bien qu'en ignore par où le passage s'est fait en réalité."

cles. Their limbs and bodies were also acted on by many muscles which now only occasionally reappear, but are normally present in the Quadrumana. At this or some earlier period, the great artery and nerve of the humerus ran through a supracondyloid foramen. The intestine gave forth a much larger diverticulum or caecum than that now existing. The foot was then prehensile, judging from the condition of the great toe in the foetus; and our progenitors, no doubt, were arboreal in their habits, and frequented some warm, forest-clad land. The males had great canine teeth, which served them as formidable weapons. At a much earlier period the uterus was double; the excreta were voided through a cloaca; and the eye was protected by a third eyelid or nictitating membrane. At a still earlier period the progenitors of man must have been aquatic in their habits; for morphology plainly tells us that our lungs consist of a modified swim-bladder, which once served as a float. The clefts on the neck in the embryo of man show where the branchiae once existed. In the lunar or weekly recurrent periods of some of our functions we apparently still retain traces of our primordial birthplace, a shore washed by the tides. At about this same early period the true kidneys were replaced by the corpora wolffiana. The heart existed as a simple pulsating vessel; and the chorda dorsalis took the place of a vertebral column. These early ancestors of man, thus seen in the dim recesses of time, must have been as simply, or even still more simply organised than the lancelet or amphioxus.

There is one other point deserving a fuller notice. It has long been known that in the vertebrate kingdom one sex bears rudiments of various accessory parts, appertaining to the reproductive system, which properly belong to the opposite sex; and it has now been ascertained that at a very early embryonic period both sexes possess true male and female glands. Hence some remote progenitor of the whole vertebrate kingdom appears to have been hermaphrodite or androgynous.[26] But here we encounter a singular difficulty. In the mammalian class the males possess rudiments of a uterus with the adjacent passage, in their vesiculae prostaticae; they bear also rudiments of mammae, and some male Marsupials have traces of a marsupial sack.[27] Other analogous facts could be added. Are we, then, to suppose that some extremely ancient mammal continued androgynous, after it had acquired the chief distinctions of its class, and therefore after it had diverged from the lower classes of the vertebrate

[26]This is the conclusion of Prof. Gegenbaur, one of the highest authorities in comparative anatomy; see 'Grundzüge der vergleich. Anat.' 1870, s. 876. The result has been arrived at chiefly from the study of the Amphibia; but it appears from the researches of Waldeyer (as quoted in 'Journal of Anat. and Phys.' 1869, p. 161), that the sexual organs of even "the higher vertebrata are, in their early condition, hermaphrodite." Similar views have long been held by some authors, though until recently without a firm basis.

[27]The male Thylacinus offers the best instance. Owen, 'Anatomy of Vertebrates,' vol. iii. p. 771.

kingdom? This seems very improbable, for we have to look to fishes, the lowest of all the classes, to find any still existent androgynous forms.[28] That various accessory parts, proper to each sex, are found in a rudimentary condition in the opposite sex, may be explained by such organs having been gradually acquired by the one sex, and then transmitted in a more or less imperfect state to the other. When we treat of sexual selection, we shall meet with innumerable instances of this form of transmission,—as in the case of the spurs, plumes, and brilliant colours, acquired for battle or ornament by male birds, and inherited by the females in an imperfect or rudimentary condition.

The possession by male mammals of functionally imperfect mammary organs is, in some respects, especially curious. The Monotremata have the proper milk-secreting glands with orifices, but no nipples; and as these animals stand at the very base of the mammalian series, it is probable that the progenitors of the class also had milk-secreting glands, but no nipples. This conclusion is supported by what is known of their manner of development; for Professor Turner informs me, on the authority of Kölliker and Langer, that in the embryo the mammary glands can be distinctly traced before the nipples are in the least visible; and the development of successive parts in the individual generally represents and accords with the development of successive beings in the same line of descent. The Marsupials differ from the Monotremata by possessing nipples; so that probably these organs were first acquired by the Marsupials, after they had diverged from, and risen above, the Monotremata, and were then transmitted to the placental mammals.[29] No one will suppose that the Marsupials still remained androgynous, after they had approximately acquired their present structure. How then are we to account for male mammals possessing mammae? It is possible that they were first developed in the females and then transferred to the males, but from what follows this is hardly probable.

It may be suggested, as another view, that long after the progenitors of the whole mammalian class had ceased to be androgynous, both sexes yielded milk, and thus nourished their young; and in the case of the Marsupials, that both sexes carried their young marsupial sacks. This will not appear altogether improbable, if we reflect that the males of existing syngnathous fishes receive

[28]Hermaphroditism has been observed in several species of Serranus, as well as in some other fishes, where it is either normal and symmetrical, or abnormal and unilateral. Dr. Zouteveen has given me references on this subject, more especially to a paper by Prof. Halbertsma, in the 'Transact. of the Dutch Acad. of Sciences,' vol. xvi. Dr. Günther doubts the fact, but it has now been recorded by too many good observers to be any longer disputed. Dr. M. Lessona writes to me, that he has verified the observations made by Cavolini on Serranus. Prof. Ercolani has recently shewn ('Accad. delle Scienze,' Bologna, Dec. 28, 1871) that eels are androgynous.

[29]Prof. Gegenbaur has shewn ('Jenaische Zeitschrift,' Bd. vii. p. 212) that two distinct types of nipples prevail throughout the several mammalian orders, but that it is quite intelligible how both could have been derived from the nipples of the Marsupials, and the latter from those of the Monotremata. See, also, a memoir by Dr. Max Huss, on the mammary glands, ibid. B. viii. p. 176.

the eggs of the females in their abdominal pouches, hatch them, and afterwards, as some believe, nourish the young;[30]—that certain other male fishes hatch the eggs within their mouths or branchial cavities;—that certain male toads take the chaplets of eggs from the females, and wind them round their own thighs, keeping them there until the tadpoles are born;—that certain male birds undertake the whole duty of incubation, and that male pigeons, as well as the females, feed their nestlings with a secretion from their crops. But the above suggestion first occurred to me from the mammary glands of male mammals being so much more perfectly developed than the rudiments of the other accessory reproductive parts, which are found in the one sex though proper to the other. The mammary glands and nipples, as they exist in male mammals, can indeed hardly be called rudimentary; they are merely not fully developed, and not functionally active. They are sympathetically affected under the influence of certain diseases, like the same organs in the female. They often secrete a few drops of milk at birth and at puberty: this latter fact occurred in the curious case, before referred to, where a young man possessed two pairs of mammae. In man and some other male mammals these organs have been known occasionally to become so well developed during maturity as to yield a fair supply of milk. Now if we suppose that during a former prolonged period male mammals aided the females in nursing their offspring,[31] and that afterwards from some cause (as from the production of a smaller number of young) the males ceased to give this aid, disuse of the organs during maturity would lead to their becoming inactive; and from two well-known principles of inheritance, this state of inactivity would probably be transmitted to the males at the corresponding age of maturity. But at an earlier age these organs would be left unaffected, so that they would be almost equally well developed in the young of both sexes.

Conclusion.—Von Baer has defined advancement or progress in the organic scale better than any one else, as resting on the amount of differentiation and specialisation of the several parts of a being,—when arrived at maturity, as I should be inclined to add. Now as organisms have become slowly adapted to diversified lines of life by means of natural selection, their parts will have become more and more differentiated and specialised for various functions from the advantage gained by the division of physiological labour. The same part appears often to have been modified first for one purpose, and then long after-

[30]Mr. Lockwood believes (as quoted in 'Quart. Journal of Science,' April, 1868, p. 269), from what he has observed of the development of Hippocampus, that the walls of the abdominal pouch of the male in some way afford nourishment. On male fishes hatching the ova in their mouths, see a very interesting paper by Prof. Wyman, in 'Proc. Boston Soc. of Nat. Hist.' Sept. 15, 1857; also Prof. Turner, in 'Journal of Anat. and Phys.' Nov. 1, 1866, p. 78. Dr. Günther has likewise described similar cases.

[31]Maddle. C. Royer has suggested a similar view in her 'Origine de l'Homme,' &c., 1870.

wards for some other and quite distinct purpose; and thus all the parts are rendered more and more complex. But each organism still retains the general type of structure of the progenitor from which it was aboriginally derived. In accordance with this view it seems, if we turn to geological evidence, that organisation on the whole has advanced throughout the world by slow and interrupted steps. In the great kingdom of the Vertebrata it has culminated in man. It must not, however, be supposed that groups of organic beings are always supplanted, and disappear as soon as they have given birth to other and more perfect groups. The latter, though victorious over their predecessors, may not have become better adapted for all places in the economy of nature. Some old forms appear to have survived from inhabiting protected sites, where they have not been exposed to very severe competition; and these often aid us in constructing our genealogies, by giving us a fair idea of former and lost populations. But we must not fall into the error of looking at the existing members of any lowly-organised group as perfect representatives of their ancient predecessors.

The most ancient progenitors in the kingdom of the Vertebrata, at which we are able to obtain an obscure glance, apparently consisted of a group of marine animals,[32] resembling the larvae of existing Ascidians. These animals probably gave rise to a group of fishes, as lowly organised as the lancelet; and from these the Ganoids, and other fishes like the Lepidosiren, must have been developed. From such fish a very small advance would carry us on to the Amphibians. We have seen that birds and reptiles were once intimately connected together; and the Monotremata now connect mammals with reptiles in a slight degree. But no one can at present say by what line of descent the three higher and related classes, namely, mammals, birds, and reptiles,

[32]The inhabitants of the seashore must be greatly affected by the tides; animals living either about the *mean* high-water mark, or about the *mean* low-water mark, pass through a complete cycle of tidal changes in a fortnight. Consequently, their food supply will undergo marked changes week by week. The vital functions of such animals, living under these conditions for many generations, can hardly fail to run their course in regular weekly periods. Now it is a mysterious fact that in the higher and now terrestrial Vertebrata, as well as in other classes, many normal and abnormal processes have one or more whole weeks as their periods; this would be rendered intelligible if the Vertebrata are descended from an animal allied to the existing tidal Ascidians. Many instances of such periodic processes might be given, as the gestation of mammals, the duration of fevers, &c. The hatching of eggs affords also a good example, for, according to Mr. Bartlett ('Land and Water,' Jan. 7, 1871), the eggs of the pigeon are hatched in two weeks; those of the fowl in three; those of the duck in four; those of the goose in five; and those of the ostrich in seven weeks. As far as we can judge, a recurrent period, if approximately of the right duration for any process or function, would not, when once gained, be liable to change; consequently it might be thus transmitted through almost any number of generations. But if the function changed, the period would have to change, and would be apt to change almost abruptly by a whole week. This conclusion, if sound, is highly remarkable; for the period of gestation in each mammal, and the hatching of each bird's eggs, and many other vital processes, thus betray to us the primordial birthplace of these animals.

were derived from the two lower vertebrate classes, namely, amphibians and fishes. In the class of mammals the steps are not difficult to conceive which led from the ancient Monotremata to the ancient Marsupials; and from these to the early progenitors of the placental mammals. We may thus ascend to the Lemuridae; and the interval is not very wide from these to the Simiadae. The Simiadae then branched off into two great stems, the New World and Old World monkeys; and from the latter, at a remote period, Man, the wonder and glory of the Universe, proceeded.

Thus we have given to man a pedigree of prodigious length, but not, it may be said, of noble quality. The world, it has often been remarked, appears as if it had long been preparing for the advent of man: and this, in one sense is strictly true, for he owes his birth to a long line of progenitors. If any single link in this chain had never existed, man would not have been exactly what he now is. Unless we wilfully close our eyes, we may, with our present knowledge, approximately recognise our parentage; nor need we feel ashamed of it. The most humble organism is something much higher than the inorganic dust under our feet; and no one with an unbiassed mind can study any living creature, however humble, without being struck with enthusiasm at its marvellous structure and properties.

ON THE DEVELOPMENT OF MAN'S INTELLECTUAL POWERS*

The greatest difficulty which presents itself, when we are driven to the above conclusion on the origin of man is the high standard of intellectual power and of moral disposition which he has attained. But every one who admits the principle of evolution, must see that the mental powers of the higher animals, which are the same in kind with those of man, though so different in degree, are capable of advancement. Thus the interval between the mental powers of one of the higher apes and of a fish, or between those of an ant and scale-insect, is immense; yet their development does not offer any special difficulty; for with our domesticated animals, the mental faculties are certainly variable, and the variations are inherited. No one doubts that they are of the utmost importance to animals in a state of nature. Therefore the conditions are favourable for their development through natural selection. The same conclusion may be extended to man; the intellect must have been all-important to him, even at a very remote period, as enabling him to invent and use language, to make

*From Charles Darwin, *The Descent of Man* (London, John Murray, 1871), Vol. 2, pp. 390-396.

weapons, tools, traps, &c., whereby with the aid of his social habits, he long ago became the most dominant of all living creatures.

A great stride in the development of the intellect will have followed, as soon as the half-art and half-instinct of language came into use; for the continued use of language will have reacted on the brain and produced an inherited effect; and this again will have reacted on the improvement of language. As Mr. Chauncey Wright[1] has well remarked, the largeness of the brain in man relatively to his body, compared with the lower animals, may be attributed in chief part to the early use of some simple form of language,—that wonderful engine which affixes signs to all sorts of objects and qualities, and excites trains of thought which would never arise from the mere impression of the senses, or if they did arise could not be followed out. The higher intellectual powers of man, such as those of ratiocination, abstraction, self-consciousness, &c., probably follow from the continued improvement and exercise of the other mental faculties.

The development of the moral qualities is a more interesting problem. The foundation lies in the social instincts, including under this term the family ties. These instincts are highly complex, and in the case of the lower animals give special tendencies towards certain definite actions; but the more important elements are love, and the distinct emotion of sympathy. Animals endowed with the social instincts take pleasure in one another's company, warn one another of danger, defend and aid one another in many ways. These instincts do not extend to all the individuals of the species, but only to those of the same community. As they are highly beneficial to the species, they have in all probability been acquired through natural selection.

A moral being is one who is capable of reflecting on his past actions and their motives—of approving of some and disapproving of others; and the fact that man is the one being who certainly deserves this designation, is the greatest of all distinctions between him and the lower animals. But in the fourth chapter I have endeavoured to shew that the moral sense follows, firstly, from the enduring and ever-present nature of the social instincts; secondly, from man's appreciation of the approbation and disapprobation of his fellows; and thirdly, from the high activity of his mental faculties, with past impressions extremely vivid; and in these latter respects he differs from the lower animals. Owing to this condition of mind, man cannot avoid looking both backwards and forwards, and comparing past impressions. Hence after some temporary desire or passion has mastered his social instincts, he reflects and compares the now weakened impression of such past impulses with the ever-present social instincts; and he then feels that sense of dissatisfaction which all unsatisfied instincts leave behind them, he therefore resolves to act differently for the future,—and this is conscience. Any instinct, permanently stronger or more

[1]'On the Limits of Natural Selection,' in the 'North American Review,' Oct. 1870, p. 295.

enduring than another, gives rise to a feeling which we express by saying that it ought to be obeyed. A pointer dog, if able to reflect on his past conduct, would say to himself, I ought (as indeed we say of him) to have pointed at that hare and not have yielded to the passing temptation of hunting it.

Social animals are impelled partly by a wish to aid the members of the their community in a general manner, but more commonly to perform certain definite actions. Man is impelled by the same general wish to aid his fellows; but has few or no special instincts. He differs also from the lower animals in the power of expressing his desires by words, which thus become a guide to the aid required and bestowed. The motive to give aid is likewise much modified in man: it no longer consists solely of a blind instinctive impulse, but is much influenced by the praise or blame of his fellows. The appreciation and the bestowal of praise and blame both rest on sympathy; and this emotion, as we have seen, is one of the most important elements of the social instincts. Sympathy, though gained as an instinct, is also much strengthened by exercise or habit. As all men desire their own happiness, praise or blame is bestowed on actions and motives, according as they lead to this end; and as happiness is an essential part of the general good, the greatest-happiness principle indirectly serves as a nearly safe standard of right and wrong. As the reasoning powers advance and experience is gained, the remoter effects of certain lines of conduct on the character of the individual, and on the general good, are perceived; and then the self-regarding virtues come within the scope of public opinion, and receive praise, and their opposites blame. But with the less civilised nations reason often errs, and many bad customs and base superstitions come within the same scope, and are then esteemed as high virtues, and their breach as heavy crimes.

The moral faculties are generally and justly esteemed as of higher value than the intellectual powers. But we should bear in mind that the activity of the mind in vividly recalling past impressions is one of the fundamental though secondary bases of conscience. This affords the strongest argument for educating and stimulating in all possible ways the intellectual faculties of every human being. No doubt a man with a torpid mind, if his social affections and sympathies are well developed, will be led to good actions, and may have a fairly sensitive conscience. But whatever renders the imagination more vivid and strengthens the habit of recalling and comparing past impressions, will make the conscience more sensitive, and may even somewhat compensate for weak social affections and sympathies.

The moral nature of man has reached its present standard, partly through the advancement of his reasoning powers and consequently of a just public opinion, but especially from his sympathies having been rendered more tender and widely diffused through the effects of habit, example, instruction, and reflection. It is not improbable that after long practice virtuous tendencies may be inherited. With the more civilised races, the conviction of the existence of an all-seeing Deity has had a potent influence on the advance of morality. Ultimately man does not accept the praise or blame of his fellows as his sole guide, though few escape this influence, but his habitual convictions, controlled by reason, afford him the safest rule. His conscience then becomes the supreme judge and monitor. Nevertheless the first foundation or origin of the moral sense lies in the social instincts, including sympathy; and these instincts no doubt were primarily gained, as in the case of the lower animals, through natural selection.

The belief in God has often been advanced as not only the greatest, but the most complete of all the distinctions between man and the lower animals. It is however impossible, as we have seen, to maintain that this belief is innate or instinctive in man. On the other hand a belief in all-pervading spiritual agencies seems to be universal; and apparently follows from a considerable advance in man's reason, and from a still greater advance in his faculties of imagination, curiosity and wonder. I am aware that the assumed instinctive belief in God has been used by many persons as an argument for His existence. But this is a rash argument, as we should thus be compelled to believe in the existence of many cruel and malignant spirits, only a little more powerful than man; for the belief in them is far more general than in a beneficent Deity. The idea of a universal and beneficent Creator does not seem to arise in the mind of man, until he has been elevated by long-continued culture.

He who believes in the advancement of man from some low organised form, will naturally ask how does this bear on the belief in the immortality of the soul. The barbarous races of man, as Sir J. Lubbock has shewn, possess no clear belief of this kind; but arguments derived from the primeval beliefs of savages are, as we have just seen, of little or no avail. Few persons feel any anxiety from the impossibility of determining at what precise period in the development of the individual, from the first trace of a minute germinal vesicle, man becomes an immortal being; and there is no greater cause for anxiety because the period cannot possibly be determined in the gradually ascending organic scale.[2]

I am aware that the conclusions arrived at in this work will be denounced by some as highly irreligious; but he who denounces them is bound to shew why it is more irreligious to explain the origin of man as a distinct species by descent from some lower form, through the laws of variation and natural selection, than to explain the birth of the individual through the laws of ordinary reproduction. The birth both of the species and of the individual are equally parts of that grand sequence of events, which our minds refuse to accept as the result of blind chance. The understanding revolts at such a conclu-

[2] The Rev. J. A. Picton gives a discussion to this effect in his 'New Theories and the Old Faith,' 1870.

sion, whether or not we are able to believe that every slight variation of structure,—the union of each pair in marriage,—the dissemination of each
seed,—and other such events, have all been ordained for some special purpose.

CHARLES DARWIN ON THE EXPRESSION OF THE EMOTIONS

DARWIN'S *The Expression of the Emotions* (1872) was originally to have been part of *The Descent of Man*, but the latter work
had grown to two large volumes, and Darwin rightly decided that it
would be better if *The Expression of the Emotions* were published as
a separate and independent work.

The Expression of the Emotions was a pioneer work and remained
so well into the twentieth century. As in almost everything else he did,
Darwin in this work was considerably ahead of his time, for it is only
in recent years that this important subject has begun to receive the attention it deserves.

The excerpt reprinted here represents the final chapter of the second
edition, posthumously published in 1890, and edited by Darwin's son,
Francis. It provides an excellent summary of Darwin's ideas as
developed in the body of the book. It is rather curious to note that
the usually careful Darwin accepts the belief that hair can turn gray
overnight from grief. The fact is that there has never been an authenticated case of this in spite of statements to the contrary, and, indeed,
no one acquainted with the physiology of hair would find it possible
to accept such a rapid change.

The universality of human emotional expressions suggested to Darwin
that this constituted yet another evidence of the fact that all the varieties
of man have descended from a single parent stock, an inference which
has been thoroughly supported by later workers.

THE EXPRESSION OF THE EMOTIONS*

I have now described, to the best of my ability, the chief expressive actions in man, and in some few of the lower animals. I have also attempted to explain the origin or development of these actions through the three principles given in the first chapter. The first of these principles is, that movements which are serviceable in gratifying some desire, or in relieving some sensation, if often repeated, become so habitual that they are performed, whether or not of any service, whenever the same desire or sensation is felt, even in a very weak degree.

Our second principle is that of antithesis. The habit of voluntarily performing opposite movements under opposite impulses has become firmly established in us by the practice of our whole lives. Hence, if certain actions have been regularly performed, in accordance with our first principle, under a certain frame of mind, there will be a strong and involuntary tendency to the performance of directly opposite actions, whether or not these are of any use, under the excitement of an opposite frame of mind.

Our third principle is the direct action of the excited nervous sytem on the body, independently of the will, and independently, in large part, of habit. Experience shows that nerve-force is generated and set free whenever the cerebro-spinal system is excited. The direction which this nerve-force follows is necessarily determined by the lines of connection between the nerve-cells, with each other and with various parts of the body. But the direction is likewise much influenced by habit; inasmuch as nerve-force passes readily along accustomed channels.

The frantic and senseless actions of an enraged man may be attributed in part to the undirected flow of nerve-force, and in part to the effects of habit, for these actions often vaguely represent the act of striking. They thus pass into gestures included under our first principle; as when an indignant man unconsciously throws himself into a fitting attitude for attacking his opponent, though without any intention of making an actual attack. We see also the influence of habit in all the emotions and sensations which are called exciting; for they have assumed this character from having habitually led to energetic action; and action affects, in an indirect manner, the respiratory and circulatory system; and the latter reacts on the brain. Whenever these emotions or sensations are even slightly felt by us, though they may not at the time lead to any exertion, our whole system is nevertheless disturbed through the force of habit and association. Other emotions and sensations are called depressing, because they have not habitually led to energetic action, excepting just at first,

*From Charles Darwin, *The Expression of the Emotions*, 2nd ed. (John Murray, London, 1890), pp. 368-387.

as in the case of extreme pain, fear, and grief, and they have ultimately caused complete exhaustion; they are consequently expressed chiefly by negative signs and by prostration. Again, there are other emotions, such as that of affection, which do not commonly lead to action of any kind, and consequently are not exhibited by any strongly marked outward signs. Affection indeed, in as far as it is a pleasurable sensation, excites the ordinary signs of pleasure.

On the other hand, many of the effects due to the excitement of the nervous system seem to be quite independent of the flow of nerve-force along the channels which have been rendered habitual by former exertions of the will. Such effects, which often reveal the state of mind of the person thus affected, cannot at present be explained; for instance, the change of colour in the hair from extreme terror or grief,—the cold sweat and the trembling of the muscles from fear,—the modified secretions of the intestinal canal,—and the failure of certain glands to act.

Notwithstanding that much remains unintelligible in our present subject, so many expressive movements and actions can be explained to a certain extent through the above three principles, that we may hope hereafter to see all explained by these or by closely analogous principles.

Actions of all kinds, if regularly accompanying any state of the mind, are at once recognised as expressive. These may consist of movements of any part of the body, as the wagging of a dog's tail, the shrugging of a man's shoulders, the erection of the hair, the exudation of perspiration, the state of the capillary circulation, laboured breathing and the use of the vocal or other sound-producing instruments. Even insects express anger, terror, jealousy, and love by their stridulation. With man the respiratory organs are of especial importance in expression, not only in a direct, but in a still higher degree in an indirect manner.

Few points are more interesting in our present subject than the extraordinarily complex chain of events which lead to certain expressive movements. Take, for instance, the oblique eyebrows of a man suffering from grief or anxiety. When infants scream loudly from hunger or pain, the circulation is affected, and the eyes tend to become gorged with blood: consequently the muscles surrounding the eyes are strongly contracted as a protection: this action, in the course of many generations, has become firmly fixed and inherited: but when, with advancing years and culture, the habit of screaming is partially repressed, the muscles round the eyes still tend to contract, whenever even slight distress is felt: of these muscles, the pyramidals of the nose are less under the control of the will than are the others, and their contraction can be checked only by that of the central fasciae of the frontal muscle: these latter fasciae draw up the inner ends of the eyebrows, and wrinkle the forehead in a peculiar manner, which we instantly recognise as the expression of grief or anxiety. Slight movements, such as these just described, or the scarcely perceptible drawing down of the corners of the mouth, are the last remnants or rudiments of strongly marked and intelligible movements. They are as full of significance to us in regard to expression, as are ordinary rudiments to the naturalist in the classification and genealogy of organic beings.

That the chief expressive actions, exhibited by man and by the lower animals, are now innate or inherited—that is, have not been learnt by the individual,—is admitted by every one. So little has learning or imitation to do with several of them that they are from the earliest days and throughout life quite beyond our control; for instance, the relaxation of the arteries of the skin in blushing, and the increased action of the heart in anger. We may see children, only two or three years old, and even those born blind, blushing from shame; and the naked scalp of a very young infant reddens from passion. Infants scream from pain directly after birth, and all their features then assume the same form as during subsequent years. These facts alone suffice to show that many of our most important expressions have not been learnt; but it is remarkable that some, which are certainly innate, require practice in the individual, before they are performed in a full and perfect manner; for instance, weeping and laughing. The inheritance of most of our expressive actions explains the fact that those born blind display them, as I hear from the Rev. R. H. Blair, equally well with those gifted with eyesight. We can thus also understand the fact that the young and the old of widely different races, both with man and animals, express the same state of mind by the same movements.

We are so familiar with the fact of young and old animals displaying their feelings in the same manner, that we hardly perceive how remarkable it is that a young puppy should wag its tail when pleased, depress its ears and uncover its canine teeth when pretending to be savage, just like an old dog; or that a kitten should arch its little back and erect its hair when frightened and angry, like an old cat. When, however, we turn to less common gestures in ourselves, which we are accustomed to look at as artificial or conventional,—such as shrugging the shoulders, as a sign of impotence, or the raising the arms with open hands and extended fingers, as a sign of wonder,—we feel perhaps too much surprise at finding that they are innate. That these and some other gestures are inherited, we may infer from their being performed by very young children, by those born blind, and by the most widely distinct races of man. We should also bear in mind that new and highly peculiar tricks, in association with certain states of the mind, are known to have arisen in certain individuals, and to have been afterwards transmitted to their offspring, in some cases, for more than one generation.

Certain other gestures which seem to us so natural that we might easily imagine that they were innate, apparently have been learnt like the words of a language. This seems to be the case with the joining of the uplifted hands, and the turning up of the eyes, in prayer. So it is with kissing as a mark of affection; but this is innate, in so far as it depends on the pleasure derived from contact with a beloved person. The evidence with respect to the inheritance of nodding and shaking the head, as signs of affirmation and negation, is doubtful; for they are not universal, yet seem too general to have been independently acquired by all the individuals of so many races.

We will now consider how far the will and consciousness have come into play in the development of the various movements of expression. As far as we can judge, only a few expressive movements, such as those just referred to, are learnt by each individual; that is, were consciously and voluntarily performed during the early years of life for some definite object, or in imitation of others, and then became habitual. The far greater number of the movements of expression, and all the more important ones, are, as we have seen, innate or inherited; and such cannot be said to depend on the will of the individual. Nevertheless, all those included under our first principle were at first voluntarily performed for a definite object,—namely, to escape some danger, to relieve some distress, or to gratify some desire. For instance, there can hardly be a doubt that the animals which fight with their teeth, have acquired the habit of drawing back their ears closely to their heads, when feeling savage, from their progenitors having voluntarily acted in this manner in order to protect their ears from being torn by their antagonists; for those animals which do not fight with their teeth do not thus express a savage state of mind. We may infer as highly probable that we ourselves have acquired the habit of contracting the muscles round the eyes, whilst crying gently, that is, without the utterance of any loud sound, from our progenitors, especially during infancy, having experienced, during the act of screaming, an uncomfortable sensation in their eyeballs. Again, some highly expressive movements result from the endeavour to check or prevent other expressive movements; thus the obliquity of the eyebrows and the drawing down of the corners of the mouth follow from the endeavour to prevent a screaming-fit from coming on, or to check it after it has come on. Here it is obvious that the consciousness and will must at first have come into play; not that we are conscious in these or in other such cases what muscles are brought into action, any more than when we perform the most ordinary voluntary movements.

With respect to the expressive movements due to the principle of antithesis, it is clear that the will has intervened, though in a remote and indirect manner. So again with the movements coming under our third principle; these, in as far as they are influenced by nerve-force readily passing along habitual channels, have been determined by former and repeated exertions of the will. The effects indirectly due to this latter agency are often combined in a complex manner, through the force of habit and association, with those directly resulting from the excitement of the cerebro-spinal system. This seems to be the case with the increased action of the heart under the influence of any strong emotion. When an animal erects its hair, assumes a threatening attitude, and utters fierce sounds, in order to terrify an enemy, we see a curious combination of movements which were originally voluntary with those that are involuntary. It is, however, possible that even strictly involuntary actions, such as the erection of the hair, may have been affected by the mysterious power of the will.

Some expressive movements may have arisen spontaneously, in association with certain states of the mind, like the tricks lately referred to, and afterwards been inherited. But I know of no evidence rendering this view probable.

The power of communication between the members of the same tribe by means of language has been of paramount importance in the development of man; and the force of language is much aided by the expressive movements of the face and body. We perceive this at once when we converse on an important subject with any person whose face is concealed. Nevertheless there are no grounds, as far as I can discover, for believing that any muscle has been developed or even modified exclusively for the sake of expression. The vocal and other sound-producing organs, by which various expressive noises are produced, seem to form a partial exception; but I have elsewhere attempted to show that these organs were first developed for sexual purposes, in order that one sex might call or charm the other. Nor can I discover grounds for believing that any inherited movement, which now serves as a means of expression, was at first voluntarily and consciously performed for this special purpose,—like some of the gestures and the finger-language used by the deaf and dumb. On the contrary, every true or inherited movement of expression seems to have had some natural and independent origin. But when once acquired, such movements may be voluntarily and consciously employed as a means of communication. Even infants, if carefully attended to, find out at a very early age that their screaming brings relief, and they soon voluntarily practise it. We may frequently see a person voluntarily raising his eyebrows to express surprise, or smiling to express pretended satisfaction and acquiescence. A man often wishes to make certain gestures conspicuous or demonstrative, and will raise his extended arms with widely opened fingers above his head, to show astonishment, or lift his shoulders to his ears, to show that he cannot or will not do something. The tendency to such movements will be strengthened or increased by their being thus voluntarily and repeatedly performed; and the effects may be inherited.

It is perhaps worth consideration whether movements at first used only by one or a few individuals to express a certain state of mind may not sometimes have spread to others, and ultimately have become universal, through the power of conscious and unconscious imitation. That there exists in man a strong tendency to imitation, independently of the conscious will, is certain. This is exhibited in the most extraordinary manner in certain brain diseases, especially at the commencement of inflammatory softening of the brain, and has been called the "echo sign." Patients thus affected imitate, without understanding, every absurd gesture which is made, and every word which is uttered near them, even in a foreign language.[1] In the case of animals, the jackal and wolf have learnt under confinement to imitate the barking of the dog. How the barking of the dog, which serves to express various emotions and desires, and which is so remarkable from having been acquired since the animal was domesticated, and from being inherited in different degrees by different breeds, was first learnt, we do not know; but may we not suspect that imitation has had something to do with its acquisition, owing to dogs having long lived in strict association with so loquacious an animal as man?

In the course of the foregoing remarks and throughout this volume, I have often felt much difficulty about the proper application of the terms, will, consciousness, and intention. Actions, which were at first voluntary, soon become habitual, and at last hereditary, and may then be performed even in opposition to the will. Although they often reveal the state of the mind, this result was not at first either intended or expected. Even such words as that "certain movements serve as a means of expression" are apt to mislead, as they imply that this was their primary purpose or object. This, however, seems rarely or never to have been the case; the movements having been at first either of some direct use, or the indirect effect of the excited state of the sensorium. An infant may scream either intentionally or instinctively to show that it wants food; but it has no wish or intention to draw its features into the peculiar form which so plainly indicates misery; yet some of the most characteristic expressions exhibited by man are derived from the act of screaming, as has been explained.

Although most of our expressive actions are innate or instinctive, as is admitted by everyone, it is a different question whether we have any instinctive power of recognising them. This has generally been assumed to be the case; but the assumption has been strongly controverted by M. Lemoine.[2] Monkeys soon learn to distinguish, not only the tones of voice of their masters, but the expression of their faces, as is asserted by a careful observer.[3] Dogs well know the difference between caressing and threatening gestures or tones; and they seem to recognise a compassionate tone. But as far as I can make out, after repeated trials, they do not understand any movement confined to the features, excepting a smile or laugh; and this they appear, at least in some cases, to recognise. This limited amount of knowledge has probably been gained, both by monkeys and dogs, through their associating harsh or kind treatment with our actions; and the knowledge certainly is not instinctive. Children, no doubt, would soon learn the movements of expression in their elders in the same manner as animals learn those of man. Moreover, when a child

[1] See the interesting facts given by Dr. Bateman on 'Aphasia,' 1870, p. 110.
[2] 'La Physionomie et la Parole,' 1865, pp. 103, 118.
[3] Rengger, 'Naturgeschichte der Säugethiere von Paraguay,' 1830 s. 55.

cries or laughs, he knows in a general manner what he is doing and what he feels; so that a very small exertion of reason would tell him what crying or laughing meant in others. But the question is, do our children acquire their knowledge of expression solely by experience through the power of association and reason?

As most of the movements of expression must have been gradually acquired, afterwards becoming instinctive, there seems to be some degree of à priori probability that their recognition would likewise have become instinctive. There is, at least, no greater difficulty in believing this than in admitting that, when a female quadruped first bears young, she knows the cry of distress of her offspring, or than in admitting that many animals instinctively recognise and fear their enemies; and of both these statements there can be no reasonable doubt. It is however extremely difficult to prove that our children instinctively recognise any expression. I attended to this point in my first-born infant, who could not have learnt anything by associating with other children, and I was convinced that he understood a smile and received pleasure from seeing one, answering it by another, at much too early an age to have learnt anything by experience. When this child was about four months old, I made in his presence many odd noises and strange grimaces, and tried to look savage; but the noises, if not too loud, as well as the grimaces, were all taken as good jokes; and I attributed this at the time to their being preceded or accompanied by smiles. When five months old, he seemed to understand a compassionate expression and tone of voice. When a few days over six months old, his nurse pretended to cry, and I saw that his face instantly assumed a melancholy expression, with the corners of the mouth strongly depressed; now this child could rarely have seen any other child crying, and never a grown-up person crying, and I should doubt whether at so early an age he could have reasoned on the subject. Therefore it seems to me that an innate feeling must have told him that the pretended crying of his nurse expressed grief; and this, through the instinct of sympathy, excited grief in him.[4]

M. Lemoine argues that, if man possessed an innate knowledge of expression, authors and artists would not have found it so difficult, as is notoriously the case, to describe and depict the characteristic signs of each particular state of mind. But this does not seem to me a valid argument. We may actually behold the expression changing in an unmistakable manner in a man or animal, and yet be quite unable, as I know from experience, to analyse the nature of the change. In the two photographs given by Duchenne of the same old

[4][Mr. Wallace ('Quarterly Journal of Science,' Jan. 1873) makes the ingenious objection that the strange expression on the nurse's face may have simply frightened the child and thus made it cry.

Compare the case of Chad Cranage, the blacksmith, in 'Adam Bede,' at whom, when he had his clean Sunday face, his little granddaughter used to cry as at a stranger.]

man . . . almost every one recognised that the one represented a true, and the other a false smile; but I have found it very difficult to decide in what the whole amount of difference consists. It has often struck me as a curious fact that so many shades of expression are instantly recognised without any conscious process of analysis on our part. No one, I believe, can clearly describe a sullen or sly expression; yet many observers are unanimous that these expressions can be recognised in the various races of man. Almost every one to whom I showed Duchenne's photograph of the young man with oblique eyebrows . . . at once declared that it expressed grief or some such feeling; yet probably not one of these persons, or one out of a thousand persons, could beforehand have told anything precise about the obliquity of the eyebrows with their inner ends puckered, or about the rectangular furrows on the forehead. So it is with many other expressions, of which I have had practical experience in the trouble requisite in instructing others what points to observe. If, then, great ignorance of details does not prevent our recognising with certainty and promptitude various expressions, I do not see how this ignorance can be advanced as an argument that our knowledge, though vague and general, is not innate.

I have endeavoured to show in considerable detail that all the chief expressions exhibited by man are the same throughout the world. This fact is interesting, as it affords a new argument in favour of the several races being descended from a single parent-stock, which must have been almost completely human in structure, and to a large extent in mind, before the period at which the races diverged from each other. No doubt similar structures, adapted for the same purpose, have often been independently acquired through variation and natural selection by distinct species; but this view will not explain close similarity between distinct species in a multitude of unimportant details. Now if we bear in mind the numerous points of structure having no relation to expression, in which all the races of man closely agree, and then add to them the numerous points, some of the highest importance and many of the most trifling value, on which the movements of expression directly or indirectly depend, it seems to me improbable in the highest degree that so much similarity, or rather identity of structure, could have been acquired by independent means. Yet this must have been the case if the races of man are descended from several aboriginally distinct species. It is far more probable that the many points of close similarity in the various races are due to inheritance from a single parent-form, which had already assumed a human character.

It is a curious, though perhaps an idle speculation, how early in the long line of our progenitors the various expressive movements, now exhibited by man, were successively acquired. The following remarks will at least serve to recall some of the chief points discussed in this volume. We may confidently believe that laughter, as a sign of pleasure or enjoyment, was practised by our progenitors long before they deserved to be called human; for very many kinds of monkeys, when pleased, utter a reiterated sound, clearly analogous to our laughter, often accompanied by vibratory movements of their jaws or lips, with the corners of the mouth drawn backwards and upwards, by the wrinkling of the cheeks, and even by the brightening of the eyes.

We may likewise infer that fear was expressed from an extremely remote period, in almost the same manner as it now is by man; namely, by trembling, the erection of the hair, cold perspiration, pallor, widely opened eyes, the relaxation of most of the muscles, and by the whole body cowering downwards or held motionless.

Suffering, if great, will from the first have caused screams or groans to be uttered, the body to be contorted, and the teeth to be ground together. But our progenitors will not have exhibited those highly expressive movements of the features which accompany screaming and crying until their circulatory and respiratory organs, and the muscles surrounding the eyes, had acquired their present structure. The shedding of tears appears to have originated through reflex action from the spasmodic contraction of the eyelids, together perhaps with the eyeballs becoming gorged with blood during the act of screaming. Therefore weeping probably came on rather late in the line of our descent; and this conclusion agrees with the fact that our nearest allies, the anthropomorphous apes, do not weep. But we must here exercise some caution, for as certain monkeys, which are not closely related to man, weep, this habit might have been developed long ago in a sub-branch of the group from which man is derived. Our early progenitors, when suffering from grief or anxiety, would not have made their eyebrows oblique, or have drawn down the corners of their mouth, until they had acquired the habit of endeavouring to restrain their screams. The expression, therefore, of grief and anxiety is eminently human.

Rage will have been expressed at a very early period by threatening or frantic gestures, by the reddening of the skin, and by glaring eyes, but not by frowning. For the habit of frowning seems to have been acquired chiefly from the corrugators being the first muscles to contract round the eyes, whenever during infancy pain, anger, or distress is felt, and there consequently is a near approach to screaming; and partly from a frown serving as a shade in difficult and intent vision. It seems probable that this shading action would not have become habitual until man had assumed a completely upright position, for monkeys do not frown when exposed to a glaring light. Our early progenitors, when enraged, would probably have exposed their teeth more freely than does man, even when giving full vent to his rage, as with the insane. We may, also, feel almost certain that they would have protruded their lips, when sulky or disappointed, in a greater degree than is the case with our own children, or even with the children of existing savage races.

Our early progenitors, when indignant or moderately angry, would not have held their heads erect, opened their chests, squared their shoulders, and clenched their fists, until they had acquired the ordinary carriage and upright attitude of man, and had learnt to fight with their fists or clubs. Until this period had arrived the antithetical gesture of shrugging the shoulders, as a sign of impotence or of patience, would not have been developed. From the same reason astonishment would not then have been expressed by raising the arms with open hands and extended fingers. Nor, judging from the actions of monkeys, would astonishment have been exhibited by a widely open mouth; but the eyes would have been opened and the eyebrows arched. Disgust would have been shown at a very early period by movements round the mouth, like those of vomiting,—that is, if the view which I have suggested respecting the source of the expression is correct, namely, that our progenitors had the power, and used it, of voluntarily and quickly rejecting any food from their stomachs which they disliked. But the more refined manner of showing contempt or disdain, by lowering the eyelids, or turning away the eyes and face, as if the despised person were not worth looking at, would not probably have been acquired until a much later period.

Of all expressions, blushing seems to be the most strictly human; yet it is common to all or nearly all the races of man, whether or not any change of colour is visible in their skin. The relaxation of the small arteries of the surface, on which blushing depends, seems to have primarily resulted from earnest attention directed to the appearance of our own persons, especially of our faces, aided by habit, inheritance, and the ready flow of nerve-force along accustomed channels; and afterwards to have been extended by the power of association to self-attention directed to moral conduct. It can hardly be doubted that many animals are capable of appreciating beautiful colours and even forms, as is shown by the pains which the individuals of one sex take in displaying their beauty before those of the opposite sex. But it does not seem possible that any animal, until its mental powers had been developed to an equal or nearly equal degree with those of man, would have closely considered and been sensitive about its own personal appearance. Therefore we may conclude that blushing originated at a very late period in the long line of our descent.

From the various facts just alluded to, and given in the course of this volume, it follows that, if the structure of our organs of respiration and circulation had differed in only a slight degree from the state in which they now exist, most of our expressions would have been wonderfully different. A very slight change in the course of the arteries and veins which run to the head, would probably have prevented the blood from accumulating in our eyeballs during violent expiration; for this occurs in extremely few quadrupeds. In this case we should not have displayed some of our most characteristic expressions. If man had breathed water by the aid of external branchiae (though the idea is hardly conceivable), instead of air through his mouth and nostrils, his features would not have expressed his feelings much more efficiently than now do his hands or limbs. Rage and disgust, however, would still have been shown by movements about the lips and mouth, and the eyes would have become brighter or duller according to the state of the circulation. If our ears had remained movable, their movements would have been highly expressive, as is the case with all the animals which fight with their teeth; and we may infer that our early progenitors thus fought, as we still uncover the canine tooth on one side when we sneer at or defy any one, and we uncover all our teeth when furiously enraged.

The movements of expression in the face and body, whatever their origin may have been, are in themselves of much importance for our welfare. They serve as the first means of communication between the mother and her infant; she smiles approval, and thus encourages her child on the right path, or frowns disapproval. We readily perceive sympathy in others by their expression; our sufferings are thus mitigated and our pleasures increased; and mutual good feeling is thus strengthened. The movements of expression give vividness and energy to our spoken words. They reveal the thoughts and intentions of others more truly than do words, which may be falsified. Whatever amount of truth the so-called science of physiognomy may contain, appears to depend, as Haller long ago remarked,[5] on different persons bringing into frequent use different facial muscles, according to their dispositions; the development of these muscles being perhaps thus increased, and the lines or furrows on the face, due to the habitual contraction, being thus rendered deeper and more conspicuous. The free expression by outward signs of an emotion intensifies it.[6] On the other hand, the repression, as far as this is possible, of all outward signs softens our emotions.[7] He who gives way to violent gestures will increase his rage; he who does not control the signs of fear will experience fear in a greater degree; and he who remains passive when overwhelmed with grief loses his best chance of recovering elasticity of mind. These results follow partly from the intimate relation which exists between almost all the emotions and their outward manifestations; and partly from the direct influence of exertion on the heart, and consequently on the brain. Even the simulation of an emotion tends to arouse it in our minds. Shakespeare, who from his wonderful knowledge of the human mind ought to be an excellent judge, says:—

> "Is it not monstrous that this player here,
> But in a fiction, in a dream of passion,
> Could force his soul so to his own conceit,

[5] Quoted by Moreau, in his edition of Lavater, 1820, tom. iv. p. 211.

[6] [In speaking of the effect of acting, Maudsley ('The Physiology of Mind,' 1876, pp. 387, 388) says that the emotion is intensified and made definite by the bodily action. Other writers have made similar remarks, e.g., Wundt, 'Essays,' 1885, p. 235. Braid found that passions can be produced by putting hypnotised people in appropriate attitudes.]

[7] Gratiolet ('De la Physionomie,' 1865, p. 66) insists on the truth of this conclusion.

That, from her working, all his visage wann'd;
Tears in his eyes, distraction in 's aspect,
A broken voice, and his whole function suiting
With forms to his conceit? And all for nothing!''

Hamlet, act. ii. sc. 2.

We have seen that the study of the theory of expression confirms to a certain limited extent the conclusion that man is derived from some lower animal form, and supports the belief of the specific or subspecific unity of the several races; but as far as my judgment serves, such confirmation was hardly needed. We have also seen that expression in itself, or the language of the emotions, as it has sometimes been called, is certainly of importance for the welfare of mankind. To understand, as far as is possible, the source or origin of the various expressions which may be hourly seen on the faces of the men around us, not to mention our domesticated animals, ought to possess much interest for us. From these several causes, we may conclude that the philosophy of our subject has well deserved the attention which it has already received from several excellent observers, and that it deserves still further attention, especially from any able physiologist.

THE GREAT DEBATE BETWEEN SCIENCE AND RELIGION AS TO MAN'S PLACE IN NATURE COMES TO A HEAD SIX MONTHS AFTER THE PUBLICATION OF DARWIN'S *ORIGIN* WHEN T. H. HUXLEY MAKES A MONKEY OUT OF A BISHOP AND SCORES A RESOUNDING VICTORY

ON Saturday, 30 June 1860, the British Association for the Advancement of Science held its annual meeting at Oxford. Huxley, who was visiting nearby, hadn't intended appearing at the meeting, knowing that Bishop Wilberforce, known to everyone as "Soapy Sam" because of his ingratiating manners, was to be there representing "the church." Wilberforce, it was generally whispered, was out to crush the Darwinists, and Huxley saw no point to attending such an occasion. But meeting a friend on the street he was persuaded not to let his own side down by absenting himself from the meeting. The friend was no less a person than Robert Chambers, the author of *The Vestiges of Creation*. The meeting place was to be the Lecture Room of the Museum, but there was such an overflow crowd that the meeting was moved to the larger west room of the Museum. Here there were gathered some 700 people or more, a large number of whom were clergymen. When Wilberforce rose to speak he was greeted with hearty applause. For this occasion he had been primed by the archenemy of Darwinsim, Richard Owen, the distinguished palaeontologist of the British Museum. In dulcet tones and well-turned periods Wilberforce spoke for more than half an hour with what one of his more sympathetic listeners described as "inimitable spirit, emptiness and unfairness." Finally, he turned to Huxley and with smiling insolence begged to know, "Was it through his grandfather or his grandmother that he claimed descent from a monkey?"

Huxley, turning to old Sir Benjamin Brodie who was seated at his side, struck his knee with his hand, and remarking, "The Lord hath delivered him into mine hands," prepared for the attack. When the great applause for the Bishop subsided, the chairman invited Huxley to speak. In a letter written 9 September 1860 to his friend Dr. Frederick Dyster, Huxley has in his own words given us an account of what he said upon that famous occasion. As one who was present wrote, "Mr. Huxley slowly and deliberately arose. A slight tall figure, stern and pale, very quiet and very grave, he stood before us and spoke those tremendous words."[1] And these were the words as recalled by Huxley some nine weeks after he had uttered them.

"Has the rumour of the Oxford row reached Tenby?—

"It was great fun—I had said that I could not see what difference it would make to my moral responsibility if I *had* an ape for a grandfather, and saponaceous Samuel thought it was a fine opportunity for chaffing a savan. However he performed the operation vulgarly & I determined to punish him—partly on that account & partly because he talked pretentious nonsense. So when I got up I spoke pretty much to the effect—that I had listened with great attention to the Lord Bishop's speech but had been unable to discover either a new fact or a new argument in it—except indeed, the question raised as to my personal predilections in the matter of ancestry—that it would not have occurred to me to bring forward such a topic as that for discussion myself, but that I was quite ready to meet the Right Rev. prelate even on that ground —If then, said I, the question is put to me would I rather have a miserable

[1] "Reminiscences of a Grandmother," *Macmillan's Magazine*, October, 1898.

ape for a grandfather or a man highly endowed by nature and possessed of great means & influence & yet who employs those faculties & that influence for the mere purpose of introducing ridicule into a grave scientific discussion—I unhesitatingly affirm my preference for the ape.

"Whereupon there was inextinguishable laughter among the people—and they listened to the rest of my argument with the greatest attention. Lubbock & Hooker spoke after me with great force & among us we shut up the bishop & his Laity.

"I happened to be in very good condition and said my say with perfect good temper & politeness—I assure you of this because all sorts of reports were spread about, e.g., that I had said I would rather be an ape than a bishop, &c.

"All the Oxford Dons were there & several hundred people in the room—so that I think Samuel will think twice before he tries a fall with men of science again.

"If he had dealt with the subject fairly and modestly I would not have treated him in this way—But the round-mouthed, oily special pleading of the man who ignorant of the subject, presumed on his position & his lawyer faculty gave me a most unmitigated contempt for him. You can't think how pleased all his confrères were. I believe I was the most popular man in Oxford for full four & twenty hours afterwards."[2]

Sir Michael Foster, the great physiologist, who was present, recalled that when Huxley rose to speak he was received coldly, with just a cheer of encouragement from his friends, the audience as a whole not joining in it, but that as he made his points the applause grew and widened, until, when he sat down, the applause was not very much less than that given to the Bishop.

As Huxley's son and biographer wrote, "The importance of the Oxford meeting lay in the open resistance that was made to authority, at a moment when even a drawn battle was hardly less effectual than acknowledged victory. Instead of being crushed under ridicule, the new theories secured a hearing, all the wider, indeed, for the startling nature of their defence."[3]

[2]By permission of the Imperial College of Science and Technology, University of London.
[3]*Life and Letters of Thomas Henry Huxley*, ed., Leonard Huxley (New York, Appleton & Co., 1901), Vol. 1, p. 204.

THOMAS HENRY HUXLEY'S *EVIDENCE AS TO MAN'S PLACE IN NATURE*, 1863.

DARWIN'S *Origin of Species* was published on the 24 November 1859. In that "Essay," as Darwin called it, the author made bare reference to man. This was a strategic omission, for Darwin anticipated trouble enough in persuading the world of the plausibility of his hypothesis, an hypothesis which postulated the modification of species by means of natural selection—a really quite revolutionary doctrine. Darwin, anxious to avoid making things any more difficult than his "Essay" was already bound to make them, kept strictly away from the subject of man. Darwin waited twelve years before he published *The Descent of Man* in 1871. In the interim the famous exchange between Huxley and Bishop Wilberforce had occurred in 1860 at the annual meeting of the British Association for the Advancement of Science, held that year at Oxford (see pp. 157-59), which resulted in a resounding victory for Darwin and evolution, an exchange the effects of which are still reverberating around the world. In addition Huxley, who had elected himself "Darwin's bulldog," was delivering lectures to working men and others with great success, and a number of these lectures were published in a series of booklets, and also in book form in 1863, the first of these being entitled *On Our Knowledge of the Causes of the Phenomena of Organic Nature* (London, Robert Hardwicke, 1863), and the second *Evidence as to Man's Place in Nature* (London, Williams & Norgate, 1863).[1] The first of these books is so rare it is hardly known. The second immediately established itself as a classic, and was later enlarged by Huxley by the addition of three new essays in the 1896 edition of his collected popular writings. The original three essays remained untouched.

Evidence as to Man's Place in Nature was the first book in which man's descent from an apelike stock was first clearly and unequivocally stated. Like Darwin's *Origin*, Huxley's little book created quite a flutter in theological and various secular orthodox dovecotes, and bats

---

[1]Both these volumes, with introductions by Ashley Montagu, have been reprinted by the University of Michigan Press.

in belfries enjoyed a regular heyday. Writing in later years, Huxley says that the Boreas of criticism blew so hard against him, he wonders how anyone who had sunk so low could ever have emerged into the relative respectability he subsequently achieved.

Huxley, in debate, had shown himself a formidable adversary, a fact which his critics were soon to discover, so that thereafter would-be critics were inclined to think again before taking him on. Huxley (1825-1895) was thirty-eight when *Man's Place in Nature* was published. When, years later, he came to write the preface to a new printing of the book, he penned the words which reflected his own feelings during its composition.

"To my observation, human nature has not sensibly changed during the last thirty years. I doubt not that there are truths as plainly obvious and as generally denied, as those contained in 'Man's Place in Nature,' now awaiting enunciation. If there is a young man of the present generation, who has taken as much trouble as I did to assure himself that they are truths, let him come out with them, without troubling his head about the barking of the dogs of St. Ernulphus. 'Veritas praevalebit' —some day; and even if she does not prevail in his time, he himself will be all the better and the wiser for having tried to help her. And let him recollect that such great reward is full payment for all his labour and pains."

To how many young men who read those ringing words must they have served as a beacon and a comfort, especially when the night was dark and impenetrable, and the orthodox sat rigid and immovable in their fortified citadels of infallibility. It took me a long time to trace St. Ernulphus and his horrible curse by serendipity to *Tristram Shandy*, at least by way of Sterne's masterpiece, while Huxley's praise of Edward Tyson led directly to the eventual writing and publication of my study of that remarkable man and his work (Ashley Montagu, *Edward Tyson, M.D., F.R.S. 1650-1708, and The Rise of Human and Comparative Anatomy in England*, Philadelphia, American Philosophical Society, 1943).

A major role played by *Man's Place in Nature* was its preparation of the way for the reception of Darwin's *Descent of Man* some eight years later. However, in the history of science, as the classic it truly is, *Evidence as to Man's Place in Nature* stands on its own merits as one of the books that played a seminal role in changing man's ideas about himself, his origin, and his evolution. As such it will always remain one of the great classics of science and humanity.

The selection reprinted here represents the middle part of Huxley's book, and shows him at his best, with a combination of expository

skill, authority, and style, which appears to have been inherited by
many subsequent Huxleys, of whom perhaps the best known are his
grandsons, Julian the biologist and Aldous the novelist.

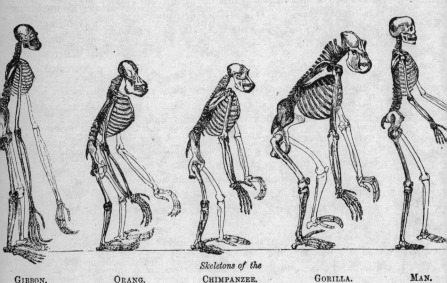

Skeletons of the

GIBBON.   ORANG.   CHIMPANZEE.   GORILLA.   MAN.

*Photographically reduced from Diagrams of the natural size (except that of the Gibbon, which was twice as large
as nature), drawn by Mr. Waterhouse Hawkins from specimens in the Museum of the Royal College of Surgeons.*

ON THE RELATIONS OF MAN TO THE LOWER ANIMALS

Multis videri poterit, majorem esse differentiam Simiae et Hominis,
quam diei et noctis; verum tamen hi, comparatione instituta inter sum-
mos Europae Heroës et Hottentottes ad Caput bonae spei degentes, dif-
ficillime sibi persuadebunt, has eosdem habere natales; vel si virginem
nobilem aulicam, maxime comtam et humanissimam, conferre vellent
cum homine sylvestri et sibi relicto, vix augurari possent, hunc et illam

*Reprinted from Thomas Henry Huxley, *Evidence as to Man's Place in Nature* (London, Williams & Norgate, 1863), pp. 76-156.

ejusdem   esse   speciei.—*Linnoei   Amoenitates   Acad.   "Anthro-*
pomorpha.†"

The question of questions for mankind—the problem which underlies all others, and is more deeply interesting than any other—is the ascertainment of the place which Man occupies in nature and of his relations to the universe of things. Whence our race has come; what are the limits of our power over nature, and of nature's power over us; to what goal we are tending; are the problems which present themselves anew and with undiminished interest to every man born into the world. Most of us, shrinking from the difficulties and dangers which beset the seeker after original answers to these riddles, are contented to ignore them altogether, or to smother the investigating spirit under the feather-bed of respected and respectable tradition. But, in every age, one or two restless spirits, blessed with that constructive genius, which can only build on a secure foundation, or cursed with the spirit of mere scepticism, are unable to follow in the well-worn and comfortable track of their forefathers and contemporaries, and unmindful of thorns and stumbling-blocks, strike out into paths of their own. The sceptics end in the infidelity which asserts the problem to be insoluble, or in the atheism which denies the existence of any orderly progress and governance of things: the men of genius propound solutions which grow into systems of Theology or of Philosophy, or veiled in musical language which suggests more than it asserts, take the shape of the Poetry of an epoch.

Each such answer to the great question, invariably asserted by the followers of its propounder, if not by himself, to be complete and final, remains in high authority and esteem, it may be for one century, or it may be for twenty: but, as invariably, Time proves each reply to have been a mere approximation to the truth—tolerable chiefly on account of the ignorance of those by whom it was accepted, and wholly intolerable when tested by the larger knowledge of their successors.

In a well-worn metaphor, a parallel is drawn between the life of man and the metamorphosis of the caterpillar into the butterfly; but the comparison may be more just as well as more novel, if for its former term we take the mental progress of the race. History shows that the human mind, fed by constant accessions of knowledge, periodically grows too large for its theoretical coverings, and bursts them asunder to appear in new habiliments, as the feeding and growing grub, at intervals, casts its too narrow skin and assumes another, itself but temporary. Truly the imago state of Man seems to be terribly distant, but every moult is a step gained, and of such there have been many.

---

†"Many may think there is a greater difference between the ape and man, than between day and night. But if such persons were to institute a comparison between the greatest heroes of Europe and the Hottentots who live at the Cape of Good Hope, they would find it difficult to believe that they could have had common ancestors: or if they were to compare a noble court lady with a wild man abandoned to himself, they would scarcely guess the two to be of the same species."

Since the revival of learning, whereby the Western races of Europe were enabled to enter upon that progress towards true knowledge, which was commenced by the philosophers of Greece, but was almost arrested in subsequent long ages of intellectual stagnation, or, at most, gyration, the human larva has been feeding vigorously, and moulting in proportion. A skin of some dimension was cast in the 16th century, and another towards the end of the 18th, while, within the last fifty years, the extraordinary growth of every department of physical science has spread among us mental food of so nutritious and stimulating a character that a new ecdysis seems imminent. But this is a process not unusually accompanied by many throes and some sickness and debility, or, it may be, by graver disturbances; so that every good citizen must feel bound to facilitate the process, and even if he have nothing but a scalpel to work withal, to ease the cracking integument to the best of his ability.

In this duty lies my excuse for the publication of these essays. For it will be admitted that some knowledge of man's position in the animate world is an indispensable preliminary to the proper understanding of his relations to the universe; and this again resolves itself, in the long run, into an inquiry into the nature and the closeness of the ties which connect him with those singular creatures whose history[1] has been sketched in the preceding pages.

The importance of such an inquiry is indeed intuitively manifest. Brought face to face with these blurred copies of himself, the least thoughtful of men is conscious of a certain shock, due perhaps, not so much to disgust at the aspect of what looks like an insulting caricature, as to the awakening of a sudden and profound mistrust of time-honoured theories and strongly-rooted prejudices regarding his own position in nature, and his relations to the underworld of life; while that which remains a dim suspicion for the unthinking, becomes a vast argument, fraught with the deepest consequences, for all who are acquainted with the recent progress of the anatomical and physiological sciences.

I now propose briefly to unfold that argument, and to set forth, in a form intelligible to those who possess no special acquaintance with anatomical science, the chief facts upon which all conclusions respecting the nature and the extent of the bonds which connect man with the brute world must be based: I shall then indicate the one immediate conclusion which, in my judgment, is justified by those facts, and I shall finally discuss the bearing of that conclusion upon the hypotheses which have been entertained respecting the Origin of Man.

The facts to which I would first direct the reader's attention, though ignored

---

[1]It will be understood that, in the preceeding Essay, I have selected for notice from the vast mass of papers which have been written upon the man-like Apes, only those which seem to me to be of special moment.

by many of the professed instructors of the public mind, are easy of demonstration and are universally agreed to by men of science; while their significance is so great, that whoso has duly pondered over them will, I think, find little to startle him in the other revelations of Biology. I refer to those facts which have been made known by the study of Development.

It is a truth of very wide, if not of universal, application, that every living creature commences its existence under a form different from and simpler than, that which it eventually attains.

The oak is a more complex thing than the little rudimentary plant contained in the acorn; the caterpillar is more complex than the egg; the butterfly than the caterpillar; and each of these beings, in passing from its rudimentary to its perfect condition, runs through a series of changes, the sum of which is called its Development. In the higher animals these changes are extremely complicated; but, within the last half century, the labours of such men as Von Baer, Rathke, Reichert, Bischoff, and Remak, have almost completely unravelled them, so that the successive stages of development which are exhibited by a Dog, for example, are now as well known to the embryologist as are the steps of the metamorphosis of the silk-worm moth to the school-boy. It will be useful to consider with attention the nature and the order of the stages of canine development, as an example of the process in the higher animals generally.

The dog, like all animals, save the very lowest (and further inquiries may not improbably remove the apparent exception), commences its existence as an egg: as a body which is, in every sense, as much an egg as that of a hen, but is devoid of that accumulation of nutritive matter which confers upon the bird's egg its exceptional size and domestic utility; and wants the shell, which would not only be useless to an animal incubated within the body of its parent, but would cut it off from access to the source of that nutriment which the young creature requires, but which the minute egg of the mammal does not contain within itself.

The Dog's egg is, in fact, a little spheroidal bag (Fig. 13), formed of a delicate transparent membrane called the vitelline membrane, and about 1/130th to 1/120th of an inch in diameter. It contains a mass of viscid nutritive matter—the *yelk*—within which is enclosed a second much more delicate spheroidal bag, called the *germinal vesicle (a)*. In this, lastly, lies a more solid rounded body, termed the *germinal spot (b)*.

The egg, or *Ovum* is originally formed within a gland, from which, in due season, it becomes detached, and passes into the living chamber fitted for its protection and maintenance during the protracted process of gestation. Here, when subjected to the required conditions, this minute and apparently insignificant particle of living matter becomes animated by a new and mysterious activity. The germinal vesicle and spot cease to be discernible (their precise fate being one of the yet unsolved problems of embryology), but the yelk becomes

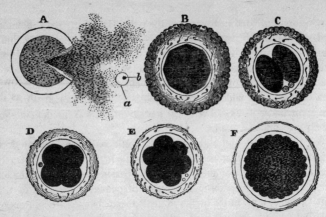

Fig. 13.—A. Egg of the Dog, with the vitelline membrane burst, so as to give exit to the yelk, the germinal vesicle (*a*), and its included spot (*b*). B. C. D. E. F. Successive changes of the yelk indicated in the text. After Bischoff.

circumferentially indented, as if an invisible knife had been drawn round it, and thus appears divided into two hemispheres (Fig. 13, C).

By the repetition of this process in various planes, these hemispheres become subdivided, so that four segments are produced (D); and these, in like manner, divide and subdivide again, until the whole yelk is converted into a mass of granules, each of which consists of a minute spheroid of yelk-substance, inclosing a central particle, the so-called *nucleus* (F). Nature, by this process, has attained much the same result as that which a human artificer arrives at by his operations in a brick-field. She takes the rough plastic material of the yelk and breaks it up into well-shaped tolerably even-sized masses—handy for building up into any part of the living edifice.

Next, the mass of organic bricks, or *cells* as they are technically called, thus formed, acquires an orderly arrangement, becoming converted into a hollow spheroid with double walls. Then, upon one side of this spheroid, appears a thickening, and, by and bye, in the centre of the area of thickening, a straight shallow groove (Fig. 14, A) marks the central line of the edifice which is to be raised, or, in other words, indicates the position of the middle line of the body of the future dog. The substance bounding the groove on each side next rises up into a fold, the rudiment of the side wall of that long cavity, which will eventually lodge the spinal marrow and the brain; and in the floor of this chamber appears a solid cellular cord, the so-called *notochord*. One end of the enclosed cavity dilates to form the head (Fig. 14, B), the other remains narrow, and eventually becomes the tail; the side walls of the body are fashioned out of the downward continuation of the walls of the groove; and from them, by and bye, grow out little buds which, by degrees, assume the shape of limbs. Watching the fashioning process stage by stage, one is forcibly reminded of the modeller in clay. Every part, every organ, is at first, as it were pinched up rudely, and sketched out in the rough; then shaped more accurately; and only, at last, receives the touches which stamp its final character.

Thus, at length, the young puppy assumes such a form as is shown in Fig. 14, C. In this condition it has a disproportionately large head, as dissimilar to that of a dog as the bud-like limbs are unlike his legs.

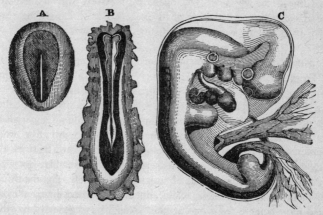

Fig. 14.—A. Earliest rudiment of the Dog. B. Rudiment further advanced, showing the foundations of the head, tail and vertebral column. D. The very young puppy, with attached ends of the yelk-sac and allantois, and invested in the amnion.

The remains of the yelk, which have not yet been applied to the nutrition and growth of the young animal, are contained in a sac attached to the rudimentary intestine, and termed the yelk sac, or *umbilical vesicle*. Two membranous bags, intended to subserve respectively the protection and nutrition of the young creature, have been developed from the skin and from the under and hinder surface of the body; the former, the so-called *amnion,* is a sac filled with fluid, which invests the whole body of the embryo, and plays the part of a sort of water-bed for it; the other, termed the *allantois,* grows out, loaded with blood-vessels, from the ventral region, and eventually applying itself to the walls of the cavity, in which the developing organism is contained, enables these vessels to become the channel by which the stream of nutriment, required to supply the wants of the offspring, is furnished to it by the parent.

The structure which is developed by the interlacement of the vessels of the offspring with those of the parent, and by means of which the former is enabled to receive nourishment and to get rid of effete matters, is termed the *Placenta*.

It would be tedious, and it is unnecessary for my present purpose, to trace the process of development further; suffice it to say, that, by a long and gradual series of changes, the rudiment here depicted and described, becomes a puppy, is born, and then, by still slower and less perceptible steps, passes into the adult Dog.

There is not much apparent resemblance between a barn-door Fowl and the Dog who protects the farm-yard. Nevertheless the student of development finds, not only that the chick commences its existence as an egg, primarily identical, in all essential respects, with that of the Dog, but that the yelk of this egg undergoes division—that the primitive groove arises, and that the contiguous parts of the germ are fashioned, by precisely similar methods, into a young chick, which at one stage of its existence, is so like the nascent Dog, that ordinary inspection would hardly distinguish the two.

The history of the development of any other vertebrate animal, Lizard, Snake, Frog, or Fish, tells the same story. There is always, to begin with, an egg having the same essential structure as that of the Dog:—the yelk of that egg always undergoes division, or *segmentation* as it is often called: the ultimate products of that segmentation constitute the building materials for the body of the young animal; and this is built up round a primitive groove, in the floor of which a notochord is developed. Furthermore, there is a period in which the young of all these animals resemble one another, not merely in outward form, but in all essentials of structure, so closely, that the differences between them are inconsiderable, while, in their subsequent course they diverge more and more widely from one another. And it is a general law, that, the more closely any animals resemble one another in adult structure, the longer and the more intimately do their embryos resemble one another: so that, for example, the embryos of a Snake and of a Lizard remain like one another longer than do those of a Snake and of a Bird; and the embryo of a Dog and of a Cat remain like one another for a far longer period than do those of a Dog and a Bird; or of a Dog and an Opossum; or even than those of a Dog and a Monkey.

Thus the study of development affords a clear test of closeness of structural affinity, and one turns with impatience to inquire what results are yielded by the study of the development of Man. Is he something apart? Does he originate in a totally different way from Dog, Bird, Frog, and Fish, thus justifying those who assert him to have no place in nature and no real affinity with the lower world of animal life? Or does he originate in a similar germ, pass through the same slow and gradually progressive modifications, depend on the same contrivances for protection and nutrition, and finally enter the world by the help of the same mechanism? The reply is not doubtful for a moment, and has not been doubtful any time these thirty years. Without question, the mode of origin and the early stages of the development of man are identical with those of the animals immediately below him in the scale:—without a doubt, in these respects, he is far nearer the Apes, than the Apes are to the Dog.

The Human ovum is about 1/125th of an inch in diameter, and might be

described in the same terms as that of the Dog, so that I need only refer to
the figure illustrative (15 A) of its structure. It leaves the organ in which it
is formed in a similar fashion and enters the organic chamber prepared for
its reception in the same way, the conditions of its development being in all
respects the same. It has not yet been possible (and only by some rare chance
can it ever be possible) to study the human ovum in so early a developmental
stage as that of yelk devision, but there is every reason to conclude that the
changes it undergoes are identical with those exhibited by the ova of other
vertebrated animals; for the formative materials of which the rudimentary
human body is composed, in the earliest conditions in which it has been
observed, are the same as those of other animals. Some of these earliest stages
are figured below and, as will be seen, they are strictly comparable to the
very early states of the Dog; the marvellous correspondence between the two
which is kept up, even for some time, as development advances, becoming
apparent by the simple comparison of the figures with those on page 167.

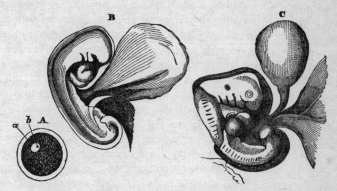

Fig. 15.—A. Human ovum (after Kölliker). *a.* germinal vesicle. *b.* germinal spot. B. A very
early condition of Man, with yelk-sac, allantois and amnion (original). C. A more advanced stage
(after Kölliker), compare Fig. 14, C.

Indeed, it is very long before the body of the young human being can be
readily discriminated from that of the young puppy; but, at a tolerably early
period, the two become distinguishable by the different form of their adjuncts,
the yelk-sac and the allantois. The former, in the Dog, becomes long and
spindle-shaped, while in Man it remains spherical: the latter, in the Dog, attains
an extremely large size, and the vascular processes which are developed from
it and eventually give rise to the formation of the placenta (taking root, as
it were, in the parental organism, so as to draw nourishment therefrom, as
the root of a tree extracts it from the soil) are arranged in an encircling zone,
while in Man, the allantois remains comparatively small, and its vascular root-
lets are eventually restricted to one disk-like spot. Hence, while the placenta

of the Dog is like a girdle, that of Man has the cake-like form, indicated by the name of the organ.

But, exactly in those respects in which the developing Man differs from the Dog, he resembles the ape, which, like man, has a spheroidal yelk-sac and a discoidal, sometimes partially lobed, placenta. So that it is only quite in the later stages of development that the young human being presents marked differences from the young ape, while the latter departs as much from the dog in its development, as the man does.

Startling as the last assertion may appear to be, it is demonstrably true, and it alone appears to me sufficient to place beyond all doubt the structural unity of man with the rest of the animal world, and more particularly and closely with the apes.

Thus, identical in the physical processes by which he originates—identical in the early stages of his formation—identical in the mode of his nutrition before and after birth, with the animals which lie immediately below him in the scale—Man, if his adult and perfect structure be compared with theirs, exhibits, as might be expected, a marvellous likeness of organization. He resembles them as they resemble one another—he differs from them as they differ from one another.—And, though these differences and resemblances cannot be weighed and measured, their value may be readily estimated; the scale or standard of judgment, touching that value being afforded and expressed by the system of classification of animals now current among zoologists.

A careful study of the resemblances and differences presented by animals has, in fact, led naturalists to arrange them into groups, or assemblages, all the members of each group presenting a certain amount of definable resemblance, and the number of points of similarity being smaller as the group is larger and *vice versâ*. Thus, all creatures which agree only in presenting the few distinctive marks of animality form the *Kingdom* ANIMALIA. The numerous animals which agree only on possessing the special characters of Vertebrates form one *Sub-kingdom* of this Kingdom. Then the Sub-kingdom VERTEBRATA is subdivided into the five *Classes,* Fishes, Amphibians, Reptiles, Birds, and Mammals, and these into smaller groups called *Orders*; these into *Families* and *Genera*; while the last are finally broken up into the smallest assemblages, which are distinguished by the possession of constant, non-sexual, characters. These ultimate groups are Species.

Every year tends to bring about a greater uniformity of opinion throughout the zoological world as to the limits and characters of these groups, great and small. At present, for example, no one has the least doubt regarding the characters of the classes Mammalia, Aves, or Reptilia; nor does the question arise whether any thoroughly well-known animal should be placed in one class or the other. Again, there is a very general agreement respecting the characters and limits of the orders of Mammals, and as to the animals which are structurally necessitated to take a place in one or another order.

No one doubts, for example, that the Sloth and the Ant-eater, the Kangaroo and the Opossum, the Tiger and the Badger, the Tapir and the Rhinoceros, are respectively members of the same orders. These successive pairs of animals may, and some do, differ from one another immensely, in such matters as the proportions and structure of their limbs; the number of their dorsal and lumbar vertebrae; the adaptation of their frames to climbing, leaping, or running; the number and form of their teeth; and the characters of their skulls and of the contained brain. But, with all these differences, they are so closely connected in all the more important and fundamental characters of their organization, and so distinctly separated by these same characters from other animals, that zoologists find it necessary to group them together as members of one order. And if any new animal were discovered, and were found to present no greater difference from the Kangaroo or from the Opossum, for example, than these animals do from one another, the zoologist would not only be logically compelled to rank it in the same order with these, but he would not think of doing otherwise.

Bearing this obvious course of zoological reasoning in mind, let us endeavour for a moment to disconnect our thinking selves from the mask of humanity; let us imagine ourselves scientific Saturnians, if you will, fairly acquainted with such animals as now inhabit the Earth, and employed in discussing the relations they bear to a new and singular "erect and featherless biped," which some enterprising traveller, overcoming the difficulties of space and gravitation, has brought from that distant planet for our inspection, well preserved, may be, in a cask of rum. We should all, at once, agree upon placing him among the mammalian vertebrates; and his lower jaw, his molars, and his brain, would leave no room for doubting the systematic position of the new genus among those mammals, whose young are nourished during gestation by means of a placenta, or what are called the "placental mammals."

Further, the most superficial study would at once convince us that, among the orders of placental mammals, neither the Whales, nor the hoofed creatures, nor the Sloths and Ant-eaters, nor the carnivorous Cats, Dogs, and Bears, still less the Rodent Rats and Rabbits, or the Insectivorous Moles and Hedgehogs, or the Bats, could claim our *Homo,* as one of themselves.

There would remain then, but one order for comparison, that of the Apes (using that word in its broadest sense), and the question for discussion would narrow itself to this—is Man so different from any of these Apes that he must form an order by himself? Or does he differ less from them than they differ from one another, and hence must take his place in the same order with them?

Being happily free from all real, or imaginary, personal interest in the results of the inquiry thus set afoot, we should proceed to weigh the arguments on one side and on the other, with as much judicial calmness as if the question related to a new Opossum. We should endeavour to ascertain, without seeking either to magnify or diminish them, all the characters by which our new Mammal differed from the Apes; and if we found that these were of less structural value than those which distinguish certain members of the Ape order from others universally admitted to be of the same order, we should undoubtedly place the newly discovered tellurian genus with them.

I now proceed to detail the facts which seem to me to leave us no choice but to adopt the last-mentioned course.

It is quite certain that the Ape which most nearly approaches man, in the totality of its organisation, is either the Chimpanzee or the Gorilla; and as it makes no practical difference, for the purposes of my present argument, which is selected for comparison, on the one hand, with Man, and on the other hand, with the rest of the Primates,[1] I shall select the latter (so far as its organisation is known)—as a brute now so celebrated in prose and verse, that all must have heard of him, and have formed some conception of his appearance. I shall take up as many of the most important points of difference between man and this remarkable creature, as the space at my disposal will allow me to discuss, and the necessities of the argument demand; and I shall inquire into the value and magnitude of these differences, when placed side by side with those which separate the Gorilla from other animals of the same order.

In the general proportions of the body and limbs there is a remarkable difference between the Gorilla and Man, which at once strikes the eye. The Gorilla's brain-case is smaller, its trunk larger, its lower limbs shorter, its upper limbs longer in proportion than those of Man.

I find that the vertebral column of a full-grown Gorilla, in the Museum of the Royal College of Surgeons, measures 27 inches along its anterior curvature, from the upper edge of the atlas, or first vertebra of the neck, to the lower extremity of the sacrum; that the arm, without the hand, is 31-1/2 inches long; that the leg, without the foot, is 26-1/2 inches long; that the hand is 9-3/4 inches long; the foot 11-1/4 inches long.

In other words, taking the length of the spinal column as 100, the arm equals 115, the leg 96, the hand 36, and the foot 41.

In the skeleton of a male Bosjesman, in the same collection, the proportions, by the same measurement, to the spinal column, taken as 100, are—the arm 78, the leg 110, the hand 26, and the foot 32. In a woman of the same race the arm is 83, and the leg 120, the hand and foot remaining the same. In a European skeleton I find the arm to be 80, the leg 117, the hand 26, the foot 35.

[1]We are not at present thoroughly acquainted with the brain of the Gorilla, and therefore, in discussing cerebral characters, I shall take that of the Chimpanzee as my highest term among the Apes.

Thus the leg is not so different as it looks at first sight, in its proportion to the spine in the Gorilla and in the Man—being very slightly shorter than the spine in the former, and between 1/10 and 1/5 longer than the spine in the latter. The foot is longer and the hand much longer in the Gorilla; but the great difference is caused by the arms, which are very much longer than the spine in the Gorilla, very much shorter than the spine in the Man.

The question now arises how are the other Apes related to the Gorilla in these respects—taking the length of the spine, measured in the same way, at 100. In an adult Chimpanzee, the arm is only 96, the leg 90, the hand 43, the foot 39—so that the hand and the leg depart more from the human proportion and the arm less, while the foot is about the same as in the Gorilla.

In the Orang, the arms are very much longer than in the Gorilla (122), while the legs are shorter (88); the foot is longer than the hand (52 and 48), and both are much longer in proportion to the spine.

In the other man-like Apes again, the Gibbons, these proportions are still further altered; the length of the arms being to that of the spinal column as 19 to 11; while the legs are also a third longer than the spinal column, so as to be longer than in Man, instead of shorter. The hand is half as long as the spinal column, and the foot, shorter than the hand, is about 5/11ths of the length of the spinal column.

Thus *Hylobates* is as much longer in the arms than the Gorilla, as the Gorilla is longer in the arms than Man; while, on the other hand, it is as much longer in the legs than the Man, as the Man is longer in the legs than the Gorilla, so that it contains within itself the extremest deviations from the average length of both pairs of limbs.[1]

The Mandrill presents a middle condition, the arms and legs being nearly equal in length, and both being shorter than the spinal column; while hand and foot have nearly the same proportions to one another and to the spine, as in Man.

In the Spider monkey (*Ateles*) the leg is longer than the spine, and the arm than the leg; and, finally, in that remarkable Lemurine form, the Indri (*Lichanotus*), the leg is about as long as the spinal column, while the arm is not more than 11/18 of its length; the hand having rather less and the foot rather more, than one third the length of the spinal column.

These examples might be greatly multiplied, but they suffice to show that, in whatever proportion of its limbs the Gorilla differs from Man, the other Apes depart still more widely from the Gorilla and that, consequently, such differences of proportion can have no ordinal value.

We may next consider the differences presented by the trunk, consisting of the vertebral column, or backbone, and the ribs and pelvis, or bony hip-

[1]See the figures of the skeletons of four anthropoid apes and man, drawn to scale, p. 162.

basin, which are connected with it, in Man and in the Gorilla respectively.

In Man, in consequence partly of the disposition of the articular surfaces of the vertebrae, and largely of the elastic tension of some of the fibrous bands, or ligaments, which connect these vertebrae together, the spinal column, as a whole, has an elegant S-like curvature, being convex forwards in the neck, concave in the back, convex in the loins, or lumbar region, and concave again in the sacral region; an arrangement which gives much elasticity to the whole backbone, and diminishes the jar communicated to the spine, and through it to the head, by locomotion in the erect position.

Furthermore, under ordinary circumstances, Man has seven vertebrae in his neck, which are called *cervical;* twelve succeed these, bearing ribs and forming the upper part of the back, whence they are termed *dorsal;* five lie in the loins, bearing no distinct, or free, ribs, and are called *lumbar;* five, united together into a great bone, excavated in front, solidly wedged in between the hip bones, to form the back of the pelvis, and known by the name of the *sacrum,* succeed these; and finally, three or four little more or less movable bones, so small as to be insignificant, constitute the *coccyx* or rudimentary tail.

In the Gorilla, the vertebral column is similarly divided into cervical, dorsal, lumbar, sacral, and coccygeal vertebrae, and the total number of cervical and dorsal vertebrae, taken together, is the same as in Man; but the development of a pair of ribs to the first lumbar vertebra, which is an exceptional occurrence in Man, is the rule in the Gorilla; and hence, as lumbar are distinguished from dorsal vertebrae only by the presence or absence of free ribs, the seventeen "dorso-lumbar" vertebrae of the Gorilla are divided into thirteen dorsal and four lumbar, while in Man they are twelve dorsal and five lumbar.

Not only, however, does Man occasionally possess thirteen pair of ribs,[1] but the Gorilla sometimes has fourteen pairs, while an Orang-Utan skeleton in the Museum of the Royal College of Surgeons has twelve dorsal and five lumbar vertebrae, as in Man. Cuvier notes the same number in a *Hylobates*. On the other hand, among the lower Apes, many possess twelve dorsal and six or seven lumbar vertebrae; the Douroucouli has fourteen dorsal and eight lumbar, and a Lemur (*Stenops tardigradus*) has fifteen dorsal and nine lumbar vertebrae.

The vertebral column of the Gorilla, as a whole, differs from that of Man in the less marked character of its curves, especially in the slighter convexity of the lumbar region. Nevertheless, the curves are present, and are quite obvi-

---

[1]"More than once," says Peter Camper, "have I met with more than six lumbar vertebrae in man. . . . Once I found thirteen ribs and four lumbar vertebrae." Fallopius noted thirteen pair of ribs and only four lumbar vertebrae; and Eustachius once found eleven dorsal vertebrae and six lumbar vertebrae.—*Oeuvres de Pierre Camper*, T. 1, p. 42. As Tyson states, his "Pygmie" had thirteen pair of ribs and five lumbar vertebrae. The question of the curves of the spinal column in the Apes requires further investigation.

ous in young skeletons of the Gorilla and Chimpanzee which have been prepared without removal of the ligaments. In young Orangs similarly preserved on the other hand, the spinal column is either straight, or even concave forwards, throughout the lumbar region.

Whether we take these characters then, or such minor ones as those which are derivable from the proportional length of the spines of the cervical vertebrae, and the like, there is no doubt whatsoever as to the marked difference between Man and the Gorilla; but there is as little, that equally marked differences, of the very same order, obtain between the Gorilla and the lower Apes.

The Pelvis, or bony girdle of the hips, of Man is a strikingly human part of his organisation; the expanded haunch bones affording support for his viscera during his habitually erect posture, and giving space for the attachment of the great muscles which enable him to assume and to preserve that attitude. In these respects the pelvis of the Gorilla differs very considerably from his (Fig. 16). But go no lower than the Gibbon, and see how vastly more he differs from the Gorilla than the latter does from Man, even in this structure. Look at the flat narrow haunch bones—the long and narrow passage—the coarse, outwardly curved, ischiatic prominences on which the Gibbon habitually rests, and which are coated by the so-called "callosities," dense patches of skin, wholly absent in the Gorilla, in the Chimpanzee, and in the Orang, as in Man!

In the lower Monkeys and in the Lemurs the difference becomes more striking still, the pelvis acquiring an altogether quadrupedal character.

But now let us turn to a nobler and more characteristic organ—that by which the human frame seems to be, and indeed is, so strongly distinguished from all others,—I mean the skull. The differences between a Gorilla's skull and a Man's are truly immense (Fig. 17). In the former, the face, formed largely by the massive jaw-bones, predominates over the brain-case, or cranium proper: in the latter, the proportions of the two are reversed. In the Man, the occipital foramen, through which passes the great nervous cord connecting the brain with the nerves of the body, is placed just behind the centre of the base of the skull, which thus becomes evenly balanced in the erect posture; in the Gorilla, it lies in the posterior third of that base. In the Man, the surface or the skull is comparatively smooth, and the supraciliary ridges or brow prominences usually project but little—while, in the Gorilla, vast crests are developed upon the skull, and the brow ridges overhang the cavernous orbits, like great penthouses.

Sections of the skulls, however, show that some of the apparent defects of the Gorilla's cranium arise, in fact, not so much from deficiency of brain-case as from excessive development of the parts of the face. The cranial cavity is not ill-shaped, and the forehead is not truly flattened or very retreating, its really well-formed curve being simply disguised by the mass of bone which is built up against it (Fig. 17).

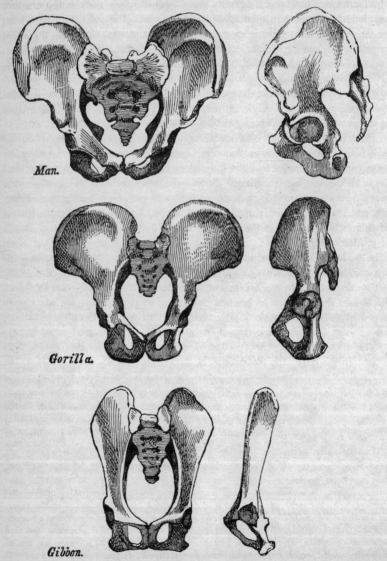

Man.

Gorilla.

Gibbon.

Fig. 16.—Front and side views of the bony pelvis of Man, the Gorilla and Gibbon: reduced from drawings made from nature, of the same absolute length, by Mr. Waterhouse Hawkins.

But the roofs of the orbits rise more obliquely into the cranial cavity, thus diminishing the space for the lower part of the anterior lobes of the brain, and the absolute capacity of the cranium is far less than that of Man. So far as I am aware, no human cranium belonging to an adult man has yet been observed with a less cubical capacity than 62 cubic inches, the smallest cranium observed in any race of men by Morton, measuring 63 cubic inches; while, on the other hand, the most capacious Gorilla skull yet measured has a content of not more than 34-1/2 cubic inches. Let us assume, for simplicity's sake, that the lowest Man's skull has twice the capacity of that of the highest Gorilla.[1]

No doubt, this is a very striking difference, but it loses much of its apparent systematic value, when viewed by the light of certain other equally indubitable facts respecting cranial capacities.

The first of these is, that the difference in the volume of the cranial cavity of different races of mankind is far greater, absolutely, than that between the lowest Man and the highest Ape, while, relatively, it is about the same. For the largest human skull measured by Morton contained 114 cubic inches, that is to say, had very nearly double the capacity of the smallest; while its absolute preponderance, of 52 cubic inches—is far greater than that by which the lowest adult male human cranium surpasses the largest of the Gorillas (62 — 34-1/2 = 27-1/2). Secondly, the adult crania of Gorillas which have as yet been measured differ among themselves by nearly one-third, the maximum capacity being 34.5 cubic inches, the minimum 24 cubic inches; and, thirdly, after making all due allowance for difference of size, the cranial capacities of some of the lower Apes fall nearly as much, relatively, below those of the higher Apes as the latter fall below Man.

---

[1] It has been affirmed that Hindoo crania sometimes contain as little as 27 ounces of water, which would give a capacity of about 46 cubic inches. The minimum capacity which I have assumed above, however, is based upon the valuable tables published by Professor R. Wagner in his *Vorstudien zu einer wissenschaftlichen Morphologie und Physiologie des menschlichen Gehrins*. As the result of the careful weighing of more than 900 human brains, Professor Wagner states that one-half weighed between 1200 and 1400 grammes, and that about two-ninths, consisting for the most part of male brains, exceed 1400 grammes. The lightest brain of an adult male, with sound mental faculties, recorded by Wagner, weighed 1020 grammes. As a gramme equals 15.4 grains, and a cubic inch of water contains 252.4 grains, this is equivalent to 62 cubic inches of water; so that as brain is heavier than water, we are perfectly safe against erring on the side of diminution in taking this as the smallest capacity of any adult male human brain. The only adult male brain, weighing as little as 970 grammes, is that of an idiot; but the brain of an adult woman, against the soundness of whose faculties nothing appears, weighed as little as 907 grammes (55.3 cubic inches of water); and Reid gives an adult female brain of still smaller capacity. The heaviest brain (1872 grammes, or about 115 cubic inches) was, however, that of a woman; next to it comes the brain of Cuvier (1861 grammes), then Byron (1807 grammes), and then an insane person (1783 grammes). The lightest adult brain recorded (720 grammes) was that of an idiotic female. The brains of five children, four years old, weighed between 1275 and 992 grammes. So that it may be safely said, that an average European child of four years old has a brain twice as large as that of an adult Gorilla.

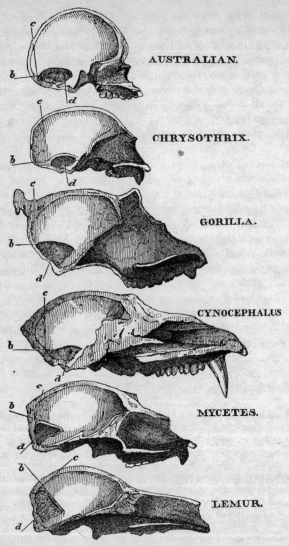

AUSTRALIAN.

CHRYSOTHRIX.

GORILLA.

CYNOCEPHALUS

MYCETES.

LEMUR.

Fig. 17.—Sections of the skulls of Man and various Apes, drawn so as to give the cerebral cavity the same length in each case, thereby displaying the varying proportions of the facial bones. The line *b* indicates the plane of the tentorium, which separates the cerebrum from the cerebellum; *d*, the axis of the occipital outlet of the skull. The extent of cerebral cavity behind *c*, which is a perpendicular erected on *b* at the point where the tentorium is attached posteriorly, indicates the degree to which the cerebrum overlaps the cerebellum—the space occupied by which is roughly indicated by the dark shading. In comparing these diagrams, it must be recollected, that figures on so small a scale as these simply exemplify the statements in the text, the proof of which is to be found in the objects themselves.

Thus, even in the important matter of cranial capacity, Men differ more widely from one another than they do from the Apes; while the lowest Apes differ as much, in proportion, from the highest, as the latter does from Man. The last proposition is still better illustrated by the study of the modifications which other parts of the cranium undergo in the Simian series.

It is the large proportional size of the facial bones and the great projection of the jaws which confers upon the Gorilla's skull its small facial angle and brutal character.

But if we consider the proportional size of the facial bones to the skull proper only, the little *Chrysothrix* (Fig. 17) differs very widely from the Gorilla, and, in the same way, as Man does; while the Baboons (*Cynocephalus,* Fig. 17) exaggerate the gross proportions of the muzzle of the great Anthropoid, so that its visage looks mild and human by comparison with theirs. The difference between the Gorilla and the Baboon is even greater than it appears at first sight; for the great facial mass of the former is largely due to a downward development of the jaws; an essentially human character, superadded upon that almost purely forward, essentially brutal, development of the same parts which characterises the Baboon, and yet more remarkably distinguishes the Lemur.

Similarly, the occipital foramen of *Mycetes* (Fig. 17), and still more of the Lemurs, is situated completely in the posterior face of the skull, or as much further back than that of the Gorilla, as that of the Gorilla is further back than that of Man; while, as if to render patent the futility of the attempt to base any broad classificatory distinction on such a character, the same group of Platyrhine, or American monkeys, to which the *Mycetes* belongs, contains the *Chrysothrix,* whose occipital foramen is situated far more forward than in any other ape, and nearly approaches the position it holds in Man.

Again, the Orang's skull is as devoid of excessively developed supraciliary prominences as a Man's, though some varieties exhibit great crests elsewhere (See p. 25); and in some of the Cebine apes and in the *Chrysothrix,* the cranium is as smooth and rounded as that of Man himself.

What is true of these leading characteristics of the skull, holds good, as may be imagined, of all minor features; so that for every constant difference between the Gorilla's skull and the Man's, a similar constant difference of the same order (that is to say, consisting in excess or defect of the same quality) may be found between the Gorilla's skull and that of some other ape. So that, for the skull, no less than for the skeleton in general, the proposition holds good, that the differences between Man and the Gorilla are of smaller value than those between the Gorilla and some other Apes.

In connection with the skull, I may speak of the teeth—organs which have a peculiar classificatory value, and whose resemblances and differences of number, form, and succession, taken as a whole, are usually regarded as more trustworthy indicators of affinity than any others.

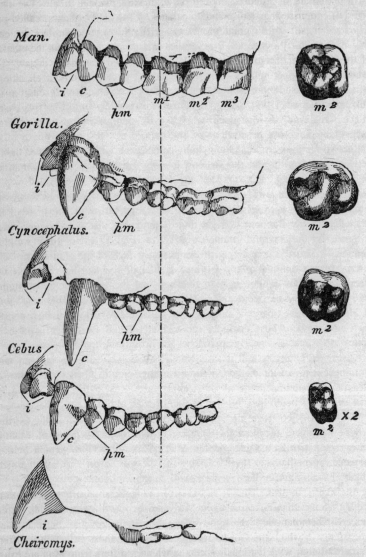

Fig. 18.—Lateral views, of the same length, of the upper jaws of various Primates. *i*, incisors; *c*, canines; *pm*, pre-molars; *m*, molars. A line is drawn through the first molar of Man, *Gorilla*, *Cynocephalus*, and *Cebus*, and the grinding surface of the second molar is shown in each, its anterior and internal angle being just above the *m* of *m²*.

Man is provided with two sets of teeth—milk teeth and permanent teeth. The former consist of four incisors, or cutting teeth; two canines, or eye-teeth; and four molars or grinders, in each jaw, making twenty in all. The latter (Fig. 18) comprise four incisors, two canines, four small grinders, called premolars or false molars, and six large grinders, or true molars in each jaw—making thirty-two in all. The internal incisors are larger than the external pair, in the upper jaw, smaller than the external pair, in the lower jaw. The crowns of the upper molars exhibit four cusps, or blunt-pointed elevations, and a ridge crosses the crown obliquely, from the inner, anterior cusp to the outer, posterior cusp (Fig. 18 m^2). The anterior lower molars have five cusps, three external and two internal. The premolars have two cusps, one internal and one external, of which the outer is the higher.

In all these respects the dentition of the Gorilla may be described in the same terms as that of Man; but in other matters it exhibits many and important differences (Fig. 18).

Thus the teeth of man constitute a regular and even series—without any break and without any marked projection of one tooth above the level of the rest; a peculiarity which, as Cuvier long ago showed, is shared by no other mammal save one—as different a creature from man as can well be imagined—namely, the long extinct *Anoplotherium*, The teeth of the Gorilla, on the contrary, exhibit a break, or interval, termed the *diastema*, in both jaws: in front of the eye-tooth, or between it and the outer incisor, in the upper jaw; behind the eye-tooth, or between it and the front false molar, in the lower jaw. Into this break in the series, in each jaw, fits the canine of the opposite jaw; the size of the eye-tooth in the Gorilla being so great that it projects, like a tusk, far beyond the general level of the other teeth. The roots of the false molar teeth of the Gorilla, again, are more complex than in Man, and the proportional size of the molars is different. The Gorilla has the crown of the hindmost grinder of the lower jaw more complex, and the order of eruption of the permanent teeth is different; the permanent canines making their appearance before the second and third molars in Man, and after them in the Gorilla.

Thus, while the teeth of the Gorilla closely resemble those of Man in number, kind, and in the general pattern of their crowns, they exhibit marked differences from those of Man in secondary respects, such as relative size, number of fangs, and order of appearance.

But, if the teeth of the Gorilla be compared with those of an Ape, no further removed from it than a *Cynocephalus*, or Baboon, it will be found that differences and resemblances of the same order are easily observable; but that many of the points in which the Gorilla resembles Man are those in which it differs from the Baboon; while various respects in which it differs from Man are exaggerated in the *Cynocephalus*. The number and the nature of the teeth remain the same in the Baboon as in the Gorilla and in Man. But the pattern of the Baboon's upper molars is quite different from that described above (Fig. 18), the canines are proportionally longer and more knifelike; the anterior premolar in the lower jaw is specially modified; the posterior molar of the lower jaw is still larger and more complex than in the Gorilla.

Passing from the old-world Apes to those of the new world, we meet with a change of much greater importance than any of these. In such a genus as *Cebus,* for example (Fig. 18), it will be found that while in some secondary points, such as the projection of the canines and the diastema, the resemblance to the great ape is preserved; in other and most important respects, the dentition is extremely different. Instead of 20 teeth in the milk set, there are 24: instead of 32 teeth in the permanent set, there are 36, the false molars being increased from eight to twelve. And in form, the crowns of the molars are very unlike those of the Gorilla, and differ far more widely from the human pattern.

The Marmosets, on the other hand, exhibit the same number of teeth as Man and the Gorilla; but, notwithstanding this, their dentition is very different, for they have four more false molars, like the other American monkeys—but as they have four fewer true molars, the total remains the same. And passing from the American apes to the Lemurs, the dentition becomes still more completely and essentially different from that of the Gorilla. The incisors begin to vary both in number and in form. The molars acquire, more and more, a many-pointed, insectivorous character, and in one Genus, the Aye-Aye *(Cheiromys),* the canines disappear, and the teeth completely simulate those of a Rodent (Fig. 18).

Hence it is obvious that, greatly as the dentition of the highest Ape differs from that of Man, it differs far more widely from that of the lower and lowest Apes.

Whatever part of the animal fabric—whatever series of muscles, whatever viscera might be selected for comparison—the result would be the same—the lower Apes and the Gorilla would differ more than the Gorilla and the Man. I cannot attempt in this place to follow out all these comparisons in detail, and indeed it is unnecessary I should do so. But certain real, or supposed, structural distinctions between man and the apes remain, upon which so much stress has been laid, that they require careful consideration, in order that the true value may be assigned to those which are real, and the emptiness of those which are fictitious may be exposed. I refer to the characters of the hand, the foot, and the brain.

Man has been defined as the only animal possessed of two hands terminating his fore limbs, and of two feet ending his hind limbs, while it has been said that all the apes possess four hands; and he has been affirmed to differ fundamentally from all the apes in the characters of his brain, which alone, it has been strangely asserted and reasserted, exhibits the structures known to anatomists as the posterior lobe, the posterior cornu of the lateral ventricle, and the hippocampus minor.

That the former proposition should have gained general acceptance is not surprising—indeed, at first sight, appearances are much in its favour; but, as for the second, one can only admire the surpassing courage of its enunciator, seeing that it is an innovation which is not only opposed to generally and justly accepted doctrines, but which is directly negatived by the testimony of all original inquirers, who have specially investigated the matter: and that it neither has been, nor can be, supported by a single anatomical preparation. It would, in fact, be unworthy of serious refutation, except for the general and natural belief that deliberate and reiterated assertions must have some foundation.

Before we can discuss the first point with advantage we must consider with some attention, and compare together, the structure of the human hand and that of the human foot, so that we may have distinct and clear ideas of what constitutes a hand and what a foot.

The external form of the human hand is familiar enough to every one. It consists of a stout wrist followed by a broad palm, formed of flesh, and tendons, and skin, binding together four bones, and dividing into four long and flexible digits, or fingers, each of which bears on the back of its last joint a broad and flattened nail. The longest cleft between any two digits is rather less than half as long as the hand. From the outer side of the base of the palm a stout digit goes off, having only two joints instead of three; so short, that it only reaches to a little beyond the middle of the first joint of the finger next it; and further remarkable by its great mobility, in consequence of which it can be directed outwards, almost at a right angle to the rest. This digit is called the *"pollex,"* or thumb; and, like the others, it bears a flat nail upon the back of its terminal joint. In consequence of the proportions and mobility of the thumb, it is what is termed "opposable"; in other words, its extremity can, with the greatest ease, be brought into contact with the extremities of any of the fingers; a property upon which the possibility of our carrying into effect the conceptions of the mind so largely depends.

The external form of the foot differs widely from that of the hand; and yet, when closely compared, the two present some singular resemblances. Thus the ankle corresponds in a manner with the wrist; the sole with the palm; the toes with the fingers; the great toe with the thumb. But the toes, or digits of the foot, are far shorter in proportion than the digits of the hand, and are less moveable, the want of mobility being most striking in the great toe—which, again, is very much larger in proportion to the other toes than the thumb to the fingers. In considering this point, however, it must not be forgotten that the civilized great toe, confined and cramped from childhood upwards, is seen to a great disadvantage, and that in uncivilized and barefooted people it retains a great amount of mobility, and even some sort of opposability. The Chinese boatmen are said to be able to pull an oar; the artisans of

Bengal to weave, and the Carajas to steal fishhooks by its help; though, after all, it must be recollected that the structure of its joints and the arrangement of its bones, necessarily render its prehensile action far less perfect than that of the thumb.

But to gain a precise conception of the resemblances and differences of the hand and foot, and of the distinctive characters of each, we must look below the skin, and compare the bony frame-work and its motor apparatus in each (Fig. 19).

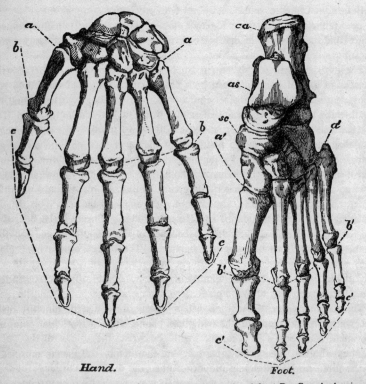

Hand.   *Foot.*

Fig. 19.—The skeleton of the Hand and Foot of Man reduced from Dr. Carter's drawings in Gray's *Anatomy*. The hand is drawn to a larger scale than the foot. The line *a a* in the hand indicates the boundary between the carpus and the metacarpus; *b b* that between the latter and the proximal phalanges; *c c* marks the ends of the distal phalanges. The line *a′ a′* in the foot indicates the boundary between the tarsus and metatarsus; *b′ b′* marks that between the metatarsus and the proximal phalanges; and *c′c′* bounds the ends of the distal phalanges; *ca*, the calcaneum; *as*, the astragalus; *sc*, the scaphoid bone in the tarsus.

The skeleton of the hand exhibits, in the region which we term the wrist, and which is technically called the *carpus*—two rows of closely fitted polygonal bones, four in each row, which are tolerably equal in size. The bones of the first row with the bones of the forearm, form the wrist joint, and are arranged side by side, no one greatly exceeding or overlapping the rest.

Three of the bones of the second row of the carpus bear the four long bones which support the palm of the hand. The fifth bone of the same character is articulated in a much more free and moveable manner than the others, with its carpal bone, and forms the base of the thumb. These are called *metacarpal* bones, and they carry the *phalanges*, or bones of the digits, of which there are two in the thumb, and three in each of the fingers.

The skeleton of the foot is very like that of the hand in some respects. Thus there are three phalanges in each of the lesser toes, and only two in the great toe, which answers to the thumb. There is a long bone, termed *metatarsal*, answering to the metacarpal, for each digit; and the *tarsus* which corresponds with the carpus, presents four short polygonal bones in a row, which correspond very closely with the four carpal bones of the second row of the hand. In other respects the foot differs very widely from the hand. Thus the great toe is the longest digit but one; and its metatarsal is far less moveably articulated with the tarsus than the metacarpal of the thumb with the carpus. But a far more important distinction lies in the fact that, instead of four more tarsal bones there are only three; and, that these three are not arranged side by side, or in one row. One of them, the *os calcis* or heel bone (*ca*), lies externally, and sends back the large projecting heel; another, the *astragalus* (*as*), rests on this by one face, and by another, forms, with the bones of the leg, the ankle joint; while a third face, directed forwards, is separated from the three inner tarsal bones of the row next the metatarsus by a bone called the *scaphoid* (*sc*).

Thus there is a fundamental difference in the structure of the foot and the hand, observable when the carpus and the tarsus are contrasted: and there are differences of degree noticeable when the proportions and the mobility of the metacarpals and metatarsals, with their respective digits, are compared together.

The same two classes of differences become obvious when the muscles of the hand are compared with those of the foot.

Three principal sets of muscles, called "flexors," bend the fingers and thumb, as in clenching the fist, and three sets,—the extensors—extend them, as in straightening the fingers. These muscles are all "long muscles"; that is to say, the fleshy part of each, lying in and being fixed to the bones of the arm, is, at the other end, continued into tendons, or rounded cords, which pass into the hand, and are ultimately fixed to the bones which are to be moved. Thus, when the fingers are bent, the fleshy parts of the flexors of the fingers, placed in the arm, contract, in virtue of their peculiar endowment as muscles; and pulling the tendinous cords, connecting with their ends, cause them to pull down the bones of the fingers towards the palm.

Not only are the principal flexors of the fingers and of the thumb long muscles, but they remain quite distinct from one another throughout their whole length.

In the foot, there are also three principal flexor muscles of the digits or toes, and three principal extensors; but one extensor and one flexor are short muscles; that is to say, their fleshy parts are not situated in the leg (which corresponds with the arm), but in the back and in the sole of the foot—regions which correspond with the back and the palm of the hand.

Again, the tendons of the long flexor of the toes, and of the long flexor of the great toe, when they reach the sole of the foot, do not remain distinct from one another, as the flexors in the palm of the hand do, but they become united and commingled in a very curious manner—while their united tendons receive an accessory muscle connected with the heel-bone.

But perhaps the most absolutely distinctive character about the muscles of the foot is the existence of what is termed the *peronoeus longus*, a long muscle fixed to the outer bone of the leg, and sending its tendon to the outer ankle, behind and below which it passes, and then crosses the foot obliquely to be attached to the base of the great toe. No muscle in the hand exactly corresponds with this, which is eminently a foot muscle.

To resume—the foot of man is distinguished from his hand by the following absolute anatomical differences:—

1. By the arrangement of the tarsal bones.
2. By having a short flexor and a short extensor muscle of the digits.
3. By possessing the muscle termed *peronoeus longus*.

And if we desire to ascertain whether the terminal division of a limb, in other Primates, is to be called a foot or a hand, it is by the presence or absence of these characters that we must be guided, and not by the mere proportions and greater or lesser mobility of the great toe, which may vary indefinitely without any fundamental alteration on the structure of the foot.

Keeping these considerations in mind, let us now turn to the limbs of the Gorilla. The terminal division of the fore limb presents no difficulty—bone for bone and muscle for muscle, are found to be arranged essentially as in man, or with such minor differences as are found as varieties in man. The Gorilla's hand is clumsier, heavier, and has a thumb somewhat shorter in proportion than that of man; but no one has ever doubted it being a true hand.

At first sight, the termination of the hind limb of the Gorilla looks very hand-like, and as it is still more so in many of the lower apes, it is not wonderful that the appellation "Quadrumana," or four-handed creatures, adopted from the older anatomists[1] by Blumenbach, and unfortunately rendered current by Cuvier, should have gained such wide acceptance as a name for the Simian group. But the most cursory anatomical investigation at once proves that the resemblance of the so-called "hind hand" to a true hand, is only skin deep, and that, in all essential respects, the hind limb of the Gorilla is as truly terminated by a foot as that of man. The tarsal bones, in all important circumstances of number, disposition, and form, resemble those of man (Fig. 20). The metatarsals and digits, on the other hand, are proportionally longer and more slender, while the great toe is not only proportionally shorter and weaker, but its metatarsal bone is united by a more moveable joint with the tarsus. At the same time, the foot is set more obliquely upon the leg than in man.

As to the muscles, there is a short flexor, a short extensor, and a *peronoeus longus*, while the tendons of the long flexors of the great toe and of the other toes are united together and with an accessory fleshy bundle.

The hind limb of the Gorilla, therefore, ends in a true foot, with a very moveable great toe. It is a prehensile foot, indeed, but is in no sense a hand; it is a foot which differs from that of man not in any fundamental character, but in mere proportions, in the degree of mobility, and in the secondary arrangement of its parts.

It must not be supposed, however, because I speak of these differences as not fundamental, that I wish to underrate their value. They are important enough in their way, the structure of the foot being in strict correlation with that of the rest of the organism in each case. Nor can it be doubted that the greater division of physiological labour in Man, so that the function of support is thrown wholly on the leg and foot, is an advance in organization of very great moment to him; but, after all, regarded anatomically, the resemblances between the foot of Man and the foot of the Gorilla are far more striking and important than the differences.

I have dwelt upon this point at length, because it is one regarding which much delusion prevails; but I might have passed it over without detriment to my argument, which only requires me to show that, be the differences between the hand and foot of Man and those of the Gorilla what they may—the differ-

---

[1] In speaking of the foot of his "Pygmie," Tyson remarks, p. 13:—

"But this part in the formation and in its function too, being liker a Hand than a Foot: for the distinguishing this sort of animals from others, I have thought whether it might not be reckoned and called rather Quadru-manus than Quadrupes, *i.e.* a four-handed rather than a four-footed animal."

As this passage was published in 1699, M. I. G. St. Hilaire is clearly in error in ascribing the invention of the term "quadrumanous" to Buffon, though "bimanous" may belong to him. Tyson uses "Quadrumanus" in several places, as at p. 91. . . . . "Our *Pygmie* is no Man, nor yet the *common Ape*, but a sort of *Animal* between both; and though a *Biped*, yet of the *Quadrumanus*-kind: though some *Men* too have been observed to use their *Feet* like *Hands* as I have seen several."

188 FRONTIERS OF ANTHROPOLOGY

between those of the Gorilla, and those of the lower Apes are much greater.

It is not necessary to descend lower in the scale than the Orang for conclusive evidence on this head.

The thumb of the Orang differs more from that of the Gorilla than the thumb of the Gorilla differs from that of Man, not only by its shortness, but by the absence of any special long flexor muscle. The carpus of the Orang, like that of most lower apes, contains nine bones, while in the Gorilla, as in Man and the Chimpanzee, there are only eight.

The Orang's foot (Fig. 20) is still more aberrant; its very long toes and short tarsus, short great toe, short and raised heel, great obliquity of articulation with the leg, and absence of a long flexor tendon to the great toe, separating it far more widely from the foot of the Gorilla than the latter is separated from that of Man.

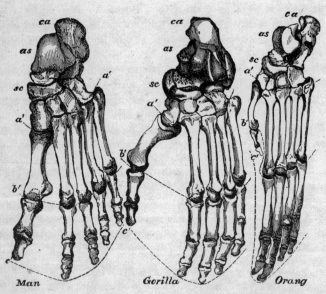

Fig. 20.—Foot of Man, Gorilla, and Orang-Utan of the same absolute length, to show the differences in proportion of each. Letters as in Fig. 19. Reduced from original drawings by Mr. Waterhouse Hawkins.

But, in some of the lower apes, the hand and foot diverge still more from those of the Gorilla, than they do in the Orang. The thumb ceases to be opposable in the American monkeys; is reduced to a mere rudiment covered by the skin in the Spider Monkey; and is directed forwards and armed with a curved claw like the other digits, in the Marmosets—so that, in all these cases, there can be no doubt but that the hand is more different from that of the Gorilla than the Gorilla's hand is from Man's.

And as to the foot, the great toe of the Marmoset is still more insignificant in proportion than that of the Orang—while in the Lemurs it is very large, and as completely thumb-like and opposable as in the Gorilla—but in these animals the second toe is often irregularly modified, and in some species the two principal bones of the tarsus, the *astragalus* and the *os calcis,* are so immensely elongated as to render the foot, so far, totally unlike that of any other mammal.

So with regard to the muscles. The short flexor of the toes of the Gorilla differs from that of Man by the circumstance that one slip of the muscle is attached, not to the heel bone, but to the tendons of the long flexors. The lower Apes depart from the Gorilla by an exaggeration of the same character, two, three, or more, slips becoming fixed to the long flexor tendons—or by a multiplication of the slips.—Again, the Gorilla differs slightly from Man in the mode of interlacing of the long flexor tendons: and the lower apes differ from the Gorilla in exhibiting yet other, sometimes very complex, arrangements of the same parts, and occasionally in the absence of the accessory fleshy bundle.

Throughout all these modifications it must be recollected that the foot loses no one of its essential characters. Every Monkey and Lemur exhibits the characteristic arrangement of tarsal bones, possesses a short flexor and short extensor muscle, and a *peronoeus longus*. Varied as the proportions and appearance of the organ may be, the terminal division of the hind limb remains, in plan and principle of construction, a foot and never, in those respects, can be confounded with a hand.

Hardly any part of the bodily frame, then, could be found better calculated to illustrate the truth that the structural differences between Man and the highest Ape are of less value than those between the highest and the lower Apes, than the hand or the foot; and yet, perhaps, there is one organ the study of which enforces the same conclusion in a still more striking manner—and that is the Brain.

But before entering upon the precise question of the amount of difference between the Ape's brain and that of Man, it is necessary that we should clearly understand what constitutes a great, and what a small difference in cerebral structure; and we shall be best enabled to do this by a brief study of the chief modifications which the brain exhibits in the series of vertebrate animals.

The brain of a fish is very small, compared with the spinal cord into which it is continued, and with the nerves which come off from it: of the segments of which it is composed—the olfactory lobes, the cerebral hemispheres, and the succeeding divisions—no one predominates so much over the rest as to obscure or cover them; and the so-called optic lobes are, frequently, the largest masses of all. In Reptiles, the mass of the brain, relatively to the spinal cord, increases and the cerebral hemispheres begin to predominate over the other parts; while in Birds this predominance is still more marked. The brain of the lowest Mammals, such as the duck-billed Platypus and the Opossums and Kangaroos, exhibits a still more definite advance in the same direction. The cerebral hemispheres have now so much increased in size as, more or less, to hide the representatives of the optic lobes, which remain comparatively small, so that the brain of a Marsupial is extremely different from that of a Bird, Reptile, or Fish. A step higher in the scale, among the placental Mammals, the structure of the brain acquires a vast modification—not that it appears much altered externally, in a Rat or in a Rabbit, from what it is in a Marsupial—nor that the proportions of its parts are much changed, but an apparently new structure is found between the cerebral hemispheres, connecting them together, as what is called the "great commissure" or "corpus callosum." The subject requires careful re-investigation, but if the currently received statements are correct, the appearance of the "corpus callosum" in the placental mammals is the greatest and most sudden modification exhibited by the brain in the whole series of vertebrated aminals—it is the greatest leap anywhere made by Nature in her brain work. For the two halves of the brain being once thus knit together, the progress of cerebral complexity is traceable through a complete series of steps from the lowest Rodent, or Insectivore, to Man; and that complexity consists, chiefly, in the disproportionate development of the cerebral hemispheres and of the cerebellum, but especially of the former, in respect to the other parts of the brain.

In the lower placental mammals, the cerebra hemispheres leave the proper upper and posterior face of the cerebellum completely visible, when the brain is viewed from above; but, in the higher forms, the hinder part of each hemisphere, separated only by the tentorium (p. 137) from the anterior face of the cerebellum, inclines backwards and downwards, and grows out, as the so-called "posterior lobe," so as at length to overlap and hide the cerebellum. In all Mammals, each cerebral hemisphere contains a cavity which is termed the "ventricle"; and as this ventricle is prolonged, on the one hand, forwards, and on the other downwards, into the substance of the hemisphere, it is said to have two horns or "cornua," an "anterior cornu," and a "descending cornu." When the posterior lobe is well developed, a third prolongation of the ventricular cavity extends into it, and is called the "posterior cornu."

In the lower and smaller forms of placental Mammals the surface of the cerebral hemispheres is either smooth or evenly rounded, or exhibits a very few grooves, which are technically termed "sulci," separating ridges or "convolutions" of the substance of the brain; and the smaller species of all orders tend to a similar smoothness of brain. But, in the higher orders, and especially the larger members of these orders, the grooves, or sulci, become extremely numerous, and the intermediate convolutions proportionately more complicated in their meanderings, until, in the Elephant, the Porpoise, the higher Apes, and Man, the cerebral surface appears a perfect labyrinth of tortuous foldings.

Where a posterior lobe exists and presents its customary cavity—the posterior cornu—it commonly happens that a particular sulcus appears upon the inner and under surface of the lobe, parallel with and beneath the floor of the cornu—which is, as it were, arched over the roof of the sulcus. It is as if the groove had been formed by indenting the floor of the posterior horn from without with a blunt instrument, so that the floor should rise as a convex eminence. Now this eminence is what has been termed the "Hippocampus minor;" the "Hippocampus major" being a larger eminence in the floor of the descending cornu. What may be the functional importance of either of these structures we know not.

As if to demonstrate, by a striking example, the impossibility of erecting any cerebral barrier between man and the apes, Nature has provided us, in the latter animals, with an almost complete series of gradations from brains little higher than that of a Rodent, to brains little lower than that of Man. And it is a remarkable circumstance, that though, so far as our present knowledge extends, there *is* one true structural break in the series of forms of Simian brains, this hiatus does not lie between Man and the man-like apes, but between the lower and the lowest Simians; or, in other words, between the old and new world apes and monkeys, and the Lemurs. Every Lemur which has yet been examined, in fact, has its cerebellum partially visible from above, and its posterior lobe, with the contained posterior cornu and hippocampus minor, more or less rudimentary. Every Marmoset, American monkey, old world monkey, Baboon, or Man-like ape, on the contrary, has its cerebellum entirely hidden, posteriorly, by the cerebral lobes, and possesses a large posterior cornu, with a well-developed hippocampus minor.

In many of these creatures, such as the Saimiri (*Chrysothrix*), the cerebral lobes overlap and extend much further behind the cerebellum, in proportion, than they do in man (Fig. 17)—and it is quite certain that, in all, the cerebellum is completely covered behind, by well developed posterior lobes. The fact can be verified by every one who possesses the skull of any old or new world monkey. For, inasmuch as the brain in all mammals completely fills the cranial cavity, it is obvious that a cast of the interior of the skull will reproduce the general form of the brain, at any rate with such minute and, for the present purpose, utterly unimportant differences as may result from the absence of the enveloping membranes of the brain in the dry skull. But if such a cast be made in plaster, and compared with a similar cast of the interior of a human skull, it will be obvious that the cast of the cerebral chamber, representing the cerebrum of the ape, as completely covers over and overlaps the cast of the cerebellar chamber, representing the cerebellum, as it does in the man (Fig. 21). A careless observer, forgetting that a soft structure like the brain loses its proper shape the moment it is taken out of the skull, may indeed mistake the uncovered condition of the cerebellum of an extracted and distorted brain for the natural relations of the parts; but his error must become patent even to himself if he try to replace the brain within the cranial chamber. To suppose that the cerebellum of an ape is naturally uncovered behind is a miscomprehension comparable only to that of one who should imagine that a man's lungs always occupy but a small portion of the thoracic cavity, because they do so when the chest is opened, and their elasticity is no longer neutralized by the pressure of the air.

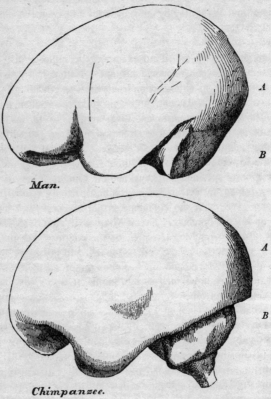

Fig. 21.—Drawings of the internal casts of a Man's and of a Chimpanzee's skull, of the same absolute length, and placed in corresponding positions, A. Cerebrum; B. Cerebellum. The former drawing is taken from a cast in the Museum of the Royal College of Surgeons, the latter from the photograph of the cast of a Chimpanzee's skull, which illustrates the paper by Mr. Marshall "On the Brain of the Chimpanzee" in the *Natural History Review* for July, 1861. The sharper definition of the lower edge of the cast of the cerebral chamber in the Chimpanzee arises from the circumstance that the tentorium remained in that skull and not in the Man's. The cast more accurately represents the brain in the Chimpanzee than in the Man; and the great backward projection of the posterior lobes of the cerebrum of the former, beyond the cerebellum, is conspicuous.

And the error is the less excusable, as it must become apparent to every one who examines a section of the skull of any ape above a Lemur, without taking the trouble to make a cast of it. For there is a very marked groove in every such skull, as in the human skull—which indicates the line of attachment of what is termed the *tentorium*—a sort of parchment-like shelf, or partition, which, in the recent state, is interposed between the cerebrum and cerebellum, and prevents the former from pressing upon the latter. (See Fig. 17.)

This groove, therefore, indicates the line of separation between that part of the cranial cavity which contains the cerebrum, and that which contains the cerebellum; and as the brain exactly fills the cavity of the skull, it is obvious that the relations of these two parts of the cranial cavity at once informs us of the relations of their contents. Now in man, in all the old world, and in all the new world Simiae, with one exception, when the face is directed forwards, this line of attachment of the tentorium, or impression for the lateral sinus, as it is technically called, is nearly horizontal, and the cerebral chamber invariably overlaps or projects behind the cerebellar chamber. In the Howler Monkey or *Mycetes* (see Fig. 17), the line passes obliquely upwards and backwards, and the cerebral overlap is almost nil; while in the Lemurs, as in the lower mammals, the line is much more inclined in the same direction, and the cerebellar chamber projects considerably beyond the cerebral.

When the gravest errors respecting points so easily settled as this question respecting the posterior lobes, can be authoritatively propounded, it is no wonder that matters of observation, of no very complex character, but still requiring a certain amount of care, should have fared worse. Any one who cannot see the posterior lobe in an ape's brain is not likely to give a very valuable opinion respecting the posterior cornu or the hippocampus minor. If a man cannot see a church, it is preposterous to take his opinion about its altar-piece or painted window—so that I do not feel bound to enter upon any discussion of these points, but content myself with assuring the reader that the posterior cornu and the hippocampus minor, have now been seen—usually, at least as well developed as in man, and often better—not only in the Chimpanzee, the Orang, and the Gibbon, but in all the genera of the old world baboons and monkeys, and in most of the new world forms, including the Marmosets.

In fact, all the abundant and trustworthy evidence (consisting of the results of careful investigations directed to the determination of these very questions, by skilled anatomists) which we now possess, leads to the conviction that, so far from the posterior lobe, the posterior cornu, and the hippocampus minor, being structures peculiar to and characteristic of man, as they have been over and over again asserted to be, even after the publication of the clearest demonstration of the reverse, it is precisely these structures which are the most marked cerebral characters common to man with the apes. They are among the most distinctly Simian peculiarities which the human organism exhibits.

As to the convolutions, the brains of the apes exhibit every stage of progress,

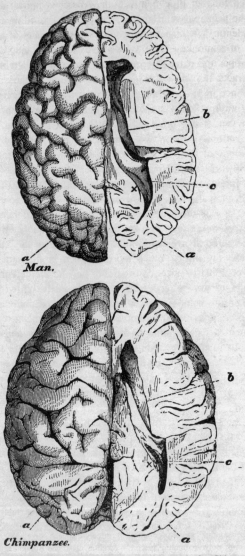

Fig. 22.—Drawings of the cerebral hemispheres of a Man and of a Chimpanzee of the same length, in order to show the relative proportions of the parts: the former taken from a specimen, which Mr. Flower, Conservator of the Museum of the Royal College of Surgeons, was good enough to dissect for me; the latter, from the photograph of a similarly dissected Chimpanzee's brain, given in Mr. Marshall's paper above referred to. *a*, posterior lobe; *b*, lateral ventricle; *c*, posterior cornu; *x*, the hippocampus minor.

from the almost smooth brain of the Marmoset, to the Orang and the Chimpanzee, which fall but little below Man. And it is most remarkable that, as soon as all the principal sulci appear, the pattern according to which they are arranged is identical with that of the corresponding sulci of man. The surface of the brain of a monkey exhibits a sort of skeleton map of man's, and in the man-like apes the details become more and more filled in, until it is only in minor characters, such as the greater excavation of the anterior lobes, the constant presence of fissures usually absent in man, and the different disposition and proportions of some convolutions, that the Chimpanzee's or the Orang's brain can be structurally distinguished from Man's.

So far as cerebral structure goes, therefore, it is clear that Man differs less from the Chimpanzee or the Orang, than these do even from the Monkeys, and that the difference between the brains of the Chimpanzee and of Man is almost insignificant, when compared with that between the Chimpanzee brain and that of a Lemur.

It must not be overlooked, however, that there is a very striking difference in absolute mass and weight between the lowest human brain and that of the highest ape—a difference which is all the more remarkable when we recollect that a full-grown Gorilla is probably pretty nearly twice as heavy as a Bosjesman, or as many an European woman. It may be doubted whether a healthy human adult brain ever weighed less than thirty-one or two ounces, or that the heaviest Gorilla brain has exceeded twenty ounces.

This is a very noteworthy circumstance, and doubtless will one day help to furnish an explanation of the great gulf which intervenes between the lowest man and the highest ape in intellectual power,[1] but it has little systematic value,

---

[1] I say *help* to furnish: for I by no means believe that it was any original difference of cerebral quality, or quantity, which caused that divergence between the human and the pithecoid stirpes, which has ended in the present enormous gulf between them. It is no doubt perfectly true, in a certain sense, that all difference of function is a result of difference of structure; or, in other words, of difference in the combination of the primary molecular forces of living substance; and, starting from this undeniable axiom, objectors occasionally, and with much seeming plausibility, argue that the vast intellectual chasm between the Ape and Man implies a corresponding structural chasm in the organs of the intellectual functions; so that, it is said, the non-discovery of such vast differences proves, not that they are absent, but that Science is incompetent to detect them. A very little consideration, however, will, I think, show the fallacy of this reasoning. Its validity hangs upon the assumption, that intellectual power depends altogether on the brain—whereas the brain is only one condition out of many on which intellectual manifestations depend; the others being, chiefly, the organs of the senses and the motor apparatuses, especially those which are concerned in prehension and in the production of articulate speech.

A man born dumb, notwithstanding his great cerebral mass and his inheritance of strong intellectual instincts, would be capable of few higher intellectual manifestations than an Orang or a Chimpanzee, if he were confined to the society of dumb associates. And yet there might not be the slightest discernible difference between his brain and that of a highly intelligent and cultivated person. The dumbness might be the result of a defective structure of the mouth, or of the tongue, or a mere defective innervation of these parts; or it might result from congenital deaf-

for the simple reason that, as may be concluded from what has been already said respecting cranial capacity, the difference in weight of brain between the highest and the lowest men is far greater, both relatively and absolutely, than that between the lowest man and the highest ape. The latter, as has been seen, is represented by, say twelve, ounces of cerebral substance absolutely, or by 32 : 20 relatively; but as the largest recorded human brain weighed between 65 and 66 ounces, the former difference is represented by more than 33 ounces absolutely, or by 65 : 32 relatively. Regarded systematically, the cerebral differences of man and apes, are not of more than generic value; his Family distinction resting chiefly on his dentition, his pelvis, and his lower limbs.

Thus, whatever system of organs be studied, the comparison of their modifications in the ape series leads to one and the same result—that the structural differences which separate Man from the Gorilla and the Chimpanzee are not so great as those which separate the Gorilla from the lower apes.

But in enunciating this important truth I must guard myself against a form of misunderstanding, which is very prevalent. I find, in fact, that those who endeavour to teach what nature so clearly shows us in this matter, are liable to have their opinions misrepresented and their phraseology garbled, until they seem to say that the structural differences between man and even the highest apes are small and insignificant. Let me take this opportunity then of distinctly asserting, on the contrary, that they are great and significant; that every bone of a Gorilla bears marks by which it might be distinguished from the corresponding bone of a Man; and that, in the present creation, at any rate, no intermediate link bridges over the gap between *Homo* and *Troglodytes*.

It would be no less wrong than absurd to deny the existence of this chasm; but it is at least equally wrong and absurd to exaggerate its magnitude and, resting on the admitted fact of its existence, to refuse to inquire whether it is wide or narrow. Remember, if you will, that there is no existing link between Man and the Gorilla, but do not forget that there is a no less sharp line of demarcation, a no less complete absence of any transitional form, between

---

ness, caused by some minute defect of the internal ear, which only a careful anatomist could discover.

The argument, that because there is an immense difference between a Man's intelligence and an Ape's, therefore, there must be an equally immense difference between their brains, appears to me to be about as well based as the reasoning by which one should endeavour to prove that, because there is a "great gulf" between a watch that keeps accurate time and another that will not go at all, there is therefore a great structural hiatus between the two watches. A hair in the balance-wheel, a little rust on a pinion, a bend in a tooth of the escapement, a something so slight that only the practised eye of the watchmaker can discover it, may be the source of all the difference.

And believing, as I do, with Cuvier, that the possession of articulate speech is the grand distinctive character of man (whether it be absolutely peculiar to him or not), I find it very easy to comprehend, that some equally inconspicuous structural difference may have been the primary cause of the immeasurable and practically infinite divergence of the Human from the Simian Stirps.

the Gorilla and the Orang, or the Orang and the Gibbon. I say, not less sharp, though it is somewhat narrower. The structural differences between Man and the Manlike apes certainly justify our regarding him as constituting a family apart from them; though, inasmuch as he differs less from them than they do from other families of the same order, there can be no justification for placing him in a distinct order.

And thus the sagacious foresight of the great lawgiver of systematic zoology, Linnaeus, becomes justified, and a century of anatomical research brings us back to his conclusion, that man is a member of the same order (for which the Linnaean term PRIMATES ought to be retained) as the Apes and Lemurs. This order is now divisible into seven families, of about equal systematic value: the first, the ANTHROPINI, contains Man alone; the second, the CATARHINI, embraces the old world apes; the third, the PLATYRHINI, all new world apes, except the Marmosets; the fourth, the ARCTOPITHECINI, contains the Marmosets; the fifth, the LEMURINI, the Lemurs—from which *Cheiromys* should probably be excluded to form a sixth distinct family, the CHEIROMYINI; while the seventh, the GALEOPITHECINI, contains only the flying Lemur *Galeopithecus*,—a strange form which almost touches on the Bats, as the *Cheiromys* puts on a Rodent clothing, and the Lemurs simulate Insectivora.

Perhaps no order of mammals presents us with so extraordinary a series of gradations as this—leading us insensibly from the crown and summit of the animal creation down to creatures, from which there is but a step, as it seems, to the lowest, smallest, and least intelligent of the placental Mammalia. It is as if nature herself had foreseen the arrogance of man, and with Roman severity had provided that his intellect, by its very triumphs, should call into prominence the slaves, admonishing the conqueror that he is but dust.

These are the chief facts, this the immediate conclusion from them to which I adverted in the commencement of this Essay. The facts, I believe, cannot be disputed; and if so, the conclusion appears to me to be inevitable.

But if Man be separated by no greater structural barrier from the brutes than they are from one another—then it seems to follow that if any process of physical causation can be discovered by which the genera and families of ordinary animals have been produced, that process of causation is amply sufficient to account for the origin of Man. In other words, if it could be shown that the Marmosets, for example, have arisen by gradual modification of the ordinary Platyrhini, or that both Marmosets and Platyrhini are modified ramifications of a primitive stock—then, there would be no rational ground for doubting that man might have originated, in the one case, by the gradual modification of a man-like ape; or, in the other case, as a ramification of the same primitive stock as those apes.

At the present moment, but one such process of physical causation has any evidence in its favour; or, in other words, there is but one hypothesis regarding

the origin of species of animals in general which has any scientific existence
—that propounded by Mr. Darwin. For Lamarck, sagacious as many of his
views were, mingled them with so much that was crude and even absurd, as
to neutralize the benefit which his originality might have effected, had he been
a more sober and cautious thinker; and though I have heard of the announce-
ment of a formula touching "the ordained continuous becoming of organic
forms," it is obvious that it is the first duty of a hypothesis to be intelligible,
and that a qua-quâ-versal proposition of this kind, which may be read backwards, or forwards, or sideways, with exactly the same amount of signification,
does not really exist, though it may seem to do so.

At the present moment, therefore, the question of the relation of man to
the lower animals resolves itself, in the end, into the larger question of the
tenability, or untenability, of Mr. Darwin's views. But here we enter upon
difficult ground, and it behoves us to define our exact position with the greatest
care.

It cannot be doubted, I think, that Mr. Darwin has satisfactorily proved that
what he terms selection, or selective modification, must occur, and does occur,
in nature; and he has also proved to superfluity that such selection is competent
to produce forms as distinct, structurally, as some genera even are. If the
animated world presented us with none but structural differences, I should have
no hesitation in saying that Mr. Darwin had demonstrated the existence of
a true physical cause, amply competent to account for the origin of living
species, and of man among the rest.

But, in addition to their structural distinctions, the species of animals and
plants, or at least a great number of them, exhibit physiological characters
—what are known as distinct species, structurally, being for the most part
either altogether incompetent to breed one with another; or if they breed, the
resulting mule, or hybrid, is unable to perpetuate its race with another hybrid
of the same kind.

A true physical cause is, however, admitted to be such only on one condition—that it shall account for all the phenomena which come within the range
of its operation. If it is inconsistent with any one phenomenon, it must be
rejected; if it fails to explain any one phenomenon, it is so far weak, so far
to be suspected; though it may have a perfect right to claim provisional
acceptance.

Now, Mr. Darwin's hypothesis is not, so far as I am aware, inconsistent
with any known biological fact; on the contrary, if admitted, the facts of
Development, of Comparative Anatomy, of Geographical Distribution, and of
Palaeontology, become connected together, and exhibit a meaning such as they
never possessed before; and I, for one, am fully convinced, that if not precisely
true, that hypothesis is as near an approximation to the truth as, for example,
the Copernican hypothesis was to the true theory of the planetary motions.

But, for all this, our acceptance of the Darwinian hypothesis must be provisional so long as one link in the chain of evidence is wanting; and so long as all the animals and plants certainly produced by selective breeding from a common stock are fertile, and their progeny are fertile with one another, that link will be wanting. For, so long, selective breeding will not be proved to be competent to do all that is required of it to produce natural species.

I have put this conclusion as strongly as possible before the reader, because the last position in which I wish to find myself is that of an advocate for Mr. Darwin's, or any other views; if by an advocate is meant one whose business it is to smooth over real difficulties, and to persuade where he cannot convince.

In justice to Mr. Darwin, however, it must be admitted that the conditions of fertility and sterility are very ill understood, and that every day's advance in knowledge leads us to regard the hiatus in his evidence as of less and less importance, when set against the multitude of facts which harmonize with, or receive an explanation from, his doctrines.

I adopt Mr. Darwin's hypothesis, therefore, subject to the production of proof that physiological species may be produced by selective breeding; just as a physical philosopher may accept the undulatory theory of light, subject to the proof of the existence of the hypothetical ether; or as the chemist adopts the atomic theory, subject to the proof of the existence of atoms; and for exactly the same reasons, namely, that it has an immense amount of primâ facie probability: that it is the only means at present within reach of reducing the chaos of observed facts to order; and lastly, that it is the most powerful instrument of investigation which has been presented to naturalists since the invention of the natural system of classification, and the commencement of the systematic study of embryology.

But even leaving Mr. Darwin's views aside, the whole analogy of natural operations furnishes so complete and crushing an argument against the intervention of any but what are termed secondary causes, in the production of all the phenomena of the universe; that, in view of the intimate relations between Man and the rest of the living world, and between the forces exerted by the latter and all other forces, I can see no excuse for doubting that all are co-ordinated terms of Nature's great progression, from the formless to the formed—from the inorganic to the organic—from blind force to conscious intellect and will.

Science has fulfilled her function when she has ascertained and enunciated truth; and were these pages addressed to men of science only, I should now close this Essay, knowing that my colleagues have learned to respect nothing but evidence, and to believe that their highest duty lies in submitting to it, however it may jar against their inclinations.

But desiring, as I do, to reach the wider circle of the intelligent public, it would be unworthy cowardice were I to ignore the repugnance with which the majority of my readers are likely to meet the conclusions to which the most careful and conscientious study I have been able to give to this matter, has led me.

On all sides I shall hear the cry—"We are men and women, not a mere better sort of apes, a little longer in the leg, more compact in the foot, and bigger in brain than your brutal Chimpanzees and Gorillas. The power of knowledge—the conscience of good and evil—the pitiful tenderness of human affections, raise us out of all real fellowship with the brutes, however closely they may seem to approximate us."

To this I can only reply that the exclamation would be most just and would have my own entire sympathy, if it were only relevant. But, it is not I who seek to base Man's dignity upon his great toe, or insinuate that we are lost if an Ape has a hippocampus minor. On the contrary, I have done my best to sweep away this vanity. I have endeavoured to show that no absolute structural line of demarcation, wider than that between the animals which immediately succeed us in the scale, can be drawn between the animal world and ourselves; and I may add the expression of my belief that the attempt to draw a psychical distinction is equally futile, and that even the highest faculties of feeling and of intellect begin to germinate in lower forms of life.[1] At the same time, no one is more strongly convinced than I am of the vastness of the gulf between civilized man and the brutes; or is more certain that whether *from* them or not, he is assuredly not *of* them. No one is less disposed to think lightly of the present dignity, or despairingly of the future hopes, of the only consciously intelligent denizen of this world.

We are indeed told by those who assume authority in these matters, that the two sets of opinions are incompatible, and that the belief in the unity of origin of man and brutes involves the brutalization and degradation of the former. But is this really so? Could not a sensible child confute by obvious arguments, the shallow rhetoricians who would force this conclusion upon us? Is it, indeed, true, that the Poet, or the Philosopher, or the Artist whose genius

[1]It is so rare a pleasure for me to find Professor Owen's opinions in entire accordance with my own, that I cannot forbear from quoting a paragraph which appeared in his Essay "On the Characters, &c., of the Class Mammalia," in the *Journal of the Proceedings of the Linnean Society of London* for 1857, but is unaccountably omitted in the "Reade Lecture" delivered before the University of Cambridge two years later, which is otherwise nearly a reprint of the paper in question. Prof. Owen writes:

"Not being able to appreciate or conceive of the distinction between the psychical phenomena of a Chimpanzee and of a Boschisman or of an Aztec, with arrested brain growth, as being of a nature so essential as to preclude a comparison between them, or as being other than a difference of degree, I cannot shut my eyes to the significance of that all-pervading similitude of structure—every tooth, every bone, strictly homologous—which makes the determination of the difference between *Homo* and *Pithecus* the anatomist's difficulty."

Surely it is a little singular, that the "anatomist," who finds it "difficult" to determine "the difference" between *Homo* and *Pithecus*, should yet range them on anatomical gounds, in distinct sub-classes.

is the glory of his age, is degraded from his high estate by the undoubted historical probability, not to say certainty, that he is the direct descendant of some naked and bestial savage, whose intelligence was just sufficient to make him a little more cunning than the Fox, and by so much more dangerous than the Tiger? Or is he bound to howl and grovel on all fours because of the wholly unquestionable fact, that he was once an egg, which no ordinary power of discrimination could distinguish from that of a Dog? Or is the philanthropist, or the saint, to give up his endeavours to lead a noble life, because the simplest study of man's nature reveals, at its foundations, all the selfish passions, and fierce appetites of the merest quadruped? Is mother-love vile because a hen shows it, or fidelity base because dogs possess it?

The common sense of the mass of mankind will answer these questions without a moment's hesitation. Healthy humanity, finding itself hard pressed to escape from real sin and degradation, will leave the brooding over speculative pollution to the cynics and the "righteous overmuch" who, disagreeing in everything else, unite in blind insensibility to the nobleness of the visible world, and in inability to appreciate the grandeur of the place Man occupies therein.

Nay more, thoughtful men, once escaped from the blinding influences of traditional prejudice, will find in the lowly stock whence Man has sprung, the best evidence of the splendour of his capacities; and will discern in his long progress through the Past, a reasonable ground of faith in his attainment of a nobler Future.

They will remember that in comparing civilised man with the animal world, one is as the Alpine traveller, who sees the mountains soaring into the sky and can hardly discern where the deep shadowed crags and roseate peaks end, and where the clouds of heaven begin. Surely the awe-struck voyager may be excused if, at first, he refuses to believe the geologist, who tells him that these glorious masses are, after all, the hardened mud of primeval seas, or the cooled slag of subterranean furnaces—of one substance with the dullest clay, but raised by inward forces to that place of proud and seemingly inaccessible glory.

But the geologist is right; and due reflection on his teachings, instead of diminishing our reverence and our wonder, adds all the force of intellectual sublimity to the mere aesthetic intuition of the uninstructed beholder.

And after passion and prejudice have died away, the same result will attend the teachings of the naturalist respecting that great Alps and Andes of the living world—Man. Our reverence for the nobility of manhood will not be lessened by the knowledge that Man is, in substance and in structure, one with the brutes; for, he alone possesses the marvellous endowment of intelligible and rational speech, whereby, in the secular period of his existence, he has slowly accumulated and organised the experience which is almost wholly lost with the cessation of every individual life in other animals; so that, now, he stands raised upon it as on a mountain top, far above the level of his humble fellows, and transfigured from his grosser nature by reflecting, here and there, a ray from the infinite source of truth.

JAMES HUNT AND THE NEGRO'S PLACE IN NATURE

JAMES HUNT (1833-1869) was one of the founders and first President of the newly formed *Anthropological Society* of London. He had broken away with some others from the *Ethnological Society* on the ground that he felt its interests were too narrow. This was the period of the Civil War in America and of heated debate in England over the issue of slavery. To resolve this issue from the "scientific" point of view Hunt chose as his Presidential Address, delivered 17 November 1863, the subject of "The Negro's Place in Nature." T. H. Huxley's book *Evidence as to Man's Place in Nature* had been published earlier that year, and Hunt, no doubt, took advantage of the popularity of that work to borrow part of its title for his own address. That address literally reverberated round the world. Hunt was thirty years of age at the time, a man of considerable learning and engaging personality. The apparatus of learning with which he paraded his "facts," and the cogency with which he presented them, made his argument irresistible, even though there is hardly an inference which he draws from his facts which would withstand more than a moment's critical examination.

The address was widely reported in the press of both England and the United States, and made a deep impression upon all who read it. When, less than six years later, Hunt died of a chill at the early age of thirty-six, one New York newspaper wrote, "Dr. Hunt, in his own clear knowledge and brave enthusiasm, was doing more for humanity, and the welfare of mankind, and for the glory of God, than all the philosophers, humanitarians, philanthropists, statesmen, and, we may say, bishops and clergy of England together."

Even though it is so utterly unsound, it was not considered so in its own time, nor for many years afterwards. One has only to survey the literature of the time to perceive how wide an influence Hunt's

*Reprinted from *Memoirs of the Anthropological Society of London* (Vol. 1), pp. 1-64.

address enjoyed. Published as it was at the height of the Civil War, it was taken up by the pro-slavery party as a rallying standard, and nothing could have been more helpful to its cause. It was, in fact, Hunt's address, as reported in the press and as published at length in all its greatly amplified sixty-four pages that set the style for the greater part of the "scientific" writing on this subject which followed for the next sixty years. It is of interest to note that during the whole of the nineteenth century virtually every writer on the subject of what we today call "race" was of the opinion that the Negro was in almost all respects inferior to the white man.

It is because Hunt's address had so great an influence in providing a pseudoscientific basis for this widely adopted opinion that his address is reprinted here. It is a document of great historic importance, and although it does not quite belong in the class of the forged *Protocols of Zion,* it has not been dissimilar in its effects. Hunt undoubtedly believed what he wrote—the authors of *The Protocols of Zion* had no illusions about the falsity of their work—but the consequences to millions of innocent people have been about the same, whereby there hangs a moral, only too obvious to draw.

The reader should not fail to pay careful attention to the notes.

I.—ON THE NEGRO'S PLACE IN NATURE.*

By James Hunt, Ph.D., F.S.A., F.R.S.L., F.A.S.L., Foreign Associate of the Anthropological Society of Paris, Honorary Fellow of the Ethnological Society of London, Corresponding Member of the Upper Hesse Society for Natural and Medical Science, etc., etc., and President of the Anthropological Society of London.

I propose in this communication to discuss the physical and mental characters of the Negro, with a view of determining not only his position in animated nature, but also the station to be assigned to him in the genus *homo*. I shall necessarily have to go over a wide field, and cannot hope to treat the subject in an exhaustive manner. I shall be amply satisfied if I succeed in directing the attention of my scientific friends to a study of this most important and hitherto nearly neglected branch of the great science of Anthropology.

It is not a little remarkable that the subject I propose to bring before you this evening is one which has never been discussed before a scientific audience

*Read Nov. 17, 1863.

in this Metropolis. In France, in America, and in Germany, the physical and mental characters of the Negro have been frequently discussed, and England alone has neglected to pay that attention to the question which its importance demands. I shall, therefore, make no apology for bringing this subject in its entirety under your consideration, although I should have preferred discussing each point in detail. I hope, however, this evening to bring before you facts and opinions that will lay a good foundation for future inquiry and discussion. Although I shall dwell chiefly on the physical, mental, and moral characters of the Negro, I shall, at the same time, not hesitate to make such practical deductions as appear to be warranted from the facts we now have at hand, and trust that a fair and open discussion of this subject may eventually be the means of removing much of the misconception which appears to prevail on this subject both in the minds of the public, and too frequently in the minds of scientific men. While, however, I shall honestly and without reservation state the conclusions at which I have arrived, I shall at the same time listen with deep attention and respect to those who differ from me, and who support their opinions by facts, by the opinions of some travellers, or by their own observations. Heretofore, however, it has happened that much human passion has been introduced, not only into public discussions, but especially into the literature on this subject. Even such a generally fair and philosophic writer as Professor Waitz has accused men of science with promulgating views which are practically in favour of the so-called "slavery" of the Confederate States of America. Many other scientific men could be named who have equally been guilty of imputing such unfair and uncharitable motives. While, on the other hand, writers thus accused retort by applying to their opponents all sorts of epithets. One author, for instance, exclaims: "How I loathe that hypocrisy which claims the same mental, moral, and physical equality for the Negro which the whites possess."* No good can come of discussion conducted in such a spirit. If we wish to discover what is the truth, we must give each other credit for honesty, and not impute base or interested motives.

In the first place, I would explain that I understand by Negro, the dark, woolly-headed African found in the neighbourhood of the Congo river. Africa contains, like every other continent, a large number of different races, and these have become very much mixed. These races may be estimated as a whole at about 150 millions, occupying a territory of between 13 and 14 millions of square miles. I shall not enter into any disquisition as to the great diversity of physical conformation that is found in different races, but shall simply say that my remarks will be confined to the typical woolly-headed Negro. Not only is there a large amount of mixed blood in Africa, but there are also appar-

---

*Negro Mania: being an examination of the falsely assumed equality of the various races of man; by John Campbell, Philadelphia, 1851, p. 11.

ently races of very different physical characters, and in as far as they aproach the typical Negro, so far will my remarks apply to them. But I shall exclude entirely from consideration all those who have European, Asiatic, Moorish or Berber blood in their veins.

My object is to attempt to determine the position which one well-defined race occupies in the genus homo, and the relation or analogy which the negro race bears to animated nature generally. We have recently heard discussions respecting Man's place in nature: but it seems to me that we err in grouping all the different races of Man under one generic name, and then compare them with the anthropoid Apes. If we wish to make any advance in discussing such a subject, we must not speak of man generally, but must select one race or species, and draw our comparison in this manner. I shall adopt this plan in comparing the Negro with the European, as represented by the German, Frenchman, or Englishman. Our object is not to support some foregone conclusion, but to endeavour to ascertain what is the truth, by a careful and conscientious examination and discussion of the facts before us. In any conclusion I may draw respecting the Negro's character, no decided opinion will be implied as to the vexed question of man's origin. If the negro could be proved to be a distinct species from the European, it would not follow that they had not the same origin—it would only render their identity of origin less likely. I shall, also, have to dwell much on the analogies existing between the Negro and the Anthropoid Apes; but these analogies do not necessarily involve relationship. The Negro race, in some of its characters, is the lowest of existing races, while in others it approaches the highest type of European: and this is the case with other savage races. We find the same thing in the Anthropoid Apes, where some species resemble man in one character, and some in another.

The father of English Ethnology, Dr. Prichard, thought that the original pair must have been Negroes, and that mankind descended from them. His words are:*—"It must be concluded that the process of nature in the human species is the transmutation of the characters of the Negro into those of the European, or the evolution of white varieties in black races of men. We have seen that there are causes existing which are capable of producing such an alteration, but we have no facts which induce us to suppose that the reverse of this change could in any circumstance be effected. This leads us to the inference that the primitive stock of men were Negroes, which has every appearance of truth." It is not a little remarkable that although Blumenbach and Prichard were both advocates for the unity of man, they materially differed in their argumentation. Blumenbach saw, in his five varieties of man, nothing but degeneracy from some ideal perfect type. Prichard, on the contrary, asserted he could imagine no arguments, or knew of no facts, to support such a conclusion. Prichard,

*Researches into the Physical History of Mankind, 1813, p. 233.

however, was not alone in this supposition; for Pallas,† Lacépède,‡ Hunter,§ Doornik,‡ and Link,¶ were also inclined to the same view. We must not dwell on such speculations; for on the present occasion we shall not touch on the origin of man: it will be enough if we assist in removing some of the misconceptions regarding the Negro-race existing in the minds of some men of science. It is too generally taught that the Negro only differs from the European in the colour of his skin and the peculiarity of his hair. The skin and hair are, however, by no means the only characters which distinguish the Negro from the European, even physically; whilst the mental and moral difference is still greater than the demonstrated physical difference. In the first place, what are the physical distinctions between the Negro and the European?

The average height of the Negro* is less than that of the European, and

†*Travels through the Southern Provinces of the Russian Empire*, in 1793-4.

‡*Vue Générale*, etc. Paris, 1822.

§*Disputatio inauguralis de Hominum Varietatibus et earum causis exponens*, etc. Joannes Hunter. Edinburgh, 1775.

‡*Wysgeerig-natuurkunding Onderzoek*, etc. Amst., 1808.

¶On this point Link (*Die Urwelt*, etc. Berlin, 1821-2) says:—"Soemmering's investigations (Die Körperliche Verschiedenheit des Negers, Frankfurt, 1785,) show how much more the Negro in his internal structure resembles the Ape than the European. The latest productions of the animal world were mammals, and it stands to reason that the most recent race should be that which is the most remote from the other mammals, and that race should be the oldest which approaches them most, namely, the Negro. Colour, also, confirms this everywhere, when we observe white and black animals of the same species. The latter always form the original stock, the former the deviation."

*"The stature of the Negro approaches the middle size. The tribes above the middle stature are probably more numerous than those below it. I know of no instances of dwarfism among Negroes, though the monuments of Egypt show that there were dwarfs among the Negroes at a very remote epoch. Nevertheless, giants and dwarfs occupy a certain place in the ideas and stories of the Negro, as well as tailed men. We know what to believe as regards the latter point. With respect to dwarfs, the Bosjesmen seem to answer the ideas of the Negroes, for they play in their stories the same part as the Hyperboreans in the traditions of ancient Greece. Obesity is exceptionally found in males of high rank, and more frequently in the women. The disposition to grow fat is less rare among the short than among the tall Negroes. The taller are frequently lank and very angular.

"On the examining the physiognomy of the Negro, I would first observe that the palpebral fissure is narrow and horizontal; but the aperture of the nostrils presents instead of a raised triangle a tranverse ellipsis; that the point of the nose is obtuse, round, and thick; that the ear is small, detached from the head, with a lobule little separated. To this must be added the cheeks stuffed by the masseters, the conformation of the jaws and lips, and the ensemble of the physiognomy of the Negro presents a singular mixture. The inferior part reflects sensuality, not to say more; above the mouth we might say it is the face of a new-born child enlarged. The absence of expression in the features produces the effect of an unfinished work. The change of colour, so significant in the white man, that mute language, but more effective than the spoken word which moves us, is almost entirely absent in our African brothers. The black veil which covers the whole, even withdraws the play of the muscles from the eye of the observer, unless it be in moments of passionate agitation.

"The eye alone enables us to judge what passes in the depth of the mind. This mirror is suf-

although there are occasionally exceptions, the skeleton of the Negro is generally heavier, and the bones larger and thicker in proportion to the muscles
than those of the European. The bones are also whiter, from the greater abundance of calcareous salts. The thorax is generally laterally compressed, and,
in thin individuals, presents a cylindrical form, and is smaller in proportion
to the extremities. The extremities of the Negro differ from other races more
by proportion than by form: the arm usually reaches below the middle of the
femur. The leg is on the whole longer, but is made to look short on account
of the ankle being only between 1-1/3 in. to 1-1/2 in. above the ground; this
character is often seen in mulattoes. The foot is flat, and the heel is both
flat and long. Burmeister has pointed out the resemblance of the foot and the
position of the toes of the Negro to those of the ape. The toes are small,

---

ficiently bright to enable us to distinguish two classes, which may be compared to the choleric
and phlegmatic temperaments. The travellers who have observed the Negro in his native country
indicate some expressive, and, so to say, national shades, which distinguish the peoples of the
Sudan. This is in harmony with the differences in features, stature, we shall speak of in the sequel.
We find thus among the authors the terms, "dignified and proud, jovial and gay, intelligent and
cunning;" also, "insignificant and inexpressive, melancholy and morose, dull and stupid." Thus
the Negro participates also in this respect largely of the nature of man in general; but it cannot
be said of him what was applied to the American, "Gentleness hovers on his lips, and ferocity
gushes from his eyes."

"The neck of the Negro is generally short; it is scarcely 8 to 9 centimetres, excepting very
tall subjects, when it attains 10 centimetres; the prominence of the larynx is rounded; the shoulders
are less powerful than in the Turanian or Aryan. The Negro prefers carrying his burden on the
head. The Negro is shrunk in the flank, the abdomen frequently relaxed; the umbilicus, situated
nearer the pubis than in the European, is slightly prominent.

"After these short remarks on the conformation of the trunk, we must fix our attention on
the limbs. We have already indicated the proportion of the parts which compose them. It now
remains to describe their particular form. The arm and the forearm of the Negro present neither
the muscular contours of the European nor the rounded shape of the American. The palm of
the hand, as well as the sole of the foot, are always of a bistre colour. The palm is narrow
and flattened; that is to say, the thenar and hypothenar eminences, as well as the tactile cushions,
are little developed. The folds of the palm are very simple and rudimentary. The fingers are elongated; of the little thickness at the ends; the nails are flat, bistre coloured, and rather widened
at the end.

"In the inferior limb we observe the fold of the buttocks less rounded, the thighs more angular
in front and specially at the back; the knees approximated; the calf usually weak, short, and
laterally compressed; the feet spread out; the heel wide and prominent; the lateral borders of
the feet straight, their anterior portion widened; the great toes short and small. The foot is rarely
highly arched; on the other hand it is elongated, and what it wants in height is made up by
the tibia, which is longer in proportion.

"This conformation of the foot of the Negro has induced a learned naturalist to take the foot
as the starting point to fix the type of races. But the particulars given by M. Simonot, on the
diversities met with in this respect among the peoples of the Senegal, which accord with the
reports of other travellers and my own observations, throw doubt upon the constancy of the conformation. On the other hand, it is certain that the type of the inferior limb, as I have described
it, is the appanage of the majority of Negroes. The flat foot is, however, also met with in a
large number of races approaching more the Aryan than the Negro; for instance, in some tribes

the first separated from the second by a free space.* Many observers have noticed the fact that the Negro frequently uses the great toe as a thumb. The knees are rather bent, the calves are little developed and the upper part of the thigh rather thin. The upper thigh-bone of the Negro has not so decided a resemblance to that of the ape as that of the bushman.† He rarely stands

---

of America and Polynesia. It is also frequent in Russia, and it frequently influences the reform of the military service in the rest of Europe. The shortening of the great toe, combined with a slight distance from the rest, has been noted in the Negro, in some races of Malaisia, and the Hottentot as a constant character approaching these peoples to the ape. The importance of the great toe is incontestable, for it is the first bone which disappears from the extremities on descending the animal series. I think it therefore necessary well to examine this point as regards the Negro. Now it is true that the great toe in the Negro rarely rises above the second, but neither is it often shorter. This applies also to the pretended lateral distance which may moreover be owing to the employment of thongs in their shoes, as done by the Arabs, for instance. It is clear that all that has been asserted relative to the opposition of the great toe of the Negro is reduced to the simple question: Is there a muscle, or at least an aponeurotic tendon, subservient to this pretended use? Nowhere, and never has anything like it been discovered in the human genus. But a slight shortening of the great toe undoubtedly exists, not merely among the Negro tribes, but also in ancient and modern Egyptians, and even in some of the most beautiful types of Caucasian females I have seen. This character is not merely constant in the ancient Egyptian statutes, it is also seen where art has fixed the characters of the ideal man, namely, in the sculptures of Greece. I am, however, as far from wishing to establish the identity of the foot of the Negro with that ideal type, as I am to class the inhabitants of Alsace among the Negroes, because many of them present the same peculiarity. (Pruner Bey. Memoire sur les Nègres, 1861.)

*"In most of the Africans the heel projects. From the skin of their feet being fit allows of greater flexibility and movement. Lawrence in his 'Lectures on Man' says, that the calves of the leg in the Negro race are very high, so as to encroach upon the hams. His observation I can fully corroborate, as well as Dr. Winterbottom's remark respecting the largeness of the feet, and the thinness and flexibility of the fingers and toes."—*Sierra Leone*, by Robert Clarke, p. 49. Mr. Louis Fraser also says, "He will pick up the most minute object with his toes; his 'great' toe is particularly flexible."

†"It is quite certain that the ape which most nearly approaches man, in the totality of its organisation, is either the chimpanzee or the gorilla; and as it makes no practical difference, for the purposes of my present argument which is selected for comparison, on the one hand, with man, and on the other hand, with the rest of the primates, I shall select the latter (so far as its organisation is known) as a brute now so celebrated in prose and verse, that all must have heard of him, and have formed some conception of his appearance. I shall take up as many of the most important points of difference between man and this remarkable creature, as the space at my disposal will allow me to discuss, and the necessities of the argument demand; and I shall inquire into the value and magnitude of these differences, when placed side by side with those which separate the gorilla from other animals of the same order. In the general proportions of the body and limbs there is a remarkable difference between the gorilla and man, which at once strikes the eye. The gorilla's brain-case is smaller, its trunk larger, its lower limbs shorter, its upper limbs longer in proportion than those of man. I find that the vertebral column of a full-grown gorilla, in the Museum of the Royal College of Surgeons, measures 27 inches along its anterior curvature, from the upper edge of the atlas or first vertebra of the neck to the lower extremity of the sacrum; that the arm, without the hand, is 31-1/2 inches long; that the leg, without the foot, is 26-1/2 inches long; that the hand is 9-3/4 inches long; the foot 11-1/4 inches long. In other words, taking the length of the spinal column as 100, the arm equals 115, the leg 96, the hand 36, and the foot 41. In the skeleton of a male Bosjesman, in the same collection, the

quite upright, his short neck and large development of the cervical muscles give great strength to the neck. The shoulders, arms, and legs are all weak in comparison to the corresponding limbs in the European. The hand is always relatively larger than in the European: the palm is flat, the thumb narrow, long, and very weak.

Dr. Pruner Bey has published the subjoined measurements* of the isolated bones in Europeans and Negroes. From Dr. Broca's careful investigations, it

---

proportions, by the same measurement, to the spinal column taken as 100, are—the arm 78, the leg 110, the hand 26, and the foot 32. In a woman of the same race the arm 83, and the leg 120, the hand and foot remaining the same. In a European skeleton I find the arm to be 80, the leg 117, the hand 26, the foot 35. Thus the leg is not so different as it looks at first sight, in its proportions to the spine in the gorilla and in the man, being very slightly shorter than the spine in the former, and between one-tenth and one-fifth longer than the spine in the latter. The foot is longer and the hand much longer in the gorilla; but the great difference is caused by the arms, which are very much longer than the spine in the gorilla, very much shorter than the spine in the man.''—*Evidence as to Man's Place in Nature*, by T. H. Huxley, 1863, p. 70.

---

* M. Pruner gives the following measures of the bones of the limbs in centimeters.

Designation of Measures	Mean Measures				Individual Measures					
	Negroes		Europeans		Negroes		Europeans			
	Males	Females	Males	Females	Man	Woman	Man	Woman	New-born Infant	Child 5 yrs. old
Total height of Skeleton	160.04	148.66	172.23	164.42	160.0	156.0	160.0	157.0	42.25	101.0
Femur	44.72	42.50	47.00	44.00	43.0	41.5	45.0	42.0	6.7	25.0
Tibia	38.09	35.33	38.76	37.71	39.0	38.5	36.0	36.0	6.0	22.0
Length of foot	24.50	21.83	25.00	23.57	23.5	21.5	24.0	23.0	"	"
Humerus	31.27	29.50	33.72	34.57	31.5	31.0	34.0	31.0	6.2	18.0
Radius	24.63	23.00	25.46	24.85	24.5	25.0	27.0	21.0	5.75	13.0
Length of hand	18.54	17.00	18.84	18.14	19.0	18.0	20.0	17.0	"	"

N.B.—''The preceding measures having been taken on skeletons, are only strictly correct as regards the isolated bones: femur, tibia, humerus, and radius. The lengths of hand and foot, and the total height of the skeleton, can only be approximative, as they are more or less modified by the mounters of the skeletons.

''By the side of the mean measures I have placed six individual measurements, viz.: a Negro and European of the same stature, and a European female and a Negress of the same height; and also a new-born European infant and a European child five years old. I wished to add a European child from thirteen to fifteen years old. It is at that age, according to M. Carus, our children most approach the Negro by the relative dimensions of their extremities.

''The skeletons of the European females, which served for measurement, are in the gallery of the museum, having been placed at my disposal by the kindness of M. Quatrefages. Nearly all of them are those of females above the middle height.''

results that the radius is decidedly longer in Negroes than in Europeans in proportion to the length of the humerus.† The proportion of the radius to the humerus, taken at 100, being in the Negro 79.40, and in the European 73.93.

The great distinguishing characters of the Negro are the following: the forehead is flat, low, and laterally compressed. The nose and whole face is flattened, and the Negro thus has a facial angle generally between 70-75 degs., occasionally only 65 degs. The nasal cavities and the orbits are spacious.‡

†*Bull de la Soc. Anthro.*, iii., p. 162.

‡*Facial cranium.*—"Before considering the anatomical details of the facial cranium, it is indispensable to note the disproportion existing between the size of the face and the cerebral cranium. This character, already indicated by Cuvier, depends chiefly on the excessive development of the jaws and the size of the cavities of the organs of sense. The orbits are large, funnel-shaped with obtuse angles; their inferior margin is thick, round, more advancing than the superior margin; the inferior is flattened; the depression lodging the lachrymal gland is very deep. The lachrymal canal is large, and almost exclusively formed by the nasal apophysis of the maxillary. The bones of the nose are short, narrow but quadrangular, very rarely triangular, and exceptionally soldered together, always joined at obtuse angles; they are sometimes on the same plane. The nasal aperture is large, of an irregular triangular form, wide, without a spine, or only the rudiment of one. The root of the depressed nose is only exceptionally in a right line with the forehead; the width of the root of the nose increases the distance between the eyes a little more in the Aryan, but less than in the Turanian race. Sometimes the nose of the Negro resembles, by its round aperture, that of the Hottentot. The cornets, especially the middle, are swelled out; the vertical lamina of the ethmoid is spread out, and the vomer stands out.

"The malar bones are neither large nor high, but are either embossed in the centre of their external surface, or distorted outwards by their inferior border. The superior jaw presents frequently in its malar apophysis a vertical pit; then the cheekbones form an angle, and their prominence appears great. When, on the contrary, the apophysis is flattened, and the inferior border of the malar is much advanced, this character, joined with the narrowness of the forehead, gives to the face a form approaching the pyramidal shape. The prominence of the external orbital apophyses of the coronal, the projection of the malar bones, and the antero-posterior direction of their frontal apophyses produce a malar angle less open than in the Aryan race; whilst, on the contrary, the lateral compression of the anterior lobe of the brain is marked by rather a right angle formed by the external wall of the orbit with the temple. The ascending apophyses of the maxillary have their internal border more or less curved according to the shape of the nose.

"Prognathism, that is to say, the inclination of the alveolar border of the superior jaw downwards and forwards from behind constitutes one of the most constant characters in the skeleton of the Negro. Three degrees are distinguished:—

"(1.) The alveolar arch, elliptic instead of parabolic, generally convex throughout, rarely concave at its external part, is alone inclined, and the teeth are vertical.

"(2.) The direction of the teeth is that of the jaw. In these two cases the superior incisors pass a little beyond the superior dental arch.

"(3.) The highest degree, which may be called double prognathism, presents itself when the inferior incisors are, like the superior, projected obliquely; then the junction of the two rows of incisors form the angle of a chisel. This latter form is not the most frequent. But in double prognathism, cases have been observed where, by a slight shortening of the horizontal rami of the inferior maxillary, the superior incisors presented upon their posterior surface triangular facettes produced by the points of the inferior incisors.

"The molar teeth of the superior jaw descend sometimes lower than the incisors, or are at least at a level with them, but rarely do the molars in the Negro participate in prognathism, as

The skull is very hard and unusually thick, enabling the Negroes to fight with, or carry heavy weights, on their heads. The coronal region is arched, but not so much developed as in the European woman. The posterior portion of the skull is increased, in proportion to that of the anterior part being diminished. But M. Gratiolet has shown that the unequal development of the anterior lobes is not the sole cause of the psychological inequalities of human races. The same scientific observer has also stated that in the superior, or frontal races, the cranial sutures close much later than in the inferior or occipital races. The frontal races he considers superior not simply from the form of the skull, but because they have an absolutely more voluminous brain. The frontal cavity being much larger than the occipital, a great loss of space is caused by the depression of the anterior region, which is not compensated for by the increase of the occipital region. From these researches it appears that in the Negro the growth of the brain is sooner arrested than in the European. This premature union of the bones of the skull may give a clue to much of the mental inferiority which is seen in the Negro race. There can be no doubt that at puberty a great change takes place in relation to psychical development; and in the

---

is the case with some Australians, or Oceanic Negroes. Never is, to my knowledge, the prognathism of the Negro confined to a simple inclination of the alveoli. I have only remarked this disposition in some female crania of the Aryan race of India.

"The palatine arch, and especially the alveolar apophyses are not merely much elongated, but more enlarged in the Negro than among the Aryans. This arch is, on the average, about sixty-five millimeteres in length in the Negro, and only fifty-eight in the Aryan.

"The inferior jaw, always more or less massive, is distinguished by a chin, retracted, generally large and rounded, rarely pointed, and by the thickness and length of its external rami. Its ascending rami are large, short, and their junction with the horizontal are rarely at right angles. The coronoid apophyses are always large, with an elliptic surface, flattened or oblique on its external half. The glenoid cavities are large and mostly of little depth. The teeth of the Negro are long, large, strikingly white, and not easily used up. The inferior molars sometimes present five tubercles, an anomaly which is sporadically found in all races of mankind. The jaw of the Negro never presented to me any trace of an intermaxillary bone (I owe to M. E. Rousseau's kindness the firm conviction of the non-existence of the intermaxillary bone in man in the normal state. His treatise places this important fact, now for ever acquired by anatomical science, beyond any doubt), though the incisive suture may be perfectly distinguished in the adult Negro at a period when the cranial sutures are mostly obliterated.

"The consistence of the cranial bones of the Negro is always considerable; but their thickness varies much, chiefly according to the volume of the cranium. Placed by the side of the Oceanian Negro, for instance, the cranium of the African would in this, as well as other respects, produce the impression of belonging to a civilised man, opposed to that of a savage, if this term be applicable to a man who, more or less, lives in a state of nature.

"Before quitting the examination of the cranium, I cannot pass over the facial angle of the Negro. It naturally varies, as in the other races, according to the greater or lesser inclination of the face, according to the development of the frontal sinuses; and, as regards the conformation of the face, it sinks, though rarely to 70°. But, on the other hand, the frontal angle of the Negro reaches to 80°. We, however, attach but a relative value to these two angles, for though the median line of the forehead is rather vertical in the Negro, the cranium is faulty, as regards the forehead, by an evident lateral contraction." (Pruner-Bey).

Negro there appears to be an arrested development of the mind exactly harmonising with the physical formation. Young Negro children are nearly as intelligent as European children; but the older they grow the less intelligent they become. They exhibit, when young, an animal liveliness for play and tricks far surpassing the European child. The young ape's skull resembles more the Negro's head than the aged ape: thus showing a striking analogy in their craniological development.

It has been pointed out that there were four forms of the human pelvis, and that they might be classified under the following heads:—The oval (European), round (American), square (Mongol), and oblong (African). The latest researches of Dr. Pruner Bey enable him to affirm that this law is perfectly applicable to the Negro. The head of the Negro is the best type of the long skull, with small development of the frontal region. The form of the pelvis is narrow, conical, or cuneiform, and small in all its diameters. Vrolik has asserted that the pelvis of the male Negro bears a great resemblance to that of the lower mammalia. With respect to the capacity of the cranium of the Negro, great difference ·of opinion has prevailed.* Tiedemann's researches,

*Dr. Pruner-Bey gives the following interesting summary of the Osteological peculiarities of the Negro race:—

Of the Cranium.—"Cerebral cranium.—The antero-posterior diameter of the cerebral cranium approaches 19 centimeters; the transversal diameter is about 13.6; the face measures, from the chin to the hair, 18 centimeters; and the distance of the zygomatic arches is 13 centimeters. I class the cranium of the Negro in the category of harmonic dolichocephali.

Cerebral Vertebrae.—"The coronal bone is rather short and narrow than receding backwards, frequently distinguished by slender superciliary arches, rarely by frontal bumps, but usually by a protuberance on the median line, which corresponds with the third primordial convolution of the brain. A slight compression is clearly marked on the two sides of the protuberance. The nasal apophysis is always more or less large, according to the conformation of the nose. The orbital apophyses, large at the base, are more curved downwards than outwards. The temporal portion of the coronal presents frequently on the top a slight dilatation, at the bottom on the contrary it is compressed. The contours vary, according to the general form of the cranium, when this is very much elongated and compressed on the sides, the coronal is more elliptic, and more parabolic when the contrary is the case. The frontal sinuses exist; they are but moderately developed as all the aerial reservoirs. The summit of the cranium presents along the sagittal suture an ogival or flattened, rarely vaulted, conformation. The great extent of the second cranial vetebra, and its predominance over the first and third, is clearly defined, specially at the posterior part where the parietals slope gently down towards the occiput, whilst their descent towards the temples is always very abrupt. In cases where the cranium of the male negro approaches the female type, the posterior descent of the parietals approaches a vertical line, and the horizontal section represents a wedge, instead of an ellipsis, which predominates in the typical form of the Negro cranium.

"When the cranium is viewed in profile, the temples appear deeply hollowed in front, flattened or elongated backwards. The anterior margins of the temporals are frequently joined to the coronal, on account of the shortening of the great alae of the sphenoid. The parietal knobs are lower and less marked in the male than in the female, and the superior semicircular lines, though well marked, reach rarely the arch of the cranium. The squamous part of the temporal is relatively low and long; its margins are irregular. The zygomatic arches are convex, rarely flattened; the meatus auditorius presents a large and usually round orifice. The greatest width of the cranium is thus

although very limited, have until recently been accepted as conclusive. He stated it as his opinion that "The brain of the Negro is, upon the whole, quite as large as that of the European and other human races; the weight of the brain, its dimensions, and the capacity of the *cavum cranii* prove this fact."* All recent researches have, however, done much to show that Tiedemann's investigations are not only unsatisfactory, but that his deduction is not warranted by the facts which we now have at hand. Blumenbach's, Knox's and Lawrence's conclusions did not accord with Tiedemann's. But the most satisfactory researches on this point are those made by the late Dr. Morton, of America, and his successor, Dr. J. A. Meigs, of Philadelphia. Dr. Meigs, in following out the researches of his predecessor, has found that in size of the brain, the Negro comes after the European, Fin, Syro-Egyptian, Mongol, Malay, Semitic, American Indian, and the Esquimaux; but that the brain of the Negro-race takes precedence of the ancient civilised races of America, the Egyptian of all periods, the Hindoo, the Hottentot, the Australian, and the

---

as frequently found at the posterior and superior angle of the squamous temporal as at the level of the parietal protuberances. Taken from this point, the cranium diminishes in breadth towards the occiput, especially when the latter projects, which is seen in most cases. There is a rather striking parallelism between the coronal and the superior part of the occipital squama; the latter being relatively small, curved, narrow, like the frontal squama and in the elliptic crania it is arched in the centre. In this case its margins intercept an obtuse angle; in the contrary case they are parabolic. The Wormian bones may be met with in the crania of Negroes, and even form a complete series along the lambdoid suture; but these cases are rare.

"The base of the cranium is always relatively narrow; that part of the occipital squama where the muscles are attached, presents sometimes a horizontal, but more frequently a slightly inclined, long, and narrow plane. In the first form the superior part of the squama rises more to a right angle towards the lambdoid suture than in the second form. The surface of the squama, marked by the imprint of the muscles, represents a truncated pyramid the base of which touches the anterior border of the great occipital foramen. This aperture, always of a more or less elongated shape, is slightly inclined from before backwards, so that its posterior border at least is above the level of the palatine arch. Its position in relation to the centre of gravity is in accord with dolichocephaly. (The distance from the occipital hole to the base of the nose and the alveolar margins of the incisors, is naturally more considerable in the Negro than in the orthognathous races; but the distance of this hole to the base of the forehead, presented only slight differences. In the brachycephalous races, on the contrary, especially in those with flattened occiput, the occipital foramen is farther back. It is, moreover, difficult to find crania in which this aperture corresponds exactly to the centre of the cranium, as asserted by some anatomists.) The condyles of the occiput are elongated, narrow, much inclined. The petrous portion of the temporal voluminous. The basilar bone is long, narrow, slightly inclined from before backwards. The development of the mastoid apophyses corresponds with the greater or lesser massiveness of the cranium; the styloid apophyses are frequently much elongated; the pterygoid apophyses are large, distant, and more or less inclined. The union of the palate with the maxillary is usually formed by an indented or undulated, instead of by a plain suture. The palate is elongated, elliptic rather than parabolic, superficial, or deep. It is only in exceptional cases that its width exceeds its length. All the apertures at the base of the cranium are very spacious. We are at the same time struck by the elliptic contours of this base and its general flatness, which renders the elevation of the borders of the occipital foramen more perceptible."

Philosophical Transactions, 1836.

Negroes of Polynesia. Thus we see that the Negro has at least six well-defined races above him, and six below him, taking the internal cavity of the skull as a test. Pruner Bey says that his own experience with the external measurements did not yield essentially different results. But we now know that it is necessary to be most cautious in accepting the capacity of the cranium simply, as any absolute test of the intellectual power of any race.

The recent researches of Huschke on this point are most significant and valuable. He gives the following mean measurements of the surface of the cranium, viz. :—

Male Negro	Male European
53206 square millimètres.	59305 square millimètres.
Female.	Women.
49868 " "	53375 " "

Relative size of three cranial vertebrae expressed in hundredths (1).

	Negro.	Negress.	Male European.	Female European.
1st Vertebra	7.7	8.1	9.7	9.68
2nd and 3rd together	92.3	91.9	90.3	90.32
	100.0	100.0	100.0	100.00
2nd Vertebra alone	75.7	76.4	72.7	74.1
3rd Vertebra	24.3	23.6	27.3	25.9
	100.0	100.0	100.0	100.0

"It is surprising," says Pruner Bey, who quotes these tables, "to observe to what a degree the mean capacity of the Negro cranium* approaches in its *ensemble* that of the European female, and particularly how much in both the middle vertebra predominates above the two others; whilst on the contrary, in the European male, the posterior vertebra, and particularly the anterior, are more developed in relation to the middle vertebra than they are in the Negro and in the European female. It should be remarked that the occipital vertebra of the Negress is more spacious than that of the Negro."

Tiedemann asserted that the brain of the Negro did not resemble that of the Oran-útan more than that of the European, except in the more symmetrical distribution of the gyri and sulci. Tiedemann also denied Sömmering's assertion that the nerves of the Negro are larger, in proportion to the brain, than in the European; but Pruner Bey has confirmed Sömmering's opinion.

There seems to be, generally, less difference between the Negro and the

Negress,* than between the European male and female: but on the other hand, the Negress, with the shortened humerus, presents a disadvantage "which one might be tempted to look at as a return to the animal form" (Pruner). Lawrence

Pruner Bey quotes the following Table respecting the cerebral cranium of the Negro.

DESIGNATION OF MEASURES	Mean Measures in Millimeters	
	Mean of 24 Negroes	Mean of 12 Negresses
1°. DIAMETER (By Compass)		
Antero-posterior	186.4	176.4
Vertical	124.8	"
Transverse Diameters — Inferior frontal	100.0	95.8
Superior frontal	113.4	108.7
Bi-temporal	125.0	119.2
Bi-auricular	112.7	108.0
Bi-parietal	134.2	130.0
Bi-mastoidian	117.7	111.6
2°. CURVES (By Metrical Tape)		
Horizontal circumference	511.7	492.5
Transversal bi-auricular curve	305.2	295.5
Vertical antero-posterior circumference	504.0	489.8
Decomposed in: 1°. Middle part — Frontal part	105.0 ⎫	108.3 ⎫
Parietal part	136.5 ⎬ 355.9	128.3 ⎬ 364.5
Occipital part	114.4 ⎭	109.9 ⎭
2°. Inferior part — Length from the occipital foramen	35.9 ⎫	34.0 ⎫
Distance from the anterior margin of the foramen to the frontal eminence	112.2 ⎬ 148.1	104.3 ⎬ 138.3
3°. OTHER MEASURES.		
Distance in a straight line from the meatus auditorius — to Nasal eminence	113.1	107.1
to occipital protuberance	110.9	107.0
Dimensions of the occipital foramen — length	35.9	34.0
breadth	30.3	28.0
4°. MILLESIMAL RATIO		
Circumferences — horizontal circumference	1000	1000
vertical	985	984
Diameters — length (antero-posterior diameter)	1000	1000
breadth (parietal diameter)	720	737
height (vertical diameter)	669	585

*See *Mémoires de la Société d'Anthropologie,* 1861.

The Negress.—"Before reviewing the chief varieties which the Negro type offers to travellers, it is necessary to cast a glance at the Negress.

"She possesses a cranium shorter, rounder, and wider in the posterior part of the middle vertebra; the parietal protuberances are more prominent, the apertures of the orbits frequently nearly circular, characters which approach her a little to the European female. As regards stature and the length of the hair, as well as in the proportions of the parts composing the inferior limb, the Negress resembles her husband more than the European female resembles her husband. As regards the latter point, it is not rare to find also in Europe, females of high stature and a muscular aspect. The features of the face do not, in the two sexes of the Sudan, present the same differences as in the Aryan race. The mammae are less rounded, but already more conical in early age. Their relaxing is rapid and excessive. This peculiarity is, however, though in a less degree, found in Oriental females in other places, and of different origin. The pelvis presents, as regards width, says,‡ "the Negro structure approaches unequivocally to that of the ape;" while Bory St. Vincent,* and Fischer† do not greatly differ in their description of the anatomy of the Negro from the facts I have adduced.

There is no doubt that the Negro brain‡ bears a great resemblance to a Euro-

---

some advantage over that of the male; the iliac bones are inclined towards the horizon, thinning towards the centre, without, however, being transparent; the haunches are rounder, steatopygy (fatty lumps on the buttocks) is only exceptionally met with. The neck of the matrix is large and elongated: the aperture of the vagina has a forward direction, despite of the inclination of the pelvis." (Pruner Bey.)

†Mr. Lawrence thus summarises the chief physical characters of the Negro "The characters of the Ethiopian variety, as observed in the genuine Negro tribes, may be thus summed up:—1. Narrow and depressed forehead; the entire cranium contracted anteriorly; the cavity less, both in its circumference and transverse measurements. 2. Occipital foramen and condyles placed farther back. 3. Large space for the temporal muscles. 4. Great development of the face. 5. Prominence of the jaws altogether, and particularly of their alveolar margins and teeth; consequent obliquity of the facial line. 6. Superior incisors slanting. 7. Chin receding. 8. Very large and strong zygomatic arch projecting towards the front. 9. Large nasal cavity. 10. Small and flattened ossa nasi, sometimes consolidated, and running into a point above."—Lectures on Physiology, Zoology, and the Natural History of Man, 1819, p. 363.

*Bory de St. Vincent (L'homme, Paris, 1827) says:—"Large; the skin black and entirely glossy, with the rete mucosum of Malpighi thicker and also black; hair black, woolly, felted together; the anterior part of the skull very narrow; flattened on the vertex, and rounded behind; eyes large, subrotund, prominent, always damp, cornea yellowish, iris tinted of a chestnut black, eyebrows very short; nose flat (nasal bones flattened); zygomatic arches protuberant; ears of moderate size and prominent; lips thick and brown; inside of the ears bright red; jaws, especially the lower one, projecting; incisor teeth procumbent; chin short, round, receding; beard rare; breasts pear-shaped, loose during milking; thighs and shanks partially curved."

†Fischer (Synopsis Mammalium, 1829-30), says:—"The brain is less, and the origins of the nerves thicker than in the American races, an opposite condition prevailing in the Japetic races; skull-cap one-ninth less ample than in the European, sutures more narrow, all the bones whiter; intermaxillary bone inclining above the chin; pelvic bones broad; muscles, blood, and bile of deep colour; foetid sweat; filthy; voice sharp and shrieking; nervous-phlegmatic temperament."

‡Pruner-Bey makes the following observations respecting the brain: "Soemmering had already observed that the peripheral nerves are larger, relative to the volume of the brain, in the Negro than in the white man. This fact is demonstrated in all its details by the beautiful preparation from the skilful hand of M. Jacquart, exhibited in the gallery of the Museum of Natural History.

"The brain, narrow and elongated, presents on its surface always a brownish tint on account of a considerable injection of venous blood. The superficial veins are very large, and resemble by their stiffness the sinus of the dura mater. The grey matter shows in the interior a clear brown colour; the white substance is yellowish. I am inclined to attribute this colour rather to the blood than to a special pigment. Melanotic patches may be met with in the meninges as elsewhere. Soemmering has observed blackish spots on the spinal marrow. The cortical layer of the grey substance of the cerebral hemispheres is of less thickness than in the European. Regarded in front the brain presents a rounded point; from the top the parts appear grosser and less varied than in the European. The convolutions, especially the anterior and the lateral, are flat and of little depth, excepting the primary convolution, the curvature of which produces the frontal eminence. In following the undulations from the front backwards, we remark less lateral deviations in the convolutions, which render the Aryan brain a real labyrinth. In the middle lobe the convolutions seem considerably raised, but they are coarse. The posterior lobe has always appeared to me flattened on the top, as the anterior at the base. Viewed in profile, it is chiefly the direction

pean female or child's brain, and thus approaches the ape far more than the European,* while the Negress approaches the ape still nearer.

With regard to the chemical constituents of the brain of the Negro, little that is positive is yet known. It has been found, however, that the grey substance of the brain of a Negro is of a darker colour than that of the European, that the whole brain has a smoky tint, and that the *pia mater* contains brown spots, which are never found in the brain of a European. M. Broca has recently

---

of the fissure of Sylvius and its interior which has occupied the attention of anatomists. (Huschke cites with reserve the observations of Van der Kolk, who places in parallel some peculiarities of this region of the Negro brain with the disposition existing in apes. This part of cerebral anatomy has as yet been little cultivated, and before arriving at conclusions we should wait until the modifications which the human brain undergoes in all the periods of its development are better known than they are at present; hence I confine myself simply to draw attention to Van der Kolk's remarks. In order to establish race characters upon such data, we should not forget what Rousseau says of the brain of Cuvier: "Multiplied convolutions were in the centre, surmounted by a mammilated exuberance, which formed an integral part of these convolutions." Are we on that account disposed to assume that this great man belonged to another race?) With regard to the former, I have never been able to observe any appreciable difference between the brain of the Negro and that of the Egyptian, which I have placed side by side in order better to study the relation of the parts externally. The superior part of the brain above the corpus callosum is relatively little elevated. The cerebellum has a less angular form than in the European; the vermis and the pineal gland are very large. Finally, the consistence of the cerebral mass is unquestionably greater in the Negro than in the white man.

"The inspection of the Negro brain shows that the convolutions of the centre are clearly marked as in the Aryan foetus of seven months (Reichert), and that the secondary details are less distinct. By its rounded apex, its less developed posterior lobe, it resembles the brain of our children; by the prominence of the parietal lobe it resembles that of our females, only that the latter is broader in the European female. The form of the cerebellum, the volume of the vermis and the pineal gland also place the Negro by the side of the Aryan child.

"Having indicated the general characters relating to the external form of the great nervous centre, I must say a word with respect to its weight and the relative proportions between cerebrum and cerebellum. The number of observations on this point is very restricted, nevertheless we obtain some important points. First, the extremes present a scarcely credible difference, were it not confirmed by the great diversity in the measurement of the horizontal circumference of the cranium. Mascagni gives 738 grammes as the weight of one brain and 1587 grammes as the weight of another. The results obtained by Soemmering and Cooper seem to approach the average weight: 1354,5 and 1458 grammes. The mean for the weight of the cerebellum compared to that of the cerebrum would be : : 13,83 : 85,93. Measurement shows that the cerebellum of the Negro, in accord with the general form, excels by 3,13 in length that of the European, which is, however, broader. Weight and measurement establish that the two sexes present less differences in both respects in the Negro race than in the Aryan race."—*Pruner Bey.*

*"The situation of the foramen magnum of the occipital bone is still a matter of dispute. Dr. Prichard thought it to be 'the same in the Negro as in the European;' and so it may be, if no allowance be made for the face. The situation of the foramen magnum of the occipital bone is not the same in the Negro as in the European. Dr. Prichard says it is exactly behind the transverse lines, bisecting the antero-posterior diameter of the base of the cranium. Supposing this measurement to be correct, which it is not, it has nothing to do with the *pose* or position of the head upon the vertebral column, which, all must know, depends on the position of the condyles of the occipital bone. A line bisecting the antero-posterior diameter of the skull, and dividing into

had an opportunity of confirming the truth of this statement.* With regard
to the convolutions, there is unanimous testimony that the convolutions of the
brain of the Negro are less numerous and more massive than in the European.
Waitz thinks that the only resemblance of the Negro's brain to that of the
ape is limited to this point.† Some observers have thought they have detected
a great resemblance between the development of the temporal lobe in the Negro
and ape; but much further observation is required on this important subject.

---

two equal parts, passes in the European head through the centre of the condyles of the occipital
bone; and the same measurement applies nearly to the antero-posterior diameter of the entire head.
Not so in the coloured races. In speaking of the base of the cranium, I am not quite sure to
which Prichard and his followers allude; for very generally in anatomical works the base of the
skull, including the upper jaw, is confounded with the true base of the skull.'' Robert Knox.
Anthropoligical Review, vol. i., p. 266. M. Broca has well pointed out the contradictions of
Prichard as to the position of the foramen magnum, and clearly establishes the fact that it is
placed further back in the Negro than in the European. *Bull. de la Soc. d'Anthropologie*, vol.
iii., p. 524.

*The following observations by M. Paul Broca on the brain of the Negro is extracted from
Bulletins de la Soc. d'Anthropologie, 1860. Before reading a manuscript addressed to the Society
by Professor Gubler, of the Faculty of Medicine, M. Broca stated the circumstances which induced
Professor Gubler to present it. A negro died in the Hospital de la Pitié. The body was brought
to the amphitheatre of Clamart, when M. Broca asked of the prosector of the hospital to examine
the brain of that body. Owing to the great heat of the month of August, the body was already
in an incipient state of decomposition, and the brain was too soft to study the convolutions. M.
Broca had, therefore, to confine himself to examining the colour of the substance. In order to
render the examination more easy, M. Broca opened at the same time the cranium of a white
subject, which was brought in the same day. The pia mater of the Negro presented in certain
spots a brown tint; nothing of the kind existed in the white subject. The white substance of the
Negro brain had a smoky tint, but it was especially in the grey substance that the brown tint
was marked. The two brains were placed in two separate vases containing the same quantity of
alcohol. After three days they were sufficiently firm to be examined. The difference of coloration
was then as decided as on the first day. In order approximately to determine the relative weight
of the two brains, they were, after the removal of the membranes, dried upon some linen during
a few minutes, and placed in the scale. The brain of the white subject weighed 1003 grammes,
that of the black weighed only 925.5 grammes, being a difference of 8.3 per 100. This individual
fact would be insignificant if it did not accord with the known data. Thus it is well known that
the measurements of the capacity of the cranium made by Meigs, according to Morton's method,
gave an average of 93-1/2 cubic inches for European and Anglo-American crania, and only 82-1/4
for Negro crania, being a difference of 11-1/4 cubic inches; that is to say, that the cranial capacity
of the Negro being represented by 100, that of the European is represented by 112. M. Broca
had preserved in alcohol the least altered portion of the Negro brain, and presented it to the
Anthropological Society; but fearing that the long contact with the alcohol might modify its coloration (which, however, it did not), he showed it when fresh to the Biological Society. Already,
some ten years ago, M. Rayer made to the same Society an analogous present: and it is known
that since Meckel in 1753 published a paper on this subject in the *Memoirs of the Prussian
Academy of Science*, many authors have stated that the brain of the Negro is notably of a darker
colour than that of the white man.''

†See Introduction to *Anthropology*, by Dr. Theodor Waitz. Edited from the first volume of
Anthropologie der Naturvölker, by J. Frederick Collingwood, Esq., F.G.S., F.R.L.S., F.A.S.L.,
Hon. Sec. of the Anthropological Society of London, Foreign Associate of the Anthropological
Society of Paris, p. 93.

The eyes are more separated than in the European, but not so much so as in the Mongol. The aperture of the eye is narrow, horizontal, and both eyes are wide apart. All the teeth, especially the last molars, are generally large, long, hard, and very white, and usually show little signs of being worn. In some Negro-skulls there has been found an extra molar in the upper jaw. There is also sometimes a space between the incisors and canine* teeth of the upper jaw. The inferior molars sometimes present in the Negro race five tubercles, and this anomaly is sporadically found in other races.† It has been noticed in the European and the Esquimaux, but is said by my friend Mr. Carter Blake to be more frequent in the Negro and Australian than in any other race. Sometimes Negroes have thirty-four instead of thirty-two teeth. The skin between the fingers, according to Van der Hoeven,* reaches higher up than in the European. The skin is also much thicker, especially on the skull, the palm of the hand, and the sole of the foot. The *rete mucosum*, which is the chief seat of coloration, presents nothing particular as regards structure.† The

*"The conical form [of the canine] I find best expressed in the Melanian races, especially the Australian. . . . It is also very well marked in the dentition of the Mozambique Negro, figured by F. Cuvier.—*Dents des Mammifères*, pl. 1;" *Owen. Odontography*, 4to., London, 1840-45, p. 452.

†"An examination of the teeth in a considerable number of African Negro crania has enabled us to draw the following conclusions:—In the African Negro the teeth are usually of large, but not excessive, size: they are regular, commonly sound, although caries is occasionally observed, and they seldom present that extreme amount of wearing down of the cutting and grinding surfaces which may be found so commonly in the Australian and Polynesian. The incisors are large, broad and thick, but not of greater absolute dimensions than in numerous individuals amongst the white varieties. The teeth do not depart from the human type in their relative proportions; for wherever the incisors and canines are of considerable size, the true molars are likewise large, and maintain that superiority which is a distinguishing feature of the teeth of Man. The lateral incisors are well formed, and in the perfect entirety of their outer angles they adhere more invariably to the human type than do the same teeth in some more civilised races. The canines are not proportionally longer or more pointed than in the white man. The premolars agree in configuration and relative size with the typical standard. The true molars are usually of large size, generally larger than in the European; the dentes sapientiae, although smaller than the other molars, are in the majority of instances of greater relative and actual dimensions, and the fangs of the last-named teeth are usually distinct in both jaws. But in the character of their grinding surfaces and their general contour, the molars of the African Negro present no departure from the typical configuration, and, as in other races, there are many instances in which a general description will not entirely apply. . . . We would observe that, according to our limited experience, the general characteristics of the African Negro dentition are best exemplified (albeit liable to exception) in the Negroes of the Western Coast. The teeth in the crania we have seen from Eastern Central Africa, and from the Mozambique, appeared to us to present less markedly the minor differences above noted. The prognathic development of the jaws also, and the consequent obliquity of implantation of the incisor teeth, though common in a varying degree to all African nations, not excluding the Egyptians, attains its greatest development in crania from the Western Coast."—F. C. Webb. *Teeth in Man and Anthropoid Apes*, p. 41.

Bijdragen tot de Natuurlijke Geschiedenis van der Negerstam, Leyden, 1842.

†M. Pruner thus speaks of the skin:—"Having now indicated the more prominent characters of the skeleton, I pass to the examination of the Negro with his integuments.

"The skin, supple and cool to the touch, presents a velvety aspect (besides the shades of colour already mentioned). Upon the abdomen such prominences form zigzags and broken fine lines; on the forearm they are seen in the form of small lozenges, and even in the extremities the skin is not altogether smooth. This aspect is partly the consequence of the great development of the glandular apparatus, indicating a great turgescence of the tissues. Thus the skin of the penis does not merely present simple folds, but mammilated eminences. The dermis is thicker than in the other races, specially of the cranium, the palm, and the sole. The epidermis of an ash-grey colour is very resisting. The rete mucosum, which is the chief seat of the coloration, presents nothing particular as regards its structure. Its contents, viz., the pigment, is deposited in a shapeless mass, or in granules, chiefly around and in the interior of the nuclei of polyhedric cells, which are disposed in numerous irregular layers. The pigment presents shades of colour according to the position of the cells. The deeper and more coloured cells are of a blackish brown, whilst those approaching more the dermis of a more or less dilute yellow resemble the serosity of the blood (Koelliker). The coloured web may be considered as the complement of the epidermis, to which it adheres more closely than to the dermis, so that it is detached in blistering, though some patches usually remain on the dermis. The colour of the cicatrices in Negroes differs according to the colour of the individual, and the time elapsed since the cicatrisation. I have observed nothing noteworthy in this respect. It is known that the lines in tattooing present a deeper colour than the skin from the materials rubbed in.

"The Negro loses a portion of the pigment on being transported to the north. It is always upon the prominent parts, such as the nose, the ears, &c., that a slight diminution is observed in dark subjects. I have, however, never observed this change in individuals with a velvety black skin which has sometimes a blueish shade. But in chronic diseases the diminution of the pigment is very perceptible; thus the Negro grows, in a certain matter, pale like the European. It is a general rule that the deeper coloured a Negro is, compared to other individuals of his tribe, the better is his health. With regard to the relation between the degree of coloration and the intellect, the accounts of travellers do not agree. Thus, Dr. Barth asserts that in the centre of the Sudan, the most glossy jet black skin belongs to the most intelligent tribes. The example of the Yaloffs seems to confirm this as regards the West. Mr. Speke, on the contrary, states with regard to the Eastern populations between Mozambique and Lake Nyassa, that the tribes of a lighter colour, though Negroes in all other respects, by far excel in activity, bravery, and intelligence their jet black brothers. Very probably both versions are correct; for we see in India, as well as Arabia, the two extremes of colour combined with the same intellectual capacities in peoples evidently congeners.

"The intensity of the colour does not depend on the geographical latitude in the tropical zone of Africa. The extremes of the chromatic scale are in juxtaposition in the principal spots, on the Senegal as well as on the Gaboon, north of the Niger and south of Lake Tsad, towards the Bay of Biaffra as in Mozambique, where M. Froberville counted thirty-one different shades of colour. Continued displacements have so much intermixed the tribes, and amalgamated entire nations, that it would be vain to determine, even by approximation, the primitive country of the true Negroes, and to derive therefrom any theory regarding the influence of geographical latitude on coloration. It is equally impossible to establish the degrees of intermixture which the representatives of the chromatic map have undergone. But, taking the deep brown or black Negro as the starting-point, can we attribute his colour to the soil, the air, the position of the sun, the great fluctuations between the diurnal and nocturnal temperature, an aliment rich in carbon such as the butter-tree, fermented liquors, &c., on one side, and the physiological reaction of the organism on the other? Must we, as regards the latter point, take in account the important part which the skin and the liver take in the respiratory functions according as we proceed from north to south? Must we admit that, in this respect, extremes meet, so that in turning to the high north, we find the coloration increase as we approach the pole? Science is as yet not in possession of the necessary facts to solve this question; experimental physiology must encounter it. As regards the etiology of the colour of the Negro, we must recur to the laws of heredity."

hair of the Negro is essentially* different from that of the European, and consists of coarse, crisp, resembling a frizzly sort of wool, growing in tufts like the wool of sheep. It is rarely more than three inches long, and generally not nearly so much.* The larynx in the Negro is not much developed, and the voice resembles sometimes the alto of an eunuch. In the male the voice is low and hoarse, and in the female it is acute and shrieking; at least, this is the opinion that has generally been given by Hamilton Smith and others: but

---

The same author makes the following remarks respecting the distribution of the pigment on the mucous membranes, the subcutaneous tissue, and the viscera:—"The pigment is in the form of black patches, found not merely upon the tongue, the velum, the conjunctivae, and the external angles of the eye, but also upon the mucous membrane of the intestinal canal, etc.

"The cellular tissue is very abundant, especially on the erectile organs. The mammae, penis, lips, ears, and nostrils. The colour of the conjunctivae, always more or less injected, is more or less yellowish; the fat is always of a wax colour. An analogous coloration is observed in all the cellular and fibrous membranes and even in the periosteum. The development of the muscles, excepting the masseters, the external muscles of the ear, the larynx, and sometimes of the temporals, are not in proportion to the weight of the bones; their colour is never of the bright red of the European, but rather of a yellowish tint, sometimes approaching the brown. M. Eschricht has found the muscles of the larynx very strong, the crico-thyroidei are especially large; he has moreover found that a portion of the fibres of these last muscles ascend to the internal surface of the thyroid cartilage. Should that be a trace of the internal crico-thyroid muscles of the hylobate apes? The visible mucous membranes of the mouth, the nostrils, etc., are of a cherry colour, excepting the lips which are bluish.

"As upon the skin, so is the glandular system much developed in the internal integument; the intestinal canal always presents a broken aspect, especially in the stomach and the colon. The intestinal mucus is very thick, especially the liver and the supra renal capsules; a venous hyperaemia seems the ordinary condition of these organs. The position of the bladder is higher than in the European. I find the seminal vesicles very large, always gorged with a turbid liquid of a slightly greyish colour, even in cases where the autopsy took place shortly after death. The penis is always of unusually large size, and I found in all bodies a small conical gland on each side at the base of the fraenum.

"The vascular apparatus is very strong; but the nervous system visibly predominates over the arterial. The small arteries present everywhere numerous flexuosities.

"The heart is powerfully organised and the right cavities are always very spacious. I have never observed here the least anomaly. The blood of the Negro (apart from anaemia and the dropsy) is always very thick, viscid, and pitchy; it rarely is projected in a jet in bleeding; it strongly adheres to the vessel, and always presents a serosity of a more or less dark yellow colour. The lungs relatively much less voluminous than the viscera of the abdomen, are usually melanose and pushed in by the stomach, the spleen, and the liver; it might be said that the latter organ usurps their place."

*Dr. Pruner-Bey has just contributed a most valuable paper to the Anthropological Society of Paris, *De la chevelure comme caractéristique des races humaines, d'après des recherches microscopiques*. A translation of this article will be found in the fourth number of the *Anthropological Review*.

*"The hair of the adult Negro is very fine, hard and elastic; generally black, exceptionally of a fiery red, resembling wool, in describing several circles from 6 to 8 millimeters. Its length in the male is usually from 9-12 centimeters. In the Negress of East Africa it rarely descends below the shoulders. These women wear the hair in small tresses, carefully greased. In the male the hair frequently has the appearance of a regular wig. Its insertion seems to follow another law in the Negro than in the white man. In the latter it presents irregular lines which converge

there appear to be exceptions, for Dr. R. Clarke† says that "a pleasing manner, soft and winning ways, with a low and musical laugh, may in strict truth be declared to be the heritage of most of the Negro women." There is a peculiarity in the Negro's voice by which he can always be distinguished. This peculiarity is so great that we can frequently discover traces of Negro blood when the eye is unable to detect it. No amount of education or time is likely ever to enable the Negro to speak the English language without this twang: even his great faculty of imitation will not enable him to do so.

Having thus briefly recapitulated the anatomical peculiarities of the Negro, we now come to the physiological* difference between the Negro and European.

---

and diverge in crossing, whilst in the former it is always circular. From this disposition frequently result separate tufts as in the Hottentot, and this peculiarity is very common among the Negresses of which I have spoken.

"The hair of the Negro is not cylindrical. Transversal sections show that its circumference is always an ellipsis, the large diameter exceeds the small diameter by 1-3rd to 3-5th. What is, moreover, remarkable, is that the large diameter, examined in different sections, does not remain parallel to itself; it turns as it were around the axis of the hair, so that the summits of these small ellipses, instead of being disposed in a straight line, describe around the hair two spiral curves (Koelliker). It is to this disposition that the crisp state of the hair of the Negro is due. With regard to the elementary microscopic structure, the hair of the Negro differs from that of other races only by its medullary portion. The central medullary and aeriferous canal which is clearly seen in hair with elliptical circumference, and of which some traces are found in the cylindric hair of Turanians, is absent in the Negro, even in those of his race which have red hair.

"In the Aryan race, the hair of the same individual presents different shades in different parts of the body, but it is certain that the hair of the Negro is finer, elliptical and crisp, and that I have never found in it any trace of a medullary canal. The Negro race has, moreover, no down upon the body; and but few hairs on the pubes and armpits. The beard comes late in the male; it is silky or slightly crisp on the upper lip, more or less frizzled on the cheeks and the chin. The eyelashes curved; the eyebrows but little furnished are generally but little arched. The contrary is, according to Dr. Barth, observed in the Mousgous."—PRUNER-BEY.

†Transactions of the Ethnological Society, vol. ii of New Series.

*Mr. Pruner Bey gives the following:—Physiological Fragments.—"The penetrating odour which the Negro exhales, has something ammoniacal and rancid; it is like the odour of the he-goat. It does not depend on the aqueous perspiration, for it is not increased by it. It is probably a volatile oil disengaged by the sebaceous follicles. This odour much diminishes by cleanliness, without, however, entirely disappearing. We are not aware whether this race-character changes by a uniform diet, as is the case with the fishers and opossum hunters in Australia.

"The observations on the temperature of the internal cavities of the Negro race are not numerous enough to draw conclusions. It is, nevertheless, useful to note the results of the researches of M. d' Abbadie. In Upper Ethiopia this celebrated traveller found at all seasons, in the buccal cavity of the Negro, a higher temperature than in individuals belonging to other races. The young Negresses always preserve in Egypt this excess of temperature; not so the young Negroes, these have the mouth warmer than young men of other races in hot weather, but colder, on the contrary, in cold weather.

"The pulse of the Negro in Egypt nearly corresponds to that of the other inhabitants, being, from 60-70 pulsations per minute. The contrary is observed in male children, from 10-13 years, and in young females from 14-20: for the former 74-96; for the latter 84-104 pulsations per minute.

"The senses of the Negro are not developed as in other races which are nearer to the state of nature, or live in a different climate. Vision does not in the Negro surpass that of the European; the flattening of the cornea renders the Negro rather presbyopic than myopic. From his inclination and talent for music, hearing seems his most developed sense; at any rate he excels, in this respect, the Egyptian. To judge from the extent of the nasal cavities, smell ought to be very acute, such, however, does not appear to be the case. This applies also to the sense of taste; the Negro is omnivorous. Touch, this general corrector of the white races, is little developed in the Negro, which accords with the flattening of the tactile cushions. But the most striking phenomenon with regard to general sensibility, is the apparent apathy of the Negro as to pain. In the most serious affections of internal organs, the Negro, arrived at a certain point, cowers on his bed (at least in the hospitals) without responding by any sign to the care of his physician. However, in a state of civilised slavery, where he has acquired some knowledge, he becomes more communicative, without, however, betraying any manifestation of pain. Bad treatment causes the Negro, the Negress, and the child to abundantly shed tears, but physical pain never provokes them. The Negro frequently resists surgical operations, but when he once submits, he fixes his eyes upon the instrument and the hand of the operator without any mark of restlessness or impatience. The lips, however, change colour and the sweat runs from him during the operation. A single example will support our view. A negress underwent the amputation of the right half of the lower jaw with the most astonishing apathy; but no sooner was the diseased part removed, than she commenced singing with a loud and sonorous voice, in spite of our remonstrances, and the wound could only be dressed after she had finished her hymn of grace.

"The phases of development present in the Negro race some peculiarities which appear to me worth notice. We know next to nothing of the embryonic state. The Negro infant is born without prognathism, with an ensemble of traits which is more or less characteristic as regards the soft parts, but which is scarcely marked in the cranium. In this respect the Negro, the Hottentot, the Australian, the Neo-Caledonian, do not indicate in the osseous system the difference which will arise later. The new born Negro child does not present the colour of the parents; it is of a red colour mixed with bistre and less vivid than that of new-born European children. This premature colour is, however, more or less deep, according to the regions of the body. From reddish it passes to slate-grey, until sooner or later, according to the climate and soil, it corresponds to the colour of the parents. In the Sudan the metamorphosis, *i.e.*, the development of the pigment, is generally completed at the end of the first year; in Egypt only at the end of three years. The hair of the Negro baby at first is rather chestnut than black; it is straight and slightly curved at the point. I was unable exactly to determine the extent of the fontanelles, but to judge from the cranium, the difference in this respect from the Aryan child is not appreciable.

"The first dentition commences nearly at the same epoch as with us. I have however, observed in Egypt cases of precocious as well as retarded dentition. Suckling continues during two years at least. After the first dentition, we already observe upon the cranium certain distinctive characters, viz.:—The median line of the forehead raised, the chin retracted, the superior jaw slightly inclined, the nose widened, the occiput prominent. Still the young Negro presents, until the time of puberty, a pleasing exterior. Puberty supervenes in girls between the ages of 10-12, and in boys between 13-15 years. It is then that the great revolution in the forms and proportions of the skeleton rapidly proceeds. This process and its results follow an inverse course as regards the cerebral and facial cranium. The jaws are enlarged without any compensation for the brain: it is not meant that there is an arrest of development—no, the difference of race manifests itself merely by a different order of increase in the growth of the respective parts. Whilst in the Aryan man the moderate increase of the jaws and the bones of the face is abundantly compensated and even surpassed by a development or rather enlargement of the brain, specially of the anterior lobe: the contrary takes place in the Negro. Great compression, chiefly lateral, produced from without inwardly by the muscles destined for animal life; small reaction in the interior on part of the brain, and we have the mould of his cranium and his brain formed as we have described it. Everything is in harmony with the organism. No doubt this mode of viewing the conformation of the Negro cranium is open for discussion.

The assumption of the unity of the species of man has been based chiefly on the asserted fact that the offspring of all the mixtures of the so called races of man are prolific. Now this is assuming what yet has to be established. At present it is only proved that the descendants of some of the different races of man are temporarily prolific; but there is the best evidence to believe that the offspring of the Negro and European are not indefinitely prolific. This ques-

---

"The course taken by the obliteration of the cranial sutures, furnishes a significative commentary to these phenomena. The medio-frontal suture as well as the lateral part of the coronal suture is in the Negro invariably closed already in early youth. In the adult Negro the union proceeds then to the middle part of the coronal suture and the sagittal suture—or as I have observed on crania in East Africa—on all sutures at once. The lambdoid suture is that which remains open longest, especially on the summit. At the base of the cranium, on the other hand, the basilo-sphenoid suture is frequently found open. As regards the incisive suture, it not only persists in the infant Negro, but is very distinct in many Negro crania of an advanced age. The obliteration of the sutures seems in the Negro race to be more rapidly effected in the female than in the male.

"Prognathism has been, and may be considered, at least partly, as the result of the action of the inferior jaw on the concentric arch of the superior jaw. At any rate, the mode of articulation of this bone with the temporal, seems much to contribute to it; for I have met with this conformation preferentially in the races in which the glenoid is large but of little depth, and the condyles of the maxillary more or less flattened, or at least elliptic; it coincides with a more or less pronounced harmony of the row of teeth. These conditions facilitate the movement of the jaw from behind forwards, whilst in the cranium with deep and contracted glenoid cavities, and with condyles more or less rounded or pointed, the movement of the jaw is preferentially vertical. I am, however, well aware of the insufficiency of this etiology, and I ask myself whether prognathism is not simply the expression of a movement towards animality. It has been thought that prolonged lactation may in the Negro favour prognathism; but I must observe that this custom prevails among many Oriental nations which are orthognathous. Moreover, it is known that the conformation is not exclusively peculiar to the African Negro. The majority of human races, whether dolicho- or brachycephalous, participate in it, as well as some civilised peoples: for instance the Peruvians, the Chinese, and Javano-Malays, at least the plurality of individuals comprising those nations. We find also exceptional cases more frequently in the ancient and modern Egyptians, less among the Jews, and less still in Western Europe. In all these cases, this conformation, however, does not exceed the first degree of three distinct degrees we have established.

"It must also be observed that the relative depression of the middle part of the face joined to the prominence of the jaws, is the essential condition of prognathism, and of the results derived from the measurement of the facial angle. We thus comprehend that the two straight lines drawn from the meatus auditorius to the forehead, and the alveolar border of the palatine suture, rarely present in favour of the latter a difference of two millimeters. This shows us that the depression of the nose in the Negro is as essential to produce prognathism, as the increase of the jaws from behind forwards. Parturition, and lactation ordinarily give but little trouble to the Negress. Her fecundity seems to be great, for she produces up to ten children; but the manners and even the institutions much reduce the number of offspring. Decline commences in the Negress between thirty-five and forty. Whilst the ugliness which accompanies age in the female is excessive, we find that in the male the hair blanches early, and at an advanced age his external aspect loses its harmony. Even in the races of the Sudan, with clear complexions and expressive features, as for instance in the Foulahs, which some hesitate to place among the Negroes, Dr. Barth remarks on the ugliness they exhibit in old age. He observes that their face has something of the ape at that period, and he makes similar observations as regards to the old ladies of the Maghis tribe, whose harmonious features when young he so much admired."

tion is one which must be dealt with separately and proved by facts. At present we find that all *primâ facie* evidence is against the assumption that permanent hybrid races can be produced, especially if the races are not very closely allied. This subject, however, merits a special discussion, and belongs to that large and important question—human hybridity. We, therefore, cannot agree with the asserted statement, especially when we find that the two scientific men who have in recent times paid the most attention to this subject—I allude to Messrs. Broca and Nott—have come to the conclusion that the offspring of the Negro and European are not indefinitely prolific. With the permission of the Society, I will enter into that question at some future day.

M. Flourens asserted that the Negro children were born white; recent observation has, however, shown that this is not the case. Benet, ex-physician of Runjeet Singh, and Dumoutier, affirm that the children are born chestnut colour. M. Pruner Bey confirms this fact from personal observation.

In the Negro race there is a great uniformity of temperament. In every people of Europe all temperaments exist; in the Negro race, we can only discover analogies for the choleric and phlegmatic temperaments. The senses of the Negro are said to be very acute, especially smell and taste; but Pruner Bey says that there has been much exaggeration as to the perfection of the senses of the Negro, and that his eye-sight in particular is very much inferior to the European. The most detestable odours delight him,* and he eats everything.

While the anatomical and physiological questions must be decided by actual facts, there still remains to investigate the psychological peculiarity of the Negro. It is here, perhaps, that the greatest amount of misconception exists in the minds of the public generally, and not unfrequently in the minds of some men of science. Wedded to the theory of a single pair for the origin of man, they attempt to show that there is in mankind no variety, nothing but uniformity.

To show I do not exaggerate on this point, I will quote the words of an esteemed friend, which he read last year at Cambridge. He says:—"For as God made of one blood all the nations of the earth, and endowed them all with the same animal, intellectual, moral, and religious nature: so has he bound them all together—in accordance with the high behest that they should increase and multiply and replenish the earth—in one common bond of universal brotherhood."

Mr. Dunn, however, it must be acknowledged, does not carry out the principles he here enunciates, for he fully admits the fact that, practically, Negro children cannot be educated with the whites. He also admits that some of the lower races are not able to conceive complex ideas, or have little power of thinking, and none of generalisation, although they have excellent memories.

---

*Mr. Louis Fraser informs me that this is not always the case, and that sometimes a Negro will leave a vessel on account of a disagreeable odour, saying, "Cap'n, your ship stink *too* much, I can't stop."

The assertion that the negro only requires an opportunity for becoming civilised, is disproved by history. The Negro race has had communication with the Egyptian, Carthaginian, and Roman civilisations, but nowhere did it become civilised. Not only has the Negro race never civilised itself, but it has never accepted any other civilisation. No people have had so much communication with Christian Europeans as the people of Africa, where Christian bishops existed for centuries.* Except some knowledge of metallurgy they possess no art; and their rude laws seem to have been borrowed and changed to suit their peculiar instincts. It is alleged that the Negro only requires early education to be equal to the European; but all experiments of this kind have proved that such is not the fact. With the negro, as with some other races of man, it has been found that the children are precocious: but that no advance in education can be made after they arrive at the age of maturity, they still continue, mentally, children. It is apparently of little consequence what amount of education they receive, the same result nearly always follows, the reflective faculties hardly appear to be at all developed. The dark races generally do not accept the civilisation which surrounds them, as is shown in the South Sea, where they remain the uncivilised race by the side of the Malays. The opinion of Dr. Channing of America, is often quoted respecting the Negro. He says:—"I would expect from the Negro race when civilised, less energy, less courage, less intellectual originality, than in ours; but more amiableness, tranquillity, gentleness, and content." Now, if it were possible to civilise them, there is no doubt they would show less energy, courage, and intellectual originality (of which they would be utterly deficient) and, as to their amiableness, tranquillity, gentleness, and content, it would be more like the tranquillity and content shown by some of our domestic animals than anything else to which we can compare it. It has been said that the present slave-holders of America "no more think of insurrection amongst their full-blooded slaves than they do of rebellion amongst their cows and horses!"* It has also been affirmed (and I believe with truth) that not a single soldier has been required to keep order in the so called "Slave States" of America.

The many assumed cases of civilised Negroes are generally not those of pure Negro blood. In the Southern States of North America, in the West Indies

*It is said that when the Negro has been with other races, he has always been a slave. This is quite true: but why has he been a slave?

*"The Southern planter, with a consciousness of superiority that would be ashamed to resort to fiction or imposition of any kind, takes off his coat and works in the same field and at the same labour as his 'slave.' The thought of the latter contesting his superiority never once enters his mind. As said by a sound statesman and gallant soldier of the South, 'we no more think of a Negro insurrection, than we do of a rebellion of our cows and horses.' The planter rules as naturally as the Negro obeys instinctively; the relation between them is natural, harmonious, and necessary, and their interests being indivisible, there can be no cause or motive, either for the abuse of power on the part of the master, or of rebellion on the part of the servant."—*Negroes and Negro "Slavery."* By J. H. Van Evrie, M.D. New York, 1861, p. 29.

and other places, it has been frequently observed that the Negroes in place of trust have European features, and some writers have supposed that these changes have been due to a gradual improvement in the Negro race, which is taking place under favourable circumstances. It is assumed that great improvement has taken place in the intellect of the Negro by education, which we much doubt. It is simply the European blood in their veins which renders them fit for places of power, and they often use this power far more cruelly than either of the pure blooded races. At the same time, there are doubtless many exceptions to this rule; depending perhaps on the amount of mixture of blood and inherited peculiarities. It has been affirmed that occasionally there are seen Negroes of pure blood who possess European features: but I believe such not to be the fact, and Pruner Bey also says that "with regard to the regular Caucasian features, with which some travellers have endowed certain Negro peoples, I must state that among many thousand Negroes who have come under my own observation, there was not one who could lay claim to it."

Instances have often been quoted of reputed European skulls with Negro characters. Such an instance there is in the College of Surgeons, another in Morton's museum, and one in Gall's collection; but if we admit these to have belonged to the pure race,* we shall only be admitting that in one character the European skull sometimes resembles that of the Negro; but there will be plenty of other characters to show that they did not belong to the same race or species, and it ought simply to caution us not to base our ideas of race or species upon one character. We know that certain species of the mammalia frequently cannot be distinguished by the form of the skeleton, and we must therefore not be surprised to find that we are unable to prove a distinction of species in mankind if we take the cranium or even skeleton as a sole test.

We now know it to be a patent fact that there are races existing which have no history, and that the Negro is one of these races. From the most remote antiquity the Negro race seems to have been what it now is.† We may be

---

*A large amount of mixture has continually been going on between the natives and the traders, especially on the rivers. The traders are not the finest specimens of their race, and much of the immorality of the settlements may be owing to this mixed blood. The following custom has existed for ages, and render most uncertain the parentage of some Africans who even come direct from the interior:—"The European stranger, however, travelling in their country, is expected to patronize their wives and daughters, and these unconscious followers of Lycurgus and Cato feel hurt, as if dishonoured, by his refusing to gratify them. The custom is very prevalent along this coast. At Gaboon, perhaps it reaches the acme; there a man will in one breath offer the choice between his wife, sister, and daughter. The women of course do as they are bid by the men, and they consider all familiarity with a white man a high honour."—*Wanderings in West Africa,* vol. 2, p.24.

†As a proof that the African has not changed during the last 2,000 years, the following description of an "Aunt Chloe" of the days of Virgil may be interesting:—

Afra genus, tota patriam testante figura,

Torta comam, labroque tumens, et fusca colorem;

pretty sure that the Negro race has been without a progressive history; and that Negroes have been for thousands of years the uncivilised race they are at this moment. Egyptian monuments depict them as such, and holding exactly the same position relative to the European. Morton* truly observes: "Negroes were numerous in Egypt, but their social position in ancient times was the same that it now is, that of servants and slaves."

Some writers have assumed that the Negro has degenerated from some higher form of civilisation, but we see no evidence to support such an assertion. We, however, fully admit that there are found traces of a higher civilisation, especially along the coasts visited, during all ages, by Europeans. The working of metals and imitation of European manufactures also exist in many parts of Africa. Indeed, there seems to be a great sameness in this respect throughout all Africa. Consul Hutchinson has given an interesting account of the finding of some implements used by the natives of Central Africa exactly resembling those used by the Anglo-Saxons.

Consul Hutchinson thus describes them:†—"You will be surprised, no doubt, to hear that I brought down with me from the tribes of Filatahs, in Central Africa, iron heads of spears with wooden shafts and iron spiked ferules, heads of javelins and arrows, double-edged swords, knives, beads for ornaments, potteryware for culinary purposes, exactly similar in pattern to those that are described by Mr. Wright, in a paper on 'Fausset Antiquities,' which he read before the British Association at Liverpool, in 1856, and which antiquities I need scarcely tell you were excavated at Canterbury, as well as proved to have been used in this country before the introduction of Christianity to our shores. Even the cowrie (the shell of the *Cypraea moneta*), which is described in Mr. Wright's paper as having been found among other relics of our Anglo-Saxon forefathers, is in this very day the currency among the Filatahs. It may perhaps increase the interest of my statement, which can be demonstrated by the articles I brought home (being deposited at the Royal Institution museum at Liverpool), when I add that they were obtained from

---

Pectore lata, jacens mammis, compressior alvo,

Cruribus exilis, spatiosa prodiga planta;

Continuis rimis calcanea scissa rigebant.

As it is the fashion to quote *Cowper on the Negro* in anthropological discussions, I append his translation of the above, which although feeble, yet conveys the spirit of the original.

"From Afric she, the swain's sole serving maid,

Whose face and form alike her birth betrayed;

With wooly locks, lips tumid, sable skin,

Wide bosom, udders flaccid, belly thin,

Legs slender, broad and most misshapen feet,

Chapped into chinks, and parched with solar heat."

Crania Aegyptiaca. Philadelphia, 1844 (eighth conclusion).

†*Transactions of the Ethn. Soc.*, vol. i, new series, p. 328.

tribes who had no record of ever having been visited by any white man previous to the time of our voyage at the end of 1854.''

There is good reason to believe that, as among all inferior races, there has been little or no migration from Africa since the earliest historical records. The European, for ever restless, has migrated to all parts of the world, and traces of him are to be found in every quarter of the globe. Everywhere we see the European as the conqueror and the dominant race, and no amount of education will ever alter the decrees of Nature's laws.

We hear much of late in this country of the equality of the Negro and European, because we have little real knowledge of the Negro; but in America the Negro is better known. As Dr. Van Evrie observes:* ''In the United States, among a people almost universally educated, and where the fact of 'equality' is almost universally understood and acted on, personally as well as politically, the advocacy of woman's 'equality,' in the sense that they (in England) argue it, or 'equality' of the Negro to the white man in any sense whatever, is inexcusable on the ground of ignorance; and those thus warring against the laws of nature and progress of society, deserve to be treated as its enemies, or as absolute maniacs, and irresponsible for the evils they seek to inflict upon it.''

It has been assumed on very insufficient evidence that the Negroes in America improve in intelligence in every generation, and that they gradually approach the European type. M. Quatrefages recently directed our attention to this point, as did Sir Charles Lyell many years ago. It is affirmed that the head and body also approach the European without any mixture of the races.

M. Quatrefages quotes the following* from M. Elisée Reclus: ''We do not intend here to touch upon the question of slavery, we would merely state a certain fact—the constant advance of Negroes in the social scale. Even in physical respects they tend gradually to approach their masters; the Negroes of the United States have no longer the same type as the African Negroes; their skin is rarely of velvet black, though nearly all their progenitors have been imported from the Coast of Guinea; their cheekbones are less prominent, their lips not so thick, nor the nose so flattened, neither is the hair so crisp, the physiognomy so brutish, the facial angle so acute as those of their brethren in the old world. In the space of one hundred and fifty years they have, as far as external appearance goes, passed one-fourth of the gulph which separates them from the white race.'' I cannot assent to this, as I believe that no improvement takes place after the second generation.

On this point Dr. Nott† has very judiciously observed: ''Sir C. Lyell, in common with tourists less eminent, but on this question not less misinformed, has somewhere stated that the Negroes in America are undergoing a manifest improvement in their physical type. He has no doubt that they will, in time,

*Negroes and ''Negro Slavery.'' New York, 1861, p. 10.
*Unité de l'Espèce Humaine. Paris, 1861.
†Types of Mankind. Philadelphia, 1857, p. 260.

show a development in skull and intellect quite equal to the whites. This unscientific assertion is disproved by the cranial measurements of Dr. Morton. That Negroes imported into, or born in, the United States become more intelligent and better developed in their physique generally than their native compatriots of Africa, every one will admit; but such intelligence is easily explained by their ceaseless contact with the whites, from whom they derive much instruction; and such physical improvement may also be readily accounted for by the increased comforts with which they are supplied. In Africa, owing to their natural improvidence, the Negroes are more frequently than not a half-starved, and therefore half-developed, race; but when they are regularly and adequately fed, they become healthier, better developed, and more humanised. Wild horses, cattle, asses, and other brutes are greatly improved in like manner by domestication; but neither climate nor food can transmute an ass into a horse, or a buffalo into an ox.''

The real facts seem to be, that the Negroes employed in domestic labour have more intelligence than those who are employed at field labour, who are nearly in the same mental condition as when they left Africa. We must bear in mind, however, that there are only some of the African tribes of Negroes who are docile and intelligent enough for domestic purposes: the Eboes are generally selected for this purpose. We see therefore in this improvement of the Negro simply the effect of education, but not of climate or other physical agents. We fully admit that the domestic Negroes are improved in intelligence in America, resulting from the imitation of the superior race by which they are surrounded; but much of the improvement in intellect is owing to the mixture of European and Negro blood. The Negro is not generally educated because it is affirmed that he is no sooner taught to read than he will take every chance of reading his master's letters; and if he be taught to write, he will soon learn to forge his master's signature. This applies with equal, and, perhaps, greater force to those free, semi-civilised Negroes who are held by some in such theoretical veneration.

I have intentionally avoided dwelling on the great diversity of physical type found in Africa, as this is foreign to our subject. There can be no doubt, however, that there is, both in North and South Africa every shade of colour and races with very different features. There are also in Central Africa some races such as the Mandingos, Fulahs, and Wolofs, who are quite distinct from the typical Negro. In these races, some of the characters found in the typical Negro are found in only a very modified degree. How many races inhabit Africa, and their relation to one another, is not the subject of present inquiry. M. Pruner Bey has very judiciously made the following observations on this point:—

"We must admit that the inferior orbital margins are frequently narrow and retreating; that the noses become longer and more prominent; that the lips turned up in some tribes are only full in others; that prognathism diminishes without however disappearing entirely; that the aperture of the eye becomes wide; that the hair short and woolly in most, grows longer; that the transverse diameter of the chest becomes enlarged; that even the pelvis, though much more rarely, acquires more rounded outlines; that the limbs acquire more harmonious proportions; that the hips, thighs, and legs become more fleshy and the foot more arched; but as regards the crowning of the work, *i.e.*, the skull, especially the cerebrum, all the variations in the Negro race remain confined within limits which deserve our attention. In the Aryan race the skull presents three fundamental types, the elongated form (producing in some exceptional cases prognathism) which approaches the limit of the Negro type; the short and round form, approaching the Turanian race; and finally, the typically beautiful oval form, which seems to have resulted from a combination of the two former. Nothing like it is to be found in the Negro. The skull is and remains elongated, it is elliptical, cuneiform, but never round; his facial bones may approach the pyramidal form by the increasing distance between the cheekbones, and may in this respect resemble the Kaffirs and the Bechuanas, but this is all." This generalisation appears to me to be in accordance with all the known facts respecting the craniological development of the chief African tribes, which thus form one great ethnic family, although composed of many distinct races.

I need not enlarge on the well-known and admitted facts respecting the intense immorality which exists amongst the Mulattoes and others of mixed blood.* There are, at the same time, perhaps, some exceptions to this general rule,

*The following extract is a striking confirmation of this remark:—"But the worst class of all is the mulatto—under which I include quadroon and octaroon. He is everywhere, like wealth, irritamenta malorum. The 'bar-sinister,' and the uneasy idea that he is despised, naturally fill him with ineffable bile and bitterness. Inferior in point of morale to Europeans, as far as regards physique to Africans, he seeks strength in making the families of his progenitors fall out. Many such men visiting England are received by virtue of their wooly hair and yellow skin into a class that would reject a fellow-countryman of similar, nay of far higher, position; and there are amongst them infamous characters, who are not found out till too late. London is fast learning to distinguish between the Asiatic Mir and the Munshi. The real African, however—so enduring are the sentimentalisms of Wilberforce and Buxton—is still to be understood."—*Wanderings in West Africa.* 1863. Vol. i. p. 271. This is by no means a modern idea, for I find the following extract from a work entitled "A new voyage to Guinea," by William Smith, Esq., appointed by the Royal African Company to survey their settlements, make discoveries, &c., in a second edition published in 1745, p. 213. Speaking of the Mulattoes of the Gold Coast at that time, this author observes: "Upon this coast are a Sort of People called MULLATOES, a race begotten by the *Europeans* upon *Negroe* Women. This Bastard Blood is a Parcel of the most profligate Villains, neither true to the *Negroes*, nor to one another; yet they assume the Name of Christians, but are indeed as great Idolators as any on the Coast. Most of the Women are public Whores to the *Europeans*, and private ones to the *Negroes*. In short, whatever is bad among the *Europeans* or Negroes are united in them; so that they are the Sink of both. They are frightfully ugly, when they grow in Years, especially the women." There is, however, an earlier description of these peoples from which the author seems to have partly borrowed his ideas. Nearly the same words are given in William Bosman's work on Guinea, published at the end of the 17th century. Is not this picture

which, however, has been observed in every country where these people exist.

Of all the questions connected with the Negro, the most difficult to settle is that of his intelligence. Amidst conflicting testimony, it is difficult to discover the truth. We may admit, however, that there are instances of the pure Negro showing great powers of memory, such as the acquirement of languages; but we must also remember that memory is one of the lowest mental powers. Numerous instances have been collected by different partisan writers to show that the Negro is equal intellectually to the European; but an examination of these cases nearly invariably leads to the conclusion that there has been much exaggeration in the statements made by writers as to the aptitudes of the Negro for education and improvement. The exhibition of cases of intelligent Negroes in the saloons of the fashionable world by so-called "philanthropists"* has

---

true of Mulattoes as a class all over the world? Bosman says (*Loc. Cit.* 141):—"Though I have been tedious in this, I hope you will pardon it; for I must own my Itch of Scribbling is not yet over, and I cannot help giving you an account of a wonderful an extraordinary sort of People, I mean the *Tapoeyers* or *Mulattoes;* a race begotten by the *Europeans* upon the *Negro* or *Mulatto*-Women. This Bastard Strain is made up of a parcel of profligate Villains, neither true to the *Negroes* nor us, nor indeed dare they trust one another; so that you very rarely see them agree together. They assume the Name of Christians, but are as great Idolators as the *Negroes* themselves. Most of the Women are public Whores to the *Europeans* and private ones to the *Negroes*, so that I can hardly give them a character so bad as they deserve. I can only tell you whatever is in its own Nature worst, in the *Europeans* and *Negroes* is united in them; so that they are the sink of both. The Men, most of which are Soldiers in our service, are clothed as we are; but the Women prink up themselves in a particular manner: Those of any Fashion wear a fine Shift, and over that a short Jacket of silk or stuff, without sleeves; which reaches from under the arms to their hips, fastened only at the shoulders. Upon their heads they wear several caps, one upon the other; the uppermost of which is of Silk, plated before and round at the top, to make it fit soft, upon all which they have a sort of Fillet, which comes twice or thrice around the Head. Thus dressed they make no small show. On the lower part of their body they are clothed as the *Negro*-Women are; and those who are poor are only distinguishable by their dress: they going naked in the upper part of their body.

"The whole Brood, when young, are far from handsome, and when old, are only fit to fright children to their beds. If a painter were obliged to paint Envy, I could wish him no better original to draw after than an old *Mulatto*-Woman. In process of time, their Bodies become speckled with white, brown, and yellow spots, like the Tigers, which they also resemble in their barbarous natures. But I shall here leave them, for fear it may be thought that I am prejudiced by hatred against 'em; but so far from that, that there is not a single person who hath anything to do with them but he must own they are not worth speaking to."

*The following words of Thomas Carlyle deserve to be recorded in every discussion on the Negro:—"Sunk in deep froth oceans of 'Benevolence,' 'Fraternity,' 'Emancipation-principle,' 'Christian Philanthropy,' and other most amiable looking, but most baseless, and in the end baleful and all-bewildering jargon, sad product of a sceptical eighteenth century, and of poor human hearts left destitute of any earnest guidance, and disbelieving that there ever was any, Christian or heathen, and reduced to believe in rosepink sentimentalism alone, and to cultivate the same under its Christian, anti-Christian, broad-brimmed, Brutus-headed, and other forms—has not the human species gone strange roads during that period? And poor Exeter Hall, cultivating the broad-brimmed form of Christian sentimentalism and long talking, and bleating and braying in that strain, has

frequently been nothing but mere imposture. In nearly every case in which the history of these cases has been investigated, it has been found that these so-called Negroes are the offspring of European and African parents. I propose on some future occasion to lay before you evidence to show, that nearly all the Negroes who are asserted to have arrived at any mental distinction had European blood in their veins: and think I shall be able to show that of the fifteen celebrated Negroes whose histories were collected by Abbé Gregoire there is not one who is of pure Negro blood. Some writers who advocate the specific difference of the Negro from the European have very injudiciously admitted that occasionally the Negro is equal in intellect to the European, but this admission has materially weakened their argument in favour of a specific difference. If this be so, let me ask those who hold such an opinion to give the name of one pure Negro who has ever distinguished himself as a man of science, as an author, a statesman, a warrior, a poet, an artist. Surely, if there is equality in the mental development of human races, some one instance can be quoted. From all the evidence we have examined, we see no reason to believe that the pure Negro even advances further in intellect than an intelligent European boy of fourteen years of age. Many writers have mentioned the precocity of the Negro children. Sir C. Lyell has observed:* "Up to fourteen years of age black children advance as fast as the whites;" and Eliot Warburton has remarked† that the modern Egyptian "when young, is remarkably precocious in intellect, and learns with facility. As he grows up, his intelligence seems to be dulled or diminished: he has no genius for discovery, and though apt in acquiring rudiments, he is incapable of generalising. He fills subordinate departments well, but appears incapable of taking or of keeping a lead." Sir C. Lyell expresses his surprise at the results of the mixture of some European blood with the Negro, and thinks "it a wonderful fact, psychologically considered, that we should be able to trace the phenomena of hybridity even into the world of intellect and reason." It would, indeed, be remarkable if all men were endowed with the same instincts; but not so wonderful if we do not accept such an unfounded hypothesis. The pure Negro seems incapable of much mental cultivation; and Archbishop Sumner's much-talked-of "improveable reason," as a distinction between men and animals, only finds a limited application in the Negro race. The reason of animals is improved to some extent by domestication and training, and this is all we can

it not worked out results? Our West India legislatings, with their spoutings, anti-spoutings, and interminable jangle and babble; our twenty millions down on the nail for blacks of our own; thirty gradual millions more, and many brave British lives to boot, in watching blacks of other people's; and now, at last, our ruined sugar estates, differential sugar duties, 'immigration loan,' and beautiful blacks sitting there up to the ears in pumpkins, and doleful whites sitting here without potatoes to eat; never, till now, I think, did the sun look down on such a jumble of human nonsenses."

Second Journey to the United States, vol. i, p. 105.

†*The Crescent and the Cross.*

say of the Negro. Dr. Madden observes: "It will be seen by all the answers the missionary gentlemen in our different settlements have given to my queries respecting the mental capacity of Negro children, that they are considered universally, in that respect, equal to European children, and by some even quicker, in their perceptions, and more lively in their powers of apprehension." To which Dr. R. Clarke adds:* "This is observable from the ages of five to twelve or thirteen years; but from that period of life to the age of eighteen or twenty, it becomes less strongly marked, and there appears to be less activity in the mental faculties."

Professor Owen gives it as his opinion† that we are unable "to appreciate or conceive of the distinction between the psychical phenomena of a Chimpanzee and of a Bosjesman, or of an Aztec with arrested brain growth;" but we are able clearly to appreciate the psychological distinction between the Negro and the Chimpanzee: just as we see that there are decided mental and moral distinctions between the European and the Negro. We fully admit, however, that the psychical distinction is simply a question of degree and not of kind.

The day is not far distant when we shall be able to analyse the mental character of the Negro far more minutely than we can do in the present infant state of psychological science.‡ In dwelling on the mental character of the Negro

*Sierra Leone, p. 34.

†Journal of the Proceedings of the Linnean Society of London, 1857, p. 20.

‡Pruner-Bey thus speaks of the Psychology of the Negro:—"The manifestations of the affective and intellectual faculties of the Negro may be placed in parallel with his physical type. Sensuality is the great lever of his propensities; from his imitative talent result the qualities which demand our esteem. The first renders him an eminently sociable being; by the second he becomes an artist of a secondary rank. Solitude is insupportable to him; song and dance are indispensable wants. Materialist in the main, he is in this respect below the more refined Chinese; but, like the latter, he prefers suicide to great privations. He preferentially selects the most violent means to attain this object; he suffocates himself by reversing his tongue towards the larynx; he throws himself from precipices; he drowns himself. He rarely takes the initiative in anything. In spiritual things he reproduces, but is not productive. It was only after having acquired the knowledge of the existence of letters among other peoples that an individual of the Vei tribe invented an alphabetic primer, the greatest effort which the Negro has ever made in the cultivation of science. The eminently imitative nature of the Negro even reveals itself in that part in which the creative faculty of every race reflects itself; viz., language. It appears to me evident that the Negro in the structure of his languages has endeavoured to produce a copy of all the systems known without attaining the perfection of any original. The same remark applies to the ideas and conceptions referring to regions of the invisible world, towards which the human mind at all times, and in all regions, soared to attempt the solution of the highest problems. The adoration of natural objects, of stones, trees, &c., of the sun, as well of the names of ancestors, demonology, the attribution of superior powers to objects made by the hand of man, divination by the inspection of entrails, human sacrifices, and anthropophagy,—for a mystical object all this found its place in the soul of the Negro, as amongst us in times past; but he surpasses the Semitic, the Aryan, and even the Chinese, in having completely forgotten the signification of the symbol. For him animals would speak the language of man if they were not too lazy. He has probably invented the fable, in approaching by the excess of his instincts, the brute to man. It is specially south of the Equator

that the Negro is heavily enchained by a fatal superstition. Living in continued fear of being bewitched, the simple suspicion of it induces him to immolate hecatombs of innocents. The *Judgment of God* of the ancient gallants of the North of Europe is not unknown to him, but he prefers poison for the ordeal of suspected persons. Moreover, the Negro takes the world as he finds it, and he neither imagines a system of cosmogony nor any spiritual theory on the attributes of a superior being. On the other hand, he readily accepts Islamism, and he probably would never oppose to the introduction of the sublime doctrine of fraternal love that desperate resistance shown by the ancient Saxons and Scandinavians.

"Another point in the psychology of the Negro remains to be examined, and it is not the least important one. I would speak of the facility with which he loses his equilibrium when passing from one extreme to the other, frequently without any appreciable motive, of that contradiction in which he presents himself in his social relations, and the excesses of which he is capable. Patient towards a master who illtreats him, he assassinates one who has cherished him. Defending his cabin with ferocious obstinacy, he would sell his children for a piece of stuff. A kneeling slave before a king of his blood, he would condemn him to death when he is tired of him. 'You please no longer men or women, old men or children, sheep or fowls,' say the Negroes of the Sudan to their Sultan, to signify to him that it is time he should execute himself. Caring little about the chastity of his daughters, and prostituting his slaves, the Negro assures himself during his absence of the fidelity of his wife by mechanical means, and he becomes an assassin on the mere suspicion of her adultery. Nevertheless, the Negress has more liberty than Islam women, and she is respected in war. Abusing the weaker sex, and deprecating her even by the difference of aliments which he gives her, he nevertheless accepts a woman as his sovereign, according prerogatives to the Queen-mother, and regulating the rights of succession as the peoples of Asia who live in a state of polyandry. A mutual exchange of the occupations of the two sexes is not rare, even among the Negroes of the Sudan. The women cultivate the soil, and the man spins cotton; he guards the fields, she goes to war. The same contradiction is observed in other things which touch the interest of the Negro. Particularly anxious about the arrangements of the interior of his cabin, he remains naked outside in the heat of the day and the comparatively excessive cold of the night. Very domestic and attached to the soil, the Negro travels over the great continent from one end to the other, either for traffic or to fulfil some religious duties. Whole nations are continually on the move, and gipsies would find their brothers among the Negro race.

"The Negro is not cruel by nature; he remains as far in this respect from the bloody refinement of the Chinese as from the atrocious proceedings of the Aryan Persians. Still the dynasties of Wadai blind their nearest male relations; the despot of the Moluwas mutilates and skins those condemned to death. The civilised Bornoui cuts off the thighs of his war prisoners, and the Mousgous skin the backs of their horses to have a firmer seat. But they do not put their slaves to the plough like some tribes of Touaregs. The punishments inflicted by the Negro on his equals, savour, however, more or less of barbarism."

"Let us not, however, forget that these excesses do not constitute the rule, and that 'the black man is to the white man what woman is to man in general, a loving being and a being of pleasure.' We cite with conviction the words of Golbery, 'the Negro is generally sober, industrious, an excellent and patient workman, not wanting skill; he governs his family with sagacity and dignity.' We also subscribe the judgment of Mungo Park, that 'the Negro is compassionate by nature,' and we may add that the Negress is even in a state of slavery capable of the greatest devotion.

"Improvidence they have in common with all human races who live in a more or less primitive state, and pride of the stronger against the weaker is not foreign to the Negro.

"The portrait which L. Magyar traces of the peoples east of Angola is not favourable. The Djambandis, though polite to strangers, are described as suspicious, false, malicious, and thievish; the Djohoes are still worse, specially vicious to strangers. They contrast with the Moluwas, who are full of attention to their guests. Most of the inhabitants of the Lobal are ferocious brigands. The judgment of Mr. Kauffmann on the Negroes of the White Nile is generally not more favourable.

we must, therefore, for the present, rely on the general observations of those *unbiassed* travellers and others who have been much associated with the Negro race. In the first place we will see what is the evidence recently published by our English consuls, who have the best opportunities of judging of the character of the people amongst whom they are placed.

Consul Hutchinson, who spent no less than eighteen years on the West coast of Africa, and who is as competent a judge as any man now living, says* that "his own observations on the African tribes tend to show that the African is not exactly the style of 'man and a brother' which mistaken enthusiasts for his civilisation depict him to be." He gives the result of a ten years' attendance at the Missionary school at Cape Palmas of one of his servants, a Kruman, and says that at the end he was asked what he knew of God? He replied: "God be very good; He made two things—one sleep and the other Sunday, when no person had to work."† Consul Hutchinson says that "the thirst for each other's blood, which seems a daily habit amongst so many of the Negro tribes in Western Africa, appears to me to be incompatible with ordinary notions of common humanity." He says that for scores of years European missionaries and English traders have mixed with them in social intercourse, yet they still cling "to their gris-gris, jujus, fetichism and cannibalism with as much pertinacity as they did many hundred years ago." He adds: "Here we have all the appliances of our arts, our science and our Christianity, doing no more good than did the wheat in the parable that was sown amongst the briars and the thorns. To attempt civilising such a race before they are humanised appears to me to be beginning at the wrong end. I have passed many a hour in cogitating and endeavouring to fabricate some sort of education likely to root out the fell spirit that dictates human sacrifices and cannibalism; but I fear years must elapse before any educational principle, in its simplest form, can produce an amendment on temperaments such as they possess."

Consul Burton considers* that M. Du Chaillu's remarks concerning the commercial shrewdness and eagerness, the greediness and rascality of the Negro, apply to him everywhere in his natural state; that an abnormal development of adhesiveness, in popular language a peculiar power of affection, is the brightest spot in the Negro character; as in children, it is somewhat tempered by caprice, especially under excitement, yet it has entitled him to the gratitude

"In social respects the Negro has at least attained the position of shepherd and agriculturist. Besides this some Negro-peoples have founded, independent of all foreign influence, a sort of civilisation and considerable states; they possess the art of metallurgy and the talent for trade to a high degree, and they well know how to profit by the foibles of their masters; their answers, for instance, are always shaped according to the desire of the questioner."

**Transactions of the Ethnological Society*, vol. i, *New Series*, p. 327.

†"All missionaries praise the African for his strict observance of the Sabbath. He would have 365 sabbaths in the year if possible, and he would as scrupulously observe them all."—*Wanderings in West Africa*, vol. i, p. 266.

**Transactions of the Ethnological Society*, vol. i, New Series, p. 317.

of many a traveller. Exaggeration, he considers, is the characteristic of the mind of both the East† and West African. He says that "they justly hold labour as an evil inferior only to death."

These are the opinions which have been published by the last two consuls who have written on the subject, and we shall now examine the evidence of some other witnesses.*

†Captain Burton thus speaks of the Coast clans of Eastern Africa:—"Supersubtle and systematic liars, they deceive where duller men would tell the truth; the lie direct is no insult, and the offensive word 'Muongo,' (liar) enters largely into every dialogue. They lie like Africans, objectlessly, needlessly, when sure of speedy detection: when fact would be more profitable than falsehood; they have not discovered with the civilised knave, that 'honesty is the best policy;' they lie till their fiction becomes subjectively fact. With them the lie is no mental exertion, no exercise of ingenuity, no concealment, nor mere perversion of the truth: it is apparently a local instinctive peculiarity in the complicated madness of poor human nature. The most solemn and religious oaths are with them empty words; they breathe an atmosphere of falsehood, manoeuvre and contrivance, wasting about the mere nothings of life—upon a pound of grain or a yard of cloth—ingenuity of iniquity enough to win and keep a crown. And they are treacherous as false; with them the salt has no signification, and gratitude is unknown even by name."—*Lake Regions of Central Africa.* By R. F. Burton. 1861. Vol. i.

*Truthful William Bosman published the following as his opinions respecting the Negroes of Guinea in 1705 (*loc. cit.*, p. 117).

"The Negroes are all, without exception, crafty, villanous and fraudulent, and very seldom to be trusted, being sure to slip no opportunity of cheating an European, nor indeed one another. A man of integrity is as rare among them as a white falcon and their fidelity seldom extends farther than to their masters; and it would be very surprising if, upon a scrutiny into their lives, we should find any of them whose perverse nature would not break out sometimes, for they indeed seem to be born and bred villains. All sorts of baseness having got such sure footing in them, that 'tis impossible to lye concealed; and herein they agree very well with what authors tell us of the Muscovites. These degenerate vices are accompanied with their sisters—Sloth and Idleness, to which they are so prone, that nothing but the utmost necessity can force them to labour. They are besides so incredibly careless and stupid, and are so little concerned at their misfortunes, that 'tis hardly to be observed, by any change in them, whether they have met with any good or ill success."

Mr. J. W. Jackson makes the following observations on the Negro (*Ethnology and Phrenology*, 1863, p. 35):—"The radical defect of the Negro is want of due nervous development. His brain is less in proportion to his body than that of any other grand division of humanity, and as a result, the involuntary and animal functions altogether preponderate. His flat foot, his long heel, his imperfect pelvis, his powerful stomach, his prognathous jaw, his enormous mouth, and his pug nose, are in perfect correspondence with his imperfectly developed brain, in which correspondently passion and affection rule principle and faculty, the basilar and posterior developments being predominant over the coronal and anterior. Except in a few unfavourable instances, however, he does not exist on the continent in his lowest form; for it is the Oceanic Negro who is the almost irreclaimable savage, while the African is the improvable barbarian type of his race. The former is useless even as a slave, while the latter is eminently valuable, because he has been broken to work and obedience, and has that hereditary aptitude for sustained toil, of which the utter savage is so generally devoid. Hence, despite his present degradation, he obviously belongs to the redeemable families of humanity. He is the labourer of the tropics, and is not going to perish out, like a wild Indian, because his buffalo grounds have been enclosed by the white faces. He has his place on the earth which none can take from him, and what we have to attempt is not his extirpation, but improvement. Hence, a study of his character and capabilities is of the

M. Du Chaillu describes the general characteristics of the tribes he visited who spoke the Mpongwe language as far superior to the Negroes of Congo. He says† "the Negroes possess an imaginative mind, are astute speakers, sharp traders, great liars, possessing great powers of dissimulation, and are far from being in many respects the stupid people they are believed to be. In everything that does not require mental labour and forethought, they seemed to me to learn almost as fast as any amongst the more intellectual races to a certain point." He further affirms that they have little power of forethought or power of reflection, and that there is "a total lack of generalisation." He also says, that although these people "are often treacherous, they have noble qualities, given to hospitality, and the women show great kindness of heart, especially when one takes into account the way they are treated."

Brehm* says that "there seems to be a complete absence of moral sentiment amongst the natives of East Sudan, who not merely excuse theft, murder, and treachery, but consider these actions as praiseworthy in man. They first learned under a Turkish ruler to distinguish murder from justifiable homicide in war. Lying and deceitfulness are considered as marks of mental superiority; and those who suffer death on the gallows are buried with the same honours as the rich merchant or the sheik."

Count Görz† narrates of the Negroes in Cuba, "Their character is very degraded; the moral feeling entirely undeveloped; all their actions proceed from animal impulse, or a cunning calculation of their own advantage. Generosity and indulgence exhibited by the white man they consider as weakness. Power imposes upon them, and excites their hatred, which would become dangerous were they not aware of their powerlessness. The only efficacious punishment for them is the whip. They delight in sowing discord; are thievish and revengeful; void of any religious feeling, they are given to the crudest superstition. Their frame, however, is well-developed and powerful; their teeth magnificent:‡ their legs slender; they digest like beasts of prey." This certainly is a severe judgment, and may be partly explained by the large amount of mixed blood in Cuba.

---

utmost importance. From temperament he is slow, but from organisation he is persistent, his lymphatic nature being sustained by a considerable amount of firmness and self-esteem. He is not skilful, his mechanical ingenuity being that of a child; nor is he capable of delicate manipulation, for which his entire organisation is too coarse. His perceptive faculties are stronger than his reflective or imaginative, and he dwells in the real rather than the ideal. He never rises from a fact to a principle, or re-creates beauty from the faultless beau-ideal of artistic conception. He has but little reverence for the past, and no very brilliant anticipation of the future, being from the overwhelming strength of his sensuous nature swallowed up in the present."

†*Transactions of the Ethnological Society*, vol. i, New Series, p. 306.

**Reise-skizzen aus Nordost-Afrika*, vol. i, pp. 162, 175. 1855.

†*Reise um die Welt (Voyage round the World)* in 1844. Stuttgard, 1853.

‡Mr. Louis Fraser says—"Their mode of mastication is very peculiar, being more like a monkey than a man."—J. H.

Colonel Hamilton Smith* thus describes the Negro. "The Negro is habitually dormant, but when roused shows his emotion by great gesticulations regardless of circumstances. War is a passion that excites in them a brutal disregard of human feelings; it entails the deliberate murder of prisoners, and victims are slain to serve the manes of departed chiefs. Even cannibalism is frequent among the tribes of the interior. Notwithstanding the listless torpidity caused by excessive heat, the perceptive faculties of the children are far from contemptible; they have a quick apprehension of the ridiculous, often surpassing the intelligence of the White, and only drop behind them about the twelfth year, when the reflective powers begin to have the ascendancy. Collectively, the untutored Negro mind is confiding and single-hearted, naturally kind and hospitable. Both sexes are easily ruled, and appreciate what is good under the guidance of common justice and prudence. Yet where so much that honours human nature remains in apathy, the typical woolly-haired races have never invented or reasoned out a theological system, discovered an alphabet, framed a grammatical language, nor made the least step in science or art. They have never comprehended what they have learned, or retained a civilisation taught them by contact with more refined nations as soon as that contact had ceased. They have at no time formed great political states, nor commenced a self-evolving civilisation. Conquest with them has been confined to kindred tribes, and produced only slaughter. Even Christianity of more than three centuries' duration in Congo has scarcely excited a progressive civilisation. Thus, even the good qualities given to the Negro by the bounty of nature, have seemed only to make him a slave trodden down by every remorseless foot, and to brand him for ages with the epithet of outcast. The marked, unceasing proof of a curse as old as the origin of society, not even deserving human forbearance, and true it is that the worst slavery is his lot even at home, for he is , there exposed to the constant peril of becoming also a victim slaughtered with the most revolting torments. Tyrant of his blood, he traffics in slavery as it were merchandise, makes war purposely to capture neighbours, and sells even his own wives and children."

Van Amringe observes of the Negro race:* "Even after having lived for centuries with the white people, from whom they have received every possible instruction for the purpose of developing an attribute which would be so serviceable to them, as well as those whom they serve, it is very far from having any virtue for which they are distinguished, or even trusted. The Canaanite (Negro) is indolent, careless, sensual, tyrannical, predatory, sullen, boisterous, and jovial. Such are the specific characteristics, and the sensual relations are founded upon them. It has been a favourite theory with some visionary

---

Unity of the Human Species, p. 190-7.
An Investigation of the Theories of the Natural History of Man. New York, 1848.

philanthropists that intermarriages of the different species would be highly favourable to the race; but we have never heard of any of them who was willing to commence the practice in their own families. There is certainly no method that could possibly be devised, which would as certainly and as expeditiously degrade the whole human family as amalgamation. If there is any hope for the improvement of the condition of the dark races, the history of mankind shows it can only be founded upon the preservation of Shemitic (White) species. This is the only species endowed with any power to drag the cumbrous dark races out of the slough in which they have been wallowing for ages."

Burmeister, an excellent observer, says:† "I need not enlarge on the long hands, slender fingers, and flat feet of the African. Any one who has ever visited a menagerie, cannot fail to have observed the long hand, slender fingers, long nails, the flat foot, the deficient calf, and compressed shank and thigh of the apes, which so much resemble in every respect the peculiarities of the Negro. I have often tried to obtain an insight into the mind of the Negro, but it never was worth the trouble; the only available result obtained was, that there is not much mental life in the Negro, and that all his thoughts and actions were merely directed to the lowest requirements of human existence. There is something in the Negro like the cunning forwardness of the monkey tribe, which renders any very familiar intercourse, such as we have with an European servant, impossible."

Carl Vogt has recently observed:* "Most of the characters of the Negro viewed externally remind us irresistibly of the ape; the short neck, the long lean limbs, the projecting pendulous belly, all this affords a glimmer of the ape beneath the human envelope, such similitudes are equally detected on examining the structure of individual parts."

Mr. Winwood Reade† says, "It must be acknowledged, that putting all exceptions aside, the women of Africa are very inferior beings. Their very virtues, with their affections and their industry, are those of well trained domestic animals. But if the women of Africa are brutal, the men of Africa are feminine. Their faces are smooth, their breasts are frequently as full as those of European women; their voices are never gruff or deep. Their fingers are long; and they can be very proud of their rosy nails. While the women are nearly always ill-shaped after their girlhood; the men have gracefully moulded limbs, and always are after a feminine type—the arms rounded, the legs elegantly formed, without too much muscular development, and the feet delicate and small." . . . . "A king of Ashanti cut off the hands of a slave, and

†R. nach Brasilien. 1857.

*Vorlesungen über den Menschen (seine Stellung in der Schöpfung und in der Geschichte der Erde). Giessen, 1863 (seventh lecture).

†Savage Africa, ch. 36.

bade her scratch his head for vermin with the stumps. If any one had accused him of barbarity he would not have understood the accusation. It was his idea of a good practical joke.''‡ He continues, ''It will be understood that the typical Negroes with whom the slavers are supplied, represent the dangerous, the destitute, and the diseased classes of African society. They may be compared to those which in England fill our jails, our workhouses, and our hospitals. So far from being equal to us, the polished inhabitants of Europe, as some ignorant people suppose, they are immeasurably below the Africans themselves. The typical Negro is the true savage of Africa, and I must paint the deformed anatomy of his mind as I have already done that of his body. The typical Negroes dwell in petty tribes where all are equal, except the women, who are slaves; where property is common, and where, consequently, there is no property at all; where one may recognise the Utopia of philosophers, and observe the saddest and basest spectacles which humanity can afford. The typical Negro, unrestrained by moral laws, spends his days in sloth and his nights in debauchery. He smokes haschisch till he stupifies his senses, or falls into convulsions; he drinks palm-wine till he brings on a loathsome disease; he abuses children, and stabs the poor brute of a woman whose hands keep him from starvation, and makes a trade of his own offspring. He swallows up his youth in premature vice; he lingers through a manhood of disease; and his tardy death is hastened by those who no longer care to find him food. Such are the 'men and brothers' for whom their friends claim, not protection, but equality! They do not merit to be called our brethren; but let us call them our children. Let us educate them carefully, and in time we may elevate them; not to our own level—that, I fear, can never be—but to the level of those from whom they have fallen.''

This last remark is made in the supposition that the typical Negro is degenerated from some higher African race; but we think such an hypothesis is not warranted by history, archaeology, or any well established facts. Mr. Reade's observations and his description does not quite agree with the accounts generally given of the Negroes in the Bights or Windward coast. Mr. Reade's terminology is far from satisfactory; all typical Negroes are Africans: but all Africans are not Negroes.

‡I know not on what authority Mr. Winwood Reade has made this assertion, but Bosman records a similar case which was perpetrated by *Anqua* about A.D. 1691. After recording innumerable cruelties, he goes on to say that one of *Anqua's* slaves touched a new coral belonging to one of his wives, ''But *Anqua* so resented this innocent freedom, that as soon as I was out of the camp, he caused both wife and slave to be put to death, drinking their blood, as he useth to do those of his enemies. For such another trivial crime, a little before, he had caused the hands of one of his wives to be cut off, after which, in derision, he used to command her to look his head for vermin, which being impossible with her stumps, afforded him no small diversion.''—*A New and Accurate Description of the Coast of Guinea*, by William Bosman, translated from the Dutch, 1705, p. 24.

Dr. Van Evrie, of New York, who has paid considerable attention to the character of the Negro, and had ample opportunities for observation, thus describes* the Negro:—"But while the analysis of a single bone or of a single feature of the Negro is thus sufficient to demonstrate the specific character, or to show the diversity of race, that great fact is still more obviously and with equal certainty revealed in the form, attitude, and other external qualities. The Negro is incapable of an erect or direct perpendicular posture. The general structure of his limbs, the form of the pelvis, the spine, the way the head is set on the shoulders, in short, the *tout ensemble* of the anatomical formation forbids an erect position. But while the whole structure is thus adapted to a slightly stooping posture, the head would seem to be the most important agency; for with any other head, or the head of any other race, it would be impossible to retain an upright position at all. But with the broad forehead and small cerebellum of the white man, it is perfectly obvious that the Negro would no longer possess a centre of gravity; and therefore, those philanthropic people who would 'educate' him into intellectual equality, or change the mental organism of the Negro, would simply render him incapable of standing on his feet, or of an upright position, on any terms. Everyone must have remarked this peculiarity in the form and attitude of the Negro. His head is thrown upwards and backwards, showing a certain though remote approximation to the quadrumana, both in its actual formation and the manner in which it is set on his shoulders. The narrow forehead and small cerebrum—the centre of the intellectual powers, and the projection of the posterior portion,—the centre of the animal functions, render the Negro head radically and widely different from that of the white man. Thus an anatomist, with the Negro and ourang-outang before him, after a careful comparison, would say, perhaps, that Nature herself had been puzzled where to place them, and had finally compromised the matter by giving them an exactly equal inclination to the form and attitude of each other."

Dr. Louis Büchner† has drawn a most graphic picture of some of the physical characters of the Negro:—"An uninterrupted series of the most various transitions and analogies connect the animal world, from the lowest to the highest. Even man, who in his spiritual pride deems himself elevated above the animal creation, is far from forming an exception to this rule. The Ethiopian race connects him by a number of the most striking analogies with the animal world. The long arms, the form of the foot, the thin calf, the long small hands, the general leanness, the undeveloped nose, the projecting jaw, the low receding forehead, the small head, the narrow pelvis, the pendulous belly, the deficient beard, the colour of the skin, the disgusting odour, the uncleanliness, the grimaces in talking, the shrieking voice, are the many marks which mani-

*On Negroes and Negro Slavery, p. 93-4-7. 1861.
†Kraft und Stoff: Force and Matter. Seventh edition.

festly exhibit the most decided approach of the Negro to the ape. That he also resembles him in his intellectual capacity, is sufficiently known and established by the best observers.''

M. Pruner Bey, one of the most eminent of living Anthropologists, has written the most complete memoir on the Negro yet published on this subject.* Many years ago he thus expressed himself† respecting the psychological character of the Negro:—''The capacity of the Negro is limited to imitation. The prevailing impulse is for sensuality and rest. No sooner are the physical wants satisfied, than all psychical efforts cease, and the body abandons itself to sexual gratification and rest. The family relations are weak; the husband or father is quite careless. Jealousy has only carnal motives, and the fidelity of the female is secured by mechanical contrivances. Drunkenness, gambling, sexual gratification, and ornamentation of the body, are the most powerful levers in the life of the Negro. The whole industry is limited to ornaments. Instead of clothing himself he ornaments his body. Like certain animals, the Negro seems apathetic under pain. The explosions of passion occur when least expected, but are not lasting. The temperament of the Negro has been called choleric, but it is only so to a certain extent. It is a momentary ebullition, followed instantly by perfect apathy. Life has for the Negro no longer any value when he cannot supply the physical wants; he never resists by increased activity, but prefers to die in a state of apathy, or he commits suicide. The Negro has no love for war; he is only driven to it by hunger. War, from passion or destructiveness, is unknown to him.''* This is a sufficiently clear

*By the kind permission of the Council, I have been able to print nearly the whole of his last Memoir on the Negro. Some portions are quoted in the text, other parts will be found in copious notes, and I have only omitted the introduction which is merely descriptive of the different African races. Feeling sure that Anthropologists will duly estimate the great value of his Treatise on the Negro, I am proud to be the means of Dr. Pruner-Bey's labours being made generally known to the English public.

†*Aegypten's Naturgeschichte.* Erlangen, 1847.

*M. Pruner-Bey also says: "It results from the examination of the organization of the Negro, that it is admirably adapted to the geographical position he occupies. The dark layer in his external integument, and its velvety character, like all blackened and rough bodies, favour the radiation of heat, and act as coolers. Experience has proved that black crape protects also the face from the solar reflection in the ascent of snow-covered mountains. The great development of the glandular system of the skin favours the secretions, refreshing the skin, and protecting it by an unctuous secretion. The thickness of all the layers of the skin protects the Negro from the night frost in his usual condition of nudity. The same considerations apply to the internal integument; the mucous membrane, with its glutinous and abundant secretion; and to all glands, without exception, which by their really enormous volume, in harmony with the excitation by heat, favour and facilitate the change, and the reproduction of organic matter so rapidly used up in the torrid zone. Do we pass beyond the limits of science, and lose ourselves in the vicious circle of teleology, if we venture to suppose that even the infantile form of the brain of the Negro may have its relative advantages? What has the noble Hindoo become under an Indian sun, drowned in a sea of spiritualism the most obscure, with his cranium, which by its admirable harmony, its graceful mould, seems exactly to resemble the organic egg which received the Divine breath of Brahma? He has, it is true, fulfilled an eminent task; but for many centuries he has been a being severed from

and truthful picture, and the following summary, with which M. Pruner Bey concluded his paper, presented to the Paris Anthropological Society, is equally to be commended for its truth and moderation. "The Negro has always appeared to me as partaking of the nature both of the child and the old man. Anatomists worthy of our confidence—Jacquart, Serres, and Huschke—have, in this sense, interpreted the details of the anatomy of the Negro. The elongated form of the cranium, the proportions of the cerebral lobes and their respective forms, the prominence of the inferior border of the orbits, the flattened nose, the rounded larynx, the less marked curves of the vertebral column, the lateral compression of the thorax and pelvis, with the vertical direction of the iliac bones, the elongated neck of the uterus, the proportion of the parts composing the extremities, the relative simplicity of the cerebral convolutions, etc., are characteristic features of the Negro race, which are found in the foetus or the infant of the Aryan race, in the different periods of development. The propensity for amusements, for physical enjoyments, for imitation, and the inconstancy of affection, are the appanage of the Negro as well as of our children. The flexuosity of the arteries, the flattening of the cornea, the weakness of the muscles, the dragging walk, and the early obliteration of the cranial sutures, the obstinacy and love of repose are met with in the Negro as in our aged men. In short, the great curve of human development, and its backward direction, appears to be sufficiently extended to appreciate the differences characterising the Negro race as opposed to our race, always taking in account the differential characters resulting from adaptation to external conditions. If our interpretation leaves open many gaps, the future may fill them up, perhaps, in the same sense. If, finally, the Negro, speaking always figuratively, partakes of the nature of the ape, it must still be admitted that it is not the most ferocious, malicious, nor the most pernicious, but rather the most patient, and frequently the most useful animal. In any case, an honourable mediocrity is his inheritance."

The general deductions we would desire to make are:—1. That there is as good reason for classifying the Negro as a distinct species from the European,

---

terrestrial regions, and of little use to his fellow beings. Let us, finally, endeavour to assign to the Negro his place in relation to the quadrumana, to which some authors seriously approximate him, and to that of other human races, which either make use of or despise the Negro. As for me, the moment that an organised being uses for standing and motion that admirable pedestal, the narrow base of which supports an enormous weight; the moment he makes use of the instrument of instruments—the hand; when he expresses his sentiments, his thoughts, his fears, and hopes by speech, I look upon it as a new order of things. While recognising the undoubted value of homologies, which form the bases of zoological science, I cannot but admire the simplicity of the means employed by creative wisdom to separate man from the anthropomorphous ape. The hair on the skin is reduced; a suture is suppressed to draw the teeth closer, and, though prognathism is developed, the lips are thickened; the iliac bones are turned aside instead of being adossed to the vertebral column; the muscles of the thumb are strengthened; the great toe is fixed; nature finally, instead of the temporal lobe, selects the anterior lobe of the brain "there to fashion the instrument of intelligence which reflects her image." (Gratiolet.)

as there is for making the ass a distinct species from the zebra; and if, in classification, we take intelligence into consideration, there is a far greater difference between the Negro and European than between the gorilla and chimpanzee. 2. That the analogies are far more numerous between the Negro and the ape, than between the European and the ape. 3. That the Negro is inferior intellectually to the European. 4. That the Negro becomes more humanised when in his natural subordination to the European than under any other circumstances. 5. That the Negro race can only be humanised and civilised by Europeans. 6. That European civilisation is not suited to the Negro's requirements or character.

No man who thoroughly investigates with an unbiassed mind, can doubt, that the Negro belongs to a distinct type. The term species, in the present state of science, is not satisfactory; but we may safely say that there is in the Negro that assemblage of evidence which would, *ipso facto,* induce an unbiassed observer to make the European and Negro two distinct types of man.

The facts I have quoted are, I believe, sufficient to establish that the Negro is intellectually inferior to the European, and that the analogies are far more numerous between the ape and Negro than between the ape and the European.

We shall not enter at length into the three last propositions. Suffice it to say, that no subject needs more attention at the present time than the position which the Negro race is fitted to hold in Nature. I have said it devolves on the student of the Science of Man to assign to each race the position which it shall hold. This is truly a momentous and most difficult problem, but one which science must not evade. As the student of mechanical science has given to the world his inductions and discoveries, so must the student of the Science of Man endeavour to deduce from actual facts principles of guidance for the relations of one race of Man to another.

It is painful to reflect on the misery which has been inflicted on the Negro race, from the prevailing ignorance of Anthropological Science, especially as regards the great question of race. By our ignorance* of the wants and aspirations of the Negro, and by a mistaken theory respecting his origin, this country has been the means of inflicting a prodigious, and, at present, totally unknown amount of mischief on these people. Our Bristol and Liverpool merchants, perhaps, helped to benefit the race when they transplanted some of them to America; and our mistaken legislature has done the Negro race much injury

---

*Dr. Van Evrie makes the following remarks respecting the imperfect accounts we have continually received of the Negro. He says (page 49): "African travellers, explorers, missionaries, &c., ignorant of the ethnology, of the physiology, of the true nature of the Negro, and moreover bitten by modern philanthropy, a disease more loathsome and fatal to the moral, than small-pox or plague to the physical nature, have been bewildered, and perverted, and rendered unfit for truthful observation or useful discovery, before they set foot on its soil or felt a single flush of its burning sun. With the monstrous conception that the Negro was a being like themselves, with the same instincts, wants, &c., the same (latent) mental capacities, all they saw, felt, or reasoned upon in Africa, was seen through this false medium, and therefore of little or no value."

by their absurd and unwarrantable attempts to prevent Africa from exporting her worthless or surplus population. All this has been done on the theoretical assumption of a mental equality of the different races or species of Man. In an attempt to benefit the Negro we have brought on him endless misery, and rendered some of the most beautiful and productive islands in the world of little more use to humanity at large, than they were before their discovery by Columbus.* But men wedded to a theory become blind to all facts, and will learn nothing from experience. All the millions of money which have been spent, and which expenditure has inflicted great hardships on our own working classes, might have been saved had we taken the trouble to investigate the character of the Negro race. Scientific men have yet to do their duty in showing what are the facts.

It may be said that some of the propositions I have advanced are in favour of the slave trade. Such, however, is not my own interpretation of these propositions. No one can be more conscious of the horrors of the "slave trade" as conducted at this time. Nothing can be worse for Africa generally than the continual capture of innocent men and women by brutal Europeans. Few things can be more horrible than the manner in which it is attempted to carry these people across the Atlantic. Nay, more, nothing can be more unjust than to sell any man, woman, or child, into "slavery", as understood by the Greeks and Romans, where the life of the slave was absolutely at the disposal of the master whenever his caprice or fancy thought fit to take it. We protest against being put forward as advocating such views.

But while I say this, I cannot shut my eyes to the fact that slavery as understood by the ancients does not exist out of Africa,* and that the highest type

*"I cannot avoid repeating that Hayti must not be held up as an example of what can be accomplished by free labour; but that it ought rather to be the beacon to warn the government of England against an experiment which may prove absolutely fatal to her colonial system. If it be not wished that a fate similar to that which has befallen Hayti should overtake our colonies, that they should be rendered wholly unproductive to the revenue of the country, and that the property invested in them should be preserved from destruction, the advisers of the Crown must pause before they listen to the ill-judged suggestions of enthusiasts; for they must banish from their minds the idea that the work of cultivation can be made productive by means of free labour. Such a thing appears to me impossible. The Negro, constituted as he is, has such an aversion to labour, and so great a propensity for indulgence and vice, that no prospect of advantage can stimulate him; and as for emulation it has not the slightest influence over him. Without force he will sink into a lethargy, and revert to his primitive savage character, and the only feasible and effectual plan to promote his civilisation is to persist in those measures which compel him to labour, inculcate morality, and tend to extirpate those vices which are inherent in the descendants of the African race."—Franklin on the Present State of Hayti.

*"No man maltreats his wild brother so much as the so-called civilised Negro. He hardly ever addresses his Kruman except by 'you jackass!' and tells him ten times a day that he considers such fellows as the dirt beneath his feet. Consequently he is hated and despised withal, as being of the same colour as, whilst assuming such excessive superiority over, his former equals. No one, also, is more hopeless about the civilisation of Africa than the semicivilised African returning to the 'home of his fathers.' One feels how hard has been his own struggle to emerge from

of the Negro race is at present to be found in the Confederate States of America. Far superior in intelligence and physique to both his brethren in Africa and to his "free" brethren in the Federal States, nowhere does the Negro attain to such a long life as in the Confederate States; and this law formerly obtained in the West India Islands before our mistaken interference. Nowhere does the Negro character shine so brightly as it does in his childish and fond attachment to his master and his family. The Negro cares far more for his master and mistress than he does for his own children after they are a few years old. I by no means join in that indiscriminate abuse of the Negro character which has been indulged in, especially by those who have only seen the Negro in his savage state, or the "emancipated" (from work?) in the West India Islands. On the contrary, there is much that is to be admired, and more that is useful in the Negro when properly and kindly treated. Brutal masters there are in every part of the world: but we must not found a law on exceptions. Scientific men, therefore, dare not close their eyes to the clear facts, as to the improvement in mind and body, as well as the general happiness, which is seen in those parts of the world in which the Negro is working in his natural subordination* to the European. In some respects, the Negro is certainly not only not inferior, but even far superior to the European. If, for instance, the European were alone in the Confederate States of America, these fertile regions would soon become a barren waste. The Negro is there able to work with impunity, and does himself and the world generally much good by his labour.†

---

barbarism. He acknowledges in his own case a selection of species, and he sees no end to the centuries before there can be a nation equal even to himself. Yet in England, and in books, he will cry up the majesty of African kings; he will give the people whom he thoroughly despises a thousand grand gifts of morals and industry, and extenuate, or rather ignore, all their faults and short-comings. I have heard a Negro assert, with the unblushing effrontery which animates a Negro speechifying in Exeter Hall, or before some learned society, that, for instance, at Lagos—a den of thieves—theft is unknown, and that men leave their money with impunity in the storehouse, or in the highway. After which he goes home, 'tongue in cheek,' despising the facility with which an Englishman and his money are parted."—*Wanderings in West Africa,* vol. i. p. 209.

*"Of late, it has become the fashion for the missionary and the lecturer to deny, in the presence of Exeter Hall, the African's recognition of the European's superiority. "The white man," writes Mr. Robert Campbell, a mulatto, "who supposes himself respected in Africa because he is white, is grievously mistaken." I distinctly assert the reverse, and every one who has studied the natural history of man, must have the same opinion. The same egregious nonsense was once propounded before the Ethnological Society—where with some ethnology there is no anthropology—by another "African". And yet the propounder, the late Mr. Consular Agent Hansen, whose death, by the bye, was an honour, and the only honour, to his life, had shaved his wool, and at the time was wearing a wig of coal-black hair, like a Cherokee's. Is imitation no sign of deference?" —*Wanderings in Western Africa,* vol. i. p. 269.

†Again, I would call attention to the noble words of Thomas Carlyle. Speaking of labour, he well says: "The thing must be done everywhere; must is the word. Only it is so terribly difficult to do, and will take generations yet, this of getting our rich European white men 'set to work!' But yours in the West Indies, my obscure black friends, your work, and the getting of you set to it, is a simple affair; and by diligence, the West Indian legislatures, and royal governors, setting

Occupations and diseases which are fatal to the Europeans, are quite harmless to the Negro. By their juxtaposition in this part of the world, they confer a material benefit on each other.

But it may be asked, "Why remove the Negro from his own country?" "Why not humanise him in Africa?" No doubt this sounds very plausible, and no pains should be spared to introduce every possible humanising influence into Africa. There is little doubt that the African is much easier humanised out of his native land away from all his savage associations; but this need not prevent us from doing all we can towards civilising him in his own country.

It has been affirmed on the best authority (although frequently denied) that domestic slaves are only sold in Africa for some crime. No one, we presume, will dare assert that there are no criminals in Africa! What shall we do with our criminals may be a problem which is occupying the attention of the political economist of Africa—like his Majesty the King of Dahomey—as well as the government of Great Britain. Is Africa not to be allowed to export her criminals, or are they so worthless and unmanageable that no people will have them? What is to be done with unruly or criminal slaves? as a king of Old Calabar said,* "You bind me down not to sell them, tell me it is wrong to kill them! What must I do with them? I will *give you some, and then you won't take them!*" Would it not be well to allow a regular export of the surplus population, instead of permitting, and indeed encouraging the butcheries of the so called King of Dahomey? The difficulties of humanising, much less of civilising, the Negro in his own country are very great; yet, if such healthy sentiments were generally diffused in this country as have been lately published in an admirable work, entitled *Wanderings in West Africa,* it is impossible to say what great results might in time be attained. This author well says, "Ever remember, that by far the greater number of the liberated were the vilest of

---

their faces fairly to the problem, will get it done. You are not 'slaves' now; nor, do I wish, if it can be avoided, to see you slaves again; but decidedly you will have to be servants to those that are born wiser than you, that are born lords of you—servants to the whites, if they are (as what mortal can doubt they are?) born wiser than you. That, you may depend on it, my obscure black friends, is and was always the law of the world, for you and for all men; to be servants, the more foolish of us to the more wise, and only sorrow, futility, and disappointment will betide both, till both in some approximate degree get to conform to the same. Heaven's laws are not repealable by earth, however earth may try—and it has been trying hard, in some directions, of late! I say, no well being, and in the end no being at all, will be possible for you or us, if the law of Heaven is not complied with. And if 'slave' mean essentially 'servant hired for life,'—for life, or by a contract of long continuance, and not easily dissoluble—I ask, whether in all human things, the 'contract of long continuance' is not precisely the contract to be desired were the right terms once found for it? Servant hired for life, were the right terms once found, which I do not pretend they are, seems to me much preferable to servant hired for the month, or by contract dissoluble in a day. An ill-situated servant that;—that servant grown to be nomadic; between whom and his master a good relation cannot easily spring up!"

*The late King Eyamba made this remark to the late Dr. Lawton in 1850, who told it to Mr. W. H. Ashmall, a Liverpool merchant who has resided for eighteen years on the West Coast of Africa, and to whom I am indebted for his approval of the chief facts contained in this paper.

criminals in their own lands, and that in their case exportation becomes, in fact, the African form of transportation."*

There is abundant evidence to show that the Negro will not work without a considerable amount of persuasion. Even Dr. R. Clarke† is obliged to admit that the Creoles of Sierra Leone "manifest the utmost contempt for agricultural pursuits, and the same feeling seems to actuate the half educated liberated African lads." Another writer observes‡ that "In Sierra Leone the christian tenderness of the British Government has tended to demoralise them. . . . . The women have become as vicious as those of Egypt, the basest of kingdoms—worse than the men, bad as they are. . . . . Theft is carried to such an extent, that no improvement is possible at Freetown."

I have stated that one of the results of my inquiry leads me to believe that English institutions are not suited to the Negro race. There seems to be a maximum testimony to show that the liberated and the creoles in our colonies are a perfectly worthless set. They accept all the vices of our civilisation with none of its duties. A recent public writer in behalf of the English colonies on the west coast of Africa well says:—"The African is far more innocent and natural a creature when he has never been brought within the range of civilised life. The liberated Africans are far superior to the rising generation —in energy, in talent, and in honest principles. To handle a hoe has now become a disgrace, and the people have lost their manhood by becoming gentlemen . . . only the ignorant can boast of the extensive freedom we have given the African. Freedom indeed we should have given, but it ought to have been qualified to suit their capacities."*

In now bringing my remarks to a close, I cannot, perhaps, do better than

---

Wanderings in West Africa, vol. i, p. 220.

†*Sierra Leone*. By Robert Clarke, p. 38.

Dr. R. Clarke speaking of the Africans of Sierra Leone, says (*Transactions of the Ethnological Society*, vol. ii, new series, p. 331)—"Servants consider it no crime to rob the white man, and so long as they are undetected they do not lose caste among their equals, although the latter may be aware of their thefts. . . . They appear to hold agricultural pursuits in contempt, preferring to obtain situations in the government offices and merchants' stores; while the young women seek employment as sempstresses, etc., seldom entering service as domestics. . . . Comparatively few of the female creoles are married, and in a colony where the marriage ceremony is held in but little esteem, and generally dispensed with, young girls live as concubines, or "sweethearts," as they phrase it (p. 332). The civilised blacks spare no expense in obtaining the best and newest style of European dress; and this love of finery too often becomes quite a passion amongst the young people, its inordinate indulgence occasionally leading to pilfering and other dishonest acts (p.326). The Africans are very litigious, and constantly summon each other on the most trivial occasions (p. 330). In one instance (of children born with supernumerary fingers) which came to my knowledge, the infant was on this account, soon after its birth, burnt alive; and, in another case, the child was destroyed by twisting its neck, when it was buried in a dung heap"(p. 333).

‡*Wanderings in West Africa*, p. 267.

*The editor of the Sierra Leone *Weekly Times*, July 30, 1862, quoted in *Wanderings in West Africa*, vol. i, p. 221.

quote the graphic picture of the present state of Africa, which has been only published during the last few weeks. There is much true science and healthy manhood in these sentiments. The work of which I speak is evidently the work of a man who has devoted much attention to the study of the great science of mankind; and I am pleased to find that my own views find ample support in the conclusions of this accomplished and scientific observer. Speaking of the Negroes of Bonny, he says:† "The slaves wore a truly miserable appearance, lean and deformed, with Krakra lepra and fearful ulcerations. It is in these places that one begins to feel a doubt touching the total suppression of slavery. The chiefs openly beg that the rules may be relaxed, in order that they may get rid of their criminals. This is at present impossible, and the effects are a reduplication of misery; we pamper our convicts, Africans torture them to death. Cheapness of the human article is another cause of immense misery to it. In some rivers a canoe crew never lasts three years. Pilfering—'Show me a black man and I will show you a thief,' say the traders—and debauchery are natural to the slave, and they must be repressed by abominable cruelties. The master thinks nothing of nailing their hands to a water-cask, of mutilating them in various ways; many lose their eyes by being peppered, after the East Indian fashion, with coarsely-powdered cayenne, their ears are cut off, or they are flogged. The whip is composed of a twisted bullock's or hippopotamus's hide, sun dried, with a sharp edge at the turns, and often wrapped with copper wire; it is less merciful even than the knout, now historical. The operation may be prolonged for hours, or for a whole day, the culprit's arms being tied to a rafter, which keeps them at full stretch, and every fifteen minutes or so, a whack that cuts away the flesh like a knife, is administered. This is a favourite treatment for guilty wives, who are also ripped up, cut to pieces, or thrown to the sharks. If a woman has twins, or becomes mother of more than four, the parent is banished, and the children are destroyed. The greatest insult is to point at a man with arm and two fingers extended, saying at the same, Nama shubra, i.e., one of twins, or a son of some lower animal. When a great man dies, all kinds of barbarities are committed; slaves are buried, or floated down the river bound to bamboo sticks and mats, till eaten piecemeal by sharks. The slave, as might be expected, is not less brutal than his lord. It amazes me to hear Englishmen plead that there is moral degradation to a Negro bought by a white man, and none when serving under a black man. The philanthropists, doubtless, think how our poorer classes at home, in the nineteenth century, would feel if hurried from liberty to eternal servitude by some nefarious African. But can any civilised sentiments belong to the miserable half-starved being, whose one scanty meal of vegetable per day is eked out with monkey and snake, cat and dog, maggot and grub; whose life is ceaseless toil, varied only by torture, and who may be destroyed at any moment

†*Wanderings in West Africa*, vol. ii, p. 280.

by a nod from his owner? When the slave once surmounted his dread of being shipped by the white man, nothing under the sun would, I believe, induce him willingly to return to what he should call his home. And, as they were, our West Indian colonies were lands of happiness compared with Oil Rivers; as for the 'Southern States,' the slave's lot is paradise when succeeding what he endures on the West Coast of Africa. I believe these to be facts, but *tant pis pour les faits*. Presently, however, the philanthropic theory shall fall, and shall be replaced by a new fabric built upon a more solid foundation.''

Finally let me observe, that it is not alone the man of science who has discerned the Negro's unfitness for civilisation as we understand it. Here is the opinion of Mr. Anthony Trollope,* who is certainly quite guiltless of ever having examined the evidence on the distinction of the Negro and European, and yet truly says of the Negroes:—''Give them their liberty, starting them well in the world at what expense you please, and at the end of six months they will come back upon your hands for the means of support. Everything must be done for them; they expect food, clothes, and instruction as to every simple act of life, as do children.''

We must for the present leave alone all questions as to the origin of the Negro, and simply take him as he exists, and not as poets or fanatics paint him. We shall then learn, that it is only by observation and experiment that we can determine the exact place in nature which the Negro race should hold, and that it is both absurd and chimerical to attempt to put him in any other.†

North America, vol. ii, p. 85. 3rd Edition. 1862.

†We believe the following opinion of Mr. George M'Henry can be confirmed by all who have narrowly watched the position of ''Free'' Negroes in the Federal States. He says that ''he has resided nearly all his life in Pennsylvania, where exists the largest community of free Negroes in the world, and he can testify to the gradual decay in their health and morals as slavery disappeared from the neighbourhood. Neither the laws of the land, nor public societies for his benefit, prevent the African from degenerating; nothing but the controlling influence of a master will keep him from sinking to that barbarous condition which is his natural state,''—*The Cotton Trade Considered in Connection with Negro Slavery in the Confederate States*, 1863, p. 259. Many other interesting and important facts, showing the superiority of the ''Slave'' over the ''Free'' Negro, will be found in this valuable work.

Another public writer, Mr. George Augustus Sala, gives the following picture (not derived from the study of Anthropology) of the Free Negroes of New York, vide *Daily Telegraph*, Jan. 2, 1864.—''Hundreds of witnesses could, if needful, be put into the box to prove how utterly puerile and irresponsible the vast majority of these poor people are. From the old slaves who crawl about the houses of their owners, fed for nothing and not worked, saying and doing what they please, and sleeping with their feet so thrust into the embers on the hearth that they scorch their toe-nails off, to the little black brats snuggling like so many guinea-pigs about the floors of southern houses; from these to the women who buy silk umbrellas instead of childbed linen, and who come roaring to their mistress for remedies if they have a sore finger or a soft corn—who will only take medicine when they are sick from her hand—and who, *as mothers, are so shamefully neglectful of, and wantonly cruel to, their children, that the white ladies are often compelled to take the little ones away from their unnatural parents to preserve their lives*—it is the same lamentable case of an inferior and impracticable race. And in the North—the free North—the land of liberty, of intellig-

APPENDIX.

After reading the foregoing paper, I was favoured with an account of Dr. Pruner-Bey's further researches since he published his first "Memoir," and as he has kindly placed them at my entire disposal, I have thought it advisable to annex a translation of M. Pruner-Bey's obliging communication.

"The gallery of the *Jardin des Plantes* has, since the publication of my *Memoir on Negroes,* received eleven more crania belonging to the same family, nine of which are those of males, and two of females. Three of the former belong to the tribe of Shir, inhabiting the banks of the White Nile; the other six are those of a Wolof, of a Thiong of Low Casamance, two of Krumans, and two of Griots. Of the two female crania, one belonged to a Negress of Saloum, and the other to a Griot.

"On comparing the subjoined table of measurements with that of the Memoir, it will be observed, that as regards the circumference, the crania of the new series are more voluminous than those of the first series. Moreover, the mean vertical diameter is here sensibly larger, whilst that of the width differs but little from that in the first series. All these new crania present the ellipsoid form; they are dolichocephalous, and more or less prognathous.

"As regards the circumference, it attains in the Shir only 490, 520, and 530 millimeters; whilst in the rest it oscillates between 530 and 75 mm. The last figure refers to the Wolof cranium, a very vigorous Negro tribe, often praised for their beauty. This cranium is very massive and coarse. The following are its chief features:—forehead low, narrow, and receding; a protuberance formed by the confluence of the superciliary arches with the glabella. Expansion of the face enormous compared with that of the forehead. Viewed in front the cranium presents the contours of a narrow lozenge. The nasal aperture corresponds, by its elliptic form, with that of the cranium. The nasal bones are

---

ence, of newspapers, and Methodist chapels, and common schools; do they fare better there? I declare that, of all the miserable and woe-begone objects I have ever beheld out of a Russian gaol or an Italian lazar-house, the free Negroes I have seen in New York are the wretchedest and most forlorn. Take away those who are coachmen or body-servants in private families, and who are clad in some kind of decent livery by the employers; take away a proportion of mulattoes and 'bright' coloured people, among which class the women are often given to tawdry finery in apparel, but seldom to personal cleanliness; take away a few, a very few old Negroes, who have made money by storekeeping, and wear broadcloth and tall hats; and the residue is a listless, decrepit, drowsy, cowering race, always going to the wall, always sliding and slinking away, always ragged, always dirty—lying and pilfering and tipsifying themselves in a feckless, shambling kind of way—horribly overgrown children—*cretins* whose *goîtres* are on their brains instead of in their throats. In the back slums of New York you meet them prowling about with baskets full of scraps and offal. When the police rout out some dilapidated tenement at the Five Points, they are sure to find Negroes lurking and snoozling among the rubbish. Let a streak of sunshine be cast across the pavement, and you are sure to find a Negro sitting on a doorstep, basking in the radiant warmth."

short and narrow; the orbits very spacious, inclined downwards and outwards; their inferior margins, of considerable thickness, advance much beyond the superior. The malar bones are very high, thick, and form a rounded prominence in front; the jaws, as well as the teeth, are very strong; the latter are, in this individual, much used up and partly carious. Chin—square, high, and wide— projects but little. Prognathism apparently inconsiderable. This Negro has, what is called, an open physiognomy. I have dwelt upon the preceding details, in order to show by an example to what extent tribes and individuals, reputed handsome, may deviate from the gross type of the great Nigritian stock, without, however, transgressing the limits which separate the African Negro from the other human races.

"Apart from the nose, which is flatter than that of the Wolof, the cranium of the Thiong, with a circumference of 550 millimeters, approaches the latter by the elongated contours of the face. The Krumans, on the contrary, present a type differing from the preceding; for their face is comparatively short, compact, and wide. Their cerebral cranium is also distinguished by the great development of the vertical diameter. It is, consequently, by these two crania that the mean of this diameter has reached the point indicated in the table.

"The three crania of the Shir Negroes, one of which is that of a young subject, demonstrate what had already been observed upon the living natives of the Nilotic region, that it is wrong to consider them more favourably organised than the western tribes. One of these crania (No. 2,919) abounds in the animal character of the face. Fortunately, its prognathism is moderate, whilst in No. 2,920 prognathism is excessive by the side of less coarse features.*

"The crania of the two Negresses did not present anything deserving particular notice."

---

*"Nature thus applies its means of compensation, even upon individuals belonging to more or less savage races, in order not to leave us in any doubt as regards the limits which physically separate man from the brute, at least as regards the form and the disposition of parts."

CEREBRAL CRANIUM	Mean Measures in Millimeters	
	Mean of 9 Negroes	Mean of 2 Negresses

1. DIAMETERS (with the Callipers)

Antero-posterior			187	178
Vertical			133	127
Transverse Diameters	Inferior frontal		99	93
	Superior frontal		115	109
	Bi-temporal		117	115
	Bi-auricular		115	108
	Bi-parietal		137	130.5
	Bi-mastoidian		121	110

2. CURVES (with the Metrical Tape)

Horizontal circumference		535	517
Transverse bi-auricular curve		321	310
Vertical antero-posterior circumference		522	489.5
Decomposed in: 1. Middle part	Frontal part	117	111.5
	Parietal part	137	125
	Occipital part	118	111
2. Inferior part	Length of the occipital hole	36	32
	Distance from the anterior border of the foramen and the frontal eminence (approximative)	114	110

3. OTHER MEASURES

Distance in a straight line from the auditory canal	to the nasal eminence	114	110
	to the occipital protuberance	113	107
Dimensions of the occipital foramen	length	36	32
	width	30.7	28

4. MILLESIMAL PROPORTIONS

Circumferences	horizontal circumference	1000	1000
	vertical circumference	975	946
Diameters	length (antero-posterior diameter)	1000	1000
	Width (bi-parietal diameter)	732	733
	Height (vertical diameter)	711	713

DESIGNATION OF MEASURES

Total length of the face, from the superciliary line to the inferior margin of the chin			135	113
Partial length of the face	from the inferior nasal spine	to the superciliary line (major length of nose)	56	54
		to fronto-nasal suture (minor length of nose)	47	44
		to inferior border of chin	74	59
Maximum length of the superior jaw from the fronto-maxillary suture to the superior alveolar arch			64	59.5
Maximum distance of the two zygomatic arches			130	124
Inferior jaw	Distance of the two angles		100	88
	From the symphysis to the angle in a straight line		99	92
	Length of the vertical branch		66	58
Orbital aperture	height		32.4	33
	width		35	35.5

————————————

BISHOP CODRINGTON ON *MANA*

ROBERT HENRY CODRINGTON (1830-1922), was English missionary to the islands of Melanesia, where he spent thirty years of his life, and wrote two important books which are classics of anthropology, *The Melanesian Languages* (Oxford, The Clarendon Press, 1885), and *The Melanesians* (Oxford, The Clarendon Press, 1891). It was in the latter work that Codrington first brought to the attention of the learned world the existence among the peoples of the Pacific of the belief in a nonindividualized supernatural power belonging to the region of the unseen, without any connection whatsoever with a belief in supreme beings, and capable of residing in almost anything. This supernatural power the Melanesians called *mana*. It is akin to the Algonquin Indian belief in *manitou*, the Iroquois *orenda*, and the Sioux *wakanda*.

Codrington's description of the belief in *mana*, in addition to being the first of its kind, contributed very considerably to the discussions that followed on the origins and development of religion. Did such a belief in an impersonal power antedate the development of the animistic belief in spiritual beings or personal spirits, or was *mana* merely one type of belief among many, having nothing whatever to do with the so-called developmental stages of religious belief? The generally accepted viewpoint today is that the latter is the correct answer to the posited question.

MANA*

The religion of the Melanesians is the expression of their conception of the supernatural, and embraces a very wide range of beliefs and practices, the limits of which it would be very difficult to define. It is equally difficult to ascertain with precision what these beliefs are. The ideas of the natives are not clear upon many points, they are not accustomed to present them in any

*Reprinted from R. H. Codrington, *The Melanesians* (Oxford, The Clarendon Press, 1891), pp. 117-121.

systematic form among themselves. An observer who should set himself the task of making systematic enquiries, must find himself baffled at the outset by the multiplicity of the languages with which he has to deal. Suppose him to have as a medium of communication a language which he and those from whom he seeks information can use freely for the ordinary purposes of life, he finds that to fail when he seeks to know what is the real meaning of those expressions which his informant must needs use in his own tongue, because he knows no equivalent for them in the common language which is employed. Or if he gives what he supposes to be an equivalent, it will often happen that he and the enquirer do not understand that word in the same sense. A missionary has his own difficulty in the fact that very much of his communication is with the young, who do not themselves know and understand very much of what their elders believe and practice. Converts are disposed to blacken generally and indiscriminately their own former state, and with greater zeal the present practices of others. There are some things they are really ashamed to speak of; and there are others which they think they ought to consider wrong, because they are associated in their memory with what they know to be really bad. Many a native Christian will roundly condemn native songs and dances, who, when questions begin to clear his mind, acknowledges that some dances are quite innocent, explains that none that he knows have any religious significance whatever, says that many songs also have nothing whatever bad in them, and writes out one or two as examples. Natives who are still heathen will speak with reserve of what still retains with them a sacred character, and a considerate missionary will respect such reserve; if he should not respect it the native may very likely fail in his respect for him, and amuse himself at his expense. Few missionaries have time to make systematic enquiries; if they do, they are likely to make them too soon, and for the whole of their after-career make whatever they observe fit into their early scheme of the native religion. Often missionaries, it is to be feared, so manage it that neither they nor the first generation of their converts really know what the old religion of the native people was. There is always with missionaries the difficulty of language; a man may speak a native language every day for years and have reason to believe he speaks it well, but it will argue ill for his real acquaintance with it if he does not find out that he makes mistakes. Resident traders, if observant, are free from some of a missionary's difficulties; but they have their own. The 'pigeon English,' which is sure to come in, carries its own deceits; 'plenty devil' serves to convey much information; a chief's grave is 'devil stones,' the dancing ground of a village is a 'devil ground,' the drums are idols, a dancing club is a 'devil stick[1].' The most intelligent

[1] It may be asserted with confidence that a belief in a devil, that is of an evil spirit, has no place whatever in the native Melanesian mind. The word has certainly not been introduced in the Solomon or Banks' Islands by missionaries, who in those groups have never used the word devil. Yet most unfortunately it has come to pass that the religious beliefs of European traders

travellers and naval officers pass their short period of observation in this atmosphere of confusion. Besides, every one, missionary and visitor, carries with him some preconceived ideas; he expects to see idols, and he sees them; images are labelled idols in museums whose makers carved them for amusement; a Solomon islander fashions the head of his lime-box stick into a grotesque figure, and it becomes the subject of a woodcut as 'a Solomon Island god.' It is extremely difficult for any one to begin enquiries without some prepossessions, which, even if he can communicate with the natives in their own language, affect his conception of the meaning of the answers he receives. The questions he puts guide the native to the answer he thinks he ought to give. The native, with very vague beliefs and notions floating in cloudy solution in his mind, finds in the questions of the European a thread on which these will precipitate themselves, and, without any intention to deceive, avails himself of the opportunity to clear his own mind while he satisfies the questioner.

Some such statement as this of the difficulties in the way of a certain knowledge of the subject is a necessary introduction to the account which is given here of the religion of the Melanesians; and it is desirable that the writer should disclaim pretension to accuracy or completeness. The general view which is presented must be taken with the particular examples of Melanesian belief and customs in matters of religion which follow.

(1) The Melanesian mind is entirely possessed by the belief in a supernatural power or influence, called almost universally *mana*[1]. This is what works to effect everything which is beyond the ordinary power of men, outside the common processes of nature; it is present in the atmosphere of life, attaches itself to persons and to things, and is manifested by results which can only be

---

have been conveyed to the natives in the word 'devil,' which they use without knowing what it means. It is much to be wished that educated Europeans would not use the word so loosely as they do.

[1] Professor Max Müller, in his Hibbert Lectures of 1878, did me the honour of quoting the following words from a letter. 'The religion of the Melanesians consists, as far as belief goes, in the persuasion that there is a supernatural power about belonging to the region of the unseen; and, as far as practice goes, in the use of means of getting this power turned to their own benefit. The notion of a Supreme Being is altogether foreign to them, or indeed of any being occupying a very elevated place in their world . . . There is a belief in a force altogether distinct from physical power, which acts in all kinds of ways for good and evil, and which it is of the greatest advantage to possess or control. This is Mana. The word is common I believe to the whole Pacific, and people have tried very hard to describe what it is in different regions. I think I know what our people mean by it, and that meaning seems to me to cover all that I hear about it elsewhere. It is a power or influence, not physical, and in a way supernatural; but it shows itself in physical force, or in any kind of power or excellence which a man possesses. This Mana is not fixed in anything, and can be conveyed in almost anything; but spirits, whether disembodied souls or supernatural beings, have it and can impart it; and it essentially belongs to personal beings to originate it, though it may act through the medium of water, or a stone, or a bone. All Melanesian religion consists, in fact, in getting this Mana for one's self, or getting it used for one's benefit—all religion, that is, as far as religious practices go, prayers and sacrifices.'

ascribed to its operation. When one has got it he can use it and direct it, but its force may break forth at some new point; the presence of it is ascertained by proof. A man comes by chance upon a stone which takes his fancy; its shape is singular, it is like something, it is certainly not a common stone, there must be *mana* in it. So he argues with himself, and he puts it to the proof; he lays it at the root of a tree to the fruit of which it has a certain resemblance, or he buries it in the ground when he plants his garden; an abundant crop on the tree or in the garden shews that he is right, the stone is *mana*[1], has that power in it. Having that power it is a vehicle to convey *mana* to other stones. In the same way certain forms of words, generally in the form of a song, have power for certain purposes; a charm of words is called a *mana*. But this power, though itself impersonal, is always connected with some person who directs it; all spirits have it, ghosts generally, some men. If a stone is found to have a supernatural power, it is because a spirit has associated itself with it; a dead man's bone has with it *mana*, because the ghost is with the bone; a man may have so close a connection with a spirit or ghost that he has *mana* in himself also, and can so direct it as to effect what he desires; a charm is powerful because the name of a spirit or ghost expressed in the form of words brings into it the power which the ghost or spirit exercises through it. Thus all conspicuous success is a proof that a man has *mana*; his influence depends on the impression made on the people's mind that he has it; he becomes a chief by virtue of it. Hence a man's power, though political or social in its character, is his *mana*; the word is naturally used in accordance with the native conception of the character of all power and influence as supernatural. If a man has been successful in fighting, it has not been his natural strength of arm, quickness of eye, or readiness of resource that has won success; he has certainly got the *mana* of a spirit or of some deceased warrior to empower him, conveyed in an amulet of a stone round his neck, or a tuft of leaves in his belt, in a tooth hung upon a finger of his bow hand, or in the form of words with which he brings supernatural assistance to his side. If a man's pigs multiply, and his gardens are productive, it is not because he is industrious and looks after his property, but because of the stones full of *mana* for pigs and yams that he possesses. Of course a yam naturally grows when planted, that is well known, but it will not be very large unless *mana* comes into play; a canoe will not be swift unless *mana* be brought to bear upon it, a net will not catch many fish, nor an arrow inflict a mortal wound.

(2) The Melanesians believe in the existence of beings personal, intelligent, full of *mana*, with a certain bodily form which is visible but not fleshly like the bodies of men. These they think to be more or less actively concerned

[1] The word *mana* is both a noun substantive and a verb; a transitive form of the verb, *manag, manahi, manangi*, means to impart *mana*, or to influence with it. An object in which *mana* resides, and a spirit which naturally has *mana*, is said to be *mana*, with the use of the verb; a man has *mana*, but cannot properly be said to be *mana*.

in the affairs of men, and they invoke and otherwise approach them. These may be called spirits; but it is most important to distinguish between spirits who are beings of an order higher than mankind, and the disembodied spirits of men, which have become in the vulgar sense of the word ghosts. From the neglect of this distinction great confusion and misunderstanding arises; and it is much to be desired that missionaries at any rate would carefully observe the distinction. Any personal object of worship among natives in all parts of the world is taken by the European observer to be a spirit or a god, or a devil; but among Melanesians at any rate it is very common to invoke departed relatives and friends, and to use religious rites addressed to them. A man therefore who is approaching with some rite his dead father, whose spirit he believes to be existing and pleased with his pious action, is thought to be worshipping a false god or deceiving spirit, and very probably is told that the being he worships does not exist. The perplexed native hears with one ear that there is no such thing as that departed spirit of a man which he venerates as a ghost but his instructor takes to be a god, and with the other that the soul never dies, and that his own spiritual interests are paramount and eternal. They themselves make a clear distinction between the existing, conscious, powerful, disembodied spirits of the dead, and other spiritual beings that never have been men at all. It is true that the two orders of beings get confused in native language and thought, but their confusion begins at one end and the confusion of their visitors at another; they think so much and constantly of ghosts that they speak of beings who were never men as ghosts; Europeans take the spirits of the lately dead for gods; less educated Europeans call them roundly devils. All Melanesians, as far as my acquaintance with them extends, believe in the existence both of spirits that never were men, and of ghosts which are the disembodied souls of men deceased: to preserve as far as possible this distinction, the supernatural beings that were never in a human body are here called *spirits*, men's spirits that have left the body are called *ghosts*[1].

---

[1]The Melanesian Mission, under the guidance of Bishop Patteson, has used in all the islands the English word God.

TO THE INCREDULITY OF THE GREATER PART OF THE LEARNED WORLD, SPENCER AND GILLEN DESCRIBE THE IGNORANCE OF PHYSIOLOGICAL PATERNITY OF THE AUSTRALIAN ABORIGINES

WALTER BALDWIN SPENCER (1860-1929), English zoologist and anthropologist, and Francis (Frank) James Gillen (1855-1912), Australian Protector of Aborigines and anthropologist, were the joint authors of one of the most famous of anthropological books, *The Native Tribes of Central Australia* (London, Macmillan, 1899). Gillen had lived at Alice Springs for many years on the most cordial terms with the aborigines, and had collected an immense amount of material on their way of life. Gillen, who was termed by Elliot Smith, "Spencer's greatest discovery," was only too glad to share his knowledge with Spencer when the latter began his studies of the Arunta and neighboring tribes in 1894. The result of their collaboration was a work which is still a model of its kind and will always remain the basic treatise on an Australian aboriginal tribe. It was in this work that Spencer and Gillen described the conception beliefs of the Arunta and their ignorance of physiological paternity. This part of their work was greeted with considerable incredulity by much of the learned world, and although such ignorance was subsequently described by Malinowski for the Trobriand Islanders,[1] the controversial debate has never ceased.[2]

Since the Australian aborigines are a highly intelligent people the puzzling question remains: How could they possibly be ignorant of the connection between intercourse and childbirth? The fact is that in highly civilized societies one occasionally encounters individuals of both sexes of normal intelligence whose knowledge of the connection between

---

[1]Bronislaw Malinowski, "Baloma: The Spirits of the Dead in the Trobriand Islands," *Journal of the Royal Anthropological Institute*, (Vol. 46, 1916), pp. 335-430; B. Malinowski, *The Sexual Life of Savages* (London, Routledge, 1919).

[2]For a detailed discussion see Ashley Montagu, *Coming Into Being Among the Australian Aborigines*, 2nd ed. (London & Boston, Routledge, 1974).

intercourse and childbirth is nonexistent. As Phillip Roberts (Wipul-
danya) of the Alawa tribe on the Roper River in the southeast corner
of Arnhem Land put it, "In recent years I have had medical training
and listened carefully to doctors who assured me that conception takes
place through fertilization of female ova by male sperm following intercourse. That story would raise a great laugh among the Alawa."[3]

Spencer himself summed the matter up for the greater number of
Australian aboriginal peoples. In a letter to Şir James Frazer dated 8
March 1898, Spencer wrote, "Amongst the Arunta and other central
tribes it is not supposed that a child is the direct result of sexual intercourse: it is the result of a spirit individual entering the woman."[4]

Since a missionary worker among the aborigines claimed to have
found that the Arunta believed in a god, Spencer in 1913 and again
in 1926 revisited Arunta country and with the aid of a number of old
informants was able to show that the claim that they numbered a god
among their many beliefs was ill-founded. Spencer was able to fill in
a large number of gaps present in the 1899 volume, and in 1927 published the revision of that work in two volumes entitled, *The Arunta:
A Study of a Stone Age People*. It is from this second edition of the
1899 work that the following excerpt is reprinted.

PROCREATIVE BELIEFS*

"The whole past history of the tribe may be said to be bound up with these
totemic ceremonies, each of which is concerned with the doings of certain
mythical ancestors who are supposed to have lived in the dim past, to which
the natives give the name of 'Alchera'.

"In the Alchera lived ancestors who, in the native mind, are so intimately
associated with the animals or plants the name of which they bear that an
Alchera man of, say, the kangaroo totem may sometimes be spoken of either
as a man-kangaroo or as a kangaroo-man. The identity of the human individual
is often sunk in that of the animal or plant from which he is supposed to
have originated. It is useless to try to get farther back than the Alchera; the
history of the tribe as known to the natives commences then.

[3]Douglas Lockwood, *I, The Aboriginal*. (Adelaide, Rigby Ltd., 1962), p. 113.

[4]R. R. Marrett and T. K. Penniman, eds., *Spencer's Scientific Correspondence* (Oxford, Clarendon Press, 1932), p. 19.

*From Baldwin Spencer and F. J. Gillen, *The Arunta: A Study of a Stone Age People* (London,
Macmillan, 1927), Vol. 1.

"Going back to this far-away time, we find ourselves in the midst of semi-human creatures endowed with powers not possessed by their living descendants and inhabiting the same country which is now inhabited by the tribe, but which was then devoid of many of its most marked features, the origin of which, such as the gaps and gorges in the Macdonnell Ranges, is attributed to these mythical Alchera ancestors.

"These Alchera men and women are represented in tradition as collected together in companies, each of which consisted of a certain number of individuals belonging to one particular totem."[1]

"Each of these Alchera ancestors is represented as carrying about with him, or her, one or more of the sacred stones, which are called by the Arunta natives Churinga, and each of these Churinga is intimately associated with the *Kuruna* or spirit part of some individual. Either where they originated and stayed, as in the case of certain of the witchetty grub people, or else where, during their wanderings, they camped for a time, there were formed what the natives call *Knanikilla*, each one of which is in reality a local totem centre. At each of these spots—and they are all well known to the old men, who pass the knowledge on from generation to generation—a certain number of Alchera ancestors went into the ground, each leaving his Churinga behind. His body died, but some natural feature, such as a rock or tree, arose to mark the spot, while his spirit part remained in the Churinga. These Churinga, as well as others that the wandering parties left behind them, were stored in *Pertalchera*, or sacred storehouses, that usually had the form of small caves and fissures in the rocks, or even a hollow tree or a carefully concealed hole in a sand-bank. The result is that, as we follow their wanderings, we find the whole country is dotted over with *Knanikilla*, or local totem centres, at each of which are deposited a number of Churinga, with *Kuruna*, or spirit individuals, associated with them. Each *Knanikilla* is, of course, connected with one totem. . . .

"As we have said, the exact spot at which a Churinga was deposited was always marked by some natural object, such as a tree or rock, and in this the spirit is supposed to take up its abode, and it is called the spirit's *Knanja*.

"We may take the following as a typical example of how each man and woman gains a totem name. Close to Alice Springs is a large and important witchetty grub totem centre or *Knanikilla*. Here there were deposited in the Alchera a large number of Churinga carried by witchetty grub men and women. There are numerous prominent rocks and boulders and certain ancient gum trees along the sides of a picturesque gap in the ranges, that are the *Knanja* trees and rocks of these spirits, which, so long as they remain in spirit form, they usually frequent. If a woman conceives a child after having been near to this gap, it is one of these spirits individuals which has entered her body,[1]

[1]*The Arunta*, vol. 1, pp. 72-73.
[1]"The spirit of *Kuruna* always enters the woman through the loins."

and therefore, quite irrespective of what the mother's or father's totem may chance to be, that child, when born, must of necessity be of the witchetty grub totem; it is, in fact, nothing else but the reincarnation of one of the witchetty grub people of the Alchera. Suppose, for example, to take a particular and actual instance, an emu woman from another locality comes to Alice Springs, and whilst there becomes aware that she has conceived a child, and then returns to her own locality before the child is born, that child, though it may be born in an emu locality, is an Udnirringita or witchetty grub. It must be, the natives say, because it entered the mother at Alice Springs, where there are only witchetty grub *Kurunas*. Had it entered her body within the limits of her own emu locality, it would as inevitably have been an emu. To take another example. Quite recently the *lubra* or wife of a witchetty grub man, she belonging to the same totem, conceived a child while on a visit to a neighbouring *Quatcha* or water locality, which lies away to the east of Alice Springs—that child's totem is water; or, again, an Alice Springs woman, when asked by us as to why her child was a witchetty grub (in this instance belonging to the same totem as both of its parents), told us that one day she was taking a drink of water near to the gap in the Ranges where the spirits dwell when suddenly she heard a child's voice crying out, '*Mia, Mia!*'—the native term for relationship, which includes that of mother. Not being anxious to have a child, she ran away as fast as she could, but to no purpose; she was fat and well favoured, and such women the *Kurunas* prefer; one of them had gone inside her, and of course it was born a witchetty grub.[1]

"The natives are quite clear upon this point. The spirit children are supposed to have a strong predilection for fat women, and prefer to choose such for their mothers, even at the risk of being born into the wrong class. . . .

"There is a curious belief in regard to one method of conception. If a man, for example, be hunting an emu and, whilst he is chasing it, it runs near to a wallaby *Knanikilla*, a wallaby *Kuruna* may go into it. If the man spears it near to the *Knanikilla* and gives some of it to his wife to eat, the wallaby *Kuruna* will go into her. She does not eat it, but, as is supposed always to be the case, it enters by her loins. Later on she becomes sick, and then knows that the *Kuruna* has given rise to a *Ratappa* inside her, which, when born, belongs to the wallaby *Knanja*. It is definitely said that she does not actually eat the *Kuruna*."[2]

"The members of each totem claim to have the power of increasing the number of the animal or plant, and in this respect the tradition connected with Undiara, the great centre of the kangaroo totem, just as the Emily Gap is the great centre of the witchetty grub totem, is of especial interest. In the Alchera,

---

[1] "*Kurunas* are also supposed to be especially fond of travelling in whirlwinds, and, on seeing one of these, which are called Uraburaba and are very frequent at certain times of the year, approaching her, a woman will at once run away."

[2] Ibid., 75-8.

as we have already described, a special kangaroo was killed by kangaroo men and its body brought to Undiara and deposited in the cave close by the waterhole. The rock ledge arose to mark the spot, and into this entered its spirit part and also the spirit parts of many other kangaroo animals (not men) who came subsequently and, as the natives say, went down into the earth here. The rock is, in fact, the *Knanja* stone of the kangaroo animals, and to them this particular rock has just the same relationship as the waterhole close by has to the men. The one is full of *Kurunas* of kangaroo animals, just as the other is full of those of men and women. The purpose of the ceremony at the present day, so say the natives, is, by means of pouring out the blood of kangaroo men upon the rock, to drive out in all directions the *Kurunas* of the kangaroo animals and so to increase the number of animals. The spirit kangaroo enters the female kangaroo in just the same way in which the spirit kangaroo man enters the kangaroo woman.

"Every animal such as a kangaroo is supposed to have a *Kuruna* or spirit part, just like a human being has. As a *Kuruna* it has no legs or arms or head, but goes into its mother and grows into a kangaroo or rat or wild dog, as the case may be. An emu *Kuruna* goes into an emu, who lays an egg containing the little emu *Kuruna*, which is very small and cannot at first be seen, but it grows into an emu inside the shell and hatches out from this just like a little kangaroo or human baby grows inside the shell and hatches out from this just like a little kangaroo or human baby grows inside its mother's *ekura*, or baby bag, and hatches out."[1]

"Churinga is the name given by the Arunta natives to certain sacred objects which, on penalty of death or very severe punishment, such as blinding by a fire-stick, are never allowed to be seen by women or uninitiated men. The term is also applied to various objects associated with the totems, but the greater number belong to that class of rounded, oval or elongated, flattened slabs of wood and stone, varying in length from six or seven feet to two or three inches, to the smaller ones of which the name bull-roarer is now commonly applied."[2]

"It must be remembered that the country occupied by the tribes, amongst whom the cult of the Churinga exists, is of great extent, so that, even in important respects, beliefs vary considerably. It is, however, possible to say that there is one fundamental Churinga belief according to which every individual possesses a special one of wood or stone with which his or her *Kuruna*, or spirit part, is intimately associated."[3]

"The original Churinga are, one and all, connected with the *Knanjas* or totems. At the present day the whole country is dotted over with *Knanikillas*, or local totem centres, and each of these has one or more sacred storehouses

[1]Ibid., 85.
[2]Ibid., 99.
[3]Ibid., 102.

in which the Churinga are kept under the charge of the head man of the local group.

"The general name for the head man, throughout most, but not all, of the totemic groups, is *Inkata,* and for the storehouse, *Pertalchera (perta,* a rock), in reference to the fact that crevices and caves in rocks are the favourite secreting places. *Pertalchera* thus signifies the Alchera rock. Each one of these contains, amongst others, the original Churinga of every individual that, in one way or another, came to be deposited there in the Alchera. With each of these, again, a *Kuruna* or spirit is associated. When the *Kuruna* goes into a woman and a child is born, the old men determine what *Kuruna* has undergone reincarnation. The Churinga is preserved in the *Pertalchera,* and there it remains in association with the *Arumburinga,* or double or the *Kuruna.* This Churinga is known as the *Churinga knanja* or *Churinga indulla-irrakura.* The *Arumburinga,* however, can travel about freely, and, in fact, often visits, and is supposed to watch over, its human representative. The spot at which the child is born and brought up, and at which it will probably spend the greater part of its life, has nothing to do with determining the resting-place of its Churinga. That remains in the storehouse or *Pertalchera* in which it was deposited in the Alchera, and to which the *Kuruna*—now called *Ulthana*—returns when the man or woman dies. In the case, for example, already quoted, in which a witchetty grub woman conceived a child in a water locality, or *Knanikilla,* twelve miles to the north of Alice Springs, where the woman's home camp is located, the child was born at the latter, but its *Churinga knanja* is deposited in the *Pertalchera* of the water group to which it belonged in the Alchera.

"So far as the possession of the *Churinga knanja* is concerned, each man and woman has a personal one; men, but not women, may possess others by inheritance. The most detailed and important traditions relating to the origin of Churinga is that associated with the Achilpa [wild-cat] totem. . . . The tradition, so far as it deals with Churinga, is shortly as follows:—

"A great Being called Numbakulla made the first Achilpa Churinga with a *Kuruna* associated with it, from which the first Achilpa man originated. Later on, he fashioned very large numbers of Churinga belonging to all *Knanjas* or totems, drawing upon each the design or designs now characteristic of the *Knanjas.* Each one of these was associated with a *Kuruna* or spirit which Numbakulla had previously made. Leaders, or *Inkatas,* of *Knanja* groups, some Achilpa (wild cat), some Erlia (emu), some Arura (kangaroo), some Unjiamba (Hakea flower), etc., were sent out with numbers of Churinga and *Kurunas* that gave rise to groups of individual men and women, each with his or her own Churinga, all of which were deposited finally in various *Pertalcheras.* According to the Achilpa tradition, the original Churinga, made by Numbakulla and afterwards by the Achilpa *Inkatas,* in the Alchera, were all stone ones called *Churinga talkara.* First of all a number of these were made, then each of them was split into two, one of which was *Atua* or *uria* (male), the other

Arragutja or *malia* (female). The pairs are now called *Chua ninga*, but the old Alchera name for them was *Unpora ninga*. According to the Achilpa tradition, the two forming a pair were tied together with hair string. Later on the *Inkata Achilpa kupitcha* transformed the female Churinga—that is, the ones with which a woman's *Kuruna* was associated—into wooden ones called *Churinga tidjanira*. Some of the latter had holes bored through them, and were called *Tidjanira alknarinja*. The women who arose, and still arise, from the *Kuruna* associated with these are called *Arragutia alknarinja*. This tradition accounts for the fact that at the present time only men have *Churinga talkara*—that is, stone ones. The stone ones are commonly spoken of collectively as *Churinga perta*, the wooden ones as *Churinga rola*. The special, personal Churinga belonging to each individual is also spoken of as his or her *Churinga knanja*. Each one of these original Churinga, wooden and stone alike, is also called *Indulla-irrakura*. In addition to these Churinga, that were carried by the Alchera ancestors, there are two other kinds. When the old *Inkatas* marched across the country they left *Kuruna*—always in pairs—in the *Tidja* (mulga) trees. In the Alchera . . . an *Oknirrabata*, wandering through the bush, would suddenly catch sight of an *Iwupa*, or spirit, in the form of a child playing about on one of the trees; it would suddenly disappear, and then the old man knew that it was one of the *Kuruna* left by the *Inkata*. Splitting a block of wood, taken from the tree, the *Oknirrabata* then fashioned from it a pair of Churinga, one associated with the male and the other with the female spirit. That tree was henceforth regarded as the *Rola knanja* of each *Kuruna* and of the human beings to whom they gave rise.

"The Churinga thus made were placed in the local *Pertalchera* and were regarded as *Indulla-irrakura*, but, in this case, the man who arose from the *Kuruna* had a wooden and not a stone Churinga.

"According to other traditions—and the traditions vary to a certain extent in different parts of the country and in different local groups—less stress is laid upon the *Inkata*, though there appears always to have been a leader of each travelling group. In some cases, as described in connection with the totems, the ancestors are stated to have arisen at a definite place and to have remained there. Each ancestor had one, and only one, original Churinga, carried either by the *Inkata* or by himself, or herself, because, quite unlike what happens at the present time, women were allowed, in the Alchera, to see and own sacred objects such as Churinga, *Nurtunjas*, and *Waningas*. When he, or she, died, that Churinga, associated with its *Kuruna*, remained behind in the *Pertalchera*, in which it had been placed for safe keeping by the *Inkata* or the Alchera ancestor. According to another widespread tradition, the spirit is supposed to drop its Churinga when it enters a woman. On the birth of a child, the mother tells her husband the position of the tree or rock near to which she believes the child entered her, and the man, accompanied by one or two of the older men, and always, if alive, by his own father—that is, the *Arunga* of the child—goes in search of the Churinga. Sometimes it is found, sometimes it is not; in the latter case a new one is made from the mulga, or some hard-wood tree, near to the *Pertalchera* of the child, and is marked by the *Arunga* with a design belonging to the child's totem. The Churinga is then placed in the *Pertalchera* and is regarded as the child's *Churinga knanja,* with which its *Kuruna* is associated.

"In some parts of the tribe, especially the Central and Northern divisions, whilst there is the same belief with regard to the existence of the original Churinga, the custom prevails of the *Arunga*—that is, the paternal grandfather of a child—going out into the scrub when a child is born, and making a wooden Churinga out of a tree close to the *Pertalchera.* This has nothing to do with the original one, which, according to this tradition, is left in the *Pertalchera.* It is called *Twanyirrika,* and is ornamented with a design belonging to the child's totem. The size—it is often a large one—and design are decided upon by the *Arunga,* but it has no *Kuruna* associated with it. A large number of these are stored in the *Pertalchera;* they are much used during totemic ceremonies, such as those shown at the *Engwura,* and it is one or more of these that are placed in the youth's hands after circumcision. The natives say, *Churinga Twanyirrika, itja Kuruna,* that is, it is a *Twanyirrika* Churinga, but has no *Kuruna.*"[1]

"Each Churinga is so closely bound up with the spirit individual that it is regarded as its representatives in the *Pertalchera.* Those of dead men are supposed to be endowed with the attributes and powers of their owner, and actually to impart these to the person who, for the time being, may, as when a fight takes place, be fortunate enough to carry one of them about with him. The Churinga is supposed to endow the possessor with courage and accuracy of aim, and also to deprive his opponent of these qualities. So firm is their belief in this, that, if two men were fighting and one of them knew that the other carried a Churinga, whilst he did not, he would certainly lose heart at once, and without doubt be beaten."[1]

"We meet in tradition with unmistakable traces of the idea that the Churinga is the dwelling-place of the spirit of the Alchera ancestor. The Achilpa belief is that the *Kuruna* or spirits were first made by Numbakulla, and, later, a Churinga for each one of them. One tradition relates that, when the Achilpa men were out hunting, they erected a sacred pole or *Nurtunja,* that they carried with them during their wanderings, and on this hung their Churinga and placed their spirit parts in them for safe keeping, taking them down when they returned to camp. Whilst this is so in regard to Alchera tradition, it must be pointed out clearly that the Arunta native, at the present day, does not regard the Churinga as the abode of his own spirit part, placed in the *Pertalchera* for safety,

[1]Ibid., 103-7.
[1]Ibid., 110.

though at the same time it is intimately associated with himself, and more especially with his *Arumburinga*, which is really the twin or double of his own *Kuruna*, and the half of the original *Kuruna* of his Alchera ancestor. If anything happens to it—if it be stolen—he mourns over it deeply, and has a vague idea that some ill may befall him, but he does not imagine that damage to the Churinga of necessity means destruction to himself. The value of the Churinga lies in the fact that each one is intimately associated with, and is, indeed, the representative of, one of the Alchera ancestors, with the attributes of which it is endowed. It is also felt that the *Arumburinga*, which spends much of its time in and around the Pertalchera, in which the Churinga is kept, may follow it, and thus the individual will lose the guardianship of the spirit."[2]

According to the Achilpa tradition, "Whilst many leaders, locally known as *Inkata, Alatunja, Chitchurta*, or *Chantchwa*, are associated with Alchera times and myths, Numbakulla, according to this tradition, is the supreme ancestor, overshadowing all others. He gave rise to all the original *Kurunas*, Churingas, and *Knanjas*, in fact to everything associated with the Alchera. He himself had no special *Knanja* or totem, but made and owned them all. During his long travels he created many of the main features of the country and decided upon the location of the central places now associated with the various *Knanjas*—Achilpa (wild cat), Erlia (emu), Arura (kangaroo), Udnirringita (witchetty grub), Irriakura (yelka), Emora (opossum), etc.

"At every such place he put his foot down, saying, *Nana, Knanja Achilpa, Erlia Arura*, etc.; here is wild cat, emu, kangaroo, etc., Knanja. Then he drew and left on some rock or ground surface what is called a *Churinga ilpintira*—that is, a special design or mark associated with the totem of that locality. Each of these designs now forms the distinctive mark or *Ilkinia* of the *Knanja* of that place."[1]

"Numbakulla thus created all the original *Kuruna* and Churinga. He himself was full of *Kuruna*: as the natives say, *Kuruna injaira oknirra, kwanala mberka Numbakulla;* there were a very large number of *Kuruna*, inside the body of Numbakulla; and again, *Kuruna aradukka* (or *aradugga*) *kwanala, Numbakulla;* the *Kuruna* came out from inside Numbakulla.[2]

"The first Churinga made by Numbakulla and placed by him on the *Churinga Ilpintira* is called *Churinga indulla-irrakura Numbakulla*.[3] All of the origi-

---

[2]Ibid., 111-12.

[1]Ibid., 356.

[2]"The word *aradugga* or *arakukka* is generally used with the meaning of coming out of, or being born, as in the phrase, *Tmerga ratappa aradugga*, the child was born yesterday. The word *knailjalugga* is more often used when speaking of a *Kuruna* coming out of, or emanating from, a Churinga; for example, when a man is shown his own *Churinga Knanja*, he is told, *Nana Churinga indulla-irrakura ingwana; unta knailjalugga*; here is your Churinga indulla-irrakura; you came out of it. The Churinga is not regarded as the body, or *mberka*, of the man: the *mberka* is supposed to be formed later when the *Kuruna*, having left the Churinga, enters a woman."

[3]*Indulla-irrakura*, totem design.

nal Alchera Churinga, made by Numbakulla and subsequently produced from them or made by the various ancestral *Inkatas* of the different *Knanjas* or totem groups, are also called *Churinga indulla-irrakura*. By the splitting of each of these original ones a pair was made. The pairs were at first tied together, and each man and woman had one of them associated with his, or her, *Kuruna* or spirit, which was originally placed in it by Numbakulla. One Churinga of each pair had an *atua* or man's spirit, the other an *arragutja* or woman's. Each Churinga had also an *Aritna churinga*, or sacred name, associated with it and its *Kuruna*, and all these names were given, originally, by Numbakulla. Later on, the *Kurunas* emanated from the Churinga, and gave rise to men and women, each of whom bore, as his or her sacred name, the one given to the Churinga by Numbakulla.

"The natives are very definite in regard to the fact that the Churinga is not the changed body (*mberga* or *mberka*) of the man or woman: the original Churinga and Kuruna were made by Numbakulla before there were any men or women."[1]

"It must be remembered that every one of the great number of *Kurunas* that gave rise to all the men and women of the various *Knanjas* was, according to this tradition, created originally by Numbakulla. Some of them, such as those associated with *Inkata Achilpa maraknirra, Inkata Achilpa oknira, Inkata Achilpa Kupitcha*,[2] Illapurinja, and the *Inkatas* of other *Knanjas*, emanated from Churinga in the Alchera and gave rise directly to human beings—without entering a woman. In all other cases the *Kuruna* entered a woman and, within her, gave rise to a child called *Ratappa*—the term applied to the child developing within the womb and also to the new-born baby. The 'spirit child' that enters a woman always does so, as a *Kuruna*, through her loins, never by way of the vulva. The *Kuruna* is described as being very small, round, like a very little pebble, and red in colour. It is shapeless and has neither arms nor legs nor head, but develops these within the mother and gives rise to a *Ratappa*. It does not enter as a *Ratappa*, but as a *Kuruna*, and only changes into the former within the womb or *ilpa*."[3]

"The natives are quite clear on the point that in the case of all the *Knanjas* originated by Numbakulla, men and women of the same *Knanja*, or totem, were arranged in pairs as mates, and married one another. It followed that, at first, all the members of one local group, men, women, and children,

---

[1]Ibid., 358-9.

[2]These terms refer to the first four Inkatas of the Alchera in order of importance, respectively, the very great Inkata, the great Inkata, the lesser Inkata, and the little Inkata.

[3]Ibid., 362-3. "The term *Ratappa* is not, strictly speaking, applied to a 'spirit-child'. The spirit is always spoken of as a *Kuruna*, and it is only after entering the mother that it gives rise to a *Ratappa*. Even at the *Ratappa* stone, so called because a small child went into the ground there, it is a *Kuruna* and not a *Ratappa* that enters a woman. The term *Kuruna* is always used in reference to the spirit itself, either before it enters the mother or after it leaves the body."

belonged to the same *Knanja*, but, when *Knanikillas* and *Knanjas* had become established and the people increased in numbers and began to move about the country, visiting different camps and assembling at various places to perform ceremonies, the *Kurunas* of one *Knanja* group entered women of another, and so the present irregular local distribution of men and women of different totems or *Knanjas* was brought about. At the same time the majority of individuals in any one locality typically belong to the *Knanja* that has its *Pertalchera* there.''[4]

''When a man or woman dies, the spirit part, or *Kuruna*, immediately leaves the body and flies away to its *Pertalchera* in the form of a little bird called *Chichurkna*, whose whistling is often heard when there has been a death in the camp. As soon as it has joined its *Arumburinga* the latter hastens from its *Knanja* tree, or rock, or from its *Pertalchera*, to the grave, to protect the body against attacks by mischievous spirits called *Eruncha*. It remains there until the *Kuru-urkna* or girdle, made of hair cut from the dead man, has been woven. During this short period of perhaps three or four days, it receives the special name of *Alknuriniata*. It then goes back to its *Knanja* tree, and the spirit of the dead man returns to the grave in the form of an *Ulthana* until the final mourning ceremony of *Urpmilchimilla* has been held, after which it returns to the *Pertalchera*, and there joins the *Arumburinga* and other spirit beings, assuming once more the form of a *Kuruna* that can enter a woman and be reborn.''[1]

From this account of the Alchera and conceptional beliefs of the Arunta the following points emerge: (1) that each individual is the incarnation of an Alchera *Kuruna* or the reincarnation of an Alchera ancestor, (2) whose spirit part or *Kuruna* enters the prospective mother directly from its *Knanja* or abode, that is, the place at which it was deposited in the Alchera, (3) generally choosing a woman as its mother whose husband is of the correct moiety, that (4) on occasion a *Kuruna* may deliberately choose to enter a woman of the ''wrong'' class and so bring it about that the living representative of an Alchera ancestor belongs to a class different from that of the ancestor whose incarnation he is, the totem, of course, remaining unchanged, (5) that the *Kuruna* therefore exhibits a certain amount of liberty of choice as to the woman, the moiety, and the class which it will enter, (6) that the *Churinga* represents the split half of the *Kuruna* of the totem ancestor, the other half being its guardian spirit, the *Arumburinga*, that (7) after his death the spirit part of an individual returns to its Churinga in the *Pertalchera*, (8) that the native does not regard the Churinga as the abode of his own spirit part, but rather of the *Arumburinga*, which watches over the *Kuruna*, the Churinga, and to a certain extent, himself, and finally (9) that intercourse does not play any causal part in the production of pregnancy, which is believed to be due to the entrance into a woman of a *Kuruna*.

There are a number of points in this account which are not very clear, and the most important of these is one that we have already encountered in our discussion of Schulze's report, namely whether the individual represents an incarnation of an Alchera spirit or the spirit part of an Alchera ancestor only, or a reincarnation of that ancestor *ab ovo usque ad mala,* soul and body. According to Spencer and Gillen's account, it would appear that the individual is, among the Arunta, regarded as a complete reincarnation of an actual Alchera ancestor, body as well as soul, though not necessarily of the *first* Alchera ancestors. The lack of clarity arises chiefly from Spencer and Gillen's careless-ness in speaking at one time as if a *Kuruna* were merely a discarnate soul, the spirit part *only* of an individual, and at another time as if it represented the complete Alchera ancestor, the reader being left to choose, unassisted, between the two alternatives afforded. Nowhere, however, in Spencer and Gil-len's account is there any explicit statement that the individual is the reincarna-tion of the spirit part *only* of an ancestor, and not also of his corporeal part. As to the native's beliefs concerning the fate of the body and of the spirit after death, according to Spencer and Gillen it would be quite obvious to him that at death the body undergoes a physical dissolution, and that the spirit must therefore leave it and return to its abode. But the native, it appears, is no Platonic dichotomist, and we must avoid any confusion which would result here from thinking him so, for the spirit which leaves the body after death is not merely the spirit of that particular body, it is a *Kuruna,* the actual being of an eternally incarnable Alchera ancestor in spirit or quasi-spirit form, a spirit soul *and* body, for the *Kuruna* is described as having a definite, though it be a somewhat amorphous, structure, "very small, round, like a very little pebble, and red in colour". Further, "it is shapeless, and has neither arms nor legs nor head, but develops these within the mother and gives rise to a *Ratappa,*" developing from a diminutive little thing, the *Kuruna,* into a baby, a *Ratappa,* within the mother.[1] It would seem then, that the *Kuruna* represents an already preformed individual who undergoes an unfolding only within the mother's womb, in which, before the entry of the *Kuruna* into her, no other soul *or* body could have been present: "the *mberka,*" that is, the body, write Spencer and Gillen, "is supposed to be formed later when the *Kuruna,* having left the Churinga, enters a woman."[2]

LEWIS HENRY MORGAN AND
CHARLES MARTIN ON THE
AMERICAN INDIAN

LEWIS HENRY MORGAN (1818-1881), the Father of American Anthropology, in the journal which he kept of his visits among various American Indian tribes from 1859 to 1862 gives an account of a meeting and conversation with Charles Martin, an itinerant French-Canadian trader, who knew many American Indian peoples intimately. Martin was one of those colorful characters who spent most of his time living and trading with American Indians, among whom he was welcomed as a friend, and for whom he had a deep personal affection. He was a man of considerable understanding and intelligence, and the report of his views on the American Indian here given by Morgan communicates, in a few words, something of the qualities of the Indian which many learned tomes have never achieved. Martin's words, "the old Indian before the advent of the white man must have been the happiest man on earth," have an especial poignancy, for they are almost certainly true. Alas.

INDIAN JOURNAL*

Rulo, Nebraska Territory
Richardson Co., June 13, 1860

Conversation with Charles Martin, Trader

I have been a trader for the last twenty years in the employ of the American Fur Company, and have visited and lived among the following, Dakotas, Otoes, Omahas, Pottawatomies of Council Bluffs, Pawnees, Arikarees (Ah-

*Reprinted from Lewis Henry Morgan, *The Indian Journals 1859-62*, ed., Leslie A. White, (Ann Arbor, University of Michigan Press, 1959), pp. 99-102.

rik-a-ra), Gros Ventres below Yellowstone, Assinaboines, (they call themselves Da-ko-ta), Crows (Up-sa-ro-ka, which means a crow), Sheyennes, Snakes (Sho-sho-nee, which means snake), Utah (U-taw they call themselves), Arapahoes (Ah-rap-a-ho they call themselves whch means tattooed breast), Ban-aks and Kaws. All these nations have their signs by which they indicate their nationality, thus the Dakota make a sign of cutting the throat by drawing the hand across the throat. Their sign is rendered by the trader in English as "cut heads." The Sheyennes are "cut arms," and they make their sign by drawing the hand or finger two or three times across the left arm. The Crows make their sign by working their hands up and down like a bird. The Dakotas are as follows, who all make the same national sign. 1, Yank-ton (Lower Band). 2, Yank-ton-ais (Upper Band). 3, Pa-bok-sa (Cut Head, Pa-head, and Bok-sa, to cut). 4, Wa-ze-koo-ta (One who shoots in the Pine). 5, Se-a-sa-pa (Black-feet, these are Blackfeet Dakotas and not the Blackfeet of the Maps [?]). 6, Onk-pa-pa. 7, Cha-ha-nump-a (Two Kettle Band). 8, Min-e-ko-zhu (Farm-ing near the Water). 9, E-ta-zip-shne (One without a Bow). 10, On-ga-lal-a (Rovers and always moving camp). 11, She-cha-hoo (Brule Dakota, Burnt Thighs). 12, Son-te. The above are given in Yankton dialect.

These are in three great divisions. 1, Son-tee. 2, Yank-ton. 3, Te-tons. The Son-tee are one. The Yankton consist of the Yankton and Yank-ton-ais. The remainder are all west of the Missouri and are called Te-tons. This is their own classification.

The Assinaboines make the cut head sign. The Blackfeet raise one foot and touch the bottom. The Snake first points his finger to himself and then waves his finger from side to side and ahead to imitate the motion of a snake. The Arapahoe touch all the fingers of the right hand upon the breast several times in quick succession to show that they are pricked or tattoed breasts. The Pawnees pass the hand edgewise over the center of the head from front to rear to show that his head is shaved, with hair along the center. The sign for a white man is the hand drawn quick across the forehead horizontally to indicate that he wears a hat. The hat is the sign of the white man. Arikaree the same as the Pawnee. The Nez Perces make the sign of the pierced nose by touching the two sides of the nostril.

Talking by Signs

There is a regular language of signs by which all the most western Indians can make themselves understood for all ordinary purposes. Martin made for me the signs for quite a long conversation. For crossing a mountain the closed hands were brought together and then stretched out horizontally to indicate a range, and then one hand is passed over the other at right angles curving upwards to indicate a crossing. That he met a white man on horseback would be made by the sign of the hat, and then two fingers in a fork on the other hand to show that he was on horseback straddle. If a mule, a motion would be made to show large ears. Martin says that without any Indian language and with these signs, he could go through these nations and travel with them and have no difficulty.

No Words of a Profane Kind

There is no swearing in an Indian language. The worst saying they can make is "you are a dog." "You are nasty" is another.

Marriage

Among all these nations the brother has most to say about the marriage of his sister. If the girl is applied for by a poor fellow, he says, "you will not marry that poor rascal. You must marry someone with plenty of horses, that he may give much horse to hunt buffalo with; or that white man and I shall always have a blanket and good clothes and horses etc." This is the way especially with the Dakotas and the Sheyennes.

Martin confirms my former position that the Indian woman has no passion, no love in our sense. She is quiescent and submissive to her husband from duty, but without active passion. Martin says that the women are not attached to their husbands in the general sense of that term as one friend is to another, and perhaps it is because of the precarious tenure of the relation. A man may put away his wife and take another whenever he pleases or have several wives at once. After the birth of a child there is a substantial separation of husband and wife for a year. The children nurse, when polygamy permits, sometimes for six years or seven, as long as they please or until they are shamed of it. That is, the boys nurse as long as they please; the girls are usually weaned at three years. I saw a boy stand on his feet and nurse sometime in Kansas last month. It was on the Sawk and Fox reservation. He must have been three years old. Martin says that where there is but one wife, the children are weaned earlier. Polygamy prevails very generally. He has known an Indian with 14 wives. He has had four at a time himself. The number of wives shows a man's wealth and influence, and not from passion. He says the Indians call the month of January the rutting month for human beings, such is the meaning of the name of the month.

An Indian never whips his wife, nor scolds her, nor pets her, but he simply says I don't like you any longer and I will throw you away. Sometimes he gives her the lodge and some horses and leaves her in it. Sometimes he sends her back to her relations. Complaints are made to the relatives on both sides but no quarrel results. She takes the children usually because the husband does not want them. The woman is not dishonored by the divorce. Another man will take her with her children just as quick if she is a proper woman and desirable.

It is clear from Martin's account that a man is expected to buy his wife with presents, usually of horses in the prairie country, and this necessarily begets an expectation and a desire to speculate or profit by the marriage of the girls in the family to which they belong.

Indian Women

Martin has had a large experience with Indian women and mentioned to me many facts which it would be perhaps injudicious to note down, although I sought them and wished to know. He says the Indian woman never or rarely kisses her children, and never her husband unless asked to do so. He says he never knew an Indian woman to have a foul breath; they are also modest and retiring, and universally industrious. He is entirely positive that they know nothing of love, and cannot be made to manifest passion. They are always the same passive and passionless creatures, but acknowledging the principle of obedience. Martin says the Indian woman really prefers an Indian husband to a white husband, as they like and approve of the Indian's ways and deport- ment the best; but they prefer to marry a white man from such motives as the certainty of more and finer clothes than an Indian can provide, and perhaps a more comfortable home and fewer hardships, but the Indian nature and temper is better adapted to her. I was surprised at what Martin said about the attachment or affections of the Indian female other than the passion of love. He says they do not become attached to him even. That if he is brought home wounded she does not manifest the least sensibility, and if he is killed she is not much affected by it. We know the Indian suppresses all emotion. If a relative returns after a hunt, or a war excursion or a long absence when he enters his home, no word is said of welcome or of pleasure. If married his wife takes off his moccasins, washes his feet and oils them if sore. She then sets food before him. After [he] has eaten, and not until he has eaten, it is polite or proper to speak to him. Then his friends and relatives begin and ask him the questions where he has been, what he has seen and what he has done, and he gives his account in due form over his pipe. Martin admitted that he was always contrary and exacting with his wives, and this I think accounts for the want of even a moderate affection for him which he discovered. The Indian female, well treated, must I think become attached to her husband, and strongly interested in his welfare.

Color of the Skin

Martin says the face and body where exposed to the sun on the prairie becomes quite dark, but that covered parts of the body of dark faced Indians are light. Speaking of the Sheyennes who have but little white blood in them, he says, none he says, the uncovered parts of their bodies are as fair as the back of his hand which was of a buff brown color. He is French Canadian, with blue eyes and chestnut hair. This is lighter than I expected. He says the forms of the Sheyennes, Crows and Sioux women are very fine, and as he says very beautiful. He seems to think the Sheyennes are about the finest Indians on the continent.

Indian Beard Plucked

Martin says he has seen Sioux and Sawks and Pawnees who had not a particle of white blood in them with heavy beards. It was plucked on the sides, and the eyebrows were plucked. The moustache was full. He says they sit for hours and work at it on their arms and face. The Indian says the white man's hair stinks, and that he is hairy like a dog. Martin says if they did not pull their beards they would become full in time. He thinks their scant beards are their own work, and besides they like to paint their faces. He says his Indian wives were continually pestering him to cut off his beard, which is yet a very full and flowing one. They said it was ugly and dirty. "You have too much to pull, but take a razor like a white man and shave it." They said "you are a good looking man and if you will shave you can get any young girl you like, etc."

Original Indian

Martin says that the three things which spoil the Indian are: 1st, the preacher, 2. the agent, and 3. the soldier. That the Indian who has seen neither, nor whisky, is a noble looking fellow, good hearted, proud and manly. He is honest, truth telling, hospitable, the best kind of a neighbor, all like brothers, and stand by each other. They fight every nation with whom they have no express treaty. These are broken by stealing horses and by retaliation. After the introduction of soldiers, and agents, and white people among them they were abused in all ways. They were made drunken, they were taken as wives and then abandoned. There are about 1,000 half breeds around Fort Laramie, and as many around Fort Randall and Fort Pierre. By these abuses the Indian is cowed down and oppressed. He also retaliates upon innocent white people for the wrongs done him in such ways as these.

At the Forts the officers high and low expect to have their Indian women, and the soldiers who are loose and free to do as they please, do the same. In this way the Indians are debased and demoralized, and learn to look upon the white man as treacherous, or at least as a devastator and the worst possible results flow from it. As to the agent I am more and more inclined to the belief that the agency system is a failure, and of but little benefit, and the only remedy I can see is to reduce the number, and leave the Indian to depend more upon himself.

Missionaries

As to the missionaries, I am not prepared to go to Martin's extent, and make the evil effects of their intercourse exceed the good. I am surprised, however, to hear the traders, who are French Catholics it must be remembered, as far as they have any religion, bear their united testimony against the missionaries, and also some of the half breeds who are the descendants of traders. I think the first and greatest blessing now which we can give the Indian is the *English language*. With this he can depend [upon] himself, and make himself understood, and show his mind to the white man. The boarding school is the only instrumentality by which this can be effectually done, and therefore I am for the missionary and his school; but as to the agent and the soldier I agree with Martin. The Agents are opposed to the missionaries and it is because they are observers of each other.

I notice that all of these Missions look out well for themselves when a reservation is broken up and a band is moved to a new home. Thus the Methodist Manual Labor School among the Shawnees secured three sections of land, the Friends Mission half a section, the Presbyterian Mission at Bellevue among the Omahas secured a section of land which covered about half of the village site. Mr. Hamilton told me that the Board had expended $25,000 at Bellevue, and that they had or would realize from their real estate received from the Indians about $20,000 which was the amount they had expended upon the new Mission building at Blackbird Hills.

At Highland the same Board has secured a section of land which is quite valuable, and I was told also that they had managed to secure Iowa Point which was a valuable village property, besides. How this was done I know not. They also told me that the children were compelled to work hard and so much of the time that the school did them but little good. There was a strong prejudice against it for this reason. It is painful to hear and see so many and such constant evidences of mi rust in the Indian mind, of white people and their motives.

[Charles] Martin

Martin gave me some account of his life, but it was too meagre to insert. He said if you take 20 white men there will be at least one soft head among them, but of 20 Indians, not one would be soft. He thinks the old Indian before the advent of the white must have been the happiest man on the earth. He was evidently a great admirer of Indian life and has a real love for it.

Martin must be 60 years old or at least 50. He brought his first wife whom he married 16 years ago down with him to this point, where she lived until last winter in January. He is now a widower and alone. His son, 15 years of age, is now in Montreal at school. I should have been glad to have seen more of him, as he is a man of intelligence and observation.

ANTHROPOLOGY INTO LITERATURE
SIR JAMES FRAZER

SIR JAMES GEORGE FRAZER (1854-1941) will always be remembered for his great work, *The Golden Bough*. This first appeared in two volumes in 1890 and the twelve-volume third edition appeared in 1935. Fraser produced many other scholarly works of great value, among them, *Totemism and Exogamy* (1910), and its supplement, *Totemica* (1937), *The Belief in Immortality and the Worship of the Dead* (3 vols., 1913-24), and *Folk Lore in the Old Testament* (3 vols., 1919), to name the most important.

Although Frazer's reputation has today suffered something of an eclipse, his influence during the last decade of the nineteenth and the first decade of the twentieth century was considerable. As a gifted writer, whose style raised the anthropology he wrote to the level of literature, Frazer contributed substantially to the popular development of interest in anthropology, especially through the abridgements of his works which appeared from time to time. But his influence went deeper than that, for not only did his works bring many readers into the ranks of professional anthropology, but because of the controversial nature of so many of his ideas, they served as a whetstone upon which many students were encouraged to sharpen their anthropological wits.

We reprint here a large part of the opening chapter of *The Golden Bough*. This will give the reader a good idea of Frazer's style both as a writer and a thinker, and will also introduce him to the problem to which the whole of the twelve volumes that followed was the attempted solution.

The second piece is a delightful account of "Some Primitive Theories of the Origin of Man," and again shows what a consummate stylist Frazer was, and how, in spite of the scholarly apparatus, he could hold one's interest.

For a biography of Frazer see R. Angus Downie, *Frazer and the Golden Bough* (London, Gollancz, 1970).

THE GOLDEN BOUGH*

CHAPTER I

THE KING OF THE WOOD

"The still glassy lake that sleeps
Beneath Aricia's trees—
Those trees in whose dim shadow
The ghastly priest doth reign,
The priest who slew the slayer,
And shall himself be slain."
MACAULAY.

§ I. *Diana and Virbius*

Who does not know Turner's picture of the Golden Bough? The scene, suffused with the golden glow of imagination in which the divine mind of Turner steeped and transfigured even the fairest natural landscape, is a dream-like vision of the little woodland lake of Nemi—"Diana's Mirror," as it was called by the ancients. No one who has seen that calm water, lapped in a green hollow of the Alban hills, can ever forget it. The two characteristic Italian villages which slumber on its banks, and the equally Italian palace whose terraced gardens descend steeply to the lake, hardly break the stillness and even the solitariness of the scene. Dian herself might still linger by this lonely shore, still haunt these woodlands wild.

In antiquity this sylvan landscape was the scene of a strange and recurring tragedy. In order to understand it aright we must try to form in our minds an accurate picture of the place where it happened; for, as we shall see later on, a subtle link subsisted between the natural beauty of the spot and the dark crimes which under the mask of religion were often perpetrated there, crimes which after the lapse of so many ages still lend a touch of melancholy to these quiet woods and waters, like a chill breath of autumn on one of those bright September days "while not a leaf seems faded."

*Reprinted from Sir James George Frazer, *The Golden Bough: The Magic Art.* 2 vols. New York, The Macmillan Co., 1935, vol. 1, pp. 1-23.

The Alban hills are a fine bold group of volcanic mountains which rise abruptly from the Campagna in full view of Rome, forming the last spur sent out by the Apennines towards the sea. Two of the extinct craters are now filled by two beautiful waters, the Alban lake and its lesser sister the lake of Nemi. Both lie far below the monastery-crowned top of Monte Cavo, the summit of the range, but yet so high above the plain that standing on the rim of the larger crater at Castel Gandolfo, where the Popes had their summer palace, you look down on the one hand into the Alban lake, and on the other away across the Campagna to where, on the western horizon, the sea flashes like a broad sheet of burnished gold in the sun.

The lake of Nemi is still as of old embowered in woods, where in spring the wild flowers flow as fresh as no doubt they did two thousand springs ago. It lies so deep down in the old crater that the calm surface of its clear water is seldom ruffled by the wind. On all sides but one the banks, thickly mantled with luxuriant vegetation, descend steeply to the water's edge. Only on the north a stretch of flat ground intervenes between the lake and the foot of the hills. This was the scene of the tragedy. Here, in the very heart of the wooded hills, under the abrupt declivity now crested by the village of Nemi, the sylvan goddess Diana had an old and famous sanctuary, the resort of pilgrims from all parts of Latium. It was known as the sacred grove of Diana Nemorensis, that is, Diana of the Wood, or, perhaps more exactly, Diana of the Woodland Glade.[1] Sometimes the lake and grove were called, after the nearest town, the lake and grove of Aricia.[1] But the town, the modern Ariccia, lay three miles away at the foot of the mountains, and separated from the lake by a long and steep descent. A spacious terrace or platform contained the sanctuary. On the north and east it was bounded by great retaining walls which cut into the hillsides and served to support them. Semicircular niches sunk in the walls and faced with columns formed a series of chapels, which in modern times have yielded a rich harvest of votive offerings. On the side of the lake the terrace rested on a mighty wall, over seven hundred feet long by thirty feet high, built in triangular buttresses, like those which we see in front of the

[1]Strictly speaking, *nemus* is a natural opening or glade in a forest. Thus Lucan says (*Pharsal.* i. 453 *sq.*) that the Druids inhabited "deep glades in sacred groves far from the haunts of men" ("*nemora alta remotis incolitis lucis*"), as the words are rendered by Haskins in his edition, who compares Propertius v. 9. 24, "*lucus ubi umbroso fecerat orbe nemus.*" But commonly *nemus* means no more than a wood or grove. See for example Lucan, *Pharsal.* iii. 396, "*procumbunt nemora et spoliantur robora silvae.*" At Nemi the sacred grove (*lucus*) formed part of the woodlands (*nemus*), as we learn from Cato, quoted by Priscian, *Inst.* iv. 21 (vol. i. p. 129, ed. M. Hertz), "*lucum Dianium in nemore Aricino,*" etc. As to the thick woods of Nemi in antiquity see Ovid, *Fasti,* iii. 263 *sq.*; *id., Metam.* xv. 485.

[1]Cato, *loc. cit.*; Ovid, *Fasti,* vi. 756; Statius, *Sylvae,* iii. I. 56; Philostratus, *Vit. Apollon.* iv. 36. A loose expression of Appian (*Bellum Civile,* v. 24) has sometimes given rise to the notion that there was a town called Nemus. But this is a mistake. See E. Desjardins, *Essai sur la Topographie du Latium* (Paris, 1854), p. 214, and on the other side, A. Bormann, *Altitalische Chorographie* (Halle, 1852), pp. 135 *sq.*

piers of bridges to break floating ice. At present this terrace-wall stands back some hundred yards from the lake; in other days its buttresses may have been lapped by the water. Compared with the extent of the sacred precinct, the temple itself was not large; but its remains prove it to have been neatly and solidly built of massive blocks of peperino, and adorned with Doric columns of the same material. Elaborate cornices of marble and friezes of terra-cotta contributed to the outward splendour of the edifice, which appears to have been further enhanced by tiles of gilt bronze.[2]

The great wealth and popularity of the sanctuary in antiquity are attested by ancient writers as well as by the remains which have come to light in modern times. In the civil war its sacred treasures went to replenish the empty coffers of Octavian,[1] who well understood the useful art of thus securing the divine assistance, if not the divine blessing, for the furtherance of his ends. But we are not told that he treated Diana on this occasion as civilly as his divine uncle Julius Caesar once treated Capitoline Jupiter himself, borrowing three thousand pounds' weight of solid gold from the god, and scrupulously paying him back with the same weight of gilt copper.[2] However, the sanctuary at Nemi recovered from this drain on its resources, for two centuries later it was still reputed one of the richest in Italy.[3] Ovid has described the walls hung with fillets and commemorative tablets;[4] and the abundance of cheap votive offerings and copper coins, which the site has yielded in our own day,

[2]The site was excavated in 1885 and 1886 by Sir John Savile Lumley, now Lord Savile, who was then English ambassador at Rome. Further excavations were conducted in 1886-1888 by Signor Luigi Boccanera, and again in 1895 by Signor Eliseo Borghi. See *Notizie degli Scavi*, 1885, pp. 159 *sq.*, 192 *sq.*, 227 *sq.*, 254 *sq.*, 317-321, 344, 428 *sq.*, 478 *sq.*; *id.* 1887, pp. 23-25, 120 *sq.*, 195-198; *id.* 1888, pp. 193 *sq.*, 392 *sq* : *id.* 1889, pp. 20-22; *id.* 1895, pp. 106-108, 206, 232, 324, 424-438; *Bulletino dell' Instituto di Corrispondenza Archeologica*, 1885, pp. 149-157, 225-242; R. Lanciani, in the *Athenaeum*, October 10, 1885, pp. 477 *sq.*; R. P. Pullan, in *Archaeologia: Miscellaneous Tracts relating to Antiquity*, l. (1887) pp. 58-65; O. Rossbach, in *Verhandlungen der vierzigsten Versammlung deutscher Philologen und Schulmänner in Görlitz* (Leipsic, 1890), pp. 147-164; G. H. Wallis, *Illustrated Catalogue of Classical Antiquities from the Site of the Temple of Diana, Nemi, Italy* (preface dated 1893). The temple measured 30 metres in length by 15.90 in breadth (*Notizie degli Scavi*, 1885, p. 193). It had columns on either side of the *pronaos* (Vitruvius, iv. 7. 4). A few votive offerings found on the site in earlier times are described in Graevius's *Thesaurus Antiquitatum Romanarum*, xii. col. 752-757. 808. For the inscriptions of Nemi and Aricia see *Corpus Inscriptionum Latinarum*, xiv. Nos. 2156-2226, 4180-4210, 4268-4275a; W. Henzen, in *Hermes*, vi. (1872) pp. 6-13; G. Tomassetti, in *Museo Italiano di Antichità Classica*, ii. (1888) coll. 481 *sqq*. Among these inscriptions the many dedications to Diana serve to identify the site beyond a doubt. The evidence of ancient writers is collected by Cluverius, *Italia Antiqua*, ii. pp. 920-935. See also H. Nissen, *Italische Landeskunde*, ii. (Berlin, 1902) pp. 588-592; and for the topography, Sir W. Gell, *The Topography of Rome and its Vicinity* (London, 1834), i. pp. 182-191, ii. pp. 112-117.

[1]Appian, *Bellum Civile*, v. 24.

[2]Seutonius, *Divus Julius*, 54. Serving his own gods thus, he naturally felt no compunction at relieving the barbarous Gaulish gods of their little savings (Seutonius, *ib.*).

[3]Appian, *loc. cit.*

[4]*Fasti*, iii. 267 *sq.*

speaks volumes for the piety and numbers, if not for the opulence and liberal-
ity, of the worshippers. Swarms of beggars used to stream forth daily from
the slums of Aricia and take their stand on the long slope up which the labour-
ing horses dragged well-to-do pilgrims to the shrine; and according to the
response which their whines and importunities met with they blew kisses or
hissed curses after the carriages as they swept rapidly down hill again.[5] Even
peoples and potentates of the East did homage to the lady of the lake by setting
up monuments in her sanctuary; and within the precinct stood shrines of the
Egyptian goddesses Isis and Bubastis, with a store of gorgeous jewellery.[1]

The retirement of the spot and the beauty of the landscape naturally tempted
some of the luxurious Roman nobles to fix their summer residences by the
lake.[2] Here Lucius Caesar had a house to which, on a day in early summer,
only two months after the murder of his illustrious namesake, he invited Cicero
to meet the assassin Brutus.[3] The emperors themselves appear to have been
partial to a retreat where they could find repose from the cares of state and
the bustle of the great city in the fresh air of the lake and the stillness of
the woods. Here Julius Caesar built himself a costly villa, but pulled it down
because it was not to his mind.[4] Here Caligula had two magnificent barges,
or rather floating palaces, launched for him on the lake;[5] and it was while

[5] Juvenal, *Sat.* iv. 117 *sq.*; Persius, *Sat.* vi. 56, with the scholiast's note; Martial, *Epigr.* ii.
19. 3, xii. 32. 10. Persius calls this part of the road the slope of Virbius. Juvenal and Martial
call it the Arician slope. But the former was probably the correct name, for at Rome also there
was a "slope of Virbius" on the Esquiline, near a sanctuary of Diana (Livy, i. 48. 6). The
double coincidence with Aricia is probably significant, as has been acutely pointed out by Mr.
A. B. Cook (*Classical Review*, xvi. (1902) p. 380, n. 3). We shall return to this later on. As
to Virbius, we shall hear more of him presently.

[1] W. Henzen, in *Hermes*, vi. (1872) pp. 6-12; *Corpus Inscriptionum Latinarum*, xiv., Nos.
2215, 2216, 2218.

[2] At the place called S. Maria, in the commune of Nemi, there have been found remains of
a magnificent villa of the first or second century, built in terraces just above the lake and adorned
with variegated marbles, frescoes, and works of art. See *Notizie degli Scavi*, 1888, pp. 194-196,
393 *sq.* The place is near the mouth of the ancient emissary, below the village of Genzano; the
vineyards beside the lake are here littered with fragments of fine marbles. In January 1901 I
visited the site in the company of Mr. St. Clair Baddeley, who has kindly furnished me with
some notes on the subject.

[3] Cicero, *Ad Atticum*, xv. 4. 5.

[4] Suetonius, *Divus Julius*, 46. From a letter of Cicero to Atticus (vi. I. 25) we infer that the
house was building in 50 B.C.

[5] Some of the timbers and fittings of these vessels were fished up from the bottom of the lake
in 1895. Especially remarkable are the beautiful bronze heads of lions and wolves with mooring-
rings in their mouths. Caligula's name (C . CAESARIS . AVG . GERMANICI) is stamped on
the leaden water-pipes, and the style of the bronzes is that of the first century. See *Notizie degli
Scavi*, 1895, pp. 361-396, 461-474; J. C. G. Boot, in *Verslagen en Mededeelingen der kon.
Akademie van Wetenschappen, Afdeeling Letterkunde*, III. Reeks, xii. deel (Amsterdam, 1895),
pp. 278-285; R. Lanciani, *New Tales of Old Rome* (London, 1901), pp. 205-214.

dallying in the woods of Nemi that the sluggard Vitellius received the tidings of revolt which woke him from his dream of pleasure and called him to arms.[6] Vespasian had a monument dedicated to his honour in the grove by the senate and people of Aricia: Trajan condescended to fill the chief magistracy of the town; and Hadrian indulged his taste for architecture by restoring a structure which had been erected in the precinct by a prince of the royal house of Parthia.[1]

Such, then, was the sanctuary of Diana at Nemi, a fitting home for the "mistress of mountains, and forests green, and lonely glades, and sounding rivers," as Catullus calls her.[2] Multitudes of her statuettes, appropriately clad in the short tunic and high buskins of a huntress, with the quiver slung over her shoulder, have been found on the spot. Some of them represent her with her bow in her hand or her hound at her side.[3] Bronze and iron spears, and images of stags and hinds, discovered within the precinct,[4] may have been offerings of huntsmen to the huntress goddess for success in the chase. Similarly the bronze tridents, which have also come to light at Nemi, were perhaps presented by fishermen who had speared fish in the lake, or maybe by hunters who had stabbed boars in the forest.[5] The wild boar was still hunted in Italy down to the end of the first century of our era; for the younger Pliny tells us how, with his usual charming affectation, he sat meditating and reading by the nets, while three fine boars fell into them.[6] Indeed, some fourteen-hundred years later boar-hunting was a favourite pastime of Pope Leo the Tenth.[1] A frieze of painted reliefs in terra-cotta, which was found in the sanctuary at Nemi, and may have adorned Diana's temple, portrays the goddess

[6]Tacitus, *Histor*. iii. 36.

[1]*Corpus Inscriptionum Latinarum*, xiv., Nos. 2213, 2216, 4191. Hadrian also had a monument in the grove dedicated to him by the senate and people of Aricia (*Notizie degli Scavi*, 1895, pp. 430 *sq*.). A bust of Caesar and a statue of Tiberius have been found on the spot. See G. H. Wallis, *Illustrated Catalogue*, p. 31; O. Rossbach, in *Verhandlungen der vierzig. Versamml. aeutscher Philologen*, p. 159.

[2]Catullus, xxxiv. 9 *sqq*.

[3]*Bulletino dell' Instituto di Corrispondenza Archeologica*, 1885, pp. 228 *sq*.; *Notizie degli Scavi*, 1887, pp. 24, 195; *id*. 1888, p. 393; O. Rossbach, in *Verhandl. d. vierzig. Versamml. deutscher Philologen*, pp. 150 note, 161; G. H. Wallis, *Illustrated Catalogue*, pp. 4, 15, 34 *sq*.

[4]*Notizie degli Scavi*, 1887, p. 195; *id*. 1888, p. 393; *Bulletino di Corr. Archeol*. 1885, p. 230; O. Rossbach, *op. cit*., pp. 150 note, 151 note, 163; G. H. Wallis, *Illustrated Catalogue*, pp. 35, 40. Greek hunters dedicated spears and javelins to Pan (*Anthologia Palatina*, vi. 57, 177). Compare W. H. D. Rouse, *Greek Votive Offerings* (Cambridge, 1902), p. 71.

[5]W. Helbig, in *Bulletino dell' Inst. di Corr. Archeol*. 1885, pp. 231 *sq*.; *Notizie degli Scavi*, 1887, p. 195; *id*. 1888, p. 393. Helbig observes that the ancients sometimes used tridents in boar-hunts.

[6]Pliny, *Epist*. i. 6. In the second century of our era the mountains and oak woods of Greece harboured numbers of wild boars. See Pausanias, i. 32. I, iii. 20. 4, v. 6. 6, vii. 26. 10. viii. 23. 9, ix. 23. 7.

[1]W. Roscoe, *Life and Pontificate of Leo the Tenth*,[3] iv. 376.

in the character of what is called the Asiatic Artemis, with wings sprouting from her waist and a lion resting its paws on each of her shoulders.[2] A few rude images of cows, oxen, horses, and pigs dug up on the site may perhaps indicate that Diana was here worshipped as the patroness of domestic animals as well as of the wild creatures of the wood.[3] In like manner her Greek counterpart Artemis was a goddess not only of game but of herds. Thus her sanctuary in the highlands of north-western Arcadia, between Clitor and Cynaethae, owned sacred cattle which were driven off by Aetolian freebooters on one of their forays.[4] When Xenophon returned from the wars and settled on his estate among the wooded hills and green meadows of the rich valley through which the Alpheus flows past Olympia, he dedicated to Artemis a little temple on the model of her great temple at Ephesus, surrounded it with a grove of all kinds of fruit-trees, and endowed it not only with a chase but also with a sacred pasture. The chase abounded in fish and game of all sorts, and the pasture sufficed to rear swine, goats, oxen, and horses; and on her yearly festival the pious soldier sacrificed to the goddess a tithe both of the cattle from the sacred pasture and of the game from the sacred chase.[5] Again, the people of Hyampolis in Phocis worshipped Artemis and thought that no cattle throve like those which they dedicated to her.[6] Perhaps then the images of cattle found in Diana's precinct at Nemi were offered to her by herdsmen to ensure her blessing on their herds. In Catholic Germany at the present time the great patron of cattle, horses, and pigs is St. Leonhard, and models of cattle, horses, and pigs are dedicated to him, sometimes in order to ensure the health and increase of the flocks and herds through the coming year, sometimes in order to obtain the recovery of sick animals.[1] And, curiously enough, like Diana of Aricia, St. Leonhard is also expected to help women in travail and to bless barren wives with offspring.[2] Nor do these points exhaust the analogy between St. Leonard and Diana of Aricia; for like the goddess the saint heals the sick; he is the patron of prisoners, as she was of runaway slaves; and his shrines, like hers, enjoyed the right of asylum.[3]

So to the last, in spite of a few villas peeping out here and there from among the trees, Nemi seems to have remained in some sense an image of what Italy had been in the far-off days when the land was still sparsely peopled

[2]O. Rossbach, *op. cit.* pp. 157 *sq.*; G. H. Wallis, *Illustrated Catalogue*, pp. 3, 31, with the plate facing p. 43.

[3]*Bulletino dell' Inst. di Corr. Archeol.* 1885, p. 153; G. H. Wallis, *Illustrated Catalogue*, p. 23.

[4]Polybius, *Hist.* iv. 18 and 19.

[5]Xenophon, *Anabasis*, v. 3. 4-13.

[6]Pausanias, x. 35. 7.

[1]R. Andree, *Votive und Weihegaben des Katholischen Volks in Süddeutschland* (Brunswick, 1904), pp. 37, 50, 152 *sqq.*

[2]R. Andree, *op. cit.* p. 41.

[3]R. Andree, *op. cit.* pp. 41-50.

with tribes of savage hunters or wandering herdsmen, when the beechwoods and oakwoods, with their deciduous foliage, reddening in autumn and bare in winter, had not yet begun, under the hand of man, to yield to the evergreens of the south, the laurel, the olive, the cypress, and the oleander, still less to those intruders of a later age, which nowadays we are apt to think of as characteristically Italian, the lemon and the orange.[4]

However, it was not merely in its natural surroundings that this ancient shrine of the sylvan goddess continued to be a type or miniature of the past. Down to the decline of Rome a custom was observed there which seems to transport us at once from civilisation to savagery. In the sacred grove there grew a certain tree round which at any time of the day, and probably far into the night, a grim figure might be seen to prowl. In his hand he carried a drawn sword, and he kept peering warily about him as if at every instant he expected to be set upon by an enemy.[1] He was a priest and a murderer; and the man for whom he looked was sooner or later to murder him and hold the priesthood in his stead. Such was the rule of the sanctuary. A candidate for the priesthood could only succeed to office by slaying the priest, and having slain him, he retained office till he was himself slain by a stronger or a craftier.

The post which he held by this precarious tenure carried with it the title of king; but surely no crowned head ever lay uneasier, or was visited by more evil dreams, than his. For year in year out, in summer and winter, in fair weather and in foul, he had to keep his lonely watch, and whenever he snatched a troubled slumber it was at the peril of his life. The least relaxation of his vigilance, the smallest abatement of his strength of limb or skill of fence, put him in jeopardy; grey hairs might seal his death-warrant. His eyes probably acquired that restless, watchful look which, among the Esquimaux of Bering Strait, is said to betray infallibly the shedder of blood; for with that people revenge is a sacred duty, and the manslayer carries his life in his hand.[2] To gentle and pious pilgrims at the shrine the sight of him might well seem to darken the fair landscape, as when a cloud suddenly blots the sun on a bright

---

[4]See V. Hehn, *Kulturpflanzen und Haustiere in ihrem übergang aus Asien*[7] (Berlin, 1902), pp. 520 *sq.*: "In the course of history the flora of the Italian peninsula assumed more and more a southern character. When the first Greeks landed in lower Italy the forests consisted predominantly of deciduous trees, the beeches reached lower down than now, when they are confined to the highest mountain regions. Centuries later in the landscapes on the walls of Pompeii we see nothing but evergreen trees, the *Laurus nobilis*, the olive, the cypress, the oleander; in the latest times of the empire and in the Middle Ages the lemon-trees and orange-trees appear, and since the discovery of America the magnolias, the agaves, and the Indian figs. There can be no question that this revolution has been brought mainly by the hand of man."

[1]ξιφήρης οὖν ἐστιν ἀεί, περισκοπῶν τὰς ἐπιφέσεισ, ἕτοιμος ἀμύνεσφαι, is Strabo's description (v. 3. 12), who may have seen him "pacing there alone."

[2]E. W. Nelson, "The Eskimo about Bering Strait," *Eighteenth Annual Report of the Bureau of American Ethnology*, Part I. (Washington, 1899) p. 293.

day. The dreamy blue of Italian skies, the dappled shade of summer woods, and the sparkle of waves in the sun, can have accorded but ill with that stern and sinister figure. Rather we picture to ourselves the scene as it may have been witnessed by a belated wayfarer on one of those wild autumn nights when the dead leaves are falling thick, and the winds seem to sing the dirge of the dying year. It is a sombre picture, set to melancholy music—the background of forest shewing black and jagged against a lowering and stormy sky, the sighing of the wind in the branches, the rustle of the withered leaves under foot, the lapping of the cold water on the shore, and in the foreground, pacing to and fro, now in twilight and now in gloom, a dark figure with a glitter of steel at the shoulder whenever the pale moon, riding clear of the cloud-rack, peers down at him through the matted boughs.

The strange rule of this priesthood has no parallel in classical antiquity, and cannot be explained from it. To find an explanation we must go farther afield. No one will probably deny that such a custom savours of a barbarous age, and, surviving into imperial times, stands out in striking isolation from the polished Italian society of the day, like a primaeval rock rising from a smooth-shaven lawn. It is the very rudeness and barbarity of the custom which allow us a hope of explaining it. For recent researches into the early history of man have revealed the essential similarity with which, under many superficial differences, the human mind has elaborated its first crude philosophy of life. Accordingly, if we can shew that a barbarous custom, like that of the priesthood of Nemi, has existed elsewhere; if we can detect the motives which led to its institution; if we can prove that these motives have operated widely, perhaps universally, in human society, producing in varied circumstances a variety of institutions specifically different but generically alike; if we can shew, lastly, that these very motives, with some of their derivative institutions, were actually at work in classical antiquity; then we may fairly infer that at a remoter age the same motives gave birth to the priesthood of Nemi. Such an inference, in default of direct evidence as to how the priesthood did actually arise, can never amount to demonstration. But it will be more or less probable according to the degree of completeness with which it fulfils the conditions I have indicated. The object of this book is, by meeting these conditions, to offer a fairly probable explanation of the priesthood of Nemi.

I begin by setting forth the few facts and legends which have come down to us on the subject. According to one story the worship of Diana at Nemi was instituted by Orestes, who, after killing Thoas, King of the Tauric Chersonese (the Crimea), fled with his sister to Italy, bringing with him the image of the Tauric Diana hidden in a faggot of sticks. After his death his bones were transported from Aricia to Rome and buried in front of the temple of Saturn, on the Capitoline slope, beside the temple of Concord. The bloody ritual which legend ascribed to the Tauric Diana is familiar to classical readers;

it is said that every stranger who landed on the shore was sacrificed on her altar. But transported to Italy, the rite assumed a milder form. Within the sanctuary at Nemi grew a certain tree of which no branch might be broken. Only a runaway slave was allowed to break off, if he could, one of its boughs. Success in the attempt entitled him to fight the priest in single combat, and if he slew him he reigned in his stead with the title of King of the Wood (*Rex Nemorensis*). According to the public opinion of the ancients the fateful branch was that Golden Bough which, at the Sibyl's bidding, Aeneas plucked before he essayed the perilous journey to the world of the dead. The flight of the slave represented, it was said, the flight of Orestes; his combat with the priest was a reminiscence of the human sacrifices once offered to the Tauric Diana. This rule of succession by the sword was observed down to imperial times; for amongst his other freaks Caligula, thinking that the priest of Nemi had held office too long, hired a more stalwart ruffian to slay him; and a Greek traveller, who visited Italy in the age of the Antonines, remarks that down to his time the priesthood was still the prize of victory in a single combat.[1]

Of the worship of Diana at Nemi some leading features can still be made out. From the votive offerings which have been found on the site, it appears that she was conceived of especially as a huntress, and further as blessing

---

[1]Servius on Virgil, *Aen.* vi. 136, " *Licet de hoc ramo hi qui de sacris Proserpinae scripsisse dicuntur, quiddam esse mysticum adfirment, publica tamen opinio hoc habet. Orestes post occisum regem Thoantem,*" etc. ; *id.* on Virgil, *Aen.* ii. 116; Valerius Flaccus, *Argonaut.* ii. 304 *sq.*; Strabo, v. 3. 12; Pausanias, ii. 27. 4; Solinus, ii. 11; Suetonius, *Caligula*, 35. The custom of breaking the branch, and its supposed connexion with the Golden Bough of Virgil, are recorded by Servius alone (on Virgil, *Aen.* vi. 136). For the title "King of the Wood" see Suetonius, *l.c.*; and compare Statius, *Sylv.* iii. I. 55 *sq.*—

"Jamque dies aderat, profugis cum regibus aptum
Fumat Aricinum Triviae nemus";
Ovid, *Fasti*, iii. 271 *sq.*—
"Regna *tenent fortesque manu, pedibusque fugaces;*
Et perit exemplo postmodo quisqu: suo";
id., Ars am. i. 259 *sq.*—
"Ecce suburbanae templum nemorale Dianae,
Partaque per gladios regna *nocente manu*";
Valerius Flaccus, *Argon.* ii. 304 sq.—
"Jam nemus Egeriae, jam te ciet altus ab alba
Juppiter et soli non mitis Aricia regi."

An archaic Greek relief, found in 1791 near the outlet of the lake, in the Vallericcia, has been sometimes thought to portray the combat between a priest and a candidate for the office. But the subject is rather the murder of Aegisthus by Orestes in presence of Clytaemnestra and Electra. See Sir W. Gell, *Topography of Rome*, ii. 116 *sq.*; O. Jahn, in *Archäologische Zeitung*, vii. (1849) coll. 113-118; Baumeister's *Denkmäler*, p. 1112; O. Rossbach, *op. cit.* pp. 148 *sq.*; R. Lanciani, *New Tales of Old Rome*, p. 204.

men and women with offspring, and granting expectant mothers an easy delivery.[1] Again, fire seems to have played a foremost part in her ritual. For during her annual festival, held on the thirteenth of August, at the hottest time of the year, her grove shone with a multitude of torches, whose ruddy glare was reflected by the lake; and throughout the length and breadth of Italy the day was kept with holy rites at every domestic hearth.[2] Bronze statuettes found in her precinct represent the goddess herself holding a torch in her raised right hand;[3] and women whose prayers had been heard by her came crowned with wreaths and bearing lighted torches to the sanctuary in fulfilment of their vows.[4] Some one unknown dedicated a perpetually burning lamp in a little shrine at Nemi for the safety of the Emperor Claudius and his family.[1] The terra-cotta lamps which have been discovered in the grove[2] may perhaps have served a like purpose for humbler persons. If so, the analogy of the custom to the Catholic practice of dedicating holy candles in churches would be obvious.[3] Further, the title of Vesta borne by Diana at Nemi[4] points clearly

[1]Thus there have been found many models of the organs of generation, both male and female, including wombs; figures of women with infants on their laps or on their arms; and couples seated side by side, the woman pregnant or carrying a child. See *Bulletino dell' Inst. di Corrisp. Archeologica*, 1885, pp. 183 *sq.*; *Notizie degli Scavi*, 1885, pp. 160, 254; *id.* 1895, p. 424; O. Rossbach, *op. cit.* p. 160; G. H. Wallis, *Illustrated Catalogue*, pp. 4, 15, 17. Another group represents a woman just after delivery, supported by the midwife, who holds the child in her lap. See Graevius, *Thesaurus Antiquitatum Romanarum*, xii. col. 808. As to the huntress Diana, see above, p. 6.

[2]Statius, *Sylvae*, iii. 1. 52-60; Gratius Faliscus, *Cynegeticon*, i. 484 *sq.* As to the date we know from the calendars (W. Warde Fowler, *The Roman Festivals of the Republic*, p. 198) and from Festus (p. 343 ed. Müller; compare Plutarch, *Quaest. Rom.* 100) that the festival of Diana on the Aventine at Rome fell on the Ides, that is, the 13th of August. Further, the Ides of August was held as the birthday of Diana at Lanuvium (*Corpus Inscriptionum Latinarum*, xiv., No. 2112; G. Wilmanns, *Exempla Inscriptionum Latinarum*, No. 319; C. G. Bruns, *Fontes Juris Romani*,[7] ed. O. Gradenwitz, p. 389; H. Dessau, *Inscriptiones Latinae Selectae*, No. 7212). Moreover, Martial (xii. 67. 2) and Ausonius (*De feriis Romanis*, 5 *sq.*) speak of the Ides of August as Diana's day. Hence we may safely conclude that the *Hecateias idus* which Statius (*l.c.*) mentions as the date of the festival of Diana at Nemi were no other than the Ides of August, all the more that the poet describes the time as the hottest of the year. Compare G. Wissowa, *Religion und Kultus der Römer* (Munich, 1902), p. 201.

[3]O. Rossbach, *op. cit.* pp. 150 note, 161. A coin of P. Clodius Turrinus (43 B.C.) portrays Diana with a long torch in either hand. See E. Babelon, *Monnaies de la Republique Romaine* (Paris, 1885), i. 355.

[4]Ovid, *Fasti*, iii. 269 *sq.*; Propertius, iii. 24. (30) 9 *sq.*, ed. Paley.

[1]*Notizie degli Scavi*, 1888, p. 193 *sq.*; O. Rossbach, *op. cit.* p. 164.

[2]*Bulletino dell' Inst. di Corrisp. Archeologica*, 1885, p. 157; *Notizie degli Scavi*, 1888, p. 393; G. H. Wallis, *Illustrated Catalogue*, pp. 24-26.

[3]On the dedication of burning lamps and candles in antiquity, see M. P. Nilsson, *Griechische Feste* (Leipsic, 1906), p. 345, note 5. As to the derivation of the Catholic from the old heathen custom, see R. Andree, *Votive und Weihegaben des Katholischen Volks in Süddeutschland* (Brunswick, 1904), p. 77.

[4]*Corpus Inscriptionum Latinarum*, xiv., No. 2213; G. Wilmanns, *Exempla Inscriptionum Latinarum*, No. 1767; H. Dessau, *Inscriptiones Latinae Selectae*, No. 3243.

to the maintenance of a perpetual holy fire in her sanctuary. A large circular basement at the north-east corner of the temple, raised on three steps and bearing traces of a mosaic pavement, probably supported a round temple of Diana in her character of Vesta, like the round temple of Vesta in the Roman Forum.[5] Here the sacred fire would seem to have been tended by Vestal Virgins, for the head of a Vestal in terra-cotta was found on the spot,[6] and the worship of a perpetual fire, cared for by holy maidens, appears to have been common in Latium from the earliest to the latest times.[7] Thus we know that among the ruins of Alba the Vestal fire was kept burning by Vestal Virgins, bound to strict chastity, until the end of the fourth century of our era.[8] There were Vestals at Tibur[1] and doubtless also at Lavinium, for the Roman consuls, praetors, and dictators had to sacrifice to Vesta at that ancient city when they entered on or laid down their office.[2]

At her annual festival, which, as we have just seen, was celebrated all over Italy on the thirteenth of August, hunting dogs were crowned and wild beasts were not molested; young people went through a purificatory ceremony in her honour; wine was brought forth, and the feast consisted of a kid, cakes served piping hot on plates of leaves, and apples still hanging in clusters on the boughs.[3] The Christian Church appears to have sanctified this great festival of the virgin goddess by adroitly converting it into the festival of the Assumption of the Blessed Virgin on the fifteenth of August.[4] The discrepancy of two days between the dates of the festivals is not a fatal argument against their identity; for a similar displacement of two days occurs in the case of St. George's festival on the twenty-third of April, which is probably identical with the ancient Roman festival of the Parilia on April twenty-first.[5] On the

[5]*Notizie degli Scavi*, 1885, p. 478; O. Rossbach, *op. cit.* p. 158; G. H. Wallis, *Illustrated Catalogue*, pp. 9 *sq*. The true character of this circular basement was first pointed out by Mr. A. B. Cook (*Classical Review*, xvi. (1902) p. 376). Previous writers had taken it for an altar or a pedestal. But the mosaic pavement and the bases of two columns which were found in position on it exclude the hypothesis of an altar and cannot easily be reconciled with that of a pedestal, for which, moreover, it appears to be too large. A rain-water gutter runs round it and then extends in the direction of the larger temple. As to the temple of Vesta at Rome see J. H. Middleton, *The Remains of Ancient Rome*, i. 297 *sq*.; O. Richter, *Topographie der Stadt Rom*[2] (Munich, 1902), pp. 88 *sq*.; G. Boni, in *Notizie degli Scavi*, May 1900, pp. 159 *sqq*.

[6]G. H. Wallis, *Illustrated Catalogue*, p. 30.

[7]J. Marquardt, *Römische Staatsverwaltung*, iii.[2] 336.

[8]Juvenal, iv. 60 *sq*.; Asconius, *In Milonianam*, p. 35, ed. Kiesseling and Schoell; Symmachus, *Epist*. ix. 128 and 129 (Migne's *Patrologia Latina*, xviii. col. 355); *Corpus Inscriptionum Latinarum*, vi., No. 2172, xiv., No. 4120; Wilmanns, *Exempla Inscriptionum Latinarum*, No. 1750. The Alban Vestals gave evidence at Milo's trial in 52 B.C. (Asconius, *l.c.*); one of them was tried for breaking her vow of chastity late in the fourth century A.D. (Symmachus, *l.c.*).

[1]*Corpus Inscriptionum Latinarum*, xiv., Nos. 3677, 3679.

[2]Servius on Virgil, *Aen*. ii. 296; Macrobius, *Saturn*. iii. 4. 11.

[3]Statius, *Sylvae*, iii. 1. 55 *sqq*.; Gratius Faliscus, *Cynegeticon*, i. 483-492.

[4]J. Rendel Harris, *The Annotators of the Codex Bezae* (London, 1901), pp. 93-102.

[5]See below, vol. ii. pp. 324 *sqq*.

reasons which prompted this conversion of the festival of the Virgin Diana into the festival of the Virgin Mary, some light is thrown by a passage in the Syriac text of *The Departure of My Lady Mary from this World*, which runs thus: "And the apostles also ordered that there should be a commemoration of the blessed one on the thirteenth of Ab [that is, August; another MS. reads the 15th of Ab], on account of the vines bearing bunches (of grapes), and on account of the trees bearing fruit, that clouds of hail, bearing stones of wrath, might not come, and the trees be broken, and their fruits, and the vines with their clusters."[6] Here the festival of the Assumption of the Virgin is definitely said to have been fixed on the thirteenth or fifteenth of August for the sake of protecting the ripening grapes and other fruits. Similarly in the Arabic text of the apocryphal work *On the Passing of the Blessed Virgin Mary*, which is attributed to the Apostle John, there occurs the following passage: "Also a festival in her honour was instituted on the fifteenth day of the month Ab [that is, August], which is the day of her passing from this world, the day on which the miracles were performed, and the time when the fruits of trees are ripening."[1] Further, in the calendars of the Syrian Church the fifteenth of August is repeatedly designated as the festival of the Mother of God "for the vines";[2] and to this day in Greece the ripening grapes and other fruits are brought to the churches to be blest by the priests on the fifteenth of August.[3] Now we hear of vineyards and plantations dedicated to Artemis,

[6]*Journal of Sacred Literature and Biblical Record*, New Series, vii. (London, 1865), "The Departure of my Lady Mary from this World," p. 153. The Greek original of the treatise was discovered by Tischendorf. This passage was kindly indicated to me by my learned friend Mr. J. Rendel Harris. He writes to me: "In these late Syrian calendars the festivals are simply taken over from the Greek and Roman calendars without any adjustment at all, as a study of the detailed saints' days shows."

[1]*Johanni Apostoli de transitu Beatae Mariae Virginis Liber:* ex recensione et cum interpretatione Maximiliani Engeri (Elberfeldae, 1854), pp. 101, 103. This and the preceding passage are both cited by the late Prof. E. Lucius in his book *Die Anfänge des Heiligenkultes in der christlichen Kirche* (Tübingen, 1904), pp. 488 *sq.*, 521. From them and from the entries in the Syrian calendars (see the next note), Lucius rightly inferred that the Assumption of the Virgin Mary had been assigned by the Church to the 15th of August with reference to the ripening of the grapes and other fruits, and that the Christian festival replaced an old heathen festival of first-fruits, which must have been held about the same time. But he appears to have overlooked the occurrence of Diana's festival on the 13th of August.

[2]N. Nilles, *Kalendarium Manuale utriusque Ecclesiae Orientalis et Occidentalis*[2] (Innsbruck, 1896-7), i. pp. 249, 480. Professor Nilles compares the blessing of the herbs *(Krautweihe)*, which still takes place in various parts of German-speaking lands on August 15th for the purpose of defeating the charms of witches.

[3]B. Schmidt, *Das Volksleben der Neugriechen* (Leipsic, 1871), p. 58. My learned friend Dr. W. H. D. Rouse, who is well acquainted with Greece, both ancient and modern, gave me similar information.

fruits offered to her, and her temple standing in an orchard.[4] Hence we may conjecture that her Italian sister Diana was also revered as a patroness of vines and fruit-trees, and that on the thirteenth of August the owners of vineyards and orchards paid their respects to her at Nemi along with other classes of the community. We have just seen that wine and apples still hanging on the boughs formed part of the festal cheer on that day; in an ancient fresco found at Ostia a statue of Diana is depicted in company with a procession of children, some of whom bear clusters of grapes;[1] and in a series of gems the goddess, is represented with a branch of fruit in one hand and a cup, which is sometimes full of fruit, in the other.[2] Catullus, too, tells us that Diana filled the husband-man's barns with a bounteous harvest.[3] In some parts of Italy and Sicily the day of the Assumption of the Virgin is still celebrated, like Diana's day of old, with illuminations and bonfires; in many Sicilian parishes the corn is then brought in sacks to the churches to be blessed, and many persons, who have a favour to ask of the Virgin, vow to abstain from one or more kinds of fruit during the first fifteen days of August.[4] Even in Scandinavia a relic of the worship of Diana survived in the custom of blessing the fruits of the earth of every sort, which in Catholic times was annually observed on the festival of the Assumption of the Virgin.[5] There is no intrinsic improbability in the view that for the sake of edification the church may have converted a real heathen festival into a nominal Christian one. Similarly in the Armenian Church "according to the express evidence of the Armenian fathers of the year 700 and later, the day of the Virgin was placed on September the fifteenth, because that was the day of Anahite, the magnificence of whose feast the Christian doctors hoped thereby to transfer to Mary."[6] This Anahite or Anaitis, as the Greeks called her, the Armenian predecessor of the Virgin Mary, was a great Oriental goddess, whose worship was exceedingly popular not only

[4]Pauly-Wissowa, *Real-Encyclop. d. class. Wissenschaften*, ii. 1342; Pausanias, vii. 18. 12; Xenophon, *Anabasis*, v. 3. 12. On the other hand the very sight of the image of Artemis at Pellene was said to render trees barren and to blight the fruits of the earth. See Plutarch, *Aratus*, 32.

[1]A. Dieterich, "Sommertag," *Archiv für Religionswissenschaft*, viii. (1905) Beiheft, pp. 108 *sqq.*, with fig. 2.

[2]Furtwängler, *Die antiken Gemmen*, iii. 231, with plates XX. 66, XXII. 18, 26, 30, 32, all cited by Mr. A. B. Cook, *Classical Review*, xvi. (1902) p. 378, note 4. Furtwängler held that these gems portray Diana of Nemi herself.

[3]Catullus, xxxiv. 17 *sqq.*

[4]G. Pitrè, *Spettacoli e Feste popolari Siciliane* (Palermo, 1881), pp. 356, 358, 360, 361, 362; G. Finamore, *Credenze, Usi e Costumi Abruzzesi* (Palermo, 1890), p. 176; G. Amalfi, *Tradizioni ed Usi nella peninsola Sorrentina* (Palermo, 1890), p. 50.

[5]Olaus Magnus, *Historia de Gentium Septentrionalium variis conditionibus*, xvi. 9.

[6]Note of Mr. F. C. Conybeare.

in Armenia but in the adjoining countries. The loose character of her rites is plainly indicated by Strabo, himself a native of these regions.[1]

Among the ancient Celts of Gaul, who, to judge by their speech, were near kinsmen of the ancient Latins, the thirteenth of August appears to have been the day when the harvest was dedicated to the harvest-god Rivos.[2] If that was so, we may conjecture that the choice of a day in mid-August for the solemn celebration of the harvest-home dates from the remote time when the ancestors of the Celtic and Italian peoples, having renounced the wandering life of the huntsman and herdsman, had settled down together in some land of fertile soil and temperate climate, where harvest fell neither so late as after the cool rainy summers of the North nor so early as before the torrid and rainless summers of southern Europe.

But Diana did not reign alone in her grove at Nemi.[3] Two lesser divinities shared her forest sanctuary. One was Egeria, the nymph of the clear water which, bubbling from the basaltic rocks, used to fall in graceful cascades into the lake at the place called Le Mole, because here were established the mills of the modern village of Nemi. The purling of the stream as it ran over the pebbles is mentioned by Ovid, who tells us that he had often drunk of its water.[4] Women with child used to sacrifice to Egeria, because she was believed, like Diana, to be able to grant them an easy delivery.[1] Tradition ran that the nymph had been the wife or mistress of the wise king Numa, that he had consorted with her in the secrecy of the sacred grove, and that the laws which he gave the Romans had been inspired by communion with her divinity.[2] Plutarch compares the legend with other tales of the loves of

[1]Strabo, xi. 8. 12, xi. 14. 16, xii. 3. 37.

[2]This is inferred from entries in the ancient Celtic calendar of which numerous fragments, engraved on bronze, were found in 1897 at Coligny near Lyons. In this calendar the month Rivros seems to mean "the harvest month" and to correspond to August. Sir John Rhys believes that the harvest-god Rivos, who is only known from this calendar, answers to the better-known Celtic god Lug. See Sir John Rhys, in *Transactions of the Third International Congress for the History of Religion* (Oxford, 1908), ii. 222 *sqq.*; and as to the Coligny calendar in general see further Sir John Rhys, "Celtae and Galli," *Proceedings of the British Academy, 1905-1906*, pp. 71 *sqq.*; *id.* "Notes on the Coligny Calendar," *Proceedings of the British Academy*, vol. iv.

[3]Dedications to Juno and Venus have been found in the grove (*Notizie degli Scavi*, 1888, p. 393; G. H. Wallis, *Illustrated Catalogue*, p. 44), also a bronze statuette of Jupiter (O. Rossbach, *op. cit.* p. 162), and a mutilated or unfinished bust supposed to represent that deity (*Notizie degli Scavi*, 1885, p. 344; G. H. Wallis, *op. cit.* p. 54).

[4]Virgil, *Aen.* vii. 762 *sqq.*; Ovid, *Fasti*, iii. 273 *sqq.*; *id.*, *Metam.* xv. 482 *sqq.*; Strabo, v. 3. 12. As to the stream, see P. Rosa, in *Monumenti ed Annali pubblic. dall' Instituto di Corrispondenza Archeologica nel 1856*, p. 7; R. Lanciani, in *Athenaeum*, October 10, 1885, p. 477. The water was diverted some years ago to supply Albano.

[1]Festus, p. 77, ed. C. O. Müller.

[2]Ovid, *Fasti*, iii. 273 *sqq.*; *id.*, *Metam.* xv. 482 *sqq.*; Cicero, *De legibus*, i. 1. 4; Livy, i. 19. 5, i. 21. 3; Plutarch, *Numa*, 4, 8, 13, 15; Dionysius Halicarn. *Antiquit. Roman.* ii. 60 *sq.*; Juvenal, *Sat.* iii. 12; Lactantius, *Divin. Inst.* i. 22; Augustine, *De civitate Dei*, vii. 35; Servius on Virgil, *Aen.* vii. 763. Ovid, Livy, Lactantius, and Augustine speak of Egeria as the wife of

goddesses for mortal men, such as the love of Cybele and the Moon for the fair youths Attis and Endymion.[3] According to some, the trysting-place of the lovers was not in the woods of Nemi but in a grove outside the dripping Porta Capena at Rome, where another sacred spring of Egeria gushed from a dark cavern.[4] Every day the Roman Vestals fetched water from this spring to wash the temple of Vesta, carrying it in earthenware pitchers on their heads.[5] In Juvenal's time the natural rock had been encased in marble, and the hallowed spot was profaned by gangs of poor Jews, who were suffered to squat, like gypsies, in the grove. We may suppose that the spring which fell into the lake of Nemi was the true original Egeria, and that when the first settlers moved down from the Alban hills to the banks of the Tiber they brought the nymph with them and found a new home for her in a grove outside the gates.[1] The remains of baths which have been discovered within the sacred precinct,[2] together with many terra-cotta models of various parts of the human body,[3] suggest that the waters of Egeria were used to heal the sick, who may have signified their hopes or testified their gratitude by dedicating likenesses of the diseased members to the goddess, in accordance with a custom which is still

---

Numa, whereas Juvenal and Servius call her his mistress. The language of Plutarch is somewhat ambiguous, but he uses the phrase γάμων θείων ἠξιωμένος (c. 4).

[3]Plutarch, *Numa*, 4.

[4]Juvenal, *Sat*. iii. 10 *sqq*.; Livy, i. 21. 3. As to the position of this grove and spring see O. Gilbert, *Geschichte und Topographie der Stadt Rom im Altertum*, i. 109 *sqq*., ii. pp. 152 *sqq*.; O. Richter, *Topographie der Stadt Rom*[2] (Munich, 1902), pp. 342 *sq*. According to the latter writer, the valley of Egeria was outside the Servian wall, at the foot of the Caelian Mount, and is now traversed by the streets Via delle Mole di S. Sisto and Via della Ferratella. He identifies the sacred spring with a copious source at the Villa Fonseca. On the other hand, Statius (*Sylvae*, v. 3. 290 *sq*.), Lactantius (*Divin. Inst*. iii. 22), and Servius (on Virgil, vii. 763) held that Numa's Egeria was not at Rome but at Nemi. The grove of Egeria is now popularly identified with a little wood called the *Bosco Sacro*, which stands in a commanding situation to the left of the Appian Way, about a mile and a half from Rome (Baedeker's *Central Italy and Rome*,[13] p. 378).

[5]Plutarch, *Numa*, 13. That they carried the water in pitchers on their heads may be inferred from Propertius. v. 4. 15 *sq*.; Ovid, *Fasti*, iii. 11-14.

[1]This is the view of A. Schwegler (*Römische Geschichte*, i. 548 note), O. Gilbert (*Geschichte und Topographie der Stadt Rom im Altertum*, i. 111), and G. Wissowa (in W. H. Roscher's *Lexikon der griech. und röm. Mythologie*, s.v. "Egeria").

[2]O. Rossbach, *op. cit.* p. 151. "The old bath" is mentioned in an inscription found on the spot (*Corpus Inscriptionum Latinarum*, xiv., No. 4190).

[3]*Notizie degli Scavi*, 1885, pp. 159 *sq*., 192, 254; *id.* 1888, p. 193; *Bulletino dell' Inst. di Corrisp. Archeologica*, 1885, pp. 153, 154 *sq*.; O. Rossbach, *op. cit.* p. 160; *Archaeologia: or Miscellaneous Tracts relating to Antiquity*, l. (1887), Pt. I. pp. 61 *sq*., 64; G. H. Wallis, *Illustrated Catalogue*, pp. 2, 4, 22. Amongst these models may be specially noted the torso of a woman clad in a long robe, with her breast cut open so as to expose the bowels. It may be the offering of a woman who suffered from some internal malady.

observed in many parts of Europe.[4] To this day it would seem that the spring retains medicinal virtues.[5]

The other of the minor deities at Nemi was Virbius. Legend had it that Virbius was the young Greek hero Hippolytus, chaste and fair, who learned the art of venery from the centaur Chiron, and spent all his days in the greenwood chasing wild beasts with the virgin huntress Artemis (the Greek counterpart of Diana) for his only comrade. Proud of her divine society, he spurned the love of women,[6] and this proved his bane. For Aphrodite, stung by his scorn, inspired his stepmother Phaedra with love of him; and when he disdained her wicked advances she falsely accused him to his father Theseus. The slander was believed, and Theseus prayed to his sire Poseidon to avenge the imagined wrong. So while Hippolytus drove in a chariot by the shore of the Saronic Gulf, the sea-god sent a fierce bull forth from the waves. The terrified horses bolted, threw Hippolytus from the chariot, and dragged him at their hoofs to death.[1] But Diana, for the love she bore Hippolytus, persuaded the leech Aesculapius to bring her fair young hunter back to life by his simples. Jupiter, indignant that a mortal man should return from the gates of death, thrust down the meddling leech himself to Hades. But Diana hid her favourite from the angry god in a thick cloud, disguised his features by adding years to his life, and then bore him far away to the dells of Nemi, where she entrusted him to the nymph Egeria, to live there, unknown and solitary, under the name of Virbius, in the depth of the Italian forest. There he reigned a king, and there he dedicated a precinct to Diana. He had a comely son, Virbius, who, undaunted by his father's fate, drove a team of fiery steeds to join the Latins in the war against Aeneas and the Trojans.[2] Virbius was worshipped as a god not only at Nemi but elsewhere; for in Campania we hear of a special priest devoted to his service.[3] Horses were excluded from the Arician grove

[4]For an example of the custom in modern times see J. J. Blunt, *Vestiges of Ancient Manners and Customs discoverable in Modern Italy and Sicily* (London, 1823), p. 135. The custom is still widespread among the Catholic population of Southern Germany. See R. Andree, *Votive and Weihegaben des Katholischen Volks in Süddeutschland* (Brunswick, 1904), pp. 94 *sqq.*, 112 *sqq.*, 123 *sqq.*

[5]R. Lanciani, in *Athenaeum*, October 10, 1885, p. 477.

[6]Xenophon, *Cyneget.* i. 2 and 11; Euripides, *Hippolytus*, 10-19. 1002 *sq.*

[1]Euripides, *Hippolytus*, 20 *sqq.*; Apollodorus, *Epitoma*, i. 18 *sq.*, ed. R. Wagner; Hyginus, *Fabulae*, 47; Ovid, *Metam.* xv. 497 *sqq.*

[2]Virgil, *Aen.* vii. 761 *sqq.*, with the commentary of Servius; Ovid, *Fasti*, iii. 263 *sqq.*, vi. 735 *sqq.*; *id.*, *Metam.* xv. 497 *sqq.*; Scholiast on Persius, *Sat.* vi. 56, p. 347 *sq.*, ed. O. Jahn; Lactantius, *Divin. Inst.* i. 17; Pausanias, ii. 27. 4; Apollodorus, iii. 10. 3; Scholiast on Pindar, *Pyth.* iii. 96. It was perhaps in his character of a serpent that Aesculapius was said to have brought the dead Hippolytus to life. See my note on Pausanias, ii. 10. 3.

[3]An inscription in the public museum at Naples mentions a *flamen Virbialis* (*Corpus Inscriptionum Latinarum*, x., No. 1493). Another inscription mentions a similar priesthood at Aricia, but the inscription is forged (Orelli, *Inscript. Latin.* No. 1457; compare H. Dessau on *Corpus Inscriptionum Latinarum*, xiv., No. 2213). The same title *flamen Virbialis* has sometimes been

and sanctuary because horses had killed Hippolytus.[4] It was unlawful to touch his image. Some thought that he was the sun.[5] "But the truth is," says Servius, "that he is a deity associated with Diana, as Attis is associated with the Mother of the Gods, and Erichthonius with Minerva, and Adonis with Venus."[1] What the nature of that association was we shall enquire presently. Here it is worth observing that in his long and chequered career this mythical personage has displayed a remarkable tenacity of life. For we can hardly doubt that the Saint Hippolytus of the Roman calendar, who was dragged by horses to death on the thirteenth of August, Diana's own day, is no other than the Greek hero of the same name, who after dying twice over as a heathen sinner has been happily resuscitated as a Christian saint.[2]

It needs no elaborate demonstration to convince us that the stories told to account for Diana's worship at Nemi are unhistorical. Clearly they belong to that large class of myths which are made up to explain the origin of a religious ritual and have no other foundation than the resemblance, real or imaginary, which may be traced between it and some foreign ritual. The incongruity of

---

wrongly read in an inscription of Gratianopolis, in Narbonensian Gaul (*Corpus Inscriptionum Latinarum*, xii., No. 2238; Orelli, *Inscript. Latin.* Nos. 2212, 4022). For the worship of Virbius we have also the testimony of Servius, on Virgil, *Aen.* vii. 776: *"Nam et Virbius inter deos colitur."*

[4] Virgil, *Aen.* vii. 779 *sq.*; Ovid, *Fasti*, iii. 265 *sq.*

[5] Servius on Virgil, *Aen.* vii. 776. Helbig proposed to identify as Virbius some bronze statuettes found at Nemi, which represent a young man naked except for a cloak thrown over his left arm, holding in his extended right hand a shallow bowl, while in his raised left hand he seems to have held a spear or staff on which he leaned. See *Bulletino dell' Inst. di Corrisp. Archeologica*, 1885, p. 229. But to this it has been objected by Rossbach (*op. cit.* p. 162) that Virbius appears to have been portrayed as an older, probably bearded man (Ovid, *Metam.* xv. 538 *sqq.*).

[1] Servius on Virgil, *Aen.* vii. 761; compare *id.* on *Aen.* vii. 84. See also Ovid, *Metam.* xv. 545 *sq.*—

"Hoc nemus inde colo de disque minoribus unus
Nomine sub dominae lateo atque accenseor illi."

[2] P. Ribadeneira, *Flos Sanctorum* (Venice, 1763), ii. 93 *sq.*; *Acta Sanctorum*, August 13, pp. 4 *sqq.* (Paris and Rome, 1867). The merit of tracing the saint's pedigree belongs to Mr. J. Rendel Harris. See his *Annotators of Codex Bezae* (London, 1901), pp. 101 *sq.* Prudentius has drawn a picture of the imaginary martyrdom which might melt the stoniest heart (*Peristeph.* xi. p. 282 *sqq.*, ed. Th. Obbarius). According to the *Acta Sanctorum* the saint shared the crown of martyrdom with twenty members of his household, of whom nineteen were beheaded, while one of them, his nurse *Concordia*, was scourged to death (*"plumbatis caesa"*). It is an odd coincidence that his Greek prototype Hippolytus dedicated just twenty horses to Aesculapius (Pausanias, ii. 27. 4); and it is another odd coincidence, if it is nothing worse, that the bones of Orestes, the other mythical hero of Nemi, were buried beside the temple of *Concordia* in Rome, and that Servius, who mentions this tradition (on Virgil, *Aen.* ii. 116), should immediately afterwards quote the words *"virgine caesa."* If we knew why the hero Hippolytus dedicated just twenty horses to the god who raised him from the dead, we might perhaps know why the saint Hippolytus went to heaven attended by a glorious company of just twenty martyrs. Bunsen courageously stood out for the historical reality of the martyr, whom he would fain identify with his namesake the well-known writer of the third century (*Hippolytus and his Age*, London, 1852, i. pp. 212 *sqq.*).

these Nemi myths is indeed transparent, since the foundation of the worship is traced now to Orestes and now to Hippolytus, according as this or that feature of the ritual has to be accounted for. The real value of such tales is that they serve to illustrate the nature of the worship by providing a standard with which to compare it; and further, that they bear witness indirectly to its venerable age by shewing that the true origin was lost in the mists of a fabulous antiquity. In the latter respect these Nemi legends are probably more to be trusted than the apparently historical tradition, vouched for by Cato the Elder, that the sacred grove was dedicated to Diana by a certain Egerius Baebius or Laevius of Tusculum, a Latin dictator, on behalf of the peoples of Tusculum, Aricia, Lanuvium, Laurentum, Cora, Tibur, Pometia, and Ardea.[1] This tradition indeed speaks for the great age of the sanctuary, since it seems to date its foundation sometime before 495 B.C., the year in which Pometia was sacked by the Romans and disappears from history.[2] But we cannot suppose that so barbarous a rule as that of the Arician priesthood was deliberately instituted by a league of civilised communities, such as the Latin cities undoubtedly were. It must have been handed down from a time beyond the memory of man, when Italy was still in a far ruder state than any known to us in the historical period. The credit of the tradition is rather shaken than confirmed by another story which ascribes the foundation of the sanctuary to a certain Manius Egerius, who gave rise to the saying, "There are many Manii at Aricia." This proverb some explained by alleging that Manius Egerius was the ancestor of a long and distinguished line, whereas others thought it meant that there were many ugly and deformed people at Aricia, and they derived the name Manius from *Mania,* a bogey or bugbear to frighten children.[3] A Roman satirist uses the name Manius as typical of the beggars who lay in wait for pilgrims on the Arician slopes.[4] These differences of opinion, together with the discrepancy between Manius Egerius of Aricia and Egerius Laevius of Tusculum, as well as the resemblance of both names to the mythical Egeria,[5] excite our suspicion. Yet the tradition recorded by Cato seems too circumstan-

[1]Cato, *Origines,* i., quoted by Priscian, *Inst.* iv. 21, vol. i. p. 129, ed. Hertz; *M. Catonis praeter librum de re rustica quae extant,* ed. H. Jordan, p. 12.

[2]Livy, ii. 25; Dionysius Halicarnas. *Antiquit. Roman.* vi. 29.

[3]Festus, p. 145, ed. C. O. Müller.

[4]Persius, *Sat.* vi. 55 *sqq.*

[5]Wissowa suggests that Manius Egerius was a half-forgotten male counterpart of Egeria (W.

tial, and its sponsor too respectable, to allow us to dismiss it as an idle fiction.[1] Rather we may suppose that it refers to some ancient restoration or reconstruction of the sanctuary, which was actually carried out by the confederate states.[2] At any rate it testifies to a belief that the grove had been from early times a common place of worship for many of the oldest cities of the country, if not for the whole Latin confederacy.[3]

SOME PRIMITIVE THEORIES OF THE ORIGIN OF MAN*
By J. G. FRAZER.

On a bright day in late autumn a good many years ago I had ascended the hill of Panopeus in Phocis to examine the ancient Greek fortifications which crest its brow. It was the first of November, but the weather was very hot; and when my work among the ruins was done, I was glad to rest under the shade of a clump of fine holly-oaks, to inhale the sweet refreshing perfume of the wild thyme which scented all the air, and to enjoy the distant prospects, rich in natural beauty, rich too in memories of the legendary and historic past.

H. Roscher's *Lexikon d. griech. und röm. Mythologie, s.v.* "Egeria"); and Dessau observes that the name Egerius *"sine dubio cohaeret cum Egerio fonte" (Corpus Inscriptionum Latinarum,* xiv. p. 204). The same view is taken by Messrs. A. B. Cook and E. Pais. Mr. Cook holds that the original form of the names was Aegerius and Aegeria, which he would interpret as "the Oak God" and "the Oak Goddess." See A. B. Cook, "The European Sky-God," *Folk-lore,* xvi. (1905) pp. 291 *sq.;* E. Pais, *Ancient Legends of Roman History,* (1906), p. 142.

[1] As Cluverius seems to do (*Italia Antiqua,* p. 931).

[2] This is substantially the view of Prof. Wissowa, who holds that the reference is to the foundation of a common altar in the grove by all the members of the league (*Religion und Kultus der Römer,* p. 199).

[3] Scholars are not agreed as to whether the list of confederate Latin cities in Cato is complete, and whether the Latin dictator he mentions was the head of the league or only of Tusculum. In regard to the former question we must remember that the passage of Cato is known to us only from Priscian, who seems to have quoted no more than suited his purpose, which was merely to illustrate a grammatical termination (*Ardeatis* for the later *Ardeas*). Probably, therefore, the original passage contained many more names of towns which Priscian did not think it needful to cite. This is the view of H. Dessau (in *Corpus Inscriptionum Latinarum,* xiv. p. 204). With regard to the second question, Mommsen held that the dictatorship in question was merely the chief magistracy of Tusculum, the presidency of the Latin league being vested in two praetors, not in a dictator (Livy, viii. 3. 9). Most scholars, however, appear to be of opinion that the dictator referred to was head of the league. See H. Jordan, *M. Catonis praeter librum de re rustica quae extant,* pp. xli. *sqq.;* J. Beloch, *Der italische Bund unter Roms Hegemonie* (Leipsic, 1880), p. 188; H. Nissen, *Italische Landeskunde,* ii. (Berlin, 1902) pp. 557 *sq.*

*From *Darwin and Modern Science,* edited by A. C. Seward (Cambridge: at the University Press, 1909), pp. 152-170.

To the south the finely-cut peak of Helicon peered over the low intervening hills. In the west loomed the mighty mass of Parnassus, its middle slopes darkened by pine-woods like shadows of clouds brooding on the mountain-side; while at its skirts nestled the ivy-mantled walls of Daulis overhanging the deep glen, whose romantic beauty accords so well with the loves and sorrows of Procne and Philomela, which Greek tradition associated with the spot. Northwards, across the broad plain to which the hill of Panopeus descends, steep and bare, the eye rested on the gap in the hills through which the Cephissus winds his tortuous way to flow under grey willows, at the foot of barren stony hills, till his turbid waters lose themselves, no longer in the vast reedy swamps of the now vanished Copaic Lake, but in the darkness of a cavern in the limestone rock. Eastward, clinging to the slopes of the bleak range of which the hill of Panopeus forms part were the ruins of Chaeronea, the birthplace of Plutarch; and out there in the plain was fought the disastrous battle which laid Greece at the feet of Macedonia. There, too, in a later age East and West met in deadly conflict, when the Roman armies under Sulla defeated the Asiatic hosts of Mithridates. Such was the landscape spread out before me on one of those farewell autumn days of almost pathetic splendour, when the departing summer seems to linger fondly, as if loth to resign to winter the enchanted mountains of Greece. Next day the scene had changed: summer was gone. A grey November mist hung low on the hills which only yesterday had shone resplendent in the sun, and under its melancholy curtain the dead flat of the Chaeronean plain, a wide treeless expanse shut in by desolate slopes, wore an aspect of chilly sadness befitting the battlefield where a nation's freedom was lost.

But crowded as the prospect from Panopeus is with memories of the past, the place itself, now so still and deserted, was once the scene of an event even more ancient and memorable, if Greek story-tellers can be trusted. For here, they say, the sage Prometheus created our first parents by fashioning them, like a potter, out of clay[1]. The very spot where he did so can still be seen. It is a forlorn little glen or rather hollow behind the hill of Panopeus, below the ruined but still stately walls and towers which crown the grey rocks of the summit. The glen, when I visited it that hot day after the long drought

[1]Pausanias, x. 4. 4. Compare Apollodorus, *Bibliotheca*, I. 7. 1; Ovid. *Metamorph*. I. 82 *sq.*; Juvenal, *Sat*. xiv. 35. According to another version of the tale, this creation of mankind took place not at Panopeus, but at Iconium in Lycaonia. After the original race of mankind had been destroyed in the great flood of Deucalion, the Greek Noah, Zeus commanded Prometheus and Athena to create men afresh by moulding images out of clay, breathing the winds into them, and making them live. See *Etymologicum Magnum, s. v.* Ἰκόνιον, pp. 470 *sq*. It is said that Prometheus fashioned the animals as well as men, giving to each kind of beast its proper nature. See Philemon, quoted by Stobaeus, *Florilegium*, II. 27. The creation of man by Prometheus is figured on ancient works of art. See J. Toutain, *Etudes de Mythologie et d'Histoire des Religions Antiques* (Paris, 1909), p. 190. According to Hesiod *(Works and Days*, 60 *sqq.)* it was Hephaestus who at the bidding of Zeus moulded the first woman cut of moist earth.

of summer, was quite dry; no water trickled down its bushy sides, but in the bottom I found a reddish crumbling earth, a relic perhaps of the clay out of which the potter Prometheus moulded the Greek Adam and Eve. In a volume dedicated to the honour of one who has done more than any other in modern times to shape the ideas of mankind as to their origin it may not be out of place to recall this crude Greek notion of the creation of the human race, and to compare or contrast it with other rudimentary speculations of primitive peoples on the same subject, if only for the sake of marking the interval which divides the childhood from the maturity of science.

The simple notion that the first man and woman were modelled out of clay by a god or other superhuman being is found in the traditions of many peoples. This is the Hebrew belief recorded in Genesis: "The Lord God formed man of the dust of the ground, and breathed into his nostrils the breath of life; and man became a living soul.[2]" To the Hebrews this derivation of our species suggested itself all the more naturally because in their language the word for "ground" (*adamah*) is in form the feminine of the word for man (*adam*)[1]. From various allusions in Babylonian literature it would seem that the Babylonians also conceived man to have been moulded out of clay[2]. According to Berosus, the Babylonian priest whose account of creation has been preserved in a Greek version, the god Bel cut off his own head, and the other gods caught the flowing blood, mixed it with earth, and fashioned men out of the bloody paste; and that, they said, is why men are so wise, because their mortal clay is tempered with divine blood.[3] In Egyptian mythology Khnoumou, the Father of the gods, is said to have moulded men out of clay.[4] We cannot doubt that such crude conceptions of the origin of our race were handed down to the civilised peoples of antiquity by their savage or barbarous forefathers. Certainly stories of the same sort are known to be current among savages and barbarians.

Thus the Australian blacks in the neighbourhood of Melbourne said that Pund-jel, the creator, cut three large sheets of bark with his big knife. On one of these he placed some clay and worked it up with his knife into a proper consistence. He then laid a portion of the clay on one of the other pieces of bark and shaped it into a human form; first he made the feet, then the legs, then the trunk, the arms, and the head. Thus he made a clay man on each of the two pieces of bark; and being well pleased with them he danced round them for joy. Next he took stringy bark from the Eucalyptus tree, made hair of it, and stuck it on the heads of his clay men. Then he looked at them

[2]Genesis ii. 7.

[1]S. R. Driver and W. H. Bennett, in their commentaries on Genesis ii. 7.

[2]H. Zimmern, in E. Schrader's *Die Keilinschriften und das Alte Testament*[3] (Berlin, 1902), p. 506.

[3]Eusebius, *Chronicon*, ed. A. Schoene, Vol. I (Berlin, 1875), col. 16.

[4]G. Maspero, *Histoire Ancienne des Peuples de l'Orient Classique*, I. (Paris, 1895), p. 128.

again, was pleased with his work, and again danced round them for joy. He then lay down on them, blew his breath hard into their mouths, their noses, and their navels; and presently they stirred, spoke, and rose up as full-grown men.[5] The Maoris of New Zealand say that Tiki made man after his own image. He took red clay, kneaded it, like the Babylonian Bel, with his own blood, fashioned it in human form, and gave the image breath. As he had made man in his own likeness he called him *Tiki-ahua* or Tiki's likeness.[6] A very generally received tradition in Tahiti was that the first human pair was made by Taaroa, the chief god. They say that after he had formed the world he created man out of red earth, which was also the food of mankind until bread-fruit was produced. Further, some say that one day Taaroa called for the man by name, and when he came he made him fall asleep. As he slept, the creator took out one of his bones (*ivi*) and made a woman of it, whom he gave to the man to be his wife, and the pair became the progenitors of mankind. This narrative was taken down from the lips of the natives in the early years of the mission to Tahiti. The missionary who records it observes: "This always appeared to me a mere recital of the Mosaic account of creation, which they had heard from some European, and I never placed any reliance on it, although they have repeatedly told me it was a tradition among them before any foreigner arrived. Some have also stated that the woman's name was Ivi, which would be by them pronounced as if written *Eve*. *Ivi* is an aboriginal word, and not only signifies a bone, but also a widow, and a victim slain in war. Notwithstanding the assertion of the natives, I am disposed to think that *Ivi*, or Eve, is the only aboriginal part of the story, as far as it respects the mother of the human race."[1] However, the same tradition has been recorded in other parts of Polynesia besides Tahiti. Thus the natives of Fakaofo or Bowditch Island say that the first man was produced out of a stone. After a time he bethought him of making a woman. So he gathered earth and moulded the figure of a woman out of it, and having done so he took a rib out of his left side and thrust it into the earthen figure, which thereupon started up a live woman. He called her Ivi (Eevee) or "rib" and took her to wife, and the whole human race sprang from this pair.[2] The Maoris also are reported

---

[5] R. Brough Smyth, *The Aborigines of Victoria* (Melbourne, 1878), I. 424. This and many of the following legends of creation have been already cited by me in a note on Pausanias, x. 4. 4 [*Pausanias's Description of Greece, translated with a Commentary* (London, 1898), Vol. v. pp. 220 *sq.*].

[6] R. Taylor, *Te Ika A Maui, or New Zealand and its Inhabitants*, Second Edition (London, 1870), p. 117. Compare E. Shortland, *Maori Religion and Mythology* (London, 1882), pp. 21 *sq.*

[1] W. Ellis, *Polynesian Researches*, Second Edition (London, 1832), I. 110 *sq. Ivi* or *iwi* is the regular word for "bone" in the various Polynesian languages. See E. Tregear, *The Maori-Polynesian Comparative Dictionary* (Wellington, New Zealand, 1891), p. 109.

[2] G. Turner, *Samoa* (London, 1884), pp. 267 *sq.*

to believe that the first woman was made out of the first man's ribs.[3] This wide diffusion of the story in Polynesia raises a doubt whether it is merely, as Ellis thought, a repetition of the Biblical narrative learned from Europeans. In Nui, or Netherland Island, it was the god Aulialia who made earthen models of a man and woman, raised them up, and made them live. He called the man Tepapa and the woman Tetata.[4]

In the Pelew Islands they say that a brother and sister made men out of clay kneaded with the blood of various animals, and that the characters of these first men and of their descendants were determined by the characters of the animals whose blood had been kneaded with the primordial clay; for instance, men who have rat's blood in them are thieves, men who have serpent's blood in them are sneaks, and men who have cock's blood in them are brave.[1] According to a Melanesian legend, told in Mota, one of the Banks Islands, the hero Qat moulded men of clay, the red clay from the marshy river-side at Vanua Lava. At first he made men and pigs just alike, but his brothers remonstrated with him, so he beat down the pigs to go on all fours and made men walk upright. Qat fashioned the first woman out of supple twigs, and when she smiled he knew she was a living woman.[2] A somewhat different version of the Melanesian story is told at Lakona, in Santa Maria. There they say that Qat and another spirit (*vui*) called Marawa both made men. Qat made them out of the wood of dracaena-trees. Six days he worked at them, carving their limbs and fitting them together. Then he allowed them six days to come to life. Three days he hid them away, and three days more he worked to make them live. He set them up and danced to them and beat his drum, and little by little they stirred, till at last they could stand all by themselves. Then Qat divided them into pairs and called each pair husband and wife. Marawa also made men out of a tree, but it was a different tree, the *tavisoviso*. He likewise worked at them six days, beat his drum, and made them live, just as Qat did. But when he saw them move, he dug a pit and buried them in it for six days, and then, when he scraped away the earth to see what they were doing, he found them all rotten and stinking. That was the origin of death.[3]

The inhabitants of Noo-hoo-roa, in the Kei Islands say that their ancestors were fashioned out of clay by the supreme god, Dooadlera, who breathed life into the clay figures.[4] The aborigines of Minahassa, in the north of Celebes,

[3] J. L. Nicholas, *Narrative of a Voyage to New Zealand* (London, 1817), I. 59, who writes "and to add still more to this strange coincidence, the general term for bone is *Hevee*."

[4] G. Turner, *Samoa*, pp. 300 *sq.*

[1] J. Kubary, "Die Religion der Pelauer," in A. Bastian's *Allerlei aus Volks und Menschenkunde* (Berlin, 1888), I. 3, 56.

[2] R. H. Codrington, *The Melanesians* (Oxford, 1891), p. 158.

[3] R. H. Codrington, *op. cit.*, pp. 157 *sq.*

[4] C. M. Pleyte, "Ethnographische Beschrijving der Kei-Eilanden," *Tijdschrift van het Nederlandsch Aardrijkskundig Genootschap*, Tweede Serie, x. (1893), p. 564.

say that two beings called Wailan Wangko and Wangi were alone on an island, on which grew a cocoa-nut tree. Said Wailan Wangko to Wangi, "Remain on earth while I climb up the tree." Said Wangi to Wailan Wangko, "Good." But then a thought occurred to Wangi and he climbed up the tree to ask Wailan Wangko why he, Wangi, should remain down there all alone. Said Wailan Wangko to Wangi, "Return and take earth and make two images, a man and a woman." Wangi did so, and both images were men who could move but could not speak. So Wangi climbed up the tree to ask Wailan Wangko, "How now? The two images are made, but they cannot speak." Said Wailan Wangko to Wangi, "Take this ginger and go and blow it on the skulls and the ears of these two images, that they may be able to speak; call the man Adam and the woman Ewa."[1] In this narrative the names of the man and woman betray European influence, but the rest of the story may be aboriginal. The Dyaks of Sakarran in British Borneo say that the first man was made by two large birds. At first they tried to make men out of trees, but in vain. Then they hewed them out of rocks, but the figures could not speak. Then they moulded a man out of damp earth and infused into his veins the red gum of the kumpang-tree. After that they called to him and he answered; they cut him and blood flowed from his wounds.[2]

The Kumis of South-Eastern India related to Captain Lewin, the Deputy Commissioner of Hill Tracts, the following tradition of the creation of man. "God made the world and the trees and the creeping things first, and after that he set to work to make one man and one woman, forming their bodies of clay; but each night, on the completion of his work, there came a great snake, which, while God was sleeping, devoured the two images. This happened twice or thrice, and God was at his wit's end, for he had to work all day, and could not finish the pair in less than twelve hours; besides, if he did not sleep, he would be no good," said Captain Lewin's informant. "If he were not obliged to sleep, there would be no death, nor would mankind be afflicted with illness. It is when he rests that the snake carries us off to this day. Well, he was at his wit's end, so at last he got up early one morning and first made a dog and put life into it, and that night, when he had finished the images, he set the dog to watch them, and when the snake came, the dog barked and frightened it away. This is the reason at this day that when a man is dying the dogs begin to howl; but I suppose God sleeps heavily

[1]N. Graafland, De Minahassa (Rotterdam, 1869), I. pp. 96 sq.

[2]Horsburgh, quoted by H. Ling Roth, The Natives of Sarawak and of British North Borneo (London, 1896), I. pp. 299 sq. Compare The Lord Bishop of Labuan, "On the Wild Tribes of the North West Coast of Borneo," Transactions of the Ethnological Society of London, New Series, II. (1863), p. 27.

now-a-days, or the snake is bolder, for men die all the same."³ The Khasis of Assam tell a similar tale.⁴

The Ewe-speaking tribes of Togo-land, in West Africa, think that God still makes men out of clay. When a little of the water with which he moistens the clay remains over, he pours it on the ground and out of that he makes the bad and disobedient people. When he wishes to make a good man he makes him out of good clay; but when he wishes to make a bad man, he employs only bad clay for the purpose. In the beginning God fashioned a man and set him on the earth; after that he fashioned a woman. The two looked at each other and began to laugh, whereupon God sent them into the world.¹ The Innuit or Esquimaux of Point Barrow, in Alaska, tell of a time when there was no man in the land, till a spirit named *á sĕ lu*, who resided at Point Barrow, made a clay man, set him up on the shore to dry, breathed into him and gave him life.² Other Esquimaux of Alaska relate how the Raven made the first woman out of clay to be a companion to the first man; he fastened watergrass to the back of the head to be hair, flapped his wings over the clay figure, and it arose, a beautiful young woman.³ The Acagchemem Indians of California said that a powerful being called Chinigchinich created man out of clay which he found on the banks of a lake; male and female created he them, and the Indians of the present day are their descendants.⁴ A priest of the Natchez Indians in Louisiana told Du Pratz "that God had kneaded some clay, such as that which potters use and had made it into a little man; and that after examining it, and finding it well formed, he blew up his work, and forthwith that little man had life, grew, acted, walked, and found himself a man perfectly well shaped." As to the mode in which the first woman was created, the priest had no information, but thought she was probably made in the same way as the first man; so Du Pratz corrected his imperfect notions by reference to Scripture.⁵ The Michoacans of Mexico said that the great god Tucapacha first made man and woman out of clay, but that when the couple went to bathe in a river they absorbed so much water that the clay of which they were composed all fell to pieces. Then the creator went to work again and moulded them afresh out of ashes, and after that he essayed a third time and made

³Capt. T. H. Lewin, *Wild Races of South-Eastern India* (London, 1870), pp. 224-26.
⁴A. Bastian, *Völkerstämme am Brahmaputra und verwandtschaftliche Nachbarn* (Berlin, 1883), p. 8; Major P. R. T. Gurdon, *The Khasis* (London, 1907), p. 106.
¹J. Spieth, *Die Ewe-Stämme, Material zur Kunde des Ewe-Volkes in Deutsch-Togo* (Berlin, 1906), pp. 828, 840.
²*Report of the International Expedition to Point Barrow* (Washington, 1885), p. 47.
³E. W. Nelson, "The Eskimo about Bering Strait," *Eighteenth Annual Report of the Bureau of American Ethnology*, Part I. (Washington, 1899), p. 454.
⁴Friar Geronimo Boscana, "Chinigchinich," appended to [A. Robinson's] *Life in California* (New York, 1846), p. 247.
⁵M. Le Page Du Pratz, *The History of Louisiana* (London, 1774), p. 330.

them of metal. This last attempt succeeded. The metal man and woman bathed in the river without falling to pieces, and by their union they became the progenitors of mankind.[6]

According to a legend of the Peruvian Indians, which was told to a Spanish priest in Cuzco about half a century after the conquest, it was in Tiahuanaco that man was first created, or at least was created afresh after the deluge. "There (in Tiahuanaco)," so runs the legend, "the Creator began to raise up the people and nations that are in that region, making one of each nation of clay, and painting the dresses that each one was to wear; those that were to wear their hair, with hair, and those that were to be shorn, with hair cut. And to each nation was given the language, that was to be spoken, and the songs to be sung, and the seeds and food that they were to sow. When the Creator had finished painting and making the said nations and figures of clay, he gave life and soul to each one, as well men as women, and ordered that they should pass under the earth. Thence each nation came up in the places to which he ordered them to go."[1]

These examples suffice to prove that the theory of the creation of man out of dust or clay has been current among savages in many parts of the world. But it is by no means the only explanation which the savage philosopher has given of the beginnings of human life on earth. Struck by the resemblances which may be traced between himself and the beasts, he has often supposed, like Darwin himself, that mankind has been developed out of lower forms of animal life. For the simple savage has none of that high notion of the transcendant dignity of man which makes so many superior persons shrink with horror from the suggestion that they are distant cousins of the brutes. He on the contrary is not too proud to own his humble relations; indeed his difficulty often is to perceive the distinction between him and them. Questioned by a missionary, a Bushman of more than average intelligence "could not state any difference between a man and a brute—he did not know but a buffalo might shoot with bows and arrows as well as a man, if it had them."[2] When the Russians first landed on one of the Alaskan islands, the natives took them for cuttle-fish "on account of the buttons on their clothes."[3] The Giliaks of the Amoor think that the outward form and size of an animal are only apparent; in substance every beast is a real man, just like a Giliak himself, only endowed with an intelligence and strength, which often surpass those of mere ordinary

[6]A. de Herrera, *General History of the vast Continent and Islands of America,* translated into English by Capt. J. Stevens (London, 1725, 1726), III. 254; Brasseur de Bourbourg, *Histoire des Nations Civilisées du Mexique et de l'Amerique-Centrale* (Paris, 1857-1859), III. 80 *sq.*; compare *id.* 1. 54 *sq.*

[1]E. J. Payne, *History of the New World called America,* I. (Oxford, 1892), p. 462.

[2]Rev. John Campbell, *Travels in South Africa* (London, 1822), II. p. 34.

[3]I. Petroff, *Report on the Population, Industries, and Resources of Alaska,* p. 145.

human beings.[4] The Borororos, an Indian tribe of Brazil, will have it that they are parrots of a gorgeous red plumage which live in their native forests. Accordingly they treat the birds as their fellow-tribesmen, keeping them in captivity, refusing to eat their flesh, and mourning for them when they die.[5]

This sense of the close relationship of man to the lower creation is the essence of totemism, that curious system of superstition which unites by a mystic bond a group of human kinsfolk to a species of animals or plants. Where that system exists in full force, the members of a totem clan identify themselves with their totem animals in a way and to an extent which we find it hard even to imagine. For example, men of the Cassowary clan in Mabuiag think that cassowaries are men or nearly so. "Cassowary, he all same as relation, he belong same family," is the account they give of their relationship with the long-legged bird. Conversely they hold that they themselves are cassowaries for all practical purposes. They pride themselves on having long thin legs like a cassowary. This reflection affords them peculiar satisfaction when they go out to fight, or to run away, as the case may be; for at such times a Cassowary man will say to himself, "My leg is long and thin, I can run and not feel tired; my legs will go quickly and the grass will not entangle them." Members of the Cassowary clan are reputed to be pugnacious, because the cassowary is a bird of very uncertain temper and can kick with extreme violence.[1] So among the Ojibways men of the Bear clan are reputed to be surly and pugnacious like bears, and men of the Crane clan to have clear ringing voices like cranes.[2] Hence the savage will often speak of his totem animal as his father or his brother, and will neither kill it himself nor allow others to do so, if he can help it. For example, if somebody were to kill a bird in the presence of a native Australian who had the bird for his totem, the black might say, "What for you kill that fellow? that my father!" or "That brother belonging to me you have killed; why did you do it?"[3] Bechuanas of the Porcupine clan are greatly afflicted if anybody hurts or kills a porcupine in their presence. They say, "They have killed our brother, our master, one of ourselves, him whom we sing of"; and so saying they piously gather the quills of their murdered brother, spit on them, and rub their eyebrows with them. They think

[4]L. Sternberg, "Die Religion der Giljaken," *Archiv für Religionswissenschaft*, VIII. (1905), p. 248.

[5]K. von den Steinen, *Unter den Naturvölkern Zentral-Brasiliens* (Berlin, 1894), pp. 352 *sq.*, 512.

[1]A. C. Haddon, "The Ethnography of the Western Tribe of Torres Straits," *Journal of the Anthropological Institute*, XIX. (1890), p. 393; *Reports of the Cambridge Anthropological Expedition to Torres Straits*, v. (Cambridge, 1904), pp. 166, 184.

[2]W. W. Warren, "History of the Ojibways," *Collections of the Minnesota Historical Society*, v. (Saint Paul, Minn. 1885), pp. 47, 49.

[3]E. Palmer, "Notes on some Australian Tribes," *Journal of the Anthropological Institute*, XIII. (1884), p. 300.

they would die if they touched its flesh. In like manner Bechuanas of the Crocodile clan call the crocodile one of themselves, their master, their brother; and they mark the ears of their cattle with a long slit like a crocodile's mouth by way of a family crest. Similarly Bechuanas of the Lion clan would not, like the members of other clans, partake of lion's flesh; for how, say they, could they eat their grandfather? If they are forced in self-defence to kill a lion, they do so with great regret and rub their eyes carefully with its skin, fearing to lose their sight if they neglected this precaution.[1] A Mandingo porter has been known to offer the whole of his month's pay to save the life of a python, because the python was his totem and he therefore regarded the reptile as his relation; he thought that if he allowed the creature to be killed, the whole of his own family would perish, probably through the vengeance to be taken by the reptile kinsfolk of the murdered serpent.[2]

Sometimes, indeed, the savage goes further and identifies the revered animal not merely with a kinsman but with himself; he imagines that one of his own more or less numerous souls, or at all events that a vital part of himself, is in the beast, so that if it is killed he must die. Thus, the Balong tribe of the Cameroons, in West Africa, think that every man has several souls, of which one is lodged in an elephant, a wild boar, a leopard, or what not. When any one comes home, feels ill, and says, "I shall soon die," and is as good as his word, his friends are of opinion that one of his souls has been shot by a hunter in a wild boar or a leopard, for example, and that that is the real cause of his death.[3] A Catholic missionary, sleeping in the hut of a chief of the Fan negroes, awoke in the middle of the night to see a huge black serpent of the most dangerous sort in the act of darting at him. He was about to shoot it when the chief stopped him, saying, "In killing that serpent, it is me that you would have killed. Fear nothing, the serpent is my *elangela*."[4] At Calabar there used to be some years ago a huge old crocodile which was well known to contain the spirit of a chief who resided in the flesh at Duke Town. Sporting Vice-Consuls, with reckless disregard of human life, from time to time made determined attempts to injure the animal, and once a peculiarly active officer succeeded in hitting it. The chief was immediately laid up with a wound in his leg. He *said* that a dog had bitten him, but few people perhaps were deceived by so flimsy a pretext.[5] Once when Mr. Partridge's canoemen

[1]T. Arbousset et F. Daumas, *Relation d'un Voyage d'Exploration au Nord-Est de la Colonie du Cap de Bonne-Espérance* (Paris, 1842), pp. 349 *sq.*, 422-24.

[2]M. le Docteur Tautain, "Notes sur les Croyances et Pratiques Religeuses des Banmanas," *Revue d'Ethnographie*, III. (1885), pp. 396 *sq.*; A. Rançon, *Dans la Haute-Gambie, Voyage d'Exploration Scientifique* (Paris, 1894), p. 445.

[3]J. Keller, "Ueber das Land und Volk der Balong," *Deutsches Kolonialblatt*, 1 Oktober, 1895, p. 484.

[4]Father Trilles, "Chez les Fang, leurs Moeurs, leur Langue, leur Religion," *Les Missions Catholiques*, XXX. (1898), p. 322.

[5]Miss Mary H. Kingsley, *Travels in West Africa* (London, 1897), pp. 538 *sq.* As to the external

were about to catch fish near an Assiga town in Southern Nigeria, the natives of the town objected, saying, "Our souls live in those fish, and if you kill them we shall die."[1] On another occasion, in the same region, an Englishman shot a hippopotamus near a native village. The same night a woman died in the village, and her friends demanded and obtained from the marksman five pounds as compensation for the murder of the woman, whose soul or second self had been in that hippopotamus.[2] Similarly at Ndolo, in the Congo region, we hear of a chief whose life was bound up with a hippopotamus, but he prudently suffered no one to fire at the animal.[3]

Amongst people who thus fail to perceive any sharp line of distinction between beasts and men it is not surprising to meet with the belief that human beings are directly descended from animals. Such a belief is often found among totemic tribes who imagine that their ancestors sprang from their totemic animals or plants; but it is by no means confined to them. Thus, to take instances, some of the Californian Indians, in whose mythology the coyote or prairie-wolf is a leading personage, think that they are descended from coyotes. At first they walked on all fours; then they began to have some members of the human body, one finger, one toe, one eye, one ear, and so on; then they got two fingers, two toes, two eyes, two ears, and so forth; till at last, progressing from period to period, they became perfect human beings. The loss of their tails, which they still deplore, was produced by the habit of sitting upright.[4] Similarly Darwin thought that "the tail has disappeared in man and the anthropomorphous apes, owing to the terminal portion having been injured by friction during a long lapse of time; the basal and embedded portion having been reduced and modified, so as to become suitable to the erect or semi-erect position."[5] The Turtle clan of the Iroquois think that they are descended from real mud turtles which used to live in a pool. One hot summer the pool dried up, and the mud turtles set out to find another. A very fat turtle, waddling after the rest in the heat, was much incommoded by the weight of his shell, till by a great effort he heaved it off altogether. After that he gradually

---

or bush souls of human beings, which in this part of Africa are supposed to be lodged in the bodies of animals, see Miss Mary H. Kingsley, *op. cit.* pp. 459-461; R. Henshaw, "Notes on the Efik belief in 'bush soul,' " *Man*, VI. (1906), pp. 121 *sq.*; J. Parkinson, "Notes on the Asaba people (Ibos) of the Niger," *Journal of the Anthropological Institute*, XXXVI. (1906), pp. 314 *sq.*

[1] Charles Partridge, *Cross River Natives* (London, 1905), pp. 225 *sq.*

[2] C. H. Robinson, *Hausaland* (London, 1896), pp. 36 *sq.*

[3] *Notes Analytiques sur les Collections Ethnographiques du Musée du Congo*, I. (Brussels, 1902-06), p. 150.

[4] H. R. Schoolcraft, *Indian Tribes of the United States*, IV. (Philadelphia, 1856), pp. 224 *sq.*; compare *id.* v. p. 217. The descent of some, not all, Indians from coyotes is mentioned also by Friar Boscana, in [A. Robinson's] *Life in California* (New York, 1846), p. 299.

[5] Charles Darwin, *The Descent of Man*, Second Edition (London, 1879), p. 60.

developed into a man and became the progenitor of the Turtle clan.[6] The Crawfish band of the Choctaws are in like manner descended from real crawfish,
which used to live under ground, only coming up occasionally through the
mud to the surface. Once a party of Choctaws smoked them out, taught them
the Choctaw language, taught them to walk on two legs, made them cut off
their toe nails and pluck the hair from their bodies, after which they adopted
them into the tribe. But the rest of their kindred, the crawfish, are crawfish
under ground to this day.[1] The Osage Indians universally believed that they
were descended from a male snail and a female beaver. A flood swept the
snail down to the Missouri and left him high and dry on the bank, where
the sun ripened him into a man. He met and married a beaver maid, and from
the pair the tribe of the Osages is descended. For a long time these Indians
retained a pious reverence for their animal ancestors and refrained from hunting
beavers, because in killing a beaver they killed a brother of the Osages. But
when white men came among them and offered high prices for beaver skins,
the Osages yielded to the temptation and took the lives of their furry brethren.[2]
The Carp clan of the Ootawak Indians are descended from the eggs of a carp
which had been deposited by the fish on the banks of a stream and warmed
by the sun.[3] The Crane clan of the Ojibways are sprung originally from a
pair of cranes, which after long wanderings settled on the rapids at the outlet
of Lake Superior, where they were changed by the Great Spirit into a man
and woman.[4] The members of two Omaha clans were originally buffaloes and
lived, oddly enough, under water, which they splashed about, making it
muddy. And at death all the members of these clans went back to their ancestors the buffaloes. So when one of them lay adying, his friends used to wrap
him up in a buffalo skin with the hair outside and say to him, "You came
hither from the animals and you are going back thither. Do not face this way
again. When you go, continue walking."[5] The Haida Indians of Queen Charlotte Islands believe that long ago the raven, who is the chief figure in the
mythology of North-West America, took a cockle from the beach and married
it; the cockle gave birth to a female child, whom the raven took to wife, and
from their union the Indians were produced.[6] The Delaware Indians called the
rattle-snake their grandfather and would on no account destroy one of these

[6]E. A. Smith, "Myths of the Iroquois," *Second Annual Report of the Bureau of Ethnology* (Washington, 1883), p. 77.
[1]Geo. Catlin, *North American Indians*[4] (London, 1844), II. p. 128.
[2]Lewis and Clarke, *Travels to the Source of the Missouri River* (London, 1815), I. 12 (Vol. I. pp. 44 *sq.* of the London reprint, 1905).
[3]*Lettres Edifiantes et Curieuses*, Nouvelle Edition, VI. (Paris, 1781), p. 171.
[4]L. H. Morgan, *Ancient Society* (London, 1877), p. 180.
[5]J. Owen Dorsey, "Omaha Sociology," *Third Annual Report of the Bureau of Ethnology* (Washington, 1884), pp. 229, 233.
[6]G. M. Dawson, *Report on the Queen Charlotte Islands* (Montreal, 1880), pp. 149 B *sq.* *(Geological Survey of Canada)*; F. Poole, *Queen Charlotte Islands*, p. 136.

reptiles, believing that were they to do so the whole race of rattle-snakes would rise up and bite them. Under the influence of the white man, however, their respect for their grandfather the rattle-snake gradually died away, till at last they killed him without compunction or ceremony whenever they met him. The writer who records the old custom observes that he had often reflected on the curious connection which appears to subsist in the mind of an Indian between man and the brute creation; "all animated nature," says he, "in whatever degree, is in their eyes a great whole, from which they have not yet ventured to separate themselves."[1]

Some of the Indians of Peru boasted of being descended from the puma or American lion; hence they adored the lion as a god and appeared at festivals like Hercules dressed in the skins of lions with the heads of the beasts fixed over their own. Others claimed to be sprung from condors and attired themselves in great black and white wings, like that enormous bird.[2] The Wanika of East Africa look upon the hyaena as one of their ancestors or as associated in some way with their origin and destiny. The death of a hyaena is mourned by the whole people, and the greatest funeral ceremonies which they perform are performed for this brute. The wake held over a chief is as nothing compared to the wake held over a hyaena; one tribe only mourns the death of its chief, but all the tribes unite to celebrate the obsequies of a hyaena.[3] Some Malagasy families claim to be descended from the babacoote (*Lichanotus brevicaudatus*), a large lemur of grave appearance and staid demeanour, which lives in the depth of the forest. When they find one of these creatures dead, his human descendants bury it solemnly, digging a grave for it, wrapping it in a shroud, and weeping and lamenting over its carcase. A doctor who had shot a babacoote was accused by the inhabitants of a Betsimisaraka village of having killed "one of their grandfathers in the forest," and to appease their indignation he had to promise not to skin the animal in the village but in a solitary place where nobody could see him.[4] Many of the Betsimisaraka believe that the curious nocturnal animal called the aye-aye (*Cheiromys madagascariensis*) "is the embodiment of their forefathers, and hence will not touch it, much less do it an injury. It is said that when one is discovered dead in the forest, these

[1] Rev. John Heckewelder, "An Account of the History, Manners, and Customs, of the Indian Nations, who once inhabited Pennsylvania and the Neighbouring States," *Transactions of the Historical and Literary Committee of the American Philosophical Society*, I. (Philadelphia, 1819), pp. 245, 247, 248.

[2] Garcilasso de la Vega, *First Part of the Royal Commentaries of the Yncas*, Vol. I. p. 323, Vol. II. p. 156 (Markham's translation).

[3] Charles New, *Life, Wanderings, and Labours in Eastern Africa* (London, 1873), p. 122.

[4] Father Abinal, "Croyances fabuleuses des Malgaches," *Les Missions Catholiques*, XII. (1880), p. 526; G. H. Smith, "Some Betsimisaraka superstitions," *The Antananarivo Annual and Madagascar Magazine*, No. 10 (Antananarivo, 1886), p. 239; H. W. Little, *Madagascar, its History and People* (London, 1884), pp. 321 *sq.*; A. van Gennep, *Tabou et Totémisme à Madagascar* (Paris, 1904), pp. 214 *sqq*.

people make a tomb for it and bury it with all the forms of a funeral. They think that if they attempt to entrap it, they will surely die in consequence."[1] Some Malagasy tribes believe themselves descended from crocodiles and accordingly they deem the formidable reptiles their brothers. If one of these scaly brothers so far forgets the ties of kinship as to devour a man, the chief of the tribe, or in his absence an old man familiar with the tribal customs, repairs at the head of the people to the edge of the water, and summons the family of the culprit to deliver him up to the arm of justice. A hook is then baited and cast into the river or lake. Next day the guilty brother or one of his family is dragged ashore, formally tried, sentenced to death, and executed. The claims of justice being thus satisfied, the dead animal is lamented and buried like a kinsman; a mound is raised over his grave and a stone marks the place of his head.[2]

Amongst the Tshi-speaking tribes of the Gold Coast in West Africa the Horse-mackerel family traces its descent from a real horse-mackerel whom an ancestor of theirs once took to wife. She lived with him happily in human shape on shore till one day a second wife, whom the man had married, cruelly taunted her with being nothing but a fish. That hurt her so much that bidding her husband farewell she returned to her old home in the sea, with her youngest child in her arms, and never came back again. But ever since the Horse-mackerel people have refrained from eating horse-mackerels, because the lost wife and mother was a fish of that sort.[3] Some of the Land Dyaks of Borneo tell a similar tale to explain a similar custom. "There is a fish which is taken in their rivers called a *puttin,* which they would on no account touch, under the idea that if they did they would be eating their relations. The tradition respecting it is, that a solitary old man went out fishing and caught a *puttin,* which he dragged out of the water and laid down in his boat. On turning round, he found it had changed into a very pretty little girl. Conceiving the idea she would make, what he had long wished for, a charming wife for his son, he took her home and educated her until she was fit to be married. She consented to be the son's wife cautioning her husband to use her well. Some time after their marriage, however, being out of temper, he struck her, when she screamed, and rushed away into the water; but not without leaving behind

[1]G. A. Shaw, "The Aye-aye," *Antananarivo Annual and Madagascar Magazine,* Vol. II (Antananarivo, 1896), pp. 201, 203 (Reprint of the Second four Numbers). Compare A. van Gennep, *Tabou et Totémisme à Madagascar,* pp. 223 *sq.*

[2]Father Abinal, "Croyances fabuleuses des Malgaches," *Les Missions Catholiques,* XII. (1880), p. 527; A. van Gennep, *Tabou et Totémisme à Madagascar,* pp. 281 *sq.*

[3]A. B. Ellis, *The Tshi-speaking Peoples of the Gold Coast of West Africa* (London, 1887), pp. 208-11. A similar tale is told by another fish family who abstain from eating the fish (*appei*) from which they take their name (A. B. Ellis, *op. cit.* pp. 211 *sq.*).

her a beautiful daughter, who became afterwards the mother of the race.''[1]

Members of a clan in Mandailing, on the west coast of Sumatra, assert that they are descended from a tiger, and at the present day, when a tiger is shot, the women of the clan are bound to offer betel to the dead beast. When members of this clan come upon the tracks of a tiger, they must, as a mark of homage, enclose them with three little sticks. Further, it is believed that the tiger will not attack or lacerate his kinsmen, the members of the clan.[2] The Battas of Central Sumatra are divided into a number of clans which have for their totems white buffaloes, goats, wild turtle-doves, dogs, cats, apes, tigers, and so forth; and one of the explanations which they give of their totems is that these creatures were their ancestors, and that their own souls after death can transmigrate into the animals.[3] In Amboyna and the neighbouring islands the inhabitants of some villages aver that they are descended from trees, such as the *Capellenia moluccana*, which had been fertilised by the *Pandion Haliaetus*. Others claim to be sprung from pigs, octopuses, crocodiles, sharks, and eels. People will not burn the wood of the trees from which they trace their descent, nor eat the flesh of the animals which they regard as their ancestors. Sicknesses of all sorts are believed to result from disregarding these taboos.[4] Similarly in Ceram persons who think they are descended from crocodiles, serpents, iguanas, and sharks will not eat the flesh of these animals.[5] Many other peoples of the Molucca Islands entertain similar beliefs and observe similar taboos.[1] Again, in Ponape, one of the Caroline Islands, ''the different families suppose themselves to stand in a certain relation to animals, and especially to fishes, and believe in their descent from them. They

[1]The Lord Bishop of Labuan, "On the Wild Tribes of the North-West Coast of Borneo," *Transactions of the Ethnological Society of London*, New Series, II. (London, 1863), pp. 26 *sq*. Such stories conform to a well-known type which may be called the Swan-Maiden type of story, or Beauty and the Beast, or Cupid and Psyche. The occurrence of stories of this type among totemic peoples, such as the Tshi-speaking negroes of the Gold Coast, who tell them to explain their totemic taboos, suggests that all such tales may have originated in totemism. I shall deal with this question elsewhere.

[2]H. Ris, "De Onderafdeeling Klein Mandailing Oeloe en Pahantan en hare Bevolking met uitzondering van de Oeloes," *Bijdragen tot de Taal- Land- en Volkenkunde van Nederlandsch-Indië*, XLVI (1896), p. 473.

[3]J. B. Neumann, "Het Pane en Bila-stroomgebied op het eiland Sumatra," *Tijdschrift van het Nederlandsch Aardrijkskundig Genootschap*, Tweede Serie, III. Afdeeling, Meer uitgebreide Artikelen, No. 2 (Amsterdam, 1886), pp. 311 *sq*.; *id. ib.* Tweede Serie, IV. Afdeeling, Meer uitgebreide Artikelen, No. 1 (Amsterdam, 1887), pp. 8 *sq*.

[4]J. G. F. Riedel, *De sluik- en kroesharige rassen tusschen Selebes en Papua* (The Hague, 1886), pp. 32, 61; G. W. W. C. Baron van Hoëvell, *Ambon en meer bepaaldelijk de Oeliasers* (Dordrecht, 1875), p. 152.

[5]J. G. F. Riedel, *op. cit.* p. 122.

[1]J. G. F. Riedel, *De sluik- en kroesharige rassen tusschen Selebes en Papua* (The Hague, 1886), pp. 253, 334, 341, 348, 412, 414, 432.

actually name these animals 'mothers'; the creatures are sacred to the family and may not be injured. Great dances, accompanied with the offering of prayers, are performed in their honour. Any person who killed such an animal would expose himself to contempt and punishment, certainly also to the vengeance of the insulted deity." Blindness is commonly supposed to be the consequence of such a sacrilege.[2]

Some of the aborigines of Western Australia believe that their ancestors were swans, ducks, or various other species of water-fowl before they were transformed into men.[3] The Dieri tribe of Central Australia, who are divided into totemic clans, explain their origin by the following legend. They say that in the beginning the earth opened in the midst of Perigundi Lake, and the totems (*murdus* or *madas*) came trooping out one after the other. Out came the crow, and the shell parakeet, and the emu, and all the rest. Being as yet imperfectly formed and without members or organs of sense, they laid themselves down on the sandhills which surrounded the lake then just as they do now. It was a bright day and the totems lay basking in the sunshine, till at last, refreshed and invigorated by it, they stood up as human beings and dispersed in all directions. That is why people of the same totem are now scattered all over the country. You may still see the island in the lake out of which the totems came trooping long ago.[4] Another Dieri legend relates how Paralina, one of the *Mura-Muras* or mythical predecessors of the Dieri, perfected mankind. He was out hunting kangaroos, when he saw four incomplete beings cowering together. So he went up to them, smoothed their bodies, stretched out their limbs, slit up their fingers and toes, formed their mouths, noses, and eyes, stuck ears on them, and blew into their ears in order that they might hear. Having perfected their organs and so produced mankind out of these rudimentary beings, he went about making men everywhere.[5] Yet another Dieri tradition sets forth how the *Mura-Mura* produced the race of man out of a species of small black lizards, which may still be met with under dry bark. To do this he divided the feet of the lizards into fingers and toes, and, applying his forefinger to the middle of their faces, created a nose; likewise he gave them human eyes, mouths and ears. He next set one of them upright, but it fell down again because of its tail; so he cut off its tail and the lizard then walked on its hind legs. That is the origin of mankind.[1]

[2]Dr. Hahl, "Mittheilungen über Sitten und rechtliche Verhältnisse auf Ponape," *Ethnologisches Notizblatt*, Vol. II. Heft 2 (Berlin, 1901), p. 10.
[3]Captain G. Grey, *A Vocabulary of the Dialects of South Western Australia*, Second Edition (London, 1840), pp. 29, 37, 61, 63, 66, 71.
[4]A. W. Howitt, *Native Tribes of South-East Australia* (London, 1904), pp. 476, 779 *sq.*
[5]A. W. Howitt, *op. cit.*, pp. 476, 780 *sq.*
[1]S. Gason, "The Manners and Customs of the Dieyerie tribe of Australian Aborigines," *Native Tribes of South Australia* (Adelaide, 1879), p. 260. This writer fell into the mistake of regarding the *Mura-Mura (Mooramoora)* as a Good-Spirit instead of as one of the mythical but more or

The Arunta tribe of Central Australia similarly tell how in the beginning mankind was developed out of various rudimentary forms of animal life. They say that in those days two beings called *Ungambikula,* that is, "out of nothing, ' or "self-existing," dwelt in the western sky. From their lofty abode they could see, far away to the east, a number of *inapertwa* creatures, that is, rudimentary human beings or incomplete men, whom it was their mission to make into real men and women. For at that time there were no real men and women; the rudimentary creatures (*inapertwa*) were of various shapes and dwelt in groups along the shore of the salt water which covered the country. These embryos, as we may call them, had no distinct limbs or organs of sight, hearing, and smell; they did not eat food, and they presented the appearance of human beings all doubled up into a rounded mass, in which only the outline of the different parts of the body could be vaguely perceived. Coming down from their home in the western sky, armed with great stone knives, the *Ungambikula* took hold of the embryos, one after the other. First of all they released the arms from the bodies, then making four clefts at the end of each arm they fashioned hands and fingers; afterwards legs, feet, and toes were added in the same way. The figure could now stand; a nose was then moulded and the nostrils bored with the fingers. A cut with the knife made the mouth, which was pulled open several times to render it flexible. A slit on each side of the face separated the upper and lower eye-lids, disclosing the eyes, which already existed behind them; and a few strokes more completed the body. Thus out of the rudimentary creatures were formed men and women. These rudimentary creatures or embryos, we are told, "were in reality stages in the transformation of various animals and plants into human beings, and thus they were naturally, when made into human beings, intimately associated with the particular animal or plant, as the case may be, of which they were the transformations—in other words, each individual of necessity belonged to a totem, the name of which was of course that of the animal or plant of which he or she was a transformation." However, it is not said that all the totemic clans of the Arunta were thus developed; no such tradition, for example, is told to explain the origin of the important Witchetty Grub clan. The clans which are positively known, or at least said, to have originated out of embryos in the way described are the Plum Tree, the Grass Seed, the Large Lizard, the Small Lizard, the Alexandra Parakeet, and the Small Rat clans. When the *Ungambikula* had thus fashioned people of these totems, they circumcised them all, except the Plum Tree men, by means of a fire-stick. After that, having

less human predecessors of the Dieri in the country. See A. W. Howitt, *Native Tribes of South-East Australia,* pp. 475 *sqq.*

done the work of creation or evolution, the *Ungambikula* turned themselves into little lizards which bear a name meaning "snappers-up of flies."[1]

This Arunta tradition of the origin of man, as Messrs. Spencer and Gillen, who have recorded it, justly observe, "is of considerable interest; it is in the first place evidently a crude attempt to describe the origin of human beings out of non-human creatures who were of various forms; some of them were representatives of animals, others of plants, but in all cases they are to be regarded as intermediate stages in the transition of an animal or plant ancestor into a human individual who bore its name as that of his or her totem."[2] In a sense these speculations of the Arunta on their own origin may be said to combine the theory of creation with the theory of evolution; for while they represent men as developed out of much simpler forms of life, they at the same time assume that this development was effected by the agency of two powerful beings, whom so far we may call creators. It is well known that at a far higher stage of culture a crude form of the evolutionary hypothesis was propounded by the Greek philosopher Empedocles. He imagined that shapeless lumps of earth and water, thrown up by the subterranean fires, developed into monstrous animals, bulls with the heads of men, men with the heads of bulls, and so forth; till at last, these hybrid forms being gradually eliminated, the various existing species of animals and men were evolved.[3] The theory of the civilised Greek of Sicily may be set beside the similar theory of the savage Arunta of Central Australia. Both represent gropings of the human mind in the dark abyss of the past; both were in a measure grotesque anticipations of the modern theory of evolution.

In this essay I have made no attempt to illustrate all the many various and divergent views which primitive man has taken of his own origin. I have confined myself to collecting examples of two radically different views, which may be distinguished as the theory of creation and the theory of evolution. According to the one, man was fashioned in his existing shape by a god or other powerful being; according to the other he was evolved by a natural process out of lower forms of animal life. Roughly speaking, these two theories still divide the civilised world between them. The partisans of each can appeal in support of their view to a large consensus of opinion; and if truth were to be decided by weighing the one consensus against the other, with *Genesis* in the one scale and *The Origin of Species* in the other, it might perhaps be found, when the scales were finally trimmed, that the balance hung very even between creation and evolution.

---

[1]Baldwin Spencer and F. J. Gillen, *Native Tribes of Central Australia* (London, 1899), pp. 388 *sq.*; compare *id.*, *Northern Tribes of Central Australia* (London, 1904), p. 150.

[2]Baldwin Spencer and F. J. Gillen, *Native Tribes of Central Australia*, pp. 391 *sq.*

[3]E. Zeller, *Die Philosophie der Griechen*, I.[4] (Leipsic, 1876), pp. 718 *sq.*; H. Ritter et L. Preller, *Historia Philosophiae Graecae et Romanae ex fontium locis contexta*[5], pp. 102 *sq.*; H. Diels, *Die Fragmente der Vorsokratiker*[2], I. (Berlin, 1906), pp. 190 *sqq.* Compare Lucretius, *De rerum natura*, V. 837 *sqq.*

ARNOLD VAN GENNEP ON THE
RITES OF PASSAGE

ARNOLD VAN GENNEP (1873-1957), Belgian anthropologist, is best remembered for his most famous and influential work, *Les Rites de Passage,* which was published in 1909, and had to wait for an English translation till 1960. The phrase "rite of passage" has become part of the English language, and a very illuminating phrase it is. This is chiefly due to the brilliant analysis by Van Gennep of the manner in which all societies treat the critical phases of life, birth, initiation, betrothal, marriage, death, and the ceremonies associated with these transitional stages from one grade into another.

We reprint here Van Gennep's final chapter of conclusions, but this hardly does justice to the book, which the reader is recommended to turn to, as well as the excellent introduction to the English translation by Professor Solon T. Kimball.[1]

CONCLUSIONS OF RITES OF PASSAGE*

Our brief examination of the ceremonies through which an individual passes on all the most important occasions of his life has now been completed. It is but a rough sketch of an immense picture, whose every detail merits careful study.

We have seen that an individual is placed in various sections of society, synchronically and in succession; in order to pass from one category to another and to join individuals in other sections, he must submit, from the day of his birth to that of his death, to ceremonies whose forms often vary but whose function is similar. Sometimes the individual stands alone and apart from all groups; sometimes, as a member of one particular group, he is separated from

---

[1]Arnold van Gennep, *The Rites of Passage,* (Chicago, University of Chicago Press, 1960).

*From Arnold van Gennep, *The Rites of Passage,* Introduction by Solon T. Kimball (Chicago, University of Chicago Press, 1960), pp. 189-194. Reprinted by permission of the University of Chicago Press.

the members of others. Two primary divisions are characteristic of all societies irrespective of time and place: the sexual separation between men and women, and the magico-religious separation between the profane and the sacred. However, some special groups—such as religious associations, totem clans, phratries, castes, and professional classes—appear in only a few societies. Within each society there is also the age group, the family, and the restricted politico-administrative and territorial unit (band, village, town). In addition to this complex world of the living, there is the world preceding life and the one which follows death.

These are the constants of social life, to which have been added particular and temporary events such as pregnancy, illnesses, dangers, journeys, etc. And always the same purpose has resulted in the same form of activity. For groups, as well as for individuals, life itself means to separate and to be reunited, to change form and condition, to die and to be reborn. It is to act and to cease, to wait and rest, and then to begin acting again, but in a different way. And there are always new thresholds to cross: the thresholds of summer and winter, of a season or a year, of a month or a night; the thresholds of birth, adolescence, maturity, and old age; the threshold of death and that of the after-life—for those who believe in it.

I am certainly not the first to have been struck by the resemblances among various components of the ceremonies discussed here. Similarities have been noted between entire rites, as well as among minor details. Thus, for example, Hartland[1] observed the resemblances between certain initiation rites and some rites of marriage; Frazer[2] perceived those between certain puberty rites and funerals; Ciszewski,[3] those among certain rites of baptism, friendship, adoption, and marriage. Diels[4] followed by Dieterich[5] and Hertz,[6] pointed out similarities among certain ceremonies of birth, marriage, and funerals, and Hertz added to the list rites for the opening of a new house (but did not present evidence) and rites of sacrifice. Goblet d'Alviella[7] pointed out the resemblance between baptism and initiation; Webster,[8] that between initiation into secret societies and the ordination of a shaman.

Hertz[9] was interested in the order of funeral rites and alluded to what he called the "transitory stage"—the period that lasts from marriage to the birth of the first child and that corresponds to the "transitory stage" of the dead

[1]Hartland, *The Legend of Perseus*, II, 335-99.

[2]Frazer, *The Golden Bough*, pp. 204-7, 209, 210 ff., 418, etc.

[3]Ciszewski, *Künstliche Verwandschaft bei den Südslaven*, pp. 1-4, 31, 36, 53, 54, 107-11, 114, etc.

[4]Hermann Diels, *Sibyllinische Blätter*, p. 48.

[5]Dieterich, *Mutter Erde*, pp. 56-57.

[6]Hertz, "La représentation collective de la mort," pp. 104, 117, 126-27.

[7]Goblet d'Alviella, "De quelques problèmes relatifs aux mystères d'Eleusis," p. 340.

[8]Webster, *Primitive Secret Societies*, p. 176.

[9]Hertz, "La représentation collective de la mort," p. 130, n. 5.

in Indonesia (especially in Borneo). But except for him, all these scholars, including Crawley,[10] saw only resemblances in particulars. For instance, the communal meal (Smith's "communion sacrifice"), union through blood, and a number of other ties of incorporation furnished the subject matter for several interesting chapters by Hartland. Certain rites of separation, like temporary seclusion and dietary and sexual taboos, Frazer and Crawley found recurring in a great many sets of ceremonies. Diels, Dieterich, and, in general, all those who have been concerned with classical religions have demonstrated the importance in these religions of the so-called rites of purification (anointing, lustration, etc.), It was inevitable that marked resemblances would appear when a specific rite, such as the exchange of blood, was isolated for analysis in a monograph and when contexts were superimposed.

A host of ethnographers and folklorists have demonstrated that among the majority of peoples, and in all sorts of ceremonies, identical rites are performed for identical purposes. In this way, and thanks first to Bastian, then to Tylor, and later to Andree, a great many unilateral theories were destroyed. Today their orientation is of interest because, in the long run, it will make possible the delineation of cultural sequences and the stages of civilization.

The purpose of this book is altogether different. Our interest lies not in the particular rites but in their essential significance and their relative positions within ceremonial wholes—that is, their order. For this reason, some rather lengthy descriptions have been included in order to demonstrate how rites of preliminary or permanent separation, transition, and incorporation are placed in relation to one another for a specific purpose. Their positions may vary, depending on whether the occasion is birth or death, initiation or marriage, but the differences lie only in matters of detail. The underlying arrangement is always the same. Beneath a multiplicity of forms, either consciously expressed or merely implied, a typical pattern always recurs: *the pattern of the rites of passage*.

The second fact to be pointed out—whose generality no one seems to have noticed previously—is the existence of transitional periods which sometimes acquire a certain autonomy. Examples of these are seen in the novitiate and the betrothal. It is this concept of transition that provides an orientation for understanding the intricacies and the order of rites preliminary to marriage.

Third, it seems important to me that the passage from one social position to another is identified with a *territorial passage*, such as the entrance into a village or a house, the movement from one room to another, or the crossing of streets and squares. This identification explains why the passage from one

[10]Crawley (*The Mystic Rose*) points out the precise similarities in the rites of marriage and funerals (p. 369) and rites of marriage and initiation (p. 326); on the last point, see also Reinach, *Cultes, mythes, et religions*, I, 309.

group to another is so often ritually expressed by passage under a portal,[1] or by an "opening of the doors." These phrases and events are seldom meant as "symbols"; for the semicivilized the passage is actually a territorial passage. In fact, the spatial separation of distinct groups is an aspect of social organization. The children live with the women up to a certain age; boys and girls live separated from married people, sometimes in a special house or section or in a special kraal; at marriage one of the two spouses, if not both, changes residence; warriors do not keep company with blacksmiths, and sometimes each professional class has its assigned place of residence.[2] In the Middle Ages the Jews were isolated in their ghettos, just as the Christians of the first centuries lived in remote sections. The territorial separation between clans may also be very definite,[3] and each Australian band camps in a specific place when on the march.[4] In short, a change of social categories involves a change of residence, and this fact is expressed by the rites of passage in their various forms.

As I have said several times, I do not maintain that all rites of birth, initiation, etc., are rites of passage only, or that all peoples have developed characteristic rites of passage for birth, initiation, and so forth. Funeral ceremonies in particular, since they depend on local beliefs concerning man's fate after death, may consist primarily of defensive procedures against the soul of the deceased and rules of prophylaxis against the contagion of death; in that case they present only a few aspects of the typical pattern. Nevertheless, it is always wise to be careful about such conclusions; the pattern may not appear in a summary description of the funeral ceremonies of a particular people, although it is clearly evident in a more detailed account. Similarly, among some peoples who do not consider the woman impure during her pregnancy and who allow anyone to be present at delivery, childbirth is only an ordinary act, painful but normal. But in that case the pattern will be transposed to the rites of childhood, or it may be included in the rites of betrothal and marriage.

The units of ceremonial life among certain peoples sometimes differ from those which are prevalent in our own and most other societies and those around which the chapters of this book have been organized. It has been pointed out, for example, that among the Todas there is a single set of ceremonies extending from the parents' adolescence to the birth of the first child and that it would be arbitrary to divide this set into ceremonies preliminary to puberty, pertaining to puberty, to marriage, to pregnancy, to delivery, to birth, and to childhood.

---

[1]Trumbull has even noted (*The Threshold Covenant*, pp. 252-57)—among the Chinese, the Greeks, the Hebrews, and others—an identification of the woman and the door.

[2][The reader will note that all these instances are not equally applicable to all societies.]

[3]See the separation of the clans in the Pueblo villages as described, among others, by Cosmos Mindeleff, *Localization of Tusayan Clans* (Nineteenth Annual Report of the Bureau of American Ethnology [1897-98], Part II [Washington, D.C.: Government Printing Office, 1900]), pp. 635-53.

[4]See, among others, Howitt, *The Native Tribes of South East Australia*, pp. 773-77 (on camping rules).

This amalgamation recurs among many other groups, but in the last analysis this effort at synthesis is not affected by it. Although the pattern of the rites of passage occurs in a different form in these instances, it is present nonetheless, and it is clearly elaborated.

Another general observation seems pertinent. The preceding analysis has shown variations in the internal division of societies, the relation of the diverse sections to one another, and the breadth of the barriers between them, which range from a simple imaginary line to a vast neutral region. Thus it would be possible to draw a diagram for each people in which the peaks of a zigzag line would represent recognized stages and the valleys the intervening periods. The apexes would sometimes be sharp peaks and sometimes flattened lines of varying length. For example, among certain peoples there are practically no betrothal rites except a meal shared at the moment of the preliminary agreement; the marriage ceremonies begin immediately afterward. Among others, on the contrary, there is a whole series of stages from the time of the betrothal (at an early age) until the newly married couple's return to ordinary life, and each of these stages possesses a certain degree of autonomy.

Whatever the intricacies of the pattern, the order from birth until death must often consists of successive stages best represented in rectilinear form. Among certain peoples like the Lushae, however, it is circular, so that all individuals go through the same endless series of rites of passage from life to death and from death to life. This extreme cyclical form of the pattern has acquired in Buddhism an ethical and philosophical significance, and for Nietszche, in his theory of the eternal return, a psychological significance.

Finally, the series of human transitions has, among some peoples, been linked to the celestial passages, the revolutions of the planets, and the phases of the moon. It is indeed a cosmic conception that relates the stages of human existence to those of plant and animal life and, by a sort of pre-scientific divination, joins them to the great rhythms of the universe.

FRANZ BOAS DEMONSTRATES THE PLASTICITY OF HUMAN TRAITS AND THE NON-FIXITY OF CERTAIN ASSUMED "RACIAL" TRAITS

FRANZ BOAS (1858-1942), American anthropologist, was for many years Professor of Anthropology at Columbia University. In his writings Boas covered the whole field of anthropology—cultural, physical, archaeological, linguistic, and statistical. He took his PhD in 1881 in physics at the University of Kiel, his dissertation being on the color of sea water. Boas came to the United States in 1884 and embarked upon a full-fledged career as an anthropologist. His contributions in all fields of anthropology have been of major importance. But if one were to single out the most significant of these it would undoubtedly be the *Report on Changes in Bodily Form of Descendants of Immigrants*, published in 1911.

The *Report* was epoch-making, for it was the first scientific study to show that, among other things, one of the most entrenched beliefs of the anthropologist, one upon which the whole system of racial classification had largely been built, namely, the shape of the head (the cephalic index), far from being fixed as was universally believed, was subject to the influences of a changed environment.

Boas' *Report* challenged so many orthodoxies, it immediately became the object of much misdirected criticism—for Boas had done his work with his usual caution and thoroughness, and his critics were all ultimately routed. For not only did Boas' work withstand their criticisms, but soon a number of independent studies began to appear which fully confirmed Boas' conclusions, and, indeed, since then those findings have been thoroughly substantiated by many studies conducted in many different parts of the world.

In that same year, 1911, Boas published another work of fundamental importance, *The Mind of Primitive Man* (New York, Macmillan). In this work Boas set out in popular form some of the findings in the *Report*, and also set before the reader the most reasonable and scientifically sound analysis of "the race problem" that had appeared up to that time. Its influence has been very considerable. The book was reprinted in 1922 and in a new edition in 1938. "The Race Problem in Modern Society" is reprinted from this latter edition in which it formed the final chapter.

CHANGES IN BODILY FORM OF DESCENDANTS OF IMMIGRANTS*
By Franz Boas

The Immigration Commission's anthropological investigation had for its object an inquiry into the assimilation of the immigrants with the American people as far as the form of the body is concerned.

On account of the magnitude of such an undertaking, it was deemed advisable to select certain important problems with a view to clearing up a few fundamental points, rather than to attack the whole problem with the prospect of not being able to give a definite answer to any of the questions involved.

An attempt was made to solve the following questions:

1. Is there a change in the type of development of the immigrant and his descendants, due to his transfer from his home surroundings to the congested parts of New York?

2. Is there a change in the type of the adult descendant of the immigrant born in this country as compared to the adult immigrant arriving on the shores of our continent?

The investigation was confined strictly to an inquiry into the physical development of members of certain races in the congested districts of New York City, only immigrants and their direct descendants being included in the study. The important problem of the selection which takes place during the period of immigration, and which is indicated by the change of type of immigrants after the panics of 1893 and 1907; the effect of rural environment and that of the climatic conditions of different parts of our country; the questions relating to the mixture of European races and of the mixture of immigrants with Americans of various types—these have not been studied.

The investigation has shown much more than was anticipated, and the results are briefly summarized in the following pages.

GENERAL RESULTS OF THE INVESTIGATION

In most of the European types that have been investigated the head form, which has always been considered one of the most stable and permanent

*From *Abstract of the Report on Changes in Bodily Form of Descendants of Immigrants* (The Immigration Commission, Washington, Government Printing Office, 1911).

characteristics of human races, undergoes far-reaching changes due to the transfer of the people from European to American soil. For instance, the east European Hebrew, who has a very round head, becomes more long-headed; the south Italian, who in Italy has an exceedingly long head, becomes more short-headed. . . .

The head form may conveniently be expressed by a number indicating the transversal diameter (or width of the head) in per cents of the diameter measured from forehead to the back of the head (or the length of the head). When the head is elongated (that is, narrow when seen from the front, and long when seen in profile), this number will be low; when it is rounded (that is, wide when seen from the front, and short when seen in profile), this number will be high. The width of the head expressed in per cents of the length of the head is about 78 per cent. among Sicilians born in Sicily and about 83 per cent. among Hebrews born in eastern Europe. Among Sicilians born in America this number rises to more than 80 per cent., while among east European Hebrews born in America it sinks to 81 per cent.

This fact is one of the most suggestive discovered in the investigation, because it shows that not even those characteristics of a race which have proved to be most permanent in their old home remain the same under the new surroundings; and we are compelled to conclude that when these features of the body change, the whole bodily and mental make-up of the immigrants may change.

These results are so definite that, while heretofore we had the right to assume that human types are stable, all the evidence is now in favor of a great plasticity of human types, and permanence of types in new surroundings appears rather as the exception than as the rule.

The disagreement of the changes in distinct types may be illustrated by Table I and figure I following, which show the head form of Sicilians and east European Hebrews of American birth in comparison with that of Sicilians and east European Hebrews of European birth.

The diagram (Table 1, p. 323) shows very clearly that the two races are quite distinct in Europe and that their descendants born in America differ from their parents in opposite directions.

In order to understand the causes which bring about these alterations of type, it is necessary to know how long a time must have elapsed since the immigration of the parents to bring about a noticeable change of type of the offspring. This investigation has been carried out mainly for the cephalic index, which during the period of growth of the individual undergoes only slight modifications. It appears in those cases that contain many individuals whose parents have been residents of America for a long time that the influence of American environment upon the descendants of immigrants increases with the time that the immigrants have lived in this country before the birth of their children.

TABLE I. CEPHALIC INDEX, OR WIDTH OF HEAD EXPRESSED IN PER CENT OF LENGTH OF HEAD, OF FOREIGN-BORN AND AMERICAN-BORN HEBREWS AND SICILIANS

MALES

Age (years)	5.	6.	7.	8.	9.	10.	11.	12.
Hebrews { Foreign-born	85.0	84.1	84.0	84.3	84.9	84.6	84.5	84.6
American-born	83.0	84.1	83.1	83.0	82.3	82.5	82.3	82.3
Sicilians { American-born	79.6	80.8	80.8	80.4	80.2	80.2	81.3	81.6
Foreign-born	80.8	79.6	79.9	78.6	78.9	80.2	79.8	78.3

Age (years)	13.	14.	15.	16.	17.	18.	19.	20 and over
Hebrews { Foreign-born	84.0	84.1	84.1	83.7	83.0	83.0	82.9	83.0
American-born	82.3	82.0	81.7	81.5	80.9	79.6	82.0	81.4
Sicilians { American-born	80.7	79.0	81.0	79.2	76.0	80.0	—	81.5
Foreign-born	79.4	78.9	78.6	76.9	76.5	77.2	78.2	77.7

FEMALES

Age (years)	4.	5.	6.	7.	8.	9.	10.	11.
Hebrews { Foreign-born	87.0	85.7	85.1	85.4	84.8	84.3	84.4	85.2
American-born	85.5	83.1	82.8	83.6	82.6	82.6	83.1	82.7
Sicilians { American-born	80.6	80.6	82.0	81.7	80.5	81.1	80.3	80.6
Foreign-born	77.0	79.6	80.2	80.0	78.9	79.6	79.8	79.2

Age (years)	12.	13.	14.	15.	16.	17.	18 and over
Hebrews { Foreign-born	84.4	85.1	83.6	83.8	83.6	84.1	83.6
American-born	82.3	81.7	81.7	82.7	82.5	80.0	82.3
Sicilians { American-born	80.3	81.1	80.6	80.0	84.2	78.7	80.3
Foreign-born	78.3	77.8	78.9	79.0	78.4	78.2	77.8

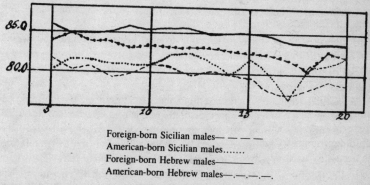

Foreign-born Sicilian males— — — —
American-born Sicilian males.......
Foreign-born Hebrew males————
American-born Hebrew males—.—.—.—.

Fig. I. Comparison of head form of American-born and foreign-born Hebrew and Sicilian males. Scale, 1 square = 0.5 unit.

The measurements of males of 5 years of age and older are indicated in this diagram. The head form, expressed by the ratio between width and length of head and its change with increasing age, is indicated by the four lines. The diagram shows that foreign-born Sicilian males have the lowest value for this ratio and the foreign-born Hebrews the highest, while the American-born Hebrews and the American-born Sicilians stand between these two extremes, and are more alike than foreign-born individuals of the same races.

We have proved this statement by comparing the features of individuals of a certain race born abroad, born in America within ten years after the arrival of the mother, and born ten years or more after the arrival of the mother. It appears that the longer the parents have been here, the greater is the divergence of the descendants from the European type. . . .

MEASUREMENTS OF DISTINCT TYPES

The features that have been studied are stature, weight, length of head, width of head, width of face, and color of hair. While it seems doubtful that changes in pigmentation occur, all the other features show notable differences. These are not in the same direction in all cases. Stature, weight, length of head, and width of head show increases in some cases, decreases in others; the width of the face decreases among all the types that have been studied, except the Scotch.

The types that have been subjected to examination are the Bohemians, Slovaks, and Hungarians, Poles, Hebrews, Sicilians, Neapolitans, and Scotch. These have been selected because they represent a number of the most distinct European types, and because they constitute a large percentage of our immigrants. The changes that have been observed may be summarized as follows:

The Bohemians, Slovaks, and Hungarians, and Poles, representing the type of central Europe, exhibit uniform changes. Among the American-born descendants of these types the stature increases and both length and width of head decrease, the latter a little more markedly than the former, so that there is also a decrease of the cephalic index. The width of the face decreases very materially.

The Hebrews show changes peculiar to themselves. Stature and weight increase; the length of the head shows a marked increase, and the width of the head decreases, so that the cephalic index decreases materially; the width of the face also decreases.

Sicilians and Neapolitans, representing the Mediterranean type of Europe, form another group which shows distinctive changes. These are less pronounced among the Neapolitans than among the Sicilians, who are also purer representatives of the Mediterranean type, notwithstanding the many mixtures of races that have occurred in Sicily and the adjoining parts of Italy. The stature of the Sicilians born in America is less than that of the foreign-born. This loss is not so marked among the Neapolitans. In both groups the length of the head decreases, the width of the head increases, and the width of the face decreases. . . .

RELATIONS BETWEEN TIME OF IMMIGRATION AND CHANGE OF TYPE

The differences in type between the American-born descendant of the immigrant and the European-born immigrant develop in early childhood and persist throughout life. This is indicated by the constant occurrence of the typical differences in the measurements of children of all ages. . . . The influence of American environment makes itself felt with increasing intensity, according to the time elapsed between the arrival of the mother and the birth of the child. In Table 8 [omitted here] and figure II we have compared the measurements of the foreign-born child, of the child born within ten years after the arrival of the mother, and of the child born ten years or more after the arrival of the mother, with the general average of children of that particular race. The table shows clearly the strong and increasing effect of American environment. . . .

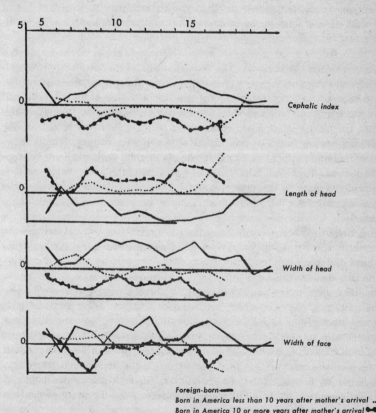

Foreign-born ●━━●
Born in America less than 10 years after mother's arrival ●●●●●
Born in America 10 or more years after mother's arrival ●━●━●

Fig. II. Comparison of head measurements of foreign-born and American-born Hebrew children.

A more detailed study of these phenomena illustrates still more clearly the increased modification of the descendants of immigrants born a long time after the arrival of their parents in America. Among the Hebrews the cephalic index of the foreign-born is practically the same, no matter how old the individual at the time of immigration. This might be expected when the immigrants are adult or nearly mature; but it is of interest to note that even children who come here one year or a few years old develop the cephalic index characteristic of foreign-born. This index ranges around 83. When we compare the value of this index with that of the index of the American-born, according to the time elapsed since their immigration, we find a sudden change. The value drops to about 82 for those born immediately after the immigration of their parents, and drops to 79 in the second generation, i.e., among the children of American-born children of immigrants. In other words, the effect of American environment makes itself felt immediately, and increases slowly with the increase of the time elapsed between the immigration of the parents, and the birth of the child.

The conditions among the Sicilians and Neapolitans are quite similar to those observed among the Hebrews. The cephalic index of the foreign-born remains throughout on almost the same level. Those born in America immediately after the arrival of their parents show an increase of the cephalic index. In this case the transition, although rapid, is not quite so sudden as among the Hebrews, probably because among the Italians born within a year before or soon after immigration, there is some doubt as to the place of birth. These uncertainties are due to the habit of the Italians to migrate back and forth between Italy and America before finally settling here, and to the indefiniteness of their answers in regard to the place of birth of the child, which sometimes had to be inferred from the age of the child and the year of immigration of the mother. As long as this uncertainty exists, which is hardly present at all in the data relating to the Hebrews, it does not seem necessary to assume any other cause for the more gradual change of the cephalic index about the time of immigration. . . .

Among the east European Hebrews the American environment, even in the congested parts of the city, has brought about a general more favorable development of the race, which is expressed in the increased height of body (stature) and weight of the children. The Italian children, on the other hand, show no such favorable influence of American environment, but rather a small loss in vigor as compared to the average condition of the immigrant children. It therefore appears that the south Italian race suffers under the influence of American city life, while the east European Hebrew develops under these conditions better than he does in his native country. It seems that the change in stature and weight increases with the time elapsed between the arrival of the mother and the birth of the child. This is indicated by the increased differences between children born more than ten years after the arrival of the mother, as compared to those born less than ten years after the arrival of the mother. . . .

PROBABLE CAUSES OF CHANGE IN TYPE

The explanation of these remarkable phenomena is not easy. Whatever their causes may be, the change in form cannot be doubted. It might, however, be claimed that the causes are no deep, physiological changes, but due to the changes of certain external factors. It is obvious that a change in the composition of the immigrants of a certain region that have arrived in America at different times might bring it about that the people who came here at different periods had distinct physical characteristics, and that those are now reflected in the descendants of the older generations when compared with those of the more recent immigrants. An investigation of this question has shown that the differences between the Bohemians, Hebrews, Sicilians, and Neapolitans, immigrating at different periods between 1860 and 1909, are so slight that they cannot account for the change of type of the descendants of immigrants. This result has been obtained first by a direct comparison of types immigrating at different periods. Furthermore, I have compared the cephalic index of all immigrants of a certain year and that of their descendants. I have tabulated in the same manner the width of face of Bohemians. It appears from these tabulations . . . that the differences which are exhibited by the whole series exist also between the immigrants who arrived here in a certain year and their descendants. The purely statistical explanation of the phenomenon may therefore be dismissed.

In order to overcome all possible objections based on the assumption of a different composition of the immigrant series and of the American-born series, I have also compared the measurements of parents and their own foreign-born and American-born children. The results of this tabulation are contained in Table 14. The figures contained in this table were obtained in the following manner: For each year the difference between father and his American-born son, father and his American-born daughter, mother and her American-born son, and mother and her American-born daughter, were determined; and these were compared with the series giving the same differences for the parents and their foreign-born children. After these differences had been obtained for each year and for the four possible combinations of sexes, the difference obtained for parents and their American-born children was compared with the difference between parents and their foreign-born children, the latter being subtracted from the former. Since the parents of both groups, foreign-born and American-born, are of the same type, when the American-born child has a larger measurement than the foreign-born child the difference of the values compared will be negative, and when the measurement of the American-born is less than that of the foreign-born the difference will be positive. The values in Table 14 were obtained by averaging the results for all ages and for all combinations of sexes. It will be seen that the results of the observations agree with·the results obtained by the generalized comparison of the foreign-born and American-born. . . . Among the Bohemians, for instance, we find the stature increased, all the other measurements decreased; among the Sicilians we find stature, length of head, and width of face decreased, while width of head and cephalic index increase. This shows clearly that an actual difference between the two groups must have developed.

TABLE 14. EXCESS DIFFERENCE BETWEEN PARENTS AND THEIR AMERICAN-BORN CHILDREN OVER DIFFERENCE BETWEEN PARENTS AND THEIR FOREIGN-BORN CHILDREN: BOHEMIANS, HEBREWS, SICILIANS, AND NEAPOLITANS

Measurements	Bohemians	Hebrews	Sicilians	Neapolitans
Stature (mm.)	−5.60	−13.10	+2.60	−11.90
Length of head (mm.)	+0.74	−1.65	+2.91	+1.56
Width of head (mm.)	+1.31	+1.52	−1.05	−0.48
Cephalic index	+0.69	+1.50	−1.78	−0.97
Width of face (mm.)	+1.04	+2.10	+1.33	+1.55

More difficult to investigate is the hypothesis that the mechanical treatment of infants may have a decided influence upon the form of the head, and that the changes in cradling and bedding which are made by immigrants almost immediately after their arrival in America account for the changes of head form. If this were true, the continued changes among the Hebrews might indicate merely that the American method of cradling is used the more frequently the longer the family has resided in this country. A number of investigators have claimed that the position of the child on the back tends to produce short-headedness, and that the position on the side tends to produce long-headedness. There is good evidence that a flattening of the occiput occurs when a very hard pillow is used and the child lies permanently on its back. This is the case, for instance, among many Indian tribes; and similar results might obtain if a swathed child were to lie permanently on its back. The prevalence of rachitis in New York would favor distortion due to pressure. While I cannot disprove the existence of such influences, I think weighty considerations are against their acceptance. If we assume that among the Hebrews the children born abroad have a lesser length of head than those born here, because they are swathed and lie more permanently on their backs than the American-born children who can move about freely, we must conclude that there is a certain compensatory decrease in the other diameters of the head of the American-born. Since this compensation is distributed in all directions, its amount in any one direction will be very small. The decrease in the width of head that has been observed is so large that it cannot be considered simply as an effect of compensation; but we have to make the additional hypothesis that the American-born children lie so much on their sides that a narrowing of the head is brought about by mechanical pressure. The same considerations hold good in all the other types. If, therefore, in one case the greater freedom of position of the child increases the length of its head, it is difficult to see why, among the Bohemians, the same causes should decrease both horizontal diameters of the head, and why, among the Sicilians, the length should decrease and the width increase. . . .

The development of the width of the face seems to my mind to show most clearly that it is not the mechanical treatment of the infant that brings about the changes in question. The cephalic index suffers a very slight decrease from the fourth year to adult life. It is therefore evident that children who arrive in America very young cannot be much affected by American environment in regard to their cephalic index. On the other hand, if we consider a measurement that increases appreciably during the period of growth, we may expect that in children born abroad but removed to America when young, the total growth may be modified by American environment. The best material for this study is presented by the Bohemians, among whom there are relatively many full-grown American-born individuals. The width of face of Bohemians, when arranged according to their age at the time of immigration, shows that there is a loss among those who came here as young children—the greater the younger they were. Continuing this comparison with the American-born, born one, two, etc., years after the arrival of their mothers, the width of face is seen to decrease still further. It appears therefore that the American environment causes a retardation of the growth of the width of face at a period when mechanical influences are no longer possible. . . .

I have not carried through the analogous investigation for stature, because in this case the increase might simply be ascribed to the better nutrition of most of the north and central European immigrants after their immigration into this country.

There is another hypothesis which might account for the observed changes of type. If it were assumed that among the descendants of immigrants born in America there are an appreciable number who are in reality children of American fathers, not of their reputed fathers, a general assimilation with the American type would occur. Socially this condition is not at all plausible, but on account of the importance of the phenomenon that we are discussing it should be considered. I do not think that any of the observations that have been made are in favor of this theory. The changes that occur in the Bohemians who arrive here as young children, the different directions of the changes in distinct types, particularly the shortening of the head of the Bohemians and of Italians, do not favor the assumption. Furthermore, if the modification were due to race mixture the similarity between fathers and American-born children should be less than the similarity between fathers and foreign-born children. There is no indication that this is the case, for the index of correlation which expresses the degree of similarity is about the same in either group. . . .

That the index of correlation is a sensitive index of similarity and, we may say, of purity of sexual relations, is shown by the correlation for color of hair between Hebrew mothers and daughters, which is exceptionally low (0.13

for 616 cases), because many mothers wear wigs, and perhaps some daughters dye their hair.

This hypothesis is also shown to be untenable by the comparisons of fathers and mothers with their own foreign-born and American-born children. These comparisons show that the differences are the same in the case of fathers and children and of mothers and children, so that obviously the same conditions must control the relations between fathers and their children and mothers and their children. In other words, the fathers must be considered as the true fathers of their children.

It seems to my mind that the changes that have been observed in the transition of Europeans to the environment of New York must be considered as analogous to those that the European rural population undergoes when it moves from the country to the city. Ammon, who was the first to observe these changes in Baden, ascribes them to the effects of natural selection, which weeds out among the south Germans that move to the city the more short-headed type, while the long-headed type survives. Livi, who made similar observations in Italy, believed that the changes are simply due to the wider range of territory from which urban populations are drawn. The more varied descent, from which the urban population is derived, brings it about that in a region inhabited by short-headed people the urban population will be more long-headed, while in a region inhabited by long-headed people it will be more short-headed, than the rural population.

I believe that this factor is of considerable importance in the development of differences between urban and rural population; but our American observations show that there is also a direct influence at work. Ammon's observations are in accord with those on our American city-born Sicilians and Neapolitans. Parallel observations made in rural districts and in various climates in America, and others made in Europe, may solve the problem whether the changes that we have observed here are only those due to the change from rural life to urban life. From this point of view the slight changes among the Scotch are also most easily intelligible, because among them there is no marked transition from one mode of life to another, most of those measured having been city dwellers and skilled tradesmen in Scotland, and continuing the same life and occupation here.

On the whole, it seems more likely that the phenomena observed in the cities of Europe and among the descendants of immigrants in America are analogous, but not the same; that both are expressions of the general plasticity of human types when living under different conditions. The variability of the Hebrew type in different parts of Europe, which has been so clearly demonstrated by Maurice Fishberg, is also in favor of this theory. Doctor Fishberg has shown that the Hebrew type in various parts of eastern Europe varies somewhat, and generally in accordance with the type of the surrounding population. He was inclined to interpret this phenomenon as due to intermixture, but it may well be an expression of the effect of environment upon the same type.

It may be possible that the wider range of intermarriages which occur in America may have an effect upon human types. The actual intermarriages in small villages in Europe are preponderantly of such character that the same strain will persist for a long period with very slight disturbance by intermixture from outside, the majority of intermarriages in small communities being generally in that community. When immigrants leave their home and settle in large cities this permanence of strain is entirely broken; and it seems at least possible that the changes which have been noticed in urban types, both in Europe and in America, may in part be due to this cause. Our present views of heredity would make it plausible that a disturbance of the established type would occur in such a case, even if the two intermarrying types are not markedly distinct. It has not been possible up to this time to investigate the material thoroughly from this point of view; but I believe the theory deserves to be followed up. Modifications in the distribution of sexes have been observed in an analogous case in the Argentine Republic, where it has been shown that in intermarriages between Spaniards and Italians the proportion of the sexes changes materially. The information contained in our material will permit us to investigate the question here suggested.

Earnest advocates of the theory of selection might claim that all these changes are due to the effects of changes in death rate among foreign-born and American-born; that either abroad or here individuals of certain types are more liable to die, and that thus these changes are gradually brought about. On the whole, it seems to my mind, the burden of proof would lie entirely on those who claim such a correlation between head index, width of face, etc., and death rate—a correlation which I think is highly improbable, and which could be proposed only to sustain the theory of selection, not on account of any available facts. I grant the desirability of settling the question by actual observations, but until these are available we may point out that the very suddenness of the changes after immigration, and the absence of changes due to selection by mortality among the adult foreign-born, would require such a complicated adjustment of cause and effect in regard to the correlation of mortality and bodily form that the theory would become untenable on account of its complexity.

It would be saying too much to claim that all the distinct European types become the same in America, without mixture, solely by the action of the new environment. First of all, we have investigated only the effect of one environment, and we have every reason to believe that a number of distinct types are developing in America. But we will set aside this point and discuss only our New York observations. Although the long-headed Sicilian becomes more round-headed in New York and the round-headed Bohemian and Hebrew more long-headed, the approach to a uniform general type cannot be established, because we do not know yet how long the changes continue and whether they would all lead to the same result. I confess I do not consider such a result likely, because the proof of the plasticity of types does not imply that the plasticity is unlimited. The history of the British types in America, of the Dutch in the East Indies, and of the Spaniards in South America favors the assumption of a strictly limited plasticity. Certainly our discussion should be based on this more conservative basis until an unexpectedly wide range of variability of types can be proved. It is one of the most important problems that arise out of our investigation to determine how far the instability or plasticity of types may extend.

Whatever the extent of these bodily changes may be, if we grant the correctness of our inferences in regard to the plasticity of human types, we are necessarily led to grant also a great plasticity of the mental make-up of human types. We have observed that features of the body which have almost obtained their final form at the time of birth show modifications of great importance in our new surroundings. We have seen that others which increase during the whole period of growth, and are therefore subject to the continued effect of the new environment, are modified even among individuals who arrive here during their childhood. From these facts we must conclude that the fundamental traits of the mind, which are closely correlated with the physical condition of the body and whose development continues over many years after physical growth has ceased, are the more subject to far-reaching changes. It is true that this is a conclusion by inference; but if we have succeeded in proving changes in the form of the body, the burden of proof will rest on those who, notwithstanding those changes, continue to claim the absolute permanence of other forms and functions of the body.

THE RACE PROBLEM IN MODERN SOCIETY*

Until the first decade of our century the opinion that race determines culture had been, in Europe at least, rather a subject of speculation of amateur historians and sociologists than a foundation of public policy. Since that time it has spread among the masses. Slogans like "blood is thicker than water," are expressions of its new emotional appeal. The earlier concept of nationality has been given a new meaning by identifying nationality with racial unity and by assuming that national characteristics are due to racial descent. It is particularly interesting to note that in the anti-Semitic movement in Germany of

*Reprinted from Franz Boas, *The Mind of Primitive Man*, revised edition (New York, Macmillan, 1938), pp. 253-272.

the time of 1880 it was not the Jew as a member of an alien race who was subject to attack, but the Jew who was not assimilated to German national life. The present policy of Germany is based on an entirely different foundation, for every person is supposed to have a definite, unalterable character according to his racial descent and this determines his political and social status. The conditions are quite analogous to the status assigned to the Negro at an earlier period, when licentiousness, shiftless laziness, lack of initiative were considered as racially determined, unescapable qualities of every Negro. It is a curious spectacle to see that serious scientists, wherever free to express themselves, have on the whole been drifting away from the opinion that race determines mental status, excepting however those biologists who have no appreciation of social factors because they are captivated by the apparent hereditary determinism of morphological forms, while among the uninformed public to which unfortunately a number of powerful European politicians belong, race prejudice has been making and is still making unchecked progress. I believe it would be an error to assume that we are free of this tendency: if nothing else the restrictions imposed upon members of certain "races," abridging their right to own real estate, to tenancy in apartment houses, membership of clubs, to their right to visit hotels and summer resorts, to admission to schools and colleges shows at least that there is no abatement of old prejudices directed against Negroes, Jews, Russians, Armenians or whatever they may be. The excuse that these exclusions are compelled by economic considerations, or by the fear of driving away from schools or colleges other social groups is merely an acknowledgment of a widespread attitude.

I may perhaps restate in briefest form the errors which underlie the theory that racial descent determines mental and social behavior. The term race, as applied to human types, is vague. It can have a biological significance only when a race represents a uniform, closely inbred group, in which all family lines are alike—as in pure breeds of domesticated animals. These conditions are never realized in human types and impossible in large populations. Investigations of morphological traits show that the extreme genetic lines represented in a so-called pure population are so different, that if found in different localities they would be counted as separate races, while the middle forms are common to races inhabiting adjoining territories, excepting the occurrence of small groups that may have been inbred for centuries. If the defenders of race theories prove that a certain kind of behavior is hereditary and wish to explain in this way that it belongs to a racial type they would have to prove that the particular kind of behavior is characterictic of all the genetic lines composing the race, that considerable variations in the behavior of different genetic lines composing the race do not occur. This proof has never been given and all the known facts contradict the possibility of uniform behavior of all the individuals and genetic lines composing the race.

Added to this is the failure to see that the many different constitutional types composing a race cannot be considered as absolutely permanent, but that the physiological and psychological reactions of the body are in a constant state of flux according to the outer and inner circumstances in which the organism finds itself.

Furthermore the varying reactions of the organism do not *create* a culture but *react* to a culture. On account of the difficulties involved in defining personality and separating the endogene and exogene elements that make up a personality it is difficult to measure the range of variation of biologically determined personalities within a race. The endogene elements can only be those determined by the structure and chemism of the body and these show a wide range of variation within each race. The claim that a race is in any way identical with a personality cannot be given.

It is not difficult to show that a very general primitive attitude of mind is involved in the identification of the characteristics of an individual with the supposed typical characteristics of the group to which he belongs. It has always found expression in the prohibition of marriage between the members of different groups and the substitution of an imputed biological difference in place of a sociological one. Examples are particularly the laws forbidding marriages between members of different religious denominations.

The diversity of local types found in Europe is a result of the intermingling of the various earlier types that lived on the continent. Since we do not know the laws of intermixture it is impossible to reconstruct the early constituent purer types, if such ever existed. . . . We may not assume on the basis of a low variability that a type is pure, for we know that some mixed types are remarkably uniform. This has been shown for American Mulattoes, Dakota Indians, and made probable for the city population of Italy.[1] It is also not certain in how far exogene elements may be partly determinants of local types or how social selection may have acted upon a heterogeneous population. In short we have no way of identifying a pure type. It must be remembered that although by inbreeding in a small local group the family lines may become alike, this is no proof of purity of type, because the ancestral forms themselves may be mixed.

Setting aside these theoretical considerations we may ask what kind of evidence is available for the claim that there is any pure race in Europe or, for that matter, in any part of the world. European national types are certainly not pure stocks. It is only necessary to look at a map illustrating the racial types of any European country—like Italy, for instance—to see that local divergence is the characteristic feature, uniformity of type the exception. Thus Dr. Ridolfo Livi, in his fundamental investigations on the anthropology of Italy, has shown that the types of the extreme north and those of the extreme south are quite distinct—the former tall, short-headed, with a considerable sprinkling of blond and blue-eyed individuals; the latter short, long-headed and remarkably dark. The transition from one type to the other is, on the whole, quite gradual; but, like isolated islands, distinct types occur here and there. The region of Lucca in Tuscany, and the district of Naples, are examples of this kind, which may be explained as due to the survival of an older stock, to the intrusion of new types, or to a peculiar influence of environment.

Historical evidence is quite in accord with the results derived from the investigation of the distribution of modern types. In the earliest times we find on the peninsula of Italy groups of heterogeneous people, the linguistic relationships of many of which have remained obscure up to the present time. From the earliest prehistoric times on, we see wave after wave of people invading Italy from the north. Very early Greeks settled in the greater part of southern Italy, and Phoenician influence was well established on the west coast of the peninsula. A lively intercourse existed between Italy and northern Africa. Slaves of Berber blood were imported, and have left their traces. Slave trade continued to bring new blood into the country until quite recent times, and Livi believes that he can trace the type of Crimean slaves who were introduced late in the Middle Ages in the region of Venice. In the course of the centuries, the migrations of Celtic and Teutonic tribes, the conquests of the Normans, the contact with Africa, have added their share to the mixture of people on the Italian peninsula.

The fates of other parts of Europe were no less diversified. The Pyrenaean Peninsula, which during the last few centuries has been one of the most isolated parts of Europe, has had a most checkered history. The earliest inhabitants of whom we know were presumably related to the Basques of the Pyrenees. These were subjected to Oriental influences in the pre-Mycenaean period, to Punic conquest, to Celtic invasions, Roman colonization, Teutonic invasions, the Moorish conquest, and later on to the peculiar selective process that accompanied the driving-out of the Moors and the Jews.

England was not exempt from the vicissitudes of this kind. It seems plausible that at a very early period the type which is now found principally in Wales and in some parts of Ireland occupied the greater portion of the islands. It was swamped by successive waves of Celtic, Roman, Anglo-Saxon and Scandinavian migration. Thus we find change everywhere.

The history of the migrations of the Goths, the invasions of the Huns, who in the short interval of one century moved their habitations from the borders of China into the very center of Europe, are proofs of the enormous changes in population that have taken place in early times.

Slow colonization has also brought about fundamental changes in blood as well as in diffusion of languages and cultures. Perhaps the most striking recent example of this change is presented by the gradual Germanization of the region east of the Elbe River, where after the Teutonic migrations, people speaking Slavic languages had settled. The gradual absorption of Celtic communities and of the Basque, in ancient times the great Roman colonization, and later the Arab conquest of North Africa, are examples of similar processes.

Intermixture in early times was not by any means confined to peoples which, although diverse in language and culture, were of fairly uniform type. On the contrary, the most diverse types of southern, northern, eastern and western Europe, not to mention the elements which poured into Europe from Asia and Africa, have been participants in this long-continued intermixture. The Jews also have been proved by physical examination as well as by blood tests to be of highly mixed origin (Brutzkus).

In Europe the belief in hereditary mental qualities of human types finds expression principally in the mutual evaluation of the cultural achievement of nations. In present-day Germany the hatred of the Government against the Jew is a relapse into cruder forms of these beliefs.

Since we have not been able to establish organically determined differences in the mental faculties of different races, such as could claim any importance as compared with the differences found in the genetic lines composing each race; since furthermore, we have seen that the alleged specific differences between the cultures of different peoples must be reduced to mental qualities common to all mankind, we may conclude that there is no need of entering into a discussion of alleged hereditary differences in mental characteristics of various branches of the White race. Much has been said and written on the hereditary character of the Italian, German, Frenchman, Irish, Jew and Gypsy, but it seems to me that not the slightest successful attempt has been made to establish causes for the behavior of a people other than historical and social conditions; and I consider it unlikely that this can ever be done. An unbiased review of the facts shows that the belief in hereditary racial characteristics and the jealous care for purity of race is based on the assumption of nonexisting conditions. Since a remote period there have been no pure races in Europe and it has never been proved that continued intermixture has brought about deterioration. It would be just as easy to claim and to prove by equally valid—or rather invalid—evidence that peoples which have had no admixture of foreign blood lacked the stimulus for cultural progress and became decadent. The history of Spain, or, outside of Europe, that of the remote villages of Kentucky and Tennessee might be given as striking examples.

The actual effects of racial mixture cannot be answered by general historical considerations. The adherents of the belief—for it is nothing else—that long-headed groups lose their bodily and mental preeminence by mixture with round heads, will never be satisfied with a proof of the improbability and impossibility of proving their cherished beliefs, for the opposite view also cannot be proved by rigid methods. The real course of race mixture in Europe will never be known accurately. We do not know anything in regard to the relative number and composition of mixed and "pure" lines; nothing in regard to the history of the mixed families. Evidently the question cannot be solved on the basis of historical data but requires the study of strictly controlled material showing the movements of population. With all this nothing in the known historical facts suggests that preservation of racial purity assures a high cultural development; else we should expect to find the highest state of culture in every small, secluded village community.

In modern times extended mixtures between different nationalities, involving migration of large masses from one country to another are rare in Europe. They occur when the rapid rise of industry in a particular locality attracts labor. This was the origin of a large Polish community in the industrial district of Westphalia. The present political terrorism directed against political opponents in Russia, Italy, Germany and other countries, and the throttling of the Jews in Germany have also led to migrations, but these are minor phenomena when compared with the oversea migration from Europe to America, South Africa and Australia. The development of the American nation through the amalgamation of diverse European nationalities, the presence of the Negro, Indian, Japanese and Chinese, and the whole ever-increasing heterogeneity of the component elements of our people, involve a number of problems to the solution of which our inquiries contribute important data.

Our previous considerations make clear the hypothetical character of many of the generally accepted assumptions, and indicate that not all of the questions involved can be answered at the present time with scientific accuracy. It is disappointing that we have to take this critical attitude, because the political question of dealing with all these groups of people is of great and immediate importance. However, it should be solved on the basis of scientific knowledge, not according to emotional clamor. Under present conditions, we seem to be called upon to formulate definite answers to questions that require the most painstaking and unbiased investigation; and the more urgent the demand for final conclusions, the more needed is a critical examination of the phenomena and of the available methods of solution.

Let us first recall to our minds the facts relating to the origins of our nation. When British immigrants first flocked to the Atlantic coast of North America, they found a continent inhabited by Indians. The population of the country was thin, and vanished rapidly before the influx of the more numerous Europeans. The settlement of the Dutch on the Hudson, of the Germans in Pennsylvania, not to speak of other nationalities, is familiar to all of us. We know that the foundations of our modern state were laid by Spaniards in the Southwest, by French in the Mississippi Basin and in the region of the Great Lakes, but that the British immigration far outnumbered that of other nationalities. In the composition of our people, the indigenous element has never played an important role, except for short periods. In regions where the settlement progressed for a long time entirely by the immigration of unmarried males of the White race, families of mixed blood have been of some importance during the period of gradual development, but they have never become sufficiently numerous in any populous part of the United States to be considered an important element in our population. Without any doubt, Indian blood flows in the veins of quite a number of our people, but the proportion is so insignificant that it may well be disregarded.

Much more important has been the introduction of the Negro, whose numbers have increased many fold, so that they form now about one-tenth of our whole nation.

More recent is the problem of the immigration of people representing all the nationalities of Europe, western Asia and northern Africa. While until late in the second half of the nineteenth century the immigrants consisted almost entirely of people of northwestern Europe, natives of Great Britain, Scandinavia, Germany, Switzerland, Holland, Belgium and France, the composition of the immigrant masses has changed completely since that time. Italians, the various Slavic peoples of Austria, Russia and the Balkan Peninsula, Hungarians, Roumanians, East European Hebrews, not to mention the numerous other nationalities, have arrived in ever-increasing numbers. For a certain length of time the immigration of Asiatic nations seemed likely to become of importance in the development of our country. There is no doubt that these people of eastern and southern Europe represent physical types distinct from the physical type of northwestern Europe; and it is clear, even to the most casual observer, that their present social standards differ fundamentally from our own.

It is often claimed that the phenomenon of mixture presented in the United States is unique; that a similar intermixture has never occurred before in the world's history; and that our nation is destined to become what some writers choose to term a "mongrel" nation in a sense that has never been equaled anywhere.

The period of immigration may now be considered closed, for the present economic and political conditions have brought it about that, as compared to the total population, immigration is insignificant.

The history of European migrations as outlined before shows that the modern transatlantic migration merely repeats in modern form the events of antiquity. The earlier migrations occurred at a period when the density of population was, comparatively speaking, small. The number of individuals concerned in the formation of the modern types of Great Britain were comparatively few as compared with the millions who have come together to form a new nation in the United States; and it is obvious that the process of amalgamation which takes place in communities that must be counted by millions differs in character from the process of amalgamation that takes place in communities that may be counted by thousands. Setting aside social barriers, which in early times as well as now undoubtedly tended to keep intermingling peoples separate, it would seem that in the more populous communities of modern times a greater permanence of the single combining elements might occur, owing to their larger numbers, which make the opportunities for segregation more favorable.

Among the early, smaller communities the process of amalgamation must have been an exceedingly rapid one. After the social distinctions had once been obliterated, pure descendants of one of the component types must have decreased greatly in number, and the fourth generation of a people consisting originally of distinct elements must have been almost homogeneous.

We may dismiss the assumption of a process of mongrelization in America different from anything that has taken place for thousands of years in Europe. Neither are we right in assuming that the phenomenon is one of a more rapid intermixture than the one prevailing in olden times. The difference is based essentially in the masses of individuals concerned in the process.

If we confine our consideration for the present to the intermixture of European types in America, it will be clear, from what has been said before, that the concern that is felt by many in regard to the continuance of racial purity of our nation is to a great extent imaginary.

Two questions stand out prominently in the study of the physical characteristics of the immigrant population. The first is the question of the selection of immigrants and the influence of environment upon them. The second is the question of the effect of intermixture.

We have been able to throw some light upon both of these.

We found that both in regard to bodily form and mental behavior the immigrants are subject to the influence of their new environment. While the causes of bodily changes and their direction are still obscure, it has been shown that the mental and social behavior of the descendants of immigrants shows in all those features that have been investigated an assimilation to American standards.

A number of data have also been obtained for a better understanding of race-mixture. Let us recall that one of the most powerful agents modifying human types is the breaking-up of the continuance of strains in small communities by a process of rapid migration, which occurs both in Europe and in America, but with much greater rapidity in our country, because the heterogeneity of descent of the people is much greater than in modern Europe.

What effect these processes may have upon the ultimate type and variability of the American people cannot be determined at the present time; but no evidence is available that would allow us to expect a lower status of the developing new types of America. Much remains to be done in the study of this subject; and considering our lack of knowledge of the most elementary facts that determine the outcome of this process, I feel that it behooves us to be most cautious in our reasoning, and particularly to refrain from all sensational formulations of the problem that are liable to add to the prevalent lack of calmness in its consideration; the more so, since the answer to these questions concerns the welfare of millions of people.

The problem is one in regard to which speculation is as easy as accurate studies are difficult. Basing our arguments on ill-fitting analogies with the animal and plant world, we may speculate on the effects of intermixture upon the development of new types—as though the mixture that is taking place in America were in any sense, except a sociological one, different from the mixtures that have taken place in Europe for thousands of years; looking for a general degradation, for reversion to remote ancestral types, or towards the evolution of a new ideal type—as fancy or personal inclination may impel us. We may enlarge on the danger of the impending submergence of the northwest European type, or glory in the prospect of its dominance over all others. Would it not be a safer course to investigate the truth or fallacy of each theory rather than excite the public mind by indulgence in the fancies of our speculations? That these are an important help in the attainment of truth, I do not deny; but they must not be promulgated before they have been subjected to a searching analysis, lest the credulous public mistake fancy for truth.

If I am not in a position to predict what the effect of mixture of distinct types may be, I feel confident that this important problem may be solved if it is taken up with sufficient energy and on a sufficiently large scale. An investigation of the anthropological data of people of distinct types—taking into consideration the similarities and dissimilarities of parents and children, the rapidity and final result of the physical and mental development of children, their vitality, the fertility of marriages of different types and in different social strata—such an investigation is bound to give us information which will allow us to answer these important questions definitely and conclusively.

The final result of race-mixture will necessarily depend upon the fertility of the present native population and of the newer immigrants. It is natural that in large cities, where nationalities separate in various quarters, a great amount of cohesion should continue for some time; but it seems likely that intermarriages between descendants of foreign nationalities will increase rapidly in later generations. Our experience with Americans born in New York whose grandparents immigrated into this country is, on the whole, that most social traces of their descent have disappeared, and that many do not even know to what nationalities their grandparents belonged. It might be expected—particularly in Western communities where frequent changes of location are common—that this would result in a rapid mixture of the descendants of various nationalities. This inquiry, which it is quite feasible to carry out in detail, seems indispensable for a clear understanding of the situation.

During the last decade studies of the population problem have made rapid strides. We refer merely to the careful analysis of population problems by Frank Lorimer and Frederick Osborn. As a result of the accumulating work it may be said that as long as the problems involved are conceived as racial problems in the usually accepted meaning of the term little progress will be made. The biological well-being of a nation is rather dependent upon the distribution of hereditary constitutional types in social classes. These are not indissolubly connected with racial types. No such relation has ever been discovered that is not adequately accounted for by historical or sociological conditions, and all the traits of personality that have ever been investigated point invariably to a high degree of pliability of the representatives of a racial group, to a greater uniformity in a mixed group subjected to similar social stresses.

At present the European nations and their descendants on other continents are deeply impressed by the fear of a threatening degeneration. Certainly, it is important to combat strictly hereditary pathological tendencies and to improve the health of the people by eugenic means as far as this is possible; but the complex conditions of modern life should receive proper consideration. Statistics show an increase of the socially weak, who become the wards of almshouses, institutions for the care of the insane, the imbecile, those afflicted by chronic diseases; and who fill our prisons and penitentiaries. We live in a period of a rapid increase in the differentiation of our population, that is of increasing variability. This would bring about an increase of the number of the weakest as well as of the strongest, without necessarily implying a lowering of the average. In many respects this seems to correspond to the actual conditions. The weak can be counted, because they are cared for by the State. The strong cannot be counted. Their presence is expressed in the greater intensity of our lives.

The aim of eugenics, namely, the improvement of constitutional health, is highly commendable, but we are still far from seeing how it can be attained. Certainly not by the panacea of many eugenists, sterilization. The decrease in the frequency of hereditary diseases by the elimination of those actually affected is so slow that an effect will not be felt for many generations; and more important than this: we do not know how often the same conditions may arise as hereditary mutations and whether the unfavorable conditions under which large classes live do not result in such mutations. The theory that recessive hereditary diseases have sprung up once only is untenable on account of its implications. It would lead us to the conclusion that we are the offspring of a number of diseased populations almost without a healthy ancestor. It is the most important and at the same time the most difficult task of our studies to find the conditions under which hereditary pathological conditions arise.

The Negro problem as it presents itself in the United States is from a biological viewpoint not essentially different from those just discussed. We have found that no proof of an inferiority of the Negro type could be given, except that it seemed barely possible that perhaps the race would not produce quite so many men of highest genius as other races, while there was nothing at all that could be interpreted as suggesting any material difference in the mental capacity of the bulk of the Negro population as compared with the bulk of the White population. There will undoubtedly be endless numbers of men and women who will be able to outrun their White competitors, and who will do better than the defectives whom we permit to drag down and retard the healthy children of our public schools.

Ethnological observation does not countenance the view that the traits observed among our poorest Negro population are in any sense racially determined. A survey of African tribes exhibits to our view cultural achievements of no mean order. To those unfamiliar with the products of native African art and industry, a walk through one of the large museums of Europe would be a revelation. Few of our American museums have made collections that exhibit this subject in any way worthily. The blacksmith, the wood carver, the weaver, the potter—these all produce ware original in form, executed with great care, and exhibiting that love of labor, and interest in the results of work, which are apparently so often lacking among the Negroes in our American surroundings. No less instructive are the records of travelers, reporting the thrift of the native villages, of the extended trade of the country, and of its markets. The power of organization as illustrated in the government of native states is of no mean order, and when wielded by men of great personality has led to the foundation of extended empires. All the different kinds of activities that we consider valuable in the citizens of our country may be found in aboriginal Africa. Neither is the wisdom of the philosopher absent. A perusal of any of the collections of African proverbs that have been published will demonstrate the homely practical philosophy of the Negro, which is often proof of sound feeling and judgment.

It would be out of place to enlarge on this subject, because the essential point that anthropology can contribute to the practical discussion of the adaptability of the Negro is a decision of the question how far the undesirable traits that are at present undoubtedly found in our Negro population are due to racial traits, and how far they are due to social surroundings for which we are responsible. To this question anthropology can give the decided answer that the traits of African culture as observed in the aboriginal home of the Negro are those of a healthy primitive people, with a considerable degree of personal initiative, with a talent for organization, with imaginative power, with technical skill and thrift. Neither is a warlike spirit absent in the race, as is proved by the mighty conquerors who overthrew states and founded new empires, and by the courage of the armies that follow the bidding of their leaders.

It may be well to state here once more with some emphasis that it would be erroneous to claim as proved that there are no differences in the mental make-up of the Negro race taken as a whole and of any other race taken as a whole, and that their activities should run in exactly the same lines. This would be a result of the varying frequency of personalities of various types. It may be that the bodily build of the Negro race taken as a whole tends to give a direction to its activities somewhat different from those of other races. An answer to this question cannot be given. There is, however, no evidence whatever that would stigmatize the Negro as of weaker build, or as subject to inclinations and powers that are opposed to our social organization. An unbiased estimate of the anthropological evidence so far brought forward does not permit us to countenance the belief in a racial inferiority which would unfit an individual of the Negro race to take his part in modern civilization. We do not know of any demand made on the human body or mind in modern life that anatomical or ethnological evidence would prove to be beyond his powers.

The traits of the American Negro are adequately explained on the basis of his history and social status. The tearing-away from the African soil and the consequent complete loss of the old standards of life, which were replaced by the dependency of slavery and by all it entailed, followed by a period of disorganization and by a severe economic struggle against heavy odds, are sufficient to explain the inferiority of the status of the race, without falling back upon the theory of hereditary inferiority.

In short, there is every reason to believe that the Negro when given facility and opportunity, will be perfectly able to fulfill the duties of citizenship as well as his White neighbor.

The anthropological discussion of the Negro problem requires also a word on the "race instinct" of the Whites, which plays a most important part in the practical aspect of the problem. Ultimately this phenomenon is a repetition of the old instinct and fear of the connubium of patricians and plebeians, of the European nobility and the common people or of the castes of India. The emotions and reasonings concerned are the same in every respect. In our case they relate particularly to the necessity of maintaining a distinct social status in order to avoid race-mixture. As in the other cases mentioned, the so-called instinct is not a physiological dislike. This is proved by the existence of our large Mulatto population, as well as by the more ready amalgamation of the Negro with Latin peoples. It is rather an expression of social conditions that are so deeply ingrained in us that they assume a strong emotional value; and this, I presume is meant when we call such feelings instinctive. The feeling certainly has nothing to do with the question of the vitality and ability of the Mulatto.

Still the questions of race mixture and of the Negro's adaptability of our environment represent a number of important problems.

I think we have reason to be ashamed to confess that the scientific study of these questions has never received the support either of our government or of any of our great scientific institutions; and it is hard to understand why we are so indifferent toward a question which is of paramount importance to the welfare of our nation. The investigations by Melville J. Herskovits on the American Negro are a valuable beginning; but we should know much more. Notwithstanding the oft-repeated assertions regarding the hereditary inferiority of the Mulatto, we know hardly anything on this subject. If his vitality is lower than that of the full-blooded Negro, this may be as much due to social as to hereditary causes. Herskovits has pointed out that contrary to conditions during the time of slavery the tendency among Mulattoes is for a lighter man to marry a darker woman and that in consequence of this the colored population tends to become darker—an undesirable condition, if we believe that a decrease of strong contrasts in racial types is desirable because it helps to weaken class-consciousness.

Our tendency to evaluate an individual according to the picture that we form of the class to which we assign him, although he may not feel any inner connection with that class, is a survival of primitive forms of thought. The characteristics of the members of the class are highly variable and the type that we construct from the most frequent characteristics supposed to belong to the class is never more than an abstraction hardly ever realized in a single individual, often not even a result of observation, but an often heard tradition that determines our judgment.

Freedom of judgment can be attained only when we learn to estimate an individual according to his own ability and character. Then we shall find, if we were to select the best of mankind, that all races and all nationalities would be represented. Then we shall treasure and cultivate the variety of forms that human thought and activity has taken, and abhor, as leading to complete stagnation, all attempts to impress one pattern of thought upon whole nations or even upon the whole world.

ALFRED KROEBER ON THE SUPERORGANIC

ALFRED LOUIS KROEBER (1876-1960), American anthropologist, and for many years Professor of Anthropology at the University of California at Berkeley, wrote and edited many classics, such as, the *Handbook of the Indians of California* (Washington, Government Printing Office, 1925) and *Anthropology* (New York, Harcourt Brace, 1923 and 1948) and numerous other works, among which one of the outstanding is his essay "The Superorganic," published in the *American Anthropologist* in 1917. This was reprinted with some stylistic revisions in 1927 by the Sociological Press of Hanover, N. H., and it is from that version of the essay that the present reprinting has been made. The revisions are so minor that it would be quite confusing to attribute the essay to the later date, when it in fact belongs to 1917, and as such its original source is given in the bibliographic note.

What Kroeber achieved in this classic essay was to show that what was essentially human about man was not an organic development so much as a superorganic one, namely, the social way of life which was transmitted not through organic particles but through learned ways of interaction, in other words, through culture or the sociocultural continuum. This is a view which is today accepted by all anthropologists, but in 1917 it had to be formulated clearly at a time when clarification in this matter was sorely needed. Kroeber, who had been a student of Boas', simply carried forward what Boas had attempted to do in his book, *The Mind of Primitive Man*, published some six years earlier in 1911 (see pp. 320-44). The important point made by Kroeber, that everything social can have existence only in the form of ideas and can be transmitted only through the mind, is fundamental.

With great respect for Francis Galton's and Karl Pearson's investigations, Kroeber nevertheless criticized them for failing to understand that while it is true that genetic factors operate in the domain of mind as well as that of the body, it does not necessarily follow that heredity is the mainspring of culture or civilization. It is quite astonishing to find how many intelligent men have fallen into this egregious error.[1] Kroeber's discussion of this error is one of the best things ever written on the subject, and has constituted one of the greatest influences in the history of the evolution of every anthropologist, whether he is aware of it or not. And so, too, one cannot help believing it contributed to the general clarification of thinking in this area.

THE SUPERORGANIC*
1917

Originally published in the "American Anthropologist," *this essay was reprinted with stylistic revisions ten years later by the Sociological Press of Hanover, New Hampshire. For many years now, the article has excited little stir among anthropologists, presumably because its contentions have largely passed into their common body of assumptions. It has however continued to*

[1]See Nicholas Pastore, *The Nature-Nurture Controversy* (New York, King's Crown Press, 1949).

*First published in the *American Anthropologist* (Vol. 19, 1917), pp. 163-213.

attract some interest among sociologists, historians, and social scientists generally, for which reason it is included here without abbreviation.

In the vista of a third of a century, the essay appears like an antireductionist proclamation of independence from the dominance of the biological explanation of sociocultural phenomena. Yet, as I look back, I cannot recall, in the two decades preceding 1917, any instances of oppression or threatened annexation by biologists. What was hanging over the study of culture, as I sense it now, was rather a diffused public opinion, a body of unaware assumptions, that left precarious the autonomous recognition of society, and still more that of culture. It was the intelligent man on the street and those who wrote for him, social philosophers like Herbert Spencer, Lester Ward, Gustve Le Bon—it was against their influence that I was protesting. The biologists, in fact, were generally ignoring society and culture. The few who did not ignore it, like Galton and Pearson, presented analyzed evidence that was handleable and might therefore be construed also in a contrary sense. Indeed, Galton has always evoked my complete respect and has been one of the largest intellectual influences on me. What the essay really protests is the blind and bland shuttling back and forth between an equivocal "race" and an equivocal "civilization"—a shuttling that is referred to at the end of one of the middle paragraphs. That confusion was certainly still prevalent at the time.

Two reservations are necessary in mid-twentieth century. First, society and culture can no longer be simply bracketed as "the social," as was customary then, in contrast to "the organic." In most contexts they are separable, and it is preferable to distinguish them. When the meaning is clearly inclusive, that fact can now be made clear by the use of "sociocultural," as is Sorokin's consistent practice. It was Bernhard Stern who pointed out in "Social Forces" in 1929 that my *"social"* in this essay was ambiguous. Ants and termites possess societies but no culture. Only man has both, necessarily always associated, though conceptually differentiable. Haziness today about the distinction is an intellectual fault only a little less gross than confusion of the organic and the superorganic. That my "superorganic" of 1917 referred essentially to culture is clear not only from all the concrete evidence cited but from the constant use of "civilization," "culture," "history," and their adjectival forms. Of the final twenty paragraphs, only three do not contain one or more occurrences of these interchangeably used terms. I should feel happier if I had been farsighted enough in 1917 consistently to say "cultural" or "sociocultural" wherever I did instead say "social" in a mistaken attempt to conform to prevalent usage—to pour new wine into the old bottle. Still I did not, I think, anywhere in the essay discuss or name "society," which fact shows that when I said "the social" I used it either in a wider sense to include culture or in a limiting sense to denote culture outright.

Second, I retract, as unwarranted reification, the references in the fourteenth, tenth, and sixth paragraphs from the last and in the final paragraph *to organic and superorganic "substances," entities, or fabrics. While it certainly is often needful to view different kinds of phenomena as of different orders and to deal with them on separate levels of apprehension, there is no need for metaphysically construing levels of conception or orders of attribute into substantial entities or different kinds of substance. Compare in this connectin No. 13 below.*

The notion expressed in the seventy-third paragraph that civilization or culture "is not mental action but a body or stream of products of mental exercise" may be contested—apart from its somewhat old-fashioned wording—but is still being argued today. We seem not yet to have attained a concise, unambiguous, inclusive, and exclusive definition of culture.

I am conscious of a degree of rhetorical ponderousness in the phrasing of the essay. I trust this will be forgiven—as it has been in the past—as a by-product of the fervor of realizations that at the time seemed both new and important. The 1927 wording has been retained unaltered except for one change of a preposition.

A way of thought characteristic of our western civilization has been the formulation of complementary antitheses, a balancing of exclusive opposites. One of these pairs of ideas with which our world has been laboring for some two thousand years is expressed in the words *body* and *soul*. Another couplet that has served its useful purpose, but which science is now often endeavoring to rid itself of, at least in certain aspects, is the distinction of the *physical* from the *mental*. A third discrimination is that of the *vital* from the *social*, or in other phraseology, of the *organic* from the *cultural*. The implicit recognition of the difference between organic qualities and processes and social qualities and processes is of long standing. The formal distinction is however recent. In fact the full import of the significance of the antithesis may be said to be only dawning upon the world. For every occasion on which some human mind sharply separates organic and social forces, there are dozens of other times when the distinction between them is not thought of, or an actual confusion of the two ideas takes place.

One reason for this current confusion of the organic and the social is the predominance, in the present phase of the history of thought, of the idea of evolution. This idea, one of the earliest, simplest, and also vaguest ever attained by the human mind, has received its strongest ground and fortification in the domain of the organic; in other words, through biological science. At the same time, there is an evolution, or growth, or gradual development, apparent also in other realms than that of plant and animal life. We have theories of stellar or cosmic evolution; and there is obvious, even to the least learned, a growth or evolution of civilization. In the nature of things there is little danger of the carrying over of the Darwinian or post-Darwinian principles of the evolution of life into the realm of burning suns and lifeless nebulae. Human civilization or progress, on the other hand, which exists only in and through living members of the species, is outwardly so similar to the evolution of plants and animals, that it has been inevitable that there should have been sweeping applications of the principles of organic development to the facts of cultural growth. This of course is reasoning by analogy, or arguing that because two things resemble each other in one point they will also be similar in others. In the absence of knowledge, such assumptions are justifiable as assumptions. Too often, however, their effect is to predetermine mental attitude, with the result that when the evidence begins to accumulate which could prove or disprove the assumption based on analogy, this evidence is no longer viewed impartially and judiciously, but is merely distributed and disposed of in such a way as not to interfere with the established conviction into which the original tentative guess has long since turned.

This is what has happened in the field of organic and social evolution. This distinction between them, which is so obvious that to former ages it seemed too commonplace to remark upon, except incidentally and indirectly, has been largely obscured in the last fifty years through the hold which thoughts connected with the idea of organic evolution have had on minds of the time. It even seems fair to say that this confusion has been greater and more general among those to whom study and scholarship are a daily pursuit than to the remainder of the world.

And yet many aspects of the difference between the organic and that in human life which is not organic, are so plain that a child can grasp them, and that all human beings, including the veriest savages, constantly employ the distinction. Everyone is aware that we are born with certain powers and that we acquire others. There is no need of argument to prove that we derive some things in our lives and make-up from nature through heredity, and that other things come to us through agencies with which heredity has nothing to do. No one has yet been found to assert that any human being is born with an inherent knowledge of the multiplication table; nor, on the other hand, to doubt that the children of a negro are born negroes through the operation of hereditary forces. Some qualities in every individual are however clearly debatable ground; and when the development of civilization as a whole and the evolution of life as a whole are compared, the distinction of the processes involved has too often been allowed to lapse.

Some millions of years ago, it is currently taught, natural selection, or some other evolutionary agency, first caused birds to appear in the world. They sprang from reptiles. Conditions were such that the struggle for existence on the earth was hard; while in the air there were safety and room. Gradually, either by a series of almost imperceptible gradations through a long line of successive generations, or by more marked and sudden leaps in a shorter period, the group of birds was evolved from its reptilian ancestors. In this development, feathers were acquired and scales lost; the grasping faculty of the front legs was converted into an ability to sustain the body in the air. The advantages of resistance enjoyed by a cold-blooded organization were given up for the equivalent or greater compensation of the superior activity that goes with warm-bloodedness. The net result of this chapter of evolutionary history was that a new power, that of aerial locomotion, was added to the sum total of faculties possessed by the highest group of animals, the vertebrates. The vertebrate animals as a whole, however, were not affected. The majority of them are without the power of flight as their ancestors were millions of years ago. The birds, in turn, had lost certain faculties which they once possessed, and presumably would still possess were it not for the acquisition of their wings.

In the last few years human beings have also attained the power of aerial locomotion. But the process by which this power was attained, and its effects on the species, are as different from those which characterized the acquisition of flight by the first birds as it is possible for them to be. Our means of flying are outside of our bodies. A bird is born with a pair of wings, but we have invented the aeroplane. The bird renounced a potential pair of hands to get his wings; we, because our new faculty is not part of our congenital make-up, keep all the organs and capacities of our forefathers but add to them the new ability. The process of the development of civilization is clearly one of accumulation: the old is retained, in spite of the incoming of the new. In organic evolution, the introduction of new features is generally possible only through the loss or modification of existing organs or faculties.

In short, the growth of new species of animals takes place through, and in fact consists of, changes in their organic constitution. As regards the growth of civilization, on the other hand, the one example cited is sufficient to show that change and progress can take place through an invention without any such constitutional alteration of the human species.

There is another way of looking at this difference. It is clear that as a new species originates, it is derived wholly from the individual or individuals that first showed the particular traits distinguishing the new species. When we say that it is derived from these individuals we mean, literally, that it is descended. In other words, the species is composed only of such individuals as contain the "blood"—the germ-plasm—of particular ancestors. Heredity is thus the indispensable means of transmission. When however an invention is made, the entire human race is capable of profiting thereby. People who have not the slightest blood kinship to the first designers of aeroplanes can fly and are flying today. Many a father has used, enjoyed, and profited by the invention of his son. In the evolution of animals, the descendant can build upon the inheritance transmitted to him from his ancestors, and may rise to higher powers and more perfect development; but the ancestor is, in the very nature of things, precluded from thus profiting from his descendant. In short, organic evolution is essentially and inevitably connected with hereditary processes; the social evolution which characterizes the progress of civilization, on the other hand, is not, or not necessarily, tied up with hereditary agencies.

The whale is not only a warm-blooded mammal, but is recognized as the remote descendant of carnivorous land animals. In some few million years, as such genealogies are usually reckoned, this animal lost his legs for running, his claws for holding and tearing, his original hair and external ears that would be useless or worse in water, and acquired fins and fluke, a cylindrical body, a layer of fat, and the power of holding his breath. There was much that the species gave up; more, on the whole, perhaps than it gained. Certainly some of its parts have degenerated. But there was one new power that it did achieve: that of roaming the ocean indefinitely.

The parallel and also contrast is in the human acquisition of the identical faculty. We do not, in gradual alteration from father to son, change our arms into flippers and grow a tail. We do not enter the water at all to navigate it. We build a boat. And what this means is that we preserve our bodies and our natal faculties intact, unaltered from those of our fathers and remotest ancestors. Our means of marine travel is outside of our natural endowment. We make it and use it: the original whale had to turn himself into a boat. It took him countless generations to attain to his present condition. All individuals that failed to conform to type left no offspring; or none that went into the blood of the whales of today.

Again, we may compare human and animal beings when groups of them reach a new and arctic environment, or when the climate of the tract where the race is established slowly becomes colder and colder. The non-human mammal species comes to have heavy hair. The polar bear is shaggy; his Sumatran relative sleek. The arctic hare is enveloped in soft fur; the jack-rabbit in comparison is shabbily thin and moth-eaten. Good furs come from the far north, and they lose in richness, in quality, and in value, in proportion as they are stripped from animals of the same species that inhabit milder regions. And this difference is racial, not individual. The jack-rabbit would quickly perish with the end of summer in Greenland; the caged polar bear suffers from temperate warmth within the massive coat which nature has fastened on him.

Now there are people who look for the same sort of inborn peculiarities in the Arctic Eskimo and Samoyed; and find them, because they look for them. That the Eskimo is furry, no one can assert: in fact, we are hairier than he. But it is asserted that he is fat-protected—like the blubber-covered seal that he lives on; and that he devours quantities of meat and oil because he needs them. The true amount of his fat, compared with that of other human beings, remains to be ascertained. He probably has more than the European; but probably no more than the normal fullblood Samoan and Hawaiian from under the tropics. And as to his diet, if this is seal and seal and seal all winter long, it is not from any congenital craving of his stomach, but because he does not know how to get himself anything else. The Alaskan miner, and the arctic and antarctic explorer, do not guzzle blubber. Wheat-flour, eggs, coffee, sugar, potatoes, canned vegetables—whatever the exigencies of their vocation and the cost of transportation permit—make up their fare. The Eskimo is only too anxious to join them; and both he and they can thrive on the one diet as on the other.

In fact, what the human inhabitant of intemperate latitudes does, is not to develop a peculiar digestive system, any more than he grows hair. He changes his environment, and thereby is able to retain his original body unaltered. He builds a closed house, which keeps out the wind and retains the heat of his body. He makes a fire or lights a lamp. He skins a seal or a caribou of the furry hide with which natural selection or other processes of organic evolution have endowed these beasts; he has his wife make him a shirt and trousers, boots and gloves, or two sets of them; he puts them on; and in a few years, or days, he is provided with the protection which it took the polar bear and the arctic hare, the sable and the ptarmigan, untold periods to acquire. What is more, his baby, and his baby's baby, and his hundredth descendant are born as naked, and unarmed physically, as he and his hundredth ancestor were born.

That this difference in method of resisting a difficult environment, as followed respectively by the polar bear species and the human Eskimo race, is absolute, need not be asserted. That the difference is deep, is unquestionable. That it is as important as it is often neglected, it is the object of this essay to establish.

It has long been the custom to say that the difference is that between body and mind; that animals have their physiques adapted to their circumstances, but that man's superior intelligence enables him to rise superior to such lowly needs. But this is not the most significant point of the difference. It is true that without the much greater mental faculties of man, he could not achieve the attainments the lack of which keeps the brute chained to the limitations of his anatomy. But the greater human intelligence in itself does not cause the differences that exist. This psychic superiority is only the indispensable condition of what is peculiarly human; civilization. Directly, it is the civilization in which every Eskimo, every Alaskan miner or arctic discoverer is reared, and not any greater inborn faculty, that leads him to build houses, ignite fire, and wear clothing. The distinction between animal and man which counts is not that of the physical and mental, which is one of relative degree, but that of the organic and social which is one of kind. The beast has mentality, and we have bodies; but in civilization man has something that no animal has.

That this distinction is actually something more than that of the physical and mental, appears from an example that may be chosen from the non-bodily: speech.

On the surface, human and animal speech, in spite of the enormously greater richness and complexity of the former, are much alike. Both express emotions, possibly ideas, in sounds formed by bodily organs and understood by the hearing individual. But the difference between the so-called language of brutes and that of men is infinitely great; as a homely illustration will set forth.

A newly-born pup is brought up in a litter of kittens by a fostering cat. Familiar anecdotes and newspaper paragraphs to the contrary, the youngster will bark and growl, not purr or miaow. He will not even try to do the latter. The first time his toe is stepped on, he will whine, not squeal, just as surely as when thoroughly angered he will bite as his never-beheld mother did, and not even attempt to claw as he has seen his foster-mother do. For half his life seclusion may keep him from sight or sound or scent of another dog. But then let a bark or a snarl reach him through the restraining wall, and he will be all attention—more than at any voice ever uttered by his cat associates. Let the bark be repeated, and interest will give way to excitement, and he will answer in kind, as certainly as, put with a bitch, the sexual impulses of his species will manifest themselves. It cannot be doubted that dog speech is ineradicably part of dog nature, as fully contained in it without training or culture, as wholly part of the dog organism, as are teeth or feet or stomach or motions or instincts. No degree of contact with cats, or deprivation of association with his own kind, can make a dog acquire cat speech, or lose his own, any more than it can cause him to switch his tail instead of wagging it, to rub his sides against his master instead of leaping against him, or to grow whiskers and carry his drooping ears erect.

Let us take a French baby, born in France of French parents, themselves descended for numerous generations from French-speaking ancestors. Let us, at once after birth, entrust the infant to a mute nurse, with instructions to let no one handle or see her charge, while she travels by the directest route to the interior heart of China. There she delivers the child to a Chinese couple, who legally adopt it, and rear it as their son. Now suppose three or ten or thirty years passed. Is it needful to discuss what the growing or grown Frenchman will speak? Not a word of French; pure Chinese, without a trace of accent and with Chinese fluency; and nothing else.

It is true that there is a common delusion, frequent even among educated people, that some hidden influence of his French-talking ancestors will survive in the adopted Chinaman: that it is only necessary to send him to France with a batch of real Chinamen, and he will acquire his mother's tongue with appreciably greater facility, fluency, correctness, and naturalness than his Mongolian companions. That a belief is common, however, is as likely to stamp it a common superstition as a common truth. And a reasonable biologist, in other words, an expert qualified to speak of heredity, will pronounce this answer to this problem in heredity, superstition. He might merely choose a politer phrase.

Now there is something deep-going here. No amount of association with Chinese would turn our young Frenchman's eyes from blue to black, or slant them, or flatten his nose, or coarsen or stiffen his wavy, oval-sectioned hair;

and yet his speech is totally that of his associates, in no measure that of his blood kin. His eyes and his nose and his hair are his from heredity; his language is non-hereditary—as much so as the length to which he allows his hair to grow, or the hole which, in conformity to fashion, he may or may not bore in his ears. It is not so much that speech is mental and facial proportions are physical; the distinction that has meaning and use is that human language is nonhereditary and social, eye-color and nose-shape hereditary and organic. By the same criterion, dog speech, and all that is vaguely called the language of animals, is in a class with men's noses, the proportions of their bones, the color of their skin, and the slope of their eyes, and not in a class with any human idiom. It is inherited, and therefore organic. By a human standard, it is not really language at all, except by the sort of metaphor that speaks of the language of the flowers.

It is true that now and then a French child would be found that under the conditions of the experiment assumed, would learn Chinese more slowly, less idiomatically, and with less power of expression, than the average Chinaman. But there would also be French babies, and as many, that would acquire the Chinese language more quickly, more fluently, with richer power of revealing their emotions and defining their ideas, than the normal Chinese. These are individual differences, which it would be absurd to deny, but which do not affect the average, and are not to the point. One Englishman speaks better English, and more of it, than another, and he may also through precocity, learn it much sooner; but one talks English no more and no less truly than the other.

There is one form of animal expression in which the influence of association has sometimes been alleged to be greater than that of heredity. This is the song of birds. There is a good deal of conflicting opinion, and apparently of evidence, on this point. Many birds have a strong inherent impulse to imitate sounds. It is also a fact that the singing of one individual stimulates the other—as with dogs, wolves, cats, frogs, and most noisy animals. That in certain species of birds capable of a complex song the full development will not often be reached in individuals raised out of hearing of their kind, may probably be admitted. But it seems to be clear that every species has a song or call distinctively its own; that this minimum is attainable without association by every normal member of the singing sex, as soon as conditions of age, food, and warmth are proper, and the requisite stimulus of noise, or silence, or sex development, is present. That there has been serious conflict of opinion as to the nature of bird song, will ultimately be found to be chiefly due to the pronouncement of opinions on the matter by those who read their own mental states and activities into animals—a common fallacy that every biological student is now carefully trained against at the outset of his career. In any event, whether one bird does or does not in some degree "learn" from another, there is no fragment of evidence that bird song is a tradition, that like human speech or human music it accumulates and develops from age to age, that it is inevitably altered from generation to generation by fashion or custom, and that it is impossible for it ever to remain the same: in other words, that it is a social thing or due to a process even remotely akin to those affecting the constituents of human civilization.

It is also true that there is in human life a series of utterances that are of the type of animal cries. A man in pain moans without purpose of communication. The sound is literally pressed from him. A person in supreme fright may shriek. We know that his cry is unintended, what the physiologist calls a reflex action. The true shriek is as liable to escape the victim pinned before the approaching engineerless train, as him who is pursued by thinking and planning enemies. The woodsman crushed by a rock forty miles from the nearest human being, will moan like the run-over city dweller surrounded by a crowd waiting for the speeding ambulance. Such cries are of a class with those of animals. In fact, really to understand the "speech" of brutes, we must think ourselves into a condition in which our utterances would be totally restricted to such instinctive cries—"inarticulate" is their general though often inaccurate designation. In an exact sense, they are not language at all.

This is precisely the point. We undoubtedly have certain activities of utterance, certain faculties and habits of sound production, that are truly parallel with those of animals; and we also have something more that is quite different and without parallel among the animals. To deny that something purely animal underlies human speech, is fatuous; but it would be equally narrow to believe that because our speech springs from an animal foundation, and originated in this foundation, it therefore is nothing but animal mentality and utterances greatly magnified. A house may be built on rock; without this base it might be impossible for it to have been erected; but no one will maintain that therefore the house is nothing but improved and glorified stone.

As a matter of fact, the purely animal element in human speech is small. Apart from laughter and crying, it finds rare utterance. Our interjections are denied by philologists as true speech, or at best but half admitted. It is a fact that they differ from full words in not being voiced, generally, to convey a meaning—nor to conceal one. But even these particles are shaped and dictated by fashion, by custom, by the type of civilization to which we belong, in short by social and not by organic elements. When I drive the hammer on my thumb instead of on the head of the nail, an involuntary "damn" may escape me as readily if I am alone in the house, as if companions stand on each side. Perhaps more readily. So far, the exclamation does not serve the purpose of speech and is not speech. But the Spaniard will say "carramba" and not "damn"; and the Frenchman, the German, the Chinaman, will avail himself of still different expression. The American says "outch" when hurt. Other nationalities do not understand this syllable. Each people has its own sound; some even two—one used by men and the other by women. A Chinaman will understand a laugh, a moan, a crying child, as well as we understand it, and as well as a dog understands the snarl of another dog. But he must learn "outch," or it is meaningless. No dog, on the other hand, ever has given utterance to a new snarl, unintelligible to other dogs, as a result of having been brought up in different associations. Even this lowest element of human speech, then, this involuntary half-speech of exclamations, is therefore shaped by social influences.

Herodotus tells of an Egyptian king, who, wishing to ascertain the parent tongue of humanity, had some infants brought up in isolation from their own kind, with only goats as companions and for sustenance. When the children, grown older, were revisited, they cried the word "bekos," or, subtracting the ending which the normalizing and sensitive Greek could not endure omitting from anything that passed his lips, more probably "bek." The king then sent to all countries to learn in what land this vocable meant something. He ascertained that in the Phrygian idiom it signified bread, and, assuming that the children were crying for food, concluded that they spoke Phrygian in voicing their "natural" human speech, and that this tongue must therefore be the original one of mankind. The king's belief in an inherent and congenital language of man, which only the blind accidents of time had distorted into a multitude of idioms, may seem simple; but naïve as it is, inquiry would reveal crowds of civilized people still adhering to it.

This however is not our moral to the tale. That lies in the fact that the one and only word attributed to the children, "bek," was, if the story has any authenticity whatsoever, only a reflection or imitation—as the commentators of Herodotus long since conjectured—of the bleating of the goats that were the children's only associates and instructors. In short, if it is allowable to deduce any inference from so apocryphal an anecdote, what it proves is that there is no natural and therefore no organic human language.

Thousands of years later another sovereign, the Mogul emperor Akbar, repeated the experiment with the intent of ascertaining the "natural" religion of mankind. His band of children were shut up in a house. When, the necessary time having elapsed, the doors were opened in the presence of the expectant and enlightened ruler, his disappointment was great: the children trooped out as dumb as deaf-mutes. Faith dies hard, however; and we may suspect that it would take a third trial, under modern chosen and controlled conditions, to satisfy some natural scientists that speech, for the human individual and for the human race, is wholly an acquired and not a hereditary thing, entirely outward and not at all inward—a social product and not an organic growth.

Human and animal speech, then, though one roots in the other, are in the nature of a different order. They resemble each other only as the flight of a bird and of an aeronaut are alike. That the analogy between them has frequently deceived, proves only the guilelessness of the human mind. The operative processes are wholly unlike; and this, to him who is desirous of understanding, is far more important than the similarity of effect. The savage and the peasant who cure by cleaning the knife and leaving the wound unattended, have observed certain indisputable facts. They know that cleanness aids, dirt on the whole impedes recovery. They know the knife as the cause, the wound as the effect; and they grasp, too, the correct principle that treatment of the cause is in general more likely to be effective than treatment of the symptom. They fail only in not inquiring into the process that may be involved. Knowing nothing of the nature of sepsis, of bacteria, of the agencies of putrefaction and retardation of healing, they fall back on agencies more familiar to themselves, and use, as best they may, the process of magic intertwined with that of medicine. They carefully scrape the knife; they oil it; they keep it bright. The facts from which they work are correct; their logic is sound enough; they merely do not distinguish between two irreconcilable processes—that of magic and that of physiological chemistry—and apply one in place of another. The student of today who reads the civilizationally moulded mind of men into the mentality of a dog or ape, or who tries to explain civilization—that is, history—by organic factors, commits an error which is less antiquated and more in fashion, but of the same kind and nature.

It is only in small measure a question of high and low as between man and animal. Many purely instinctive activities of the beasts lead to far more complex and difficult achievements than some of the analogous customs of this or that human nation. The beaver is a better architect than many a savage tribe. He fells larger trees, he drags them farther, he builds a closer house; he constructs it both below and above water; and he does what many nations never attempt to do: he makes himself a suitable topography for a habitat by erecting a dam. But the essential point is not that after all a man can do more than a beaver, or a beaver as much as a man; it is that what a beaver accomplishes he does by one means, and a man by another. The rudest savage, who builds but a shack of a wind-pierced hut, can be taught, innumerable times has been taught, to saw and nail together boards, to mortar stone on stone, to sink foundations, to rear an iron frame. All human history concerns itself primarily with just such changes. What were the ancestors of ourselves, of us steel-building Europeans and Americans, but hut-dwelling savages of a few thousand years ago—a period so short that it may barely suffice for the formation of an occasional new species of organism? And on the other side, who would be so rash as to affirm that ten thousand generations of example and instruction would convert the beaver from what he is into a carpenter or a bricklayer—or, allowing for his physical deficiency in the lack of hands, into a planning engineer?

The divergence between social and organic forces is perhaps not fully grasped until the mentality of the so-called social insects, the bees and ants, is thoroughly realized. Social the ant is, in the sense that she associates; but she is so far from being social in the sense of possessing civilization, of being influenced by non-organic forces, that she would better be known as the antisocial animal. The marvelous powers of the ant cannot be underestimated. There is no one to whom the full exploitation of their understanding will be of more service than to the historian. But he will not use this understanding by applying his knowledge of ant mentality to man. He will use it to fortify and render precise by intelligent contrast, his conception of the agencies that mould human civilization. Ant society is as little a true society, in the human sense, as a caricature is a portrait.

Take a few ant eggs of the proper sexes—unhatched eggs, freshly laid. Blot out every individual and every other egg of the species. Give the pair a little attention as regards warmth, moisture, protection, and food. The whole of ant "society," every one of the abilities, powers, accomplishments, and activities of the species, each "thought" that it has ever had, will be reproduced, and reproduced without diminution, in one generation. But place on a desert island or in a circumvallation two or three hundred human infants of the best stock from the highest class of the most civilized nation; furnish them the necessary incubation and nourishment; leave them in total isolation from their kind; and what shall we have? The civilization from which they were torn? One tenth of it? No, not any fraction; nor a fraction of the civilizational attainments of the rudest savage tribe. Only a pair or a troop of mutes, without arts, knowledge, fire, without order or religion. Civilization would be wiped out within these confines—not disintegrated, not cut to the quick, but obliterated in one sweep. Heredity saves for the ant all that she has, from generation to generation. But heredity does not maintain, and has not maintained, because it cannot maintain, one particle of the civilization which is the specifically human thing.

The mental activity of the animals is partly instinctive, partly based on individual experience; the content, at least, of our own minds comes to us through tradition, in the widest sense of the word. Instinct is what is "pricked in"; an unalterable pattern inherent in the goods; indelible and inextinguishable, because the design is nothing but the warp and the woof, coming ready-made from the loom of heredity.

But tradition, what is "given through," handed along, from one to another, is only a message. It must of course be carried; but the messenger after all is extrinsic to the news. So, a letter must be written; but as its significance is in the meaning of the words, as the value of a note is not in the fiber of the paper but in the characters inscribed on its surface, so tradition is something super-added to the organisms that bear it, imposed upon them, external to them. And as the same shred can bear any one of thousands of inscriptions, of the most diverse force and value, and can even be tolerably razed and reinscribed, so it is with the human organism and the countless contents that civilization can pour into it. The essential difference between animal and man, in this illustration, is not that the latter has finer grain or the chaster quality of material; it is that his structure and nature and texture are such that he is inscribable, and that the animal is not. Chemically and physically, there is little difference between a lump of pulp and a sheet of paper. Chemically and physically, it is of slight consequence to trouble about such minute difference. But chemically and physically there is still less difference between the treasury note stamped with "one" and that stamped with "thousand"; and yet less between the check with an honored signature and that written with the same pen, the same ink, the same strokes even, by a forger. The difference that counts between the valid and the counterfeit check, is not the broader or the narrow line, the continuous curve of a letter in place of the broken one, but the purely social one that one signer has a valid account in the bank and the other has not; which fact is surely extrinsic to the paper and even to the ink upon it.

Exactly parallel to this is the relation of the instinctive and traditional, the organic and the social. The animal, so far as social influences are concerned, is as unsuitable as a dish of porridge is for writing material; or when like the beach sand, it is inscribable, by domestication, it can retain no permanent impression, as a species. Hence it has no society, and therefore no history. Man, however, comprises two aspects: he is an organic substance, that can be viewed as a substance, and he is also a tablet that is written upon. One aspect is as valid and as justifiable as another; but it is a cardinal mistake to confuse the two views.

The mason builds in granite and roofs with slate. The child learning its letters knows nothing of the qualities of its slate, but puzzles whether to write c or k. The mineralogist gives no precedence to one of the stones over the other; each has a constitution, a structure, properties, and uses. The educator ignores the granite; but, though he uses the slate, he does not therefore rate it higher, or deny the serviceability of the other material; he takes his substance as he finds it. His problem is whether the child should begin with words or letters; at what age, for what hours, in what sequence, and under what conditions, its education toward literacy should commence. To decide these issues upon crystallogical evidence because his pupils write upon a variety of stone would be as futile as if the geologist were to employ his knowledge of rocks for inferences as to the soundest principles of pedagogy.

So, if the student of human achievement were to try to withdraw from the observation of the natural historian and the mechanical philosopher the human beings upon whom is inscribed the civilization which he himself investigates, he would be ridiculous. And when on the other hand, the biologist proposes to rewrite history, in whole or in part, through the medium of heredity, he reveals himself in little more favorable light, though he would have the sanction of some precedent.

There have been many attempts to make precise the distinction between instinct and civilization, between the organic and the social, between animal and man. Man as the clothing animal, the fire-using animal, the tool-using or tool-making animal, the speaking animal, are all summations that contain some approximation. But for the conception of the discrimination that is at once most complete and most compact, we must go back, as for the first precise expression of so many of the ideas with which we operate, to the unique mind that impelled Aristotle. "Man is a political animal." The word political has changed in import. We use instead the Latin term social. This, both philosopher and philologist tell us, is what the great Greek would have said were he speaking in English today. Man is a social animal, then; a social organism. He has organic constitution; but he has also civilization. To ignore one element is as short-sighted as to overlook the other; to convert one into the other, if each has its reality, is negation. With this basic formulation more than two thousand years old, and known to all the generations, there is something puny, as well as obstinately destructive, in the endeavor to abrogate the distinction, or to hinder its completest fruition. The attempt today to treat the social as organic, to understand civilization as hereditary, is as essentially narrow as the alleged mediaeval inclination to withdraw man from the realm of nature and from the ken of the scientist because he was believed to possess an immaterial soul.

But unfortunately the denials, and for every denial a dozen confusions, still persist. They pervade the popular mind; and thence they rise, again and again, into the thoughts of avowed and recognized science. It seems, even, that in a hundred years we have retrograded. A century and two centuries ago, with a generous impulse, the leaders of thought devoted their energies, and the leaders of men their lives, to the cause that all men are equal. With all that this idea involves, and with its correctness, we need not here concern ourselves; but it certainly implied the proposition of equality of racial capacity. Possibly our ancestors were able to maintain this liberal stand because its full practical imports did not yet face them. But, whatever the reason, we have certainly gone back, in America and in Europe and in their colonies, in our application of the assumption; and we have receded too in our theoretic analysis of the evidence. Hereditary racial differences of ability pass as approved doctrine, in many quarters. There are men of eminent learning who would be surprised to know that serious doubts were held in the matter.

And yet, it must be maintained that little really satisfactory evidence has been produced to support the assumption that the differences which one nation shows from another—let alone the superiority of one people to another—are racially inherent, that is organically founded. It does not matter how distinguished the minds are that have held such differences to be hereditary—they have in the main only taken their conviction for granted. The sociologist or anthropologist can, and occasionally does, turn the case inside out with equal justification; and he then sees every event, every inequality, the whole course of human history, confirming his thesis that the distinctions between one group of men and another, past and present, are due to social influences and not to organic causes. Real proof, to be sure, is as wanting on one side as on the other. Experiment, under conditions that would yield satisfying evidence, would be difficult, costly, and perhaps contrary to law. A repetition of Akbar's interesting trial, or some modification of it, intelligently directed and followed out, would yield results of the greatest value; but it would scarcely yet be tolerated by a civilized government.

There have been some attempts to investigate so-called racial distinctions with the apparatus of experimental psychology. The results incline superficially toward confirmation of organic differences. But too much stress may not as yet be laid on this conclusion, because what such investigations have above all revealed is that social agencies are so tremendously influential on every one of us that it is difficult to find any test which, if distinctive racial faculties were inborn, would fairly reveal the degree to which they are inborn.

It is also well to remember that the problem of whether the human races are or are not in themselves identical, has innumerable practical bearings, which relate to conditions of life and to views that have emotional relations, so that an impartially abstract predisposition is rather rarely to be encountered. It is practically futile, for instance, even to touch upon the question with most Americans from the Southern states, or those tinged by Southern influences, no matter what their education or standing in the world. The actual social cleavage which is fundamental to all life in the South, and which is conceived of mainly as a race question, is so overshadowing and inevitable, that it compels, for the individual almost as firmly as for his group, a certain line of action, an unalterable and conscious course of conduct; and it could not well be otherwise than that opinions which flagrantly clash with one's habitual activities and with their associated ideals, should arouse hostility. It is then but natural if the Southerner frequently receives the profession of racial equality, when it can be made to carry the conviction of sincerity to him, as an affront; and that he often meets even the most abstract, impersonal, and judicial consideration of the issues involved, with resentment, or, where this is checked by courtesy, with internal dissatisfaction.

The attitude of the Englishman in India, of the continental European in his colonies, is perhaps less extremely manifested; but all accounts indicate that it is no less settled.

On the other hand, the avowed and thoroughgoing Socialist or Internationalist must take the opposite stand, however unsympathetic it may be to him personally, or renounce the aspirations that he holds dear. His inclination therefore, if generally less clearly defined, is no less predetermined and persistent.

Impartiality is thus not to be expected in this great case, except in some measure on the part of really detached and therefore uninfluential students; so that the maximum of assertion and rancor, and minimum of evidence, which prevail, are to be accepted as regrettable indeed, but as unavoidable and scarcely to be censured.

The problem, being in the present state of our knowledge unprovable, is really also not arguable. What is possible, however, is to realize that a complete and consistent explanation can be given, for so-called racial differences, on a basis of purely civilizational and non-organic causes; and to attain also to the recognition that the mere fact of the world in general assuming that such differences between one people and another are inborn and ineradicable except by breeding, is no evidence in favor of the assumption being true.

The final argument, that one can actually *see* such national peculiarities born into each generation, and that it is unnecessary to verify the assumption because its truth is obvious to every one, has the least weight of all. It is of a kind with the contention that might be made that this planet is after all the fixed central point of the cosmic system because everyone can see for himself that the sun and stars move and that our earth stands still. The champions of the Copernican doctrine had this in their favor: they dealt with phenomena to which exactitude was readily applicable, about which verifiable or disprovable predictions could be made, which an explanation either fitted or did not fit. In the domain of human history this is not possible, or has not yet been found possible; so that an equal neatness of demonstration, a definitiveness of proof, a close tallying of theory with the facts to the exclusion of all rival theories, is not to be hoped for at present. But there is almost as fundamental a shifting of mental and emotional point of view, as absolute a turning upside down of attitude involved when the current thought of today is asked to view civilization as a nonorganic affair, as when the Copernican doctrine challenged the prior conviction of the world.

Most ethnologists, at any rate, are convinced that the overwhelming mass of historical and miscalled racial facts that are now attributed to obscure organic causes, or at most are in dispute, will ultimately be viewed by everyone as social and as best intelligible in their social relations. That there may be a residuum in which hereditary influences have been operative, it would be dogmatic to deny; but even this residuum of organic agencies will perhaps be found to be operative in quite other manners than those which are customarily adduced at present.

The opinion may further be uncompromisingly maintained, that for the historian—him who wishes to understand any sort of social phenomena—it is an unavoidable necessity, today, to disregard the organic as such and to deal only with the social. For the larger number who are not professional students of civilization, insistence upon these articles would be an unreasonable demand, under our present inability to substantiate them by proof. On the other hand, the social as something distinct from the organic is an old enough concept, and is a plain enough phenomenon about us in daily life, to warrant the claim that it cannot be outright dispensed with. It is perhaps too much to expect any one wedded, deliberately or unknowingly, to organic explanations, to discard these wholly in the face of such incomplete evidence as is available to the contrary of these explanations. But it does seem justifiable to stand unhesitatingly on the proposition that civilization and heredity are two things that operate in separate ways; that therefore any outright substitution of one for the other in the explanation of human group phenomena is crass; and that the refusal to recognize at least the possibility of an explanation of human achievement totally different from the prevailing tendency toward a biological explanation, is an act of illiberality. When once such recognition, of the rationality of this attitude of mind which is diametrically opposed to the current one, shall have become general, far more progress will have been made on the road towards a useful agreement as to the truth, than by any present attempts to win converts by argument.

One of the minds endowed with as eminent power of perception and formulation as any of the last generation, Gustave Le Bon, whose name ranks high even if his regardless fearlessness has gained him but little of an avowed following, has carried the interpretation of the social as organic to its consistent consequence. His *Psychology of Peoples* is an attempt to explain civilization on the basis of race. Le Bon is really an historian of unusually keen sensitiveness and perspicacity. But his professed attempt to resolve the civilizational materials with which he deals, directly into organic factors, leads him on the one hand to renounce his skilful interpretations of history until only intermittent flashes remain; and on the other hand, to rest his professed solutions ultimately on such mystic essences as the "soul of a race." As a scientific concept or tool, a race soul is as intangible and useless as a phrase of mediaeval philosophy, and on a par with Le Bon's ready declaration that the individual is to the race as the cell is to the body. If instead of soul of the race, the distinguished Frenchman had said spirit of civilization, or tendency or character of culture, his pronouncements would have commanded less appeal, because seeming vaguer; but he would not have had to rest his thought upon a supernatural idea antagonistic to the body of science to which he was trying to attach his work; and if nonmechanistic, his efforts at explanation would at least have earned the respect of historians.

As a matter of fact, Le Bon clearly operates with social phenomena, however insistently he gives them organic names and proclaims that he has resolved them organically. That "not the 18 Brumaire but the soul of his race established Napoleon," is biologically, and under any aspect of the science that deals with mechanical causality, a meaningless statement; but it becomes excellent history as soon as for "race" we substitute "civilization," and of course take "soul" in a metaphorical sense.

When he says that "cross breeding destroys an ancient civilization" he affirms only what many a biologist would be ready to maintain. When he adds:

"because it destroys the soul of the people that possess it," he gives a reason that must inspire a scientist with a shudder. But if we change "cross breeding," that is, the mixture of sharply differentiated organic types, into "sudden contact or conflict of ideals," that is, mixture of sharply differentiated social types, the profound effect of such an event is indisputable.

Again, Le Bon asserts that the effect of environment is great on new races, on races forming through cross breeding of peoples of contrary heredities; and that in ancient races solidly established by heredity the effect of environment is nearly nil. It is obvious that in an old and firm civilization the actively changing effect of geographical environment must be small because the civilization has long since had ample opportunity to utilize the environment for its needs; but that on the other hand when the civilization is new—whether because of its transportation, because of its proceeding fusion from several elements, or from mere internal development—the renewing of relationship between itself and the surrounding physical geography must go on at a rapid rate. Here again good history is turned into bad science by a confusion that seems almost deliberately perverse.

A people is guided far more by its dead than by its living, Le Bon says. He is trying to establish the importance of heredity on national careers. What, though unrecognized by himself, lies at the bottom of his thought, is the truth that every civilization rests in the past, that however much its ancient elements are no longer living as such, they nevertheless form its trunk and body, around which the live sap-wood of the day is only a shell and a surface. That imposed education, a formal and conscious thing, can not give the substance of a new or another civilization to a people, is a verity that Le Bon has seized with vigor. But when he deduces this maxim as an inference from the unbridgeable abyss that externally exists between races, he rests an obvious fact, which no person of discrimination has yet disputed, upon a mystical assertion.

It might nearly have been foreseen, after the above citations, that Le Bon would lay the "character" of his "races" to "accumulation by heredity." It has already been shown that if there is anything that heredity does not do, it is to accumulate. If, on the other hand, there is any one method by which civilization may be defined as operating, it is precisely that of accumulation. We add the power of flight, the understanding of the mechanism of the aeroplane, to our previous accomplishments and knowledges. The bird does not; he has given up his legs and toes for wings. It may be true that the bird is on the whole a higher organism than his reptilian ancestor, that he has traveled farther on the road of development. But his advance has been achieved by a transmutation of qualities, a conversion of organs and faculties, not by an increasing summation of them.

The whole theory of heredity by acquirement rests upon the confusion of these two so diverse processes, that of heredity and that of civilization. It has been nourished, perhaps, by unsatisfied needs of biological science, but it has never obtained the slightest unchallengeable verification from biology, and has in fact long been assailed, by a sound an vigorous instinct, as well as in consequence of the failure of observation and experiment, from within that science. It is a doctrine that is the constant blazon of the dilettante who knows something of both history and life, but has no care to understand the workings of either. Le Bon's studies being an attempt to explain one by the other, his utilization, sooner or later, of the doctrine of heredity by acquisition or accumulation, could almost have been predicted.

From a different and less aggressive temperament springs the wail that Lester Ward has voiced for a wide and aspiringly earnest element. Heredity by acquirement must take place, he argues, or there would be no hope of permanent progress for humanity. To believe that what we have gained will not be at least in part implanted in our children, removes the incentive to effort. All the labor bestowed upon the youth of the world would be in vain. Mental qualities are not subject to natural selection; hence they must be accumulated in man by acquirement and fixed by heredity. This view may be heard again and again from people who have arrived at the attitude through their own reflections, who have probably never read Ward directly or indirectly, and whose world seems to crash when its foundation of heredity is shaken. It is, if not a deep view, a common one; and for that reason Ward's formulation is, however worthless intrinsically, representative and significant. It reveals the tenacity, the insistence, with which many conscientious intellects of the day will not and can not see the social except through the glass of the organic. That this habit of mind can itself be depressing, that it forever prelimits development and eternally chains the future to the poverties and paucities of the present, does not dawn upon its devotees; is in fact probably the fixity which gives it its emotional hold.

It would seem probable that the greatest of the champions of acquired heredity, Herbert Spencer, was led to his stand by a similar motive. The precise method by which organic evolution takes place is after all essentially a biological problem, and not a philosophical one. Spencer, however, like Comte, was a sociologist as much as a philosopher. That he should have contested so stubbornly what in itself is a technical question of biology, is hardly intelligible except on the supposition that he felt the question to bear vitally on his principles; and that, in spite of his happy coinage of the term which has been prefixed as title to the present essay, he did not adequately conceive of human society as holding a specific content that is non-organic.

When R. R. Marett, in opening his *Anthropology*—one of the most stimulating books produced in this field—defines the science as "the whole history of man as fired and pervaded by the idea of evolution," and adds that "anthropology is the child of Darwin—Darwinism makes it possible," he is unfortunately depicting the recent condition of this science with some truth; but as a program or an ideal his delineation must be challenged. Anthropology may be biology; it may be history; it may be an attempt to ascertain the relations of the two; but as history, the study of the social, shot through with the idea of organic evolution, it would be a jumble of diverse methods, and therefore no science in any sense of the term.

Of all the comminglings of the cultural with the vital, that which has crystallized under the name of the eugenics movement is the most widely known and of directest appeal. As a constructive program for national progress, eugenics is a confusion of the purposes to breed better men and to give men better ideals; an organic device to attain the social; a biological short cut to a moral end. It contains the inherent impossibility of all short cuts. It is more refined but no less vain than the short cut which the savage follows, when, to avoid the trouble and danger of killing his foe in the body, he pierces, in safety and amid objurgations uttered in the convenience of his own home, a miniature image addressed by the name of the enemy. Eugenics, so far as it is more than an endeavor at social hygiene in a new field, is a fallacy; a mirage like the philosopher's stone, the elixir of life, the ring of Solomon, or the material efficacy of prayer. There is little to argue about it. If social phenomena are only or mainly organic, eugenics is right, and there is nothing more to be said. If the social is something more than the organic, eugenics is an error of unclear thought.

Galton, the founder of the eugenics propaganda, was one of the most truly imaginative intellects produced by his country. Pearson, its distinguished living protagonist with scientific weapons, possesses one of the keenest minds of the generation. Hundreds of men of ability and eminence have professed themselves converts. It is plain that a simple fallacy must have presented itself in an envelope of enticing complications to be acceptable to them. Such men have not confounded important things that are intrinsically distinct, without a good reason. The explanation that Galton, Pearson, and the majority of the most creative of their followers were professional biologists, and therefore inclined to see the world through the lenses of the organic, is insufficient. Mere interest in one factor does not lead thinking minds practically to deny the existence of other factors. What then is the reason of the confusion into which they have precipitated themselves?

The cause seems to be a failure to distinguish between the social and the mental. All civilization in a sense exists only in the mind. Gunpowder, textile arts, machinery, laws, telephones are not themselves transmitted from man to man or from generation to generation, at least not permanently. It is the perception, the knowledge and understanding of them, their *ideas* in the Platonic sense, that are passed along. Everything social can have existence only through mentality. Of course, civilization is not mental action itself; it is carried by men, without being in them. But its relation to mind, its absolute rooting in human faculty, is obvious.

What, then, has occurred is that biology, which correlates and often identifies the "physical" and the mental, has gone one natural but as yet unjustified step further, and assumed the social as mental; whence the explanation of civilization in physiological and mechanical terms was an unavoidable consequence.

Now, the correlation by modern science of the physical and mental is certainly correct. That is, it is justifiable as a method which can be consistently employed toward a coherent explanation of phenomena, and which leads to intellectually satisfactory and practically useful results. The correlation of the two sets of phenomena is made, or admitted, by all psychologists; it clearly holds for all faculties and instincts; and it has some definite physiological and chemical corroboration, though of a more crude and less completely established kind than is sometimes imagined. At any rate, this correlation is an unchallenged axiom of those who concern themselves with science: all mental equipment and all mental activity have an organic basis. And that is sufficient for present purposes.

This inseparability of physical and mental must be true also in the field of heredity. It is well known that where instincts are definite or specialized, as in insects, they are inherited as absolutely as are organs or structure. It is a matter of common experience that our own mental traits vary as much and as frequently tally with those of ancestors, as physical features. There is no logical reason, and nothing in the observation of daily life, that operates against the belief that an irascible temper is as heritable as the red hair with which it is traditionally associated, and that certain forms of musical aptitude may be as wholly congenital as blue eyes.

Of course there is much false inference in these matters, as regards man, through the interpretation of accomplishment as evidence of the degree of faculty. The discrimination of the two is not always easy; it frequently requires painstakingly acquired knowledge of facts, as well as careful judgment; and popular reasoning is likely to be scant of both. A powerful congenital faculty may establish the father successfully in a pursuit. This in turn may give an environmental influence, or a deliberate training, that will elevate the mediocre son, so far as his attainments are concerned, far above what his unaided natural faculties would have secured for him, and above many another individual of greater inherent capacities. The earning of a million is normally an indication of ability; but it normally requires intenser ability to earn a million after starting with nothing than to begin with a million received as a gift and increase it to three. That a musician is more frequently the son of a musician than not, at least when relative numbers are taken into account, is in itself no evidence at all that musical talent is heritable, for we know of purely social influences, such as Hindu caste, which attain similar results with far greater regularity than any one can assert heredity plus social influences to bring about among ourselves.

But it would be as unreasonable to exaggerate this caution into an outright denial of mental heredity, as to disregard it entirely.

There is then nothing in an off-hand survey of the situation to lead to a disbelief, and a large body of common experience to confirm the conviction, that characters of mind are subject to heredity much like traits of the body.

In addition, there is some proof, which, although not extensive, is hard to resist. Galton, in a fairly large series of records, has found the amount of regression—a quantitative index of the potency of heredity—to be the same for artistic faculty as for bodily stature. In another work he has investigated the blood relatives of eminent men, with the finding that eminence occurs among them with a frequency and in a degree exactly like the influence of heredity in respect to physical characters. Pearson has ascertained that the correlation—the degree of resemblance, quantitatively expressed, of phenomena available in numbers—between brothers is substantially the same for conscientiousness as for the shape of the head, for intellectual ability as for hair color, and so forth for other mental or moral and physical qualities. There is of course the possibility that in the data that underlie these results, as well as Galton's, there has been some confounding of temper with bad manners, of native intelligence with training of the intellect, of congenital artistic faculty with cultivated taste. But the attention of those who have made the records seems to have been pretty definitely directed to innate individual traits. Further, all the coefficients or figures for the inheritance of these psychic characteristics agree as closely as could be expected with the corresponding ones relating to bodily features. The case may therefore be fairly regarded as substantially proved, at least until new evidence is available.

In spite of a wide acceptance of these demonstrations, especially by those predisposed to sympathize with biological progress, they have also met with some opposition, and with more ignoring than their bearing on a question of general interest warranted. In part this negative attitude may be due to a persistence of religious beliefs, in the main already superseded but not yet defunct, that center around the old concept of the soul, and which see in every linkage of mind and body an effacement of the cherished distinction of body and soul. But this belated conservatism will not account for all the failure of the Galton-Pearson demonstrations to meet universal acceptance or arouse wide enthusiasms.

The remainder of the opposition has been caused by Galton, Pearson, and their adherents themselves, who have not confined themselves to their well-supported conclusions, but have pressed on to further inferences that rest only on assertion. That heredity operates in the domain of mind as well as that of the body, is one thing; that therefore heredity is the mainspring of civilization, is an entirely different proposition, without necessary connection and without established connection with the former conclusion. To maintain both doctrines, the second as a necessary corollary of the first, has been the habit of the biological school; and the consequence has been that those whose intellectual inclinations were otherwise, or who followed another method of research, have avowedly or tacitly rejected both propositions.

The reason why mental heredity has so little if anything to do with civilization, is that civilization is not mental action but a body or stream of products of mental exercise. Mental activity, as biologists have dealt with it, being organic, any demonstration concerning it consequently proves nothing whatever as to social events. Mentality relates to the individual. The social or cultural, on the other hand, is in its essence nonindividual. Civilization, as such, begins only where the individual ends; and whoever does not in some measure perceive this fact, even though only as a brute and rootless one, can find no meaning in civilization, and history for him must be only a wearying jumble, or an opportunity for the exercise of art.

All biology necessarily has this direct reference to the individual. A social mind is as meaningless a nonentity as a social body. There can be only one kind of organicness: the organic on another plane would no longer be organic. The Darwinian doctrine relates, it is true, to the race; but the race, except as an abstraction, is only a collection of individuals; and the bases of this doctrine, heredity, variation, and competition, deal with the relation of individual to individual, from individual, and against individual. The whole key of the success of the Mendelian methods of studying heredity lies in isolating traits and isolating individuals.

But a thousand individuals do not make a society. They are the potential basis of a society; but they do not themselves cause it; and they are also the basis of a thousand other potential societies.

The findings of biology as to heredity, mental and physical alike, may then, in fact must be, accepted without reservation. But that therefore civilization can be understood by psychological analysis, or explained by observations or experiments in heredity, or, to revert to a concrete example, that the destiny of nations can be predicted from an analysis of the organic constitution of their members, assumes that society is merely a collection of individuals; that civilization is only an aggregate of psychic activities and not also an entity beyond them; in short, that the social can be wholly resolved into the mental as it is thought this resolves into the physical.

It is accordingly in this point of the tempting leap from the individually mental to the culturally social which presupposes but does not contain mentality, that the source of the distracting transferences of the organic into the social is to be sought. A more exact examination of the relation of the two is therefore desirable.

In a brilliant essay written, under Pearsonian influence, on heredity in twins, Thorndike arrives anew, and by a convincing use of statistical evidence, at the conclusion that so far as the individual is concerned heredity is everything and environment nothing; that the success of our path in life is essentially determined at birth; that the problem of whether each one of us shall outstrip his fellows or lag behind them, is settled when the parental germ cells unite, and already long closed when the child emerges from the womb, all our careers run under the light of the sun being nothing but an unwinding, longer or shorter according to accident beyond our control, of the thread rolled on the spool before the beginning of our existence.

This finding is not only thoroughly elucidated by the author, but has the support of our common experience in life. No one can deny some measure of truth to the proverbial sow's ear that cannot be made into a silk purse. Every one numbers among his acquaintance individuals of energy, of address and skill, of what seems an uncanny prescience, or of a strength of character, that leave no doubts in our judgment that whatever their lot of birth, they would have risen above their fellows and have been marked men and women. And on the other hand, we also admit regretfully the maladroit and sluggish, the incompetent and commonplace, who, born in any station, would have been of the mediocrities or unfortunates of their time and class. That Napoleon, set in another land and era, would not have conquered a continent, is sufficiently certain. The contrary affirmation may with fairness, it seems, be said to evince an absence of understanding of history. But the belief that under other circumstances this eternal beacon flame might have remained a household lamp, that his forces would never have been called forth. that a slight change of the accidents of epoch, place, or surroundings might have left him a prosperous and contented peasant, a shopkeeper or a bureaucrat, a routine captain retired on a pension—to maintain this argues a lack or a perverted suppression of knowledge of human nature. It is important to realize that congenital differences may have but limited effect on the course of civilization. But it is equally important to realize that we may and must concede the existence of such differences and their inextinguishability.

According to a saying that is almost proverbial, and true to the degree that such commonplaces can be true, the modern schoolboy knows more than Aristotle; but this fact, if a thousand times so, does not in the least endow him with a fraction of the intellect of the great Greek. Socially—because knowledge must be a social circumstance—it is knowledge, and not the greater development of one individual or another, that counts; just as, to measure the true force of the greatness of the person, the psychologist or genetist disregards the state of general enlightenment, the varying degree of civilizational development, to make his comparisons. A hundred Aristotles among our cave-dwelling ancestors would have been Aristotles in their birthright no less; but they would have contributed far less to the advance of the science than a dozen plodding mediocrities in the twentieth century. A super-Archimedes in the ice age would have invented neither firearms nor the telegraph. Bach born in the Congo instead of Saxony could have composed not even a fragment of choral or sonata, though we can be equally confident that he would have outshone his compatriots in some manner of music. Whether or not a Bach ever had birth in Africa, is another question—one to which a negative answer cannot be given merely because no Bach has ever appeared there, a question that in fairness we must admit to be unanswered but in regard to which the student of civilization, until some demonstration has been made, can make but one reply and pursue only one course: to assume, not as an end but as a condition of method, that there have been such individuals; that genius and ability occur with substantially regular frequency, and that all races or large enough groups of men average substantially alike and the same in qualities.

These are extreme cases, whose clearness is little likely to arouse opposition. Normally, the differences between individuals are less imposing, the types of society more similar, and the two elements involved are separable only by the exercise of some discrimination. It is then that the confusions begin. But if the factor of society and that of natal personality are distinct in the glaring examples, they are at least distinguishable in the more subtly shaded and intricate ones; provided only we wish to keep them apart.

If this is true, it follows that all so-called inventors of appliances or discoverers of thoughts of note were unusually able men, endowed from before birth with superior faculties, which the psychologist can hope to analyze and define, the physiologist to correlate with functions of organs, and the genetic biologist to investigate in their hereditary origins until he attains not only system and law but verifiable power of prediction. And, on the other hand, the content of the invention or discovery springs in no way from the make-up of the great man, or that of his ancestors, but is a product purely of the civilization into which he with millions of others is born as a meaningless and regularly recurring event. Whether he in his person becomes inventor, explorer, imitator, or user, is an affair of forces that the sciences of mechanistic causality are concerned with. Whether his invention is that of the cannon or the bow, his achievement a musical scale or a system of harmony, his formulation that of the soul or that of the categorical imperative, is not explainable by the medium of mechanistic science—at least, not by methods now at the command of biological science—but finds its meaning only in such operations with the material of civilization as history and the social sciences are occupied with.

Darwin, whose name has been cited so frequently in the preceding pages, provides a beautiful exemplification of these principles. To deny this great man genius, mental eminence, inherent superiority to the mass of the human herd, would be fatuous. In Galton's famous classification, he would probably attain, by general opinion, at least to grade G, perhaps to the still higher—the highest —grade X. That is, he was an individual born with capacities such as but fourteen, or more likely one, or still fewer, persons in every million possess. In short, he would have towered intellectually above his fellows in any society.

On the other side, no one can sanely believe that the distinction of Darwin's greatest accomplishment, the formulation of the doctrine of evolution by natural selection, would now stand to his credit had he been born fifty years sooner or later. If later, he would have been infallibly anticipated by Wallace, for one thing; by others, if an early death had cut off Wallace. That his restless mind would have evolved something noteworthy is as likely as it is away from the point: the distinction of the particular discovery which he did make, would not have been his. Put on earth by contrary supposition, a half-century earlier, his central idea would not have come to him as it failed to come to his brilliant predecessor, the evolutionist Lamarck. Or, it would have risen in his own mind, as it did in all its essentials in that of Aristotle, only to be discarded as logically possible indeed, but as unworthy of actual consideration. Or, finally, the thought might indeed have germinated and grown in him, but been ignored and forgotten by the world, a mere unfruitful accident, until European civilization was prepared, a few decades later, and hungry as well as prepared, to use it—when its rediscovery and not its barren formal discovery would have been the event of historical significance. That this last possibility is no idle conjecture is evidenced by its actual taking place in the case of one of the greatest of Darwin's contemporaries, his then unknown brother in arms, Gregor Mendel.

It is inconceivable that the independent occurrence of the idea of selection as the motive force of organic evolution, synchronously in the minds of Darwin and Wallace, should have been an affair of pure chance. The immediate acceptance of the idea by the world, proves nothing as to the intrinsic truth of the concept; but it does establish the readiness of the world, that is of the civilization of the time, for the doctrine. And if civilization was prepared and hungry for the doctrine, the enunciation seems to have been destined to come almost precisely when it did come. Darwin carried with himself the germ of the idea of natural selection for twenty long years before he dared put forward the hypothesis which previously he had felt would be received with hostility, and which he must have thought insufficiently armed. It was only the briefer expression of the same insight by Wallace that led Darwin to publicity. Can it be imagined, if Wallace had met death at sea among the Malay islands, and Darwin, unspurred by his competitor colleague's activity, had carried his theory in hesitant privacy a few years longer and then suddenly succumbed to mortal illness, that we of the civilized world of today should have lived all our intellectual lives without a definite mechanism for evolution and therefore without any active employment of the evolutionary idea—that our biologists would be still standing where Linnaeus, Cuvier, or at most Lamarck stood? If so, the great currents of history would be absolutely conditioned by the lodgment or dislodgment of a bacillus in a particular human frame on a certain day; which conviction would certify to as much understanding as we should credit to him, who, finding in the high Andes the ultimate source of the tiny streamlet farthest removed in tortuous miles from the Atlantic ocean, should set his foot in the bubbling spring and believe that so long as he held it there the Amazon ceased to drain a continent and to pour its tide into the sea.

No. Wallace's crowding on Darwin's heels so that his too was a share, though a minor one, of the glory of the discovery, evidences that behind him trod still others, unnamed and perhaps forever themselves unconscious; and that had the leader or his second fallen by one of the innumerable accidents to which individuals are subject, the followers, one or several or many, would have pressed forward, would have been pressed forward, it would be better to say, and done their work—immediately, as history reckons time.

The failure of Mendel's revolutionizing experiments in exact heredity to achieve the least recognition during their author's life, and for years after, has already been alluded to as an instance of the inexorable fate in store for the discoverer who anticipates his time. He is fortunate indeed if he is permitted to live out his lot in obscurity; and to escape the crucifixion which seemed a meet punishment for the first circumnavigator of Africa who saw the sun on his north. It has been said that Mendel's essay, in which are contained most of the vital principles of the branch of science that now bears his name, was published in a remote and little known source, and therefore failed for a generation to come to the notice of biologists. The last assertion may be challenged as unproved and inherently improbable. It is far more likely that biologist after biologist saw the essay, that some even read it, but that, one and all, it remained meaningless to them—not because they were unusually stupid men, but because they lacked the transcendent superiority of the occasional individual to see issues that lie ahead of those with which the world of their day is wrestling. Slowly, however, time rolled on and a change of content of thought was preparing. Darwin himself had been concerned with the origin and nature of variations. When the first shock of overpowering novelty of his central discovery had begun to be assimilated by scientific conscience, this variation question trended to the front. The investigations of De Vries and Bateson, though their recognized outcome seemed only a destructive analysis of one of the pillars of Darwinism, were accumulating knowledge as to the actual operation of heredity. And then suddenly in 1900, with dramatic eclat, three students, independently and "within a few weeks of each other," discovered the discovery of Mendel, confirmed its conclusions with experience of their own, and a new science was launched on a career of splendid fulfillment.

There may be those who see in these pulsing events only a meaningless play of capricious fortuitousness; but there will be others to whom they reveal a glimpse of a great and inspiring inevitability which rises as far above the accidents of personality as the march of the heavens transcends the wavering contacts of random footprints on clouds of earth. Wipe out the perception of De Vries, Correns, and Tschermak, and it is yet clear that before another year had rolled around, the principles of Mendelian heredity would have been proclaimed to an according world, and by six rather than three discerning minds. That Mendel lived in the nineteenth century instead of the twentieth, and published in 1865, is a fact that proved of the greatest and perhaps regrettable influence on his personal fortunes. As a matter of history, his life and discovery are of no more moment, except as a foreshadowing anticipation, than the billions of woes and gratifications, of peaceful citizen lives or bloody deaths, that have been the fate of men. Mendelian heredity does not date from 1865. It was discovered in 1900 because it could have been discovered only then, and because it infallibly must have been discovered then—given the state of European civilization.

The history of inventions is a chain of parallel instances. An examination of patent office records, in any other than a commercial or anecdotic spirit, would alone reveal the inexorability that prevails in the advance of civilization. The right to the monopoly of the manufacture of the telephone was long in litigation; the ultimate decision rested on an interval of hours between the recording of concurrent descriptions by Alexander Bell and Elisha Gray. Though it is part of our vulgar thinking to dismiss such conflicts as evidences of unscrupulous cupidity and legal inadequacy or as melodramatic coincidence, it behooves the historian to see beyond such childlike plays of the intellect.

The discovery of oxygen is credited to both Priestley and Scheele; its liquefaction to Cailletet as well as to Pictet whose results were attained in the same month of 1877 and announced in one session. Kant as well as La Place can lay claim to the promulgation of the nebular hypothesis. Neptune was predicted by Adams and by Leverrier; the computation of the one, and the publication of that of the other, had precedence by a few months.

For the invention of the steamboat, glory is claimed by their countrymen or partisans for Fulton, Jouffroy, Rumsey, Stevens, Symmington, and others; of the telegraph, for Steinheil and Morse; in photography Talbot was the rival of Daguerre and Niepce. The doubly flanged rail devised by Stevens was reinvented by Vignolet. Aluminum was first practically reduced by the processes of Hall, Heroult, and Cowles. Leibnitz in 1684 as well as Newton in 1687 formulated calculus. Anaesthetics, both ether and nitrous oxide, were discovered in 1845 and 1846, by no less than four men of one nationality. So independent were their achievements, so similar even in details and so closely contemporaneous, that polemics, lawsuits, and political agitation ensued for many years, and there was not one of the four but whose career was embittered, if not ruined, by the animosities arising from the indistinguishability of the priority. Even the south pole, never before trodden by the foot of human beings, was at last reached twice in one summer.

A volume could be written, with but few years' toil, filled with endlessly repeating but ever new accumulation of such instances. When we cease to look upon invention or discovery as some mysterious inherent faculty of individual minds which are randomly dropped in space and time by fate; when we center our attention on the plainer relation of one such advancing step to the others; when, in short, interest shifts from individually biographic elements—which can be only dramatically artistic, didactically moralizing, or psychologically interpretable—and attaches whole heartedly to the social or civilizational, evidence on this point will be infinite in quantity, and the presence of majestic forces or sequences pervading civilization will be irresistibly evident.

Knowing the civilization of an age and a land, we can then substantially affirm that its distinctive discoveries, in this or that field of activity, were not directly contingent upon the personality of the actual inventors that graced the period, but would have been made without them; and that, conversely, had the great illuminating minds of other centuries and climates been born in the civilization referred to, instead of their own, its first achievements would probably have fallen to their lot. Ericsson or Galvani eight thousand years ago might have polished or bored the first stone; and in turn the hand and mind whose operation set in inception the neolithic age of human culture, would, if held in its infancy in unchanging catalepsy from that time until today, now be devising wireless telephones and nitrogen extractors.

Some reservations must be admitted to this principle. It is far from established, rather the contrary, that extraordinary ability, however equal in intensity, is identical in direction. It is highly unlikely that Beethoven put in Newton's cradle would have worked out calculus, or the latter have given the symphony its final form. We can and evidently must admit congenital faculties that are fairly specialized. Everything shows that the elementary mental faculties such as memory, interest, and abstraction, are by nature uneven in individuals of equivalent ability but distinctive bent; and this in spite of cultivation. The educator who proclaimed his ability to convert a native memory for absolute numbers or for mathematical formulas into an equally strong retention of single tones or of complex melodies, would be distrusted. But it does not essentially matter if the originating faculty is one or several in mind. If Eli Whitney could not have formulated the difference between the subjective and the objective and Kant in his place would have failed to devise a practical cotton gin, Watt or Fulton or Morse or Stephenson could in the place of the former, have accomplished his achievement, and Aristotle or Aquinas the task of the latter. It is possibly not even quite accurate to maintain that the individualities of the unknown inventor or inventors of the bow and arrow and those of firearms could have been interchanged, for the first production of the bow necessarily involved mechanical and even manual faculty, while the discovery of gunpowder and of its applicability to weapons may have required the different ability to perceive certain peculiar qualities of a more highly dynamic or chemical nature.

In short, it is a debatable point, though one of the greatest psychological interest, how far human faculty is divisible and subdivisible into distinct kinds. But the matter is not vital in the present connection, for there will hardly be any one rash enough to maintain that there exist as many distinguishable faculties as there are separate human beings; which in fact would be to assert that abilities do not differ in intensity or degree but only in direction or kind; in short, that while no two men were alike, all were equal in potential capacity. If this view is not correct, then it matters little whether the kinds of ability are several or many, because in any case they will be very few compared with the endless number of human organisms; because there will accordingly be so many individuals possessing each faculty, that every age must contain persons with low and mediocre and high measure of intensity of each; and the extraordinary men of one sort in one period will therefore still be substitutable for those of another time in the manner indicated.

If, therefore, anyone's interpretation of mentality is disturbed by some of the particular equivalences that have been suggested, he can easily find others that seem more just, without dissenting from the underlying principle that the march of history, or as it is current custom to name it, the progress of civilization, is independent of the birth of particular personalities; since these apparently averaging substantially alike, both as regards genius and normality, at all times and places, furnish the same substratum for the social.

Here, then, we have an interpretation which allows to the individual, and through him to heredity, all that the science of the organic can legitimately claim on the strength of its actual accomplishments; and which also yields the fullest scope to the social in its own distinctive field. The accomplishment of the individual measured against other individuals depends, if not wholly then mainly, on his organic constitution as compounded by his heredity. The accomplishments of a group, relative to other groups, are little or not influenced by heredity because sufficiently large groups average much alike in organic makeup.

This identity of average is incontestable for some instances of the same nations in closely successive ages—as Athens in 550 and 450, or Germany in 1800 and 1900—during which brief periods their hereditary composition could not have altered to a small fraction of the degree in which cultural achievement varied; it is certainly probable even for people of the same blood separated by long intervals of time and wide divergences of civilization; and it is, while neither proved nor disproved, likely to be nearly true, as suggested before, for the most distant races.

The difference between the accomplishments of one group of men and those of another group is therefore of another order from the difference between the faculties of one person and another. It is through this distinction that one of the essential qualities of the nature of the social is to be found.

The physiological and the mental are bonded as aspects of the same thing, one resolvable into the other; the social is, directly considered, not resolvable into the mental. That it exists only after mentality of a certain kind is in action, has led to confusion of the two, and even their identification. The error of this identification, is a fault that tends to pervade modern thinking about civilization, and which must be overcome by self-discipline before our understanding of this order of phenomena that fill and color our lives can become either clear or serviceable.

If the relation of the individual to culture here outlined is a true one, a conflicting view sometimes held and already alluded to, is unentertainable. This view is the opinion that all personalities are, while not identical, potentially equal in capacity, their varying degrees of accomplishment being due solely to different measures of accord with the social environment with which they are in touch. This view has perhaps been rarely formulated as a generic principle; but it seems to underlie, though usually vaguely and by implication only, many tendencies toward social and educational reform, and is therefore likely to find formal enunciation at some time.

This assumption, which would certainly be of extensive practical application if it could be verified, seems to rest ultimately on a dim but profound perception of the influence of civilization. More completely though this influence of civilization is upon national fortunes than upon individual careers, it nevertheless must influence these latter also. Mohammedanism—a social phenomenon—in stifling the imitative possibilities of the pictorial and plastic arts, has obviously affected the civilization of many peoples; but it must also have altered the careers of many persons born in three continents during a thousand years. Special talents which these men and women possessed for delineative representation may have been suppressed without equal compensation in other directions, in those whose endowment was unique. Of such individuals it is true that the social forces to which they were subject depressed each of them from successful attainment to more mediocre. And without question the same environment elevated many an individual to high rank above his fellows whose special abilities, in some other age and country, would have been repressed to his private disadvantage. The personality born with those qualities that lead to highly successful leadership of religious brigands, for instance, is undoubtedly assured of a more prosperous and contented career in Morocco than in Holland of today.

Even within one nationally limited sphere of civilization, similar results are necessarily bound to occur. The natural logician or administrator born into a caste of fisherman or street sweepers is not likely to achieve the satisfaction in life, and certainly not the success, that would have been his lot had his parents been Brahmins or Kshatriyas; and what is true formally of India holds substantially for Europe.

But, that a social environment may somewhat affect the fortunes and career of the individual as measured against other individuals, does not prove that the individual is wholly the product of circumstances outside of himself, any more than the opposite is true that a civilization is only the sum total of the products of a group of organically shaped minds. The concrete effect of each individual upon civilization is determined by civilization itself. Civilization appears even in some cases and in some measure to influence the effect of the individual's native activities upon himself. But to proceed from these realizations to the inference that all the degree and quality of accomplishment by the individual is the result of his moulding by the society that encompasses him, is assumption, extreme at that, and at variance with observation.

Therefore it is possible to hold the historical or civilizational interpretation of social phenomena without proceeding to occupy the position that the human beings that are the given channels through which civilization courses, are only and wholly the products of its stream. Because culture rests on the specific human faculty, it does not follow that this faculty, the thing in man that is supra-animal, is of social determination. The line between the social and the organic may not be randomly or hastily drawn. The threshold between the endowment that renders the flow and continuance of civilization possible and that which prohibits even its inception, is the demarcation—doubtful enough once, in all probability, but gaping for a longer period than our knowledge covers—between the social itself, however, the entity that we call civilization, and the non-social, the pre-social or organic, is the diversity of quality or order which exists between animal and man conjointly on the one hand, and the products of the interactions of human beings on the other. In the previous pages the mental has already been subtracted from the social and added to the physically organic which is subject to the influence of heredity. In the same way it is necessary to eliminate the factor of individual capacity from the consideration of civilization. But this elimination means its transfer to the group of organically conceivable phenomena, not its denial. In fact nothing is further from the path of a just prosecution of the understanding of history than such a negation of differences of degree of the faculties of individual men.

In short, social science, if we may take that word as equivalent to history, does not deny individuality any more than it denies the individual. It does refuse to deal with either individuality or individual as such. And it bases this refusal solely on denial of the validity of either factor for the achievement of its proper aims.

It is true that historical events can also be viewed mechanically, and expressed ultimately in terms of physics and chemistry. Genius may prove definable in unit characters or the constitution of chromosomes, and its particular achievements in osmotic or electric reactions of nerve cells. The day may come when what took place in the tissue of Darwin's brain when he first thought the concept of natural selection, can be profitably studied, or even approximately ascertained, by the physiologist and chemist. Such an achievement, destructive as it may seem to those whom revelation appeals, would be not only defensible but of enormous interest, and possibly of utility. Only, it would not be history; nor a step toward history or social science.

To know the precise reactions in Darwin's nervous system at the moment when the thought of natural selection flashed upon him in 1838, would involve a genuine triumph of science. But it would mean nothing historically, since history is concerned with the relation of doctrines such as that of natural selection to other concepts and social phenomena, and not with the relation of Darwin himself to social phenomena or other phenomena. This is not the current view of history; but, on the other hand, the current view rests on the endlessly recurring but obviously illogical assumption that because without individuals civilization could not exist, civilization therefore is only a sum total of the psychic operations of a mass of individuals.

As, then, there are two lines of intellectual endeavor in history and in science, each with its separate aim and set of methods; so also two wholly disparate evolutions must be recognized: that of the substance which we call organic and that of the phenomena called social. Social evolution is without antecedents in the beginnings of organic evolution. It commences late in the development of life—long after vertebrates, after mammals, after the primates even, are established. Its exact point of origin we do not know, and perhaps shall never know; but we can limit the range within which it falls. This origin occurred in a series of organic forms more advanced, in general mental faculty, than the gorilla, and much less developed than the first known race that is unanimously accepted as having been human, the man of Neanderthal and Le Moustier. In point of time, these first carriers of the rudiments of civilization must antedate the Neanderthal race by far, but must be posterior to other extinct human ancestors of the approximate intellectual level of the modern gorilla and chimpanzee.

The beginning of social evolution, of the civilization which is the subject of history, thus coincides with that of mystery of the popular mind: the missing link. But the term "link" is misleading. It implies a continuous chain. But with the unknown bearers of the primeval and gradually manifesting beginnings of civilization, there took place a profound alteration rather than an improved passing of the existing. A new factor has arisen which was to work out its own independent consequences, slowly and of little apparent import at first, but gathering weight, and dignity, and influence; a factor that had passed beyond natural selection, that was no longer wholly dependent on any agency of organic evolution, and that, however rocked and swayed by the oscillations of the heredity that underlay it, nevertheless floated unimmersibly upon it.

The dawn of the social thus is not a link in a chain, not a step in a path, but a leap to another plane. It may be likened to the first occurrence of life in the hitherto lifeless universe, the hour when that one of infinite chemical combinations took place which put the organic into existence, and made it that from this moment on there should be two worlds in place of one. Atomic qualities and movements were not interfered with when that seemingly slight event took place; the majesty of the mechanical laws of the cosmos was not diminished; but something new was inextinguishably added to the history of this planet.

One might compare the inception of civilization to the end of the process of slowly heating water. The expansion of the liquid goes on a long time. Its alteration can be observed by the thermometer as well as in bulk, in its solvent power as well as in its internal agitation. But it remains water. Finally, however, the boiling point is attained. Steam is produced: the rate of enlargement of volume is increased a thousand fold; and in place of a glistening, percolating fluid, a volatile gas diffuses invisibly. Neither the laws of physics nor those of chemistry are violated; nature is not set aside, but yet a saltation has taken place: the slow transitions that accumulated from zero to one hundred have been transcended in an instant, and a condition of substance with new properties and new possibilities of effect is in existence.

Such, in some manner, must have been the result of the appearance of this new thing, civilization. We need not consider that it abolished the course of development of life. It certainly has not in any measure done away with its own substratum of the organic. And there is no reason to believe that it was born full fledged. All these incidents and manners of the inception of the social are after all of little consequence to an understanding of its specific nature, and of the relation of that nature to the character of the organic substance that preceded in absolute time and still supports it. The point is, there was an addition of something new in kind, an initiation of that which was to run a course of its own.

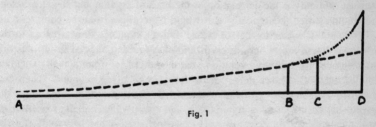

Fig. 1

We may sketch the relation which exists between the evolutions of the organic and of the social (fig. I). A line progressing with the flow of time, rises slowly, but gatheringly. At a certain point, another line begins to diverge from it, insensibly at first, but ascending ever farther above it on its own course; until, at the moment where the curtain of the present cuts off our view, each is advancing, but far from the other, and uninfluenced by it.

In this illustration, the continuous line denotes the level inorganic; the broken line, the evolution of the organic; the line of dots, the development of civilization. Height above the base is degree of advancement, whether that be complexity, heterogeneity, degree of coördination, or anything else. A is the beginning of time on this earth as revealed to our understandings. B marks the point of the true missing link, of the first human precursor, the first animal that carried and accumulated tradition. C would denote the state reached by what we are accustomed to call primitive man, that Neanderthal *homo* who was our forefather in culture if not in blood; and D, the present moment.

It is inevitable that if there is foundation for the contentions that have been set forth, an arguing from one of these lines to the other must be futile. To assert, because the upper line has risen rapidly just before it is cut off, that the one below it must also have ascended proportionally more in this period than in any before, is obviously uncompelling. That our institutions, our knowledge, the exercising of our minds, have advanced dizzyingly in twenty thousand years is no reason that our bodies and brains, our mental equipment and its physiological basis, have advanced in any corresponding measure as is sometimes argued by scientists and generally taken for granted by men at large. If anything, it might be an evidence that the lower, organic line has fallen off in its rate of ascent. The bodies and minds in this line have continued to carry civilization; but this civilization has met the struggle of the world in such a way that much of the stress has been directed away from these bodies and minds. We do not argue that the progress of organic evolution is *prima facie* indication that inorganic matter is more complex, more advanced in its combinations, or in any sense "higher," than it was fifty million years ago; much less that organic evolution has taken place through an inorganic evolution as cause. And no more can we infer from social development to a progress of the hereditary forms of life.

In fact, not only is the correlation of the lines of organic and social development as unjustified theoretically as it would be to argue from the compressibility or weight of water to that of steam; but all evidence directs us as to the conviction that in recent periods civilization has raced at a speed so far outstripping the pace of hereditary evolution, that the latter has, if not actually standing still, afforded all the seeming, relatively, of making no progress. There are a hundred elements of civilization where there was one in the time when the Neanderthal skull enclosed a living brain; and not only the content of civilization but the complexity of its organization has increased a hundred-fold. But the body and the associated mind of that early man have not attained a point a hundred times, nor even twice, as fine, as efficient, as delicate, or as strong, as they were then; it is doubtful if they have improved by a fifth. There are, it is true, those who make the contrary assertion. Yet it seems the fair-minded must avow that such assertions rest not on objective interpretation of the facts, but on a wish to find a correlation, a desire to make the thread of evolution a single, unbranching one, to see the social only as organic.

Here, then, we have to come to our conclusion; and here we rest. The mind and the body are but facets of the same organic material or activity; the social substance—or unsubstantial fabric, if one prefers the phrase—the thing that we call civilization, transcends them for all its being rooted in life. The processes of civilizational activity are almost unknown to us. The factors that govern their workings are unresolved. The forces and principles of mechanistic science can indeed analyze our civilization; but in so doing they destroy its essence, and leave us without understanding of the very thing which we seek. The historian as yet can do little but picture. He traces and he connects what seems far removed; he balances; he integrates; but he does not really explain, nor does he transmute phenomena into something else. His method is not mechanistic; but neither can the physicist or physiologist deal with historical material and leave it to civilization nor convert it into concepts of life and leave nothing else to be done. What we all are able to do is to realize this gap, to be impressed by it with humility, and to go our paths on its respective sides without self-deluding boasts that the chasm has been bridged.

WHAT INFORMED SPECULATION CAN DO. CARVETH READ, UTTERLY NEGLECTED AND FORGOTTEN, BUT WHOSE IDEAS HAVE BEEN COMPLETELY CONFIRMED FIFTY YEARS LATER

CARVETH READ (1848-1931), English logician and philosopher, was Professor of Philosophy at University College, London for many years until 1922. His principal interest, however, was anthropology, a subject on which he wrote many excellent papers, and a delightful book, *The Origin of Man and His Superstitions* (Cambridge University Press, 1920). In 1925 this was enlarged and published in two separate volumes, *Man and His Superstitions* and *The Origin of Man.* The latter volume formed the first part of the original 1920 volume, and while this first part was appreciably enlarged to form *The Origin of Man,* all the ideas are present in the 1920 version.

Read recognized the crucial role of the adoption of meat-eating and the hunting activities this necessitated as the major factor in the differentiation of man from the apes. Once an ape begins hunting, the adaptive advantages are all with those who can stalk and run bipedally, who can manufacture implements with which to bring down the quarry at a distance, make snares, communicate with his fellow hunters over a distance by chopped up segments of sounds upon which conventionalized meanings have been imposed, and develop an ability for rapid problem-solving—in short, all those traits that make a primate human.[1] Read discusses all these traits, and even in the matter of the period at which man differentiated he gets incredibly nearer the correct age than did any anthropologist up to a few years ago. In passing it is also worthy of note that Read saw how unsatisfactory the phrase "the survival of the fittest" was, and how it served to convey the wrong idea about the process of natural selection. It is, of course, "the survival of the fit," not "the fittest," that more accurately describes that process, for should conditions rapidly change the "fittest" are left high and dry, while those who have retained a certain plasticity are more likely to be able to adjust to the changed conditions than the overspecialized.

As a professional logician and philosopher with a beautifully acute mind,[2] Read was not afraid of drawing inferences from the facts, and constructing the necessary hypotheses. In section three of his first chapter reprinted here, he discusses this matter in a manner which I hope will encourage the reader to go out to his book.

AN HYPOTHESIS CONCERNING OUR ORIGIN*

§1. MAN WAS DIFFERENTIATED FROM THE ANTHROPOIDS BY BECOMING A HUNTER

That the human species, as we now see it, with its several races, Mongolian, Negro, Mediterranean, represents a Family of the Primates is generally agreed; and there is evidence that the Family formerly comprised other species that have become extinct. Our nearest surviving zoological relatives are the gorilla and chimpanzee, the orang and (at a still further remove) the siamang and gibbons; and in spite of the fundamental anatomical resemblance between those

[1] See Ashley Montagu, *The Human Revolution* (New York, Bantam Books, 1967); William S. Laughlin, "Hunting: An Integrating Biobehavior System and Its Evolutionary Importance," in *Man the Hunter*, ed. Richard B. Lee and Irven DeVore (Chicago, Aldine Publishing Co., 1968), pp. 304-320.

[2] See his *Logic: Inductive and Deductive* (London, Black, 1920); *The Metaphysics of Nature* (London, Black, 1906); *Natural and Social Morals* (London, Black, 1909).

*From Carveth Read, *The Origin of Man* (Cambridge University Press, 1925), pp. 1-10. Reprinted by permission of Cambridge University Press.

apes and ourselves, our differences from them are so great that we cannot wonder at the incredulity with which the doctrine of our consanguinity was first received. Even A. R. Wallace thought that the descent of the *Hominidae* could not be explained by natural causes; yet we cannot regard our existence as a sort of miracle.

It is the differences between Man and his nearest relatives that have to be accounted for; by derivation from a common stock only his resemblance to them can be understood: heredity explains his nature only in so far as he is an ape. The differences in detail are, indeed, innumerable; but taking the chief of them, and assuming that minor characters are correlated with these, it is the argument of this essay that they may all be traced to the predominating influence of one variation operating amongst the original anthropoid conditions. I do not deny that other causes may have co-operated, but propose to consider how far that one will carry us toward an explanation of the facts, namely, all that we know of the characteristic physical and moral nature of Man. The determining variation was the adoption of a flesh diet and the habits of a hunter in order to obtain it. Without the adoption of a flesh diet there could have been no hunting; but a flesh diet obtained without hunting (supposing it possible) could have done nothing for the evolution of our Family. The adoption of the hunting life, therefore, was the essential change upon which everything else depended. We need not suppose that a whole ancestral species varied in this way; it may have been enough that a few of the common anthropoid stock should do so, provided that the variation was advantageous and was inherited.

Such a change from the frugivorous to the hunting life must have occurred at some time, since Man is everywhere more or less carnivorous, and agriculture is a comparatively recent discovery; the earliest known men were hunters; weapons are amongst the earliest known artifacts. And it is not improbable that the change began at the anthropoid level; because, although extant anthropoids are mainly frugivorous, yet they occasionally eat birds' eggs and young birds; the gorilla is said to eat small mammals, and in confinement they all readily take flesh-food; whilst other Primates (*Cebidae,* macaques and baboons) eat insects, arachnids, worms, frogs, lizards, birds; and the crab-eating macaque (*M. cynomolgus*) collects a large portion of its food upon the Malay littoral. Why, then, should not one ape have betaken itself to hunting? Variety of diet, moreover, is not peculiar to the Primates: it is found in other Orders—marsupials, bats, rodents; whilst amongst carnivora the bears are nearly all omnivorous—the Arctic bear feeding chiefly on seals, porpoises and fish, the grizzly and the American black bear being extensively carnivorous but also consuming a good deal of vegetable food, the brown bear in its many varieties adapting its diet to the region in which it lives, and the Indian sloth bear *(Melursus)* confining itself to fruit, insects and honey.

We are not to suppose that our early ancestors became at once exclusively carnivorous: so sudden a change might have put too great a strain on their digestive economy. Even amongst hunting tribes a mixed diet is the rule; and everywhere the women collect and consume fruits and roots. But if at first omnivorous, our ancestor (I conjecture) soon preferred to attack mammals and advanced at a remote date to the killing of the biggest game found in his habitat. Everywhere savage hunters do so now: the little Semang kills the tiger, rhinoceros, elephant and buffalo; and thousands of years ago, in Europe, men slew the reindeer and mammoth, the horse and the bison, the hyaena and the cave-bear. It is true they had weapons and snares, whilst the first hunters had only hands and teeth. These however were formidable weapons of aggression; and their power must have greatly increased if a number of apes cooperated in the chase, forming a hunting-pack, as a sort of wolf-ape (Lycopithecus).

In a friendly communication it has been said that the great difficulty of the above hypothesis lies at the beginning of the adventure, in the first change of the feeding habit and the good success of it. I admit this. The gait of a gorilla or chimpanzee upon the ground (the orang is still more arboreal) is an awkward shuffle in which they help themselves along with their long arms; in open forest they move faster, swinging themselves forward by the lower boughs of trees. But neither plan is well adapted to hunting. Upper Oligocene (if our differentiation began then) had just the same mode of progression on the ground as those now extant; but these supply the only clue to their habit; and if it was somewhat similar, they were not at such a disadvantage with their contemporaries as they would be if they had to contend with the herbivora and carnivora of our day. For, according to Prof. Osborne, animals of the Lower Miocene, both herbivora and carnivora, were clumsy and slow-moving[1]. The average pace of the Mammalia, herbivores, carnivores and ourselves, has greatly improved during the last two or three million years: a natural result of competition. Again, what we know of the anthropoid style of fighting suggests that it is a poor preparation for attacking prey. Mr. Hornaday says that orangs in captivity are quarrelsome and, when fighting, try (1) to seize and bite an adversary's fingers, (2) attack his face and try to bite his lips[2]. Similarly, the chimpanzee, fighting with a leopard, tries to seize its paws and bite the claws off. If our progenitor naturally fought in this way, he must have adopted some other plan in attacking (say) one of the primitive hornless deer—must have found the throat or spine; but this he may have learnt in capturing smaller prey. It is not improbable that the adventure of hunting for animal food was attempted more than once by Primates and failed, but once, in a happy conjuncture of circumstances, was successful.

The change from a fruit-eating to a hunting life, subserved the great utility of opening fresh supplies of food; and possibly a shortage in the normal supply of the old customary diet was the immediate occasion of the new habit. If

[1] The Age of Mammals, p. 249.
[2] Mind and Manners of Wild Animals, p. 272.

our ape lived near the northern limits of the tropical forest and a fall of temperature there took place, such as to reduce (especially in winter) the yield of fruit and other nutritious vegetation on which he had mainly subsisted, famine may have driven him more frequently to attack other animals[3]; whilst more southerly anthropoids, not suffering from the change of climate, continued in their ancient manner of life. In Central Europe, during the Miocene period, the climate altered from subtropical to temperate with corresponding changes in fauna and flora; hence it formerly occurred to me that perhaps the decisive change in the life of our Family occurred there and then. Good judges, however, put the probable date of the great differentiation much earlier, in the Oligocene[1]. Indeed the occurrence of a chimpanzee (*Dryopithecus*) in a Miocene formation of Europe may be held to indicate that the anthropoid stock had already broken up. But in the Oligocene I cannot find that any extensive change of climate has been detected. As, however, not much is known of

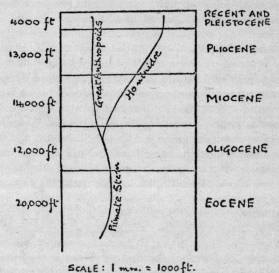

SCALE : 1 mm. = 1000 ft.

[3]Suggested to me by Mr. G. A. Garfitt.

[1]Estimated duration of the Cainozoic Period, assuming that the thickness of the deposits is about 63,000 feet, and that deposits accumulate at the rate of 1 foot in 100 years. Drawn to the scale of 1 mm. to 100,000 years. The estimate is given and explained by Prof. Sollas in the *Quarterly Journal of the Geological Society* (1909), LXV. The "tree" is based on that given by Sir A. Keith in *The Antiquity of Man*, p. 509.

If we suppose the differentiation of the *Hominidae* to have begun before the close of the Oligocene, about (say) 3,500,000 years are allowed for the evolution of the existing species of Man. All these reckonings are provisional.

the condition of Central Asia at that time, it is possible that a considerable elevation of land took place there. The Himalayas, indeed, attained their present elevation only in the Pliocene; but the area had been rising for a very long time; and if it reached in the Oligocene the height of only five or six thousand feet, that may have sufficed to reduce in the area affected the supply of the customary anthropoid food so far as to make hunting a profitable or necessary alternative.

Awaiting adequate evidence for such conjectures, there remains, in the last resort, "spontaneous" variation: that is to say, from causes which are at present beyond our knowledge, the fateful ape did in fact prefer animal food so decisively as to begin the hunting for it. That being granted, the rest of the history was inevitable. The new pursuit was of a nature to engross the animal's whole attention and coordinate all his faculties; and to maintain and reinforce it, his structure in body and mind may reasonably be supposed to have undergone rapid modification by natural selection; because those individuals that were in any organ or faculty adapted to the new life had an advantage which might be inherited and gradually increased[1].

§2. NATURAL SELECTION

Having thus appealed to the principle of natural selection as controlling the evolution of Man, I must explain what is to be understood by it. In the first place, it has nothing to do with the causes of variation. Much interesting and instructive work has been done by Biologists upon the structure of cytoplasm and the possible results of combination and recombination among its constituents, chromosomes and genes, and upon the conditions which increase or decrease variation in resulting generations. But that in some way variations occur is here assumed, and we are concerned only with what happens to them afterwards. Nor do the Mendelian laws of inheritance affect this problem; for

---

[1]That Man was from the first a hunter has been suggested by several authors; but the consequences of the assumption have never (as far as I know) been worked out. A. R. Wallace, in *Darwinism*, p. 459, has the following passage: "The anthropoid apes, as well as most of the monkey tribe, are essentially arboreal in their structure, whereas the great distinctive character of man is his special adaptation to terrestrial locomotion. We can hardly suppose, therefore, that he originated in a forest region, where fruits to be obtained by climbing are the chief vegetable food. It is more probable that he began his existence on the open plains on high plateaux of the temperate or sub-tropical zone, where the seeds of indigenous cereals, numerous herbivora, rodents, game-birds, with fishes and molluscs in the lakes and rivers and seas supplied him with an abundance of varied food. In such a region he would develop skill as a hunter, trapper or fisherman, and later as a herdsman and cultivator—a succession of which we find indications in the palaeolithic and neolithic races of Europe."

Prof. MacBride, in his popular introduction to *Zoology*, p. 84, also traces the specialisation of Man to the hunting life.

My friend Mr. Thomas Whittaker has sent me the following extract from Comte's *Politique Positive*, I, pp. 604-5: "L'obligation de se nourrir d'une proie qu'il faut atteindre et vaincre, perfectionne à la fois tous les attributs animaux, tant intérieurs qu'extérieurs. Son influence envers

in whatever way an animal is constituted by inheritance, having been born it must either live or die; and it is with this alternative that natural selection is concerned. If the animal is not sufficiently adapted to the conditions of life, interuterine, natal and environmental, climatic or biological, to live at least until the age of propagation, it must die without offspring: it is eliminated.

But it has been urged that the condition of such elimination is not well expressed by the phrase "survival of the fittest." Not only the fittest but many less fit can, and do, normally survive; for that they need only reach a certain standard of fitness. So much is plainly true. What shall be the standard of the least unfit, however, must depend upon the severity of the conditions of life, competition for food and mates, self-maintenance against enemies, rivals, disease and whatever else may be inimical to their welfare. After such a change of life as I have supposed on the part of our ancestral ape, the struggle probably was very severe, and the standard of fitness was very high.

Further, it has been urged that many characters that seem to us very important in the classification of animals, or in the determination of human races, cannot be shown to have any survival value, and therefore cannot be explained by natural selection; and this also seems to be true. What adaptation is involved in the distinction between long-heads and round-heads, upon which Anthropologists have done so much careful statistical work? What survival value can be assigned to the Negro's heel, or to the Kalmuck's slanting eye, or to the remarkable differences in the hair-section of our conspicuous races? But it is not with such characters that we have to do in explaining the adaptation of Man to the life of a hunter. Consider the erect gait, the modification of legs and feet, of arms and hands, social life, language, intelligence, the discipline of the pack. These are the things that I attribute to natural selection; and will anyone deny that they are adaptations to the hunting-life of Man and conditions of all his development?

---

les sens et les muscles est trop évidente pour exiger ici aucun examen. Par sa réaction habituelle sur les plus hautes fonctions du cerveau, elle développe également l'intelligence et l'activité, dont le premier essor lui est toujours dû, même chez notre espèce. A tous ces titres, cette nécessité modifie aussi les races qui en sont victimes, d'après les efforts moins énergiques, mais plus continus, qu'elle y provoque pour leur défense. Dans les deux cas, et surtout quant à l'attaque, elle détermine même les premières habitudes de co-opération active, au moins temporaire. Bornées à la simple famille chez les espèces insociables, ces ligues peuvent ailleurs embrasser quelquefois de nombreuses troupes. Ainsi commencent, parmi les animaux, des impulsions et des aptitudes qui ne pouvaient se développer que d'après la continuité propre à la race la plus sociable et la plus intelligente. Enfin, la condition carnassière doit aussi être appreciée dans sa réaction organique. Une plus forte excitation, une digestion moins laborieuse et plus rapide, une assimilation plus complète produisant un sang plus stimulant: telles sont ses propriétés physiologiques. Toutes concourent à développer les fonctions supérieures, soit en augmentant l'énergie de leurs organes, soit en procurant plus de temps pour leur exercice."

For the views of Mr. Ch. Morris in *Man and His Ancestors* (New York, 1900) see the Preface to this edition.

§3. An hypothesis is an inference from the facts it is presented to explain. Hypothetical reasoning is almost universal in science and very common in every-day life; yet it is often regarded with a dull suspicion that can only result from misunderstanding. The form of such reasoning seems to be deductive; the hypothesis is stated, and the facts seem to be inferred from it; and our frequent resort to this mode of stating a case led Whewell to remark that "Man is prone to become a deductive thinker." But the truth is that the argument is inductive: the form of statement turns the psychology of it upside down; for the argument really is that the hypothesis may be inferred from the facts. What usually (perhaps always) happens, I believe, is that one or a few facts may suggest a common cause, or schema, as their explanation; then this explanation is constituted an hypothesis, and one goes on to show how, if true, it will lead to all the given facts and to as many others as possible within the sphere of investigation. But in saying that a few facts suggest a common cause, we mean that this cause may be inferred from them; and, extending it to more and more facts, we mean that it may be inferred from them also. The facts from which this hunting hypothesis were first inferred by me were the modification of our legs and arms from those of the simian type, the upright gait, intelligence, social organization (like that of wolves) and freedom of movement beyond the tropical forest[1]. These changes are such as might be expected to follow if an anthropoid ape should have become a hunter. Then, assuming that one did so, certain other changes (as below) may be deduced; that is to say, from these further changes also the original hunting life may be inferred.

Since each of these inferences is from an effect to a possible cause, none of them is conclusive. When an effect is conceived in a general way, it often happens that it may be explained by more than one cause. But each inference raises some probability in favour of the cause, and as one instance is added to another the probability increases; and at the same time the probability that any other cause would explain all the facts equally well grows less and less. As we cannot attach any numerical values to the probabilities severally, we cannot exactly estimate their value altogether. Each reader must make his own estimate as best he can. For my part I think the total probability may fairly be put at more than a half.

It is a great advantage in verifying an hypothesis when other hypotheses to the same purpose have been advanced, and it is possible to refute them; for it may then appear that not only is the hypothesis in some degree probable, but that, as the alternatives go down one by one, it is probably the only valid one. But in the present case no such help is offered; for (as far as I know) there is no other hypothesis (limited to the natural order) that attempts to explain how the human race came to exist.

[1] *Metaphysics of Nature*, ch. xv, §3.

To refute the argument one may show (1) that the hypothesis cannot be inferred with any probability from this, that and the other stated fact; (2) that there are other differences between ourselves and the anthropoids (of equal weight with those I mention) from which the hypothesis cannot be inferred; (3) that some change other than the adoption of the hunting life, would, in the conditions of some anthropoid's life, explain all the facts equally well or better. I invite attention to these considerations.

If the problem of the causes of our differentiation is to be dealt with at all, there is no other method at our command except such an accumulation of probable inferences from the known facts of our present condition in comparison with that of the apes. The subject is not open to observation or experiment. It has been said that the true method is to compare all that we know of primitive Man, fossil Man and so forth. I have taken account of these things so far as they throw any light upon the inquiry; but consider how little we know of fossil Man and his congeners. Suppose we found in the later Miocene a complete skeleton of a Primate with human-like characters: it would be a new species; no one could be confident that it stood in the line of our ancestry. Suppose we should find a complete series of skeletons, one for every 200,000 years from the end of the Pliocene back to the Oligocene, and that experts should agree that they represented the "orthogenic" evolution of *Homo sapiens*: we should hardly be any nearer a solution of our present problem. For the remains would not show the conditions under which the differentiation began and was maintained, but would merely add to the data upon which an hypothesis might be constructed. In short nothing can be done in the matter except by thinking, by trying to think what is most probably indicated by all the facts within our knowledge. The leaders of scientific investigation do not shrink (I observe) from thinking courageously or even audaciously. But a good many people, relying too much on their own experience, adopt the sentiment of that mighty verse:

Thinking is but an idle waste of thought.

W. H. R. RIVERS ON THE PSYCHOLOGICAL "GIVING-UP" SYNDROME AS A FACTOR IN THE DEPOPULATION OF ABORIGINAL PEOPLES

WHEN white peoples enter into permanent contact with aboriginal peoples, it has been repeatedly observed that there is a sudden and precipitate fall in the aboriginal birthrate. This had first become evident to William Halse Rivers (1864-1922), the English anthropologist, during his visits to Melanesia in 1908 and 1914. Rivers' sudden death at the early age of fifty-eight was a great loss, for he was that rare scientist and thinker who fully understood the dangers of specialization for both the scientist and society. In passing it may be of interest to note that Rivers' maternal uncle was James Hunt (see pp. 202-53), founder and first President of the Anthropological Society of London. In addition to the achievement of such an uncle, Rivers, among his many other distinguished accomplishments, was the first to recognize and describe with Elliot Smith and T. H. Pear, during the First World War "shell shock," as a distinct clinical entity. In the year of his death —1922—Rivers' edited volume, *Essays on the Depopulation of Melanesia,* appeared and included the essay reprinted here.

Rivers here speaks quite forthrightly of the disastrous role that missionaries played in the destruction of aboriginal peoples, and he correctly diagnoses the disorder as "loss of heart." It is today known as "the giving-up syndrome," and has been described by several observers in quite considerable detail for the Australian aborigines,[1] and was a principal factor in the extinction of the noble-hearted Tasmanians.[2] Rivers, who was an experienced physician, psychiatrist, and trained experimental physiologist, was the first to understand the mechanism by which the fall in the birthrate could be induced, principally by loss of interest in continuing to be and by stress. The mechanism is now

[1] See A. Lommel, "Modern Culture Influences on the Aborigines," *Oceania* (Vol. 21, 1950), pp. 16-17; R. M. Berndt, "Influence of European Culture on Australian Aborigines," *Oceania* (Vol. 21, 1951), pp. 229-235; B. Pentony, "Psychological Cause of Depopulation of Primitive Groups," *Oceania* (Vol. 24, 1953), pp. 142-145.

[2] C. Turnbull, *Black War*. Melbourne, F. W. Cheshire, 1948.

reasonably well understood, and was first described by the distinguished American physiologist Walter B. Cannon (1871-1945) in his classic paper "Voodoo Death," published in 1942 and reprinted in this volume (pp. 519-532).

THE PSYCHOLOGICAL FACTOR*
By W. H. R. RIVERS

The papers by members of the Melanesian Mission and other workers in Melanesia published in this book show conclusively that this great archipelago is undergoing a process of depopulation. In some parts the decline is taking place so rapidly that at no distant date the islands will wholly lose their native inhabitants unless something is done to stay its progress. I propose to begin my contribution to this volume by recounting some facts concerning this dying out of the people noted by myself during visits to Melanesia in 1908 and 1914.

In the New Hebrides the loss of native population is especially great and is progressing rapidly. Not long ago Fate, or Sandwich Island, had a considerable population in which, as usual in Melanesia, it was possible to distinguish between the bush-people and those living near the coast. Now the bush-people have wholly disappeared and the few survivors of the coastal districts have left the main island and live on one or other of the small islands, such as Eretap and Erekor, which fringe its coasts. In the island of Epi further north, the numbers of the people are said to be rapidly declining. Still farther north the shores of the island of Aore are strewn with sherds of pottery which show the former presence of a population of considerable size; now just three inhabitants survive. In Espiritu Santo, usually known as Santo, the largest island of the New Hebrides, the inhabitants of several villages on the west coast have entirely disappeared and their places have been taken by a few wretched people who have moved down from the interior. The little island of Tangoa was formerly the site of three villages, each of which must have been a community of considerable size, for the people are said to have had different dialects. Now all the people of the island live in one small village. At the southern end of Santo the people of Vulua twenty years ago numbered at least 200 according to the estimate of the Rev. F. G. Bowie, the missionary of the district. Now there is only a miserable handful of people, herded together in one village with hardly any children, and they will soon be altogether extinct.

*From W. H. R. Rivers, editor, *Essays on the Depopulation of Melanesia* (Cambridge University Press, 1922), pp. 84-113. Reprinted by permission of Cambridge University Press.

In the Banks and Torres Islands to the north of the New Hebrides the decrease in numbers has been very great. According to a recent estimate of the Rev. R. Godfrey the population of these islands has been reduced by at least one half during the last twenty years. Another member of the Melanesian Mission, the Rev. R. E. Tempest, gives the following figures showing the decrease during the last two or three years:

	1917	1918	1920
Mota	384	——	315
Motalava (Motlav)	697	——	568
Merelava (Merlav)	——	506	467
Gaua (Santa Maria)			
7 villages	——	229	215
Ureparapara	——	169	150

The rapid decrease is ascribed by Mr. Tempest to the inhabitants having been recruited to work in the plantations, chiefly of Espiritu Santo.

In the Santa Cruz group, large islands which are said to have been well peopled are now uninhabited, the decline here having been especially great during the last few years. In the Solomon Islands, the tale is less pitiful, but here also the population of many islands is diminishing so rapidly that unless something is done to stay the decline, it will soon share the fate which has already overtaken so many parts of the New Hebrides.

The Rev. C. E. Fox of the Melanesian Mission has given a striking picture of the decrease of population in San Cristoval in the Solomons. The Spaniards in 1546[1] spoke of the large population of the island. At Wango in 1887 H. G. Guppy[2] estimated the population at about 500; now there are less than 100. From one hill-top Mr. Fox was shown the sites of forty-six once flourishing villages of which only three are now inhabited.

Since my visit to Melanesia in 1914 the archipelago has been visited by the severe epidemic of influenza which, here as elsewhere in the Pacific, has done much to hasten the process by which the people of Oceania are disappearing.

The rapidity of the decay at the present time has been brought home to myself by two instances which, though of no great value as evidence, may yet be cited in illustration. During a visit in 1908 I gained a large amount of valuable information from two men, fairly young and apparently full of life and vigour, one a Polynesian living in Melanesia, the other a native of the Banks Islands. I looked forward to their help in future visits to their islands, but before I had had time to record the knowledge they had shared with me,

[1] *The Discovery of the Solomon Islands*, London, Hakluyt Soc., 1901.
[2] *The Solomon Islands and their Natives*, London, 1887, p. 57.

I heard that both were dead. In 1914 I was again in Melanesia and obtained from a still younger native a most important account of a district in the island of Ambrim, whose people had been almost entirely uprooted and destroyed by a volcanic catastrophe. Before I have been able to put this fragment of vanishing knowledge upon record, I hear that the witness is already dead, a victim to the scourge of dysentery.

Various causes have been given in this volume to account for the dying out of the people, different factors having been stressed by different authors. I propose to attempt a more complete survey of the causes which lead to decrease of population.

Before beginning this survey it will be well to deal briefly with a supposed fact which has frequently been brought forward as a means of accounting for the decrease of the population of Melanesia. It has been supposed that the Melanesians were already a dying people before the European invasion, and that their decline was due to faults inherent in their own culture. In the first place there is no evidence of any value that the people were decreasing in number before the advent of Europeans. Mr. Durrad has dealt with this topic in his contribution to this volume and has failed to find such evidence. It may be true that here and there the people already showed signs of diminution on the arrival of the missionaries[1]. It must be remembered, however, that the people had already been subject for many years to certain European influences, such as that of the sandal-wood hunters, which were far from being of a harmless kind.

When apologists for the effects of their own civilisation give reasons for the supposed original decadence, these often bear their own refutation on the face. Thus, one writer blames the heathen custom of polygamy, but in the same paragraph states that the practice is confined to the few. As if a custom confined to the few could ever be the cause of the dying out of a whole people. As a matter of fact, the polygamy of Melanesia is very different from that of Africa, being so exceptional and the number of wives so small as to have no appreciable influence upon the people, whether for good or evil.

Another cause which has been put forward is the special kind of consanguineous union known as the cross-cousin marriage. This is a marriage between the children of a brother and sister which takes place habitually, while marriage between the children of two brothers or of two sisters is strictly forbidden. This marriage is orthodox in several parts of Melanesia and is especially frequent and important in Fiji. This subject was fully investigated by the Commis-

---

[1]In some cases this decrease in early times is almost certain. Thus, there is little doubt that the northern end of Ysabel in the Solomons was decimated by the activity of the head-hunters of Ruviana and Eddystone, but this decrease was purely local and had no appreciable influence on the general population of Melanesia.

sion which more than twenty years ago inquired into the decrease of the native population of Fiji. In their *Report*,[1] which forms a storehouse of most valuable facts concerning the topics of this book, it is shown conclusively that this factor had not contributed towards Fijian decadence, but rather that these consanguineous marriages were more fruitful than marriage between wholly unrelated persons.

I shall deal presently with native customs in relation to our subject and hope to show that it is rather the indiscriminate and undiscriminating interference with them which stands forth prominently among the causes of decay.

I can now consider the conditions to which real efficacy in the process of destruction can be assigned. In studying this subject the first point to bear in mind is the double character of the factors upon which fluctuation of population depends, a double character which holds good of Melanesia as of more civilised parts of the world. Diminution of population may be due to increase of the death-rate to decrease of the birth-rate, or to both combined. I can bring forward evidence to show that both factors have been active in Melanesia. I will begin with the conditions which have affected the death-rate.

In a subject in which we can find little on which to pride ourselves, it is satisfactory to be able to exclude one cause of depopulation which has contributed in no small measure to the disappearance of native races in other parts of the world. There has been no deliberate attempt to exterminate the people such as has disgraced the history of our relations with regions more suited to European habitation than the sweltering and unhealthy islands of Melanesia. The injurious influences due to European rulers and settlers have been unwitting. Owing to the need for the labour of those accustomed to the tropics, it has always been in the interests of the settlers that the native population shall be alive and healthy. In so far as native decay is due to European influence we have to lay the blame on ignorance and lack of foresight, not on any deliberate wish to destroy.

In considering the death of a people as of an individual, it is natural to think first of disease. Disease is the name we give to a group of processes by which the size of population is adjusted so as to enable it best to utilise the available means of subsistence. Before the arrival of Europeans, Melanesia had its own diseases, by means of which Nature helped to keep the population within bounds. Everything goes to show that the population of Melanesia was well within the limits which the country was capable of supporting, but it is not so certain that it was far within this capacity in relation to the very simple means the people possessed for exploiting its resources. So far as we can tell, there had been set up a state of equilibrium between the size of the population and the available resources of the country. Recent knowledge goes to show

[1]*Report of the Commission appointed to inquire into the Decrease of the Native Population (Colony of Fiji)*, Suva, 1896.

that the diseases due to infective parasites tend to set up a state of tolerance and habituation which renders a people less prone to succumb to their ravages, and there is no reason to suppose that Melanesia was any exception in this respect. Thus the people are largely habituated to the malaria which certainly existed among them before the coming of European influence.

Into this community thus adapted to the infective agents of their own country, the invaders brought a number of new diseases: measles, dysentery, probably tubercle and influenza, and last but unfortunately far from least potent, venereal disease. These maladies had effects far more severe than those they bring upon ourselves, partly because they found a virgin soil, partly because the native therapeutic ideas were not adapted to the new diseases, so that remedies were often used which actually increased their harmfulness. Many of these introduced diseases are still drawing a large toll on the numbers and energies of the people, the two which seem to be exerting the most deadly influence, so far as my observations show, being dysentery and tubercle.

A second group of introduced causes of destruction is composed of what may be called the social poisons, such as alcohol and opium. Though it is possible that the people use tobacco somewhat to excess, the only poison which needs to be considered in Melanesia is alcohol. In certain parts of Melanesia there is no question that it has exerted in the past and is still exerting a most deleterious influence, but it is satisfactory to be able to say that its noxious influence has been reduced to negligible importance in those parts of the archipelago wholly subject to British rule, where it is penal to sell or give alcohol to a native. Alcohol is still, however, potent as a cause of disease and death in the New Hebrides. In those islands there are regulations against the sale of alcohol to natives, but under the present Condominium Government they are not obeyed.

A third direct cause of increase of death-rate is the introduction of fire-arms, by means of which the comparatively harmless warfare of the natives is given a far more deadly turn. This cause is still active to some extent in the New Hebrides owing to breaking of the regulations of the Condominium Government, but fire-arms have never had great importance as an instrument of destruction in Melanesia.

I come to a more serious cause when I consider European influence upon native customs. I begin with one which excites perennial interest whenever native welfare is discussed. Before the advent of Europeans the people of some islands went wholly nude or wore only garments, if they can be so called, which fulfilled neither of the two chief purposes for which the clothing of civilised people is designed. In other parts the native clothing consisted of petticoats, loin-cloths, or other simple garments thoroughly adapted to the necessities of the climate. One of the first results of European influence was the adoption of the clothing of the visitors, and clothes were adopted in such a manner as to accentuate the evils which they necessarily brought with them.

The Melanesian is not uncleanly. He bathes frequently, and where he preserves his native mode of clothing, his ablutions are amply sufficient for cleanliness. When he wears European garments, he fails to adopt measures, such as the frequent change of clothing, which then become necessary. He continues to bathe in his clothes, and instead of changing his garments frequently, wears them continuously till they are ragged, and even when new clothing is obtained, it is put over the old.

It is a great mistake, often made, to blame the missionaries for this use of foreign clothing. It is true that its use was directly encouraged by the early missionaries, but this encouragement was unnecessary. To the native, trousers and coats are the distinctive mark of the white man, and nothing short of prohibition could have prevented their use. Where we can now see the missionaries to have been at fault is that they did not recognise the evil of the innovation and set themselves steadily to minimise it. They should have insisted upon attention to the elementary principles of the hygiene which the use of clothes involves.

At the present time the influence of missionaries is steadily directed to this end. Having been privileged to live among missionaries of different schools of thought in Melanesia, I can testify that no subject is more frequently discussed and more thoroughly and anxiously considered than how to lessen the use and injurious influence of European clothing.

Another modification of native custom, which is less widely recognised, but in my experience quite as much in need of consideration at the present time, is housing. The native Melanesian house is usually rain-proof and of good proportions, while owing to its mode of construction it is well ventilated and thoroughly adapted to the climate. Instead of being content with houses of similar construction or with houses of the kind used by Europeans living in other tropical countries, settlers have built houses with thick walls and very imperfect means of ventilation. These have in some cases been copied by the natives, or even built by the missionaries for the use of their followers. Such buildings might have been specially devised for the propagation of tubercle, and if they are allowed to be built will certainly increase the already far too heavy ravages of this disease.

The modifications of housing and clothing which I have just considered touch especially the material side of life. I have now to consider a number of modifications and interferences with native custom which I believe to have been quite as important, if not more important, in the production of native decadence. When Melanesia became subject to Europeans, magistrates and missionaries were sent to rule and direct the lives of the people. They found in existence a number of institutions and customs which were, or seemed to them to be, contrary to the principles of morality. Such customs were usually forbidden without any inquiry into their real nature, without knowledge of the part they took in native life, and without any attempt to discriminate between their good and bad elements. Thus, in the Solomon Islands the rulers stopped the special kind of warfare known as head-hunting, without at all appreciating the vast place it took in the religious and ceremonial lives of the people, without realising the gap it would leave in their daily interests, a blank far more extensive than that due to the mere cessation of a mode of warfare. Again, in Fiji, the custom according to which the men of the community slept apart from the women in a special house, a widespread custom in Melanesia, seemed to the missionaries contrary to the ideals of the Christian family, and the custom was stopped or discouraged without it being realised that the segregation of the sexes formed an effectual check on too free intercourse between them.

In the New Hebrides again, the missionaries put an end to, or where they did not destroy, treated with a barely veiled contempt, a highly complicated organisation arising out of beliefs connected with the cult of dead ancestors. In some cases it was apparent enough that the institution with all its elaborate ceremonial was heathen and prejudiced church attendance, while elsewhere stress was laid on occasional revels and dances which gave opportunity for licence. It was not recognised that in forbidding or discouraging without inquiry, they were destroying institutions which had the most far-reaching ramifications through the social and economical life of the people. I have called attention to this subject elsewhere in an essay on "The Government of Subject Peoples," included in the Cambridge collection of essays entitled *Science and the Nation*[1]. I have there pointed out that if these and similar institutions had been studied before they were destroyed or discouraged, it would have been found possible to discriminate between those features which were noxious and needed repression or amendment, and those which were beneficial to the welfare of the community. Even when their destruction was deemed necessary, something could have been done to replace the social sanctions of which the people were thus deprived. The point I wish to emphasise is that through this unintelligent and undiscriminating action towards native institutions, the people were deprived of nearly all that gave interest to their lives. I have now to suggest that this loss of interest forms one of the reasons, if indeed it be not the most potent of all the reasons, to which the native decadence is due.

It may at first sight seem far-fetched to suppose that such a factor as loss of interest in life could ever produce the dying out of a people, but my own observations have led me to the conclusion that its influence is so great that it can hardly be overrated. I venture therefore to consider it at some length.

When you inquire of those who have lived long in Melanesia concerning the illness and mortality of the natives, you are struck by the frequency of reference to the ease with which the native dies. Over and over again one is told of a native who seemed hale and well until, after a day or two of some apparently trivial illness, he gives up the ghost without any of the signs

[1]Cambridge Univ. Press, 1917, p. 302.

which among ourselves usually give ample warning of the impending fate. A native who is ill loses heart at once. He has no desire to live, and perhaps announces that he is going to die when the onlooker can see no ground for his belief.

The matter becomes more easy to understand if we consider the ease with which the people are killed by magic or as the result of the infraction of a taboo. The evidence is overwhelming that such people as the Melanesians will sicken and die in a few hours or days as the result of the belief that an enemy has chosen them as the victim of his spells, or that they have, wittingly or unwittingly, offended against some religious taboo. If people who are interested in life and do not wish to die can be killed in a few days or even hours by a mere belief, how much more easy it is to understand that a people who have lost all interest in life should become the prey of any morbid agency acting through the body as well as through the mind. It is this evidence of the enormous influence of the mind upon the body among the Melanesians and other lowly peoples that first led me to attach so much importance to loss of interest as the primary cause of their dying out. Once this belief has been formulated, there is seen to be much definite evidence in Melanesia to support it.

Certain islands and districts of Melanesia show a degree of vitality in striking contrast with the rest. These exceptional cases fall into two classes: one includes those islands or parts of islands where the people have so far been fierce and strong enough to withstand European influence. There are still certain parts in Melanesia which as yet the footprint of the white man has not reached, and others where, after successful encounters with punitive expeditions, the people still believe themselves to be a match for the invader. Here the old zest and interest in life persist and the people are still vigorous and abundant.

The other group of peoples who show signs of vitality are those who have adopted Christianity, not merely because it is the religion of the powerful white man, but with a whole-hearted enthusiasm which has given them a renewed interest in life. Here the numbers are increasing after an initial drop. Christianity and the occupations connected with it have given the people a new interest to replace that of their indigenous culture, and with this interest has come the desire to live.

The special point I wish to make in my contribution to this book is that interest in life is the primary factor in the welfare of a people. The new diseases and poisons, the innovations in clothing, housing and feeding, are only the immediate causes of mortality. It is the loss of interest in life underlying these more obvious causes which gives them their potency for evil and allows them to work such ravages upon life and health.

I can pass to the second of the two groups of influences by which a people decline in number, having so far dealt only with those which increase the death-rate. I have now to consider those which produce decline by diminishing the birth-rate and will begin by stating briefly the evidence that this factor has played and is playing a part in the dying out of the Melanesians. This evidence has been gained by a mode of inquiry adopted originally for purely scientific purposes. When in Torres Straits with Dr. Haddon twenty-four years ago, I discovered that the people preserved in their memories with great fidelity a full and accurate record of their descent and relationships[1]. It was possible to collect pedigrees so ample in all collateral lines that they could serve as a source of statistical inquiry into such features as the average size of a family, infant mortality, and other subjects which furnish the basis for conclusions concerning fluctuations of population. I have found this interest in genealogy wherever I have worked, and the collection of pedigrees has always formed the basis of my ethnographic inquiries. In Melanesia this instrument shows conclusively that the fall in numbers is due quite as much to decrease of the birth-rate as to increase of the death-rate.

I will begin with the evidence from the Solomon Islands. I have a large collection of pedigrees from two islands of the group, Eddystone Island and Vella Lavella. The result of the analysis of these pedigrees is given in the two following tables, which make it possible to compare, if only in a rough manner, the fertility of the present with that of preceding generations. The tables record in percentages the size of the family, the proportion of childless marriages, and other data for three successive generations. The chief difficulty arose in dealing with the third or present generation, for its marriages evidently include a number which, though childless or with only a small family at present, may be expected to result in offspring, or more offspring, in time. A certain number of marriages, viz. 9.1 per cent. of this generation were therefore set aside as doubtful, as shown in the eighth column of the table. It is possible that a certain number of the marriages included in the childless category of the fourth column may also become fruitful, and there may also be a slight increase in the figures recording the number of children per marriage. Thus, though the record of childless marriages only includes cases where it seemed safe to assume that the marriage would be permanently sterile, the figure is probably somewhat larger than it would be if the record could be taken ten years hence. Similarly, the figures giving the size of the family in this generation would also show some increase.

The division into generations was necessarily rough, but was effected before any attempt was made to estimate fertility. The objections which I have considered do not apply to the comparison of the two earlier generations, though there is the possibility that persons of the earlier generation may have been altogether omitted from the pedigrees because, owing to the absence of children, they were not of social importance, so that their existence had been for-

[1] See *Journ. Anthrop. Inst.* 1900, XXX. p. 74; and *Sociological Review*, 1910, III. p. 1.

gotten. It is possible that this factor may have come into action to some extent
in the pedigrees from Vella Lavella, but it is improbable that it has had any
influence on the Eddystone figures, for these were collected from several
sources and verified in many ways. It is possible that persons who failed to
marry may have been omitted, but improbable that persons who married would
have escaped record.

Table I. Eddystone Island.

Generation	Total No. of marriages	Total No. of children	Childless marriages in %	Marriages with			Number of children doubtful	Children who died young in %	
				1 or 2 children	3 to 5 children	6 or more children		M	F
I	207	447	19.4	43.5	32.8	4.3	—	6.4	4.5
II	295	379	46.1	29.0	18.9	3.3	2.7	18.5	8.1
III	110	72	52.7	32.7	5.5	0	9.1	31.1	14.8

Table II. Vella Lavella.

Generation	Total No. of marriages	Total No. of children	Childless marriages in %	Marriages with			No. of children doubtful	Children who died young	
				1 or 2 children	3 to 5 children	6 or more children		M	F
I	116	279	12.1	4.2	41.4	4.3	—	1.7	2.7
II	209	297	35.4	37.8	21.1	1.4	4.3	6.3	3.7
III	57	15	71.9	22.8	0	0	5.3	25.0	28.6

The Eddystone figures are more satisfactory than those of Vella Lavella in
many respects, for they are based on a fairly complete genealogical record
of the whole population of the island, whereas the pedigrees of Vella Lavella
are only samples collected here and there from a population very much larger
than that of Eddystone.

The Eddystone figures show decisively how great has been the influence
of some factor or factors leading to decrease in the size of the family. Childless
marriages increased in frequency from 19.4 to 46.1 per cent. in passing from
the first to the second generation. As I have already mentioned the increase
to 52.7 per cent. in the present generation may possibly be illusory owing

to certain families being still incomplete, but this factor cannot possibly explain the great increase in the number of childless marriages in the earlier generation. Equally striking are the figures showing the total number of children recorded for each generation in the pedigrees. Whereas two generations ago, 207 marriages produced 447 children, or well over two children per marriage, the figures for the following generation were 379 children from 295 marriages or an average of less than a child and a half per marriage. In the present generation the record is even worse, only 72 children having been born from 110 marriages, or less than one child per marriage. This figure may be expected, however, to become somewhat larger when recent marriages have produced their full effect upon the population.

The figures recording the size of the family are equally depressing. They show a striking decrease in the number of families of more than five. The last two columns give the infant mortality of the two sexes. It is a question whether children who died young may not have been in many cases forgotten in the case of the earliest generation and therefore omitted when the pedigrees were collected, and in this case the increase in infant mortality would not be as great as represented in the table. It will be noted that the mortality is definitely greater in the case of male children, but here again there is the possibility that male children who died young would be remembered better and that some female children who died in infancy may have been forgotten and therefore omitted.

The record of the island of Vella Lavella in the Solomons is similar in its nature but shows an even more serious decrease of fertility. As I have already mentioned, however, the record is less trustworthy. The island is much larger than Eddystone and the figures given in the table are derived from random samples taken from various villages of the coast. The record differs from that of Eddystone in that the number of childless marriages has shown a progressive increase to the present day, but as I did not know the people and their circumstances as I knew them in Eddystone no great significance should be attached to the figure for the present generation. It is significant, however, that the proportion of childless marriages two generations ago,viz. 12.1 per cent., does not differ greatly from the Eddystone figure.

Especially noteworthy is the total disappearance of families of more than two children in the present generation of Vella Lavella. Equally striking is the great diminution in the total number of children in this generation, the names of only fifteen children from marriages of this generation being recorded.

The two islands which show this striking fall in birth-rate are of especial interest in that in them, and especially in Eddystone, the chief factors to which the dying out of peoples is usually ascribed are absent. In Eddystone, about which a residence of several months enables me to speak with confidence, there is no record of any very severe epidemics. Tubercle and dysentery, the two most deadly diseases in Melanesia, do not appear to be, or to have been, especially active; and though both the chief forms of venereal disease exist in the island, they do not seem to have done any great amount of mischief. The island has never had a white missionary; the people still wear their native dress and live in houses of native build. Alcohol is little known and other poisons not at all, while any effect of fire-arms on mortality is negligible. Few of the people have left the island as labour or for any other reason. All the factors to which other writers in this book ascribe the decrease of the population of Melanesia are practically absent, and yet we have a striking diminution of population, due in the main to decrease of the birth-rate.

If now we pass from material to mental factors, the decrease in the birth-rate becomes easier to understand. No one could be long in Eddystone without recognising how great is the people's lack of interest in life and to what an extent the zest has gone out of their lives. This lack of interest is largely due to the abolition of head-hunting by the British Government. This practice formed the centre of a social and religious institution which took an all-pervading part in the lives of the people. The heads sought in the head-hunting expeditions were needed in order to propitiate the ancestral ghosts on such occasions as building a new house for a chief or making a new canoe, while they were also offered in sacrifice at the funeral of a chief. Moreover, head-hunting was not only necessary for the due performance of the religious rites of the people, but it stood in the closest relation to pursuits of an economic kind. The actual head-hunting expedition only lasted a few weeks, and the actual fighting often only a few hours, but this was only the culminating point of a process lasting over years. It was the rule that new canoes should be made for an expedition to obtain heads, and the manufacture of these meant work of an interesting kind lasting certainly for many months, probably for years. The process of canoe-building was accompanied throughout by rites and feasts which not only excited the liveliest interest but also acted as stimuli to various activities of horticulture and pig-breeding. As the date fixed for the expedition approached other rites and feasts were held, and these were still more frequent and on a larger scale after the return of a successful expedition. In stopping the practice of head-hunting the rulers from an alien culture were abolishing an institution which had its roots in the religion of the people and spread its branches throughout nearly every aspect of their culture, and by this action they deprived the people of the greater part of their interest in life, while at the same time they undermined the religion of the people without any attempt to put another in its place.

The other region of Melanesia where, through the application of the genealogical method, I am able to demonstrate the existence of a greatly lowered birth-rate is the New Hebrides. During my visit to that group in 1914 I did not stay in any one place long enough to collect a full genealogical record, as in Eddystone, but I obtained sample pedigrees in various islands which show clearly a state of affairs similar to that of the Solomons. I have already mentioned the people of Vulua in Espiritu Santo as an example of a people who have almost disappeared, and a pedigree obtained from one of the survivors well illustrates the chief factor to which their disappearance is due. About eighty years ago, when Santo was hardly touched by outside influences, a man of Vulua named Rathati married. He had four children whose marriages gave Rathati fifteen grandchildren, of whom my informant, a man verging towards middle age, was the sole survivor. Of the fifteen grandchildren of Rathati ten grew to adult age and married, but only two of these unions produced offspring: in one case a boy who died in infancy, while in the other case there were three children. All three of these children, the only great-grandchildren of Rathati, reached adult age and married, but none had offspring, so that a family which was once rapidly growing in numbers is now closing its career with a monotonous record of sterile marriages.

Another pedigree shows a man of Tasariki in Santo to have had five children whose marriages produced nine grandchildren. Six of these grandchildren married, but only two have been fruitful and in each of these cases the family is limited to one. Childless marriages are of frequent occurrence in other pedigrees collected in the New Hebrides, showing that there, as in the Solomons, lowered birth-rate must rank with enhanced death-rate as an important factor in the disappearance of the people.

I need only consider here very briefly the agencies to which this fall in birth-rate is due. It is well known that certain forms of venereal disease will produce sterility, and it is noteworthy that the dying out of the people of Vulua is ascribed by their neighbours to the ravages of this disease brought by returning labourers from Queensland. There is little doubt, however, that if we take Melanesia as a whole, causes of this kind are trivial or of slight importance as compared with voluntary restriction. Throughout Melanesia the people are acquainted with various means of producing abortion and also practise measures which they believe to prevent conception, and processes of this kind almost certainly form the main agencies in lowering the birth-rate. We have here only another effect of the loss of interest in life which I have held to be so potent in enhancing mortality. The people say themselves: "Why should we bring children into the world only to work for the white man?" Measures which, before the coming of the European, were used chiefly to prevent illegitimacy have become the instrument of racial suicide.

It is satisfactory that before I leave this subject I am able to point to a brighter side. I have already said that in certain parts of Melanesia the downward movement has been arrested and that the people now show signs of growth. I mentioned also that this was occurring especially in islands where the people have really taken to their hearts the lessons of their Christian teachers. I collected pedigrees from several Christian islands and they tell a tale vastly different from the miserable record of Vulua. A man of Makura named Masosopo, who married about seventy years ago, had three children and nine grandchildren, and there are already fourteen great-grandchildren, with a prospect of more to come, a striking contrast with the impending disappearance of the Vulua family. A couple who married about the same time in Nguna now have twenty-three descendants living and thriving, while in other islands I have records of families from eight to ten in number.

The teachings of the missionaries concerning the evils of racial suicide may possibly have contributed in some degree to this recovery, though I doubt whether in general they have been aware of the part which voluntary restriction has taken. I believe that their influence has lain much more in the fact that the religion they have taught has given the people a renewed interest in life which has again made it worth while to bring children into the world.

Until now I have said nothing of a cause of depopulation which has been especially active in Melanesia. The causes I have so far considered have been treated under two headings, according as they have enhanced the death-rate or lowered the birth-rate. The labour-traffic which I have now to consider is more complex and involves both of these factors.

In dealing with this cause of depopulation it is well that it is possible to begin by distinguishing between the traffic as it was and as it is. It would be difficult to exaggerate the evil influence of the process by which the natives of Melanesia were taken to Australia and elsewhere to labour for the white man. It forms one of the blackest of civilisation's crimes. Not least among its evils was the manner of its ending, when large numbers of people who had learnt by many years' experience to adapt themselves to civilised ways were, in the process of so-called repatriation, thrust back into savagery without help of any kind. The misery thus caused and the resulting disaffection not only underlie most of the open troubles in the recent history of Melanesia, but by the production of a state of helplessness and hopelessness have contributed as much as any other factors to the decline of the population.

I must not, however, dwell on the crimes and mistakes of the past. Our object in this book is to call attention to existing evils in the hope that they may be remedied before it is too late. At the present time Melanesians are only recruited as labourers to work within the confines of Melanesia, and both the recruitment and the conditions of labour are subject to Government control. Its grosser evils have been removed, at any rate in those parts of Melanesia which are wholly governed by Great Britain, though it would appear that there are still very grave defects in those parts of Melanesia under the control of the Condominium Government. But however closely and wisely the traffic is controlled, the removal from their own homes of the younger men, and still more of the younger women, of a declining population is not a factor which can tend to arrest the decline or convert it into a movement in the opposite direction. Even in its improved form, and limited to Melanesia though it be, the labour traffic continues to act as a cause of depopulation. It acts directly by taking men and women away from their homes when they should be marrying and producing children, while other evils are that, as at present conducted, the traffic tends to spread disease and to undermine an influence which I believe to be at the present time the most potent for good in Melanesia, the work of the missionaries. Moreover, the use of natives as labourers on plantations fails to give that interest in life which, as I have tried to show, forms the most essential factor in maintaining the health of a people.

Thus far in this contribution I have been dealing with the causes to which the dying out of the Melanesian people must be ascribed. To use medical language suitable to such a state of affairs as that recorded in this volume, I have been attempting to make a diagnosis. It is now time to turn to treatment and inquire what can be done to arrest the decline and make the Melanesians again a thriving and vigorous people. If I am right in my diagnosis that the chief cause of decline is lack of interest, it is not difficult to see the general lines upon which successful treatment must be based.

I shall pass, therefore, with a mere mention those lines of treatment, dictated by the ordinary principles of hygiene, by means of which faults of clothing, housing and feeding may be remedied, and shall confine my attention to the factor which I believe to stand first and foremost among the causes of the dying out of the Melanesian—the loss of interest in life from which at present he is suffering.

The main problem of treatment is how far it is possible to restore the old interests, or maintain them where they have not yet been destroyed, and how far they must be replaced by others. As I have already mentioned, there are still certain parts of Melanesia where the old life still persists with but little change. It would be an interesting experiment to see how far it is possible in these cases to maintain the old interests and make them the foundation on which to build a culture which would not conflict with the ethical and social ideals of the people who have come to be their rulers.

To most of the writers in this volume, and probably to most of its readers, such an experiment would not appeal, for it is naturally to the total replacement of the old religious interests by new that they will look for the remedy. It may be instructive, however, to consider for a moment how far it would be possible to modify the old customs and institutions of the people; to preserve enough to maintain interest while removing all those features which conflict with the ideals of modern civilisation. For this purpose I will take an extreme case and consider whether it would have been possible to have modified such a practice as the head-hunting of the Solomons. At first sight it might seem a hopeless task, and so it would be if one attended only to the outward practice obvious to the European observer and ignored the meaning which the institution of head-hunting bears to those who practice it. If we turn to this inner meaning, the case becomes less difficult. The essential motive for the head-hunting of

Melanesia is the belief that on various important occasions, and especially on occasions connected with the chiefs, a human head is necessary as an offering to the ancestral ghosts. There is little doubt that the custom is a relic of an earlier practice of human sacrifice, and the head-hunting of the Solomons was but little removed from this, for till recently it was the custom to bring home from expeditions captives who were killed when some important ceremony created the need for a head. In other parts of the world there is reason to believe that, where human beings were formerly sacrificed, the place of the human victim has been taken by an animal, and even that the place of a human head has been taken by that of an animal. I have no doubt that it would have been possible to effect such a substitution in the Solomons, that officials with the necessary knowledge of native custom and belief, and with some degree of sympathy with them, could have brought about such a substitution and thus avoided the loss of life and money which has accompanied the suppression of head-hunting in the Solomons. At the same time they would have kept up the interest of the people in their native institutions until such time as the march of events produced new interests, including new religious interests, connected with the culture which was being brought to bear upon their lives.

The substitution of the head of a pig for that of a human being would not, however, wholly solve the problem. I have already mentioned that the chief stimulus to the making of canoes in Eddystone Island came out of the practice of head-hunting. The substitution of a porcine for a human head, while satisfying many of the ceremonial needs, would leave no motive for the manufacture of new canoes and the maintenance of this industry. Here it would be necessary to provide some new motive for the making of canoes. This might be found in the introduction of canoe races as elements in the ceremonial connected with the ancestral offerings, while to this might be added economic motives connected with fishing or trade. It is probable that in such a process of substitution the native canoe would be displaced by the boat of European build, but much as this would be regretted by the anthropologist or the artist, this form of craft would be probably fully as efficacious in maintaining interest and zest in life and would thus contribute to the purpose which the writers of this volume have before them. Only, it is essential that the change should grow naturally out of native institutions and should not be forced upon the people without their consent and without any attempt to rouse their interest.

In this brief sketch of the lines upon which native customs might be modified so as to bring them into harmony with European culture I have already mentioned incidentally the introduction of new economic interests. I must now consider this subject more explicitly. In former days the chief need of the people outside their own island or district was for certain weapons and for kinds of food which did not flourish at home. Here it is noteworthy that the need for food from without was often connected with religion. Thus, one of the chief reasons why the people of Eddystone went elsewhere for the taro which did not flourish in their own island was its inclusion among the foods which should be used in certain ceremonial feasts, an example which shows how motives due to trade and the interest arising therefrom are often closely connected with religion. If religious interest flags, other interests, which might at first sight seem wholly devoid of any connection with it, will flag also.

At the present time the natives of Melanesia have acquired certain new needs through their contact with European influence, especially the need for tobacco and calico, while in many parts external influence has produced a liking for rice and other introduced foods which have had a most destructive influence on native horticulture. In order to obtain the articles thus needed the Melanesian has to do a certain amont of work, chiefly that involved in the collection and drying of coconuts to make copra. This takes little of his time and has in it little or nothing to arouse interest.

One of the chief needs of Melanesia is that the native shall be given a real interest in the economic development of his country. The Melanesian is a keen trader and there are cases in the New Hebrides in which he has shown much ability when he has entered as an ordinary trader into competition with the European. There is no question that if he were given a fair chance, he could take an important part in any organisation which had as its object the encouragement of native industry. Until recently the missionary societies of Melanesia have made no attempt at industrial development, either to encourage the old industries or to introduce new, and the Government has done even less in this direction. The only neighbouring region of Oceania where any progress in this direction has been made is in Torres Straits, where "The Papuan Industries Company" has endeavoured to give to the natives that share in the management of the industries of their country which is the best means of bringing back the old interest and zest in life. In other parts of the world, and pre-eminently in West Africa, such movements have had the most striking success and there is no reason why the success should not be as great in Melanesia.

It is doubtful, however, whether the modification of native custom and the replacement of old economic interests by new will be sufficient to allow the Melanesian to enter once more upon an upward course of progress. The old life of the people was permeated through and through by interests of a religious kind, based on a profound belief in continued existence after death and in the influence of the dead upon the welfare of the living. Experience has amply shown that Christianity is capable of giving the people an interest in life which can take the place of that due to their indigenous religion. Even if it were thought desirable to maintain the native religion in a modified form, it is highly improbable that there will be found people of our own culture sufficiently self-sacrificing to guide the progress of the people in the way which comes so naturally to the missionaries of the Christian religion. But if this religion is to help in the restoration of the material welfare of the people it is essential that its leaders shall recognise the difficulties which beset their path and should have a definite policy in connection with these difficulties.

Few things have done more harm in the past than the absence of such a policy and the consequent doubt and uncertainty concerning the attitude towards native institutions. Where one missionary has seen nothing but the work of the devil in some native institution and has willed its complete destruction, another, perhaps even of the same Mission, has seen in it a means of preparing the ground for the truth and has, to some extent at least, encouraged its activities. Faced with this difference of attitude the native has in his doubt been led into dissimulation. He has tried to combine the guidance which should have come from those whose business it should be to understand the religious practices they were displacing. If a new gospel is to be taken with success to such a people as the Melanesian, it is essential that the indigenous point of view shall be understood and that the misunderstanding to which the new views are inevitably subject shall be appreciated. Even if it were decided utterly to destroy the old religion there is no way in which these difficulties can be met so successfully as by a study of the old religion and of the mental attitude upon which the old religious practices rested, for this attitude must inevitably influence the reception of the new religion. If, on the other hand, it be decided to preserve such elements of the old religion as are not in conflict with the new, this study is even more essential. How can it be possible to decide whether a native practice shall be preserved unless the nature of the practice is thoroughly understood and its relations with other aspects of the native culture realised[1]? Whatever the policy adopted towards the indigenous religion, it is of the utmost importance that this religion shall be understood and that, even if no concerted effort to study native religions is made, attempts in this direction made by individual missionaries shall be encouraged.

Another question of policy which must be faced concerns the attitude which the missionary is to take towards economic development. I have already pointed out the close relation between religion and economics in the indigenous society of Melanesia. Such institutions as the Sukwe of the Banks Islands[2] or the ancestor-cult of the Solomons stand in the closest relation to economic needs and cannot be modified or abolished without producing far-reaching changes in the social and economic life of the people. These are only individual instances of a feature of early forms of human culture according to which they show a far greater interdependence of different aspects of social life than exists among ourselves. Even in our own society a new law intended by legislators to act upon some one branch of social life often produces changes of a far-

---

[1] I have dealt with this subject in its relation to government in the paper already quoted, "The Government of Subject Peoples," published in Science and the Nation, Cambridge Univ. Press, 1917, p. 302.

[2] See History of Melanesian Society, Cambridge, 1914, I. p. 140.

reaching kind on other aspects which were wholly unforeseen when the law was passed. Such interdependence is even greater in such simple societies as those of Melanesia, and it is very unlikely that this interdependence will cease with the introduction of new customs from without. The economic life of the people of Melanesia is being profoundly modified by external influence, but it is doubtful whether the close relation between economic and religious interests will disappear. It is essential that the missionary shall face this problem and make up his mind concerning the attitude he is going to adopt towards the economic life of the people. In the past many of the best missionaries of all denominations have set their faces against mixing economic problems with their religion. It has seemed to them that in so doing the spiritual side of religion must inevitably suffer, and no one who has had the opportunity of observing sporadic examples of the mixture can fail to sympathise with them. It must be recognised, however, that there is a problem and that it is in urgent need of settlement. If, as seems natural, economic development is made the business of the civil power, while the missionary occupies himself wholly with religion, there will be endless opportunities for conflict. The best course is one in which Government and missionary societies join in common council to decide how they can avert the disappearance of the Melanesian. The lesson of this article is that something must be done, and done quickly, to give him that renewed interest in life to which the health of peoples is mainly due.

KARL PEARSON FINDS THE ALIEN JEWISH POPULATION OF LONDON SOMEWHAT INFERIOR TO THE NATIVE POPULATION

KARL PEARSON (1857-1936), English biometrician and anthropologist, was for many years Professor of Mathematics and Biometry, and first Galton Professor at University College, in the University of London. Pearson was a man of extraordinary ability and wide learning, covering the fields of folklore, mathematics, statistics, biology, and the behavioral sciences, to mention but a few. If he was not a genius he was very close to being one. After being called to the bar he was appointed Professor of Mathematics at University College at the age of twenty-seven. At the age of thirty-five he produced one of the most widely read and influential books on science ever written, *The Grammar of Science*,[1] an acknowledged classic which will always remain among the best and most readable of such works. He was one of the founders of modern statistics and of statistical biology. Among his 650 published works his *Life of Francis Galton*, 3 vols., (Cambridge University Press, 1914-1930), is one of the finest biographies of a scientific man extant.[2]

In his younger days Pearson was a socialist, but as he grew older he became rather more of a Tory than one would ever have expected him to be. He was a man of complete integrity, rather a cold fish, and a "very superior person" who hardly deigned to communicate with his colleagues in other departments at University College. He was as far from being a bigot as could be imagined, and yet, strange as it may seem, his firm belief in the scientific powers of statistics caused him to become, for all practical purposes, a scientific bigot of the worst kind. It is for this reason that the following excerpt from his detailed study of the Jewish population of London, and the conclusions he drew from it, is reprinted here. That the views expressed here by Pearson and his collaborator were not new with him is evident from certain passages which are here reprinted from *The Grammar of Science*.

In 1884 Francis Galton wrote to the Swiss botanist, Alphonse de Candolle, "It strikes me that the Jews are *specialized* for a parasitical existence upon other nations, and that there is need of evidence that they are capable of fulfilling the varied duties of a civilised nation by themselves."[3] Pearson, Galton's disciple and admirer, some four decades later sought to provide that "evidence" in the monograph which is excerpted here. He concluded, with his mentor, that "alien Jews will not be absorbed by, and at the same time strengthen the existing population; they will develop into a parasitic race."[4]

It is very strange that Jewish children from the same Polish and Russian backgrounds when reared in individual Israeli homes have an average IQ of 105, and when reared in a kibbutz have an average IQ of 115.[5] Must be the climate!

The amusing thing about Pearson's conclusions—if such conclusions can ever be amusing—is that undoubtedly the most creative and gifted

---

[1]Karl Pearson, *The Grammar of Science* (London, Walter Scott, 1892). See the Everyman Library edition, New York, Dutton, 1937.

[2]For a biography of Pearson by his son see E. S. Pearson, *Karl Pearson* (Cambridge University Press, 1938).

[3]See Karl Pearson, *The Life, Letters and Labours of Francis Galton*, Vol. 2 (Cambridge University Press, 1924), p. 209.

[4]Karl Pearson and Margaret Moul, "The Problem of Alien Immigration Into Great Britain, Illustrated by an Examination of Russian and Polish Jewish Children." *Annals of Eugenics* (Vol. 1, 1925), p. 125.

[5]B. S. Bloom, Letter to the editor, *Harvard Educational Review* (Vol. 39, 1969), pp. 419-421.

element, as measured by achievement, in the population of England today is represented by those Jews who grew up in the very environments in which Pearson's investigations were conducted! The disproportionate number of distinguished individuals of second and third generation Jewish origin now domiciled in England would probably have caused Pearson some surprise even though the facts might not have caused him to question his prejudices.[6]

KARL PEARSON SOLILOQUIZES AS SCIENTIST AND SOCIALIST ON THE FATE OF "SUPERANNUATED RACES"*

"It is not a matter of indifference to other nations that the intellect of any people should lie fallow, or that any folk should not take its part in the labour of research. It cannot be indifferent to mankind as a whole whether the occupants of a country leave its fields untilled and its natural resources undeveloped. It is a false view of human solidarity, a weak humanitarianism, not a true humanism, which regrets that a capable and stalwart race of white men should replace a dark-skinned tribe which can neither utilize its land for the full benefit of mankind, nor contribute its quota to the common stock of human knowledge.[1] The struggle of civilized man against uncivilized man and against nature produces a certain partial 'solidarity of humanity' which involves a prohibition against any individual community wasting the resources of mankind."

The best comment on these words was, I think, made at about the time Pearson wrote them, namely in February, 1890, by Alice James, sister to William and Henry James, who, in her diary about the English wrote of their "profound ineradicable in the bone and sinew conviction that outlying regions are their preserves, that they alone of human races

[6]For a discussion of Pearson along these lines see Nicholas Pastore, *The Nature-Nurture Controversy* (New York, King's Crown Press, 1949).

*Reprinted from Karl Pearson, *The Grammar of Science* (London, Walter Scott, 1892), p. 310.

[1]This sentence must not be taken to justify a brutalizing destruction of human life. The anti-social effects of such a mode of accelerating the survival of the fittest may go far to destroy the preponderating fitness of the survivor. At the same time, there is cause for human satisfaction in the replacement of the aborigines throughout America and Australia by white races of far higher civilization. (Pearson's footnote).

massacre savages out of pure virtue. It would ill-become an American to reflect upon the treatment of aboriginal races; but I never heard it suggested that our hideous dealings with the Indians was brotherly love masquerading under the disguise of pure cussedness."[2]

The "bone and sinew" conviction of the superiority of the English to all other people, was something that virtually every Englishman, including those of the lowest class, took for granted. Pearson, without being aware of it, was simply repeating the prejudices of his predecessors and mistaking them for the laws of nature—*that* is the definition, often, of a scientist and a practical man.

THE PROBLEM OF ALIEN IMMIGRATION INTO GREAT BRITAIN, ILLUSTRATED BY AN EXAMINATION OF RUSSIAN AND POLISH JEWISH CHILDREN.*
By KARL PEARSON and MARGARET MOUL.

Introductory.

The purport of this memoir is to discuss whether it is desirable in an already crowded country like Great Britain to permit indiscriminate immigration, or, if the conclusion be that it is not, on what grounds discrimination should be based. If there is to be discrimination it may be based on purely quantitative considerations—such as largely rule at present admission of immigrants into the United States, where percentages of each racial element only are admitted per month; or it may be based solely on qualitative considerations—all immigrants up to a certain level of mentality, physique or health may be admitted. Here again the question of standard for admission is a very important one. It may be fixed so high that practically few are admitted, but the few may be those who are so much above the average intelligence of a nation, that they are a national gain. Or a community may admit individuals of special craft capacity, as, for example, the Huguenot silk-weavers, German clock-makers, Italian tunnel-workers, or Dutch engravers. We cannot disregard the advantages which in the past such immigrants have brought not only to our handicrafts, but to our arts. The argument for the admission of such immigrants has, we fear, been misused in the past in order to obtain a supply of cheap labour, because the foreign immigrants have not been subjected to any rigid entrance tests.

[2]*The Diary of Alice James*, ed. Leon Edel (New York, Dodd, Mead & Co., 1964), p. 88.
*Reprinted from *Annals of Eugenics* (Vol. 1, 1925), pp. 5-9, 126-7.

In the present state of psychological and medical knowledge it should not be hard to establish a standard of admission, which would insure that only immigrants of good physique and high mentality gained entrance. But here from the standpoint of national eugenics two problems arise for which at present we know little in the way of solution. The first problem is concerned with the relation between the new immigrant and our climate; he may be intellectually and physically above the average of the existing population, but that does not demonstrate that he or his stock can maintain those advantages permanently with a very much changed environment. We are quite certain that the superior Scandinavian or German workman does not necessarily degenerate in our climate—it is not too unlike his own—but this becomes far less certain in the case of the Armenian or the Arab. It may be unwise to disregard race entirely when a standard of physique and intelligence has been established.

The second problem is even more difficult of solution: an immigrant may pass the highest standard we can select; he may be quite fitted to our climate, but other difficulties arise. Will he blend with our population? Let us put on one side any idea that we ourselves are a pure race; we are a nation of ineradicable hybrids. But there are limits to successful hybridism, and at present we understand very little about them. By both intelligence and physique there are Japanese and Chinese well above any immigration standard likely to be enforced; both races appear to readily adapt themselves to our climate. But would a stream of the most intelligent Japanese into Great Britain—or for the matter of that a stream of the most intelligent Englishmen into Japan—be really desirable for either nation? If the immigrants do not blend with the old population, but maintain themselves as a group apart, we reach a nation within a nation, the immigrants if many tend to have divergent interests, and if few may become parasitic; in both cases arises a source of real national danger. On the other hand, if the immigrants do blend, science has at present little to tell us of the value of the resulting hybrids. Too little work has been devoted to the study of human hybrids, and what has been done has too often been biased from the standpoint of the observer, who has started more or less pledged to a narrow view-point or to some hereditary theory. How little we know about the F_1 generation of English and Japanese; and still less about F_2 and F_3! We have really no idea whether the maintenance of a high grade of intelligence and of physique is possible. We know as little at present about the ultimate value of Eurasian and Africander crosses.

Such a slight sketch as the above may, perhaps, suffice to convince the reader of the thorny problems of immigration into already settled countries. The student of national eugenics desires in every way to improve and strengthen his own nation. He would do this by intra-national selection for parentage, and by the admission wherever and whenever possible to superior brains and muscles into his own country; but while he naturally objects entirely to indiscriminate immigration, he has to confess that a mere test of superior mentality and physique may not be adequate in the case of the more widely divergent races. We simply have not the knowledge at present requisite to set a value on the hybrids which may result from crosses even of the physically and mentally best in Caucasian, Oriental and African races*. It is perfectly idle to talk in these matters either of pride of race or of the common humanity of all mankind. The reasons that can be given for admitting orientals as permanent immigrants into a densely populated occidental country apply equally to the admission of occidentals into oriental countries. When it comes to settling or resettling a sparsely peopled country, then it is possible to find out whether the individual is a real humanitarian or not, according as he thinks only of his own race, or of the actual suitability of other races, as judged by their culture and their adaptation to the proposed environment. From this standpoint it is probable that the Japanese would be far more valuable than men of Nordic race in many of the Pacific islands, and that the Hindoo and still more the Chinaman might, to the great advantage of general world progress, replace the negro in many districts of Africa.

In the years preceding the Great War the question of indiscriminate immigration—especially that of the Polish and Russian Jews into the East End of London, and the poorer quarters of other large towns in Great Britain—had become a very vital one. It was asserted on the one hand that the immigrants were a useful class of hard workers fully up to the level of the English workman in physique and intelligence, and on the other hand these immigrants were painted in lurid colours as weaklings, persons with a low standard of life and of cleanliness, under-bidding native workers in sweated trades and spreading anarchic doctrines, so that the continued inflow of this population was leading not only to economic distress, but to a spread of doctrines incompatible with the stability of our social and political systems.

It was very obvious to the onlooker that whatever might be the real facts of the situation, those facts were not available for the calm discussion of the case. The partizans of cheap labour and the partizans of monopolistic trades-unionism were both undoubtedly acting from personal and party inspirations, and there was no one whose business it really was to find the true answer to the question of whether Great Britain could assimilate to its national profit this mass of new and untested material.

The whole problem of immigration is fundamental for the rational teaching of national eugenics. What purpose would there be in endeavouring to legislate

*For many years past the Galton Laboratory has been crossing the "nordic" Pommeranian with the "oriental" Pekinese even to the F_8 and F_{10} generations. Smaller and larger types than either of the original stocks have resulted, but neither in mentality nor physique has a strain equal to the pure dogs been evolved, and there has been some tendency to physical and mental defects; due probably to the considerable divergence in skeletal form of the originals. The skeletal differences between the Japanese and our Nordic races are probably as great, but the analogy can only serve as a caution, not as an argument.

for a superior breed of men, if at any moment it could be swamped by the influx of immigrants of an inferior race, hastening to profit by the higher civilisation of an improved humanity? To the eugenist permission for indiscriminate immigration is and must be destructive of all true progress. Such progress is only possible where intra-racial selection is combined with a large measure of isolation. No sane man, however, doubts that at various periods of English history our nation has been markedly strengthened by foreign immigration. The Huguenots brought us a most valuable element, the Dutch a second, and, I think, we may add to these invasions, that of the Germans of 1848—the "Achtundvierziger"—many of whom were indeed of Jewish extraction. But these special cases do not prove the general desirability of free immigration. They prove the value of it, if the immigrants are men of high mentality and firm purpose. In the cases referred to we had to deal with men of marked character and originality; men often of peculiar craftsmanship, driven from their homes by religious or political persecution, mostly coming from as high a civilisation as our own, if not indeed from a higher one. They were capable of blending and have largely blended with our own racial elements. Except for antiquarian interest we no more trouble about their origin than we worry whether a fellow countryman is mainly of Anglo-Saxon, Danish or Norman blood. It was undoubtedly from the standpoint thus outlined that the members of the Eugenics Laboratory started their investigations into the most recent sources of immigration into this country. They recognised no wider principle than that of national welfare. If a man be a good Englishman in the first place, and in the second be sound in body and mind, then his religion is his own private concern; he may, for aught we have to do with the matter, be a good Christian, a good Jew or a good Freethinker. The only sound doctrine on such a theme is that of Lessing's fine old Hebrew Nathan der Weise: seek the man beneath the Moslem, Christian, Jew.

We did not select the Polish and Russian immigrants because they were Jews, but because they formed a large and accessible body of immigrants who could be worked relatively easily from one centre. Everybody recognises the services of the English Jew to our national welfare. He has contributed honourably to politics—to both the legal and civil executives—to finance, to commerce, to literature, to the arts, and to science. We have known him at school; we have known him at college, and worked with him and alongside him in after life. The differences are no greater than in the case of a Catholic fellow-subject. In the University of London the portraits on its walls indicate how large and distinguished a part both as benefactor and *alumnus* has been taken by the English Jew.

But the English Jew has been theoretically a free man for a century, and practically one for a much longer time. In the case of the Russian and Polish Jews there has been more or less continuous oppression, nay a veritable selection going on for a much longer period. Such a treatment does not necessarily leave the best elements of a race surviving. It is likely indeed to weed out the mentally and physically fitter individuals, who alone may have had the courage to resist their oppressors. We can sympathise with a man who has suffered hard treatment, but that in itself is not an adequate eugenic reason for granting him citizenship in a crowded country. For that citizenship we demand physical and mental fitness; we need the possibility of an ultimate blending and we need full sympathy with our national habits and ideals. Those of us who had occasion to travel during air-raids on London will not lightly forget the sights and sounds we encountered among the Yiddish-speaking population who sought refuge in the tube stations. But that is only an isolated aspect of the problem; we know also of acts of great courage among Jews of Russo-Polish origin. We know further of brilliant achievements and university distinctions gained by recent immigrants or their children. No satisfactory conclusions can be reached by citing individual instances which may tell one way or the other. There is only one solution to a problem of this kind, and it lies in the cold light of statistical inquiry. And, we will venture to say it, we believe there is no institution more capable of impartial statistical inquiry than the Galton Laboratory. We have no axes to grind, we have no governing body to propitiate by well-advertised discoveries; we are paid by nobody to reach results of a given bias. We have no electors, no subscribers to encounter in the market-place. We firmly believe that we have no political, no religious and no social prejudices, because we find ourselves abused incidentally by each group and organ in turn. We rejoice in numbers and figures for their own sake and, subject to human fallibility, collect our data—as all scientists must do—to find out the truth that is in them. The tradition of the Laboratory has always been that until data are reduced and analysed no member of the staff holds the slightest opinion as to what might, ought or will come out of them. And we can safely assert that until a year ago no one engaged on this work had any idea of what our judgment on the alien Jewish population was likely to be. Let us once more emphasise the fact that we did not take the group of Russian and Polish Jews for investigation because it was a non-Christian immigration, or because these people were racially remote, or because their traditions are against blending with their hosts. We do not dismiss these points as unworthy of serious consideration, we believe them to be nationally of importance. But we propose to lay no weight on them here, but to consider merely the question of whether a mental and physical immigration test is desirable. We could equally well have answered the question on an alien Italian or alien Greek population had such been available. But the bulk of the immigration from 1906 onwards was Russian and Polish, and the difficult question of indiscriminate immigration in 1908 turned largely on the alien Jews. Over them the fight waxed hottest, and about them the most unblushing statements were made without any firm basis in fact. Yet owing to the concentration of Jewish alien children in the Jews' Free School, it was possible to reach the best of them in fairly adequate numbers with moderate ease.

The hot controversy over the alien Jewish population rendered a careful statistical inquiry essential; and this not only from the standpoint of the Gentile Englishman, but also from that of the English Jew. In the former case the problem was: Are these newcomers worthy compatriots? In the latter case it was a question not only of worthy compatriots, but of worthy members of a religious society. The late Lord Rothschild did immense service for Jewish, in particular alien Jewish education, by the support he gave to that wonderful institution, the Jews' Free School in Aldgate. But both he and other English Jews admitted the gravity of our problem by contributing to the fund we had to raise in order to carry through the work. The scheme was to examine physically, mentally and medically the children of the Jews' Free School; and then with the assistance of "field-workers" or home visitors report on the home conditions of their parents. We enlisted the friendly aid of the Headmaster of the school, Mr. L. G. Bowman, who gave us all the information in his power; we have also to thank the Headmistress and the staff for much assistance. The London County Council permitted medical officers appointed by the Laboratory, of whom one was a Jew and the other a Gentile, to examine in more detail the children in association with their own medical men. A special examination was made of the children's eyesight by ophthalmologists of our own selecting; and three Jewish ladies each with a knowledge of Yiddish and German, and having experience in the inquiry work which precedes the distribution of Jewish charities, visited the homes and filled in our schedules. We can safely say that while it has probably been impossible to avoid errors, they are not biased errors. Our recorders and observers were sympathetic and for the most part Jews. We found on every side help, suggestion and kindness, and we desire to state emphatically how much we owe not only to the staff of the Jews' Free School, not only to the authorities of the London County Council, but to the medical men and the field-workers. While, however, we owe to their assistance the data, we desire to state expressly that they are in no way responsible for its reduction or interpretation; that is the work of the Eugenics Laboratory and has been conducted by the usual methods of modern statistical inquiry*.

In certain directions only we met with difficulty. Perhaps the only serious case was the examination of eyesight. Examination of the accurate character we attempted took a long time, and the girls—even some of the elder ones—became nervous and there were even hysterical threatenings. This experience was unexpected, it had not been found with Gentile children, and

*We have to thank Mrs. Mary Curwen, formerly assistant in the Laboratory, for aid in the preparation of sorting-cards and for the preparation of some of the tables.

was not the case with the Jewish boys. We had therefore—except for mere
vision tests—to limit ourselves to the boys. Even in this case owing to the
time and therefore expense involved we did not succeed in taking a sample
of more than about 500 cases. It is large enough however to base certain conclusions upon. Our data were collected on three schedules:

(a) the ordinary London County Council medical school inspection card (C);

(b) a schedule (A) to be filled in at the school and largely covering information provided by the staff, or the additional medical examiners;

(c) a schedule (B) to be filled in by the field-workers.

Ultimately schedules (a), (b) and (c) were clipped together and formed the
dossier of the individual child.

About 600 such dossiers were obtained for boys and nearly the like number
for girls. These provide a fair random sample of the population.

[In the matter of intelligence] there is no substantial difference between boys
and girls, the percentages being, if anything, somewhat in favour of the latter.
Speaking therefore not of knowledge but of mother-wit we are able to assert
reasonable equality between gentile boys and girls. This equality seems wholly
wanting in the case of alien Jews. We have now to obtain a comparable distribution for the Gentile boys. We think it may be found in Gilby's observations
published some years ago on a number of London County Council Schools,
the teachers using Pearson's scale*. His investigations were on boys only, and
he found the following percentages:

Very Able	Capable	Intelligent	Slow	Dull	Very Dull and Mentally Defective
3.4%	21.7%	31.0%	23.6%	12.7%	7.6%

Here, as in all investigations with this scale, the average or median is a
little to one or other side of the dichotomic line between Intelligent and Slow.
Returning to Table CXLII we will take our true average at the middle of the
Average Group, and reckon the 22.5% below the true average as "slow."
If we now divide the "above average" into two equal groups of 12.5% each,
reckoning the upper as "capable" and the lower as the upper part of intelligent,
we get a London School Scheme from the Pioneer Survey which agrees very
well with Gilby's, namely:

	Very Able and Capable	Intelligent	Slow	Dull and Very Dull
L.C.C. Survey	22.5%	35.0%	22.5%	20.0%
Gilby	25.1	31.0	23.6	20.3

*Biometrika, Vol. VIII, pp. 94-108.

The object of thus bringing the L.C.C. Survey into line with Gilby's is solely to enable us to consider, by applying the same rule, the distribution of Intelligence in the different grades of London Schools as given in our Table LX. Doing this we reach the following distributions†:

Table CXLIV. *Distribution of Intelligence in London Schools*.

	Boys				Girls			
	Very Able and capable	Intelligent	Slow	Dull and Very Dull	Very Able and Capable	Intelligent	Slow	Dull and Very Dull
Gentiles, Better Schools	18.6%	34.8%	23.1%	23.5%	13.9%	34.6%	25.0%	26.5%
Gentiles, Medium Schools	21.3	37.2	24.7	16.8	12.4	41.4	32.5	13.7
Gentiles, Poor Schools	15.6	32.3	23.5	28.6	15.8	37.2	29.4	17.6
Gentiles, Gilby's Data	25.1	31.0	23.6	20.3	—	—	—	—
Gentiles, Alien Jews	16.0	36.2	34.7	13.1	7.5	25.5	37.8	29.2

†A total of 5761 records made directly on the Pearson scale in L.C.C. schools gave:

Concluding Remarks on Parts I and II of this Memoir. An examination of this table shows us at once that the Jewish girls have less intelligence than the Gentile girls in any type of Council School. The comparison of the Gentile and Jewish boys is less clear cut; the latter may be judged somewhat less intelligent than Gilby's sample, which was classified by the same scale as the alien Jewish boys. They are not as good as the boys of the medium or average schools, but are better than the boys of the poor type of school. What is definitely clear, however, is that our alien Jewish boys do *not* form from the standpoint of intelligence a group markedly superior to the natives. But that is the sole condition under which we are prepared to admit that immigration should be allowed. Taken *on the average*, and regarding both sexes, this alien Jewish population is somewhat inferior physically and mentally to the native population. It is not so markedly inferior as some of those who wish to stop *all* immigration are inclined to assert. But we have to face the facts; we know and admit that some of the children of these alien Jews from the academic standpoint have done brilliantly, whether they have the staying powers of the native race is another question*. No breeder of cattle, however, would purchase an entire herd because he anticipated finding one or two fine specimens included in it; still less would he do it, if his byres and pastures were already

Very Able and Capable	Intelligent	Slow	Dull and Very Dull
22.86%	42.77%	22.68%	11.69%

These results are distinctly superior to those for the Jewish children.

*A member of an eastern race said to the senior author of this paper recently: "It puzzles me when I see how late in life you English can work; all I have to do, must be done before I am fifty."

full. He would certainly select those animals only which would strengthen his own stock, and these alone he would find place for.

The law of patriotism for a crowded country surely must be to admit not those who merely reach our own average—and *a fortiori* not those who fall below—but only those who can give us, either physically or mentally, what we do not possess or possess only in inadequate quantity.

Let us set a standard for immigrants, say 25% higher than the mental and physical averages of the native population—and in the present state of our medical, physical and psychological anthropometry this is not an idle dream—and let us allow none to enter who fails to reach this standard. The writers of this paper are not against all immigration into this already crowded country. The ancestors of the men who pride themselves on being English to-day were all at one time immigrants; it is not for us to cast the first stone against newcomers, solely because they are newcomers. But the test for the immigrant in the old days was a severe one; it was power physical and mental to retain their hold on the land they seized. So came Celts, Saxons, Norsemen, Danes and Normans in succession and built up the nation of which we are proud. Nor do we criticise the alien Jewish immigration simply because it is Jewish; we took the alien Jews to study, because they were the chief immigrants of that day and material was readily available. We know what the world owes to Jewish philosophers, to Jewish musicians and to Jewish writers. We should have stood by Reuchlin when he cried: "Print rather than burn the Jewish books." Our chief fear in checking indiscriminate Jewish immigration is not that Britain may lose a supply of cheap labour, but that we may exclude a future Spinoza, a Mendelssohn, a Heine or an Einstein. Yet approaching the problem sympathetically and as we hope without bias, we cannot see that unrestricted immigration has been an advantage to this country. At first sight it seems a hard judgment. If we accept some of these Polish and Russian Jews as reaching a proper immigration standard, are we to leave the majority of them to suffer the hardships, possibly the tortures they have met with in Eastern Europe? Assuredly this is not the only alternative. There are lands less crowded than our own; there are populations physically and mentally below the level of these alien Jews. If Palestine be such a land, then the associations of the past are an invaluable aid. But if it be such a land the Jewish immigrant must go as the Danes went to Yorkshire, with a spade in one hand and a weapon in the other. For it is not town-workers, but fruit and corn-growers that are needed, and the Arab race will not indefinitely allow soil to the man who cannot defend it and himself. If Palestine fulfil not our immigration conditions, then surely the wisdom of our statesmen might find another home for the bulk of these persecuted Jews than the crowded cities of Western Europe? The welfare of our own country is bound up with the maintenance and improvement of its stock, and our researches do not indicate that this will follow the unrestricted admission of either Jewish or any other type of immigrant.

THE IDEA THAT WAR IS NATURAL ANATOMIZED AND DECENTLY INTERRED

ALBERT FREDERICK POLLARD (1869-1948) was Professor of History at University College, in the University of London, from 1903 to 1931. His essay "The War of Nature and a Peace of Mind" appeared in the Christmas number of *Vincula*, the University of London Students Journal, on 14 December 1925, at which time I read it, and finished in a frenzy of enthusiasm (as Shelley once wrote of a similar "read"). This essay had an influence upon me out of all proportion to its length, and there is hardly a sentence in it which I have not borrowed for my own writings in the fifty years that have elapsed.

Pollard's essay strikes me as one of the sanest and soundest critiques of the idea that war is "natural" in the literature of the subject. It says more in a few words than most of the innumerable tomes that have been devoted to the discussion of war have managed to say. It was the direct inspiration of my own study, "The Nature of War and the Myth of Nature," *The Scientific Monthly* (Vol. 54, 1942), pp. 342-353.

And what is the moral of this story? It is that when professors are invited to contribute to student papers they should jump at the opportunity, for they will there sow seeds that may later bear piquant fruit.

In the same issue of *Vincula* in which this essay appeared there was published a letter of mine on "The Colour Question" which ended with the words, referring to the editor's comment in a previous issue, "That 'The world cannot be divided among races so fundamentally different and be a place of peace or liberty, etc.' is, I think, a great fallacy. Naturally, however, whilst nations sign Peace Treaties with one hand, and with the other build super-submarines, simple ideals will not suffice." Alas!

THE WAR OF NATURE AND A PEACE OF MIND.*

The Editor has asked me to produce a Christmas "vox" a little more appropriate to the season than the refrain that "war is natural," which distracted readers of the Armistice number of VINCULA; and I am tempted to accept his invitation by the fact that a lecture I gave on the first day of term after the War broke out dealt with this, its fundamental (1) issue. The refrain is familiar enough: it was the burden of the opening chapters of that notorious book, "Germany and the Next War," in which Bernhardi in 1911 expressed and fortified the German will-to-war. He wrote to protest against "the aspirations for peace, which seem to dominate our age and threaten to poison the soul of the German people": "war," he declared, "is a biological necessity"; it "is as necessary as the struggle of the elements in Nature"; it "gives a biologically just decision, since its decisions rest on the very nature of things." "The whole idea" of arbitration "represents a presumptuous encroachment on the natural laws of development," for "what is right is decided by the arbitrament of war." He, too, invokes Darwin and "the plant world and the animal world" to prove this "universal law of Nature." (2)

Nevertheless, the statement that "war is natural" has no meaning, and any comment on it must be mainly speculation as to what those who make it imagine they mean when they repeat the words. "Natural" to whom, when, and under what conditions? "Let dogs delight to bark and bite, it is their nature to." Is it the nature, too, of men of science? What is nature? By nature, says Aristotle, some men are slaves; by nature, retorts Cicero, all men are free. In nature, says Hobbes, "the life of man is solitary, poor, nasty, brutish, and short": it is a condition of "war of every man against every man," in which "the notions of right and wrong, justice and injustice, have no place," and "force and fraud are the two cardinal virtues." "The state all men naturally are in," replies Locke, is "a state of perfect freedom to order their actions . . . as they think fit, within the bounds of the law of nature . . . a state also of equality." Nature, writes Wordsworth, "to me was all in all"; she "never did betray the heart that loved her." Nature, rejoins Tennyson, "red in tooth and claw, shrieks against the creed of man." It was one of Voltaire's least irreligious gibes against the religion of men that, if God made men after His own image, they had repaid the compliment. They do the same with nature: some discern nothing but good, others little but evil. Some see red, others see God; it all depends upon the kingdom that is within them.

Nature is as you like it. "Natural" may mean anything; but what may mean

*Reprinted from *Vincula* (University of London Students Journal, December 14, 1925, pp. 60-61.

(1) See my *Commonwealth at War*, pp. 2-8.

(2) English translation, popular edition, 16th impression, pp. 14, 18, 20, 23-4, 30, 34.

anything, in fact means nothing. War, it appears, is equally vague: it is natural, we are told, because "all nature fights, even trees and flowers, although their actions are not visible to the naked eye." Are these warlike actions of trees and flowers forward or rearguard actions? It would be useful to know whether it is offensive or defensive war that is natural. The sun and the moon, we suppose, declare war with great regularity because they get into opposition every month. Parties in the House of Commons are perpetually at war because they are opposed. The police wage war because they are a force; for "naturally" if we use force against a criminal, we must needs make war upon other communities. War, indeed, will last for ever, because men will never "cease to struggle." So the League of Nations has obviously failed whenever a stern parent is caught in the act of chastising a peccant child; and "fighting" will go on without end because drowning men will fight for life, doctors will fight disease, and women will fight for places at drapery sales. And this is war!

But these flowers that bloom in the verbal spring have nothing to do with the logical case. Life is indeed a struggle in which the only armistice is death. But that did not prevent the saving of millions of lives by the Armistice of 1918; and "war" in most of the arguments to prove it "natural" is an anaemic analogy. We only get confusion of mind by confounding "war" with "struggle" and "fighting" with "force"; and we get into deeper depths by confusing the "nature" of suns and moons, of cats and dogs, of brutes and men, of prehistoric and civilized man, of Kurds and Welsh, of prize-fighters and peace-makers. The fact that die-hard theologians and die-hard scientists alone agree that human nature does not change might seem a case of the meeting of extremes, were not prejudice predominant in both. Human nature has changed beyond all recognition, and continues to change with ever-increasing momentum. Is the nature of neolithic man the nature of man to-day? Even in English medieval history it was "natural" (and indeed legal) for all claims to real property to be tried by battle, and trial by jury was an artificial creation; which is "natural" to-day? For centuries longer it was "natural" to burn heretics for heresy, wage wars of religion, torture persons accused of treason, kill prisoners of war, put the whole population of places taken by assault to death. As late as the 19th century it was "natural" for people to crowd to see men, and even women, publicly hanged. Down to 1914 it seemed "natural" to German students and French politicians to fight duels with swords and pistols. Would it seem natural to the readers of VINCULA or to Mr. Baldwin and Mr. Ramsay Macdonald? It seemed "natural" to Turks to massacre Armenians. Is massacre therefore natural to us? Is war "natural" on the Canadian frontier, where peace without armaments has reigned for a hundred years, because armaments have made war seem "natural" in Alsace?

Those who assert that "war is natural" forget that every particle of civilisation has been achieved by the repeal, repudiation, and suppression of that "nature" which they are pleased to regard as an everlasting, universal law; and that human society depends upon the maintenance of control by the mind over the brute in man. The evolution of that control of mind over "nature" is the content of history beside which everything else sinks into insignificance. It is, perhaps, "natural" for the specialist in the means of human destruction to ignore it, and to contend that what he regards as artificial can never withstand his "nature." One might retort that modern war is as artificial as modern civilisation. It is waged by highly artificial entities, namely States; it is fought by highly artificial weapons, bombs and submarines and poison gas; it often arises from artificial motives and is sometimes conducted for artificial ends. War, as we know it, is made by man and not by nature; "the fault, dear Brutus, lies not in our stars, but in ourselves."

I need not delay over the nature of war in A.D. 2025, except to remark that it is not much wiser to forecast its methods to-day than it would have been in 1814 to forecast those of the last great war: our prevision may possibly be keener, but there is no reason to suppose that scientific invention will be more sluggish than it was in the nineteenth century. But I should like to demur to the assumption that scientific invention had much to do with either the winning or losing of the late war. Competition was so keen on both sides that in the long run inventions cancelled out. There was a ding-dong race in air craft; at one time submarines came perilously near success; and if the result had depended on scientific invention the Germans would have won. As it was, they neutralized enormous odds in numbers to such an extent that for four years the principal front hardly shifted on an average more than half a dozen miles in either direction. The Allied victory was due not to scientific superiority but to the economic exhaustion of the foe, and to the fact that in Foch's decisive campaign America was pouring more fresh troops into the line of battle in a month than the Germans could raise in a year.

It was, in fact, confidence in "reeking tube and iron shard" that led the Germans from peace and security into war and disaster; and civilisation is being faced with the same alternative. Peace, like war, is as you like it—to be or not to be. We need not take *au pied de la lettre* the threats of what destructive science may do, for in war the effectiveness of defence keeps closely in touch with that of offence and often outruns it. But it is the nature of artificial war to exact intolerable sacrifice without producing satisfaction; and for the sake of argument we may admit the contention that it is coming within the range of possibility that man might—in this "natural" course of things—destroy the human race. The late war came as the climax to an age in which the growth of man's control over physical forces outran his control over human passions; and it is the creed of "natural war" that man, controlling the forces of nature can never control himself.

There looms a day of judgement, a day of judgement pronounced by man upon himself as having committed suicide because he was not fit to live. For we come to a common issue between a common mind to live and common "nature" to kill. If there is Armageddon all will be taken, none will be left, and Fate will be common to victors and vanquished, rich and poor, all the nations, and both the hemispheres. To learn lest we perish is the logic of the League of Nations; learn to destroy is the teaching of "natural" war. Whether mankind survives depends less on its science than on its humanity, upon whether we trust an increasing control over physical forces to men with a decreasing sense of responsibility for their use, and whether we regard as more "natural" the war we think rooted in Nature or the peace we owe to our mind.

WILLIAM ERNEST CASTLE ON RACE AND HALF-CASTES

WILLIAM ERNEST CASTLE (1867-1962) was one of the founding fathers of genetics in the United States. He graduated from Harvard and served on its faculty as zoology instructor and professor from 1897 to 1936. He was the author of a number of distinguished books, among them *Heredity in Relation to Evolution and Animal Breeding* (1911), *Genetics and Eugenics* (1916), *Mammalian Genetics* (1940), and many scientific papers on heredity and evolution.

In the contribution reprinted here Castle writes authoritatively, simply, and clearly on the problem of what used to be called "the half-caste." It is something of a measure of the progress that has been made in this connection that the term is today hardly ever heard. But when Castle wrote, in the twenties, this was a matter very much on the racists' agenda. "Mongrelization" is something they held before their audience as a sure evidence of the degeneration of the good old Anglo-Saxon stock. Books like Madison Grant's *The Passing of the Great Race* (1916), and his *The Alien in Our Midst* (1930), Lothrop Stoddard's *The Rising Tide of Color* (1920), and many others all testified to the imminent destruction of The Great White Race by race mixture or, to use the polite word, "miscegenation."

Castle's article was by way of being a rejoinder to these nonsensical racist claims. In its quiet way it exerted a considerable influence upon the thinking of many young scientists who read it, and it is for that reason and also because it constitutes one of the best things ever written on the subject that it is reprinted here.

BIOLOGICAL AND SOCIAL CONSEQUENCES OF RACE-CROSSING*
W. E. CASTLE

What constitute the essential differences between human races seems to be a question difficult for anthropologists to agree upon but from a biologist's point of view those appear to be on safe ground who base racial distinctions on easily recognizable and measureable differences perpetuated by heredity irrespective of the environment. See Hooton, 1926. It is still a moot question how races originate, not merely in man, but also among the lower animals and plants. At one time natural selection was thought to be an all-sufficient explanation of the matter, but the more carefully the question is studied and the more exact and experimental in character the data which enter into its solution, the more fully do we become convinced that forms of life are rarely static, that organic change is the rule rather than the exception. Change is inevitable and is not limited to useful or adaptive variations. Natural selection undoubtedly determines the survival of decidedly useful variations, which arise for any reason, and also the extinction of those which are positively harmful, but a host of other variations fall in neither of these categories and survive among the descendants as a matter of course, quite unaffected by natural selection.

The experimental study of evolution indicates that genetic (herditary) variations are all the time arising, and with especial frequency in such organisms as are bisexual and cross-fertilized.

In a state of nature no species can for long be separated by geographical barriers into non-interbreeding groups, without the origin of specific or racial differences between such groups. This is because new variations are from time to time originating in each group, and if chance is an element in the origin of variations, it would be a rare event for the same variation to appear simultaneously in two geographically separated groups. Hence such groups become different irrespective of the action of natural selection. Hence the maple, sassafras, chestnut and oak trees of Asia have become specifically different from those of North America since the land connection between the two continents disappeared, although the species found in one continent will grow perfectly well in the other. Also the reindeer of Eurasia is different from the caribou of Alaska, although the two are still enough alike to interbreed and produce fertile hybrids. For a like reason the North American Indians are racially dis-

¹This paper, prepared at the suggestion of Dr. Hrdlička, is based largely on an article published under the same title in The Journal of Heredity, Vol. 15, Sept. 1924. Thanks are due to the editor of that journal for permission to use the material here.

*Reprinted from *American Journal of Physical Anthropology*, Vol. ix, No. 2 (April-June, 1926), pp. 145-156.

tinct from the Mongolians, their nearest of kin among human races. Time and isolation have made them different.

When isolated groups of flowering plants have become specifically distinct, they often show a tendency to remain distinct even if subsequently they are brought into the same territory. One may have become earlier or later than the other in its time of flowering, or structural or physiological differences may have arisen which make cross fertilization between the two difficult. Similarly in the higher animals (particularly among birds and mammals) a psychological element enters into the maintenance of group differences. The individual prefers to mate only in his own group and with his own kind, but circumstances may overcome racial antipathy and the overpowering impulse of sex bring about mixed unions when mates of the same race are not available. Thousands of mules are produced annually by matings between a mare and a jackass, but it often requires considerable finesse on the breeder's part to bring them about, and if asses and horses of both sexes were turned loose together on a range, it is doubtful whether a mule would be produced once in a century.

In mankind, where the race differences are less profound, so far as the physiology of reproduction is concerned, the psychological element in the maintenance of racial differences is even greater. In a population mixed in its racial composition, differences in language, religion, dress, or social customs, often keep the racially different elements distinct for centuries. The castes of India are a case in point. Since there are no biological obstacles to crossing between the most diverse human races, when such crossing does occur, it is in disregard of social conventions, race pride and race prejudice. Naturally therefore it occurs between antisocial and outcast specimens of the respective races, or else between conquerors and slaves. The social status of the children is thus bound to be low, their educational opportunities poor, their moral background bad.

There is a school of writers who insist that mixed races are inferior just because they are mixed. They cite the poor cultural attainments of the mixed races of the West Indies and of certain South American countries, maintaining that the half-breeds have all the vices of both parent races but the virtues of neither. They compare the cultural attainments of the southern U. S. with those of the northern U. S., much to the disadvantage of the former, and ascribe the difference wholly to the presence of the mulatto. They overlook or ignore a number of other factors which enter into the question, such as the kind of individuals who contracted the mixed matings and the character of the physical inheritance of their offspring, the conditions under which the children of mixed race were reared, the nature of their intellectual and moral education, the character of their economic and industrial opportunities, their ability to share in the equal protection of the law. Does the half-breed, in any community of the world in which he is numerous, have an equal chance to make a man of himself, as compared with the sons of the dominant race? I think not. Can we then fairly consider him racially inferior just because his racial attainments are less? Attainments imply opportunities as well as abilities.

Writers who appeal to race prejudice are very much in vogue. Their task is easy. We inherit from a long line of animal ancestors the group instinct, loyalty to the herd against the rest of creation. It is not difficult to persuade us that our group of races is the best group, our particular race the best race and all others inferior. There was a time when divine revelation was relied upon to establish the claim to the status of "chosen people," but now it is sufficient to write "science says." Would it not be well to inquire into the credentials of a "science," which so confidently proclaims one race superior and another inferior, and all mixtures worse than either? Is it really *science*, truth established by adequate evidence, or is it *assumption* backed up by loud voiced assertion? I share the views in this connection of Dr. Hooton as recently expressed in Science. He says (p. 76)

"A third group of writers on racial subjects, usually not professional anthropologists, associates cultural and psychological characteristics with physical types on wholly insufficient evidence. These race propagandists commonly attribute to the physical subdivision of mankind to which they imagine that they themselves belong all or most of the superior qualities of mankind, physical, mental and moral. They talk of the psychological characteristics of this or that race as if they were objective tangible properties, scientifically demonstrated. Starting from an *a priori* assumption that physical types have psychological correlates, they attempt to refer every manifestation of the psychological qualities assumed to be the exclusive property of this or that race to the physical type in question. Great men of whatever period are claimed to be members of the favored race on the basis of their achievements and sometimes with a total disregard of physical criteria. In no case has any serious effort been made by such ethnomaniacs to isolate a pure racial type and to study either its mental qualities or its material culture. The fact that most if not all peoples are racially mixed is consistently ignored. While some of the conclusions of such writers may be correct, none of them have been scientifically established."

A commendable attempt to obtain experimental evidence on the effects of race crossing was made a few years ago by Dr. Alfred Mjoen who crossed dissimilar races of rabbits. His general conclusion was that racial crossing tends to produce physical deterioration both in rabbits and in humans. He admitted the impracticability of investigating the question critically in human populations and for that reason resorted to experiments with rabbits for critical evidence. He offers the results of two sets of experiments in one of which two different races of rabbits were crossed, in the other three. The evidences which he observes of physical deterioration are: 1. Increased size in F_1 (first hybrid generation), greater than that of either parent. This is regarded as a "weakness" because "abnormal." 2. Decreased size of some individuals in F_4 (fourth hybrid generation), which are smaller than either ancestor of pure race. Other individuals of F_4 are intermediate in size between the uncrossed ancestors. 3. Diminished fertility and increased mortality in the young in F_4 as compared with earlier generations. 4. Failure of the sexual instinct in many F_4 individuals. 5. Asymmetrical carriage of the ears, one erect, one pendant, among cross-breeds between lop-eared and albino rabbits.

The increased size of F_4 individuals is a phenomenon familiar to animal and plant breeders and frequently utilized by them. It is regularly attended by unusual vigor of growth and resistance to disease as well as by high fecundity. I have never before seen it mentioned as an evidence of physical deterioration. If it is "deterioration" to be "abnormal," all superior individuals have "deteriorated," because they are "abnormal." The races with which Dr. Mjoen started were "abnormal" as compared with the ancestral wild rabbit of Europe, all being medium to large sized (3400-4300 grams). The weights given for the F_1 individuals are 4160 and 4645 grams respectively. In F_4 weights are given for eight individuals, ranging from 2560 to 3850 grams. The smallest of these is well above the average weight of wild rabbits and so "abnormal." Is it an evidence of "deterioration" that some of these are less "abnormal" than their immediate ancestors, or that the group is more variable than the F_1 generation?

The diminished fertility of F_4 individuals and the increased mortality of their young more probably resulted from unsanitary environment than from the mixed racial nature of the parents. The animals are reported to have been kept in this generation one or two males in a common hutch with eight females. Rabbits cannot be bred successfully in such crowded quarters and it is not surprising that only one litter of young was obtained in a period of six months. Failure of the sexual instinct and inability to produce viable young are well known consequences of an inadequate or unbalanced diet but not of race crossing in any species of animal that ever I heard of.

The asymmetrical carriage of the ears which Dr. Mjoen regards as "the most distinct outward sign of a disharmonic crossing that can well be imagined," and which he observes among three of his cross-bred rabbits, is a feature not confined to cross-breeds but of frequent occurrence among rabbits of large size, irrespective of race. Ear size in rabbits is closely correlated with body size, as I have shown elsewhere. When the ears are long, the muscles at their base are often unable to hold the ears erect, and they may lop over both to the same side, or one may lop over while the other remains upright. Ossification at the base of the ear adapts itself to this abnormal relation, as observed by Darwin (*Animals and Plants*) and the condition thus becomes permanent. The purest races of large rabbits, such as Flemish Giants and pure bred lop-eared rabbits, often show this asymmetrical ear carriage. Breeders naturally consider it a defect and in lop-eared rabbits seek to correct it in the young by mechanical means, such as manipulation with the hands to separate the connective tissue beneath the skin which joins the ears together. Books on rabbit-keeping figure leather caps to be placed over the top of the head of the young lop-eared rabbits to hold the ears apart and down. It is evident, therefore, that the asymmetrical ear carriage of Dr. Mjoen's rabbits was not due to their cross-bred state, since this same condition is found in uncrossed individuals of one, at least, of his "pure races."

From an experience of more than twenty years in the breeding of rabbits, in the course of which I have crossed nearly all known breeds, some of which differed much more in size and other characters than did those used by Dr. Mjoen, I am satisfied that there are no breeds of domestic rabbits so distinct racially that their hybrids show the slightest diminution in fertility or vigor, as compared with the uncrossed races. Breeds of rabbits show no more racial distinctness than breeds of cattle, which are so frequently crossed in the most enlightened agricultural practice, without any indications of diminished fertility being observed.

Dr. Mjoen's conclusions rest on insufficient and uncritical observations. It would not be necessary to point this out to an experienced geneticist, but the sociologist is perhaps entitled to a biological rating of these observations.

ORGANIC MISFITS

Dr. Mjoen's argument, if I understand him rightly, assumes that all inheritance in rabbits and in men is Mendelian, and that if this is so all possible recombinations of the inherited characters will occur in F_2 and later generations. Among these recombinations, he thinks, are sure to be many organic misfits, such as small legs on large bodies. It might be supposed that in the evolution of existing races organic misfits had been eliminated by natural selection, and therefore, that surviving types are superior types which could only be made worse by intercrossing, since the frequency of organic misfits must be increased by such crossing.

The question of the production of skeletal misfits in crossing the largest with the smallest known races of rabbits, I have subjected to an extensive and intensive experimental investigation, but I have failed to observe any indication of the occurrence of misfits either in F_1 or F_2. There is a remarkable constancy in the degree of correlation between part and part within the body, quite irrespective of size. The genetic agencies which control the size of particular parts are identical with the agencies which control the size of the body as a whole. From an intimate study of the subject I am able to deny categorically Dr. Mjoen's assumption that there is inheritance, independent of general body size, of types of bone structure which regulate "the way or mode of jumping and holding—carrying—the body."

Why, it might be asked, if nature abhors race crossing, does she do so much of it? Why is it that distinct races of the same species of animal occur only where geographical isolation exists? Why does she go to such pains to ensure cross fertilization rather than self fertilization or close fertilization?

· Are there such things as "harmonic" and "disharmonic" race crossings? It is assumed in Dr. Mjoen's argument that some combinations of inherited characters are better than others, have greater survival value, and for that reason are found in existing races. As race crossing brings about recombination of inherited characters, it is to be expected on genetic principles that mixed races will be more variable than unmixed races. Is such variability a disadvantage? Yes, if all *new* combinations are inferior to those which previously existed. This Dr. Mjoen seems to assume to be true in certain cases, as in Norwegian-Lapp crosses, which he regards as "disharmonic." From his viewpoint any infusion of Lapp characters into the Norwegian complex is deterioration. Perhaps the Lapp might reasonably take a similar view of the situation. Race pride and race prejudice narrow down to just that view of all alien stocks. But to an outside observer it is conceivable that *some* inherited characters of the Lapp might be combined with other inherited characters of the Norwegian to produce meritorious racial combinations, which would be viewed with satisfaction both by the intelligent Lapp and by the intelligent Norwegian. When these combinations had gained such recognition, Dr. Mjoen would doubtless designate them "harmonic race crossings."

Now is there any way, other than trial and error, by which harmonic can be distinguished from disharmonic race crossing? I doubt it. I doubt whether there is any race of human beings whose genetic qualities are all inherently bad. I doubt whether there is any human race so "superior" that it is incapable of improvement. Dr. Mjoen is looking for some simple "blood test" chemical or serological which will show whether a proposed mating, either inter-racial or intra-racial, is "harmonic" or "disharmonic." I doubt whether he finds it. The methods of genetic analysis of inherited qualities are far in advance of chemical knowledge of the material determiners of those inherited qualities. We may reasonably expect to learn more from a study of the genetic qualities of races and individuals and their mode of inheritance than from blood tests.

RACE CROSSING AND SOCIAL INHERITANCE

I doubt whether there are any race combinations which are, so far as biological qualities are concerned, inherently either harmonic or disharmonic, that is productive of better or worse genetic combinations. Both better and worse should theoretically result, if all inherited characters follow Mendel's law in transmission. A more variable population would then result, which should be on the whole more adaptable to a new or changing environment either physical or social. Is it not possible that the racially mixed character of the populations of France, Germany, England and the United States have been one factor in their adaptability to social and economic changes?

If all inheritance of human traits were simple Mendelian inheritance, and natural selection were unlimited in its action among human populations, then unrestricted racial intercrossing might be recommended. But in the light of our present knowledge, few would recommend it. For, in the first place, much that is best in human existence is a matter of social inheritance, not of biological inheritance. Race crossing disturbs social inheritance. That is one of its worst features. And, limiting our attention to biological characters only, few of them follow the simple Mendelian law, with presence or absence of single characters, dominance or elimination. Most inherited characters are blending (the Mendelian interpretation of which is in terms of multiple factors). When parents differ in a trait, the offspring commonly possess an intermediate degree of it. This is true of stature, weight, and, I think, of general mental powers. Neither parent is devoid of stature or weight or is without mental ability. The children as a rule are intermediate between their parents as regards such traits. It is so in racial crosses, except for the complication of hybrid vigor or "heterosis" in the F_1 generation, a well known occurrence both in animal and human crosses. When two races cross which differ in stature, the children may surpass either parent in this respect, as Dr. Mjoen has observed. But the "overgrowth," as he well calls it, does not persist into later generations. It disappears, as heterosis disappears, and the population of later generations will be intermediate in character, though probably more variable than either uncrossed race. This is the outcome in numerous careful experimental investigations among animals, and may confidently be predicted as the result with similar characters in the crossing of human races.

When traits blend in human crosses, deterioration is not to be expected as a consequence, but rather an intermediate degree of the characters involved. Whether from a purely biological standpoint a particular race cross is considered desirable or undesirable will depend on whether a greater or less degree of the characters under consideration is desired.

RACE CROSSING IN THE UNITED STATES

Consider for a moment the physical (not social) consequences in the United States of a cross between African black races and European whites, an experiment which has been made on a considerable scale. The white race has less skin pigment and more intelligence. The first difference will not be disputed, the second can be claimed at least on the basis of past racial accomplishment. As regards skin color the F_1 hybrids are intermediate; as regards intelligence it is not so easy to judge, since their environment has commonly been that of the blacks, but it will be generally admitted that they are superior in this respect to the blacks and that this has been a factor in their social advancement which has been more rapid than that of the blacks. Repeated backcrosses with whites, if permitted, might be expected to result in an approximation to the skin color and level of intelligence of the whites in a few generations. Similarly back-crosses with the blacks would naturally result in an approximation to their physical and mental standards. Matings of F_1 individuals *inter se* would continue indefinitely a race varying about intermediate standards, but varying more widely than either uncrossed race.

So far as biological considerations are concerned, there is no race problem in the United States. If social considerations were not much more-powerful than biological ones, the future population of the United States would certainly be highly variable in skin color and intelligence, passing by scarcely perceptible gradations from a pure black type of the present "black belt" to a pure white type such as would result from a mixing of European races. But the social considerations *are* of much more importance than biological ones in this connection, and the racial future of the United States cannot be predicted from the latter alone.

MIXED RACES FROM INFERIOR STOCKS

Dr. Mjoen would like to believe that the mixed race constituent of Norway's population will die out of itself, because he finds that it coexists with bad physical and social states of the population. He seeks biological support of this hope in animal experiments, but will not find it, I think, if those experiments are made critical and interpreted without bias. He should investigate also the social environment under which race crossing occurs and in which the hybrids are forced to live. In these, if I mistake not, rather than in any mysterious biological disharmonies, will be found the explanation of the alleged greater prevalence of tuberculosis, drunkenness, theft and other social evils among the mixed population. He should inquire what sort of individuals contract mixed marriages, and under what conditions. Are they the best or the worst of their respective races? Do those who contract such marriages do so from deliberate choice or only because they can find no eligible mates among their own people? Are they individuals of force of character with passions well under control, or are they of the feebler sort, yielding readily to impulse and with unbridled passions? Is it to be expected that a cross between poor specimens of two races will result in anything but poor offspring? It is illogical to ascribe the poor quality of a mixed race to the fact that it is a mixture, provided that the original ingredients are poor. How could it well be otherwise?

Consider also the social environment in which race crossing usually occurs and in which the hybrids grow up. Crossing occurs clandestinely or, if in legalized wedlock, between individuals lost to shame. For parties to such matings are despised by both races and their children are social outcasts. Their social opportunities are decidedly limited. Is it any wonder that their social attainments are limited and that they show lack of the ordinary social inhibitions? It is not necessary to invoke biological disharmonies in order to explain the poor results of many race mixtures. Social agencies afford a sufficient explanation.

OUTLOOK FOR THE MULATTOES

Let us consider further, in this connection, the black-white race mixture in the United States. According to Willcox, about nine-tenths of the present population of the United States consists of whites without admixture of African blood, the other tenth consisting of blacks or black-white hybrids, known as mulattoes. If there were free intercrossing of all elements of the population, the proportion of mixed bloods should steadily increase, but this has not been the case in the past and is not likely to be in the future. At the first United States Census in 1790, according to Willcox, the negroes and mulattoes constituted about one-fifth of the total population, or twice the proportion they now represent. Instead of the increase which random matings would produce, there has been a steady decrease in the proportion of blacks and mulattoes. This has been due in part to white immigration, in part to a lower rate of increase among the blacks, but chiefly to a strong social prejudice among the whites against mixed marriages, which in many States has found expression in legislation against miscegenation, and in all States takes the effective form of a strong public sentiment against it. This same public sentiment insists on classifying as black every individual who is known to have or is suspected of having any trace of negro blood in his veins. The consequence is that marriages between whites and blacks or mulattoes are at present extremely rare and clandestine unions are uncommon.

So far as back-crossing of mulattoes with blacks is concerned, this probably does not occur with random frequency, since pure-blooded negroes on one hand and mulattoes on the other, have each a degree of group consciousness which tends to keep them apart. The mulattoes as a rule are more intelligent and have enjoyed better educational advantages so that they find more ready employment in urban life as porters, janitors, or even in clerical or professional occupations. But with urban life goes a reduced birth rate among blacks as well as whites. The prospect is that, if things go on as they now are, the mulattoes will not amalgamate either with the whites or with the blacks, but will form a separate but diminishing proportion of the total population. The blacks are holding their own in certain rural sections of the South, but elsewhere are going back numerically. No complete amalgamation of blacks with whites is to be anticipated, simply because of social impediments, though no biological barrier whatever is discoverable.

INDIAN-WHITE CROSSES

Another distant racial cross which has been made on a considerable scale in North America is that between European whites and North American Indians. To be sure, the number of hybrids resulting from this cross is insignificant compared with that of the mulattoes, but it is sufficient to be instructive as a biological and social experiment. The early English colonists kept close to the coast and steadfastly refused to associate with the "savages," but the French in Canada were more disposed to roam the woods. Their young men explored the interior of the continent, lived with the Indians as trappers and hunters and often took Indian wives. Thus a half-breed population grew up of hardy adventurous frontiersmen. It would be difficult to find in them evidences of physical or intellectual degeneracy, other than those entailed by the introduced vices of the white race.

Within the United States, the settlement of the Mississippi Valley took place so rapidly that it amounted to a complete dispossession of the Indian tribes found there. These moved bodily westward to "reservations" beyond the great river. Accordingly there was little opportunity for race mixture. Nevertheless, renegade whites, who had reason to lose their identity temporarily, often joined the Indians on their reservations. As the reservation lands became valuable through the occupation of the surrounding territory by whites, the "squaw men" and their half-breed children found it an economic advantage to be members of the tribe. So when later the wild Indians were domesticated and "given lands in severalty," the individuals of mixed race often found themselves wealthy land owners. This gave them social advantages which resulted in frequent marriage alliances with the whites. For there is no strong social prejudice against the red man such as exists against the black man, recently a slave. Consequently the pureblooded Indians are a rapidly vanishing element of the population of the United States, and those of mixed race are being rapidly assimilated in the white population, frequently attaining positions of influence and authority. The difference in results following crossing with the black and with the red races in the United States are not referable to any biological harmonies or disharmonies existing in the respective cases but wholly to the social attitude of the whites, which is hostile in one case, indifferent in the other.

A further illustration of the surpassing importance of social over biological considerations in race-crossing is seen in the attitude of the Pacific Coast States towards Chinese and Japanese intermixture. No one questions the virility of these races or their biological fitness. Their cultural attainments are very high and antedate our own. Hybrids between these races and white races, so far as our information goes, are of high quality physically and intellectually. Yet public opinion is unalterably opposed to Oriental immigration or race mixture, not on biological grounds, but purely on social, economic, or political grounds.

So far as a biologist can see, human race problems are not biological problems any more than rabbit crosses are social problems. The rabbit breeder does not cross his selected races of rabbits unless he desires to improve upon what he has. The sociologist who is satisfied with human society as now constituted may reasonably decry race crossing. But let him do so on social grounds only. He will wait in vain, if he waits to see mixed races vanish from any biological unfitness.

THE RACISTS, EUGENISTS, AND HEREDITARIANS ANATOMIZED

GEORGE AMOS DORSEY (1868-1931), American anthropologist, was a singularly well-rounded anthropologist and thinker. His specialty was the American Indian, and to American Indian studies he made many first-rate contributions. In 1929 his book *Civilization: Man's Own Show* (Harper & Bros.) appeared and immediately became a bestseller in America and abroad. It remains a remarkably fine example of popular exposition and is still very much worth reading. In the preceding year the essay here reprinted, "Race and Civilization," appeared in the volume edited by the historian Charles A. Beard, *Whither Mankind*. This book had a wide sale, the distinction of its seventeen contributors, among them Bertrand Russell, John Dewey, James Harvey Robinson, Havelock Ellis, Sidney and Beatrice Webb, Lewis Mumford, and Carl Van Doren, serving to make it a memorable volume.

Dorsey's contribution is one of the earliest and remains one of the best critical examinations of the views of the racists, eugenists, and hereditarians of the first three decades of the twentieth century. Its arguments are as forcibly relevant today as they were when they were made nearly half a century ago. I have never seen a reference to this article, but I am quite sure that it must have exerted a considerable influence upon those who read it, and thus contributed to the general clarification of thinking on the subject of "race" and "heredity," two words so confusing that contributions like Dorsey's will, it seems, always be necessary to serve as correctives to the quanta of misinformation for which they stand. Dorsey makes this brilliantly clear in this really quite delightful anatomy.

RACE AND CIVILIZATION*
By GEORGE A. DORSEY

Race is the garment we are born in and is set in our biologic or blood inheritance; civilization—or culture, to use a more comprehensive term—is the garment we learn to wear and depends on physical and social environment: time, place, parents, teachers, society. The author of this chapter holds, in common with his fellow-anthropologists, that no necessary or innate connection between race and civilization has yet been proved, and that while such connection is conceivable it is highly improbable. He holds further that there is no warrant for the assumption that certain races are "higher" than others, or that there are any "pure" races, or that race mixtures or "hybrid races" are biologically (or culturally) inferior; or even that any existing classification of mankind according to biologic or heritable features and psychologic or cultural traits has any permanent scientific merit or furnishes any real clue as to how peoples and cultures are genetically related.

I

And yet a group of writers, not inappropriately termed "heredity mongers," not only make such assumptions but assert that race and civilization are innately related, and use their assumptions and assertions as arguments for political legislation and social reform. In fact, the amount of false biology, infantile logic, and bad faith that these heredity mongers bring to bear on our enormously complicated and complex racial and cultural problems is unbelievable. Wittingly or unwittingly, they juggle biologic, psychologic, and cultural factors to suit their convenience, and pour forth flimsy arguments based on dogmatic

*Reprinted from Charles A. Beard, Ed., *Whither Mankind* (New York, Longmans, Green & Co., 1928), pp. 229-263.

and unfounded assumptions as scientific facts to gratify their race phobia. They demand attention solely because of their prominence or academic standing, or because as "best sellers" they attempt to mould American civilization in ways biologically unwarranted and socially false and misleading.

Race phobia is as old as human nature and springs from the same primitive impulse: *We* are the People. Race phobia in its modern form[1] began (in 1854) with Count Arthur de Gobineau's "Essay on the Inequality of the Races of Man," which undertook to prove that the decisive factor in civilization was race, or physical structure; that national development depended on keeping the race pure; and that the "Aryan" race only had founded a really great civilization. Max Müller, in his work on Aryan tongues, indirectly and unwittingly helped establish the idea of an Aryan race; and in spite of the fact that Aryan tongues are spoken by peoples of India and of diverse racial type, "Aryan" came to be synonymous with Blumenbach's European or Caucasian race, and especially with the blond peoples of North Europe—the Teutons or "Nordic" race.

The World War produced a recrudescence of race phobia that has not yet run its course or possibly yet reached the height of its virulence. But the original "Aryan" race has been resolved into three "races" represented by the blond Teuton, the heavy Slav, and the darker Italian—or, the Nordic, Alpine, and Mediterranean. Due to the flood of emotion which swept this country during the war, the "Teutonic" race quite gave way to a Nordic obsession or an Anglo-Saxon myth. This virtual abandonment of the Aryan for a Nordic idea was largely due to the "Foundations of the Nineteenth Century" by the Scotsman, Houston Stewart Chamberlain, who deserted his country for Germany. Schultz's "Race or Mongrel" (1908) definitely brought the Nordic idea to America.

With Madison Grant's "The Passing of the Great Race" (1916) the doctrine of a specific Nordic race was definitely let loose on the public. That doctrine has already been put to work in America in keeping the Nordic stock "pure" by restricting immigration of "inferior" races, and is now being invoked by the eugenics cult to make it purer by encouraging "superior" people to outbreed their "inferiors" and by discouraging inferior people from breeding at all. Nonsense of course; but potentially so dangerous that a critical examination of the doctrine and its inferences is properly a part of this discussion of race and civilization.

Grant's book alone, in spite of its formidable display of "authorities" (especially prepared by a Columbia student as window dressing for a later edition), could not have reached its vogue without the endorsement of a great name—Professor Henry Fairfield Osborn. He wrote a preface to two editions.

[1] The complete history of this movement is beautifully told in Part I of Professor F. H. Hankins' "The Racial Basis of Civilization: A Critique of the Nordic Doctrine."

How ruthlessly Professor Osborn argues and how well he knows "facts" (quite unknown to anthropologists) is best revealed by the following extracts from his letter to the *New York Times*, April 8, 1924:

> The Northern races, as is well known to anthropologists, include all those peoples which originally occupied the western plateau of Asia and traversed Northern Europe, certainly as early as 12,000 B.C. In the country which they occupied the conditions of life were hard, the struggle for existence severe, and this gave rise to their principal virtues, as well as to their faults, to their fighting qualities and to their love of strong drink. . . . They invaded the countries to the South, not only as conquerors but as contributors of strong moral and intellectual elements to more or less decadent civilizations. Through the Nordic tide which flowed into Italy came the ancestors of Raphael, Leonardo da Vinci, Galileo, Titian; also according to Günther, of Giotto, Donatello, Botticelli, Andrea del Sarto, Petrarch and Tasso. . . . Columbus from his portraits and from busts, authentic or not, was clearly of Nordic ancestry. Kossuth was a Calvinist and of noble family, and there is a presumption in favor of his being a Nordic; Kosciusko and Pulaski were members of a Polish nobility which at that time was largely Nordic. Coligny, Colbert, Richelieu, Lafayette, and Rochambeau, beyond all question were of French (Norman) Nordic nobility, and in modern France we observe that two of the leaders in the recent great struggle, Joffre and Foch, are both Nordic, while Clemenceau and Poincaré are of Alpine blood. France includes among her great artists Rodin, of Nordic origin; among her leading literary men, Lamartine, Racine, Anatole France, all Nordics. The intellectual influence of the Northern race is also apparent in Spain where it appears in her greatest man of letters, Cervantes; also in Portugal in the poet-hero Camoëns, whose ancestors were Gothic. Of the fighting stock of Italy, Napoleon, although born in Corsica, was descended from the old Lombard nobility, of Nordic origin, and it is probable that Garibaldi with his Teutonic name was largely of Northern stock. . . .

"*Columbus from his portraits and from busts, authentic or not, was clearly of Nordic ancestry.*" This sentence seems worth requoting—even italicizing; comment would be superfluous.

In the first preface to Grant's book, Professor Osborn asserts that race plays a larger part than language or nationality in moulding human destiny: "Race implies heredity and heredity implies all the moral, social, and intellectual characteristics and traits which are the springs of politics and government. . . . Thus the racial history of Europe . . . might be paraphrased as the heredity history of Europe." He then speaks of "the gradual dying out among our people of those hereditary traits through which the principles of our religious, political, and social foundations were laid down and their insidious replacement by traits of less noble character.''

By the time of the writing of the preface to the second edition, the United States had entered the World War. Professor Osborn found that it was the ''Anglo-Saxon branch of the Nordic race'' that was ''again showing itself to be that upon which the nation must chiefly depend for leadership, for courage, for loyalty, for unity and harmony of action, for self-sacrifice and devotion to an ideal. . . . In the new world that we are working and fighting for, the world of liberty, of justice, and of humanity, we shall save democracy only when democracy discovers its own aristocracy as in the days when our Republic was founded.'' Professor Osborn is plainly in the grip of race phobia.

With Professor Osborn so baselessly dogmatic we need not be surprised if Grant asserts anything he wants as *evidence*, but when he claims that ''modern anthropology has demonstrated that racial lines are not only absolutely independent of both national and linguistic groupings, but that in many cases these racial lines cut through them at sharp angles and correspond closely with the divisions of social cleavage,'' he claims something that no living anthropologist admits as demonstrated.

Equally unfounded in observable fact is his claim that ''the great lesson of the science of race is the immutability of somatological or bodily characters, with which is closely associated the immutability of psychical predispositions and impulses. This continuity of inheritance has a most important bearing on the theory of democracy and still more upon that of socialism, for it naturally tends to reduce the relative importance of environment.''

Does Grant know what a ''race'' is? Or the result of hybridization? Or whether there are ''higher'' races? Let this quotation answer: ''Whether we like to admit it or not, the result of the mixture of two races, in the long run, gives us a race reverting to the more ancient, generalized, and lower type. The cross between a white man and an Indian is an Indian; the cross between a white man and a Negro is a Negro; the cross between a white man and a Hindu is a Hindu; and the cross between any of the three European races and a Jew is a Jew.''

But ''mix'' they will, especially ''women of the better classes.'' In fact, man's ''perverse predisposition to mismate'' is one of the greatest difficulties in classifying man!

Yet in spite of these ''difficulties''—and he has not named half of them— Grant ''easily and surely'' finds a Nordic, Alpine, and Mediterranean race. With equal ease he finds racial ''aptitudes.'' His three European races ''vary intellectually and morally just as they do physically. Moral, intellectual and spiritual attributes are as persistent as physical characters and are transmitted substantially unchanged from generation to generation. . . . Each race differs in the relative proportion of what we may term good and bad strains, just as nations do.''

Thus the Alpine race, although ''submissive to authority both political and religious, being usually Roman Catholics in western Europe, tends toward democracy.'' But the Nordics are ''a race of soldiers, sailors, adventurers, and explorers, but above all, of rulers, organizers, and aristocrats in sharp contrast to the essentially peasant and democratic character of the Alpines . . . domineering, individualistic, self-reliant and jealous of their personal freedom both in political and religious systems and as a result they are usually Protestants. Chivalry and knighthood and their still surviving but greatly impaired counterparts are peculiarly Nordic traits, and feudalism, class distinctions, and race pride among Europeans are traceable for the most part to the north.''

No Brahman of Benares, London, or Boston ever looked down upon a pariah from a dizzier height than that from which Grant looks down upon the whole non-Nordic race of human outcasts. And what is the point of this false science? To serve as a basis for the ethics of a Gorilla, to warn us that ''we Americans must realize that the altruistic ideals which have controlled our social development during the past century and the maudlin sentimentalism that has made America 'an asylum for the oppressed,' are sweeping the nation toward a racial abyss. If the Melting Pot is allowed to boil without control and we continue to follow our national motto and deliberately blind ourselves to all 'distinctions of race, creed, or color,' the type of native American of Colonial descent will become as extinct as the Athenian of the age of Pericles, and the Viking of the days of Rollo.''

One is reminded in this connection of a remark of John Langdon-Davies in his ''The New Age of Faith'': ''If America had set out to attract Dantes and Benedetto Croces she would have had no alien problem at all, but the fact is she set out to attract cheap labor and as a result she has got Chicago.''

Professor William McDougall's ''Is America Safe for Democracy?'' might be ignored except for the fact that it is based on lectures entitled ''Anthropology and History, or the Influence of Anthropologic Constitution on the Destinies of Nations,'' given at the Lowell Institute when he was Professor of Psychology in Harvard University; that he cites ''evidence'' that our ''social stratification'' is ''positively correlated with a corresponding stratification of innate moral and intellectual quality''; and that ''the upper social strata as compared with the lower contain a larger proportion of persons of superior natural endowments.'' ''Every human being, every community of human beings, every populace, inherits from its ancestry a stock of innate qualities which enable it to enjoy, to sustain, to promote, a civilization of a certain degree of complexity.''

From the following we may learn Professor McDougall's idea of ''evidence": "The colored men of the Northern States showed distinct superiority to those of the South, in respect of their performance in the army intelligence-tests. Have they not a larger proportion of white blood? I do not know, but I suspect it. . . . We have pretty good evidence that capacity for intellectual growth is inborn in different degrees, that it is hereditary, and also that it is closely correlated with social status." Also that "just as that peculiarity which enables a man to become a great mathematician (or a great musician) is certainly innate and hereditary, so also the development of the highest moral character only proceeds upon the basis of a hitherto undefined innate and hereditary peculiarity."

After an "it seems," Professor McDougall finds "good reason" to add to his "hypothesis" an "assumption," namely, that the "herd instinct" is relatively stronger in the Mediterranean than in the Nordic peoples, and that the "Nordic race" is more curious and less sociable!

Alfred Edward Wiggam, in his "The New Decalogue of Science" and "The Fruit of the Family Tree," has broadcasted more false views about race and civilization than any other one man. He is *the* spokesman of the Nordic faction, the silver-tongued champion of the eugenics cult, and popularizer of genetics *par excellence*. He even ventures the assumption that had Jesus been among us he "would have been President of the First Eugenics Congress"! And he would re-write the Golden Rule: "Do unto the born and the unborn as you would have the born and the unborn do unto you." That, by the way, is the "biologist's conception of the brotherhood of man" and "the final reconciliation of science and the Bible."

Mr. Wiggam, it need hardly be added, has no doubt about his "biology" when he speaks of the "integrity of the racial blood." Unless we keep the blood currents of our race "rich, regnant, and alive," there can be "no ethics, religion, art, democracy, idealism, philosophy," nor can "any other dream of man long succeed."

Mr. Wiggam's biologic "evidence"? Certain Darwinian generalizations, a microscope, sweet peas, guinea-pigs, human stud books, fruit flies, biometric calculations; but he "cannot present the highly technical proof." Why should he, when "every biologist knows that intelligence is inherited, energy is inherited, insanity is inherited, emotional possibilities are inherited, a man's inner character is inherited"? And if what "every biologist knows" is not proof enough, the curious are invited to examine Woods' "Royal Families of Europe," Thorndike's twins, and the conduct of our Pilgrim forefathers!

Why pile up "evidence"? Because in the past two decades we have admitted to America "at least two million oppressed peoples of other lands, of lower intellectual ability than our ten million or more Negroes already on hand." Because Brigham's interpretation of army intelligence tests "gives ample evidence that especially the Nordic elements of our population are being forced out by other races whose representatives in this country are of distinctly lower average mental alertness and of less social coherence and political capacity." — (Wiggam, by the way, nowhere alludes to the fact that these same tests showed that New York State Negroes had a higher intelligence rating than the Nordics of Alabama.) "This (Nordic race) has contributed a vast share of all political wisdom and scientific discovery to the modern world."

Lothrop Stoddard's "The Rising Tide of Color" is appropriately introduced by Madison Grant, who presents the great Nordic race and Stoddard as its prophet. Certainly no fair-skinned man can read that introduction and not be proud of his Nordic ancestors. They and they alone saved civilization on four separate occasions, and, if that great race ever passes, civilization passes with it! Then what? "An unstable and bastardized population, where worth and merit would have no inherent right to leadership and among which a new and darker age would blot out our racial inheritance." But that catastrophe cannot happen if the Nordic race will get together, shake off the shackles of its inveterate altruism, discard the vain phantom of internationalism, and reassert the pride of race and the right of merit to rule! "Democratic ideals among an homogeneous population of Nordic blood, as in England or America, is one thing, but it is quite another for the white man to share his blood with, or intrust his ideals to, brown, yellow, black, or red men."

Dr. Ellsworth Huntington assumes to be an authority on race and civilization problems, and, while he solves them in terms of climatic changes, he is also a confirmed Nordic propagandist. Were he not connected with Yale University, and did he not pretend to set forth "fundamental facts, principles and relationships" fit for use in "classes in human geography, sociology, oriental and biblical history, and the philosophy of history," we might pass by his "The Pulse of Progress." While climate in a way, according to Dr. Huntington, is intimately related to civilization, civilization and race are innately related. For example, "would any amount of training ever make the *average* Chinese as good a boatman as the *average* Eskimo, or could the average Eskimo by any possibility be as careful and patient a farmer as the Chinese?" After posing other questions equally absurd, a "thoughtful answer," we are led to infer, would be that there is "such thing as innate mental differences between one race and another"; at any rate "the vast majority of people believe in biological differences in the mentality of different races"—as though such belief were in itself of any weight in any court of science.

But Dr. Huntington knows that anthropologists do not believe in such differences. How get rid of them? By a trick worthy of a shifty lawyer: "The people who chiefly question this (innate mental differences) are a relatively small group of scientific men, *especially those who belong to races that are not dominant*, and a rather large group of persons with strong philanthropic and religious tendencies." (Italics mine.) He is referring, of course, especially to Professor Franz Boas, whose "Mind of Primitive Man," although a classic in anthropological literature for seventeen years, has never, so far as I know, been mentioned by Osborn, Grant, McDougall, Wiggam, or Huntington. That "relatively small group" presumably also includes three other leading American anthropologists of international reputation, Robert H. Lowie, Alfred L. Kroeber, and A. A. Goldenweiser. Imagine a Nordic physicist thumbing his nose at the hypothesis of relativity because propounded by a man who belongs to a race that is not dominant! And yet Dr. Huntington knows so little of the history of the Jews that he speaks of them as a "pure" stock, and accounts for their being the most religious nation by "a long eugenic process which began with the patriarchs and culminated in Jesus."

Edwin M. East is a professor in Harvard University, and by profession one of those geneticists who, in the words of his preface to his "Mankind at the Crossroads," as a result of their labors "with fruit flies and guinea-pigs, with sweet peas and corn, with thousands of animals and plants, have made heredity no longer a mystery but an exact science to be ranked close behind physics and chemistry in definiteness of conception"! Professor East talks much of genes and chromosomes, and has no doubt of the laws of inheritance—at least in sweet peas. There is nothing mysterious about the *how* of inheritance, he tells us; in fact "a superficial acquaintance with Mendelism is expected today of every schoolboy . . . but what the scientists appear to have neglected to tell the general public is how these facts [which every schoolboy should know] affect the human race directly and personally." He will tell us.

Not only are "mental attributes inherited" but "great gaps separate the races. There are huge series of hereditary units possessed exclusively by each. Thus the white race has developed intellectual qualities superior to the black race, *though the black race can resist malaria much better than the white*." (Italics mine.)

Professor East quotes McDougall with approval, and finds Stoddard one of the ablest writers on the "doctrine"—that world supremacy is imperilled and that there is a very real danger of the colored races supplanting the white race. Therein lie the crossroads. The finest families are hardly replacing themselves—the incompetents are taking their place. What is the answer? Not restriction of immigration but eugenics—"parentage must not be haphazard."

Not content with his crossroads puzzle, Professor East returns to the fight to save the world for the elect in his "Heredity and Human Affairs." "Thoughtful members of society" can get one version of biological determinism from "newspaper men and professors of journalism, from certain retired lawyers and bartenders, from preachers and social workers, who write out of the fullness of their hearts"; or "another version from the works of Morgan, of Bateson, of Conklin, of Guyer, who write out of a fullness of critical experience which has made genetics a science." Why no mention of Pearl or Jennings—lack of critical experience? But he does quote Wiggam approvingly.

Between writing his "Crossroads" and his "Heredity" Professor East evidently heard of Professor Boas, for "Heredity" has a chapter on an analysis of Boas' investigations on changes in head shape in the children of certain immigrants. But still no overt mention of "The Mind of Primitive Man"; only this: "Today the Jews retaliate by proclaiming the Nordic race a myth."

Professor East's logic in establishing a point is typical of the heredity mongers. Thus, speaking of Alain Locke's "The New Negro," his "wide experience in making genetic judgments" forces him to conclude that "the developed germ-plasm causing the making of this book is nine-tenths white at least." Or, paraphrasing Professor Osborn, whether Locke's skin color is authentic or not, his germ-plasm must be at least nine-tenths Nordic!

Professor East not only knows how heredity works but what is inherited. "The physical differences between races are extraordinary . . . the mental differences are just as great. We cannot suppose that nature has produced the red man, the brown man, the white man, the black man, the pigmy and the giant, and has stopped there. No matter what value one may assign to precept and example in moulding the mind of man, his mentality is due fundamentally to his hereditary endowment, to his inborn traits"!

And yet Professor East would dismiss with contempt anyone still unconvinced that genetics can solve any problem in heredity—all is "crystal clear" except to fools and knaves. For Christianity, which he characterizes as "a little geocentric universe created as a kind of preserve for the *Hominidae*," he would substitute "something infinitely more grand and glorious," science —the science of genetics, whose proved facts are so simple and obvious that "there is no difficulty whatever in accounting for the emergent individuals like Carlyle and Lincoln in otherwise undistinguished families." With genetics elevated to the rank of religion, we can dispense with obstetrical societies, aseptic surgery, prenatal clinics, certified milk stations, public hospitals, higher wages, slum renovation, and all such social amenities—they favor the survival of the poor, are "unsound biologically," and nullify the "natural elimination of the unfit." Nature eliminated the unfit—why shouldn't we? Down with civilization, back to the jungle, and long live the new religion, genetics!

The chief difference between these heredity mongers and the Ku Klux Klan is the difference between kid gloves and a nightgown—they have the same ethics. There is no problem of race and civilization; they know. Their only problem is salvage: how may the Great race, the Anglo-Saxon branch of the Nordic race, be saved and perpetuated in all its "purity," with all its "genius for democracy" and other inherent virtues.

In fact, between the religious prejudice of a Bryan's ignorance and the class prejudice of a McDougall, Grant, East, or Osborn, there is little to choose and less to excuse. Bryan had Genesis to support him, Grant has Osborn, both have McDougall, all three are endorsed by Wiggam, who is endorsed by East. All of them, by stooping to loose reasoning, easily find what they want. To build hypotheses on assumptions and use them as facts from which they can, by faulty logic, draw as much proof as they need to support a dogma is bad enough, but to put on blinders and deny observed facts is to prostitute science and put scientists in the fundamentalist boat.

If these words seem harsh, let us isolate one more passage as typical of the "science" of the whole Nordic group. Professor Osborn in his preface to the second edition of "The Passing of the Great Race" says: "It should be remembered also that many of the dark-haired, dark-eyed youths of Plattsburg and other volunteer training camps are often three-fourths or seven-eighths Nordic, *because it only requires a single dark-eyed ancestor to lend the dark hair and eye color to an otherwise pure Nordic strain*." (Italics mine.) Professor Osborn in effect says that if I, a pure "Anglo-Saxon of the Nordic race," marry a female of the "Mediterranean race," my son may have dark eyes and hair, but he will have the courage, loyalty, self-sacrifice and idealism of my branch of the Nordic race! I need hardly say that neither Davenport himself, nor Castle, nor Walter, nor Morgan, nor any geneticist who prefers his science to his infantile beliefs, would agree to such a conclusion or ever pretended to find any evidence for such a principle of inheritance.

Or, turn to Professor Osborn's well known "Men of the Old Stone Age" for further light on his idea of heredity and his reasoning when he is forced to solve a problem in heredity. In trying to account for the great change in the Cro-Magnon "race" between the Aurignacian and Magdalenian periods, he says: "It is probable that in the genial climate of the Riviera these men (Cro-Magnon race) obtained their finest development; the country was admirably protected from the cold winds of the north, refuges were abandoned, and game by no means scarce, to judge by the quantity of animal bones found in the caves. Under such conditions of life the race enjoyed a fine physical development and dispersed widely"; in fact, became "one of the finest the world has ever seen."

But by the Magdalenian period this superb race had become something else, and Professor Osborn accounts for it by change in physical environment —"very severe climatic conditions." But if mere environment change can account for a difference in cranial capacity as great as that between *Pithecanthropus erectus* and a modern Nordic, and a difference in stature as great as that between a Pygmy and a modern Frenchman, what becomes of *heredity*, and what becomes of the doctrine of racial purity and the theory of the germ-plasm? And yet these Nordic "fans" accuse anthropologists of over-emphasizing environment, or sneer them out of court with a gesture of contempt.

II

Geneticists give one version of heredity, says Professor East; bartenders, preachers, journalists, etc., another. I offer still others. And turn first to the biological laboratory of Johns Hopkins University, directed by Professor H. S. Jennings, specialist in genetics, authority on heredity.

Professor Jennings says that heredity is neither an entity nor a force which does anything, and that we would be better off without the concept. As for "unit characters" about which East is so certain, "there is no such thing. . . . At least fifty genes must work together to produce a single feature such as red eye" in the humble fruit fly. That is, there are fifty or more separate ways in which an insect's eye character can be altered. Predictable characters are extremely few. No pair of parents can be certain of the character of their prospective offspring. Nor is it true that a given set of genes must produce just one set of characters and no other. In other words, inheritance is not foreordained. "Characters are not inherited at all; certain material which will produce a particular character under certain conditions is inherited."

Knowledge of the natural history of the oyster is useless in predicting the behavior and social organization of ants; the natural history of neither enables us to predict man's behavior—"only knowledge of the biology of man himself is relevant." Thus, as Jennings points out, the difference in stature between Jones and Smith may be due to heredity; that between the same Jones and Brown, to environment.

Well, if there are no inferior races, how about the eugenic programme to wipe out defective germ-plasm, which in some unexplained manner seems to have become so prevalent even inside the Nordic race itself? Professor Jennings thinks that possibly some cases of insanity belong to the small group in which the known number of single gene defects is so serious as to justify measures to stop their propagation. But the defects of such individuals, along with those with thyroid deficiency, etc., are "mingled with similar defects that are due primarily to environmental conditions, operating on special gene-combinations, so that it is difficult to know whether the stoppage of propagation in these classes gets rid of the main cause of the defects."

As for mental characteristics, "the rules for their inheritance are little known." Are they innate? They "are the organism's reaction to the varying environment, differing under different environments." From which an outsider might infer that at least one outstanding geneticist knows little of the inheritance of so-called mental characters and thinks they are due primarily to environment.

Raymond Pearl, Professor of Biology and Director of the Biologic Institute of Johns Hopkins University, is also a geneticist, and not without honor in his own country. He maintains (in "The Biology of Superiority," *American Mercury*, November, 1927) that the science of genetics has not yet produced a superior pod of beans or flock of hens. He characterizes eugenics literature as "a mingled mass of ill-grounded and uncritical sociology, economics, anthropology, and politics, full of emotional appeals to class and race prejudices, solemnly put forth as science, and unfortunately accepted as such by the public." Eugenics has fallen into disrepute "because of the ill-advised zeal with which some of its more ardent devotees have assigned such complex and heterogeneous phenomena as poverty, insanity, crime, prostitution, cancer, etc., to the operation of either single genes or to other simple and utterly hypothetical Mendelian mechanisms."

There is "no support to the view that the somatic (physical) characters of the offspring can be predicted from a knowledge of the somatic characters of the parents." The eugenists' claim that "like produces like" and that "superior people will have superior children" is contrary to the established facts of genetics and in the long run does the cause harm. He asks eugenics to clean house, and throw away the "old-fashioned rubbish which has accumulated in the attic."

"The epoch-making achievement of genetics during the last quarter of a century," he declares, "is the complete, comprehensive and general demonstration that heredity does *not* mean that like produces like." And yet the public teaching, legislative enactments, and moral fervor of the eugenists are "plainly based upon a pre-Mendelian genetics, as outworn and useless as the rind of yesterday's melon."

In his "Differential Fertility," in the *Quarterly Review of Biology*, Professor Pearl emphasizes still further his disagreement with "the eugenic condemnation of whole social or economic classes," directly or by inference; such condemnation is "unwarranted by anything now known. It has yet to be demonstrated that either poverty or lack of membership in a social aristocracy are biologically inherited traits."

And, finally, the dean of geneticists—certainly qualified to express an opinion on the relations of genetics and human affairs—Professor Thomas Hunt Morgan, in his "Evolution and Genetics," is "inclined to think" that considerable individual differences are "probably" genetic. But, he insists, there is:

> . . . no real scientific evidence of the kind that we are familiar with in other animals and in plants. I will even venture to go so far as to suppose that the average of the human race might be improved by eliminating a few of the extreme disorders, however they may have arisen. In fact, this is attempted at present on a somewhat extensive scale by the segregation into asylums of the insane and feeble-minded. I should hesitate to recommend the incarceration of all their relatives if the character is suspected of being recessive, or of their children if a dominant. . . . Least of all should we feel any assurance in deciding genetic superiority or inferiority as applied to whole races, by which is meant not races in a biological sense but social or political groups bound together by physical conditions, by religious sentiments, or by political organizations. . . . If it is unjust "to condemn a whole *people*"

. . . how much more hazardous is it, as some sensational writers have not hesitated to do, to pass judgment as to the relative inferiority or superiority of different *races*.

If within each human social group the geneticist finds it impossible to discover, with any reasonable certainty, the genetic basis of behavior, the problems must seem extraordinarily difficult when groups are contrasted with each other where the differences are obviously connected not only with material advantages and disadvantages resulting from location, climate, soil, and mineral wealth, but with traditions, customs, religions, taboos, conventions, and prejudices. A little goodwill might seem more fitting in treating these complicated questions than the attitude adopted by some of the modern race-propagandists.

I offer still another version of genetics, from the physiological laboratory of the University of Chicago, directed by Professor A. J. Carlson. In his address at the Third Race Betterment Conference, Professor Carlson was skeptical even of the fatter hogs and faster horses that have been produced by selection and controlled breeding: "Have we thereby secured a better hog and a better horse? We know many factors that injure the individual, and a few that injure the race, but in our almost complete ignorance of the mechanisms of race improvement, we seem impotent on the positive side." But even if we knew how to improve the "race," we are still far from agreement as to the goal: "Is the super model of *homo sapiens* to be constructed on the line of a Mussolini, a Gandhi, an Einstein, a Dempsey, a Darwin, or a Henry Ford? Is he to be 'wet' or 'dry'? Should he be white, black, yellow, brown, pink, or gray? Should he be six or sixty feet tall? Should he be a more rational or a more emotional machine? Is he to be a pacifist or a man fitted to wage bigger and better wars? Are we to aim at a better co-ordinated society of masters and slaves or a democracy?"

As Professor Carlson points out, man has reached his present state of development almost without any conscious direction whatsoever based on accumulated experience. We do not know what our forebears ate and drank and how much, nor how they worked, rested, and loved, and without that knowledge we are hardly entitled to label our way of living or our artificial environment "favorable" or "unfavorable." What is known today of the influence of diet, work, behavior, environment, etc., on physiological processes tends merely to limit or permit full development of individual growth and functions, and hence is not significant in relation to race betterment. "The only clear instances we have of rapid modification of the germ plasm by experimental (drugs) or environmental means seem to be injurious or destructive. Man today is like a curious and clumsy and very ignorant child tinkering with the watch; will he tomorrow contrive a superior mechanism? The lesson for the present seems clear: *The germ plasm can be injured; some phases of the present man-made environment seem to enhance such injury*. Are the ablest, the strongest, the wisest men merely grave-diggers in disguise?''

I offer still another version of genetics, this time from an insane asylum. Professor A. Myerson, neurologist and psychiatrist, author of ''The Psychology of Mental Disorders,'' has especially investigated the question of heredity in relation to mental diseases and feeble-mindedness. Is feeble-mindedness inherited—or ''intelligence''? And how about the Jukes, etc., of whom so many thousand pages have been written?

The Jukes, Kilikaks, etc., are bad enough, Myerson says, but ''it has not been proved that they are really feeble-minded; nor even if they are feeble-minded has it been proved that they are typical of the bulk of cases of feeble-mindedness.'' While psychoses such as dementia praecox and manic depressive *may* run in families, even such diseases ''appear as isolated characteristics of one individual and cannot be linked up with mental disease of the family, or appear without any hereditary linking up which is worthy of the name. . . . A few cases of three-generation disease are recorded, only one or two where four generations were mentally sick. It appears that mental disease, like physical disease, either destroys the stock which it attacks, or there is final recovery.'' But even if a father has a psychosis and his son or daughter is feeble-minded, ''there is no known hereditary bond between the two states.''

After paying his respects to the ''surprisingly omniscient way'' certain people pass judgment on the dead as well as the quick, Dr. Myerson admits that he finds it hard to ''evaluate individuals after a close study and after a long acquaintance with mental and physical disease. . . . Much of feeble-mindedness is environmental in origin, much is hereditary, but the most is of unknown origin, and may represent the inexplainable downward movement of intelligence, just as genius represents its inexplainable upward movement.'' Eugenics ''needs research more than legislation . . . It does not yet need publicity so much as it needs scientists and scientific work . . . We are still far away from real understanding of the bulk of mental diseases and of feeble-mindedness, and no amount of statistical evaluation of improper data will bring us light.''

III

Well, how about the far-famed ''intelligence tests'' made on millions of army recruits and since on millions of school children of various ''races''? Do they not prove innate connection between race and intelligence, do they not definitely prove that the Great race is greatest in innate ability? These tests have been a mighty arsenal of ammunition for the heredity mongers, cited again and again as proof that races differ in innate mental capacity.

But what do the tests test—''intelligence''? What is intelligence? Whatever it is, the outstanding fact brought out in the tests is that it is astoundingly scarce. Why this is so is well put by Dr. Myerson. Few people, comparatively speaking, are really interested in matters beyond their immediate concerns, or have any intellectual interest at all. Most people lead a parochial existence, absorbed in their own problems of livelihood, sex, and pleasure. They read little beyond the innately interesting things, and avoid real mental exertion. They forget readily the fragments of culture which reached them in school and which bob up now and then in newspaper and magazine. And yet, while the average adult may rank lower in "intelligence" than a bright child, he "ranks much higher in qualities that tests cannot evaluate—experience in life, sober judgment, special efficiency, etc."

And that is just what the tests do not test—ability to learn from experience.

The tests may furnish samples of knowledge, but there is no way whereby inborn capacity for intelligent behavior can be directly measured. At best they can only give a measure of behavior. Any test, to serve as measure of innate capacity, must be made on individuals who have been subjected to the same social environment. The really significant thing brought out in the army tests was the enormous variation in the same "racial" strains and amongst individuals of practically the same environment. What they have not shown is that there is anything in the anatomical make-up, physiological processes, or chromosomes of a son of the chief of the *Mano Nera* of Catania which will pre-dispose him, on the East Side of New York or the West Side of Chicago, to follow in the footsteps of his illustrious parent. That such a youth at the age of twenty, reared in a New York or Chicago Little Italy atmosphere, should not rate highly in an examination paper prepared by a one hundred per cent American schoolteacher, is to be expected. Whatever the tests showed, they did not measure capacity to learn, and they are therefore, so far as criteria of innate "racial" capacity are concerned, worthless.

IV

The last version of genetics—the problem of innate relation of race and civilization—I shall offer, is that of the anthropologists, of those whose life business it is to study mankind in the making, man's genetic history, his cultural achievements. Are these two necessarily related?

Professor A. C. Haddon of Cambridge University, in "The Races of Man," says: "A classification based on culture may be of interest to the sociologist, but it is obviously one which can have no prime importance in regard to genetic relationship, though it may indicate the influence of peoples upon one another. There is no such thing as racial culture. The culture of any given people is primarily dependent upon their mode of life, which is in itself largely an expression of geographical conditions."

With that dictum, I need hardly add, I am in complete agreement—as are, I believe, practically all living anthropologists. Professor Haddon is not of the, or a, non-dominant "race"; he belongs to the "Anglo-Saxon branch of the Nordic Race"!

Professor Franz Boas, in the chapter on Race Problems in the United States in his "Mind of Primitive Man," specifically raises the question as to how far the undesirable traits that are today found in our Negro population are innate, and how far they are due to social surroundings for which we are responsible. In answer to that question he emphasizes the fact, known to every ethnologist, that the culture of the African Negroes is that of a healthy primitive people with much personal initiative, talent for organization, and with imaginative power, technical skill, and thrift. "Neither is a warlike spirit absent in the race, as is proved by the mighty conquerors who overthrew states and founded new empires, and by the courage of the armies that follow the bidding of their leaders. There is nothing to prove that licentiousness, shiftless laziness, lack of initiative, are fundamental characteristics of the race. Everything points out that these qualities are the result of social conditions rather than of hereditary traits."

Boas thinks, however, that there may be differences in the mental make-up of the Negro and other races. But there is "no evidence whatever that would stigmatize the Negro as of weaker build, or as subject to inclinations and powers that are opposed to our social organization. An unbiassed estimate of the anthropological evidence so far brought forward does not permit us to countenance the belief in a racial inferiority which would unfit an individual of the Negro race to take his part in modern civilization . . . In short, there is every reason to believe that the Negro, when given facility and opportunity, will be perfectly able to fulfil the duties of citizenship as well as his white neighbor."

In an article on "The Question of Racial Purity" in the *American Mercury*, Professor Boas insists even more strongly that "nobody has ever given satisfactory proof of an inherent inequality of races."

Professor Robert E. Lowie states his opinion as to the existence of innate racial capacity thus: "As to the existence of superior races, I am an agnostic open to conviction. All evolutionists admit that at some point an organic change of fundamental significance occurred. It is *conceivable* that the Bushmen and Negritos, Pygmies and Negroes are organically below the remainder of living human types, and that differences of one sort or another even divide more closely related stocks."

Between Boas' "nobody has ever given satisfactory proof," or Lowie's "it is *conceivable*," and the flat-footed assertions of those who assume to know races as such and to classify them according to innate virtues or traits, there is not the difference between Tweedledum and Tweedledee but a gulf. That gulf is so wide that, it may confidently be asserted, no one yet has definitely and conclusively associated, either for individual or for race, any innate connection between physical structure and cultural trait or "mental faculty."

Physical features are, within certain limits, heritable traits, and something is known of the laws which govern their transmission. Such innate factors are rooted in biology, the same for man as for other species of animals. To classify mankind by the way they look, or by their physical features or anatomical traits, is one thing; to classify men by what they do is an entirely different thing. As the behavior of an individual depends, certainly in some measure, upon the training he receives at the hands of parents, playmates, teachers, and social environment in general, so the cultural behavior of families, groups, tribes, and nations is dependent upon historic and psychological factors never in any way proved to be heritable traits.

Indeed there is no evidence that man's capacity to learn human behavior has increased in the slightest since he definitely left the trees and became man. During that long period, variously reckoned from 50,000 to 250,000 years, due to factors little understood as yet, fairly distinct physical types have come to be formed in different parts of the world, physical types marked by varying proportions of anatomical features, character of hair, pigmentation of skin and eye, etc. Human culture has varied from one generation to another. Just as every normal newborn "Nordic," Jew, or Negro born in New York City in 1928 inherits in general the features of his near ancestors, so he is heir to a culture environment or stage of civilization unlike anything the world has seen before. What that youngster will be twenty, forty, or sixty years hence, no one can possibly predict, because no one can possibly predict the social and conditioning factors which will play upon him and to which he will learn to respond, not because of his physical inheritance but because of his common human inheritance of a capacity to learn any human language or culture.

The outstanding fact about human beings is individual variation of physical type. Equally striking is the capacity of every normal newborn to learn or acquire human behavior. Why one individual of a family, or why one family in a group of families more or less closely related by blood, achieves different results culturally, is a problem that is yet far from solution, but the primary factors in that problem seem to be psychologic rather than biologic. That is to say, so far as we know at the present time, the factors which make for, say, a given state of culture among the aborigines of Australia at any given time are the incidence of geographic and physical environment and the antecedent historic and psychologic factors which made that culture what it is. What any individual, family, or physical type could or would do under different geographic and social environmental conditions is something which no one at present is warranted in asserting dogmatically. *Conceivably*, the Australian, or the Bushman, Negrito, or Pygmy, for any evidence we have to the contrary, could learn to behave like a Nordic if he were reared in a Nordic environment. What is too often left out of account is that the Nordic social environment makes it difficult, if not impossible, for the alleged inferior to develop to the fullest his innate capacity.

V

There is no such thing as racial culture or Nordic civilization. Is there such a thing as race or Nordic race? Obviously, Nordic, Alpine, Caucasian, Mongolian, etc., are merely abstract terms, convenient, as Haddon says, only to the extent that they help us appreciate broad facts. "A race type exists mainly in our own minds." What are the "broad facts"?

Of the dozens of attempted classifications of man by anatomical traits, no two agree. Presumably never will agree, because there are no outstanding, sharply defined physical traits by which groups of mankind can be partitioned off from one another. To classify human beings by shape of head is one thing, by stature another, by pigmentation of skin or eyes another, by color and character of hair still another. Any classification made on any one of these traits is to classify mankind by such a trait and by no other. But there is always overlapping. When the attempt is made to classify man by a combination of two or more of these traits, hopeless confusion results. When the attempt is made to combine as many as five physical traits, the proportion of "pure" types becomes, as Ripley says, almost infinitesimal. "We are thus reduced to the extremity in which my friend, Dr. Ammon of Baden, found himself, when I wrote asking for photographs of a pure Alpine type from the Black Forest. He has measured thousands of heads, and yet he answered that he really had not been able to find a perfect specimen in all details. All his round-headed men were either blond, or tall, or narrow-nosed, or something else that they ought not to be."

Possibly the difficulty in finding a satisfactory classification of man on the basis of heritable traits is because the influence of environment on innate structure is not yet known. We do not yet know why men vary in stature, in amount of pigmentation, in head form, etc., nor how permanent are such variations. No anthropologist has succeeded in isolating a pure race or type, presumably because there is no such thing. Hence the probability that races in a strict sense of the term do not exist, or if they did once, cannot be distinguished because of inter-breeding.

But there are pronounced differences between, for example, the tall blond of Northern Europe and the diminutive Pygmy of Africa, or between the European in general and the native of Australia. Why they differ, or the extent to which these differences would persist under changed environment, is not known; nor, I repeat, is any inherent connection between these physical differences and psychologic or cultural abilities known.

Only in a very limited sense, then, can we say that "racial inheritance" has any significance. Traits common to every individual of a race, and which set him off from every individual of other races, may be spoken of as hereditary racial traits. Thus we may speak of the black skin and kinky hair of the African Negro as hereditary racial traits. All Negroes have these traits. But shape of head and size of brain cannot be spoken of as traits which set off Negroes from Whites, because there is great overlapping amongst the two groups in these respects. Such overlapping of types found everywhere today is presumably due to intermixture, but we are not, as Boas points out, on that account entitled to assume that extreme physical types represent pure races. Thus the classification of Europeans into Northern or Nordic, Central or Alpine, and Southern or Mediterranean, in no sense represents *races* but merely extreme forms of three physical characters: stature, skin color, and head form. The extremes of these forms are not typical of a "race," much less of a pure race; they are only the extremes in an unbroken series from the North to the South of Europe. Anyone not content with three European races can have thirty-three, or in fact as many as he wants.

The argument put forth by our racial purity propagandists falls to the ground. There is no evidence for pure races, no evidence that the extreme forms of any type represent the purest, nor any evidence for the assumption that inter-breeding of different types in any respect lowers their capacity for culture or civilization. Nowhere does the ethnologist find evidence of correlation of racial achievement and supposed race purity; nor is there any substantial proof of inherent lack of mentality or capacity for intelligence in any race or racial type. On the contrary, all that we know of human history makes the claim for racial inferiority seem improbable.

Race and civilization, then, are not interchangeable terms. No classification of mankind by blood will coincide with classification by language or culture. No one language or culture belongs to any distinct physical type. Hence every attempt to classify mankind from a combined physical and cultural or linguistic point of view has failed, and must inevitably fail.

Perhaps the best known attempt to combine blood and culture is the classification of F. Müller, who, basing his classification on hair, discovered two great races (woolly-haired and straight-haired), and within these, minor divisions based on linguistics. But as the laws governing the inheritance of language and culture are based on psychologic and historic factors, and the laws which govern physical inheritance are biologic, his classification has only historic interest.

Early classifications of mankind were geographical—a race to a continent. Thus Linnaeus found four varieties of man: European White, Asiatic Yellow, American Red, and African Black. Blumenbach (1775) added a fifth: the Oceanic or Brown. That was the classification which I learned in school, and is still embodied in our Federal laws as Caucasian, Mongolian, Ethiopian, American, Malayan. Cuvier (1800) hung his three "races" on the sons of Noah: Shem, Ham, and Japheth.

Thereafter it was a perpetual open season for race hunting, with widely varying results. Haeckel could only find twelve races in 1873, but a few years later succeeded in finding thirty-four. Topinard found sixteen in 1878, and a few years later discovered three more. Deniker also had difficulty with his count, but in 1900 decided there were six "grand divisions," seventeen "divisions," and twenty-nine "races." Why these differences? Because, as Blumenbach had observed, "the innumerable varieties of mankind run into one another by insensible degrees"; because, as Pritchard in his "Natural History of Man" said, "the different races of man are not distinguishable from each other by strongly marked and permanent distinctions. All the diversities which exist are variable, and pass into each other by insensible gradations."

Races do not exist; classifications of mankind do. And Kroeber's, in his "Anthropology," or Haddon's, in his "The Races of Man," are as good as any, and have the merit of being up to date.

Personally, the simple scheme proposed by Boas many years ago is the classification I like best. It is easily remembered and requires no stretch of the imagination. Boas finds two great forms or groups of the human species in which skin color, shape of hair, form of face and nose, and body proportions, are characteristically distinct. The Negroid, represented geographically as the Indian Ocean, is contrasted with the Mongoloid, or Pacific Ocean group. The Negroid form is dark-skinned, frizzled-haired, flat-nosed, as opposed to the light-skinned, straight-haired, high-nosed Mongoloid division. Boas does not pretend, of course, that these two groups represent pronounced and sharply contrasted forms of humanity, or that there are not individuals in one group that in certain respects differ more from their own group than from some of those in the opposite group. The Mongoloid group is found in both Americas, Asia, and Europe; the Negroid in Africa, and presumably once in the whole of Southern Asia and the islands on the West side of the Indian Ocean.

Outside of these two great divisions of mankind are certain pronounced physical types, such as the North Europeans, the Australians, and the Pygmies, but how they are genetically related to one or the other of the two main groups of mankind is not known. Europeans differ in pigmentation from the Negroid more than from the Mongoloid type, but in form of hair, proportions of body, and form of eye and cheeks, are not so different from the Negroid as from the Mongoloid. The Australian natives in certain respects are rather sharply set off from the rest of mankind, and possibly represent a type differentiated early in the history of the human race. The Pygmy people are found irregularly distributed in many parts of Africa, the Andaman Islands, Malay Peninsula, the Philippines, and New Guinea, and in early times were possibly more widely distributed. They form in themselves a distinct, definite, and wholly unsolved problem in the genesis of the human species.

Europeans presumably came into their physical characteristics in Europe or nearby Asia. But the difference between the skin color of the European and the Mongoloid group is neither so pronounced as is commonly supposed nor so common as to make it a distinguishing mark of race. Many Asiatics have a skin quite as white as the average European. Boas has even found among the Haida Indians of British Columbia, white skins, brownish red hair, and light brown eyes. The Indian tribes of the Upper Mississippi had also a very light complexion, yet the Yuma Indians of Southern California are often as dark in skin color as the lighter skinned Negroes. Thus the most we can say is that the very light-skinned European represents an extreme variant of pigment deficiency, in itself characteristic of the whole Mongoloid group. While blond hair is not found among the Mongoloids, yet reddish brown hair is common. The European nose varies among Europeans, and in line with similar variants in the Mongoloid group. From these and other considerations Boas believes the European type to represent nothing more than a recent specialization of the Mongoloid group.

If no definite innate connection between physical type and cultural capacity can be discovered, and if there is no agreement as to the genetic relationship of the varying physical types of mankind, it seems hardly worth while to inquire whether some races or types are, anatomically speaking, lower than others; yet inasmuch as it is a favorite diversion of certain geneticists to arrange races according to the supposed distance from their animal ancestor, let us see what basis there is in observed fact for the existence of "higher" and "lower" races.

The real point brought out by all such graded series is that the gap between man in general and his anthropoid progenitor is wide, but qualitative rather than quantitative. The Negro, to be sure, has a broad and flat nose and a protruding jaw, which seems to bring him nearer the anthropoid than the European. But while the European and the Mongoloid have the largest brains, the European shares with the native Australian the doubtful honor of remaining the hairiest of the human race, a peculiarly animal-like trait. The red lip, one of our most human characteristics, is most strongly developed in the Negro. Again, in proportion of limbs the Negro is most human—that is, has diverged most from ape-like forms.

In other words, divergence from animal ancestor has developed in varying directions in varying types. Such differences are at best purely anatomical. We have no reason to infer that they have anything to do with "mental faculty." We have been misled by associating features that seem to us brutish, with brutality. Karl Pearson, after extended inquiry into the whole subject, expressed his conviction that there is little relation between physical and psychical characters in man. Nor could Manouvrier, the great French anatomist, discover any direct connection between anatomical characteristics and mental ability.

How about size of brain? True, whatever difference there is between Europeans and Mongoloids or Negroids favors in general the Europeans, but this difference in itself is no proof of increase in ability. If the majority of eminent men have had large brains, so too have the majority of murderers. Some of the most eminent men of Europe have had very small brains. Dr. Franklin

Mall, who specially investigated brain weights, concluded that, because of the great variability of individuals of each race, racial differences, if they exist, are exceedingly difficult to discover. But even if we could assume that ability is inherent in brain capacity, the most we could say is that the European is likely to produce more men of commanding genius than the African. As a matter of fact, there is no distinct gap between European and Negro brains. They distinctly overlap in size; only in Europe there are a few who reach a size not found in Africa. We have neither anatomical nor psychological evidence that the European or so-called white race is physically the highest type of man.

As for the three alleged European races—Nordic, Alpine, and Mediterranean—they simply do not exist other than as abstract conveniences. The Alpine type, for example, includes such diverse languages and cultures as French, German, Italian, and Slav. There is good reason to believe that these peoples are related in blood and sprang from common ancestors; today they are far apart in language and culture.

How, then, can we account for the fact that the European has developed a civilization which has encompassed the globe and which makes all other civilizations appear fundamental or in a state of arrested development? And if the culture of the European is superior to all others, why is it not because of innate capacity?

The ethnologist, familiar through long personal contact with so-called savages, and accustomed to view his own civilization objectively and hence more or less unemotionally, has no difficulty in seeing the fallacy implicit in such questions as I have just posed. And is grateful when a philosopher comes to his aid, as does Professor John Dewey, in saying that "the present civilized mind is virtually taken as a standard and the savage mind is measured off on this fixed scale. It is no wonder that the outcome is negative: that primitive mind is described in terms of 'lack,' 'absence'; its traits are incapacities." Then there was the visitor to a savage tribe who wrote of its Manners and Customs: "Customs, beastly; Manners, none."

The fallacy I spoke of above is in the "lack," "absence." I may lack a dress suit: that does not necessarily mean I cannot afford one or cannot learn to wear one; it may only mean that I, as King of the Cannibal Islands, have no need or desire for a dress suit—or having seen one, devoutly hope Customs and Manners will never force me or my kind into one.

The answer to the *why* of present white supremacy must be sought in a historic review of human achievement. We cannot assign dates to the beginnings of human culture. Even in the remote past there were certain fundamental inventions and beginnings of culture known to all peoples.

Only a few thousand years ago we find types of culture approximating civilization beginning to develop on an extensive scale in Asia. In the course of time these higher types of culture—or civilization—fluctuated, moved about from one people to another. Civilization seemed to ebb and flow, now here, now there. At the dawn of recorded history the contrast between so-called civilized peoples and savage peoples was about as sharp as it is today. But throughout this vast land area there was constant conflict, civilized peoples often being vanquished only to have their culture taken up and carried on by their conquerors, as was the case with the Mongol Manchu conquerors of China. Centres of civilization shifted from one part of Asia to another. Meanwhile, the ancestors of modern Europeans possessed culture in no wise superior to that of primitive man, or of savage man today who has not yet come in contact with modern civilization.

What was the origin of this ancient Asiatic civilization? Does it indicate a special kind of genius or any special innate capacity? Seemingly not. The peoples of Asia were fortunate in their social environment. Asiatic civilization was the product of the genius of no one people; each contributed something toward general progress and the general fund. The more we know of the history of this civilization, the more abundant become the proofs that culture was disseminated from one people to another whenever and wherever tribes or nations came in contact, neither race nor language nor distance limiting the diffusion of culture. Hamitic, Semitic, Aryan, and Mongol alike made invaluable contributions, each offering of its genius.

Meanwhile, on the more isolated continent of America, in at least three centres, a high culture developed. In the highlands of Peru and Mexico, and in the Ohio Valley, we find highly developed political organizations and elaborate divisions of labor and an intricate organization. Huge public works requiring the co-operation of master minds and swarms of people were undertaken and successfully carried through. Many animals and plants extremely valuable to man were domesticated; the art of writing was invented.

As Professor A. C. Tozzer, in his "Social Origins and Social Continuities," says: "The Maya calendar functioned without the loss of a day for 2000 years, until it was broken up by Spanish priests. Marginal corrections were applied to take care of the variation in the year and the true solar year—a means more accurate than our method of leap year. It was not until 1582 that the Julian day was invented, which corresponds to the Maya day count—2000 years after the same principles had been adopted by the Mayas."

The ancient civilization of the New is not the ancient civilization of the Old World, but its general status was almost as high. There were differences, but the nature of these differences is essentially the same as that between the ancient Asiatic and the ancient European culture—simply a difference in time. One reached a certain stage a few hundred or a few thousand years in advance of the other. Natural causes, in which we may include the vast land area and a more abundant natural supply of animals, especially the horse, cow, elephant, and dromedary, and plants suitable for domestication—these seem to have been the chief factors which predetermined that the development of human culture was to make more rapid progress in the Old than in the New World. There is nothing strange in the course of such a race for cultural supremacy. Europe alone in the last two thousand years furnishes innumerable parallels, not only in one people arriving at a destination sooner than another, but in the phenomenon so often presented in Asia two or three thousand years ago, of the van of progress being assumed now by one people, now by another. Thus the lead in civilization has been held by Greece, Rome, Byzantine, Bulgaria, the Moors, Portugal, Spain, France, and Holland, to go no further. Of two children born at the same time, the difference in their progress by the age of fifty is likely to be much greater than the difference between them at the age of ten; and in each case it is possible generally to evaluate the factors which accelerate or retard their development, rather than to account for them by hereditary or innate inferior or superior capacity.

Applying this argument to human history, we are justified in concluding that, considering the vast age of the human species, a difference of a few centuries in becoming what we call "civilized" is to be accounted for on purely historical grounds, and not on any real or fancied innate capacity.

But, it may be argued, when we contrast modern European civilization with that of the primitive peoples of Africa and the peoples of other areas equally backward, we find a difference more fundamental than can be accounted for by the mere element of time. I can find no valid ground on which to base this argument. Modern competition—that is, the clash between the European, who has objectified and perfected his methods of warfare and transportation, and primitive peoples—is along unfair lines; primitive man cannot compete with the power of the white man's machine. Further, primitive tribes in certain parts of the world, as in America and Siberia, have been swamped by the crowds of alien white immigrants they have had no time to assimilate. The average American Indian had no more chance of holding his own against the Europeans than had the Chinese armies a few years ago, equipped with bow and arrows, against the bullets of the British.

In short, a peculiar sequence of historical causes has had infinitely more to do in furthering the rapid growth of civilization amongst some people than amongst others; and this growth is due to these historical causes rather than to innate faculty.

Even granting as we must the actual cultural superiority of the Whites or Europeans, the weakness of the argument for correlation of race faculty and civilization becomes apparent when we try to evaluate the relative parts played in culture history by the several divisions of the European or Caucasian race. Thus Kroeber would award the palm to the Mediterranean branch for its long-continued lead in productivity and having reared the largest portion of the structure of existing civilization:

To it belonged the Egyptians; the Cretans and other Aegeans; the

Semitic strain in the Babylonians; the Phoenicians and Hebrews; and a large element in the populations of classic Greece and Italy, as well as the originators of Mohammedanism. With the Hindus added as probably nearly related, the dark whites have a clear lead.

The next largest share civilization would owe to the Alpine-Armenoid broad-headed Caucasian branch. This may have included the Sumerians, if they were not Mediterranean; comprised the Hittites; and contributed important strains to the other peoples of Western Asia and Greece and Italy.

By comparison, the Nordic branch looms insignificant. Up to a thousand years ago the Nordic peoples had indeed contributed ferment and unsettling, but scarcely a single new culture element, certainly not a new element of importance and permanence. For centuries after that, the centre of European civilization remained in Mediterranean Italy or Alpine France. It is only after A.D. 1500 that any claim for a shift of this centre to the Nordic populations could be alleged. In fact, most of the national and cultural supremacy of the Nordic peoples, so far as it is real, falls within the last two hundred years. Against this, the Mediterraneans and Alpines have a record of leading in civilizational creativeness for at least six thousand years.

I am in entire accord with Tozzer's conclusions that:

There is no present evidence, physical, psychological, or cultural, to prove that contemporaneous savages are fundamentally different in mind, body, or estate from the sophisticated human product of civilization. The savage is "bone of our bone and flesh of our flesh." He is, in short, a "poor relation, but our own." . . .

Savages the world over have come to possess in some form every basic institution of civilized society. There is no reason to believe that they owe such social institutions to precept, example, or imitation of the so-called "Higher Cultures." On the contrary, these "Higher Cultures" owe much to the institutions from which they have been derived. . . .

The evolution of institutions may, like physical life, have had many mutations. . . . They are characterized by many spontaneous growths, individual creations of life-forms (the product of the workings of the mind). . . . Similarity of nomenclature does not always mean either identity of structure or a common history.

The savage in his customs and social organization manifests a genius for diversification, a skill in practical adaptation, and a willingness and often a surprising ability to modify and to improve which make it unsafe to assume that primitive man is either stagnant or degenerate. Any modern group of savages with health and unmolested by the grosser benefits of civilization may have the potentiality to work out for itself an abundant spiritual and material enrichment.

All of the defects behind the so-called irrational follies of the savage, evidenced in superstition, credulity, suspicion, and vanity, are the common inheritance of all mankind. The same psychological principles are behind the same psychological weaknesses both in savage and in civilized life. They are actively functioning among the ignorant of the civilized peoples and are by no means atrophied in those human groups which have been most constantly exposed to education. . . .

If we compare the relation between opportunity and achievement of the savage and of his more cultured brother, we soon realize that, from this point of view, our superiority is very doubtful. The complexity of institutions is not a measure of their validity, nor is the multiplication of inventive devices a true criterion of progress.

The savage is a rational being, morally sound, and in every respect worthy of a place in the "Universal Brotherhood of Man."

For "savages" read Hottentots, Chinese, Japanese, Russians, Sicilians, Mexicans, Greeks, Jews, Choctaws, and I am still in complete accord.

In conclusion, then, we may say that judgments of cultural capacity—or, specifically, the capacity to enter into American civilization—based on the known contribution of this or that race to civilization, or judgments of races through sampling of individuals in so-called intelligence tests, are inconclusive and for practical purposes worthless. Nor have we any reason to believe that further mixture with our present sub-stratum by immigrants from any part of Europe or Asia will destroy the integrity of our race, hybridize it, or in any way lower it. Such racial mixtures as we have in America today are in no essential different from race mixtures which have been going on for thousands of years in Europe and Asia, and which we have no reason to believe have ever resulted in inferior races or in breaking up civilization.

Our problems, then, are not those of race and civilization, but of too little understanding and too much prejudice. Result: too many aliens in our midst socially unadjusted. Answer: less race phobia, more intelligent understanding of the nature of civilization. Like human behavior, civilization is made and not born. Like life itself, it must be nourished day by day, ceaselessly, with new energy and new materials, or it sickens and dies.

THE SOLUTION OF THE PROBLEM OF THE INFERTILITY OF THE UNMARRIED IN NONLITERATE SOCIETIES

FOR many years anthropologists had been puzzled by the fact that in nonliterate societies childbirth out of wedlock and for some years after puberty was exceedingly rare. All sorts of theories were offered for this interesting phenomenon: contraception, the free mixing of lovers, and the immunological effects to which this led, and so on. Malinowski, in his book *The Sexual Life of Savages* (London, 1929), had brought the subject into prominence once more in his account of the Trobriand Islanders, but long before that, as a result of the stimulus of Malinowski's lectures, I had begun working on a solution to the problem. As a result, largely, of the work of L. Mirskaia and F. A. E. Crew ["Maturity in the Female Mouse," *Proceedings of the Royal Society of Edinburgh*, (Vol. 50, 1920), pp. 179-186], in which they showed that the female mouse took some time before ovulation occurred in the development of the estrus cycle, in other words, that the early estrus cycles were anovulatory. I suspected that this was probably the explanation in the human female also. This was happily quickly confirmed by the work of Carl G. Hartman in 1931, although his work was done on the rhesus monkey. I was able to validate these findings by citing the data on nonliterate and other peoples. This was published as "Adolescent Sterility," *Quarterly Review of Biology* (Vol. 14, 1939), pp. 13-34, 192-219, and subsequently in the book of that title in 1945, and enlarged as *The Reproductive Development of the Female* (New York, Julian Press, 1957).

The fact is that the human female from the appearance of the first menstruation (menarche) is not usually capable of conception. There is, on the average, a period of three years during which the menstrual cycles of the human female are anovulatory. This is now known as the adolescent sterility period, and it is because of this fact that females in nonliterate societies are rarely observed to bear children before they are married, and usually not for some years afterwards.

The fact that such a period of infertility in the postpubertal female escaped the attention of millennia of generations of mankind is not difficult to understand. Nor is it difficult to surmise how the belief evolved that the first menstruation represents a mark of the female's arrival at the procreative stage of development. It is very likely that it had been independently noted that women remained sterile before they menstruated, and that after the first menstruation they menstruated periodically, and it was only during their menstrual life that they were capable of bearing children, for after the final cessation of menstruation (menopause) they were no longer capable of bearing children. Hence, the appearance of menstruation was taken to be the sign of the ability to procreate. But as Mirskaia and Crew were able to show for the mouse, Hartman for the rhesus monkey, and Ashley Montagu for the human female, the physiological facts are quite otherwise.

The fact that in almost all nonliterate societies the female is married at or immediately after she attains menarche renders possible a sexual history for the person very different and much less trying than that which the person experiences in literate societies. In nonliterate societies premarital intercourse is usually, though not always, permitted. Since there is rarely any danger of pregnancy occurring before menarche, the problem of children out of wedlock seldom arises. On the other hand, cultures in which marriage is postponed till some years after menarche, that is, until, the postmenarcheal nubile period (17-20 years), cannot permit premarital intercourse owing to the fact that the birth of many children out of wedlock would have a socially disrupting effect—for undoubtedly many of them would be born during the menarche-nubility interval. Hence, this additional impediment in such societies toward the recognition of an adolescent sterility interval.

ON THE RELATIVE STERILITY OF THE ADOLESCENT ORGANISM*
CARL G. HARTMAN

The literature of adolescence is chiefly psychological. Anatomical and physiological studies on the adolescent organism are extremely sporadic and uncorrelated. A recent conference of "experts" served chiefly to emphasize our ignorance of the subject.

One of the prevailing notions concerning adolescence is that it is a very restricted period of time marked by sudden, almost explosive changes in bodily structure and function. The immature organism is represented as becoming all

*Reprinted from *Science* (Vol. 74, August 28, 1931), pp. 226-27.

at once mature; the boy becomes a man, the girl a woman, almost as if by a change of clothing. The illusion is probably due to the popular as well as gynecological notion that the first menstruation, which certainly is a definitely demarcated event, is equivalent to the attainment of full maturity. It can, however, easily be shown that puberty and maturity are neither synonymous nor synchronous. The interval of time between the two in man, monkey and rat is about what one would expect with the application of Donaldson's law of equivalent ages: three years, one year and one month, respectively, for man, monkey and rat.

The Carnegie colony of rhesus monkeys has had fifteen females whose every menstrual cycle from the very first was observed. An excellent opportunity was thus afforded for studying the phenomena of adolescence, as affecting body growth, certain changes in the secondary sex characters and changes in the ovaries and genital tract. The sex skin becomes redder and redder and at the same time greatly swollen, almost to pathological proportions at times. Such swellings are extremely rare in mature animals. Furthermore, the menstrual cycles of the young females are extremely irregular in length and duration, and there is a very low incidence of ovulatory as compared with non-ovulatory cycles.

Now, these fifteen females averaged 3,350 grams in weight at the first menses. Most of them were mated soon after puberty, but not a single female conceived before attaining a weight of 4,370 grams. The average weight at first conception of nine of these females was 5,000 grams; hence it is apparent that many menstrual cycles passed between the first menses and the first conception, despite frequent matings in the interval. The interval may be estimated at about a year of time.

The same gradual unfolding of maturity holds true for such good breeders as the rat and the mouse. Slonaker's studies on spontaneous activities in the rat[1] show a gradual increase in the peak of the cyclic activity to the maximum which is maintained during the reproductive life of the individual. This "staircase" phenomenon of adolescence indicates a gradual though saltatory increase in the effect of the ovarian hormone. It is very likely that the first cycles of moderately high activity were unaccompanied by ovulation, though I know of no studies on the rat to bear this out.

With regard to the mouse we are somewhat more fortunate. That puberty and maturity are distinct phenomena separated by a considerable interval of time was established for the mouse by Mirskaia and Crew.[2] In a series of experiments pregnancy followed first matings in only 24 per cent. of cases, whereas the same mice were 80 to 90 per cent. fertile with later matings. Puberty is defined by these authors as the ability to elaborate functional

[1]*Am. Jour. Physiol.*, 1904, on.
[2]Proc. Roy. Soc., Edinburgh, 1930.

gametes and to possess the physical ability and the desire to play the appropriate rôle in mating; maturity, on the other hand, is defined as the stage of maximum fertility ratio and the ability to produce viable offspring and to rear them.

In this definition, ovulation is included as one of the criteria of puberty. To my notion maturity, the end of adolescence, is marked by the first ovulation and the preparation of a receptive uterus capable of carrying the offspring to term; puberty is indicated by the first manifestations of gonadal activity and marks the beginning of adolescence. The threshold for the hormones causing the latter changes (sex color, menstruation, cyclic variations in spontaneous activity, cornification and opening of the vagina), according to various species are much lower than the changes culminating in ovulation and conception.

The onset of menstruation in girls is, of course, a momentous event. Nevertheless, though the mores of a given people may force "effective marriage" upon them at this moment, there is much indication that, by and large, nature herself prevents motherhood supervening during an important series of preparatory years.

The reader will naturally recall the case of India in this connection and the lurid picture of child mothers conjured up by Katherine Mayo in her notorious "Mother India." This propagandist would have us believe: "The Indian girl, in common practise, looks for motherhood nine months after reaching puberty, or anywhere between the ages of 14 and 8. The latter is extreme, though in some sections not exceptional, the former is well above the average."

In characteristic fashion, Mrs. Mayo fails to continue her quotation from the Appendix VII of the 1921 Indian Census, where we read that, though cohabitation begins with puberty, "in the majority of cases the first child is born the third year of effective marriage." Alden Clark[3] has pointed out, furthermore, that returns from maternity hospitals place the first parturition at 18.3 to 19.4 years. At the Madras Maternity Hospital only 10 out of 3,000 cases were under 15! Besides, we learn also from the 1921 census that only 399 out of 1,000 girls were married at 15, which would seem to indicate the average age at menarche is over 15 rather than under 13!

Among gynecologists Dr. Henry Vignes seems to be the only one to recognize the principle suggested in this paper. He says in his "Physiologie Gynécologique" (Paris, 1929), p. 55: "The onset of menstruation does not mean the capacity for conception; many girls who are just beginning to menstruate conceive with difficulty. Godin says that the age of maturity (nubilité), when the individual is capable of reproducing, is about five years after puberty." Dr. Vignes, moreover, kindly sent me a copy of the article "Nubilité" by Mondière in "Le Dictionnaire des Sciences Anthropologiques"

[3]*Atlantic Monthly*, February, 1928.

(1890?). This gynecologist spent some years in Cochin-China, where he gathered certain data (first menses, first parturition, number of children, menopause, etc.) concerning 960 Annamite, 106 Chinese and 87 Cambodian women. He found that the first menstruation took place on the average at 16-1/4 years in the Annamites, at 16-1/2 in the Chinese, at 16-10/12 in the Cambodians; the first parturition in these groups at 20-1/2, 16-10/12 and 22-1/2 years, respectively, despite their early marriages. He therefore concludes: "Maturity (nubilité) is often confused with puberty, which is a very different thing, for maturity signifies the faculty of normal reproduction."

This interval between the appearance of the first manifestations of sexual activity and the ability to conceive doubtless explains the Trobiand Islanders' ignorance and denial of physiological paternity and the corollary thereof, a matriarchal form of society, as set forth by Malinowsky in his "Sexual Life of Savages" (London and New York, 1929). Contact with white man has not yet made any headway in convincing the natives that sexual intercourse has any relation to procreation.

Malinowsky is, nevertheless, well-nigh baffled by the fact that despite the absolutely unrestrained and promiscuous sex life of the young Trobiander from childhood on, pregnancy among young unmarried girls is extremely rare—perhaps one per cent. "Can there by any physiological law," the author asks, "which makes conception less likely when women begin their sexual life young, lead it indefatigably, and mix their lovers freely?"

It seems highly reasonable that Malinowsky's predicament is explained by the facts presented in this paper, namely, that the first menstruation (*puberty*) marks merely an early manifestation of a train of events (*adolescence*) which only after three or four years on the average lead to ovulation and conception, the proof of *maturity*.

MALINOWSKI ON METHOD AND FUNCTIONALISM

BRONISLAW KASPAR MALINOWSKI (1884-1942), Polish-English anthropologist, was one of the most brilliant anthropologists of our time. A magnificent teacher, master of half a dozen languages, and an artist in the use of English, a language which he acquired largely through reading Frazer's *The Golden Bough*. It was this work which led him to give up all thought of a career in mathematics and physics, in which he had taken the PhD at the University of Cracow, and to formally pursue the study of anthropology. In 1913 Malinowski published his now classical study on *The Family Among the Australian Aborigines*, and in 1914 he set out for New Guinea where he was to do his first field work. Out of this came his study "The Natives of Mailu" (1915), and for this report and his book on the Australian aborigines he was awarded, in 1916, the DSc degree by the University of London. In June 1915 he went to the Trobriands in North-Western Melanesia, where he remained till May 1916. A second visit lasted from October 1917 to October 1918. The eighteen months he spent among the Trobriand Islanders provided him with enough material for a half dozen or more works which have since become classics of anthropology. The first of these, published in 1922, was *Argonauts of the Western Pacific*, a fascinating and detailed study of an intertribal closed-circuit form of economic exchange practiced among and within the neighboring island groups. The quality of this first full-length study of a native institution was sufficient to establish Malinowski's reputation as a distinguished and original anthropologist.

Through the study of this institution, in all its functional interrelations, Malinowski was able to give the world a well-rounded insightful picture into the so-called savage and his society, and to place him squarely within it as a living, interesting, human being. This had never really been achieved before in quite so professional a way.

In 1926 Malinowski published a critical examination of the views of W. H. R. Rivers and Sidney Hartland, in the light of his own field-work on crime, punishment, and law in nonliterate societies; this was entitled *Crime and Custom in Savage Society*. In the same year he published the article on "Anthropology" in the 13th edition of the *Encyclopaedia Britannica*, in which for the first time he set out his views on what he called "the functional method" in anthropology. In 1927 *Sex and Repression in Savage Society* appeared. In this work Malinowski, again on the basis of his own fieldwork, was able to show that Freud's conception of the oedipus complex was not a universal phenomenon, since it did not exist among the Trobrianders. In 1919 appeared *The Sexual Life of Savages*, with a new printing in 1932 to which Malinowski added the "Special Foreword" which is here reprinted, because it gives an excellent account of the author's view of anthropological method and especially of his view of the functional method in anthropology.

Functionalism has had a very refreshing influence upon anthropological thinking in its emphasis upon anthropological facts as interrelated to each other within the society, and the manner in which these in turn are related to the physical environment. This is a view which has been successfully absorbed into the main body of anthropological thinking, much to the benefit of the science.[1]

SPECIAL FOREWARD TO THE
THIRD EDITION*

I am writing this somewhat lengthy Foreword to the new edition of *The Sexual Life of Savages* because the book has been a disappointment to me, and that in spite of a reception on the whole extremely benevolent and encouraging. The book has appeared in four languages, with separate English and American editions; other translations are being prepared; the reviewers have been invariably kind and pleasant—and yet I am not satisfied. No author, I expect, ever is satisfied that his book has been taken in the spirit in which it was given, or understood as it was meant to be understood, and this is, of course, always the author's own fault.

I am disappointed in the reception of this book because I wanted it to be regarded as an achievement in field-work and in methods of exposition, an achievement—or perhaps an experiment—to be questioned, discussed, criticized, rejected in parts, but not to be ignored. But this experimental and ambitious aim has not, so far as I can judge, received the attention which I wished it to receive.

So that I want to take the opportunity of explaining this aim, that is of stating the significance of the functional method in field-work and in the synthetic description of ethnographic material.

Sex as a Cultural Force.

My object in publishing this monograph was to demonstrate the main principle of the functional method: I wanted to show that only a synthesis of facts concerning sex can give a correct idea of what sexual life means to a people. The effect of the book, on the other hand, was that merely sensational details were picked out, and wondered or laughed at, while the synthesis, the integra-

---

[1]For a critical examination of the work of Malinowski see Raymond Firth, editor, *Man and Culture: An Evaluation of the Life and Work of Malinowski* (New York, Humanities Press, 1957).

*From *The Sexual Life of Savages in North-Western Melanesia* (London, George Routledge & Sons, 1932), pp. xix-xliv. Reprinted by permission of Routledge & Kegan Paul, Ltd.

tion of details, the correlation of aspects, the whole functional mechanism in short was missed.

I intended to give a concrete example showing that a subject like sex cannot be treated except in its institutional setting, and through its manifestations in other aspects of culture. Love, sexual approaches, eroticism, combined with love-magic and the mythology of love, are but a part of customary courtship in the Trobriands. Courtship, again, is a phase, a preparatory phase, of marriage, and marriage but one side of family life. The family itself ramifies into the clan, into the relations between matrilineal and patriarchal kindred; and all these subjects, so intimately bound up with one another, constitute really one big system of kinship, a system which controls the social relations of the tribesmen with each other, dominates their economics, pervades their magic and mythology, and enters into their religion and even into their artistic productions.

So that, starting with the problem of sex, I was led to give a full account of the kinship system, and of its function within the Trobriand culture. I have left out, or, rather, I have only briefly indicated, the linguistic aspect of the question—the ill-omened kinship nomenclatures—a subject so wildly over-discussed, so often exaggerated in records of field-work, that one is sometimes led to suspect that it is nothing but an avenue to anthropological insanity. This aspect of kinship I have reserved for publication in a separate volume, hoping that by an overdose of terminological documentation and linguistic detail I can administer a cathartic cure to social anthropology.

My main aim in this book, however, was to show that from whichever side you approach it, the problem of sex, family, and kinship presents an organic unity which cannot be disrupted. I somehow feel that the synthetic or constructive part of my book did not "get across". Havelock Ellis saw the significance of my main argument and commented on it in the Preface. Bertrand Russell fully appreciated the functional significance of the Trobriand facts as regards paternity and made use of them in his pioneering work on *Marriage and Morals*. A brilliant American writer, Floyd Dell, used my evidence with a clear grasp of the essentials in his *Love in the Machine Age*—a book which I should like everyone to read. But apparently most other readers have not been aware of the wider purpose of my book. What has aroused general interest has been sensational details—the notorious ignorance of primitive paternity, the technicalities of love-making, certain aspects of love-magic (a subject unquestionably attractive), and one or two eccentricities of the so-called matriarchal system.

The Ignorance of Paternity and the Social Dynamics of a Native Doctrine.

The "ignorance of paternity" seems to be the most popular subject in this book. And here I feel that most of those who have commented upon my material have missed two points. First of all, the Trobrianders do not suffer from a specific complaint, an *ignorantia paternitatis*. What we actually find among them is a complicated attitude towards the facts of maternity and paternity. Into this attitude there enter certain elements of positive knowledge, certain gaps in embryological information. These cognitive ingredients again are overlaid by beliefs of an animistic nature, and influenced by the moral and legal principles of the community and by the sentimental leanings of the individual.

The second point which I should like emphatically to make here is that in this book I am not pronouncing any opinion as to whether there was any "original ignorance of paternity" throughout primitive mankind and whether the Trobrianders still suffer from it; or whether what they believe is the result of the direct influence of the matrilineal system of social organization upon their physiological knowledge. I have contributed towards the confusion perhaps by committing myself in a previous publication to the view that the Trobrianders represent the state of "original ignorance". This was as early as 1916, when, in an article published in the *Journal of the Royal Anthropological Institute*, I gave the preliminary statement about the Trobrianders' beliefs concerning reincarnation and procreative processes. I still believe that most of what I said there was plausible, but as a field-worker I should have made my theoretical conjectures entirely distinct from my descriptions of fact, and there is no doubt that I committed myself then to certain evolutionary views, which at present I regard as irrelevant, even though unimpeachable.

An Evolutionist's Recantation.

This, I think, is a good opportunity of making a clean breast of it in the form of a recantation. In 1916 I defended the evolutionary thesis of Sidney Hartland about the universal ignorance of paternity in primitive mankind. I also tried to prove that the Trobrianders as well as a number of other peoples in New Guinea and Central Australia are still under the sway of this primitive ignorance of paternity.

In 1923 and again in 1927 I reiterated "my firm conviction that the ignorance of paternity is an original feature of primitive psychology, and that in all speculations about the origins of marriage and the evolution of sexual customs, we must bear in mind this fundamental ignorance".[1] But the reader of Chapter VII of this book, which appeared in 1929, will find no such statements about "origins", "primeval states", and other fundamentals of evolutionism, not even echoes of them. The fact is that I have ceased to be a fundamentalist of evolutionary method, and I would rather discountenance any speculations about the "origins" of marriage or anything else than contribute to them even

[1] *The Father in Primitive Psychology*, p. 93. Cf. also "The Psychology of Sex in Primitive Societies", *Psyche*, Oct., 1923.

indirectly. So that the complete elimination of all evolutionary or reconstructive attitudes from this book is not merely the outcome of a greater puritanism in method, the maintenance of the sacred rule in all exposition which makes the statement of fact kept clear from any conjectural opinions. The change in my presentation of material is also due to the fact that I have grown more and more indifferent to the problems of origins—origins, that is, conceived in the naïve way in which I treated them in my previous utterances. In 1916 I was still interested in the question: "Is this state of ignorance primitive, is it simply the absence of knowledge, due to insufficient observation and inference, or is it a secondary phenomenon, due to an obscuring of the primitive knowledge by superimposed animistic ideas?"[1] Now this problem and problems of this type have become meaningless to me. The original state of any knowledge or any belief or any ignorance must have no doubt been a complete blank. Pithecanthropus as it became man had not even language to express its interests. Evolution in this case as in any other was a gradual growth and differentiation of ideas, customs, institutions.

Professions of a Disguised Antiquarian.

I still believe in evolution, but what appears to me really relevant is not how things started or how they followed one another, but rather the statement of the elements and factors which control the growth of culture and of social organization. In the present case I would ask what were the social and moral forces which could have contributed to the development of embryological knowledge or its obscuring? Under what circumstances was man likely to become aware about physiological paternity and what are the constellations which would place this knowledge on a very distant plane of interest? Now such questions, however reconstructively we put them, can only be empirically answered by the study of the mechanisms which still can be observed in present-day stone-age communities.

If we find out that ideas about procreation are invariably correlated with the reckoning of kinship; if we can establish that in patriarchal societies there is generally greater emphasis on female chastity, hence a greater opportunity for empirical correlation between the sexual act and pregnancy; if, again, we find that in patriarchal communities the father's procreative share is emotionally more important—we learn a great deal about the mechanisms of the process by which sexual relations and knowledge, marriage, and kinship must have evolved. And such information is the real foundation on which all our speculations about the development of domestic institutions have to rest. Such speculations may, at times even must, go beyond the strictly empirical basis. As long as we are aware that we move in the realm of hypothesis, of probabilities,

[1]"Baloma," *Journal of the Royal Anthropological Institute*, 1916, p. 413.

of things imagined or tentatively reconstructed, there is no harm in flights of speculative antiquarianism.

My indifference to the past and to its reconstruction is therefore not a matter of tense, so to speak; the past will always be most attractive to the antiquarian, and every anthropologist is an antiquarian, myself certainly so. My indifference to certain types of evolutionism is a matter of method. I wish the past to be reconstructed on the foundations of sound scientific method, and science teaches us above all that we can reconstruct only when we know the regularities of a process, when we know laws of growth, development, and correlation. As long as we are ignorant of these laws and regularities, we can have only flights of imagination and not a scientific reconstruction. After we have established the laws of a process, we can then, within limits, reconstruct the past.

The Sentimental Charm, The Philosophic Interest, and The Scientific Value of Anthropology.

If I had to balance sentiment, imagination, and reason I should definitely state that romantically, that is allowing sentiment to dominate my imagination, I am a full-blooded antiquarian. Philosophically, that is allowing my reason to be swayed by imagination, the facts of anthropology attract me mainly as the best means of knowing myself. But scientifically I have to claim that unless we use the comparative method from the functional point of view, and through this obtain the laws of correlation, of cultural process, and of the relationship between various aspects of human civilization, we shall inevitably be building all our vast edifices of reconstructive hypothesis or philosophical reflection on sand.

Cuvier was able to reconstruct his antediluvian monster from a tiny bone only because he knew the correlation of the bone to the rest of the skeleton. It is in the relation between a detail of structure to the whole that its meaning and its reconstructive virtue lies, and in the science of culture to tear out a custom which belongs to a certain context, which is part of it, the very existence of which would determine all the work which it does within that context —to tear it out, to dote upon it in a collectioneering or curio-hunting spirit, leads nowhere. And in the item of culture which we study, in the doctrine of bodily identity as derived from procreation, it is only the significance of this doctrine as a basis of matrilineal descent, as determining the father's relationship to the child, and as entering more or less directly into most aspects of kinship, that we find its significance.

The hunt for origins then should lead us to the study of laws of structure, of laws of process. In recanting my evolutionary adherence to the dogma of "primitive ignorance", I am not altogether renegade from evolutionism. I still believe in evolution, I am still interested in origins, in the process of development, only I see more and more clearly that answers to any evolutionary questions must lead directly to the empirical study of the facts and institutions, the past development of which we wish to reconstruct.

The Trobriand Belief in Reincarnation.

Returning to my present views as compared to my previous interests, I have to recant my affirmation that "if we are at all justified in speaking of certain 'primitive' conditions of mind, the ignorance in question is such a primitive condition".[1] I recant this statement precisely because I do not think that we are justified in speaking about "primitive views of man" or of anything else, using *primitive* in the absolute sense of the word. But I fully abide by my view that "a state of ignorance similar to that found in the Trobriands obtains among a wide range of the Papuo-Melanesians of New Guinea".[2] I also abide by my view that what with the laxity in sexual conduct and its early beginning in life, the natives of the Trobriands have extremely unpropitious conditions for any empirical observations on embryology.

I said in 1916 that had the Trobrianders had favourable opportunities, they probably would have obtained a much clearer insight into the facts of impregnation than they actually have. "Given such (favourable) conditions, the natives would probably have discovered the causal connection (between copulation and pregnancy), because the native mind works according to the same rules as ours; his powers of observation are keen, whenever he is interested, and the concept of cause and effect is not unknown to him."[1] I am still convinced that there is nothing extraordinary in the Trobrianders' incomplete realization of embryological facts.

The Trobrianders' Ignorance of Relativity.

Let me here briefly justify this theoretical conviction. I think it is rather inconsistent to get excited about the faulty knowledge of the Trobrianders when it comes to processes of sexual fertilization, while we are perfectly satisfied that they possess no real knowledge as to processes of nutrition, or metabolism, the causes of disease and health, or any other subject of natural history—that they have no correct knowledge and cannot have it. These natives, in fact, do not know very much about Einstein's theory of relativity, nor about the Newtonian laws of motion, nor yet about the systems of Copernicus and Keppler. Their knowledge of astronomy and physics is limited, their beliefs concerning anatomy and physiology crude. On botany and geology we would not

[1]*Baloma*, p. 418.
[2]Op. cit., p. 414.
[1]Op. cit., pp. 417, 148.

expect them to give us any scientifically valid observations. Why, then, do we demand full and precise ideas on embryology? It would be much more incredible if the natives "knew the connection between sexual intercourse and pregnancy", as we are so often told about one tribe or another. The verb "know" in this context cannot mean "to possess correct knowledge", it must always cover a great confusion of the elements of knowledge and ignorance.

Every open-minded reader can see from the relevant chapters of this book that the natives have a knowledge, however incomplete, of the correlation between sexual intercourse and pregnancy. Their strong matrilineal principles of law make the recognition of paternity a remote question to them, and the supernatural version of the causes of childbirth has the strongest hold on their imagination and the greatest influence on their institutional life.

The Social Function of Procreative Ideas.

I have given in this book the native theory of bodily and spiritual identity derived from procreation. I have shown how the scanty gleanings of physical and physiological fact are overshadowed by mythological beliefs concerning the reincarnation of spirits—beliefs which are embedded in their whole animistic system. My account is an answer to the questions: What are the actual facts of the Trobrianders' knowledge, beliefs, ignorances, institutionalized attitudes about maternity, paternity, and the physiological and spiritual foundations of kinship? Incidentally, my account is a methodological challenge for future field-work. It constitutes a demand that in future we should have neither affirmations nor denials, in an empty wholesale verbal fashion, of native "ignorance" or "knowledge", but instead, full concrete descriptions of what they know, how they interpret it, and how it is all connected with their conduct and their institutions.

There is then nothing miraculous or even unexpected in the Trobriand configuration of belief, moral conduct, embryological knowledge, and social institution as regards paternity. We might feel incredulous if we were told we could find there *perfect knowledge* or *absolute ignorance*. This is exactly what we do not find in the Trobriands. The search for such clear-cut, absolute facts in black and white seems to me always futile. The functional method insists on the complexity of sociological facts; on the concatenation of various often apparently contradictory elements in one belief or conviction; on the dynamic working of such a conviction within the social system; and on the expression of social attitudes and beliefs in traditionally standardized behaviour.

The functional method, therefore, not merely leads the theory-maker to a reframing of facts, above all it drives the field-worker to new types of observation. It is thus a theory which, begun in field-work, leads back to field-work again.

As we have seen, the functional method develops the interest in the relations between isolated customs, institutions, and aspects of culture. All the ligatures which connect social and moral forces, dogmatic beliefs, ritual acts, cannot be reconstructed from the armchair—they must be discovered in the study of a native community as it lives its beliefs and as it does or does not practise its moral and legal rules.

The Functional School.

I have been speaking of the *functional method* as if it were an old-established school of anthropology. Let me confess at once: the magnificent title of the Functional School of Anthropology has been bestowed by myself, in a way on myself, and to a large extent out of my own sense of irresponsibility. The claim that there is, or perhaps that there ought to be, a new school based on a new conception of culture and that this school should be called "functional", was made first in the article s.v. "Anthropology" in the 13th edition of *The Encyclopaedia Britannica* (1926). Among the various tendencies of modern anthropology, I there claimed a special place for "the Functional Analysis of Culture". And I briefly defined this method as follows: "This type of theory aims at the explanation of anthropological facts at all levels of development by their function, by the part which they play within the integral system of culture, by the manner in which they are related to each other within the system, and by the manner in which this system is related to the physical surroundings. It aims at the understanding of the nature of culture, rather than at conjectural reconstructions of its evolution or of past historical events."[1]

I was fully aware then that I was speaking of a New Movement, which hardly existed, and that in a way I was making myself into the captain, the general staff, and the body of privates of an army which was not yet there. The only thing which I can claim in extenuation of this act of self-appointment was that it was not done without some sense of humour.

> "Oh, I am the cook and the captain bold,
> And the mate of the *Nancy* brig:
> And the bo'sun tight
> And the midship mite
> And the crew of the captain's gig. . . ."

(. . . and, as many of my colleagues would suggest, for the same reason . . .).
But the "Functional School" has come to stay. It is now generally admitted

[1]This article has been reprinted in the 14th edition of *The Encyclopaedia Britannica*, s.v. "Social Anthropology."

that such a school is needed. As to myself, from the very outset of my anthropological work, I felt it was high time to precipitate into existence, to consolidate and define a tendency which, old as the hills in all studies of human culture and society, has only gradually been coming to the fore, a tendency, however, which imperatively demanded explicit recognition and reorganization. The reason for this need of a rapid crystallizing of principles is the fact that at present specialized and scientifically competent field-work among primitive peoples has to be done against time: it must be accomplished within the next few decades or never. Now the modern specialist in the field becomes aware at once that in order to do his work effectively and within the short space of time which he has at his disposal, he has to develop methods, principles, and theories of a different type to those which were sufficient for the long-stay amateur or the old travelling curio-hunter. The rapid collecting of really relevant documents, the possibility during a sojourn of necessity all too short, of obtaining correct and reliable information directly from native sources, requires a special theoretical grounding.

The Functional Method as the Theory of Field-work.

Modern field-work therefore needs a theory of a purely empirical nature, a theory which does not go beyond inductive evidence, but which provides for a clear understanding of how human culture in its primitive forms works. The field-worker is bound to make mistakes, and to frame his material within a wrong perspective if he is under the obsession of any reconstructive diffusionist or evolutionary doctrines.

The scientific field-worker should study the culture of his tribe in its own right so to speak, and as a self-contained reality. The comparative work as well as reconstructive speculations on his material can be done later on from the armchair. The observations on what exists, on how it works, and what it means to the natives—the full reality of culture as it works in full swing—this has to be seized and related by the man in the field. No one will be able to accomplish it after he has left his tribe, not even the man himself.

And here a very important point has to be made: while without a theory in the right empirical sense, that is, a theory which serves to guide and orientate the observer, no effective field-work can be done, conjectural and reconstructive theories have a directly bad influence on field-work. The reconstructive theorist, whether evolutionary or diffusionist, is bound to regard every element of culture as extraneous to the context in which it is found. For the evolutionist is mainly interested in a fact as a survival of a past stage, while the diffusionist sees in it above all a mechanically conveyed importation from another geographical region. The one places it in a past time, the other in a distant space. But both remove the fact far from the actual surroundings where it now lives.

Thus every element of culture, the idea, the custom, the form of organization, the word, has to be torn out of its context and fitted into some imaginary scheme.

How the Discovery of "Group Marriage" followed its Invention.

It is this isolating of loose items or "traits", this dissecting of culture which makes the reconstructive attitude dangerous in the field. Thus, take an apparently innocent, theoretical pastime: speculations about the "origins of marriage". One school, and a very powerful school, believes in group marriage, that is, in a state when individual marriage was unknown and instead of that human beings were sexually united into group marriage—something very immoral, terribly prurient, in fact, so unthinkable that it has never been clearly defined! Can you imagine Morgan, the respectable Puritan of New England, entering into details of his own famous hypothesis, "group marriage," explaining how it really took place? The fact is that Morgan never did analyse or define his fundamental categories of primitive organization: "promiscuity," "group marriage," "consanguine family," and so on. This was, perhaps, excusable, certainly comprehensible, in a man of his moral outlook and with a lack of sociological training. He was a pioneer, in many ways a great pioneer, but he was not a schooled student of human society. What is really shocking to the modern sociologist is that not one of his numerous followers ever exercised his creative imagination sufficiently to give us a clear vision and definition of those imaginary modes of human mating.

But postulated and affirmed they were, and they became an obsession to the amateur field-worker as well as to the theoretical student.

"Numerous instances" of "group marriage" were found all over the world and brought triumphantly to Morgan and laid at his puritanic doorstep. Thus we have the famous *pirrauru* institution of Central Australia made into a "form of group marriage". This was done by tearing the *pirrauru* out of its context, failing completely to inquire into its non-sexual aspects, and over-emphasizing its sexual side. By identifying in the special puritanic euphemism *sexual relations* with *marital relations, pirrauru* was made into "an actually existing form of group marriage". In reality this is neither marriage nor a group relationship, but a form of seriatim cicisbeism (cf. my *Family among the Australian Aborigines*, ch. v, 1913). And all this happened because the writers who were describing it were looking for "traces of group marriage", and were not interested in a full all-round description of the working institutions as they really existed and functioned within a concrete and complex sociological context. In Central Australia individual marriage, which is real marriage, does exist. The question which our first-hand observers should have answered is: "What is the relation between the *pirrauru* institution and marriage; what actual services do the *pirrauru* partners render to one another besides occasional mutual sexual enjoyment?'' Such an analysis would have shown that while marriage in Central Australia is a domestic, ceremonial, legal, religious, and procreative institution, the *pirrauru* is mainly a legalized sexual relationship.

The Passing of Rites de Passage.

Another typical dangerous label is that of *rites de passage*. Valuable as M. Van Gennep's contribution has been, it was mainly a formal scheme not based on the real functional analysis of the various rites lumped together because of their formal similarity. The essence of an initiation ceremony lies in its sociological, educational, and religious significance. The analysis of secret societies and initiation ceremonies given by Schurtz, Cunow, and Hutton Webster were made in a much more functional spirit and are therefore more useful than the formal classifications under the several sub-headings of *rites de passage*. Yet innumerable field-workers have been gripped by the clever label, and very good material such as that of Rattray's, or of Junod, is vitiated by the formalism of its setting.

''Classificatory systems of kinship,'' mother-right, and father-right, the dual organization, the clan system, solar or lunar mythology—all these are labels manufactured often by armchair theorists who never saw the enlivening actuality of native tribal life, and had a tendency towards the abstract and detached formulation of cultural realities. Many an amateur field-worker, again, fascinated by the learned-sounding title, hypnotized into the belief that in order to be scientific you have to go far away from what is under your nose, used these labels in at times a ridiculously inadequate and naïve fashion.

Sex is not Everything.

I have been speaking of sex because this is the subject matter of the present book. Any other topic would have led us to the same conclusions and I could exemplify the synthetic principle of the Functional School on the problems of nutrition, of economic pursuits, of religious and magical beliefs, or on any other anthropological theme. To take nutrition as an example, food becomes in all primitive—and, of course, in all civilized—societies, a centre of social grouping, a basis of systems of value, and the nucleus of ritual acts and religious beliefs. We need only remember that the central rite of our own religion is a nutritive act.

Everything which refers to food should be studied in a synthetic manner, by analysing the integration of social grouping, of systems of value, and of ritualism round this main biological need and mental interest of man. No culture can be understood unless all its nutritive institutions are worked out in direct reference to the preparing and eating of food, to the quest for food, to its distribution and storage. It is one of the remarkable paradoxes of social science that while a whole school of economic metaphysics has erected the importance of material interests—which in the last instance are always food interests—into the dogma of materialistic determination of all historical process, neither anthropology nor any other special branch of social science has devoted any serious attention to food. The anthropological foundations of Marxism or of anti-Marxism are still to be laid down.

Again, while sex has been discussed and is being discussed *ad nauseam*, while the psycho-analytic school are reducing everything to the sexual impulse, no one as far as I know has thought of devoting the same amount of attention and emphasis to the twin interest, that in food—to nutrition, the other need of the human organism, as fundamental as procreation. Nutrition is, of course, being studied by biologists, by hygienists, and by medical men, but, on the one hand, to study the physiology of nutrition without its cultural setting con- stitutes a great loss to both aspects of the subject, and, on the other hand, the whole of the science of culture is sterile as long as the second great founda- tion of human society, the quest for food, is not brought fully to the attention of anthropologists.

The functional school, which ultimately aims at tracing all cultural phenomena to the essential wants of the human organism, is bound to remedy this evil. As a matter of fact, Dr. A. I. Richards, in her work, *Food in Savage Society*, dealing with the sociology of nutrition and which is shortly to be pub- lished, has made an important contribution to this subject. It is to be hoped that her pioneering lead will be soon followed by others of this school.

The Study of Primitive Economics.

But functionalism does not hinge only on sex or food or on both of these. The functional method recognizes perhaps above all that the satisfaction of biological needs implies and develops a system of derivative requirements. Man living under conditions of culture obtains his bread indirectly through co- operation and exchange. He has to procure it in complicated economic pursuits. Culture therefore creates new requirements, requirements for implements, weapons, and means of transport, for social co-operation, for institutions which ensure an ordinary and lawful working of human groups and which allow of organized co-operation.

The function therefore of many features of human culture is not the direct satisfaction of nutritive or sexual needs, but rather the satisfaction of what might be called *instrumental needs*, that is, needs for instruments, for means to an end, the end being the biological well-being of the individual, the pro- creation of the species, and also the spiritual development of the personality and the establishment of a give-and-take in social co-operation. Instrumental needs, again, that is the body of artifacts and social organization, imply other requirements. The whole production is based on knowledge, while social organization is based on morality, religion, and magic. We have, therefore, cultural wants of a yet higher degree of derivation, and I like to call them *integrative needs*.

Some preparatory work in the direction of coping with the instrumental aspect of culture has been done by economists and anthropologists, in the discussion of the economic organization of primitive peoples. The extraordinary preconceptions as to the simplicity of primitive economic organization has led to the later theories of the four or five stages of economic development. The only problem known to early anthropology and comparative economics was the problem of sequence in occupational stages. Did hunting precede a pastoral life, or did agriculture come first? Was the tilling of the soil invented by women, by men, or by priests? These and such like were the questions discussed by Liszt, by Schmoller, by Wagner, and even in the recent works of Hahn and Max Schmidt.

A certain over-simplification of the problem still dominates the pioneering attempts of Karl Bücher, from which really modern discussions on primitive economics begin. Dr. R. W. Firth's book on *The Primitive Economics of the Maori* is perhaps the first full monograph treating primitive economics from the functional point of view. And an analysis of that book—which welds together magic and economic activities, aesthetic interests and incentives to labour, economic values and religious ideas—an analysis of Dr. Firth's arguments would show us quite as well as an analysis of the present book what functionalism really means. In writing my *Argonauts of the Western Pacific*, I was made to realize also how the study of one economic institution inevitably forces us to place it within the general context of tribal economics, and to trace out its relations to other social aspects of the community. The real definition of such an institution as the inter-tribal trading round Eastern New Guinea is really made not by this or that activity but by establishing the relation between magic, mythology, social organization, purely commercial interests, and a half ceremonial, half aesthetic system of values, built round objects whose primary function was adornment, but which soon became simply repositories of a traditional and competitive principle of value.

I wish only briefly to indicate here that the functional theory is not merely the statement that what functions must have a function, but that it leads us to an analysis of the nature of culture and of cultural processes. Since I have given a preliminary outline of such a functional theory of culture (article s.v. "Culture" in the *American Encyclopaedia of the Social Sciences*, edited by Edwin Seligman and Alvin Johnson), it will be enough for me to refer to it, indicating here merely the width and scope of modern anthropological work on functional lines.

Returning, however, to the present book, let me once more illustrate by another example the point which I was making at the outset, viz. that the little curiosities or self-contained facts and stories which were picked out and discussed are in themselves of little consequence, and that the real significance becomes only apparent if we place them within their institutionalized context.

The Antiquarian Aspect of Culture.

I shall take the one aspect of primitive culture which is usually regarded as leading an independent existence, detached from present-day concerns, idle and useless—except perhaps as a form of stimulating pastime or entertainment. I mean folk-lore, the body of stories, legends and myths related by a tribe. The current view is that myths are a mere intellectual hobby, a sort of cross-word puzzle of primitive man. Folk-lore, we are told, contains "the earliest attempts to exercise reason, imagination, and memory . . . Myths are stories which, however marvellous and improbable to us, are, nevertheless, related in all good faith because they are intended, or believed by the teller, to *explain* by means of something concrete and intelligible, an *abstract* idea or such *vague* and *difficult* conceptions as Creation, Death, distinctions of race or animal species, the different occupations of men and women; the origins of rites and customs, or striking natural objects or prehistoric monuments; the meaning of the names of persons or places. Such stories are sometimes described as *aetiological* because their *purpose is to explain why something exists or happens*." (The italics are mine.) I have quoted here from the last edition but one of *Notes and Queries*,[1] a statement written, in collaboration with the late Miss C. S. Burne, by one of our greatest authorities, Professor J. L. Myres, than whom no one is more competent to summarize the views of the classical anthropology of to-day.

And yet this statement cannot be accepted by those holding functional points of view—and it is the functionalist who is entitled to judge it because this statement concerns the function of myth. We read about "explanations", "abstract ideas", the relation of myth to "vague and difficult conceptions". Mythology then would be a primitive form of science. It would be, in fact, an incomplete or warped science, because, while our own science is an integral part of modern culture, the foundation of our technology, the source of our philosophic, even of our religious inspiration, mythology or primitive science would of necessity remain idle and unconnected with primitive economics or pragmatic *Weltanschauung* for the very simple reason that it is not knowledge but fancy. The function of folk-lore, then, according to modern anthropologists, would be to provide primitive man with a fanciful, useless, and completely self-contained system of warped scientific explanations.

Is such a functional definition of myth acceptable? Certainly not. The functionalist field-worker finds that myths are by no means told when questions

[1] *Notes and Queries on Anthropology*, 4th ed., 1912, p. 210.

of "why" or "for what reason" arise. They are not used as exercises of intelligence, imagination, or memory. In the first place they are not mere stories idly told. Myths to the native are enacted in ritual, in public ceremony, in dramatic performances. His sacred tradition lives to him in his sacramental acts, in his magical performances, in his social order and his moral outlook. It is not of the nature of fiction, such as we cultivate in our novels or moving pictures, or even in our drama. It is not a scientific doctrine such as we apply in present-day theory and carry out in practice. It is to the native a living reality believed to have once happened in primeval times and to have established a social, moral, and physical order.

This perhaps may seem a mere modified restatement of the previous quotation. But there is a fundamental difference between explaining, such as a scientific instructor does, and laying down a sacred rule as is done by the modern religious teacher who "explains" the doctrine of original sin by reference to the Biblical myth of Adam and Eve. To confuse mythological causality, which is essentially dogmatic, religious, and mystical, with scientific causality, is an epistemological and logical mistake, which has, however, dominated most of the work done on mythology.

The Functional Character of Myth.

Glance at the myths of Central Australia. Are they mere stories to the natives? They are danced, enacted, performed ritually at initiation and during the Intichiuma ceremonies. This re-enactment of mythology influences rain and wind and the growth of plants. The myths constitute the charter of the totemic order, of the local rights, of the rules of descent, inheritance, and sexual relationship. They are the foundation of magical technique and the guarantee of magical effectiveness. Indirectly they also influence the economics of this tribe. But in all this, myth does not function as a real science, but as a charter of moral and social order, as the precedent on which modern life must be built if it is to be good and effective.

Exactly the same applies to the legends of the Polynesians with the long pedigrees forming the foundation of the aristocratic order of their society; to the mythology of West Africa or of North America; or for that matter to our own myth about Adam and Eve and the Garden of Eden. The myths of the Old Testament are the foundation of our doctrines of moral responsibility and original sin, of our patriarchal order of kinship, and of many of our ideas about social duty and personal conduct; they are the basis of our Christian views of human nature and of the relation between man and God. The stories of the New Testament, again, are to the Roman Catholics the very backbone of their main religious rite, the Holy Mass. Whenever a new religion is founded by a Joseph Smith or a Mrs. Eddy, by a Stalin or a Mussolini, some special myth has to be created, revived, or reinterpreted, in order to give a supernatural validity to the new religion. Would we regard such modern myth as in any way equivalent to science? Certainly not. But if our myths are not science, why should we assume that primitive myths are so? Since the function of both is the same, their nature is identical, and they must be studied by anthropologists from the same point of view.

The Myth of Incest in the Trobriands.

But let us turn once more to the present book. We have a moving and dramatic myth of primitive incest which lies at the foundation of Trobriand folklore and which is deeply associated with their social organization, above all, with the powerful taboo on brother and sister relationship. Does this myth *explain* anything? Perhaps incest? But incest is strictly forbidden; it is to the natives an almost unthinkable event, the occurrence of which they do not even want to admit. They cannot tell stories in explanation of things to them unthinkable.

A moral lesson the myth does contain: the death of the two incestuous lovers is a precedent and a pattern, but a moral lesson is not an explanation. The myth also contains no exercises in imagination; such an exercise would be really repugnant to the natives when it comes to incest; nor in memory, since whenever incest occurs they try hard to forget it. The reader of the present volume will see that the function of the myth of Kumilabwaga is to provide the charter for love-magic, to show how through the power of spell and rite even the strong repulsion of incest can be broken. The myth also contains a potential excuse for such transgressions of incestuous and exogamous rules as sometimes occur, and it sanctions the forces which give an exclusiveness in the practice of magic to certain communities.

But what is the net and practical result of our functional reformulation of mythology? Here, again, it is not a mere verbal resetting. Whereas the older conception of myth encouraged the field-worker to do nothing but note down stories and find out what they "explain", the functionalist has a much harder task. He has to study the myth in its concrete embodiment. Are certain stories enacted ritually; are others constantly referred to in discussions of moral and social rules; are, again, others told invariably on certain occasions? All such problems can only be worked out in that most difficult type of field-work which consists in living native life side by side with the natives, in following them into their concerns and activities, and not merely taking down statements on paper. The relation between myth and magic, for instance, can be learned best in seeing magical rites enacted. The function of the present myth, the myth of love and of love-magic, I was able to grasp mainly by listening to echoes of dramatic occurrences, by following up village gossip and being aware of what actually was happening in the villages. The myth of Iwa and Kumilabwaga lives in the love-making and the courtship of the Trobrianders; in the relations between brother and sister, and between those who are allowed to mate; also in the rivalries between the community of Iwa and that of Kumilabwaga.

We have thus shown that the most antiquarian side of primitive culture appears alive, active, dynamic, once we study it in relation to the full context of tribal life, and not merely as a set of stories written down by the ethnographer in his note-book.

The Function of Material Culture.

We may rest confident that the other aspects of culture are also imbued with function, that means, with the capacity to go on working, to satisfy the needs, to be correlated with human wants. The field-worker in his observations sees every implement constantly used. In his study of material culture, therefore, he is quickly weaned from the vision of Museum specimens ranged in comparative or diffusionist series. He becomes impressed with the fact that it is in the manual use of a material object that we find its prima facie significance to the natives. He also finds that the manual use of a weapon, a tool, a magical gewgaw, or a religious image, shades imperceptibly into what might be called mental or spiritual use; that is, that material objects are deeply embedded in the beliefs, customary attitudes, and types of social organization of a tribe.

Take again material objects of more directly sociological character, such as dwellings, means of locomotion, places of magical or religious worship, arrangements for public gatherings, schemes of human settlement—the field-worker who wishes to squeeze the full meaning out of the physical matter, out of the shaped environment of his tribe, is more and more driven to the study of function. And by function here I mean the manner in which a house, or a canoe, or a ceremonial site is correlated with the bodily and spiritual needs of the tribesmen. Thus even in material culture, the simple interest in technology or in typological arrangements on the pattern of a museum case, must give way in field-work to the economics of human possessions, to the sociological concatenations of the monuments of a tribe, to the magical, religious, mythological, and spiritual significance of every object which man produces, owns, and uses.

Functional field-work consists always in the study of concatenations or the correlation of aspects in actual usage. And by usage I mean not merely manipulation, not merely the direct or instrumental satisfaction of needs, but the bodily attitudes in the widest behaviouristic sense in which body embraces mind; that is the ideas, beliefs, and values which centre round an object.

Obviously the explanation of customs must go on the same lines. A custom, that is a traditionally standardized habit, or as a modern physiologist would call it, conditioned reflex, is always an integral part of a bigger compound.

Detailed analysis of social organization and culture would show us that most customs, in fact all customs, integrate into a number of institutions.

But I cannot enter any further into such detailed analysis. I have given enough references to my other writings, especially to my two concise but comprehensive statements in the American *Encyclopaedia of the Social Sciences* (s.v. "Culture") and in the *Encyclopaedia Britannica* (s.v. "Anthropology", 13th edition, reprinted as "Social Anthropology" in the 14th edition). I have not been able here to give a full definition of what I understand by Functional Method. I have tried rather to stimulate the reader or perhaps to intrigue him. If I have succeeded in that, the purpose of this rambling foreword has been fulfilled.

RUTH BENEDICT ON THE INDIVIDUAL AND CULTURE

RUTH FULTON BENEDICT (1887-1948), American anthropologist, taught for many years in the Department of Anthropology at Columbia University. She was a woman of great beauty, a poet, and a sensitive writer. Her most famous work, *Patterns of Culture*, published in 1934, is an anthropological classic and in our own time has perhaps been more widely read than any other anthropological work. It has sold over a million copies.

The last chapter of *Patterns of Culture* is reprinted here because it distills the essence, as it were, of the best of her own teacher's thought, namely Franz Boas, purified through the alembic of a poet's mind. Boas, on one occasion, remarked to Benedict that he wished he could write as she did, but knew that he never could. In this last chapter, "The Individual and the Pattern of Culture," Benedict is at pains to show that the plasticity of human nature is such that culture can mold human beings to an almost infinite variety of forms. In an earlier part of the book she likens culture to a great arc, from which every culture selects some aspects. Traits which are integrated into a society are not haphazardly there, but exist in relation to a definite gestalt or configuration, and for the purpose of her purely descriptive analysis, she borrows from Nietzsche two contrasting ways of arriving at the values of existence as that philosopher saw them through his studies of Greek tragedy. One was the Dionysian, in which the aim was to break through the boundaries imposed by the senses, to achieve excess. The other was the Apollonian, the distrust of excess, the keeping of the middle path, commitment to tradition and opposition to individualism. Benedict saw the Pueblo Indians, and American Indians as a whole, as Dionysian. As an example of the Dionysian approach to life's values Benedict discussed the people of Dobu, an island in the D'Entrecasteaux group off the southern shore of New Guinea, described as a lawless and treacherous people, who put a premium upon ill-will and treachery.

Benedict did not claim that all societies are describable from such an Apollonian-Dionysian viewpoint, nor did she claim to have said the last word upon this type of analysis. What she achieved was a fresh and transitional way of looking at some cultures, and by contrasting them through the Apollonian-Dionysian refracting-glass she caused them, like the colors seen through a spectroscope, to be more finely perceived. This she achieved, even though her presentation of the three cultures with which she deals, the Zuni of the Southwest, the Kwakiutl of the Northwest-Pacific, and the Dobuans of Melanesia, has been criticized on the grounds that her original sources were not quite as accurate as could have been desired. A further criticism was that some of Benedict's assertions were rather extravagant, such, for example, as her statement that, "suicide was too violent an act . . . for the Pueblos to contemplate," since suicide does sometimes occur among Pueblo Indians. There were other criticisms. Legitimate as these criticisms are, they nevertheless make little difference to the effect of her book as a whole, and this last chapter, here reprinted, a final chapter which is, as it were, in itself a short course in cultural anthropology.

THE INDIVIDUAL AND THE PATTERN OF CULTURE*

The large corporate behaviour we have discussed is nevertheless the behaviour of individuals. It is the world with which each person is severally presented, the world from which he must make his individual life. Accounts of any civilization condensed into a few dozen pages must necessarily throw into relief the group standards and describe individual behaviour as it exemplifies the motivations of that culture. The exigencies of the situation are misleading only when this necessity is read off as implying that he is submerged in an overpowering ocean.

*From *Patterns of Culture* (Boston, Houghton-Mifflin Co., 1934), pp. 251-278. Reprinted by permission of Houghton-Mifflin Company.

There is no proper antagonism between the rôle of society and that of the individual. One of the most misleading misconceptions due to this nineteenth-century dualism was the idea that what was subtracted from society was added to the individual and what was subtracted from the individual was added to society. Philosophies of freedom, political creeds of *laissez faire*, revolutions that have unseated dynasties, have been built on this dualism. The quarrel in anthropological theory between the importance of the culture pattern and of the individual is only a small ripple from this fundamental conception of the nature of society.

In reality, society and the individual are not antagonists. His culture provides the raw material of which the individual makes his life. If it is meagre, the individual suffers; if it is rich, the individual has the chance to rise to his opportunity. Every private interest of every man and woman is served by the enrichment of the traditional stores of his civilization. The richest musical sensitivity can operate only within the equipment and standards of its tradition. It will add, perhaps importantly, to that tradition, but its achievement remains in proportion to the instruments and musical theory which the culture has provided. In the same fashion a talent for observation expends itself in some Melanesian tribe upon the negligible borders of the magico-religious field. For a realization of its potentialities it is dependent upon the development of scientific methodology, and it has no fruition unless the culture has elaborated the necessary concepts and tools.

The man in the street still thinks in terms of a necessary antagonism between society and the individual. In large measure this is because in our civilization the regulative activities of society are singled out, and we tend to identify society with the restrictions the law imposes upon us. The law lays down the number of miles per hour that I may drive an automobile. If it takes this restriction away, I am by that much the freer. This basis for a fundamental antagonism between society and the individual is naïve indeed when it is extended as a basic philosophical and political notion. Society is only incidentally and in certain situations regulative, and law is not equivalent to the social order. In the simpler homogeneous cultures collective habit or custom may quite supersede the necessity for any development of formal legal authority. American Indians sometimes say: 'In the old days, there were no fights about hunting grounds or fishing territories. There was no law then, so everybody did what was right.' The phrasing makes it clear that in their old life they did not think of themselves as submitting to a social control imposed upon them from without. Even in our civilization the law is never more than a crude implement of society, and one it is often enough necessary to check in its arrogant career. It is never to be read off as if it were the equivalent of the social order.

Society in its full sense as we have discussed it in this volume is never an entity separable from the individuals who compose it. No individual can arrive even at the threshold of his potentialities without a culture in which he participates. Conversely, no civilization has in it any element which in the last analysis is not the contribution of an individual. Where else could any trait come from except from the behaviour of a man or a woman or a child?

It is largely because of the traditional acceptance of a conflict between society and the individual, that emphasis upon cultural behaviour is so often interpreted as a denial of the autonomy of the individual. The reading of Sumner's *Folkways* usually rouses a protest at the limitations such an interpretation places upon the scope and initiative of the individual. Anthropology is often believed to be a counsel of despair which makes untenable a beneficent human illusion. But no anthropologist with a background of experience of other cultures has ever believed that individuals were automatons, mechanically carrying out the decrees of their civilization. No culture yet observed has been able to eradicate the differences in the temperaments of the persons who compose it. It is always a give-and-take. The problem of the individual is not clarified by stressing the antagonism between culture and the individual, but by stressing their mutual reinforcement. This rapport is so close that it is not possible to discuss patterns of culture without considering specifically their relation to individual psychology.

We have seen that any society selects some segment of the arc of possible human behaviour, and in so far as it achieves integration its institutions tend to further the expression of its selected segment and to inhibit opposite expressions. But these opposite expressions are the congenial responses, nevertheless, of a certain proportion of the carriers of that culture. We have already discussed the reasons for believing that this selection is primarily cultural and not biological. We cannot, therefore, even on theoretical grounds imagine that all the congenial responses of all its people will be equally served by the institutions of any culture. To understand the behaviour of the individual, it is not merely necessary to relate his personal life-history to his endowments, and to measure these against an arbitrarily selected normality. It is necessary also to relate his congenial responses to the behaviour that is singled out in the institutions of his culture.

The vast proportion of all individuals who are born into any society always and whatever the idiosyncrasies of its institutions, assume, as we have seen, the behaviour dictated by that society. This fact is always interpreted by the carriers of that culture as being due to the fact that their particular institutions reflect an ultimate and universal sanity. The actual reason is quite different. Most people are shaped to the form of their culture because of the enormous malleability of their original endowment. They are plastic to the moulding force of the society into which they are born. It does not matter whether, with the Northwest Coast, it requires delusions of self-reference, or with our own civilization the amassing of possessions. In any case the great mass of individuals take quite readily the form that is presented to them.

They do not all, however, find it equally congenial, and those are favoured and fortunate whose potentialities most nearly coincide with the type of behaviour selected by their society. Those who, in a situation in which they are frustrated, naturally seek ways of putting the occasion out of sight as expeditiously as possible are well served in Pueblo culture. Southwest institutions, as we have seen, minimize the situations in which serious frustration can arise, and when it cannot be avoided, as in death, they provide means to put it behind them with all speed.

On the other hand, those who react to frustration as to an insult and whose first thought is to get even are amply provided for on the Northwest Coast. They may extend their native reaction to situations in which their paddle breaks or their canoe overturns or to the loss of relatives by death. They rise from their first reaction of sulking to thrust back in return, to 'fight' with property or with weapons. Those who can assuage despair by the act of bringing shame to others can register freely and without conflict in this society, because their proclivities are deeply channelled in their culture. In Dobu those whose first impulse is to select a victim and project their misery upon him in procedures of punishment are equally fortunate.

It happens that none of the three cultures we have described meets frustration in a realistic manner by stressing the resumption of the original and interrupted experience. It might even seem that in the case of death this is impossible. But the institutions of many cultures nevertheless attempt nothing less. Some of the forms the restitution takes are repugnant to us, but that only makes it clearer that in cultures where frustration is handled by giving rein to this potential behaviour, the institutions of that society carry this course to extraordinary lengths. Among the Eskimo, when one man has killed another, the family of the man who has been murdered may take the murderer to replace the loss within its own group. The murderer then becomes the husband of the woman who has been widowed by his act. This is an emphasis upon restitution that ignores all other aspects of the situation—those which seem to us the only important ones; but when tradition selects some such objective it is quite in character that it should disregard all else.

Restitution may be carried out in mourning situations in ways that are less uncongenial to the standards of Western civilization. Among certain of the Central Algonkian Indians south of the Great Lakes the usual procedure was adoption. Upon the death of a child a similar child was put into his place. This similarity was determined in all sorts of ways: often a captive brought in from a raid was taken into the family in the full sense and given all the privileges and the tenderness that had originally been given to the dead child. Or quite as often it was the child's closest playmate, or a child from another related settlement who resembled the dead child in height and features. In such cases the family from which the child was chosen was supposed to be pleased, and indeed in most cases it was by no means the great step that it would be under our institutions. The child had always recognized many 'mothers' and many homes where he was on familiar footing. The new allegiance made him thoroughly at home in still another household. From the point of view of the bereaved parents, the situation had been met by a restitution of the *status quo* that existed before the death of their child.

Persons who primarily mourn the situation rather than the lost individual are provided for in these cultures to a degree which is unimaginable under our institutions. We recognize the possibility of such solace, but we are careful to minimize its connection with the original loss. We do not use it as a mourning technique, and individuals who would be well satisfied with such a solution are left unsupported until the difficult crisis is past.

There is another possible attitude toward frustration. It is the precise opposite of the Pueblo attitude, and we have described it among the other Dionysian reactions of the Plains Indians. Instead of trying to get past the experience with the least possible discomfiture, it finds relief in the most extravagant expression of grief. The Indians of the plains capitalized the utmost indulgences and exacted violent demonstrations of emotion as a matter of course.

In any group of individuals we can recognize those to whom these different reactions to frustration and grief are congenial: ignoring it, indulging it by uninhibited expression, getting even, punishing a victim, and seeking restitution of the original situation. In the psychiatric records of our own society, some of these impulses are recognized as bad ways of dealing with the situation, some as good. The bad ones are said to lead to maladjustments and insanities, the good ones to adequate social functioning. It is clear, however, that the correlation does not lie between any one 'bad' tendency and abnormality in any absolute sense. The desire to run away from grief, to leave it behind at all costs, does not foster psychotic behaviour where, as among the Pueblos, it is mapped out by institutions and supported by every attitude of the group. The Pueblos are not a neurotic people. Their culture gives the impression of fostering mental health. Similarly, the paranoid attitudes so violently expressed among the Kwakiutl are known in psychiatric theory derived from our own civilization as thoroughly 'bad'; that is, they lead in various ways to the breakdown of personality. But it is just those individuals among the Kwakiutl who find it congenial to give the freest expression to these attitudes who nevertheless are the leaders of Kwakiutl society and find greatest personal fulfilment in its culture.

Obviously, adequate personal adjustment does not depend upon following certain motivations and eschewing others. The correlation is in a different direction. Just as those are favoured whose congenial responses are closest to that behaviour which characterizes their society, so those are disoriented whose congenial responses fall in that arc of behaviour which is not capitalized by their culture. These abnormals are those who are not supported by the institutions of their civilization. They are the exceptions who have not easily taken the traditional forms of their culture.

For a valid comparative psychiatry, these disoriented persons who have failed to adapt themselves adequately to their cultures are of first importance. The issue in psychiatry has been too often confused by starting from a fixed list of symptoms instead of from the study of those whose characteristic reactions are denied validity in their society.

The tribes we have described have all of them their non-participating 'abnormal' individuals. The individual in Dobu who was thoroughly disoriented was the man who was naturally friendly and found activity an end in itself. He was a pleasant fellow who did not seek to overthrow his fellows or to punish them. He worked for anyone who asked him, and he was tireless in carrying out their commands. He was not filled by a terror of the dark like his fellows, and he did not, as they did, utterly inhibit simple public responses of friendliness toward women closely related, like a wife or sister. He often patted them playfully in public. In any other Dobuan this was scandalous behaviour, but in him it was regarded as merely silly. The village treated him in a kindly enough fashion, not taking advantage of him or making a sport of ridiculing him, but he was definitely regarded as one who was outside the game.

The behaviour congenial to the Dobuan simpleton has been made the ideal in certain periods of our own civilization, and there are still vocations in which his responses are accepted in most Western communities. Especially if a woman is in question, she is well provided for even today in our *mores*, and functions honourably in her family and community. The fact that the Dobuan could not function in his culture was not a consequence of the particular responses that were congenial to him, but of the chasm between them and the cultural pattern.

Most ethnologists have had similar experiences in recognizing that the persons who are put outside the pale of society with contempt are not those who would be placed there by another culture. Lowie found among the Crow Indians of the plains a man of exceptional knowledge of his cultural forms. He was interested in considering these objectively and in correlating different facets. He had an interest in genealogical facts and was invaluable on points of history. Altogether he was an ideal interpreter of Crow life. These traits, however, were not those which were the password to honour among the Crow. He had a definite shrinking from physical danger, and bravado was the tribal virtue. To make matters worse he had attempted to gain recognition by claiming a war honour which was fraudulent. He was proved not to have brought in, as he claimed, a picketed horse from the enemy's camp. To lay false claim to war honours was a paramount sin among the Crow, and by the general opinion, constantly reiterated, he was regarded as irresponsible and incompetent.

Such situations can be paralleled with the attitude in our civilization toward a man who does not succeed in regarding personal possessions as supremely important. Our hobo population is constantly fed by those to whom the accumulation of property is not a sufficient motivation. In case these individuals ally themselves with the hoboes, public opinion regards them as potentially vicious, as indeed because of the asocial situation into which they are thrust they readily become. In case, however, these men compensate by emphasizing their artistic temperament and become members of expatriated groups of petty artists, opinion regards them not as vicious but as silly. In any case they are unsupported by the forms of their society, and the effort to express themselves satisfactorily is ordinarily a greater task than they can achieve.

The dilemma of such an individual is often most successfully solved by doing violence to his strongest natural impulses and accepting the rôle the culture honours. In case he is a person to whom social recognition is necessary, it is ordinarily his only possible course. One of the most striking individuals in Zuñi had accepted this necessity. In a society that thoroughly distrusts authority of any sort, he had a native personal magnetism that singled him out in any group. In a society that exalts moderation and the easiest way, he was turbulent and could act violently upon occasion. In a society that praises a pliant personality that 'talks lots'—that is, that chatters in a friendly fashion—he was scornful and aloof. Zuñi's only reaction to such personalities is to brand them as witches. He was said to have been seen peering through a window from outside, and this is a sure mark of a witch. At any rate, he got drunk one day and boasted that they could not kill him. He was taken before the war priests who hung him by his thumbs from the rafters till he should confess to his witchcraft. This is the usual procedure in a charge of witchcraft. However, he dispatched a messenger to the government troops. When they came, his shoulders were already crippled for life, and the officer of the law was left with no recourse but to imprison the war priests who had been responsible for the enormity. One of these war priests was probably the most respected and important person in recent Zuñi history, and when he returned after imprisonment in the state penitentiary he never resumed his priestly offices. He regarded his power as broken. It was a revenge that is probably unique in Zuñi history. It involved, of course, a challenge to the priesthoods, against whom the witch by his act openly aligned himself.

The course of his life in the forty years that followed this defiance was not, however, what we might easily predict. A witch is not barred from his membership in cult groups because he has been condemned, and the way to recognition lay through such activity. He possessed a remarkable verbal memory and a sweet singing voice. He learned unbelievable stores of mythology, of esoteric ritual, of cult songs. Many hundreds of pages of stories and ritual poetry were taken down from his dictation before he died, and he regarded his songs as much more extensive. He became indispensable in ceremonial life and before he died was the governor of Zuñi. The congenial bent of his personality threw him into irreconcilable conflict with his society, and he solved his dilemma by turning an incidental talent to account. As we might well expect, he was not a happy man. As governor of Zuñi, and high in his cult groups, a marked man in his community, he was obsessed by death. He was a cheated man in the midst of a mildly happy populace.

It is easy to imagine the life he might have lived among the Plains Indians, where every institution favoured the traits that were native to him. The personal authority, the turbulence, the scorn, would all have been honoured in the career he could have made his own. The unhappiness that was inseparable from his temperament as a successful priest and governor of Zuñi would have had no place as a war chief of the Cheyenne; it was not a function of the traits of his native endowment but of the standards of the culture in which he found no outlet for his native responses.

The individuals we have so far discussed are not in any sense psychopathic. They illustrate the dilemma of the individual whose congenial drives are not provided for in the institutions of his culture. This dilemma becomes of psychiatric importance when the behaviour in question is regarded as categorically abnormal in a society. Western civilization tends to regard even a mild homosexual as an abnormal. The clinical picture of homosexuality stresses the neuroses and psychoses to which it gives rise, and emphasizes almost equally the inadequate functioning of the invert and his behaviour. We have only to turn to other cultures, however, to realize that homosexuals have by no means been uniformly inadequate to the social situation. They have not always failed to function. In some societies they have even been especially acclaimed. Plato's *Republic* is, of course, the most convincing statement of the honourable estate of homosexuality. It is presented as a major means to the good life, and Plato's high ethical evaluation of this response was upheld in the customary behaviour of Greece at that period.

The American Indians do not make Plato's high moral claims for homosexuality, but homosexuals are often regarded as exceptionally able. In most of North America there exists the institution of the *berdache*, as the French called them. These men-women were men who at puberty or thereafter took the dress and the occupations of women. Sometimes they married other men and lived with them. Sometimes they were men with no inversion, persons of weak sexual endowment who chose this rôle to avoid the jeers of the women. The berdaches were never regarded as of first-rate supernatural power, as similar men-women were in Siberia, but rather as leaders in women's occupations, good healers in certain diseases, or, among certain tribes, as the genial organizers of social affairs. They were usually, in spite of the manner in which they were accepted, regarded with a certain embarrassment. It was thought slightly ridiculous to address as 'she' a person who was known to be a man and who, as in Zuñi, would be buried on the men's side of the cemetery. But they were socially placed. The emphasis in most tribes was upon the fact that men who took over women's occupations excelled by reason of their strength and initiative and were therefore leaders in women's techniques and in the accumulation of those forms of property made by women. One of the best known of all the Zuñis of a generation ago was the man-woman We-wha, who was, in the words of his friend, Mrs. Stevenson, 'certainly the strongest person in Zuñi, both mentally and physically.' His remarkable memory for ritual made him a chief personage on ceremonial occasions, and his strength and intelligence made him a leader in all kinds of crafts.

The men-women of Zuñi are not all strong, self-reliant personages. Some of them take this refuge to protect themselves against their inability to take part in men's activities. One is almost a simpleton, and one, hardly more than a little boy, has delicate features like a girl's. There are obviously several reasons why a person becomes a berdache in Zuñi, but whatever the reason, men who have chosen openly to assume women's dress have the same chance as any other persons to establish themselves as functioning members of the society. Their response is socially recognized. If they have native ability, they can give it scope; if they are weak creatures, they fail in terms of their weakness of character, not in terms of their inversion.

The Indian institution of the berdache was most strongly developed on the plains. The Dakota had a saying, 'fine possessions like a berdache's,' and it was the epitome of praise for any woman's household possessions. A berdache had two strings to his bow, he was supreme in women's techniques, and he could also support his *ménage* by the man's activity of hunting. Therefore no one was richer. When especially fine beadwork or dressed skins were desired for ceremonial occasions, the berdache's work was sought in preference to any other's. It was his social adequacy that was stressed above all else. As in Zuñi, the attitude toward him is ambivalent and touched with malaise in the face of a recognized incongruity. Social scorn, however, was visited not upon the berdache but upon the man who lived with him. The latter was regarded as a weak man who had chosen an easy berth instead of the recognized goals of their culture; he did not contribute to the household, which was already a model for all households through the sole efforts of the berdache. His sexual adjustment was not singled out in the judgment that was passed upon him, but in terms of his economic adjustment he was an outcast.

When the homosexual response is regarded as a perversion, however, the invert is immediately exposed to all the conflicts to which aberrants are always exposed. His guilt, his sense of inadequacy, his failures, are consequences of the disrepute which social tradition visits upon him, and few people can achieve a satisfactory life unsupported by the standards of their society. The adjustments that society demands of them would strain any man's vitality, and the consequences of this conflict we identify with their homosexuality.

Trance is a similar abnormality in our society. Even a very mild mystic is aberrant in Western civilization. In order to study trance or catalepsy within our own social groups, we have to go to the case histories of the abnormal.

Therefore the correlation between trance experience and the neurotic and psychotic seems perfect. As in the case of the homosexual, however, it is a local correlation characteristic of our century. Even in our own cultural background other eras give different results. In the Middle Ages when Catholicism made the ecstatic experience the mark of sainthood, the trance experience was greatly valued, and those to whom the response was congenial, instead of being overwhelmed by a catastrophe as in our century, were given confidence in the pursuit of their careers. It was a validation of ambitions, not a stigma of insanity. Individuals who were susceptible to trance, therefore, succeeded or failed in terms of their native capacities, but since trance experience was highly valued, a great leader was very likely to be capable of it.

Among primitive peoples, trance and catalepsy have been honoured in the extreme. Some of the Indian tribes of California accorded prestige principally to those who passed through certain trance experiences. Not all of these tribes believed that it was exclusively women who were so blessed, but among the Shasta this was the convention. Their shamans were women, and they were accorded the greatest prestige in the community. They were chosen because of their constitutional liability to trance and allied manifestations. One day the woman who was so destined, while she was about her usual work, fell suddenly to the ground. She had heard a voice speaking to her in tones of the greatest intensity. Turning, she had seen a man with drawn bow and arrow. He commanded her to sing on pain of being shot through the heart by his arrow, but under the stress of the experience she fell senseless. Her family gathered. She was lying rigid, hardly breathing. They knew that for some time she had had dreams of a special character which indicated a shamanistic calling, dreams of escaping grizzly bears, falling off cliffs or trees, or of being surrounded by swarms of yellow-jackets. The community knew therefore what to expect. After a few hours the woman began to moan gently and to roll about upon the ground, trembling violently. She was supposed to be repeating the song which she had been told to sing and which during the trance had been taught her by the spirit. As she revived, her moaning became more and more clearly the spirit's song until at last she called out the name of the spirit itself, and immediately blood oozed from her mouth.

When the woman had come to herself after the first encounter with her spirit, she danced that night her first initiatory shaman's dance. For three nights she danced, holding herself by a rope that was swung from the ceiling. On the third night she had to receive in her body her power from her spirit. She was dancing, and as she felt the approach of the moment she called out, 'He will shoot me, he will shoot me.' Her friends stood close, for when she reeled in a kind of cataleptic seizure, they had to seize her before she fell or she would die. From this time on she had in her body a visible materialization of her spirit's power, an icicle-like object which in her dances thereafter she would exhibit, producing it from one part of her body and returning it to another part. From this time on she continued to validate her supernatural power by further cataleptic demonstrations, and she was called upon in great emergencies of life and death, for curing and for divination and for counsel. She became, in other words, by this procedure a woman of great power and importance.

It is clear that, far from regarding cataleptic seizures as blots upon the family escutcheon and as evidences of dreaded disease, cultural approval had seized upon them and made of them the pathway to authority over one's fellows. They were the outstanding characteristic of the most respected social type, the type which functioned with most honour and reward in the community. It was precisely the cataleptic individuals who in this culture were singled out for authority and leadership.

The possible usefulness of 'abnormal' types in a social structure, provided they are types that are culturally selected by that group, is illustrated from every part of the world. The shamans of Siberia dominate their communities. According to the ideas of these peoples, they are individuals who by submission to the will of the spirits have been cured of a grievous illness—the onset of the seizures—and have acquired by this means great supernatural power and incomparable vigour and health. Some, during the period of the call, are violently insane for several years; others irresponsible to the point where they have to be constantly watched lest they wander off in the snow and freeze to death; others ill and emaciated to the point of death, sometimes with bloody sweat. It is the shamanistic practice which constitutes their cure, and the extreme exertion of a Siberian séance leaves them, they claim, rested and able to enter immediately upon a similar performance. Cataleptic seizures are regarded as an essential part of any shamanistic performance.

A good description of the neurotic condition of the shaman and the attention given him by his society is an old one by Canon Callaway, recorded in the words of an old Zulu of South Africa:

> The condition of a man who is about to become a diviner is this; at first he is apparently robust, but in the process of time he begins to be delicate, not having any real disease, but being delicate. He habitually avoids certain kinds of food, choosing what he likes, and he does not eat much of that; he is continually complaining of pains in different parts of his body. And he tells them that he has dreamt that he was carried away by a river. He dreams of many things, and his body is muddied [as a river] and he becomes a house of dreams. He dreams constantly of many things, and on awaking tells his friends, 'My body is muddied today; I dreamt many men were killing me, and I escaped I know not how. On waking one part of my body felt different from other parts; it was no longer alike all over.' At last that man is very ill, and they go to the diviners to enquire.

The diviners do not at once see that he is about to have a soft head [that is, the sensitivity associated with shamanism]. It is difficult for them to see the truth; they continually talk nonsense and make false statements, until all the man's cattle are devoured at their command, they saying that the spirit of his people demands cattle, that it may eat food. At length all the man's property is expended, he still being ill; and they no longer know what to do, for he has no more cattle, and his friends help him in such things as he needs.

At length a diviner comes and says that all the others are wrong. He says, 'He is possessed by the spirits. There is nothing else. They move in him, being divided into two parties; some say, "No, we do not wish our child injured. We do not wish it." It is for that reason he does not get well. If you bar the way against the spirits, you will be killing him. For he will not be a diviner; neither will he ever be a man again.'

So the man may be ill two years without getting better; perhaps even longer than that. He is confined to his house. This continues till his hair falls off. And his body is dry and scurfy; he does not like to anoint himself. He shows that he is about to be a diviner by yawning again and again, and by sneezing continually. It is apparent also from his being very fond of snuff; not allowing any long time to pass without taking some. And people begin to see that he has had what is good given to him.

After that he is ill; he has convulsions, and when water has been poured on him they then cease for a time. He habitually sheds tears, at first slight, then at last he weeps aloud and when the people are asleep he is heard making a noise and wakes the people by his singing; he has composed a song, and the men and women awake and go to sing in concert with him. All the people of the village are troubled by want of sleep; for a man who is becoming a diviner causes great trouble, for he does not sleep, but works constantly with his brain; his sleep is merely by snatches, and he wakes up singing many songs; and people who are near quit their villages by night when they hear him singing aloud and go to sing in concert. Perhaps he sings till morning, no one having slept. And then he leaps about the house like a frog; and the house becomes too small for him, and he goes out leaping and singing, and shaking like a reed in the water, and dripping with perspiration.

In this state of things they daily expect his death; he is now but skin and bones, and they think that tomorrow's sun will not leave him alive. At this time many cattle are eaten, for the people encourage his becoming a diviner. At length [in a dream] an ancient ancestral spirit is pointed out to him. This spirit says to him, 'Go to So-and-so and he will churn for you an emetic [the medicine the drinking of which is a part of shamanistic initiation] that you may be a diviner altogether.' Then he is quiet a few days, having gone to the diviner to have the medicine churned for him; and he comes back quite another man, being now cleansed and a diviner indeed.

Thereafter for life, when he is possessed by his spirits, he foretells events and finds lost articles.

It is clear that culture may value and make socially available even highly unstable human types. If it chooses to treat their peculiarities as the most valued variants of human behaviour, the individuals in question will rise to the occasion and perform their social rôles without reference to our usual ideas of the types who can make social adjustments and those who cannot. Those who function inadequately in any society are not those with certain fixed 'abnormal' traits, but may well be those whose responses have received no support in the institutions of their culture. The weakness of these aberrants is in great measure illusory. It springs, not from the fact that they are lacking in necessary vigour, but that they are individuals whose native responses are not reaffirmed by society. They are, as Sapir phrases it, 'alienated from an impossible world.'

The person unsupported by the standards of his time and place and left naked to the winds of ridicule has been unforgettably drawn in European literature in the figure of Don Quixote. Cervantes turned upon a tradition still honoured in the abstract the limelight of a changed set of practical standards, and his poor old man, the orthodox upholder of the romantic chivalry of another generation, became a simpleton. The windmills with which he tilted were the serious antagonists of a hardly vanished world, but to tilt with them when the world no longer called them serious was to rave. He loved his Dulcinea in the best traditional manner of chivalry, but another version of love was fashionable for the moment, and his fervour was counted to him for madness.

These contrasting worlds which, in the primitive cultures we have considered, are separated from one another in space, in modern Occidental history more often succeed one another in time. The major issue is the same in either case, but the importance of understanding the phenomenon is far greater in the modern world where we cannot escape if we would from the succession of configurations in time. When each culture is a world in itself, relatively stable like the Eskimo culture, for example, and geographically isolated from all others, the issue is academic. But our civilization must deal with cultural standards that go down under our eyes and new ones that arise from a shadow upon the horizon. We must be willing to take account of changing normalities even when the question is of the morality in which we were bred. Just as we are handicapped in dealing with ethical problems so long as we hold to an absolute definition of morality, so we are handicapped in dealing with human society so long as we identify our local normalities with the inevitable necessities of existence.

No society has yet attempted a self-conscious direction of the process by which its new normalities are created in the next generation. Dewey has pointed out how possible and yet how drastic such social engineering would be. For some traditional arrangements it is obvious that very high prices are paid, reckoned in terms of human suffering and frustration. If these arrangements presented themselves to us merely as arrangements and not as categorical imperatives, our reasonable course would be to adapt them by whatever means to rationally selected goals. What we do instead is to ridicule our Don Quixotes, the ludicrous embodiments of an outmoded tradition, and continue to regard our own as final and prescribed in the nature of things.

In the meantime the therapeutic problem of dealing with our psychopaths of this type is often misunderstood. Their alienation from the actual world can often be more intelligently handled than by insisting that they adopt the modes that are alien to them. Two other courses are always possible. In the first place, the misfit individual may cultivate a greater objective interest in his own preferences and learn how to manage with greater equanimity his deviation from the type. If he learns to recognize the extent to which his suffering has been due to his lack of support in a traditional ethos, he may gradually educate himself to accept his degree of difference with less suffering. Both the exaggerated emotional disturbances of the manic depressive and the seclusion of the schizophrenic add certain values to existence which are not open to those differently constituted. The unsupported individual who valiantly accepts his favourite and native virtues may attain a feasible course of behaviour that makes it unnecessary for him to take refuge in a private world he has fashioned for himself. He may gradually achieve a more independent and less tortured attitude toward his deviations and upon this attitude he may be able to build an adequately functioning existence.

In the second place, an increased tolerance in society toward its less usual types must keep pace with the self-education of the patient. The possibilities in this direction are endless. Tradition is as neurotic as any patient; its overgrown fear of deviation from its fortuitous standards conforms to all the usual definitions of the psychopathic. This fear does not depend upon observation of the limits within which conformity is necessary to the social good. Much more deviation is allowed to the individual in some cultures than in others, and those in which much is allowed cannot be shown to suffer from their peculiarity. It is probable that social orders of the future will carry this tolerance and encouragement of individual difference much further than any cultures of which we have experience.

The American tendency at the present time leans so far to the opposite extreme that it is not easy for us to picture the changes that such an attitude would bring about. Middletown is a typical example of our usual urban fear of seeming in however slight an act different from our neighbours. Eccentricity is more feared than parasitism. Every sacrifice of time and tranquillity is made in order that no one in the family may have any taint of nonconformity attached to him. Children in school make their great tragedies out of not wearing a certain kind of stockings, not joining a certain dancing-class, not driving a certain car. The fear of being different is the dominating motivation recorded in Middletown.

The psychopathic toll that such a motivation exacts is evident in every institution for mental diseases in our country. In a society in which it existed only as a minor motive among many others, the psychiatric picture would be a very different one. At all events, there can be no reasonable doubt that one of the most effective ways in which to deal with the staggering burden of psychopathic tragedies in America at the present time is by means of an educational program which fosters tolerance in society and a kind of self-respect and independence that is foreign to Middletown and our urban traditions.

Not all psychopaths, of course, are individuals whose native responses are at variance with those of their civilization. Another large group are those who are merely inadequate and who are strongly enough motivated so that their failure is more than they can bear. In a society in which the will-to-power is most highly rewarded, those who fail may not be those who are differently constituted, but simply those who are insufficiently endowed. The inferiority complex takes a great toll of suffering in our society. It is not necessary that sufferers of this type have a history of frustration in the sense that strong native bents have been inhibited; their frustration is often enough only the reflection of their inability to reach a certain goal. There is a cultural implication here, too, in that the traditional goal may be accessible to large numbers or to very few, and in proportion as success is obsessive and is limited to the few, a greater and greater number will be liable to the extreme penalties of maladjustment.

To a certain extent, therefore, civilization in setting higher and possibly more worth-while goals may increase the number of its abnormals. But the point may very easily be overemphasized, for very small changes in social attitudes may far outweigh this correlation. On the whole, since the social possibilities of tolerance and recognition of individual difference are so little explored in practice, pessimism seems premature. Certainly other quite different social factors which we have just discussed are more directly responsible for the great proportion of our neurotics and psychotics, and with these other factors civilizations could, if they would, deal without necessary intrinsic loss.

We have been considering individuals from the point of view of their ability to function adequately in their society. This adequate functioning is one of the ways in which normality is clinically defined. It is also defined in terms of fixed symptoms, and the tendency is to identify normality with the statistically average. In practice this average is one arrived at in the laboratory, and deviations from it are defined as abnormal.

From the point of view of a single culture this procedure is very useful. It shows the clinical picture of the civilization and gives considerable information about its socially approved behaviour. To generalize this as an absolute normal, however, is a different matter. As we have seen, the range of normality in different cultures does not coincide. Some, like Zuñi and the Kwakiutl, are so far removed from each other that they overlap only slightly. The statistically determined normal on the Northwest Coast would be far outside the extreme boundaries of abnormality in the Pueblos. The normal Kwakiutl rivalry contest would only be understood as madness in Zuñi, and the traditional Zuñi indifference to dominance and the humiliation of others would be the fatuousness of a simpleton in a man of noble family on the Northwest Coast. Aberrant behaviour in either culture could never be determined in relation to any least common denominator of behaviour. Any society, according to its major preoccupations, may increase and intensify even hysterical, epileptic, or paranoid symptoms, at the same time relying socially in a greater and greater degree upon the very individuals who display them.

This fact is important in psychiatry because it makes clear another group of abnormals which probably exists in every culture: the abnormals who represent the extreme development of the local cultural type. This group is socially in the opposite situation from the group we have discussed, those whose responses are at variance with their cultural standards. Society, instead of exposing the former group at every point, supports them in their furthest aberrations. They have a licence which they may almost endlessly exploit. For this reason these persons almost never fall within the scope of any contemporary psychiatry. They are unlikely to be described even in the most careful manuals of the generation that fosters them. Yet from the point of view of another generation or culture they are ordinarily the most bizarre of the psychopathic types of the period.

The Puritan divines of New England in the eighteenth century were the last persons whom contemporary opinion in the colonies regarded as psychopathic. Few prestige groups in any culture have been allowed such complete intellectual and emotional dictatorship as they were. They were the voice of God. Yet to a modern observer it is they, not the confused and tormented women they put to death as witches, who were the psychoneurotics of Puritan New England. A sense of guilt as extreme as they portrayed and demanded both in their own conversion experiences and in those of their converts is found in a slightly saner civilization only in institutions for mental diseases. They admitted no salvation without a conviction of sin that prostrated the victim, sometimes for years, with remorse and terrible anguish. It was the duty of the minister to put the fear of hell into the heart of even the youngest child, and to exact of every convert emotional acceptance of his damnation if God saw fit to damn him. It does not matter where we turn among the records of New England Puritan churches of this period, whether to those dealing with witches or with unsaved children not yet in their teens or with such themes as damnation and predestination, we are faced with the fact that the group of people who carried out to the greatest extreme and in the fullest honour the cultural doctrine of the moment are by the slightly altered standards of our generation the victims of intolerable aberrations. From the point of view of a comparative psychiatry they fall in the category of the abnormal.

In our own generation extreme forms of ego-gratification are culturally supported in a similar fashion. Arrogant and unbridled egoists as family men, as officers of the law and in business, have been again and again portrayed by novelists and dramatists, and they are familiar in every community. Like the behaviour of Puritan divines, their courses of action are often more asocial than those of the inmates of penitentiaries. In terms of the suffering and frustration that they spread about them there is probably no comparison. There is very possibly at least as great a degree of mental warping. Yet they are entrusted with positions of great influence and importance and are as a rule fathers of families. Their impress both upon their own children and upon the structure of our society is indelible. They are not described in our manuals of psychiatry because they are supported by every tenet of our civilization. They are sure of themselves in real life in a way that is possible only to those who are oriented to the points of the compass laid down in their own culture. Nevertheless a future psychiatry may well ransack our novels and letters and public records for illumination upon a type of abnormality to which it would not otherwise give credence. In every society it is among this very group of the culturally encouraged and fortified that some of the most extreme types of human behaviour are fostered.

Social thinking at the present time has no more important task before it than that of taking adequate account of cultural relativity. In the fields of both sociology and psychology the implications are fundamental, and modern thought about contacts of peoples and about our changing standards is greatly in need of sane and scientific direction. The sophisticated modern temper has made of social relativity, even in the small area which it has recognized, a doctrine of despair. It has pointed out its incongruity with the orthodox dreams of permanence and ideality and with the individual's illusions of autonomy. It has argued that if human experience must give up these, the nutshell of existence is empty. But to interpret our dilemma in these terms is to be guilty of an anachronism. It is only the inevitable cultural lag that makes us insist that the old must be discovered again in the new, that there is no solution but to find the old certainty and stability in the new plasticity. The recognition of cultural relativity carries with it its own values, which need not be those of the absolutist philosophies. It challenges customary opinions and causes those who have been bred to them acute discomfort. It rouses pessimism because it throws old formulas into confusion, not because it contains anything intrinsically difficult. As soon as the new opinion is embraced as customary belief, it will be another trusted bulwark of the good life. We shall arrive then at a more realistic social faith, accepting as grounds of hope and as new bases for tolerance the coexisting and equally valid patterns of life which mankind has created for itself from the raw materials of existence.

CASHIERING THE IDEA OF RACE

JULIAN SORELL HUXLEY (1887-), English biologist and publicist, and grandson of Thomas Henry Huxley, and Alfred Cort Haddon (1885-1940), English anthropologist, founder of the department of anthropology at Cambridge University, leader of the Cambridge Anthropological Expedition to the Torres Straits in 1898, and author of numerous works of distinction in anthropology, in reaction to the rise of Nazism and the elevation of racism as a political dogma in Germany in the early thirties, combined their knowledge and skills to produce a book, *We Europeans* (1936), to expose the vicious mythology which later led to the death of so many millions of human beings under the most unspeakably inhuman conditions. As Huxley and Haddon said in the last paragraph of their book, "Racialism is a myth, and a dangerous myth at that."[1]

In the excerpt from *We Europeans* reprinted here, after having pointed out the errors and fallacious inferences drawn by racists concerning the diversity of mankind, Huxley and Haddon came out boldly for dropping the term "race" altogether from the scientific vocabulary, and using instead the noncommittal term, "ethnic group." This suggestion was immediately adopted by some anthropologists, but not by many others who completely failed to understand the meaning of this recommendation. Some described it as an "evasion," an "artful dodge," "a mere substitute," and so on, failing to see that far from being any of these things it was in fact the demolition of a term for a myth masquerading as a fact.[2]

---

[1] It was from that sentence that I took the title for my own book on the subject, *Man's Most Dangerous Myth: The Fallacy of Race* (New York, Columbia University Press, 1942, fourth edition, World Publishing Co., 1964).

[2] For a full discussion of the meaning of the term "ethnic group" and an examination of the futile objections to it, see Ashley Montagu, *Man's Most Dangerous Myth: The Fallacy of Race*, pp. 372-80.

Huxley especially has in many of his writings pointed out the importance of terminology, and all scientists agree in principle, but when, in practice, they are confronted with terms that have been embarrassed by false meanings and emotion they not infrequently put up a surprising show of resistance against any suggestion that such terms should be dropped from the vocabulary. It is as if they had made a heavy emotional investment in the term which they could be persuaded to give up only with the greatest reluctance.

Nevertheless, such progress as has been made in the replacement of the term "race" by the noncommittal "ethnic group," is due largely to the discussion initiated by Huxley and Haddon, and which was the direct inspiration for the next contribution.

WE EUROPEANS*

Man, as we have seen, is unique in the extent to which the expression of the characteristics most important to him as a species—intelligence, mentality, and temperament—can be influenced by the character of his environment. He is also unique in respect of his purely biological variation. The nature of such biological variation we must briefly consider.

In most wild species of animals, especially those with wide distribution, two types of genetic phenomena are found. In the first place, a population from any one locality presents relatively little range of variability. Of this, some is non-genetic, due to environmental and nutritional differences, but a large amount is due to differences in genetic composition between different individuals. Usually this genetic variability is continuous, due to gene-differences with slight and quantitative effects, so that some individuals are slightly darker, others slightly lighter than the mean, some slightly bigger, others slightly smaller, and so on. Occasionally, however, larger or more definite individual differences occur, as for instance between the blue and the white types of Arctic fox, or between the normal and so-called bridled variety of the guillemot, which latter has a white spectacle mark round the eye. Such differences usually depend on differences in very few genes, and often involve only one.

Besides differences of this kind, there are differences distinguishing populations from different localities. These are often quite marked, and constitute

*From J. S. Huxley and A. C. Haddon, *We Europeans* (New York, Harper & Bros., 1936), pp. 74-84. Reprinted by permission of A. D. Peters and Company.

the diagnostic characters of "geographical races," or as they are now usually and more satisfactorily called, *sub-species*. Well-marked sub-species may be connected with each other by every gradation, or they may be sharply distinct. Gradation is usually found when the range of the two is continuous, discontinuity when the ranges are isolated. The latter is most clearly manifested in island races, for instance the St. Kilda wren, or the British pied wagtail.

A third kind of variation may sometimes be recognized, as when markedly different sub-species (or mutually fertile species) have overlapping ranges. Then, while the two types present constant and characteristic differences over most of the ranges along the region of overlap, individuals are found with every possible combination of these characters. Classical examples of this are the Eastern and Western flickers (woodpeckers) of North America, and the hoodie and carrion crows of Northern Europe. This effect seems to be produced when considerable differentiation has taken place in the two types while isolated, and when after this they extend their ranges so as to meet. Interbreeding then produces every variety of Mendelian recombination. This type of variation, due to the wholesale crossing of distinct and differentiated types, is much rarer in animals than the geographical variation due to the divergent differentiation of groups wholly or largely isolated from each other geographically.

In man, conditions are quite different. In this, as in numerous other respects, man is a unique animal. In the first place, his tendency to migrate from one more or less permanent habitat to another[1] is much stronger than in any other animal and has become progressively more manifested in the later stages of his history. In the second place, for reasons which are not wholly clear, physical differentiation of local types has been able to go much farther than in almost any other wild species without leading to the development of mutual sterility—i.e. to fully differentiated species, sterile *inter se*. An African pigmy, a Chinese, and a typical Scandinavian Nordic, in spite of their striking differences, are mutually fertile.

The result is that crossing of types with the production of much variation by recombination is incomparably more frequent in man than in any other species. This crossing has occurred between the major as well as the minor subdivisions of man, between groups that show large physical differences as well as between those that approximate in type. The great majority of native Africans, the reader may be surprised to learn, are not pure Negroes, but have an admixture of Caucasian genes from crosses with Hamitic stocks. India is more of a racial melting-pot than the United States. Mongolian invasions from the east have left their physical traces in Eastern Europe. There is a gradient of increasing concentration of mongol genes, from Prussia eastward across

[1]As contrasted with the *seasonal* migration found e.g. in birds, or the *reproductive* migration of various fish.

European Russia into Central Asia. How the subdivisions of man may have originated, and what names should be applied to them, we will consider in the next chapter. But however they originated and whatever degree of difference they may show, they have been intercrossing for tens of thousands of years, and this fact has had various important results.

On simple Mendelian principles, the first result of a cross between groups differing in average physical type will be to increase variability by producing a large number of hitherto non-existent recombinations, quite different from either of the original types or from the intermediate between them.

Next, it should be remembered that after crossing, selection may play a very important rôle. For instance, it appears that after the irruption of light-skinned conquerors from temperate latitudes into more tropical areas inhabited by darker-skinned peoples, natural selection has seen to it that combinations with darker skins survive while those with fair skin tend to die out.[2] This seems to have been the case for instance in Greece and in India. In India especially, the social selection brought about via the caste system seems to have exerted pressure for the retention in the highest castes of the general features of the conquering group—"Aryan" as they used to be called and perhaps rightly in that particular land—but there seems little doubt that the genes for these are now associated with a different set of pigmentation-genes from those present in the original invaders. Similarly in Greece today, the average distribution of genes and the most frequent types of gene-combination, must be very different not only from those found either in the Achaeans or in the indigenous Pelasgian population before the irruption of the former in the second millennium B.C., but also from those characteristic of the mixed population in early classical times.

It must further be emphasized that, after crossing, the various gene-combinations will, in the absence of selection, automatically maintain themselves in proportions which depend on the proportions of the different genes originally contributed to the cross.[3] There will not be a uniform mixed type, but the same general tendency to form recombinations will occur, generation after generation. Those who have been to Sicily know how types immediately classifiable as "Greek," "Moorish," and "Norman," and those with certain negroid characters, still crop up strikingly in the more mixed general population after centuries of crossing. The same phenomenon occurs in Britain, where we still find men of well-marked Mediterranean type, dark and small and swarthy. In Germany too men with dark and fair hair, round and long head, tall and stumpy stature, regularly recur as segregation-types from the mixture

---

[2]This is so even when there has been counter-selection of a social nature against dark skin, e.g. in the higher castes of India. These are on the average much lighter in skin-colour than the lower castes, but are clearly darker than the original stock from which they trace descent.

[3]This can be established as a direct consequence of neo-Mendelian theory. See Hogben, *Genetic Principles in Medicine and Social Science*, p. 148.

of Nordic, Eurasiatic (Alpine) and the numerous other stocks which constitute the general population. There is no sign of a tendency towards a uniform blend. An excellent example of this is given by the two hundred inhabitants of Pitcairn Island, all descended since 1788 from a cross between Tahitians and the British-born mutineers of the *Bounty*. These have recently been investigated for the American Museum. It was found that the population comprises a large number of recombinations, ranging from predominantly Tahitian to predominantly European, although no pure British or pure Tahitian types now exist. It is an interesting fact that the language spoken is also composite: in this case, however, degenerate English predominates, and in addition to Tahitian elements, words coined on Pitcairn itself (or possibly, modified slang or obsolete English words) are found.

In addition to the variation produced by the crossing of already differentiated groups, which in man thus appears to be basic and not merely of the secondary importance that it assumes in other species, the general variability inherent in most animal populations is also to be found in *Homo sapiens*. For instance, some at all events, of the variation in stature, proportions, pigmentation, intelligence, etc., which are to be found in all human groups must be ascribed to this factor. We may stress the fact that the main types of body-build and temperament recur in all ethnic groups, black, white, brown or yellow.

It will thus be clear that the picture of the hereditary constitution of human groups which can now be drawn in the light of modern genetics is very different from any which could be framed in the pre-Mendelian era. Populations differ from each other with respect to the genes which they possess. Sometimes certain genes are wholly absent from a group—e.g. that for light eye-colour among Central African tribes, or for frizzy hair among the Eskimo. Most frequently, however, the difference is a quantitative one, in regard to the proportions of genes present and in the frequency of certain main types of gene combinations. This is eminently characteristic of the populations of Western Europe.

Crossing between moderately or strikingly differentiated types is frequent as the aftermath of large-scale migration and gives rise to many previously unrealized gene-combinations. Infiltrative individual migration also takes place very frequently and leads to the steady diffusion of genes from one region to another. There is no such thing as blending, causing gene-recombinations to disappear gradually after crossing: in the absence of selection the various types of gene combination will tend to recur in the same proportion, generation after generation.

It follows that practically all human groups are of decidedly mixed origin. Within any one group we should therefore expect the variation due to recombination to be great. This last point is of great importance. The expectation of the anthropologist of the Darwinian era, when the *a priori* idea of blending inheritance was in fashion, was of groups with well-marked characteristics, and a small range of variation chiefly affecting quantitative characters. The expectation of the Mendelian geneticist, knowing the facts of inheritance and the migratory habits of man, is of groups possessing a large range of variation, often concerned with striking characters of a qualitative nature as well as with quantitative ones; such groups can only be distinguished from each other by statistical methods. In such groups the *mean values* for characters, though still useful, no longer have the same theoretical importance. The *range of variation* of characters is of far greater practical importance, as is also the range of qualitatively different recombination-types. The two resultant "racial" or ethnic concepts are fundamentally dissimilar.

To these considerations derived from the modern study of inheritance may be added others due to the historical progress of ethnology. The modern outlook had its beginnings in the Renaissance. In its growth, the exploration of the planet, first geographical and then scientific, went hand in hand with the liberation of thought and the transformation of social and economic structure. In the earliest part of this modern period, the voyages of the great explorers and of the traders and colonizers who succeeded them brought home to man a new realization of the variety of the human race and the marked distinction between its types. The red man of the New World, the black man of Africa, the yellow man of the far East, the brown man of the East Indies—it was the *differences* between human types which impressed themselves upon general thought.

The patient labours of anthropological science during the last hundred years or so, however, have given us a wholly different picture. The different main types exist, but they are vaguer and less well-defined than was at first thought. Within each main type there are geographical trends of variation and there are connecting links even between the most distinct major types. Quite apart from the results of very recent crossings, almost every gradation exists between the Negro and the European along several different lines, via Hamite, Semite and Mediterranean; every gradation exists between the white man and the yellow, through East Central Europe, across Russia, to Mongolia and China; every gradation exists between the yellow man and the already mixed dark brown Asiatic. Even among the Eskimo and the pigmies we find evidence of crossing with other types. The same process, of course, is continuing today and at an increasing rate. New links, often along new racial lines, are yearly being forged between Negro and white in countries like the United States, Brazil, Portugal and Africa; new links between yellow and white and between brown and white in various parts of the world; new links between yellow and brown all over the East.

We can thus no longer think of common ancestry, a single original stock, as the essential badge of a "race." What residuum of truth there is in this idea is purely quantitative. Two Englishmen, for instance, are almost certain to have more ancestors in common than an Englishman and a Negro. For the sharply defined qualitative notion of common ancestry we must substitute the statistical idea of the probable number of common ancestors which two members of a group may be expected to share in going back a certain period of time. Being quantitative and statistical, this concept cannot provide any sharp definition of race, nor do justice to the results of recombination. If, however, concrete values for the probability could be obtained for various groups (which would be a matter of great practical difficulty), it would provide a "co-efficient of common ancestry" which could serve as the only possible measure of their biological relationship.

The result is that the popular and scientific views of "race" no longer coincide. The word "race," as applied scientifically to human groupings, has lost any sharpness of meaning. Today it is hardly definable in scientific terms, except as an abstract concept which *may*, under certain conditions, very different from those now prevalent, have been realized approximately in the past, and *might*, under certain other but equally different conditions, be realized in the distant future.

In spite of the work of the geneticist and anthropologist there is still a lamentable confusion between the ideas of *race, culture* and *nation*. In this respect anthropologists themselves have not been blameless, and therefore the deplorable amount of loose thinking on the part of writers, politicians and the general public is not surprising. In the circumstances, it is very desirable that the term *race* as applied to human groups should be dropped from the vocabulary of science. Its employment as a scientific term had a dual origin. In part, it represents merely the taking over of a popular term, in part the attempt to apply the biological concept of "variety" or "geographical race" to man. But the popular term is so loose that it turns out to be unworkable, and the scientific analysis of human populations shows that the variation of man has taken place on lines quite different from those characteristic of other animals. In other animals, the term *sub-species* has been substituted for "race." In man, migration and crossing have produced such a fluid state of affairs that no such clear-cut term, as applied to existing conditions, is permissible. What we observe is the relative isolation of groups, their migration and their crossing. In what follows the word *race* will be deliberately avoided, and the term (*ethnic*) *group* or *people* employed for all general purposes.

Scientifically, there are only two methods of treatment which can be used for the genetic definition of human groups. One is to define them by means of the characters which they exhibit, the other to define them by means of the genes which they contain. In both cases the procedure must be primarily quantitative. In any group, certain characters or genes may be totally absent, and when this is so we can make a qualitative distinction. But usually the distinction will be quantitative. The characters or genes which are present will be present in different proportions in different groups: their most frequent combinations will also differ from one group to the next. It is only by means of this quantitative difference in representation that in the main we can hope to define the difference between one group and another.

The method of characters and the method of genes differ in their scientific value and in their practicability. It is much easier to attempt a classification in terms of characters, and indeed this is the only method that is immediately practicable (as well as a necessary first step towards the classification in terms of genes).

But it is less satisfactory from the scientific point of view. This is partly because apparently similar characters may be determined by different genes, and conversely because the same gene in combination with different constellations of other genes may produce very different characters. It is also less satisfactory because a character is always the result of an interaction between constitution and environment. To disentangle the genetically unimportant effects of environment from the genetically essential action of genes is difficult in all organisms and especially so in man, where the social and cultural environment—unique characters of the human species—play predominant parts. Until we have invented a method for distinguishing the effects of social environment from those of genetic constitution, we shall be wholly unable to say anything of the least scientific value on such vital topics as the possible genetic differences in intelligence, initiative and aptitude which may distinguish different human groups.

Having thus cleared the ground for further discussion, we may proceed to consider the concrete phenomena of the apparently genetic differences between different groups, as they actually occur in man.

THE CONCEPT OF "RACE" IS CHALLENGED

THE paper which follows, when it was delivered as a lecture before the American Association of Physical Anthropologists meeting at the University of Chicago 7 April 1941, was entitled "The Meaninglessness of the Anthropological Conception of Race." It was found utterly meaningless by the professional physical anthropologists attending the meeting, but not by some of the students who were present. The Chairman of the Department of Anthropology at the University of Chicago, Professor Fay Cooper-Cole, at that time rose to state that he didn't see that it really made any difference whether Shakespeare was written by Shakespeare or by another man of that name. I have never quite seen the relevance of that remark to what had preceded it. In any event, an axiom of orthodoxy had been challenged, and the heresy and the heretic were condemned. But the heresies of yesterday have a way of becoming the orthodoxies of today, and while not all physical anthropologists agree that the concept of "race" is something of a whited sepulcher, most no longer accept it as uncritically as they did.

The suggestion that because it is so confused and confusing and embarrassed by emotion, the term "race" should be dropped altogether, and some such noncommittal term as "ethnic group" be used to indicate that here is something that requires investigation rather than taken for granted, has still found little favor among anthropologists, although it is interesting to find it more and more frequently used by journalists and other well-informed and critically-minded persons.

THE CONCEPT OF RACE IN THE HUMAN SPECIES IN THE LIGHT OF GENETICS*

It is said that when the theory of evolution was first announced it was received by the wife of the Canon of Worcester Cathedral with the remark, "Descended from the apes! My dear, we will hope it is not true. But if it is, let us pray that it may not become generally known."

I rather feel that the attempt to deprive the anthropologist of his belief in race is a piece of cruelty akin to that which sought to deprive the Canon's wife of her belief in special creation. Indeed, the anthropological conception of race and the belief in special creation have much in common. The prevailing attitude of mind is illustrated by the remark of a colleague who, when I gave him an account of the paper I proposed to present at this meeting replied, somewhat like the Canon's wife, "My dear, I always thought that there was such a thing as race." I believe he had spoken more correctly had he said that he had always taken the idea for granted. Certainly, I had always taken the idea for granted, and I think all of us have done so. Indeed, the idea of race is one of the most fundamental, if not *the* most fundamental of the concepts with which the anthropologist has habitually worked. To question the validity of this fundamental concept upon which we were intellectually brought up as if it were an axiom, was something which simply never occurred to one. One doesn't question the axioms upon which one's science, and one's activity in it, are based—at least, not usually. One simply takes them for granted.

*This paper, originally a lecture delivered before the American Association of Physical Anthropologists in Chicago on April 7, 1941, is reprinted from the *Journal of Heredity* (Vol. 23, 1941), pp. 243-247.

But in science, as in life, it is a good practice, from time to time, to hang a question mark on the things one takes most for granted. In science such questioning is important because without it there is a very real danger that certain erroneous or arbitrary ideas which may originally have been used merely as a convenience, may become so fortified by technicality and so dignified by time that their original infirmities may be wholly concealed.

Early Views

Blumenbach, in 1775 and in later years, foresaw this danger with respect to the usage of the term "race," and warned that it was merely to be used as a convenience helpful to the memory and no more. Herder, who was the first philosopher to make extensive use of Blumenbach's work wrote, in 1784 in his *Ideen zur Philosophie der Geschichte der Menschheit*, "I could wish the distinctions between the human species, that have been made from a laudable zeal for discriminating science, not carried beyond the due bounds. Some for instance have thought fit, to employ the term *races* for four or five divisions, originally made in consequence of country or complexion: but I see no reason for this appellation. Race refers to a difference of origin, which in this case does not exist, or in each of these countries, and under each of these complexions, comprises the most different races. . . . In short, there are neither four or five races, nor exclusive varieties, on this Earth. Complexions run into each other: forms follow the genetic character: and upon the whole, all are at last but shades of the same great picture, extending through all ages, and over all parts of the Earth. They belong not, therefore, so properly to systematic natural history, as to the physicogeographical history of man." When the last word has come to be said upon this subject it will, I am convinced, be very much in the words of Blumenbach and Herder. Meanwhile I propose to make a step in this direction here by showing that the concept of race is nothing but a whited sepulchre, a conception which in the light of modern experimental genetics is utterly erroneous and meaningless, and that it should therefore be dropped from the vocabulary of the anthropologist, for it has done an infinite amount of harm and no good at all.

The development of the idea of race may be clearly traced from the scholastic naturalization of Aristotle's doctrine of the Predicables of Genus, Species, Difference, Property, and Accident. From thence it may be directly traced to the early days of the Age of Enlightenment when Linnaeus, in 1735, took over the concepts of Class, Species and Genus from the theologians to serve him as systematic tools. The term race was actually first introduced into the literature of Natural History by Buffon who, in the year 1749, used it to describe six groups of man.

The term merely represented an extension of the Aristotelian conception of Species, that is to say, it was a subdivision of a species. Buffon recognized that all human beings belonged to a single species, as did Linnaeus, and he considered it merely *convenient*, and I emphasize the word convenient, as did Blumenbach after him, to distinguish between certain geographic groups of man. Thus, at the very outset the term was understood to be purely arbitrary and a simple convenience.

The Aristotelian conception of Species, the theological doctrine of special creation and the Natural History of the Age of Enlightenment, as represented particularly by Cuvier's brilliant conception of Unity of Type, namely the idea that animals can be grouped and classified upon the basis of assemblages of structural characters which, more or less, they have in common, these three conceptions fitted together extremely well and together yielded the idea of the Fixity of Species. An idea which, in spite of every indication to the contrary in the years which followed, was gradually extended to the concept of race.

The Darwinian contribution was to show that species were not as fixed as was formerly believed, and that under the action of Natural Selection one species might give rise to another, that all animal forms might change in this way. It is, however, important to remember that Darwin conceived of evolution as a process involving continuous materials which, without the operation of Natural Selection, would remain unchanged. Hence under the Darwinian conception of species it was still possible to think of species as relatively fixed and immutable, with the modification that under the slow action of Natural Selection they were capable of change. For the nineteenth century anthropologist, therefore, it was possible to think of race, not as Buffon or Blumenbach did in the eighteenth century as an arbitrary convenience in classification, but as Cuvier at the beginning of the nineteenth century had done for all animals, as groups which could be classified upon the basis of the fact that they possessed an aggregate of common physical characters, and as Darwin later postulated, as groups which varied only under the conditions of Natural Selection, but which otherwise remained unchanged.

This is essentially a scholastic conception of species with the one additive fundamental difference that a species is considered to be no longer fixed and immutable. As far as the anthropological conception of race is concerned, the anthropologist who can afford to pass by the findings of experimental genetics, still thinks of race as the scholastics thought of species, as a knowable fixed whole the essence of which could be defined *per genus, species, propria et differentia*.

In fact, what the anthropologist has done has been to take a very crude eighteenth century notion which was originally offered as no more than an arbitrary convenience, and having erected a tremendous terminology and methodology about it, has deceived himself in the belief that he was dealing with an objective reality.

Reality of Race Differences

For nearly two centuries anthropologists have been directing their attention principally towards the task of establishing criteria by whose means races of mankind might be defined. All have taken completely for granted the one thing which required to be proven, namely, that the concept of race corresponded with a reality which could actually be measured and verified and descriptively set out so that it could be seen to be a fact. In short, that the anthropological conception of race is true which states that there exist in nature groups of human beings comprised of individuals each of whom possesses a certain' aggregate of characters which individually and collectively serve to distinguish them from the individuals in all other groups.

Stated in plain English this is the conception of race which most anthropologists have held and which practically everyone else, except the geneticist, accepts. When, as in recent years, some anthropologists have admitted that the concept cannot be strictly applied in any systematic sense, they have thought to escape the consequences of that fact by calling the term a "general" one, and have proceeded to play the old game of blind man's buff with a sublimity which is almost enviable. For it is not vouchsafed to everybody to appreciate in its full grandeur the doctrine here implied. The feeling of dissatisfaction with which most anthropologists have viewed the many laborious attempts at classification of human races has not, on the whole, succeeded in generating the unloyal suspicion that something was probably wrong somewhere. If there was a fault, it was generally supposed, it lay not with the anthropologist but with the material, with the human beings themselves who were the subject of classification and who always varied so much that it was difficult to put them into the group where they were conceived to belong, and this was definitely a nuisance, but happily one which could be overcome by the simple expedient of "averaging"—the principal task of the student of "race."

Race No Omelette

The process of averaging the characters of a given group, knocking the individuals together, giving them a good stirring, and then serving the resulting omelette as a "race" is essentially the anthropological process of race-making. It may be good cooking but it is not science, since it serves to confuse rather than to clarify. When an omelette is done it has a fairly uniform character, though the ingredients which have gone into its making may have been variable. This is what the anthropological conception of "race" is. It is an omelette which corresponds to nothing in nature. It is an indigestible dish conjured into being by an anthropological chef from a number of ingredients which are extremely variable in the characters which they present. The omelette called "race" has no existence outside the statistical frying-pan in which it has been reduced by the heat of the anthropological imagination.

It is this omelette conception of "race" which is so meaningless—meaningless because it is inapplicable to anything real. When anthropologists begin to realize that the proper description of a group does not consist in the process of making an omelette of it, but in the description of the character of the variability of the elements comprising it, its ingredients, they will discover that the fault lies not with the materials but with the conceptual tool with which they have approached its study.

That many differences exist between different groups of human beings is obvious, but the anthropological conception of these is erroneous, and the anthropological approach to the study of their relationships is unscientific and pre-Mendelian. Taxonomic exercises in the classification of assemblages of phenotypical characters will never succeed in elucidating the relationships of different groups of mankind to one another for the simple reason that it is not assemblages of characters which undergo change in the formation of the individual and of the group, but single units which influence the development of those characters. One of the great persisting errors involved in the anthropological conception of race has been due to the steady refusal to recognize this fact. The fact that it is not possible to classify the various groups of mankind by means of the characters which anthropologists customarily use, because these characters do not behave as pre-Mendelian anthropologists think that they should behave, namely, as complexes of characters which are relatively fixed and are transmitted as complexes. Those characters instead behave in a totally different manner as the expressions of many independent units which have entered into their formation.

The materials of evolution are not represented by continuous aggregates which in turn determine particular aggregates of characters, but by discontinuous packages of chemicals, each of which is independent in its action and may be only partially responsible for the ultimate form of any character. These chemical packages are the genes, with which most anthropologists are still scarcely on terms of a bowing acquaintance. These genes retain both their independence and their individual character more or less indefinitely, although they are probably all inherently variable and, in time, capable of mutation. For these reasons any conception of race which operates as if inheritance were a matter of the transmission of gross aggregates of characters is meaningless.

The principal agencies of evolutionary change in man are primarily gene variability and gene mutation, that is to say, through the rearrangement of gene combinations in consequence of the operation of many secondary factors, physical and social, and change in the character of genes themselves. In order to appreciate the meaning of the variety presented by mankind today it is indispensably necessary to understand the manner in which these agencies work. Thus, in man, it is practically certain that some forms of hair, and skin color, are due to mutation, while still other forms are due to various combinations of these mutant forms with one another as also with non-mutant forms. The rate of mutation for different genes in man is unknown, though it has been calculated that the gene for normal clotting mutates, for example, to the gene for haemophilia is one out of every 50,000 individuals per generation. It is highly probable, for example, that such a mutation occurred in the person of Queen Victoria's father, a fact which in the long run may perhaps prove her chief claim to fame. Mutation of the blood group genes is, however, known to be very slow, and it is unlikely that such mutations have occurred since the apes and man set out upon their divergent evolutionary paths. Mutation of skin color genes is also very slow, while mutation of hair form genes is relatively frequent.

If we are ever to understand how the differing groups of mankind came to possess such characters as distinguish the more geographically isolated of them, and those of the less isolated more recently mixed, and therefore less distinguishable, groups, it should be obvious that we shall never succeed in doing so if we make omelettes of the very ingredients, the genes, which it should be our purpose to isolate and map. We must study the frequencies with which such genes occur in different groups. If, roughly speaking, we assign one gene to every component of the human body it should be fairly clear that as regards the structure of man we are dealing with many thousands of genes. If we consider the newer genetic concepts which recognize that the adult individual represents the end-point in an interaction between all these genes, the complexities become even greater. The morphological characters which anthropologists have relied upon for their "racial" classifications have been very few indeed, involving a minute fraction of the great number of genes which it would actually be necessary to consider in attempting to make any real, that is to say, genetically analytic, classification of mankind.

To sum up, the indictment against the anthropological conception of race is (1) that it is artificial; (2) that it does not agree with the facts; (3) that it leads to confusion and the perpetuation of error, and finally, that for all these reasons it is meaningless, or rather more accurately such meaning as it possesses is false. Being so weighed down with false meaning it were better that the term were dropped altogether than that any attempt should be made to give it a new meaning.

If it be agreed that the human species is one and that it consists of a group of populations which, more or less, replace each other geographically or ecologically and of which the neighboring ones intergrade or hybridize wherever they are in contact, or are potentially capable of doing so, then it should be obvious that the task of the student interested in the character of these populations must lie in the study of the frequency distribution of the genes which characterize them—and not in the study of entities which have no meaning.

In conclusion, let me say that I realize how unsatisfactory this paper is, and that I cannot expect to have convinced you, within the short space of fifteen minutes, of the meaninglessness of the anthropological concept of race. It may be that a notion so many times attacked during recent years is now passed beyond the reach both of scientific judgment and mortal malice, but in any event, may I be so bold as to hope that you will not feel as the Canon's wife felt about the threat to her belief in special creation?

*   *   *

This article was the subject of an unusual and gratifying procedure. The editor of the Journal of Heredity, *Dr. Robert C. Cook, considered it important enough to append to it the following editorial comments, which because of their interest are reprinted here.*

Dr. Ashley Montagu's interesting history of the term race, shows certain ways it has outgrown any usefulness, even becoming a menace. Some of his views may draw fire from geneticists, for humankind differs greatly in many characteristics variously distributed. If these differences are real enough to allow objective groupings of people, such groups will differ just as much whether we call them "races" as to invent a new term. If Dr. Montagu's idol smashing helps to clear the air it has served a very useful purpose.

The laboratory scientist shuns the market place and the politician's rostrum. Unfortunately folks accustomed to reach for a microphone refuse to stay out of the laboratory if they see a chance to gain even reluctant support for their pet nostrum. Because "race" is a word which inflames the emotions, much fanatical nonsense has been spoken and written about it. "Class" is another word called upon to carry an impossible genetic load, as the history of the eugenics movement testifies. Strange perversions, allegedly sanctioned by careful laboratory research, perplex and enslave millions of people.

Research workers in those sciences which may become social dynamite through perversion or prostitution of conclusions, may have to defend the integrity of their science whether they like it or not. This is emphasized in the depths of biological absurdity recently reached by champions of "racism" (a derivative word with very ugly connotations). Even the Norwegians have been read out of the Aryan fold by the dark-moustached "protector" of destiny-freighted blonds. The color of Norwegian hair and eyes has not changed. Rugged Norse individualism has made it impossible for the most "nordic" group in the world to accept the Procrustean savagery of the "new order."

With racism thus divorced by its leading proponent from shape of head and color of hair, eyes, and skin, it is essential that anthropologists and biologists clarify their own minds and inform lay people what actually are the differences between the human races. The study of human relationships through an analysis of gene distributions is as yet limited mainly to the blood groups and to P.T.C. taste reaction. The technique offers a hopeful approach which needs to be further explored.

As far as research and observation have been able to prove, the chromosome number of all the human races is the same, and all of the five, seven, or ten races (depending on who we follow) are inter-fertile. The blood of all races is built of the same pattern of agglutinins and antigens, and the appropriate blood type from one race can be transfused into any of the others without untoward effect. Thus in spite of the unquestionable physical differences (and less measurable mental and emotional differences) between groups of people, an imposing substrate of similarity underlies these differences. This must serve as a foundation for a world order willing to accept the differences as a challenge to developing useful specializations and not as a fatuous excuse for the enslavement or exploitation of one "race," class or nation by another.

A PHYSIOLOGIST EXPLAINS THE MECHANISM OF "VOODOO" DEATH

WALTER BRADFORD CANNON (1871-1945), one of America's greatest physiologists, author of the classical *Bodily Changes in Pain, Hunger, Fear and Rage* (2nd ed., 1919), and the *Wisdom of the Body* (1932), and as an outcome of his studies during the First World War, *Traumatic Shock* (1923), in the contribution which here follows offered the first explanation of the phenomenon of what has come to be called "Voodoo" death.

Anthropologists and others had observed and reported the strange fact that members of aboriginal populations who have been "hexed" by a magician or as a result of having broken some taboo which is invariably followed by death, will simply lie down and within anything from a day to a few weeks waste away and die. No physician can prevent such death, but a native sorcerer can, by convincing the victim that the proper spells have been cast and that he has therefore been relieved of the curse, bring such a dying person back to life as if, literally, by magic.

The phenomenon is actually one of shock, the physiology of which is now very much more fully understood than it was a generation ago. The mechanism of death is much the same as it is in death from wound shock, except that the initiating cause in "Voodoo" death is anxiety or fear, resulting in a gradual failure of circulation and its attendant damage to tissues and the final failure of the heart.[1]

"VOODOO" DEATH*
By WALTER B. CANNON

In records of anthropologists and others who have lived with primitive people in widely scattered parts of the world is the testimony that when subjected to spells or sorcery or the use of "black magic" men may be brought to death. Among the natives of South America and Africa, Australia, New Zealand, and the islands of the Pacific, as well as among the negroes of nearby Haiti, "voodoo" death has been reported by apparently competent observers. The phenomenon is so extraordinary and so foreign to the experience of civilized people that it seems incredible; certainly if it is authentic it deserves careful consideration. I propose to recite instances of this mode of death, to inquire whether reports of the phenomenon are trustworthy, and to examine a possible explanation of it if it should prove to be real.

First, with regard to South America. Apparently Soares de Souza (1587) was first to observe instances of death among the Tupinambás Indians, death induced by fright when men were condemned and sentenced by a so-called "medicine man." Likewise Varnhagen (1875) remarks that generally among Brazilian Indian tribes, the members, lacking knowledge, accept without question whatever is told them. Thus the chief or medicine man gains the reputation of exercising supernatural power. And by intimidation or by terrifying augury or prediction he may cause death from fear.

There is like testimony from Africa. Leonard (1906) has written an account of the Lower Niger and its tribes in which he declares:

> I have seen more than one hardened old Haussa soldier dying steadily and by inches because he believed himself to be bewitched; no nourishment or medicines that were given to him had the slightest effect either

[1] For a good discussion of the microphysiology of shock see William Schumer and Richard Sperling, "Shock and Its Effect on the Cell," *Journal of the American Medical Association* (Vol. 205, 1968), pp. 215-219.

*Reproduced by permission of the American Anthropological Association from the *American Anthropologist*, 44 (2), 1942, pp. 169-181.

to check the mischief or to improve his condition in any way, and nothing was able to divert him from a fate which he considered inevitable. In the same way, and under very similar conditions, I have seen Kru-men and others die in spite of every effort that was made to save them, simply because they had made up their minds, not (as we thought at the time) to die, but that being in the clutch of malignant demons they were bound to die.

Another instance of death wrought by superstitious fear in an African tribe is reported by Merolla in his voyage to the Congo in 1682 (cited by Pinkerton, 1814). A young negro on a journey lodged in a friend's house for the night. The friend had prepared for their breakfast a wild hen, a food strictly banned by a rule which must be inviolably observed by the immature. The young fellow demanded whether it was indeed a wild hen, and when the host answered "No," he ate of it heartily and proceeded on his way. A few years later, when the two met again, the old friend asked the younger man if he would eat a wild hen. He answered that he had been solemnly charged by a wizard not to eat that food. Thereupon the host began to laugh and asked him why he refused it now after having eaten it at his table before. On hearing this news the negro immediately began to tremble, so greatly was he possessed by fear, and in less than twenty-four hours was dead.

Also in New Zealand there are tales of death induced by ghostly power. In Brown's *New Zealand and Its Aborigines* (1845) there is an account of a Maori woman who, having eaten some fruit, was told that it had been taken from a tabooed place; she exclaimed that the sanctity of the chief had been profaned and that his spirit would kill her. This incident occurred in the afternoon; the next day about 12 o'clock she was dead. According to Tregear (1890) the *tapu* (taboo) among the Maoris of New Zealand is an awful weapon. "I have seen a strong young man die," he declares, "the same day he was tapued; the victims die under it as though their strength ran out as water." It appears that among these aborigines superstitions associated with their sacred chiefs are a true though purely imaginary barrier; transgression of that barrier entails the death of the transgressor whenever he becomes aware of what he has done. It is a fatal power of the imagination working through unmitigated terror.

Dr. S. M. Lambert of the Western Pacific Health Service of the Rockefeller Foundation wrote to me that on several occasions he had seen evidence of death from fear. In one case there was a startling recovery. At a Mission at Mona Mona in North Queensland were many native converts, but on the outskirts of the Mission was a group of non-converts including one Nebo, a famous witch doctor. The chief helper of the missionary was Rob, a native who had been converted. When Dr. Lambert arrived at the Mission he learned that Rob was in distress and that the missionary wanted him examined. Dr. Lambert made the examination, and found no fever, no complaint of pain, no symptoms or signs of disease. He was impressed, however, by the obvious indications that Rob was seriously ill and extremely weak. From the missionary he learned that Rob had had a bone pointed at him by Nebo and was convinced that in consequence he must die. Thereupon Dr. Lambert and the missionary went for Nebo, threatened him sharply that his supply of food would be shut off if anything happened to Rob and that he and his people would be driven away from the Mission. At once Nebo agreed to go with them to see Rob. He leaned over Rob's bed and told the sick man that it was all a mistake, a mere joke—indeed, that he had not pointed a bone at him at all. The relief, Dr. Lambert testifies, was almost instantaneous; that evening Rob was back at work, quite happy again, and in full possession of his physical strength.

A question which naturally arises is whether those who have testified to the reality of "voodoo" death have exercised good critical judgment. Although the sorcerer or medicine-man or chief may tacitly possess or may assume the ability to kill by bone-pointing or by another form of black magic, may he not preserve his reputation for supernatural power by the use of poison? Especially when death has been reported to have occurred after the taking of food may not the fatal result be due to action of poisonous substances not commonly known except to priests and wizards? Obviously, the possible use of poisons must be excluded before "voodoo" death can be accepted as an actual consequence of sorcery or witchcraft. Also it is essential to rule out instances of bold claims of supernatural power when in fact death resulted from natural causes; this precaution is particularly important because of the common belief among aborigines that illness is due to malevolence. I have endeavored to learn definitely whether poisoning and spurious claims can quite certainly be excluded from instances of death, attributed to magic power, by addressing enquiries to medically trained observers.

Dr. Lambert, already mentioned as a representative of the Rockefeller Foundation, wrote to me concerning the experience of Dr. P. S. Clarke with Kanakas working on the sugar plantations of North Queensland. One day a Kanaka came to his hospital and told him he would die in a few days because a spell had been put upon him and nothing could be done to counteract it. The man had been known by Dr. Clarke for some time. He was given a very thorough examination, including an examination of the stool and the urine. All was found normal, but as he lay in bed he gradually grew weaker. Dr. Clarke called upon the foreman of the Kanakas to come to the hospital to give the man assurance, but on reaching the foot of the bed, the foreman leaned over, looked at the patient, and then turned to Dr. Clarke saying, "Yes, doctor, close up him he die" (i.e., he is nearly dead). The next day, at 11 o'clock in the morning, he ceased to live. A postmortem examination revealed nothing that could in any way account for the fatal outcome.

Another observer with medical training, Dr. W. E. Roth (1897), who served for three years as government surgeon among the primitive people of north-central Queensland, has also given pertinent testimony. "So rooted sometimes is this belief on the part of the patient," Roth wrote, "that some enemy has 'pointed' the bone at him, that he will actually lie down to die, and succeed in the attempt, even at the expense of refusing food and succour within his reach: I have myself witnessed three or four such cases."

Dr. J. B. Cleland, Professor of Pathology at the University of Adelaide, has written to me that he has no doubt that from time to time the natives of the Australian bush do die as a result of a bone being pointed at them, and that such death may not be associated with any of the ordinary lethal injuries. In an article which included a section on death from malignant psychic influences, Dr. Cleland (1928) mentions a fine, robust tribesman in central Australia who was injured in the fleshy part of the thigh by a spear that had been enchanted. The man slowly pined away and died, without any surgical complication which could be detected. Dr. Cleland cites a number of physicians who have referred to the fatal effects of bone pointing and other terrifying acts. In his letter to me he wrote, "Poisoning is, I think, entirely ruled out in such cases among our Australian natives. There are very few poisonous plants available and I doubt whether it has ever entered the mind of the central Australian natives that such might be used on human beings."

Dr. Herbert Basedow (1925), in his book, *The Australian Aboriginal*, has presented a vivid picture of the first horrifying effect of bone pointing on the ignorant, superstitious and credulous natives, and the later more calm acceptance of their mortal fate:

> The man who discovers that he is being boned by any enemy is, indeed, a pitiable sight. He stands aghast, with his eyes staring at the treacherous pointer, and with his hands lifted as though to ward off the lethal medium, which he imagines is pouring into his body. His cheeks blanch and his eyes become glassy and the expression of his face becomes horribly distorted. . . . He attempts to shriek but usually the sound chokes in his throat, and all that one might see is froth at his mouth. His body begins to tremble and the muscles twist involuntarily. He sways backwards and falls to the ground, and after a short time appears to be in a swoon; but soon after he writhes as if in mortal agony, and covering his face with his hands, begins to moan. After a while he becomes very composed and crawls to his wurley. From this time onwards he sickens and frets, refusing to eat and keeping aloof from the daily affairs of the tribe. Unless help is forthcoming in the shape of a counter-charm administered by the hands of the Nangarri, or medicine-man, his death is only a matter of a comparatively short time. If the coming of the medicine-man is opportune he might be saved.

The Nangarri, when persuaded to exercise his powers, goes through an elaborate ceremony and finally steps toward the awestricken relatives, holding in his fingers a small article—a stick, a bone, a pebble, or a talon—which, he avows, he has taken from the ''boned'' man and which was the cause of the affliction. And now, since it is removed, the victim has nothing to fear. The effect, Dr. Basedow declares, is astounding. The victim, until that moment far on the road to death, raises his head and gazes in wonderment at the object held by the medicine-man. He even lifts himself into a sitting position and calls for water to drink. The crisis is passed, and the recovery is speedy and complete. Without the Nangarri's intervention the boned fellow, according to Dr. Basedow, would certainly have fretted himself to death. The implicit faith which a native cherishes in the magical powers of his tribal magician is said to result in cures which exceed anything recorded by the faith-healing disciples of more cultured communities.

Perhaps the most complete account of the influence of the tribal taboo on the fate of a person subjected to its terrific potency has come from W. L. Warner, who worked among primitive aborigines in the Northern Territory of Australia. In order to provide a background for his testimony I quote from William James' *Principles of Psychology* (1905):

> A man's social me is the recognition which he gets from his mates. We are not only gregarious animals, liking to be in sight of our fellows, but we have an innate propensity to get ourselves noticed, and noticed favorably, by our kind. No more fiendish punishment could be devised, were such a thing physically possible, than that one should be turned loose in society and remain absolutely unnoticed by all the members thereof. If no one turned round when we entered, answered when we spoke, or minded what we did, but if every person we met ''cut us dead,'' and acted as if we were non-existing things, a kind of rage and impotent despair would ere long well up in us, from which the cruellest bodily tortures would be a relief; for these would make us feel that, however bad might be our plight, we had not sunk to such a depth as to be unworthy of attention at all.

Now to return to the observations of Warner regarding the aborigines of northern Australia, creatures too ignorant, he assured me, to know about poisons. There are two definite movements of the social group, he declares, in the process by which black magic becomes effective on the victim of sorcery. In the first movement the community contracts; all people who stand in kinship relation with him withdraw their sustaining support. This means everyone he knows—all his fellows—completely change their attitudes towards him and place him in a new category. He is now viewed as one who is more nearly in the realm of the sacred and tabu than in the world of the ordinary where the community finds itself. The organization of his social life has collapsed and, no longer a member of a group, he is alone and isolated. The doomed man is in a situation from which the only escape is by death. During the death illness which ensues, the group acts with all the outreachings and complexities of its organization and with countless stimuli to suggest death positively to the victim, who is in a highly suggestible state. In addition to the social pressure upon him the victim himself, as a rule, not only makes no effort to live and to stay a part of his group but actually, through the multiple suggestions which he receives, coöperates in the withdrawal from it. He becomes what the attitude of his fellow tribesmen wills him to be. Thus he assists in committing a kind of suicide.

Before death takes place, the second movement of the community occurs, which is a return to the victim in order to subject him to the fateful ritual of mourning. The purpose of the community now, as a social unit with its ceremonial leader, who is a person of very near kin to the victim, is at last to cut him off entirely from the ordinary world and ultimately to place him in his proper position in the sacred totemic world of the dead. The victim, on his part, reciprocates this feeling.

The effect of the double movement in the society, first away from the victim and then back, with all the compulsive forces of one of its most powerful rituals, is obviously drastic. Warner (1941) writes:

> An analogous situation in our society is hard to imagine. If all a man's near kin, his father, mother, brothers and sisters, wife, children, business associates, friends and all the other members of the society should suddenly withdraw themselves because of some dramatic circumstance, refusing to take any attitude but one of taboo and looking at the man as one already dead, and then after some little time perform over him a sacred ceremony which is believed with certainty to guide him out of the land of the living into that of the dead, the enormous suggestive power of this two-fold movement of the community, after it has had its attitudes crystallized, can be somewhat understood by ourselves.

The social environment as a support to morale is probably much more important and impressive among primitive people, because of their profound ignorance and insecurity in a haunted world, than among educated people living in civilized and well protected communities. Dr. S. D. Porteus, physician and psychologist, has studied savage life extensively in the Pacific islands and in Africa; he writes:

> Music and dance are primitive man's chief defenses against loneliness. By these he reminds himself that in his wilderness there are other minds seconding his own . . . in the dance he sees himself multiplied in his fellows, his action mirrored in theirs. There are in his life very few

other occasions in which he can take part in concerted action and find partners. . . . The native aboriginal is above all fear-ridden. Devils haunt to seize the unwary; their malevolent magic shadows his waking moments, he believes that medicine men know how to make themselves invisible so that they may cut out his kidney fat, then sew him up and rub his tongue with a magic stone to induce forgetfulness, and thereafter he is a living corpse, devoted to death. . . . So desperate is this fear that if a man imagines that he has been subjected to the bone pointing magic of the enemy he will straight away lie down and die.

Testimony similar to the foregoing, from Brazil, Africa, New Zealand and Australia, was found in reports from the Hawaiian Islands, British Guiana and Haiti. What attitude is justified in the presence of this accumulation of evidence? In a letter from Professor Lévi-Bruhl, the French ethnologist long interested in aboriginal tribes and their customs, he remarked that answers which he had received from inquiries could be summed up as follows. The ethnologists, basing their judgment on a large number of reports, quite independent of one another and gathered from groups in all parts of the world, admit that there are instances indicating that the belief that one has been subjected to sorcery, and in consequence is inevitably condemned to death, does actually result in death in the course of time. On the contrary, physiologists and physicians—men who have had no acquaintance with ethnological conditions —are inclined to consider the phenomenon as impossible and raise doubts regarding clear and definite testimony.

Before denying that "voodoo" death is within the realm of possibility, let us consider the general features of the specimen reports mentioned in foregoing paragraphs. First, there is the elemental fact that the phenomenon is characteristically noted among aborigines—among human beings so primitive, so superstitious, so ignorant that they are bewildered strangers in a hostile world. Instead of knowledge they have a fertile and unrestricted imagination which fills their environment with all manner of evil spirits capable of affecting their lives disastrously. As Dr. Porteus pointed out, only by engaging in communal activities are they able to develop sufficient *esprit de corps* to render themselves resistant to the mysterious and malicious influences which can vitiate their lives. Associated with these circumstances is the fixed assurance that because of certain conditions, such as being subject to bone pointing or other magic, or failing to observe sacred tribal regulations, death is sure to supervene. This is a belief so firmly held by all members of the tribe that the individual not only has that conviction himself but is obsessed by the knowledge that all his fellows likewise hold it. Thereby he becomes a pariah, wholly deprived of the confidence and social support of the tribe. In his isolation the malicious spirits which he believes are all about him and capable of irresistibly and calamitously maltreating him, exert supremely their evil power. Amid this mysterious murk of grim and ominous fatality what has been called "the gravest known extremity of fear," that of an immediate threat of death, fills the terrified victim with powerless misery.

In his terror he refuses both food and drink, a fact which many observers have noted and which, as we shall see later, is highly significant for a possible understanding of the slow onset of weakness. The victim "pines away"; his strength runs out like water, to paraphrase words already quoted from one graphic account; and in the course of a day or two he succumbs.

The question which now arises is whether an ominous and persistent state of fear can end the life of a man. Fear, as is well known, is one of the most deeply rooted and dominant of the emotions. Often, only with difficulty can it be eradicated. Associated with it are profound physiological disturbances, widespread throughout the organism. There is evidence that some of these disturbances, if they are lasting, can work harmfully. In order to elucidate that evidence I must first indicate that great fear and great rage have similar effects in the body. Each of these powerful emotions is associated with ingrained instincts—the instinct to attack, if rage is present, the instinct to run away or escape, if fear is present. Throughout the long history of human beings and lower animals these two emotions and their related instincts have served effectively in the struggle for existence. When they are roused they bring into action an elemental division of the nervous system, the so-called sympathetic or sympathico-adrenal division, which exercises a control over internal organs, and also over the blood vessels. As a rule the sympathetic division acts to maintain a relatively constant state in the flowing blood and lymph, i.e., the "internal environment" of our living parts. It acts thus in strenuous muscular effort; for example, liberating sugar from the liver, accelerating the heart, contracting certain blood vessels, discharging adrenaline and dilating the bronchioles. All these changes render the animal more efficient in physical struggle, for they supply essential conditions for continuous action of laboring muscles. Since they occur in association with the strong emotions, rage and fear, they can reasonably be interpreted as preparatory for the intense struggle which the instincts to attack or to escape may involve. If these powerful emotions prevail, and the bodily forces are fully mobilized for action, and if this state of extreme perturbation continues in uncontrolled possession of the organism for a considerable period, without the occurrence of action, dire results may ensue (cf. Cannon, 1929).

When, under brief ether anesthesia, the cerebral cortex of a cat is quickly destroyed so that the animal no longer has the benefit of the organs of intelligence, there is a remarkable display of the activities of lower, primary centers of behavior, those of emotional expression. This decorticate condition is similar to that produced in man when consciousness is abolished by the use of nitrous oxide; he is then decorticated by chemical means. Commonly the emotional expression of joy is released (nitrous oxide is usually known as "laughing gas"), but it may be that of sorrow (it might as well be called "weeping gas"). Similarly, ether anesthesia, if light, may release the expression of rage. In the sham rage of the decorticate cat there is a supreme exhibition of intense emotional activity. The hairs stand on end, sweat exudes from the toe pads, the heart rate may rise from about 150 beats per minute to twice that number, the blood pressure is greatly elevated, and the concentration of sugar in the blood soars to five times the normal. This excessive activity of the sympathico-adrenal system rarely lasts, however, more than three or four hours. By that time, without any loss of blood or any other event to explain the outcome, the decorticate remnant of the animal, in which this acme of emotional display has prevailed, ceases to exist.

What is the cause of the demise? It is clear that the rapidly fatal result is due to a persistent excessive activity of the sympathico-adrenal system. One of my associates, Philip Bard (1928), noted that when the signs of emotional excitement failed to appear, the decorticate preparation might continue to survive for long periods; indeed, its existence might have to be ended by the experimenter. Further evidence was obtained by another of my associates, Norman E. Freeman (1933), who produced sham rage in animals from which the sympathetic nerves had been removed. In these circumstances the behavior was similar in all respects to the behavior described above, excepting the manifestations dependent upon sympathetic innervation. The remarkable fact appeared that animals deprived of their sympathetic nerves and exhibiting sham rage, so far as was possible, continued to exist for many hours without any sign of breakdown. Here were experiments highly pertinent to the present inquiry.

What effect on the organism is produced by a lasting and intense action of the sympathico-adrenal system? In observations by Bard, he found that a prominent and significant change which became manifest in animals displaying sham rage was a gradual fall of blood pressure towards the end of the display, from the high levels of the early stages to the low level seen in fatal wound shock. In Freeman's research he produced evidence that this fall of pressure was due to a reduction of the volume of circulating blood. This is the condition which during World War I was found to be the reason for the low blood pressure observed in badly wounded men—the blood volume is reduced until it becomes insufficient for the maintenance of an adequate circulation (see Cannon, 1923). Thereupon deterioration occurs in the heart, and also in the nerve centers which hold the blood vessels in moderate contraction. A vicious circle is then established; the low blood pressure damages the very organs which are necessary for the maintenance of an adequate circulation, and as they are damaged they are less and less able to keep the blood circulating to an effective degree. In sham rage, as in wound shock, death can be explained as due to a failure of essential organs to receive a sufficient supply of blood or, specifically, a sufficient supply of oxygen, to maintain their functions.

The gradual reduction of blood volume in sham rage can be explained by the action of the sympathico-adrenal system in causing a persistent constriction of the small arterioles in certain parts of the body. If adrenaline, which constricts the blood vessels precisely as nerve impulses constrict them, is continuously injected at a rate which produces the vasoconstriction of strong emotional states, the blood volume is reduced to the degree seen in sham rage. Freeman, Freedman and Miller (1941) performed that experiment. They employed in some instances no more adrenaline than is secreted in response to reflex stimulation of the adrenal gland, and they found not only marked reduction of the blood plasma but also a concentration of blood corpuscles as shown by the percentage increase of hemoglobin. It should be remembered, however, that in addition to this circulating vasoconstrictor agent there are in the normal functioning of the sympathico-adrenal system the constrictor effects on blood vessels of nerve impulses and the cöoperation of another circulating chemical substance besides adrenaline, viz., sympathin. These three agents, working together in times of great emotional stress, might well produce the results which Freeman and his collaborators observed when they injected adrenaline alone. In the presence of the usual blood pressure, organs of primary importance, e.g., the heart and the brain are not subjected to constriction of their vessels, and therefore they are, continuously supplied with blood. But this advantage is secured at the deprivation of peripheral structures and especially the abdominal viscera. In these less essential parts, where constriction of the arterioles occurs, the capillaries are ill-supplied with oxygen. The very thin walls of capillaries are sensitive to oxygen want and when they do not receive an adequate supply they become more and more permeable to the fluid part of the blood. Thereupon the plasma escapes into the perivascular spaces. A similar condition occurs in the wound shock of human beings. The escape of the plasma from the blood vessels leaves the red corpuscles more concentrated. During World War I we found that the concentration of corpuscles in skin areas might be increased as much as fifty per cent (cf. Cannon, Fraser and Hooper, 1917).

A condition well known as likely to be harmful to the wounded was a prolonged lack of food or water. Freeman, Morison and Sawyer (1933) found that loss of fluid from the body, resulting in a state of dehydration, excited the sympathico-adrenal system; thus again a vicious circle may be started, the low blood volume of the dehydrated condition being intensified by further loss through capillaries which have been made increasingly permeable.

The foregoing paragraphs have revealed how a persistent and profound emotional state may induce a disastrous fall of blood pressure, ending in death. Lack of food and drink would collaborate with the damaging emotional effects, to induce the fatal outcome. These are the conditions which, as we have seen, are prevalent in persons who have been reported as dying as a consequence of sorcery. They go without food or water as they, in their isolation, wait in fear for their impending death. In these circumstances they might well die from a true state of shock, in the surgical sense—a shock induced by prolonged and tense emotion.

It is pertinent to mention here that Wallace, a surgeon of large experience in World War I, testified (1919) to having seen cases of shock in which neither trauma nor any of the known accentuating factors of shock could account for the disastrous condition. Sometimes the wounds were so trivial that they could not be reasonably regarded as the cause of the shock state; sometimes the visible injuries were negligible. He cites two illustrative instances. One was a man who was buried by the explosion of a shell in a cellar; the other was blown up by a buried shell over which he had lighted a fire. In both the circumstances were favorable for terrifying experience. In both all the classic symptoms of shock were present. The condition lasted more than 48 hours, and treatment was of no avail. A *postmortem* examination did not reveal any gross injury. Another remarkable case which may be cited was studied by Freeman at the Massachusetts General Hospital. A woman of 43 years underwent a complete hysterectomy because of uterine bleeding. Although her emotional instability was recognized, she appeared to stand the operation well. Special precautions were taken, however, to avoid loss of blood, and in addition she was given fluid intravenously when the operation was completed. That night she was sweating, and refused to speak. The next morning her blood pressure had fallen to near the shock level, her heart rate was 150 beats per minute, her skin was cold and clammy and the measured blood flow through the vessels of her hand was very slight. There was no bleeding to account for her desperate condition, which was diagnosed as shock brought on by fear. When one understands the utter strangeness, to an inexperienced layman, of a hospital and its elaborate surgical ritual, and the distressing invasion of the body with knives and metal retractors, the wonder is that not more patients exhibit signs of deep anxiety. In this instance a calm and reassuring attitude on the part of the surgeon resulted in a change of attitude in the patient, with recovery of a normal state. That the attitude of the patient is of significant importance for a favorable outcome of an operation is firmly believed by the well-known American surgeon, Dr. J. M. T. Finney, for many years Professor of Surgery at the Johns Hopkins Medical School. He (1934) has publicly testified, on the basis of serious experiences, that if any person came to him for a major operation, and expressed fear of the result, he invariably refused to operate. Some other surgeon must assume the risk!

Further evidence of the possibility of a fatal outcome from profound emotional strain was reported by Mira (1939) in recounting his experiences as a psychiatrist in the Spanish War of 1936-39. In patients who suffered from what he called "malignant anxiety", he observed signs of anguish and perplexity, accompanied by a permanently rapid pulse (more than 120 beats per minute, and a very rapid respiration (about three times the normal resting rate). These conditions indicated a perturbed state deeply involving the sympathico-adrenal complex. As predisposing conditions Mira mentioned "a previous lability of the sympathetic system" and "a severe mental shock experienced in conditions of physical exhaustion due to lack of food, fatigue, sleeplessness, etc." The lack of food appears to have attended lack of water, for the urine was concentrated and extremely acid. Towards the end the anguish still remained, but inactivity changed to restlessness. No focal symptoms were observed. In fatal cases death occurred in three or four days. *Postmortem* examination revealed brain hemorrhages in some cases, but, excepting an increased pressure, the cerebrospinal fluid showed a normal state. The combination of lack of food and water, anxiety, very rapid pulse and respiration, associated with a shocking experience having persistent effects, would fit well with fatal conditions reported from primitive tribes.

The suggestion which I offer, therefore, is that "voodoo death" may be real, and that it may be explained as due to shocking emotional stress—to obvious or repressed terror. A satisfactory hypothesis is one which allows observations to be made which may determine whether or not it is correct. Fortunately, tests of a relatively simple type can be used to learn whether the suggestion as to the nature of "voodoo death" is justifiable. The pulse towards the end would be rapid and "thready." The skin would be cool and moist. A count of the red blood corpuscles, or even simpler, a determination by means of a hematocrit of the ratio of corpuscles to plasma in a small sample of blood from skin vessels would help to tell whether shock is present; for the "red count" would be high and the hematocrit also would reveal "hemoconcentration." The blood pressure would be low. The blood sugar would be increased, but the measure of it might be too difficult in the field. If in the future, however, any observer has opportunity to see an instance of "voodoo death," it is to be hoped that he will conduct the simpler tests before the victim's last gasp.

REFERENCES

Bard, P. *A diencephalic mechanism for the expression of rage with special reference to the sympathetic nervous system* (American Journal Physiology, 1928, *84*), pp. 490-513.

Basedow, H. *The Australian Aboriginal* (Adelaide, 1925), pp. 178-179.

Brown, W. *New Zealand and Its Aborigines* (London, 1845), p. 76.

Cannon, W. B. *Traumatic Shock* (New York, 1923).

Cannon, W. B. *Bodily Changes in Pain, Hunger, Fear and Rage* (New York, 1929).

Cannon, W. B., John Fraser and A. N. Hooper. *Report No. 2 of the Special Investigation Committee on Surgical Shock and Allied Conditions, Medical Research Committee, on Some Alterations in the Distribution and Character of the Blood in Wound Conditions* (London, 1917), pp. 24-40.

Cleland, J. B. (Journal of Tropical Medicine and Hygiene, 1928, *31*), p. 233.

Finney, J. M. T. *Discussion of papers on shock*. (Annals of Surgery, 1934, *100*), p. 746.

Freeman, N. E. *Decrease in blood volume after prolonged hyperactivity of the sympathetic nervous system* (American Journal of Physiology, 1933, *103*), pp. 185-202.

Freeman, N.E., H. Freedman and C. C. Miller. *The production of shock by the prolonged continuous injection of adrenalin in unanesthetized dogs* (American Journal of Physiology, 1941, *131*), pp. 545-553.

Freeman, N. E., R. S. Morison and M. E. MacK. Sawyer. *The effect of dehydration on adrenal secretion and its relation to shock* (American Journal Physiology, 1933, *104*), pp. 628-635.

James, W. *Principles of Psychology* (New York, 1905), pp. 179-180.

Leonard, A. G. *The Lower Niger and Its Tribes* (London, 1906), p. 257 *et seq*.

Mira, F. *Psychiatric experience in the Spanish war*. (British Medical Journal, 1939, i), pp. 1217-1220.

Pinkerton, J. *Voyages and Travels* (1814, *16*), p. 237 *et seq*.

Porteus, S. D. *Personal communication*.

Roth, W. E. *Ethnological Studies among the North-West-Central Queensland Aborigines* (Brisbane and London, 1897), p. 154.

Soares de Souza, G. *Tratado Descriptivo do Brasil in 1587* (Rio de Janeiro, 1879), pp. 292-293.

Tregear, E. *Journal of the Anthropological Institute* (1890, *19*), p. 100.

Varnhagen, F. A. *Historia Geral do Brasil* (1875, *1*), pp. 42-43.

Wallace, Sir Cuthbert. *Introduction to Report No. 26 to Medical Research Committee, on Traumatic Toxaemia as a Factor in Shock* (London, 1919), p. 7.

Warner, W. L. *A Black Civilization, a Social Study of an Australian Tribe* (New York and London, 1941), p. 242.

WHY THE MENTAL CAPACITIES OF THE VARIOUS ETHNIC GROUPS OF MANKIND ARE PROBABLY PRETTY MUCH OF A MUCHNESS

PROFESSOR THEODOSIUS DOBZHANSKY (1900-) and Ashley Montagu (1905-) are said to regard their paper "Natural Selection and the Mental Capacities of Mankind" as one of the most important of their works. This opinion does not appear to be shared by the rest of the scientific community, to judge from the infrequency with which reference is made to this contribution. It may have had a greater impact than the authors are aware. However that may be, in this paper a geneticist with anthropological interests and an anthropologist with genetical interests combine their knowledge and thinking to examine the kind of selective pressures that were probably operative upon men, no matter how distantly separated by both time and geography, during the course of their evolution.

In foodgathering, and in foodgathering-hunting communities, the state in which mankind lived for several million years, the challenges of the environment and the selective pressures must have been very much the same everywhere. Hence, there would have been no selection for different kinds of specific abilities in one group as compared with another sufficient to bring about significant differences within each group for intelligence—intelligence defined as the ability to make the most appropriately successful response to the challenge of the particular situation. Dobzhansky and Montagu concluded, therefore, that whatever differences may exist in potentialities for intelligence among the different groups of mankind, they cannot be of any major significance. It is a view which has been strangely ignored in discussions of "race." One cannot help wondering why.

NATURAL SELECTION AND THE MENTAL CAPACITIES OF MANKIND*

TH. DOBZHANSKY and ASHLEY MONTAGU

The fundamental mechanisms of the transmission of heredity from parents to offspring are surprisingly uniform in most diverse organisms. Their uniformity is perhaps the most remarkable fact disclosed by genetics. The laws discovered by Mendel apply to human genes just as much as to those of the maize plant, and the processes of cellular division and germ cell maturation in man are not very different from those in a grasshopper. The similarity of the mechanisms of heredity on the individual level is reflected on the population level in a similarity of the basic causative factors of organic evolution throughout the living world. Mutation, selection, and genetic drift are important in the evolution of man as well as in amoebae and in bacteria. Wherever sexuality and cross-fertilization are established as exclusive or predominant methods of reproduction, the field of hereditary variability increases enormously as compared with asexual or self-fertilizing organisms. Isolating mechanisms which prevent interbreeding and fusion of species of mammals are operative also among insects.

Nevertheless, the universality of basic genetic mechanisms and of evolutionary agents permits a variety of evolutionary patterns to exist not only in different lines of descent but even at different times in the same line of descent. It is evident that the evolutionary pattern in the dog species under domestication is not the same as in the wild ancestors of the domestic dogs or in the now

*Reprinted from *Science* (Vol. 105, June 6, 1947), pp. 587-90.

living wild relatives. Widespread occurrence of reduplication of chromosome complements (polyploidy) in the evolution of plants introduces complexities which are not found in the animal kingdom, where polyploidy is infrequent. Evolutionary situations among parasites and among cave inhabitants are clearly different from those in free-living forms. Detection and analysis of differences in the evolutionary patterns in different organisms is one of the important tasks of modern evolutionists.

It can scarcely be doubted that man's biological heredity is transmitted by mechanisms similar to those encountered in other animals and in plants. Likewise, there is no reason to believe that the evolutionary development of man has involved causative factors other than those operative in the evolution of other organisms. The evolutionary changes that occurred before the pre-human could become human, as well as those which supervened since the attainment of the human estate, can be described causally only in terms of mutation, selection, genetic drift, and hybridization—familiar processes throughout the living world. This reasoning, indisputable in the purely biological context, becomes a fallacy, however, when used, as it often has been, to justify narrow biologism in dealing with human material.

The specific human features of the evolutionary pattern of man cannot be ignored. Man is a unique product of evolution in that he, far more than any other creature, has escaped from the bondage of the physical and the biological into the multiform social environment. This remarkable development introduces a third dimension in addition to those of the external and internal environments—a dimension which many biologists, in considering the evolution of man, tend to neglect. The most important setting of human evolution is the human social environment. As stated above, this can influence evolutionary changes only through the media of mutation, selection, genetic drift, and hybridization. Nevertheless, there can be no genuine clarity in our understanding of man's biological nature until the role of the social factor in the development of the human species is understood. A biologist approaching the problems of human evolution must never lose sight of the truth stated more than 2,000 years ago by Aristotle: "Man is by nature a political animal."

In the words of Fisher, "For rational systems of evolution, that is, for theories which make at least the most familiar facts intelligible to the reason, we must turn to those that make progressive adaptation the driving force of the process." It is evident that man by means of his reasoning abilities, by becoming a "political animal," has achieved a mastery of the world's varying environments quite unprecedented in the history of organic evolution. The system of genes which has permitted the development of the specifically human mental capacities has thus become the foundation and the paramount influence in all subsequent evolution of the human stock. An animal becomes adapted to its environment by evolving certain genetically determined physical and behavioral traits; the adaptation of man consists chiefly in developing his inventiveness, a quality to which his physical heredity predisposes him and which his social heredity provides him with the means of realizing. To the degree to which this is so, man is unique. As far as his physical responses to the world are concerned, he is almost wholly emancipated from dependence upon inherited biological dispositions, uniquely improving upon the latter by the process of learning that which his social heredity (culture) makes available to him. Man possesses much more efficient means of achieving immediate or long-term adaptation than any other biological species: namely, through learned responses or novel inventions and improvisations.

In general, two types of biological adaptation in evolution can be distinguished. One is genetic specialization and genetically controlled fixity of traits. The second consists in the ability to respond to a given range of environmental situations by evolving traits favorable in these particular situations; this presupposes genetically controlled plasticity of traits. It is known, for example, that the composition of the blood which is most favorable for life at high altitudes is somewhat different from that which suffices at sea level. A species which ranges from sea level to high altitudes on a mountain range may become differentiated into several altitudinal races, each having a fixed blood composition favored by natural selection at the particular altitude at which it lives; or a genotype may be selected which permits an individual to respond to changes in the atmospheric pressure by definite alterations in the composition of the blood. It is well known that heredity determines in its possessor not the presence or absence of certain traits but, rather, the responses of the organisms to its environments. The responses may be more or less rigidly fixed, so that approximately the same traits develop in all environments in which life is possible. On the other hand, the responses may differ in different environments. Fixity or plasticity of a trait is, therefore, genetically controlled.

Whether the evolutionary adaptation in a given phyletic line will occur chiefly by way of genetic fixity or by way of genetically controlled plasticity of traits will depend on circumstances. In the first place, evolutionary changes are compounded by mutational steps, and consequently the kind of change that takes place is always determined by the composition of the store of mutational variability which happens to be available in the species populations. Secondly, fixity or plasticity of traits is controlled by natural selection. Having a trait fixed by heredity and hence appearing in the development of an individual regardless of environmental variations is, in general, of benefit to organisms whose milieu remains uniform and static except for rare and freakish deviations. Conversely, organisms which inhabit changeable environments are benefited by having their traits plastic and modified by each recurrent configuration of environmental agents in a way most favorable for the survival of the carrier of the trait in question.

Comparative anatomy and embryology show that a fairly general trend in organic evolution seems to be from environmental dependence toward fixation of the basic features of the bodily structure and function. The appearance of these structural features in the embryonic development of higher organisms is, in general, more nearly autonomous and independent of the environment than in lower forms. The development becomes "buffered" against environmental and genetic shocks. If, however, the mode of life of a species happens to be such that it is, of necessity, exposed to a wide range of environments, it becomes desirable to vary some structures and functions in accordance with the circumstances that confront an individual or a strain at a given time and place. Genetic structures which permit adaptive plasticity of traits become, then, obviously advantageous for survival and so are fostered by natural selection.

The social environments that human beings have created everywhere are notable not only for their extreme complexity but also for the rapid changes to which immediate adjustment is demanded. Adjustment occurs chiefly in the psychical realm and has little or nothing to do with physical traits. In view of the fact that from the very beginning of human evolution the changes in the human environment have been not only rapid but diverse and manifold, genetic fixation of behavioral traits in man would have been decidedly unfavorable for survival of individuals as well as of the species as a whole. Success of the individual in most human societies has depended and continues to depend upon his ability rapidly to evolve behavior patterns which fit him to the kaleidoscope of the conditions he encounters. He is best off if he submits to some, compromises with some, rebels against others, and escapes from still other situations. Individuals who display a relatively greater fixity of response than their fellows suffer under most forms of human society and tend to fall by the way. Suppleness, plasticity, and, most important of all, ability to profit by experience and education are required. No other species is comparable to man in its capacity to acquire new behavior patterns and discard old ones in consequence of training. Considered socially as well as biologically, man's outstanding capacity is his educability. The survival value of this capacity is manifest, and therefore the possibility of its development through natural selection is evident.

It should be made clear at this point that the replacement of fixity of behavior by genetically controlled plasticity is not a necessary consequence of all forms of social organization. The quaint attempts to glorify insect societies as examples deserving emulation on the part of man ignore the fact that the behavior of an individual among social insects is remarkable precisely because of the rigidity of its genetic fixation. The perfection of the organized societies of ants, termites, bees, and other insects is indeed wonderful, and the activities of their members may strike an observer very forcibly by their objective purposefulness. This purposefulness is retained, however, only in environments in which the species normally lives. The ability of an ant to adjust its activities to situations not encountered in the normal habitats of its species is very limited. On the other hand, social organizations on the human level are built on the principle that an individual is able to alter his behavior to fit any situation, whether previously experienced or new.

This difference between human and insect societies is, of course, not surprising. Adaptive plasticity of behavior can develop only on the basis of a vastly more complex nervous system than is sufficient for adaptive fixity. The genetic differences between human and insect societies furnish a striking illustration of the two types of evolutionary adaptations—those achieved through genetically controlled plasticity of behavioral traits and those attained through genetic specialization and fixation of behavior.

The genetically controlled plasticity of mental traits is, biologically speaking, the most typical and uniquely human characteristic. It is very probable that the survival value of this characteristic in human evolution has been considerable for a long time, as measured in terms of human historical scales. Just when this characteristic first appeared is, of course, conjectural. Here it is of interest to note that the most marked phylogenetic trend in the evolution of man has been the special development of the brain, and that the characteristic human plasticity of mental traits seems to be associated with the exceptionally large brain size. The brain of, for example, the Lower or Middle Pleistocene fossil forms of man was, grossly at least, scarcely distinguishable from that of modern man. The average Neanderthaloid brain was somewhat larger than that of modern man, though slightly different in shape. More important than the evidence derived from brain size is the testimony of cultural development. The Middle Acheulean handiwork of Swanscombe man of several hundred thousand years ago and the beautiful Mousterian cultural artifacts associated with Neanderthal man indicate the existence of minds of a high order of development.

The cultural evidence thus suggests that the essentially human organization of the mental capacities emerged quite early in the evolution of man. However that may be, the possession of the gene system, which conditions educability rather than behavioral fixity, is a common property of all living mankind. In other words, educability is truly a species character of man, *Homo sapiens*. This does not mean, of course, that the evolutionary process has run its course and that natural selection has introduced no changes in the genetic structure of the human species since the attainment of the human status. Nor do we wish to imply that no genetic variations in mental equipment exist at our time level. On the contrary, it seems likely that with the attainment of human status that part of man's genetic system which is related to mental potentialities did not cease to be labile and subject to change.

This brings us face to face with the old problem of the likelihood that significant genetic differences in the mental capacities of the various ethnic groups of mankind exist. The physical and, even more, the social environments of men who live in different countries are quite diversified. Therefore, it has often been argued, natural selection would be expected to differentiate the human species into local races differing in psychic traits. Populations of different countries may differ in skin color, head shape, and other somatic characters. Why, then, should they be alike in mental traits?

It will be through investigation rather than speculation that the problem of the possible existence of average differences in the mental make-up of human populations of different geographical origins will eventually be settled. Arguments based on analogies are precarious, especially where evolutionary patterns are concerned. If human races differ in structural traits, it does not necessarily follow that they must also differ in mental ones. Race differences arise chiefly because of the differential action of natural selection on geographically separated populations. In the case of man, however, the structural and mental traits are quite likely to be influenced by selection in different ways.

The very complex problem of the origin of racial differentiations in structural traits does not directly concern us here. Suffice it to say that racial differences in traits such as the blood groups may conceivably have been brought about by genetic drift in populations of limited effective size. Other racial traits are genetically too complex and too consistently present in populations of some large territories and absent in other territories to be accounted for by genetic drift alone. Differences in skin color, hair form, nose shape, etc. are almost certainly products of natural selection. The lack of reliable knowledge of the adaptive significance of these traits is perhaps the greatest gap in our understanding of the evolutionary biology of man. Nevertheless, it is at least a plausible working hypothesis that these and similar traits have, or at any rate had in the past, differential survival values in the environments of different parts of the world.

By contrast, the survival value of a higher development of mental capacities in man is obvious. Furthermore, natural selection seemingly favors such a development everywhere. In the ordinary course of events in almost all societies those persons are likely to be favored who show wisdom, maturity of judgment, and ability to get along with people—qualities which may assume different forms in different cultures. Those are the qualities of the plastic personality, not a single trait but a general condition, and this is the condition which appears to have been at a premium in practically all human societies.

In human societies conditions have been neither rigid nor stable enough to permit the selective breeding of genetic types adapted to different statuses or forms of social organization. Such rigidity and stability do not obtain in any society. On the other hand, the outstanding fact about human societies is that they do change and do so more or less rapidly. The rate of change was possibly comparatively slow in earlier societies, as the rate of change in present-day nonliterate societies may be, when compared to the rate characterizing occidental societies. In any event, rapid changes in behavior are demanded of the person at all levels of social organization even when the society is at its most stable. Life at any level of social development in human societies is a pretty complex business, and it is met and handled most efficiently by those who exhibit the greatest capacity for adaptability, plasticity.

It is this very plasticity of his mental traits which confers upon man the unique position which he occupies in the animal kingdom. Its acquisition freed him from the constraint of a limited range of biologically predetermined responses. He became capable of acting in a more or less regulative manner upon his physical environment instead of being largely regulated by it. The process of natural selection in all climes and at all times have favored genotypes which permit greater and greater educability and plasticity of mental traits under the influence of the uniquely social environments to which man has been continuously exposed.

The effect of natural selection in man has probably been to render genotypic differences in personality traits, as between individuals and particularly as between races, relatively unimportant compared to their phenotypic plasticity. Instead of having his responses genetically fixed as in other animal species, man is a species that invents its own responses, and it is out of this unique ability to invent, to improvise, his responses that his cultures are born.

LESLIE WHITE ON THE CONCEPT OF CULTURE[1]

LESLIE A. WHITE (1900-   ), American anthropologist, for many years Professor of Anthropology at the University of Michigan, in this essay provides one of the most cogent clarifications of the meaning of the anthropological concept of culture to be found in any language. It is reprinted not alone for this reason, but also because it has had a considerable influence upon most thinkers in this field, and because it will always remain one of the most readable and helpful elucidations of the most fundamental of all anthropological concepts.[1]

---

[1]See also White's *The Study of Culture: A Study of Man and Civilization* (New York, Farrar, Straus & Co., 1949), and his *The Evolution of Culture: The Development of Civilization to the Fall of Rome* (New York, McGraw-Hill Book Co., 1959).

THE CONCEPT OF CULTURE*
LESLIE A. WHITE

Virtually all cultural anthropologists take it for granted, no doubt, that *culture* is the basic and central concept of their science. There is, however, a disturbing lack of agreement as to what they mean by this term. To some, culture is learned behavior. To others, it is not behavior at all, but an abstraction from behavior—whatever that is. Stone axes and pottery bowls are culture to some anthropologists, but no material object can be culture to others. Culture exists only in the mind, according to some; it consists of observable things and events in the external world to others. Some anthropologists think of culture as consisting of ideas, but they are divided upon the question of their locus: some say they are in the minds of the peoples studied, others hold that they are in the minds of ethnologists. We go on to "culture in a psychic defense mechanism," "culture consists of *n* different social signals correlated with *m* different responses," "culture is a Rohrschach of a society," and so on, to confusion and bewilderment. One wonders what physics would be like if it had as many and as varied conceptions of energy!

There was a time, however, when there was a high degree of uniformity of comprehension and use of the term culture. During the closing decades of the nineteenth century and the early years of the twentieth, the great majority of cultural anthropologists, we believe, held to the conception expressed by E. B. Tylor, in 1871, in the opening lines of *Primitive Culture*: "Culture . . . is that complex whole which includes knowledge, belief, art, morals, law, custom, and any other capabilities and habits acquired by man as a member of society." Tylor does not make it explicit in this statement that culture is the peculiar possession of man; but it is therein implied, and in other places he makes this point clear and explicit (Tylor 1881:54, 123, where he deals with the "great mental gap between us and the animals"). Culture, to Tylor, was the name of all things and events peculiar to the human species. Specifically, he enumerates beliefs, customs, objects—"hatchet, adze, chisel," and so on—and techniques—"wood-chopping, fishing. . . , shooting and spearing game, fire-making," and so on (Tylor 1913:5-6).

The Tylorian conception of culture prevailed in anthropology generally for decades. In 1920, Robert H. Lowie began *Primitive Society* by quoting "Tylor's famous definition." In recent years, however, conceptions and definitions of culture have multiplied and varied to a great degree. One of the most highly favored of these is that *culture is an abstraction*. This is the conclusion reached by Kroeber and Kluckhohn in their exhaustive review of the subject:

*Reproduced by permission of the American Anthropological Association from *American Anthropologist*, 61 (2), 1959, pp. 227-51.

Culture: a Critical Review of Concepts and History (1952:155, 169). It is the definition given by Beals and Hoijer in their textbook, *An Introduction to Anthropology* (1953:210, 219, 507, 535). In a more recent work, however, *Cultural Anthropology* (1958:16, 427), Felix M. Keesing defines culture as "the totality of learned, socially transmitted behavior."

Much of the discussion of the concept of culture in recent years has been concerned with a distinction between culture and human behavior. For a long time many anthropologists were quite content to define culture as behavior, peculiar to the human species, acquired by learning, and transmitted from one individual, group, or generation to another by mechanisms of social inheritance. But eventually some began to object to this and to make the point that culture is not itself behavior, but is an abstraction from behavior. Culture, say Kroeber and Kluckhohn (1952:155), "is an abstraction from concrete human behavior, but it is not itself behavior." Beals and Hoijer (1953:210, 219) and others take the same view.[1]

Those who define culture as an abstraction do not tell us what they mean by this term. They appear to take it for granted (1) that they themselves know what they mean by "abstraction," and (2) that others, also, will understand. We believe that neither of these suppositions is well founded; we shall return to a consideration of this concept later in this essay. But whatever an abstraction in general may be to these anthropologists, when culture becomes an "abstraction" it becomes imperceptible, imponderable, and not wholly real. According to Linton, "culture itself is intangible and cannot be directly apprehended even by the individuals who participate in it" (1936:288-89). Herskovits also calls culture "intangible" (1945:150). Anthropologists in the imaginary symposium reported by Kluckhohn and Kelly (1945:79, 81) argue that "one can see" such things as individuals and their actions and interactions, but "has anyone ever seen 'culture'?" Beals and Hoijer (1953:210) say that "the anthropologist cannot observe culture directly; . . ."

If culture as an abstraction is intangible, imperceptible, does it exist, is it real? Ralph Linton (1936:363) raises this question in all seriousness: "If it [culture] can be said to exist at all. . . ." Radcliffe-Brown (1940:2) declares that the word culture "denotes, not any concrete reality, but an abstraction, and as it is commonly used a vague abstraction." And Spiro (1951:24) says that according to the predominant "position of contemporary anthropology . . . culture has no ontological reality. . . ."

Thus when culture becomes an abstraction it not only becomes invisible and imponderable; it virtually ceases to exist. It would be difficult to construct a less adequate conception of culture. Why, then, have prominent and influential anthropologists turned to the "abstraction" conception of culture?

[1] One of the earliest instances of regarding culture as an abstraction is Murdock's statement: "realizing that culture is merely an abstraction from observed likenesses in the behavior of individuals . . ." (1937:xi).

A clue to the reason—if, indeed, it is not an implicit statement of the reason itself—is given by Kroeber and Kluckhohn (1952:155):

> Since behavior is the first-hand and outright material of the science of psychology, and culture is not—being of concern only secondarily, as an influence on this material—it is natural that psychologists and psychologizing sociologists should see behavior as primary in their field, and then extend this view farther to apply to the field of culture also.

The reasoning is simple and direct: if culture is behavior, then (1) culture becomes the subject matter of psychology, since behavior is the proper subject matter of psychology; culture would then become the property of psychologists and "psychologizing sociologists"; and (2) nonbiological anthropology would be left without a subject matter. The danger was real and imminent; the situation, critical. What was to be done?

The solution proposed by Kroeber and Kluckhohn was neat and simple: let the psychologists have behavior; anthropologists will keep for themselves abstractions from behavior. These abstractions become and constitute *culture*.

But in this rendering unto Caesar, anthropologists have given the psychologists the better part of the bargain, for they have surrendered unto them real things and events, locatable and observable, directly or indirectly, in the real external world, in terrestrial time and space, and have kept for themselves only intangible, imponderable abstractions that "have no ontological reality." But at least, and at last, they have a subject matter—however insubstantial and unobservable—of their own!

Whether or not this has been the principal reason for defining culture as "not behavior, but abstractions from behavior," is perhaps a question; we feel, however, that Kroeber and Kluckhohn have made themselves fairly clear. But whatever the reason, or reasons—for there may have been several—may have been for the distinction, the question whether culture is to be regarded as behavior or as abstractions from it is, we believe, the central issue in recent attempts to hammer out an adequate, usable, fruitful, and enduring conception of culture.

The present writer is no more inclined to surrender culture to the psychologists than are Kroeber and Kluckhohn; indeed, few anthropologists have taken greater pains to distinguish psychological problems from culturological problems than he has.[2] But he does not wish to exchange the hard substance of culture for its wraith, either. No science can have a subject matter that consists

---

[2] Several of the essays in *The Science of Culture* (1949)—"Culturological vs. Psychological Interpretations of Human Behavior," "Cultural Determinants of *Mind*," "Genius: Its Causes and Incidence," "Ikhnaton: The Great Man vs. the Culture Process," "The Definition and Prohibition of Incest," etc.—deal with this distinction.

of intangible, invisible, imponderable, ontologically unreal "abstractions"; a science must have real stars, real mammals, foxes, crystals, cells, phonemes, gamma rays, and culture traits to work with.[3] We believe that we can offer an analysis of the situation that will distinguish between psychology, the scientific study of behavior on the one hand, and culturology, the scientific study of culture, on the other, and at the same time give a real, substantial subject matter to each.

Science makes a dichotomy between the mind of the observer and the external world[4]—things and events having their locus outside the mind of this observer. The scientist makes contact with the external world with and through his senses, forming percepts. These percepts are translated into concepts which are manipulated in a process called thinking[5] in such a way as to form premises, propositions, generalizations, conclusions, and so on. The validity of these premises, propositions, and conclusions is established by testing them in terms of experience of the external world (Einstein 1936:350). This is the way science proceeds and does its work.

The first step in scientific procedure is to observe, or more generally to experience, the external world in a sensory manner. The next step—after percepts have been translated into concepts—is the classification of things and events perceived or experienced. Things and events of the external world are thus divided into classes of various kinds: acids, metals, stones, liquids, mammals, stars, atoms, corpuscles, and so on. Now it turns out that there is a class of phenomena, one of enormous importance in the study of man, for which science has as yet no name: this is the class of things and events consisting of or dependent upon symboling.[6] It is one of the most remarkable facts

[3] I made this point in my review of Kroeber and Kluckhohn, "Culture: a Critical Review etc." (1954:464-65). At about the same time Huxley was writing (1955:15-16): "If anthropology is a science, then for anthropologists culture must be defined, not philosophically or metaphysically, nor as an abstraction, nor in purely subjective terms, but as something which can be investigated by the methods of scientific inquiry, a phenomenal process occurring in space and time."

[4] "The belief in an external world independent of the perceiving subject is the basis of all natural science," says Einstein (1934:6).

[5] Thinking, in science, means "operations with concepts, and the creation and use of definite functional relations between them, and the co-ordination of sense experiences to these concepts," according to Einstein (1936:350). Einstein has much to say in this essay about the manner and process of scientific thinking.

[6] By "symboling" we mean bestowing meaning upon a thing or an act, or grasping and appreciating meanings thus bestowed. Holy water is a good example of such meanings. The attribute of holiness is bestowed upon the water by a human being, and it may be comprehended and appreciated by other human beings. Articulate speech is the most characteristic and important form of symboling. Symboling is trafficking in nonsensory meanings, i.e., meanings which, like the holiness of sacramental water, cannot be comprehended with the senses alone. Symboling is a kind of behavior. Only man is capable of symboling.

We have discussed this concept rather fully in "The Symbol: the Origin and Basis of Human Behavior," originally published in The Philosophy of Science, Vol. 7, pp. 451-63, 1940. It has

in the recent history of science that this important class has no name, but the fact remains that it does not. And the reason why it does not is because these things and events have always been considered and designated, not merely and simply as the things and events that they are, in and of themselves, but always as things and events in a particular context.

A thing is what it is; "a rose is a rose is a rose." Acts are not first of all ethical acts or economic acts or erotic acts. An act is an act. An act becomes an ethical datum or an economic datum or an erotic datum when—and only when—it is considered in an ethical, economic, or erotic context. Is a Chinese porcelain vase a scientific specimen, an object of art, an article of commerce, or an exhibit in a lawsuit? The answer is obvious. Acutally, of course, to call it a "Chinese porcelain vase" is already to put it into a particular context; it would be better first of all to say "a glazed form of fired clay is a glazed form of fired clay." As a Chinese porcelain vase, it becomes an object of art, a scientific specimen, or an article of merchandise when, and only when, it is considered in an esthetic, scientific, or commercial context.

Let us return now to the class of things and events that consist of or are dependent upon symboling: a spoken word, a stone axe, a fetich, avoiding one's mother-in-law, loathing milk, saying a prayer, sprinkling holy water, a pottery bowl, casting a vote, remembering the sabbath to keep it holy—"and any other capabilities and habits [and things] acquired by man as a member of [human] society" (Tylor 1913:1). They are what they are: things and acts dependent upon symboling.

We may consider these things-and-events-dependent-upon-symboling in a number of contexts: astronomical, physical, chemical, anatomical, physiological, psychological, and culturological, and, consequently, they become astronomic, physical, chemical, anatomical, physiological, psychological, and culturological phenomena in turn. All things and events dependent upon symboling are dependent also upon solar energy which sustains all life on this planet; this is the astronomic context. These things and events may be considered and interpreted in terms of the anatomical, neurological, and physiological processes of the human beings who exhibit them. They may be considered and interpreted also in terms of their relationship to human organisms, i.e., in a somatic context. And they may be considered in an extrasomatic context, i.e., in terms of their relationship to other like things and events rather than in relationship to human organisms.

When things and events dependent upon symboling are considered and inter-

---

been reprinted in slightly revised form in *The Science of Culture*. It has also been reprinted in Etc., A Review of General Semantics, Vol. 1, pp. 229-37, 1944; *Language, Meaning, and Maturity*, S. I. Hayakawa ed. (New York, 1954); *Readings in Anthropology*, E. Adamson Hoebel et al. eds. (New York, 1955); *Readings in Introductory Anthropology*, Elman R. Service ed. (Ann Arbor, Mich., 1956); *Sociological Theory*, Lewis A. Coser and Bernard Rosenberg eds. (New York, 1957); and in *Readings in the Ways of Mankind*, Walter Goldschmidt ed. (1957).

preted in terms of their relationship to human organisms, i.e., in a somatic context, they may properly be called *human behavior*, and the science, *psychology*. When things and events dependent upon symboling are considered and interpreted in an extrasomatic context, i.e., in terms of their relationships to one another rather than to human organisms, we may call them *culture*, and the science, *culturology*. This analysis is expressed diagrammatically in Fig. 1.

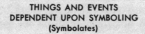

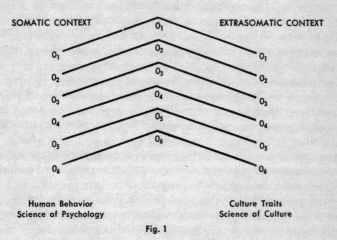

Fig. 1

In the middle of the diagram we have a vertical column of circles, O_1, O_2, O_3, etc., which stand for things (objects) and events (acts) dependent upon symboling. These things and events constitute a distinct class of phenomena in the realm of nature. Since they have had heretofore no name we have ventured to give them one: *symbolates*. We fully appreciate the hazards of coining terms, but this all-important class of phenomena needs a name to distinguish it from other classes. If we were physicists we might call them "Gamma phenomena." But we are not physicists, and we believe a simple word would be better—or at least more acceptable—than a Greek letter. In coining our term we have followed a well-established precedent: if an *isolate* is something that results from the process or action of isolating, then something that results from the action or process of symboling might well be called a symbolate. The particular word with which we designate this class of phenomena is not of paramount importance, and perhaps a better term than symbolate can be found. But it is of paramount importance that this class has a name.

A thing or event dependent upon symboling—a symbolate—is just what it is, but it may become significant in any one of a number of contexts. As we have already seen, it may be significant in an astronomic context: the performance of a ritual requires the expenditure of energy which has come from the sun. But within the sciences of man we may distinguish two significant contexts: the somatic and the extrasomatic. Symbolates may be considered and interpreted in terms of their relationship to the human organism, or they may be considered in terms of their relationships to one another, quite apart from their relationship to the human organism. Let us illustrate with some examples.

I smoke a cigarette, cast a vote, decorate a pottery bowl, avoid my mother-in-law, say a prayer, or chip an arrowhead. Each one of these acts is dependent upon the process of symboling;[7] each therefore is a symbolate. As a scientist, I may consider these acts (events) in terms of their relationships to me, to my organism; or, I may treat them in terms of their relationships to one another, to other symbolates, quite apart from their relationship to my organism.

In the first type of interpretation I consider the symbolate in terms of its relationship to my bodily structure: the structure and functions of my hand, for example; or to my stereoscopic, chromatic vision; or to my needs, desires, hopes, fears, imagination, habit formation, overt reactions, satisfactions, and so forth. How do I feel when I avoid my mother-in-law or cast a ballot? What is my attitude toward the act? What is my conception of it? Is the act accompanied by heightened emotional tone, or do I perform it in a mechanical, perfunctory manner? And so on. We may call these acts *human behavior*; our concern is *psychological*.

What we have said of acts (events) will apply to objects (things) also. What is my conception of a pottery bowl, a ground axe, a crucifix, roast pork, whisky, holy water, cement? What is my attitude and how do I react toward each of these things? In short, what is the nature of the relationship between each of these things and my own organism? We do not customarily call these things human behavior, but they are the embodiments of human behavior; the difference between a nodule of flint and a stone axe is the factor of human labor. An axe, bowl, crucifix—or a haircut—is congealed human labor. We have then a class of objects dependent upon symboling that have a significance in terms of their relationship to the human organism. The scientific consideration and interpretation of this relationship is *psychology*.

But we may treat symbolates in terms of their relationships to one another,

[7]"How is chipping an arrowhead dependent upon symboling?" it might be asked. I have answered this question in "On the Use of Tools by Primates" (Journal of Comparative Psychology, Vol. 34, pp. 369-74, 1942; reprinted in White, *The Science of Culture*; in *Man in Contemporary Society*, prepared by the Contemporary Civilization staff of Columbia University (New York, 1955); and in *Readings in Introductory Anthropology*, E. R. Service ed. (Ann Arbor, Mich., 1956). There is a fundamental difference between the tool process in the human species and the tool process among subhuman primates. This difference is due to symboling.

quite apart from their relationship to the human organism. Thus, in the case of the avoidance of a mother-in-law, we would consider it in terms of its relationship to other symbolates, or symbolate clusters, such as customs of marriage—monogamy, polygyny, polyandry—place of residence of a couple after marriage, division of labor between the sexes, mode of subsistence, domestic architecture, degree of cultural development, etc. Or, if we are concerned with voting we would consider it in terms of forms of political organization (tribal, state), kind of government (democratic, monarchical, fascist); age, sex, or property qualifications; political parties and so on. In this context our symbolates become *culture*—culture traits or trait clusters, i.e., institutions, customs, codes, etc., and the scientific concern is *culturology*.

It would be the same with objects as with acts. If we were concerned with a hoe we would regard it in terms of its relationships to other symbolates in an extrasomatic context: to other instruments employed in subsistence, the digging stick and plow in particular; or to customs of division of labor between the sexes; the stage of cultural development, etc. We would be concerned with the relationship between a digital computer and the degree of development of mathematics, the stage of technological development, division of labor, the social organization within which it is used (corporation, military organization, astronomical laboratory), and so on.

Thus we see that we have two quite different kinds of sciencing[8] with regard to things and events—objects and acts—dependent upon symboling. If we treat them in terms of their relationship to the human organism, i.e., in an organismic, or somatic context, these things and events become *human behavior* and we are doing *psychology*. If, however, we treat them in terms of their relationship to one another, quite apart from their relationship to human organisms, i.e., in an extrasomatic, or extraorganismic, context, the things and events become *culture*—cultural elements or culture traits—and we are doing *culturology*. Human psychology and culturology have the same phenomena as their subject matter: things and events dependent upon symboling (symbolates). The difference between the two sciences derives from the difference between the contexts in which their common subject matter is treated.[9]

The analysis and distinction that we have made with regard to things and events dependent upon symboling in general is precisely like the one that linguists have been making for decades with regard to a particular kind of these things and events, namely, words.

A word is a thing (a sound or combination of sounds, or marks made upon some substance) or an act dependent upon symboling. Words are just what they are: words. But they are significant to scientific students of words in two

---

[8]"Sciencing," too, is a kind of behavior. See our essay, "Science is *Sciencing*" (Philosophy of Science, Vol. 5, pp. 369-89, 1938; reprinted in *The Science of Culture*).

[9]Importance of context may be illustrated by contrasting attitudes toward one and the same class of women: as mothers they are revered; as mothers-in-law, reviled.

different contexts: somatic or organismic, and extrasomatic or extraorganismic. This distinction has been expressed customarily with the terms *la langue* and *la parole*, or language and speech.[10]

Words in a somatic context constitute a kind of human behavior: speech behavior. The scientific study of words in a somatic context is the psychology (plus physiology, perhaps, and anatomy) of speech. It is concerned with the relationship between words and the human organism: how the words are produced and uttered, the meanings of words, attitudes toward words, perception of and response to words, and so on.

In the extrasomatic context, words are considered in terms of their relationships to one another, quite apart from their relationship to the human organism. The scientific concern here is linguistics, or the science of language. Phonetics, phonemics, syntax, lexicon, grammar, dialectic variation, evolution or historical change, etc., indicate particular focuses, or emphases, within the science of linguistics.

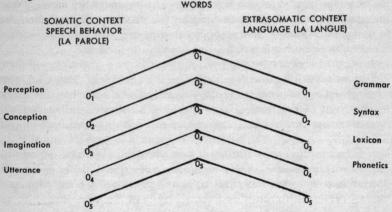

WORDS

SOMATIC CONTEXT SPEECH BEHAVIOR (LA PAROLE)

EXTRASOMATIC CONTEXT LANGUAGE (LA LANGUE)

Perception — O_1 — O_1 — Grammar

Conception — O_2 — O_2 — Syntax

Imagination — O_3 — O_3 — Lexicon

Utterance — O_4 — O_4 — Phonetics

The difference between these two sciences may be illustrated by citing two books: *The Psychology of Language* by Walter B. Pillsbury and Clarence L. Meader (New York, 1928), and *Language* by Leonard Boomfield (New York, 1933). In the former we find chapter titles such as "The Speech Organs," "The Senses Involved in Speech," "Mental Processes in Speech," etc. In

[10]"According to [Ferdinand] de Sassure the study of human speech is not the subject matter of *one* science but of two sciences. . . . De Sassure drew a sharp line between *la langue* and *la parole*. Language (*la langue*) is universal, whereas the process of speech (*la parole*) . . . is individual" (Cassirer 1944:122). Huxley (1955:16), citing Cassirer's discussion of de Sassure's distinction between *la langue* and *la parole*, speaks of the former as "the super-individual system of grammar and syntax," and of the latter as "the actual words or way of speaking used by particular individuals." He goes on to say that "we find the *same distinction in every cultural activity*—in law, . . . ; in art . . . in social structure. . . ; in science . . ." (emphasis ours).

the latter the chapter headings are "The Phoneme," "Phonetic Structure," "Grammatical Forms," "Sentence-Types," etc. We illustrate the distinction between these two sciences in Fig. 2.

Figures 1 and 2 are fundamentally alike. In each case we are concerned with a class of things and events dependent upon symboling. In Fig. 1, we are concerned with a general class: symbolates; in Fig. 2 we are dealing with a particular class: words (a subclass of the class symbolates). In each case we refer the things and events to a somatic context on the one hand, and to an extrasomatic context on the other, for purposes of consideration and interpretation. And in each case we have two distinct kinds of science, or sciencing: the psychology of human behavior or of speech; and the science of culture or of language.

Culture, then, is a class of things and events, dependent upon symboling, considered in an extrasomatic context. This definition rescues cultural anthropology from intangible, imperceptible, and ontologically unreal abstractions and provides it with a real, substantial, observable subject matter. And it distinguishes sharply between behavior—behaving organisms—and culture; between the science of psychology and the science of culture.

It might be objected that every science should have a certain class of things per se as its subject matter, not things-in-a-certain-context. Atoms are atoms and mammals are mammals, it might be argued, and as such are the subject matter of physics and mammalogy, respectively, regardless of context. Why therefore should cultural anthropology have its subject matter defined in terms of things in context rather than in terms of things in themselves? At first glance this argument might appear to be a cogent one, but actually it has but little force. What the scientist wants to do is to make intelligible the phenomena that confront him. And very frequently the significant thing about phenomena is the context in which they are found. Even in the so-called natural sciences we have a science of organisms-in-a-certain-context: parasitology, a science of organisms playing a certain role in the realm of living things. And within the realm of man-and-culture we have dozens of examples of things and events whose significance depends upon context rather than upon the inherent qualities of the phenomena themselves. An adult male of a certain animal species is called a man. But a man is a man, not a slave; a man becomes a slave only when he enters a certain context. So it is with commodities: corn and cotton are articles of use-value, but they were not commodities—articles produced for sale at a profit—in aboriginal Hopi culture; corn and cotton become commodities only when they enter a certain socioeconomic context. A cow is a cow, but she may become a medium of exchange, money (*pecus*, pecuniary) in one context, food in another, mechanical power (Cartwright used a cow as motive power for his first power loom) in another, and a sacred object of worship (India) in still another. We do not have a science of cows, but we do have scientific studies of mediums of exchange, of mechanical power, and of sacred objects in each of which cows may be significant. And so we have a science of symboled things and events in an extrasomatic context.

If we define culture as consisting of real things and events observable, directly or indirectly, in the external world, where do these things and events exist and have their being? What is the locus of culture? The answer is: the things and events that comprise culture have their existence, in space and time, (1) within human organisms, i.e., concepts, beliefs, emotions, attitudes; (2) within processes of social interaction among human beings; and (3) within material objects (axes, factories, railroads, pottery bowls) lying outside human organisms but within the patterns of social interaction among them.[11] The locus of culture is thus intraorganismal, interorganismal, and extraorganismal (see Fig. 3).

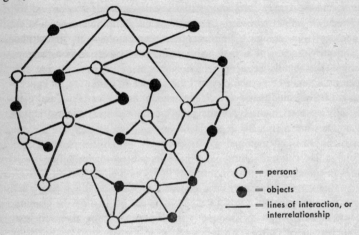

O = persons

● = objects

—— = lines of interaction, or interrelationship

Fig. 3 The locus of culture.

But, someone might object, you have said that culture consists of extrasomatic phenomena and now you tell me that culture exists, in part, within human organisms. Is this not a contradiction? The answer is, No, it is not a contradiction; it is a misunderstanding. We did not say that culture consists of extrasomatic things and events, i.e., phenomena whose locus is outside human organisms. What we said is that culture consists of things and events considered within an extrasomatic context. This is quite a different thing.

Every cultural element has two aspects: subjective and objective. It might

[11]"The true locus of culture," says Sapir (1932:236), "is in the interactions of . . . individuals and, on the subjective side, in the world of meanings which each one of these individuals may unconsciously abstract for himself from his participation in these interactions." This statement is like ours except that it omits objects: material culture.

appear that stone axes are "objective," and ideas and attitudes are "subjective." But this is a superficial and inadequate view. An axe has a subjective component; it would be meaningless without a concept and an attitude. On the other hand, a concept or an attitude would be meaningless without overt expression, in behavior or speech (which is a form of behavior). Every cultural element, every culture trait, therefore, has a subjective and an objective aspect. But conceptions, attitudes, and sentiments—phenomena that have their locus within the human organism—may be considered for purposes of scientific interpretation in an extrasomatic context, i.e., in terms of their relation to other symboled things and events rather than in terms of their relationship to the human organism. Thus, we may consider the subjective aspect of the mother-in-law taboo, i.e., the conceptions and attitudes involved, in terms of their relationship, not to the human organism, but to other symbolates such as forms of marriage and the family, place of residence after marriage, and so on. On the other hand, we may consider the axe in terms of its relationship to the human organism—its meaning; the person's conception of it; his attitude toward it—rather than to other symboled things and events such as arrows, hoes, and customs regulating the division of labor in society.

We shall now pass in review a number of conceptions of culture, or conceptions with regard to culture, widely current in ethnological literature, and comment critically upon each one from the standpoint of the conception of culture set forth in this paper.

Culture Consists of Ideas

Some anthropologists like to define culture in terms of ideas only. The reason for this, apparently, is the notion that ideas are both basic and primary, that they are prime movers and as such originate behavior which in turn may produce objects such as pottery bowls. "Culture consists of ideas," says Taylor (1948:98-110, passim), it "is a mental phenomenon . . . not . . . material objects or observable behavior. . . . For example, there is present in an Indian's mind the idea of a dance. This is the trait of culture. This idea influences his body so that he behaves in a certain way," i.e., he dances.

This conception of sociocultural reality is a naive one. It is based upon a primitive, prescientific, and now obsolete metaphysics and psychology. It was Thought-Woman among the Keresan Pueblo Indians who brought about events by thinking and willing them to happen. Ptah created Egyptian culture by objectifying his thoughts. And God said "Let there be light," and there was light. But we no longer explain the origin and development of culture by simply saying that it has resulted from man's ideas. To be sure, an idea was involved in the invention of firearms, but we have explained nothing when we say that firearms are the fruit of thought, because the ideas themselves have not been accounted for. Why did the idea occur when and where it did rather than at some other time and place? And, actually, ideas—matter of fact, realistic ideas—enter the mind from the outside world. It was working with soils that gave man, or woman, the idea of pottery; the calendar is a by-product of intensive agriculture. Culture does indeed consist in part of ideas; but attitudes, overt acts, and objects are culture, also.

We return now to the presently popular definition: "culture is an abstraction, or consists of abstractions." As we observed earlier, those who define culture in these terms do not tell us what they mean by "abstraction," and there is reason to believe that they are not very clear as to what they do mean by it. They make it emphatically clear, however, that an abstraction is not an observable thing or event. The fact that doubts have been raised as to the "reality" of an abstraction indicates that those who use this term are not sure what "it means," i.e., what they mean by it. We do have some clues, however.

Culture is "basically a form or pattern or way," say Kroeber and Kluckhohn (1952:155, 169), "even a culture trait is an abstraction. A trait is an 'ideal type' because no two pots are identical nor are two marriage ceremonies ever held in precisely the same way." The culture trait "pot" therefore appears to be the ideal form of which each particular pot is an exemplification—a sort of Platonic idea, or ideal. Each and every pot, they reason, is real; but the "ideal" is never realized in any particular pot. It is like the "typical American man": 5'8-1/2" high, weighs 164.378 pounds, is married, has 2.3 children, and so on. This is, we suppose, what they mean by an abstraction. If so, we know it well: it is a conception in the mind of the observer, the scientist.

There is a slightly different way of looking at an "abstraction." No two marriage ceremonies are ever held in precisely the same way. Well, let us tabulate a large sample of marriage ceremonies. We find that 100 percent contain element a (mutual acceptance of spouses). Ninety-nine percent contain element b. Elements c, d, and e appear in only 96, 94, and 89 percent, respectively, of the cases. We construct a distribution curve and determine an average or norm about which all particular instances are distributed. This is the typical marriage ceremony. But, like the typical American who has 2.3 children, this ideal is never fully and perfectly realized in any actual instance. It is an "abstraction," that is, a conception, worked out by the scientific observer and which exists in his own mind.

The failure to recognize the fact that abstractions are conceptions has led to confusion both as to their locus and their reality. Recognition of the fact that the so-called abstractions of science (such as a "rigid body" in physical theory; rigid bodies do not exist in actuality) are conceptions in the mind of the scientist clears up both these points: cultural "abstractions" are conceptions ("ideas") in the mind of the anthropologist. And as for their "ontological reality," conceptions are none the less real for being in the minds of men—nothing is more real, for example, than an hallucination.

This point was well made by Bidney (1954:488-89) in his review of *Culture, a Critical Review etc.*:

> The real crux of the problem centers about what is meant by abstraction and what is its ontological import. Some anthropologists maintain that they are dealing only with logical abstractions and that culture has no reality other than that of an abstraction, but they can hardly expect other social scientists to agree with them, conceding that the objects of their sciences have no ontological, objective reality. *Thus Kroeber and Kluckhohn have confused the concept culture, which is a logical construct, with the actual existential culture* . . . [emphasis ours].

It is interesting to note in this connection that one anthropological theorist, Cornelius Osgood (1951:208; 1940), has defined culture explicitly as consisting of ideas in the minds of anthropologists: "Culture consists of all ideas of the manufactures, behavior, and ideas of the aggregate of human beings which have been directly observed or communicated to one's mind and of which one is conscious." Spiro (1951:24), also, holds that "culture is a logical construct, abstracted from human behavior, and as such, it exists only in the mind of *the investigator*" (Spiro's emphasis).

There Is No Such Thing As "Material" Culture

Those who define culture in terms of ideas, or as an abstraction, or as behavior, find themselves obliged logically to declare that material objects are not, and cannot be, culture. "Strictly speaking," says Hoebel (1956:176), "material culture is really not culture at all." Taylor (1948:102, 98) goes farther: ". . . the concept of 'material culture' is fallacious" because "culture is a mental phenomenon." Beals and Hoijer (1953:210): ". . . culture is an abstraction from behavior and not to be confused with acts of behavior or with material artifacts, such as tools. . . ." This denial of material culture is rather awkward in view of the long established tradition among ethnographers, archeologists, and museum curators of calling tools, masks, fetiches, and so on, "material culture."[12]

Our definition extricates us from this dilemma. As we have already seen, it would not be absurd to speak of sandals or pottery bowls as behavior; their significant attribute is not mere deer hide or clay, but human labor; they are

[12]It is interesting to note that Durkheim (1951:313-14), who uses the term "society" when many an American anthropologist would say culture, or sociocultural system, remarks that "it is not true that society is made up only of individuals; it also includes material things, which play an essential role in the common life." He cites as examples such things as houses, instruments and machines used in industry, etc. "Social life . . . is thus crystallized . . . and fixed on material supports . . . externalized. . . ."

congelations of human labor. But in our definition, symboling is the common factor in ideas, attitudes, acts, and objects. There are three kinds of symbolates: (1) ideas and attitudes, (2) overt acts, and (3) material objects. All may be considered in an extrasomatic context; all are to be reckoned as culture. This conception brings us back to long established usage in cultural anthropology: "Culture is that which is described in an ethnographic monograph."

Reification of Culture

There is a kind of conception of culture held by some anthropologists that is much deplored by others who call it "reification." As one who has been especially singled out as a "reifier" of culture,[13] I may say that the term is singularly inappropriate. To reify is to make a thing of that which is not a thing, such as hope, honesty, or freedom. But it is not I who have made culture things. I have merely found real things and events in the external world which are distinguishable as a class by being dependent upon symboling, and which may be treated in an extrasomatic context, and I have called these things and events culture. This is precisely what E. B. Tylor did. It is what Lowie, Wissler, and most early American anthropologists have done. To Durkheim (1938:xliii) "the proposition which states that social facts [i.e., culture traits] are to be treated as things" lay "at the very basis of our method." It is not we who have reified culture; the elements comprising culture, according to our definition, were things to start with.

To be sure, if culture is defined as consisting of intangible, imponderable, ontologically unreal "abstractions," then to transform these wraiths into real, substantial bodies would indeed be to reify them. But we do not subscribe to such a definition.

Culture: A Process Sui Generis

"Culture is a thing *sui generis* . . ." said Lowie many years ago (1917:66, 17). This view has been held also by Kroeber, Durkheim, and others (for citation of examples see White 1949:89-94). It has been misunderstood and opposed by many. But what Lowie meant by this statement is made clear in the rest of the passage cited above (1917:66): "Culture is a thing *sui generis* which can be explained only in terms of itself . . . the ethnologist . . . will account for a given cultural fact by merging it in a group of cultural facts or by demonstrating some other cultural fact out of which it has been developed." For example, the custom of reckoning descent patrilineally may be explained in terms of customs of division of labor between the sexes, cus-

---

[13]Max Gluckman "reifies structure in precisely the way that White reifies culture . . ." says Murdock (1951:470). Strong (1953:392) feels that "White reifies, and at times almost deifies, culture. . . ." See, also, Herrick 1956:196.

toms of residence—patrilocal, matrilocal, or neolocal—of a married couple; mode of subsistence; rules of inheritance, and so on. Or, to express it in terms of our definition of culture: "a symbolate in an extrasomatic context (i.e., a culture trait) is to be explained in terms of its relationship to other symbolates in the same context."

This conception of culture, like "reification" with which it is closely related, has been much misunderstood and opposed. In general, 'it has been regarded as "mystical." How can culture grow and develop by itself? ("Culture . . . seems to grow of itself"; Redfield 1941:134.) "It seems hardly necessary," says Boas (1928:235), "to consider culture a mystic entity that exists outside the society of its individual carriers, and that moves by its own force." Bidney (1946:535) brands this view of culture as a "mystical metaphysics of fate." And it has been opposed by Benedict (1934:231), Hooton (1939:370), Spiro (1951:23), and others.

But no one has ever said that culture is an entity that exists and moves by, and of, itself, quite apart from people. Nor has anyone ever said, as far as we know, that the origin, nature, and functions of culture can be understood without taking the human species into consideration. Obviously, if one is to understand culture in these aspects he must consider the biological nature of man. What has been asserted is that, given culture, its variations in time and place, and its processes of change are to be explained in terms of culture itself. This is precisely what Lowie meant when he said that "culture is a thing [process would have been a better term] *sui generis*," as the above quotation from him (1917:66) makes clear. A consideration of the human organism, individually or collectively, is irrelevant to an explanation of processes of culture change. "This is not mysticism," says Lowie (1917:66), "but sound scientific method." And, as everyone knows, scholars have been working in accordance with this principle of interpretation for decades. One does not need to take human organisms into account in a scientific explanation of the evolution of currency, writing, or of Gothic art. The steam engine and textile machinery were introduced into Japan during the closing decades of the nineteenth century and certain changes in social structure followed; we add nothing to our explanation of these events by remarking that human beings were involved. Of course they were. And they were not irrelevant to the events which took place, but they are irrelevant to an explanation of these events.

It Is People, Not Culture, That Does Things

"Culture does not 'work,' 'move,' 'change,' but is worked, is moved, is changed. It is people who do things," says Lynd (1939:39). He supports this argument with the bold assertion that "culture does not enamel its fingernails . . . but people do . . ." (ibid.). He might have clinched it by demonstrating that culture has no fingernails.

The view that "it is people, not cultures, that do things" is widely held among anthropologists. Boas (1928:236) tells us that "the forces that bring about the changes are active in the individuals composing the social group, not in the abstract culture." Hallowell (1945:175) remarks that "in a literal sense cultures never have met nor will ever meet. What is meant is that peoples meet and that, as a result of the processes of social interaction, acculturation—modifications in the mode of life of one or both peoples—may take place. Individuals are the dynamic centers of this process of interaction." And Radcliffe-Brown (1940:10-11) pours fine scorn on the notion that cultures, rather than peoples, interact:

> A few years ago, as a result perhaps of re-defining social anthropology as the study, not of society, but of culture, we were asked to abandon this kind of investigation in favor of what is now called the study of "culture contact." In place of the study of the formation of new composite societies, we are supposed to regard what is happening in Africa as a process in which an entity called African culture comes into contact with an entity called European or Western culture, and a third new entity is produced . . . which is to be described as Westernized African culture. To me this seems a fantastic reification of abstractions. European culture is an abstraction and so is the culture of an African tribe. I find it fantastic to imagine these two abstractions coming into contact and by an act of generation producing a third abstraction.

We call this view, that people rather than culture do things, the fallacy of pseudo-realism. Of course culture does not and could not exist independently of people.[14] But, as we have pointed out earlier, cultural processes can be explained without taking human organisms into account; a consideration of human organisms is irrelevant to the solution of certain problems of culture. Whether the practice of mummification in pre-Columbian Peru was indigenous or the result of Egyptian influence is an example of a kind of problem that does not require a consideration of human organisms. To be sure the practice of mummification, its invention in Peru, or its diffusion from Egypt to the Andean highlands, could not have taken place without the action of real, flesh-and-blood human beings. Neither could Einstein have worked out the theory of relativity without breathing, but we do not need to take his respiration into account when we trace the history, or explain the development, of this theory.

Those who argue that it is people, not culture, that do this or that mistake a description of what they see for an explanation of these events. Seated in the Senate gallery they see men making laws; in the shipyards men are building

---

[14]"To be sure, these cultural events could not have taken place had it not been for human organisms . . . the culturologist knows full well that culture traits do not go walking about like disembodied souls interacting with each other . . ." (White, *The Science of Culture*, pp. 99-100).

freighters; in the laboratory human beings are isolating enzymes; in the fields they are planting corn, and so on. And, for them, a description of these events, as they observe them, is a simple explanation of them: it is people who pass laws, build freighters, plant corn, and isolate enzymes. This is a simple and naive form of anthropocentrism.

A scientific explanation is more sophisticated. If a person speaks Chinese, or avoids his mother-in-law, loathes milk, observes matrilocal residence, places the bodies of the dead on scaffolds, writes symphonies, or isolates enzymes, it is because he has been born into, or at least reared within, an extrasomatic tradition that we call culture which contains these elements. A people's behavior is a response to, a function of, their culture. The culture is the independent, the behavior the dependent, variable; as the culture varies so will the behavior. This is, of course, a commonplace that is usually expounded and demonstrated during the first two weeks of an introductory course in anthropology. It is indeed people who treat disease with prayers and charms or with vaccines and antibiotics. But the question, "Why does one people use charms while another uses vaccines?" is not explained by saying that "this people does this, that people does that." It is precisely this proposition that needs to be explained: why do they do what they do? The scientific explanation does not take the people into account at all. And as for the question, Why does one extrasomatic tradition use charms while another uses vaccines, this also is one to which a consideration of people, of human organisms, is irrelevant; it is answered culturologically: culture, as Lowie has observed, is to be explained in terms of culture.

Culture "cannot be realistically disconnected from those organizations of ideas and feelings which constitute the individual," i.e., culture cannot be realistically disconnected from individuals, says Sapir (1932:233). He is quite right, of course; in actuality culture is inseparable from human beings. But if culture cannot be realistically (in actuality) disconnected from individuals it most certainly can be disconnected in logical (scientific) analysis, and no one has done a better job of "disconnecting" than Edward Sapir: there is not a single Indian—or even a nerve, muscle, or sense organ—in his monograph, *Southern Paiute, a Shoshonean Language* (1930). Nor are there any people roaming about in his *Time Perspective in Aboriginal American Culture* (1916). "Science must abstract some elements and neglect others," says Morris Cohen (1931:226) "because *not all things that exist together are relevant to each other*" (emphasis ours). Comprehension and appreciation of this fact would be an enormous asset to ethnological theory. "Citizenship cannot be realistically disconnected from eye color," i.e., every citizen has eyes and every eye has a color. But, in the United States at least, color of eyes is not relevant to citizenship: "things that exist together are not always relevant to each other."

And so it is perfectly true, as Hallowell, Radcliffe-Brown, and others say, that "it is *peoples* who meet and interact." But this should not keep us from confining our attention, in the solution of certain problems, to symbolates in an extrasomatic context: to tools, utensils, customs, beliefs, and attitudes; in short, to culture. The meeting and mixing of European culture with African culture and the production thereby of a mixture, Euro-African culture, may seem "a fantastic reification of abstractions" to Radcliffe-Brown and others. But anthropologists have been concerned with problems of this sort for decades and will continue to deal with them. The intermingling of customs, technologies, and ideologies is just as valid a scientific problem as the intermingling of human organisms or genes.

We have not asserted, nor do we imply, that anthropologists in general have failed to treat culture as a process sui generis, i.e., without taking human organisms into account; many, if not most, cultural anthropologists have in fact done this. But some of them, when they turn to theory, deny the validity of this kind of interpretation. Radcliffe-Brown himself provides us with examples of purely culturological problems and culturological solutions thereof—in "The Social Organization of Australian Tribes" (1930-31), "The Mother's Brother in South Africa" (1924), etc. But when he dons the philosopher's cap he denies that this procedure is scientifically valid.[15]

However, some anthropologists have recognized, on the theoretical level, that culture can be scientifically studied without taking human organisms into account, that a consideration of human organisms is irrelevant to the solution of problems dealing with extrasomatic traditions. We have cited a number—Tylor, Durkheim, Kroeber, Lowie, et al.—who have done this.[16] But we may add one or two new references here. "The best hope . . . for parsimonious description and 'explanation' of cultural phenomena," say Kroeber and Kluckhohn (1952:167) "seems to rest in the study of cultural forms and processes as such, largely . . . abstracted from individuals and personalities." And Steward (1955:46) remarks that "certain aspects of a modern culture can best be studied quite apart from individual behavior. The structure and function of a system of money, banking, and credit, for example, represents supraindividual aspects of culture." Also, he says: "form of government, legal system, economic institutions, religious organizations, educational systems," and so on, "have aspects which are national . . . in scope and which must be understood apart from the behavior of the individuals connected with them" (ibid.:47).

There is nothing new about this; anthropologists and other social scientists have been doing this for decades. But it seems to be difficult for some of them to accept this as a matter of theory and principle as well as of actual practice.

[15]Cf. White, *The Science of Culture*, pp. 96-98, for further discussion of this point.
[16]In our essays "The Expansion of the Scope of Science" and "The Science of Culture," in *The Science of Culture*.

It Takes Two or More to Make a Culture

There is a conception, not uncommon in ethnological theory, that whether a phenomenon is an element of culture or not depends upon whether it is expressed by one, two, or "several" individuals. Thus Linton (1945:35) says that "any item of behavior . . . which is peculiar to a single individual in a society is not to be considered as a part of the society's culture. . . . Thus a new technique for weaving baskets would not be classed as a part of culture as long as it was known only to one person." Wissler (1929:358), Osgood (1951:207-08), Malinowski (1941:73), Durkheim (1938:lvi), et al., have subscribed to this view.

Two objections may be raised against this conception of culture: (1) if plurality of expression of learned behavior be the significant distinction between culture and not-culture, then the chimpanzees described by Wolfgang Köhler in *The Mentality of Apes* (New York, 1925) had culture, for innovations made by a single individual were often quickly adopted by the whole group. Other subhuman species also would have culture according to this criterion. (2) The second objection is: if expression by one person is not enough to qualify an act as a cultural element, how many persons will be required? Linton (1936:274) says that "as soon as this new thing has been transmitted to and is shared by even one other individual in the society, it must be reckoned as a part of culture." Osgood (1951:208) requires "two or more." Durkheim (1938:lvi) needs "several individuals, at the very least." Wissler (1929:358) says that an item does not rise to the level of a culture trait until a standardized procedure is established in the group. And Malinowski (1941:73) states that a "cultural fact starts when an individual interest becomes transformed into public, common, and transferable systems of organized endeavor."

Obviously such a conception does not meet the requirements of science. What agreement could one find on the point at which an "individual interest becomes transformed into public, common, and transferable systems of organized endeavor"? Or, suppose an ornithologist said that if there were but one specimen of a kind of bird it could not be a carrier pigeon or a whooping crane, but that if there were an indefinite number then they could be pigeons or cranes. Or, suppose a physicist said that if there were but one atom of a certain element that it could not be copper, but if there were "a lot of such atoms" then it might properly be called copper. One wants a definition that says that item *x* belongs to class *y* or it does not, regardless of how many items of *x* there may be (and a class, in logic, may have only one member, or even none).

Our definition meets the requirements of a scientific definition: an item—a conception or belief, an act, or an object—is to be reckoned an element of culture (1) if it is dependent upon symboling, and (2) when it is considered in an extrasomatic context. To be sure, all cultural elements exist in a social context; but so do such nonhuman (not dependent upon symboling) traits as grooming, suckling, and mating exist in a social matrix. But it is not sociality, duality, or plurality that distinguishes a human, or cultural, phenomenon from a nonhuman or noncultural phenomenon. The distinguishing characteristic is symboling. Secondly, whether a thing or an event can be considered in an extrasomatic context does not depend upon whether there is only one such thing or event, or two, or "several." A thing or event may be properly considered an element of culture even if it is the only member of its class, just as an atom of copper would still be an atom of copper even if it were the only one of its kind in the cosmos.

And, of course, we might have pointed out in the first place that the notion that an act or an idea in human society might be wholly the work of a single individual is an illusion, another one of the sorry pitfalls of anthropocentrism. Every member of human society is of course always subjected to sociocultural stimulation from the members of his group. Whatever a man does as a human being, and much of what he does as a mere animal, is a function of his group as well as of his organism. Any human act, even in its first expression in the person of a single individual, is a group product to begin with.[17]

Culture as "Characteristic" Traits

"Culture may be defined," says Boas (1938:159), "as the totality of the mental and physical reactions and activities that *characterize* the behavior of the individuals composing a social group . . ." (emphasis ours). Herskovits (1948:28) tells us that "when culture is closely analyzed, we find but a series of patterned reactions that characterize the behavior of the individuals who constitute a given group." (Just what "close analysis" has to do with this conception is not clear.) Sapir (1917:442): "The mass of typical reactions called culture. . . ." This view has, of course, been held by others.

Two objections may be raised against this conception of culture: (1) how does one determine which traits characterize a group and which traits do not—how does one draw the line between the two classes, culture and not-culture? And, (2) if we call the traits that characterize a group *culture*, what are we to call those traits that do not characterize it?

It seems probable that anthropologists who hold this view are really thinking of *a* culture, or cultures, plural, rather than of culture in general, culture as a particular kind of phenomena. Thus, "French culture" might be distinguished

[17]More than one hundred years ago Karl Marx wrote: "Man is in the most literal sense of the word a *zoon politikon*, not only a social animal, but an animal which can develop into an individual only in society. Production by isolated individuals outside of society . . . is as great an absurdity as the idea of the development of language without individuals living together and talking to one another," *A Contribution to the Critique of Political Economy* (Charles H. Kerr & Co., Chicago, 1904), p. 268.

from "English culture" by those traits which characterize each. But if, on the one hand, the French and the English may be distinguished from each other by differences of traits, they will on the other hand be found to be very similar to each other in their possession of like traits. And the traits that resemble each other are just as much a part of the "way of life" of each people as the traits that differ. Why should only one class be called culture?

These difficulties and uncertainties are done away with by our conception of culture: culture consists of all of the ways of life of each people which are dependent upon symboling and which are considered in an extrasomatic context. If one wished to distinguish the English from the French on the basis of their respective culture traits he could easily specify "those traits which characterize" the people in question. But he would not assert that nontypical traits were not culture.

In this connection we may note a very interesting distinction drawn by Sapir (1917:442) between the behavior of individuals and "culture."

It is always the individual that really thinks and acts and dreams and revolts. Those of his thoughts, acts, dreams, and rebellions that somehow contribute in sensible degree to the modification or retention of the mass of typical reactions called culture we term social data; *the rest, though they do not, psychologically considered, in the least differ from these, we term individual and pass by as of no historical or social moment* [i.e., they are not culture]. It is highly important to note that the differentiation of these two types of reaction is essentially arbitrary, resting, as it does, entirely on a principle of selection. The selection depends on the adoption of a scale of values. Needless to say, the threshold of the social (or historical) [i.e., cultural] *versus* the individual shifts according to the philosophy of the evaluator or interpreter. I find it utterly inconceivable to draw a sharp and eternally valid dividing line between them [emphases ours].

Sapir finds himself confronted by a plurality, or aggregation, of individuals. (He would have preferred this wording rather than "society," we believe, for he speaks of "a theoretical [fictitious?] community of human beings" adding that "the term 'society' itself is a cultural construct"; Sapir, 1932:236.) These individuals do things: dream, think, act, and revolt. And "it is always the individual," not society or culture, who does these things. What Sapir finds then is: individuals and their behavior; nothing more.

Some of the behavior of individuals is culture, says Sapir. But other elements of their behavior are non-culture, although, as he says, psychologically considered they do not differ in the slightest from those elements which he calls culture. The line thus drawn between "culture" and "not-culture" is purely arbitrary, and depends upon the subjective evaluation of the one who is drawing the line.

A conception of culture could hardly be less satisfactory than this one. It says, in effect: "culture is the name that we give to some of the behavior of some individuals, the selection being arbitrary and made in accordance with subjective criteria."

In the essay from which we have been quoting, "Do We Need a Superorganic?" (1917), Sapir is opposing the culturological point of view presented by Kroeber in "The Superorganic" (1917). He (Sapir) virtually makes culture disappear; it is dissolved into the totality of the reactions of individuals. Culture becomes, as he has elsewhere called it, a "statistical fiction" (Sapir 1932:237). If there is no significant reality that one can call culture, then there can be no science of culture. Sapir's argument was skillful and persuasive. But it was also unsound, or at least misleading.

Sapir's argument was persuasive because he bolstered it with authentic, demonstrable fact. It was unsound or misleading because he makes it appear that the only significant distinction between the behavior of individuals and culture is the one that he had made.

It is perfectly true that the elements which comprise the human behavior of individuals and the elements which comprise culture are identical classes of things and events. All are symbolates—dependent upon man's unique ability to symbol. It is true, also, that "psychologically considered," they are all alike. But Sapir overlooks, and by his argument effectively obscures, the fact that there are two fundamentally different kinds of contexts in which these "thinkings, actings, dreamings, and revolts" can be considered for purposes of scientific interpretation and explanation: the somatic and the extrasomatic. Considered in a somatic context, i.e., in terms of their relationship to the human organism, these acts dependent upon symboling constitute *human behavior*. Considered in an extrasomatic context, i.e., in terms of their relationships to one another, these acts constitute *culture*. Instead, therefore, of arbitrarily putting some in the category of culture and the rest in the category human behavior, we put all acts, thoughts, and things dependent upon symboling in either one context or the other, somatic or extrasomatic, depending upon the nature of our problem.

Summary

Among the many significant classes of things and events distinguishable by science there is one for which science has had no name. This is the class of phenomena dependent upon symboling, a faculty peculiar to the human species. We have proposed that things and events dependent upon symboling be called symbolates. The particular designation of this class is not as important, however, as that it be given a name of some kind in order that its distinction from other classes be made explicit.

Things and events dependent upon symboling comprise ideas, beliefs, attitudes, sentiments, acts, patterns of behavior, customs, codes, institutions, works and forms of art, languages, tools, implements, machines, utensils, ornaments, fetiches, charms, and so on.

Things and events dependent upon symboling may be, and traditionally have been, referred to two fundamentally different contexts for purposes of observation, analysis, and explanation. These two contexts may properly and appropriately be called somatic and extrasomatic. When an act, object, idea or attitude is considered in the somatic context it is the relationship between that thing or event and the human organism that is significant. Things and events dependent upon symboling considered in the somatic context may properly be called human behavior—at least, ideas, attitudes, and acts may; stone axes and pottery bowls are not customarily called behavior, but their significance is derived from the fact that they have been produced by human labor; they are, in fact, congelations of human behavior. When things and events are considered in the extrasomatic context they are regarded in terms of the interrelationships among themselves rather than in terms of their relationship to the human organism, individually or collectively. Culture is the name of things and events dependent upon symboling considered in an extrasomatic context.

Our analysis and distinctions have these advantages. The distinctions made are clear cut and fundamental. Culture is clearly distinguished from human behavior. Culture has been defined as all sciences must define their subject matter, namely, in terms of real things and events, observable directly or indirectly in the actual world that we live in. Our conception rescues anthropology from the incubus of intangible, imperceptible, imponderable "abstractions" that have no ontological reality.

Our definition extricates us, also, from the dilemmas in which many other conceptions place us, such as whether culture consists of ideas and whether these ideas have their locus in the minds of peoples studied or in the minds of anthropologists; whether material objects can or cannot be culture; whether a trait must be shared by two, three, or several people in order to count as culture; whether traits have to characterize a people or not in order to be culture; whether culture is a reification or not, and whether a culture can enamel its fingernails.

Our distinction between human behavior and culture, between psychology and culturology, is precisely like the one that has been in use for decades between speech and language, between the psychology of speech and the science of linguistics. If it is valid for the one it is valid for the other.

Finally, our distinction and definition is in very close accord with anthropological tradition. This is what Tylor meant by culture as a reading of *Primitive Culture* will make clear. It is the one that has actually been used by almost all nonbiological anthropologists. What is it that scientific field workers among primitive peoples have studied and described in their monographs? Answer: real observable things and events dependent upon symboling. It can hardly be said that they were studying and describing imperceptible, intangible, imponderable, ontologically unreal abstractions. To be sure, the field worker may be interested in things and events in their somatic context, in which case he would be doing psychology (as he would be if he considered words in their somatic context). And anthropology, as this term is actually used, embraces a number of different kinds of studies: anatomical, physiological, genetic, psychological, psychoanalytic, and culturological. But this does not mean that the distinction between psychology and culturology is not fundamental. It is.

The thesis presented in this paper is no novelty. It is not a radical departure from anthropological tradition. On the contrary, it is in a very real sense and to a great extent, a return to tradition, the tradition established by Tylor and followed in practice by countless anthropologists since his day. We have merely given it concise and overt verbal expression.

REFERENCES

BEALS, RALPH L., and HARRY HOIJER 1953 An introduction to anthropology. New York, The Macmillan Co.
BENEDICT, RUTH 1934 Patterns of culture. Boston and New York, Houghton, Mifflin Co.
BIDNEY, DAVID 1946 The concept of cultural crisis. American Anthropologist 48:534-552.
——— 1954 Culture: a critical review of concepts and definitions, by Kroeber and Kluckhohn. American Journal of Sociology 59:488-489.
BOAS, FRANZ 1928 Anthropology and modern life. New York, W. W. Norton and Co., Inc.
——— 1938 The mind of primitive man, revised edition. New York, The Macmillan Co.
CASSIRER, ERNST 1944 An essay on man. New Haven, Yale University Press.
COHEN, MORRIS R. 1931 Fictions. Encyclopedia of the Social Sciences 7:225-228. New York, The Macmillan Co.
DURKHEIM, EMILE 1938 The rules of sociological method, George E. G. Catlin ed. Chicago, The University of Chicago Press.
——— 1951 Suicide, a study in sociology, George Simpson ed. Glencoe, Ill., The Free Press.
EINSTEIN, ALBERT 1934 The world as I see it. New York, Covici, Friede.
——— 1936 Physics and reality. Journal of the Franklin Institute 221:313-347, in German; 349-382 in English.
HALLOWELL, A. IRVING 1945 Sociopsychological aspects of acculturation. In The science of man in the world crisis, Ralph Linton ed. New York, Columbia University Press.
HERRICK, C. JUDSON 1956 The evolution of human nature. Austin, University of Texas Press.
HERSKOVITS, MELVILLE J. 1945 The processes of cultural change. In The science of man in the world crisis, Ralph Linton ed. New York, Columbia University Press.
——— 1948 Man and his works. New York, Alfred A. Knopf.
HOEBEL, E. ADAMSON 1956 The nature of culture. In Man, culture and society, Harry L. Shapiro ed. New York, Oxford University Press.
HOOTON, EARNEST A. 1939 Crime and the man. Cambridge, Mass., Harvard University Press.

HUXLEY, JULIAN S. 1955 Evolution, cultural and biological. Yearbook of Anthropology, Wm. L. Thomas, Jr. ed.

KEESING, FELIX M. 1958 Cultural anthropology. New York, Rinehart and Co., Inc.

KLUCKHOHN, CLYDE, and WM. H. KELLY 1945 The concept of culture. *In* The science of man in the world crisis, Ralph Linton ed. New York, Columbia University Press.

KROEBER, A. L. 1917 The superorganic. American Anthropologist 19:163-213; reprinted in The nature of culture. Chicago, University of Chicago Press.

KROEBER, A. L., and CLYDE KLUCKHOHN 1952 Culture, a critical review of concepts and definitions. Papers of the Peabody Museum of American Archaeology and Ethnology, Harvard University, 47(1):1-223. Cambridge, Mass.

LINTON, RALPH 1936 The study of man. New York, D. Appleton-Century Co.

―――― 1945 The cultural background of personality. New York, D. Appleton-Century Co.

LOWIE, ROBERT H. 1917 Culture and ethnology. New York, Boni and Liverright.

LYND, ROBERT S. 1939 Knowledge for what? Princeton, N. J., Princeton University Press.

MALINOWSKI, BRONISLAW 1941 Man's culture and man's behavior. Sigma Xi Quarterly 29:170-196.

MURDOCK, GEORGE P. 1937 Editorial preface to Studies in the science of society, presented to Albert Galloway Keller. New Haven, Conn., Yale University Press.

―――― 1951 British social anthropology. American Anthropologist 53:465-473.

OSGOOD, CORNELIUS 1940 Ingalik material culture. Yale University Publications in Anthropology No. 22.

―――― 1951 Culture: its impirical and non-empirical character. Southwestern Journal of Anthropology 7:202-214.

RADCLIFFE-BROWN, A. R. 1924 The mother's brother in South Africa. South African Journal of Science, 21:542-555. Reprinted in Structure and function in primitive society.

―――― 1930-31 The social organization of Australian tribes. Oceania 1:34-63; 206-246; 322-341; 426-456.

―――― 1940 On social structure. Journal of the Royal Anthropological Institute 70:1-12; reprinted in Structure and function in primitive society. Glencoe, Ill., The Free Press.

―――― 1952 Structure and function in primitive society. Glencoe, Ill., The Free Press.

REDFIELD, ROBERT 1941 The folk culture of Yucatan. Chicago, The University of Chicago Press.

SAPIR, EDWARD 1916 Time perspective in aboriginal American culture. Canada Department of Mines, Geological Survey Memoir 90. Ottawa.

―――― 1917 Do we need a superorganic? American Anthropologist 19:441-447.

―――― 1930 Southern Paiute, a Shoshonean language. Proceedings of the American Academy of Arts and Sciences 65:1-296.

―――― 1932 Cultural anthropology and psychiatry. Journal of Abnormal and Social Psychology 27:229-242.

SPIRO, MELFORD E. 1951 Culture and personality. Psychiatry 14:19-46.

STEWARD, JULIAN H. 1955 Theory of culture change. Urbana, Ill., University of Illinois Press.

STRONG, WM. DUNCAN 1953 Historical approach in anthropology. *In* Anthropology today, A. L. Kroeber ed. Chicago, The University of Chicago Press, pp. 386-397.

TAYLOR, WALTER W. 1948 A study of archeology. American Anthropological Association Memoir No. 69.

TYLOR, EDWARD B. 1881 Anthropology. London.

―――― 1913 Primitive culture. 5th ed., London.

WHITE, LESLIE A. 1949 The science of culture. New York, Farrar, Straus and Cudahy; paperbound, 1958, New York, The Grove Press.

―――― 1954 Culture: a critical review of concepts and definitions, by Kroeber and Kluckhohn. American Anthropologist 56:461-468.

WISSLER, CLARK 1929 Introduction to social anthropology. New York, Henry Holt and Co.

THE NEW PHYSICAL ANTHROPOLOGY: THE CORRELATION BETWEEN CULTURE, ENVIRONMENT, AND BIOLOGY IN THE EVOLUTION OF MAN

FRANK B. LIVINGSTONE (1928-) is Professor of Anthropology at the University of Michigan. In 1958 he published this highly significant study of the relation of a particular genetic disorder, sickle-cell anemia, its distribution and frequency, to the cultural habits of peoples among whom it is found, the environment in which it occurs, and the genetic forms the disorder takes.

This classic contribution to our understanding of the complex interrelation between disease, genes, and culture was really the first to show how finely interwoven those relationships are in the total ecological picture into which man together with all other living things fits.

The major vector of malaria, the mosquito *Anopheles gambiae*, has to have certain environmental conditions at its disposal, if it is to breed. These are described by Livingstone. He shows that such conditions could not have developed among hunting peoples, and that, therefore, prehistoric man was probably wholly free of the disease, and hence, since there would have been no selective advantage to the sickle-cell gene (sicklemia), its frequency, when present, would have been low.

It is only with the development of agriculture that the conditions are made available for the mosquito to multiply and flourish and live off the blood of human beings, whom they parasitize with the *Plasmodium falciparum* in the areas studied. Those who carry a double dose (are homozygous) for the sickle-cell gene tend, after infestation, to die very early in life. Those who carry only one gene (are heterozygous) for sickle-cell anemia possess an adaptive advantage, and are resistant to the attacks of *P. falciparum*. Hence, a high frequency of such single-gene heterozygotes is maintained in such malarious populations. The sickle-cell gene, therefore, may be regarded as an evolutionary response to a special challenge of the environment, a challenge largely produced by man by his "blundering" upon a stage without much if any understanding of the roles of the other players in relation to himself.

It is a thought, not without some poignancy, that at one time in man's prehistory mosquitoes lived on amicable terms with man, and took their meals off other host animals, until, as Livingstone says, man "blundered upon the scene" and disturbed the ecologic balance by killing off the host animal(s).

In any event, this tale of the manner in which a disease, an infection by parasitization, and the adaptive response to this genetically within a population comes about, constitutes one of the most dramatic and interesting chapters in the history of anthropology.

ANTHROPOLOGICAL IMPLICATIONS
OF SICKLE CELL GENE DISTRIBUTION
IN WEST AFRICA*
FRANK B. LIVINGSTONE

During the past fifteen years, data on the frequency of the sickle cell gene have accumulated to such an extent that its world distribution can now be outlined in considerable detail. Frequencies of more than 20 percent of the sickle cell trait have been found in populations across a broad belt of tropical Africa from the Gambia to Mozambique. Similar high frequencies have been found in Greece, South Turkey, and India. At first it appeared that there were isolated "pockets" of high frequencies in India and Greece, but more recently the sickle cell gene has been found to be widely distributed in both countries (Choremis and Zannos 1956; Sukumaran, Sanghvi, and Vyas 1956). Moreover, between these countries where high frequencies are found, there are intermediate frequencies, in Sicily, Algeria, Tunisia, Yemen, Palestine, and Kuwait. Thus, the sickle cell gene is found in a large and rather continuous region of the Old World and in populations which have recently emigrated from this region, while it is almost completely absent from an even larger region of the Old World which stretches from Northern Europe to Australia.

When the broad outlines of the distribution of the sickle cell gene first began to emerge, several investigators attempted to explain various aspects of this distribution by migration and mixture. Lehmann and Raper (1949) attempted to show that the differences in the frequency of the sickle cell gene among the Bantu tribes of Uganda were due to varying degrees of Hamitic admixture; Brain (1953) and Lehmann (1954) postulated migrations from Asia to account for the distribution of the sickle cell gene in Africa; and Singer (1953), using

*Reproduced by permission of the American Anthropological Association from *American Anthropologist*, 60 (3), 1958, pp. 533-62.

an age-area type of argument, postulated that the sickle cell gene arose by mutation near Mt. Ruwenzori and diffused from there. However, it was recognized early in the development of the sickle cell problem that regardless of the extent to which migration and mixture explained the distribution pattern of a sickle cell gene, its high frequencies in various widely scattered areas raised some additional and striking problems in human population genetics.

Since persons who are homozygous for the sickle cell gene very rarely reproduce, there is a constant loss of sickle cell genes in each generation. In order for the gene to attain frequencies of .1 to .2, which are equivalent to about 20 to 40 percent of the sickle cell trait, there must be some mechanism which is compensating for this loss. In other words, there must be some factor which is tending to increase the number of sickle cell genes in the population. Neel (1951) first pointed out that there are two outstanding possibilities; either the sickle cell gene is arising frequently by mutation, or the heterozygote for the sickle cell gene possesses a selective advantage over the normal homozygote which offsets the selective disadvantage of the sickle cell homozygote (balanced polymorphism). Since the evidence (Vandepitte et al. 1955) indicated that the mutation rate was not sufficient to maintain the high frequencies, selection in favor of individuals with the sickle cell trait seemed to be implicated as the factor which was maintaining them.

When Allison (1954a; 1954b; 1954c) advanced the hypothesis that the heterozygote for the sickle cell gene possessed a relative immunity to falciparum malaria, he marshalled the first clear evidence for the mechanism by which selection maintained the observed high frequencies. In addition to experiments on sicklers and nonsicklers which seemed to show that the sicklers could cope more easily with a malarial infection, Allison (1954b) also showed that the tribal frequencies of the sickle cell gene in Uganda and other parts of East Africa could be explained as well by his malaria hypothesis as by varying degrees of Hamitic admixture. Thus, Allison's work showed that selection must be taken into consideration in any attempt to explain the distribution of the sickle cell gene.

Although selection has undoubtedly played a major role in determining the frequencies of the sickle cell gene in the populations of the world, in many areas other factors in addition to selection may well be involved. Allison (1954b) has shown that most of the tribes of East Africa seem to have frequencies of the sickle cell trait which are in approximate equilibrium with the amount of malaria present, but there appear to be many populations in West Africa and elsewhere for which this is not so. It will be the purpose of this paper to show how the distribution of the sickle cell gene in West Africa is the result of the interaction of two factors, selection and gene flow. Gene flow will be used here to include both migration and mixture; the term migration is used where the gene flow involves the movement of breeding populations or large segments of them, and mixture where the breeding populations remain rather stationary and the gene flow involves the exchange of individuals between them. Of course, any actual situation is usually a combination of these two "polar" concepts.

According to modern genetic theory as developed by Wright and others, there are five factors which can contribute to gene frequency change: selection, mutation, gene drift, gene flow, and selective mating. Strictly speaking, an attempt to explain the distribution of any gene must take into consideration all five. However, three of these factors—mutation, gene drift, and selective mating—are thought to have had relatively little effect on the features of the distribution of the sickle cell gene in West Africa which this paper will attempt to explain, and thus will not be discussed at any length in this paper.

The general plan of the paper will be as follows. First, the distribution of the sickle cell gene in West Africa will be plotted; then an attempt will be made to correlate this distribution with that of falciparum malaria in West Africa. It will be assumed that the high frequencies of the sickle cell gene are in equilibrium with the particular endemicity of malaria in which they are found. Thus, by comparing these two distributions we can determine where the frequencies of the sickle cell gene appear to be explained by selection (i.e. are in equilibrium), and we can also determine where the frequencies appear to be very far from equilibrium and hence where other factors in addition to selection appear to be involved. The rest of the paper will then be concerned with the populations which do not appear to be in equilibrium. In order to explain why the frequencies of the sickle cell gene in these populations are not in equilibrium with the present-day endimicity of malaria, it is necessary to have some idea of the ethnic and culture history of West Africa. The literature on the culture history of West Africa is rather sparse, so the major part of this paper will be an attempt to infer its broad outlines from the distribution of language and of certain domesticated plants in West Africa.

The Distribution of the Sickle Cell Gene in West Africa

In the following compilation of data on the distribution of the sickle cell gene in West Africa, several early publications of surveys have been omitted. In all of these reports, the tribe of the persons tested is not given, and the reports could thus contain subjects from several breeding populations with very different frequencies of the sickle cell gene. Data by tribe are available for the areas covered by these surveys, except for part of Evans' (1944) survey. His sample from the Cameroons has been included since there are no other data from this area.

Where the same tribe has been tested by different investigators, differences in the frequency of the sickle cell trait have been tested by a chi-square test. If the differences were not significant, the results have been combined. However, for several large tribes which extend over considerable distances and into several different countries, the samples have been kept separate when they were obtained in different countries.

For the surveys in which paper electrophoresis or other biochemical tests were done on the bloods, all individuals who would have been positive for the sickle cell test were counted as positive without regard to whether they appeared to be homozygous or heterozygous for the sickle cell gene. Thus, the frequency of the sickle cell trait, as used in this paper, includes both heterozygotes and any living homozygotes for the sickle cell gene. However, recent studies (Lehmann and Raper 1956) indicate that homozygotes for the sickle cell gene rarely survive the first years of life, so that most likely very few homozygotes are included in the tribal samples. Throughout the discussion, sickle cell trait frequencies will be used instead of gene frequencies, since the trait frequencies are used by most investigators and hence their significance is more easily comprehended. Since very few homozygotes are included in the samples, the gene frequency would be close to one-half the trait frequency in all cases.

Except for the Ivory Coast, Dahomey, and the Cameroons, the compilation is by tribe. The Dahomey and Cameroons samples have been included in an effort to fill up large gaps in the distribution in areas where tribal investigations are nonexistent. These samples have combined several tribes and thus have probably combined data from isolates which differ significantly from one another in the frequency of the sickle cell trait. Since they are also quite small samples, this paper will not consider them in detail.

Due to the lack of investigations, and also to the multiplicity of small tribes which inhabit the Ivory Coast, the tribal samples from there are all rather small. Since the frequency of the sickle cell trait is 0 percent in Liberia to the west of the Ivory Coast and greater than 20 percent in Ghana to the east, the Ivory Coast is an area of crucial concern to this study. For this reason, the tribal samples have been combined into larger linguistic units to increase the sample sizes and thus give them more reliability. The tribes which have been combined are very closely related, since in most cases they speak the same language with only dialectic differences between them. Although the individual tribal samples are small, there is no indication that this procedure has combined tribes which have very different frequencies of the sickle cell trait.

TABLE 1

THE FREQUENCIES OF THE SICKLE CELL TRAIT IN THE TRIBES OF WEST AFRICA

Country Tribe	Investigations*	Number	Number	Sickle Cell Trait (%)
Senegal				
Wolof (Oulof)	16, 18	2277	151	6.63

Lebu (Lebou)	16, 18	522	31	5.94
Serer	16, 18	1515	50	3.30
Soce	16	70	11	15.71
Fulani (Peul)	16, 18	299	27	9.03
Tukulor (Toucouleur)	16, 18	634	60	9.46
Dyola	18, 19	39	2	5.13
Mandiago	16, 18, 19	101	1	0.99
Gambia				
Mandingo-Western Division	2	167	18	10.78
Mandingo-Keneba	2	240	15	6.25
Mandingo-Jali	2	115	7	6.09
Mandingo-Mandjar	2	59	10	16.95
Mandingo-Tankular	2	132	32	24.24
Fulani (Fula)	2	127	24	18.90
Dyola (Jola)	2	312	53	16.99
Wolof (Jolloff)	2	104	18	17.31
Saracole (Serahuli)	2	96	8	8.33
Bainunka	2	90	15	16.67
Portuguese Guinea				
Papel	24	500	15	3.00
Mandiago (Mandjaca)	15	500	16	3.20
Balante (Balanta)	15	500	25	5.00
Feloop (Felupe)	15	466	6	1.72
Baiote	15	473	6	1.27
Nalu	15	501	14	2.79
Saracole	15	286	24	8.39
Mandingo (Mandinga)	15	500	75	15.00
Biafada (Beafada)	15	505	77	15.25
Pajadinca	15	358	66	18.44
Fulani (Fula-Foro)	15	500	115	23.00
Fulani (Fula-Preto)	15	430	108	25.12
French Guinea				
Fulani (Foula)	15, 16, 18	682	109	15.98
Susu	5, 18, 19	48	15	31.25
Kissi	19	18	4	22.22
Loma-Kpelle (Toma-Guerze)	19	40	8	20.00
Sierra Leone				
Creole	2	42	10	23.81
Timne	2	52	15	28.95
Mende	2, 23	1124	330	29.36
Liberia				
Kissi	17	298	58	19.46
Mende	17	77	13	16.88

Gbandi	17	352	54	15.34
Vai	17	93	13	13.98
Kpelle	17	982	128	13.03
Loma	17	511	65	12.72
Gola	17	183	22	12.02
Belle	17	29	3	10.34
Bassa	17	811	58	7.15
Dei	17	53	2	3.77
Mano	17	709	15	2.12
Gio	17	428	9	2.10
Grebo	17	69	1	1.45
Krahn	17	154	1	0.65
Kru	17	148	1	0.68
Webbo	17	77	0	0.00
French Sudan				
Moor (Maure)	18, 19	70	4	5.71
Saracole	16, 18	196	16	9.18
Bambara	16, 18	262	27	10.31
Mandingo (Malinke)	18, 19	50	8	16.00
Fulani (Peul)	20	152	22	14.47
Songhai	20	100	11	11.00
Ivory Coast				
Senufo	5, 19	33	8	24.24
Agni-Boule	5, 19	53	7	13.21
Dan-Gouro	5, 19	30	0	0.00
Lagoon	5, 19	48	2	4.17
Bete	5, 19	53	1	.89
Bakwe	5, 19	63	1	1.59
Upper Volta				
Samogo	20	120	8	6.67
Bobofing	5, 19, 22	232	57	24.57
Lobi	5, 19	15	3	20.00
Mossi	5, 19, 20	207	24	11.59
Gurma	5, 19, 20	34	3	8.82
Gurunsi	5, 19	14	1	7.14
Ghana				
Mossi (Moshie)	10, 11	121	5	4.13
Dagarti	11	97	11	11.34
Dagomba	11	71	3	4.23
Ewe	2, 10, 11	232	54	23.28
Fanti	2, 10, 11	204	48	23.53
Ga	2, 10, 11	367	67	18.26
Twi	2, 10	111	24	21.62

Frafra	9	680	66	9.71
Ashanti	2	102	23	22.55
French Togoland				
Kabre	4	1104	109	9.87
Dahomey				
Dahomeans	5, 19	55	5	9.09
Niger				
Djerma (Zabrama)	2, 19	69	15	21.74
Tuareg	3	93	5	5.38
Nigeria				
Yoruba	7, 13, 25	3477	853	24.53
Igalla	25	155	28	18.06
Ibo	2	51	11	21.57
Cameroons	12	138	21	15.22
Kerikeri	14	159	17	10.69
Fulani	14	184	31	16.85
Hausa	1, 6, 14	611	107	17.51
Lake Chad				
Mobur (Mobeur)	21	273	49	17.95
Kanembu (Kanembou)	21	76	17	22.37
Mangawa	21	58	12	20.69
Sugurti (Sougourti)	21	37	6	16.22

* References are as follows:

1—Adamson (1951)
2—Allison (1956)
3—Barnicot, Ikin, and Mourant (1954)
4—Bezon (1955)
5—Binson, Neel, and Zuelzer (unpublished)
6—Bruce-Chwatt (unpublished)
7—Charles and Archibald (unpublished)
8—Colbourne, Edington, and Hughes (1950)
9—Colbourne and Edington (1956)
10—Edington and Lehmann (1954)
11—Edington and Lehmann (1956)
12—EUVANS (1944)
13—Jelliffe and Humphreys (1952)
14—Jelliffe (1954)
15—Leite and Ré (1955)
16—Linhard (1952)
17—Livingstone (1958)
18—Neel, Hiernaux, Linhard, Robinson Zuelzer, and Livingstone (1956)
19— Pales and Linhard (1951)
20—Pales and Serere (1953)
21—Pales, Galais, Gert, and Fourquet (1955)
22—Raoult (unpublished)
23—Rose and Suliman (1955)
24—Trincao, Pinto, Almeida, and Gouveia (1950)
25—Walters and Lehmann (1956)

Table 1 shows the frequency of the sickle cell trait for West Africa by tribe and also by country. For the purposes of further discussion, the spelling of all tribal names has been standardized. On Table 1 the names used by the original investigators are shown in parentheses after the standardized name.

The distribution of the frequency of the sickle cell trait in West Africa is shown on Figure 1. In order to make the general configuration of the distribution more easily visualized, the frequencies have been grouped into five categories: 0-2, 2-8, 8-15, 15-22, and greater than 22 percent. The frequency of the sickle cell trait can be seen to exhibit extreme variability, sometimes over very short distances. In many cases there are significant differences in the frequency of the trait even within the same tribe. For example, the Fulani have frequencies ranging from 8 to 25 percent, and the Mandingo in the Gambia vary from 6 to 28 percent. Although this great variability impedes generalizing about the distribution, some significant generalizations can nevertheless be made.

Generally, the higher frequencies tend to be toward the south, and, despite many exceptions, there is some indication of a north-south gradient in the frequency of the sickle cell trait. The distribution of falciparum malaria follows a similar gradient, and, in addition, all the populations which have sickle cell trait frequencies greater than 15 percent inhabit areas where malaria is either hyperendemic or holoendemic.

In an environment in which malaria is hyperendemic or holoendemic, the disease is transmitted throughout most of the year, so that the individuals are continually being reinfected. The average number of infective bites per person per year is always greater than about 5, and in some areas ranges up to 100 or more. Thus, infants are infected with malaria shortly after birth, and for about the first five years of life every child is engaged in a mortal struggle with the parasite. During these years the parasite rate (i.e., the percentage of individuals harboring malaria parasites) is close to 100 percent and there is a considerable mortality from the disease. Those individuals who survive this struggle have a solid immunity to malaria. In later years they are being continually reinfected with malaria but are able to keep their infection at a sub-clinical level. The parasite rate then decreases among older children and is lowest in adults. In holoendemic malaria the adult parasite rate will be about 20 percent and the adults will almost never have any clinical symptoms of malaria, while in hyperendemic malaria the adult parasite rate will be somewhat higher and the adults will sometimes have clinical symptoms, usually chills and fever. However, in both these conditions there is seldom any adult mortality from malaria.

It is in an environment in which malaria is either hyperendemic or holoendemic that the heterozygote for the sickle cell gene has been postulated to have a selective advantage over the normal homozygote. Allison (1954a) and Raper (1955) have shown that, although sicklers are infected with falciparum malaria almost as readily as nonsicklers, in the younger age groups the very high densities of parasites are not found as often among sicklers. In addition, Raper (1956) has shown that the sicklers do not suffer from cerebral malaria and blackwater fever as much as nonsicklers. Since these are the complications of falciparum malaria which result in death, the sicklers had a lower mortality rate from falciparum malaria. In addition, I have postulated (1957a) that if the sickling females did not have as heavy falciparum infections of the placenta as did normal females, they would have a higher net reproduction rate and hence this could be another mechanism by which malaria was maintaining the high frequencies of the sickle cell gene. Although the evidence is not conclusive, it seems for the most part favorable to this hypothesis. When the evidence for both these mechanisms is considered as a whole, it seems to be conclusive that malaria is the major cause of the high frequencies of the sickle cell gene. One would therefore expect to find high frequencies of the sickle cell trait in areas in which malaria is either hyperendemic or holoendemic.

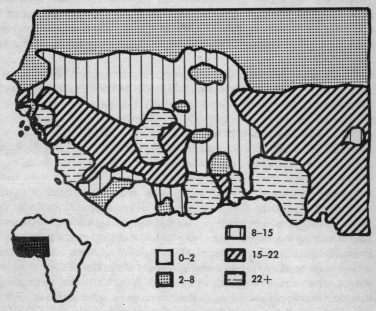

8–15
0–2
15–22
2–8
22+

Fig. 1 The distribution of the frequency of the sickle cell trait in West Africa.

From about the latitude of the Gambia south, West Africa is almost entirely characterized by hyperendemic or holoendemic malaria; hence, high frequencies of the sickle cell trait would be expected. However, there are many populations in this region with very low frequencies of the trait. The majority of them are found in three areas: (1) Coastal Portuguese Guinea, (2) Eastern

Liberia and the Western Ivory Coast, (3) Northern Ghana. The low frequency populations which are found in Northern Ghana differ from those in the other two areas by having high frequencies of the gene which is responsible for Hemoglobin C. This gene is an allele of the sickle cell gene (Ranney 1954), so that in Northern Ghana the sickle cell locus is a tri-allelic system. Since the selective values associated with the various phenotypes of this system are not known at present, the equilibrium frequencies for these populations cannot be ascertained (see Allison 1957 for further discussion of this problem). Thus, one cannot say whether or not these populations are in equilibrium for this locus. The rest of this paper will therefore be concerned with the two areas, Coastal Portuguese Guinea and Eastern Liberia-Western Ivory Coast, where the Hemoglobin C gene is almost completely absent (Neel et al. 1956).

Cambournac (1950) in Coastal Portuguese Guinea and Young and Johnson (1949) in Eastern Liberia found malaria to be either hyperendemic or holoendemic in these areas where low frequencies of the sickle cell trait are found. Thus, these frequencies appear to be very far from equilibrium, and hence do not seem to be explained by the factor of selection alone. An attempt will now be made to show how the explanation involves the two factors, selection and gene flow. More specifically, two hypotheses will be advanced to explain these low frequencies:

(1) The sickle cell gene has been present in some parts of West Africa for a considerable time, but, due to the comparative isolation of the low frequency populations in Portuguese Guinea and Eastern Liberia, is only now being introduced to them.

(2) The environmental conditions responsible for the high frequencies of the sickle cell gene have been present for a relatively short time among these populations, so that the spread of the sickle cell gene is only now following the spread of the selective advantage of the gene.

In order to demonstrate these propositions, two general types of evidence will now be considered; first, the distribution of language in West Africa, from which an attempt will be made to ascertain the general outlines of the migrations which have occurred there; then, the archeological evidence and the distributions of certain domesticated plants in West Africa, from which an attempt will be made to determine the broad outlines of the culture history of the area. From a consideration of the culture history of West Africa and the relationship between culture patterns and the endemicity of malaria, the spread of the selective advantage of the sickle cell gene will be inferred.

The Distribution of Language in West Africa

In the following discussion Greenberg's (1955) classification of African languages will be used, since it is the most recent and also the most widely accepted. In addition, Greenberg is attempting to make a "genetic" classification of African languages. Languages are said to be genetically related when their similarities are due to their development from a common ancestral language. It is this type of linguistic relationship which is most likely to have biological significance, since the ancestors of the speakers of genetically related languages were probably once members of the same breeding population and thus biologically related. Greenberg's classification is concerned with the larger linguistic families of Africa and the larger subgroupings within these families. Since it will be necessary at times to separate the languages into smaller subgroups, other sources will be used, but only when these agree with Greenberg's overall classification.

Except for the Songhai, Hausa, Kerikeri, Tuareg, Moor, and the tribes around Lake Chad, all the tribes listed on Table 1 speak languages belonging to the Niger-Congo family. The exceptions noted above speak either Songhai, Central Saharan, or Afro-Asiatic languages. These tribes are in the northern and eastern parts of West Africa and a considerable distance from the two low frequency areas of the sickle cell trait with which we are concerned. Therefore, this discussion will be concerned only with the Niger-Congo languages.

Figure 2 shows the language distribution in West Africa, both by family and by subfamily within Niger-Congo. The Niger-Congo family contains seven subfamilies: (1) West Atlantic, (2) Mande, (3) Gur, (4) Kwa, (5) Ijo, (6) Central Group, (7) Adamawa-Eastern. All of these subfamilies have some member languages in West Africa, but, with the exception of the Adamawa-Eastern speakers in northern Central Africa, the Niger-Congo languages in Central, East, and South Africa all belong to a single subfamily (Central Group) and even to a single subgroup (Bantu) within that subfamily.

Because of the great linguistic diversity in West Africa, this area appears to have been inhabited for a relatively long time by speakers of Niger-Congo. On the other hand, because of the similarity of language in the area inhabited by the Bantu peoples, this area has undoubtedly been peopled by a relatively recent spread of those peoples. As Greenberg (1955:40) states:

> If the view of the position of the Bantu languages presented here is accepted, there are certain historical conclusions of considerable significance which follow. When Sapir demonstrated that the Algonkian languages were related to the Wiyot and Yurok languages of California, it was clear that, if this demonstration was accepted, it constituted a powerful argument for the movement of the Algonkian-speaking peoples from the west to the east. Here we have not two languages, but twenty-three separate stocks all in the same general area of Nigeria and the Cameroons. The evidence thus becomes strong for the movement of the Bantu-speaking peoples from this area southeastwards. The usual assumption has been a movement directly south from the great lake region of East Africa. It will also follow that this is a relatively recent

movement, a conclusion which has generally been accepted on the basis of the wide extension of the Bantu languages and the relatively small differentiation among them.

In discussing the archeological and ethnological evidence, an attempt will be made to give reasons for the relatively recent spread of the Bantu from Nigeria, as well as to show that this other evidence seems to support the linguistic evidence.

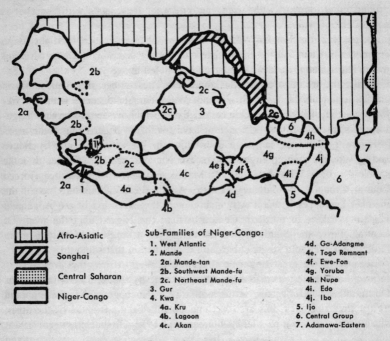

Fig. 2 The distribution of language in West Africa.

In West Africa west of Nigeria, there are four subfamilies of Niger-Congo: West Atlantic, Mande, Gur, and Kwa. With the exception of the rather recent movement of the Fulani pastoralists across the entire length of West Africa, the West Atlantic languages are all located along the coastal fringe of West Africa. The Kwa languages are distributed along the Guinea Coast from Liberia to Central Nigeria, with the great majority of them located in the tropical rain forest. In the central part of West Africa, in two large blocks, are the Mande languages on the west and the Gur languages on the east. These languages are for the most part located in the Sudan, although several Mande groups have penetrated the tropical rain forest in Sierra Leone, Liberia, and the Ivory Coast.

The tribes with low frequencies of the sickle cell trait in Portuguese Guinea speak West Atlantic languages, but some Mandingo groups in the Gambia, who speak a Mande language, also have relatively low frequencies. In Eastern Liberia and the Western Ivory Coast, the tribes with low sickling frequencies include speakers of Kwa and Mande languages. Thus, with the exception of Gur, all these subfamilies include some languages whose speakers are far from equilibrium with respect to the sickle cell gene. Since these subfamilies also include some languages whose speakers have high frequencies of the sickle cell trait and seem to be close to equilibrium, the frequency of the trait is not correlated with language. This seems to indicate that the gene has been introduced into this part of West Africa since these subfamilies of Niger-Congo began to separate. However, since there is considerable linguistic diversity within the subfamilies, their separation occurred long ago.

Although there is no correlation of the frequency of the sickle cell trait with the linguistic subfamilies in this part of West Africa, the tribes with low frequencies in both Portuguese Guinea and Eastern Liberia seem to be the indigenous inhabitants of West Africa who have been forced back into these areas by later migrants from the east. The distribution of the West Atlantic languages along the coast with some isolated pockets in the interior indicates that the speakers of these languages were once more widespread and have been forced back to the coast by more recent invaders (Forde 1953). This retreat of the West Atlantic speakers is documented to some extent, and there is general agreement that the general trend of migration has been toward the west. Of course, the West Atlantic peoples probably occupied the coastal regions at an early time also, but their present concentration there results from their displacement from a wider area by invaders from the east.

Several authorities state that the Baga, who now inhabit the coastal regions of French Guinea, originally inhabited the Futa Djallon, which is the highland area of Central French Guinea. The Baga were forced out of there by the Susu, who were in turn forced out by the Fulani (Houis 1950; Demougeot 1944; Joire 1952). This forcing back of the West Atlantic speakers was also noted by Beranger-Ferand (1879:285) in the Casamance River area of the French Senegal. He divides the populations of this region into three groups:

A. Peuplades primitives (Feloupes, Bagnouns).

B. Peuplades envahissantes (Balantes, Mandingues, Peuls).

C. Peuplades adventives (Ouolofs, Saracoles, Toucouleur, Mandiagos, Machouins, Taumas, Vachelons).

He then states that A are the indigenous inhabitants; B are the fighters who conquered; and C are the traders or farmers who infiltrated in small groups. In Gambia the same migrations have been noted by Southorn (1952) and Reeve (1912). Reeve (1912:17) states:

The only relics that are to be found today of the primitive negro race which originally occupied the forest belt between the Senegal and the Rio Grande are the Serreres on the coast, north of the Saloum River, who are pagans and were cannibals; the Feloops, Floops, or Flups, as called by early voyagers, but now, ín the valley of the Gambia, known as the Jolahs, occupying the territory between the seacoast and the head-waters of the Vintang Creek, about one hundred miles inland; the Patch-aris or Pakaris in the Middle Valley, and the Bassaris including the Kunyadis, in the Upper Valley. These will be again referred to, and it is evident, from the chronicles of the different writers on the subject of slavery in this part of West Africa, that it was these Arcadians and forest dwellers, with their simple manners and customs of sustaining life from the products of the forest, field, and streams, who supplied the bulk of the trade, under the pretext that they worshipped idols, and therefore were considered to be outside the pale of humanity by the races that had adopted the Koran.

Thus, it can be seen that these writers agree that the Feloops, who have one of the lowest frequencies of the sickle cell trait, are one of the indigenous tribes. In addition, Reeve states that the Serer, who also have a low frequency of the trait, are the indigenous inhabitants in the north and in the past were hunters and gatherers and not agriculturalists. It should also be noted that Leite and Ré (1955), who tested the tribes of the Portuguese Guinea for sickling, give a similar explanation for the differences in the frequency of the sickle cell trait which they found.

The tribes with low sickling frequencies in Eastern Liberia and the Western Ivory Coast include speakers of Mande languages and of Kwa languages. All of the speakers of Kru and Lagoon languages, which belong to the Kwa sub-family, have very low frequencies of the sickle cell trait, and the positives for the trait who do occur among these peoples are in the eastern tribes where they are in contact with the Agni, Baoule, and other Akan speakers. On the other hand, the Kwa speakers who are to the east of the Kru and Lagoon peoples all have relatively high frequencies of the sickle cell trait. Viard (1934) states that the Guere, who speak a Kru language, came from the east, and Yenou (1954) makes a similar statement for the Alladians, who speak a Lagoon language. Since the linguistic relationships point to the east, these statements are probably true. Much has been written about the migrations of the Akan, Ewe, Ga, and other Kwa speakers who are to the east of the Kru and Lagoon speakers, and most authorities agree that the general direction of migration of these tribes has been to the southwest. Since the Lagoon languages are quite similar to the Togo Remnant languages (Bertho 1950), it seems that the speakers of these languages were forced back into peripheral areas by the Akan peoples (i.e., Ashanti, Fanti, Agni, Baoule), when they migrated to Southern Ghana. The movement of the Agni and Baoule into the Ivory Coast is quite recent—17th century according to most authorities. Thus, it seems that some Kwa speakers were more widespread through the tropical rain forest when the later Kwa migrants entered it and were then forced back by these later migrants. Since the later migrants have high frequencies of the sickle cell trait, it appears that they introduced the sickle cell gene into this part of West Africa.

In addition to the Kru and Lagoon-speaking peoples, there are several tribes with low sickling frequencies who speak Mande languages in Eastern Liberia and the western Ivory Coast. These are the Mano, Gio, Dan, Gouro, and other smaller groups. At the border between the Mano and the Kpelle, the frequency of the sickle cell trait increases sharply. Although these peoples both speak Mande languages, they belong to different subgroups of the Mande subfamily (Prost 1953). Kpelle is related to Mende and Susu to the northwest in Sierra Leone, and this tribe has undoubtedly come into Liberia from that direction. However, Mano and the other Mande languages whose speakers have low frequencies of the sickle cell trait are related to several Mande languages in the Upper Volta Province of French West Africa and also to a Mande language in Nigeria. Vendeix (1924) states that the Dan, and Tauxier (1924) that the Gouro, came into their present habitats from the northeast. Donner (1939) states that the Dan came from the north into the forest and forced the Kru peoples ahead of them. It would thus appear that these Mande tribes with low sickling frequencies came into their present location by a different route than that of their Mande neighbors to the northwest in Liberia and Sierra Leone. The Bobofing, who speak a language related to these Mande languages whose speakers have low sickling frequencies, have 25 percent of the sickle cell trait and are some distance to the northeast of the Dan and Gouro; so that it seems that the sickle cell gene was introduced after the separation of these languages. The Mandingo are to the north of the Mano, Dan, and Gouro, and between them and the Bobofing. From the 12th to 15th centuries A.D. when the Mali Empire, which was ruled by the Mandingos, was at its height, these people are known to have expanded out from their original homeland. It would appear that this expansion of the Mandingo forced the Mano, Dan, and Gouro into the forest and separated them from their relatives to the northeast.

The two areas of low frequencies of the sickle cell trait thus seem to be inhabited by peoples who have been forced back into these peripheral areas by later migrants from the east and northeast. However, this does not mean to imply that all the later migrants had the sickle cell gene. It is possible that the Kwa migrants to Southern Ghana introduced the gene into this part of West Africa by migration; but along the West Atlantic coastal fringe, the sickle cell gene seems to have spread in the past by mixture, and is still spreading in this manner today.

In the Central Ivory Coast on the border of the Kru and Lagoon peoples on the west and the Akan peoples on the east, there is a sharp increase in the frequency of the sickle cell trait. Since all the Kwa peoples from the Akan east to the Ibo in Nigeria have very high frequencies of the trait, it seems that these peoples possessed the sickle cell gene when they migrated into these regions from the east and northeast. However, along the Atlantic Coast of West Africa from the Senegal to Central Liberia, the gene does not seem to have been introduced by large-scale migration. The highest frequencies of the sickle cell trait in this region are found in the Gambia and in Sierra Leone, which are also the two places where Mande peoples have penetrated to the seacoast in large numbers. Since the Mande peoples were the migrants from the east, it would appear that they introduced the sickle cell gene into this part of Africa. However, the smooth gradient in the frequency of the trait in Sierra Leone and Liberia seems to indicate that the gene was introduced after the original Mande migrations. Starting with the Susu in northwest Sierra Leone who have a sickling frequency of 31 percent and proceeding southeastward, there is a smooth gradient in frequency which is not correlated with language. The speakers of Southwest Mande-fu languages, the Mende in Sierra Leone, the Mende in Liberia, the Gbandi, Loma, and Kpelle, have 29, 17, 15, 13, and 13 percent, respectively, while the West Atlantic speakers, the Timne, Kissi, and Gola, have 29, 19, and 12 percent respectively. The Vai, who speak a Mande-tan language and are the latest immigrants from the interior (McCulloch 1950), have a frequency of 14 percent, which is also in agreement with this gradient. In Portuguese Guinea, where the Mande peoples have not penetrated in great numbers, there is also a smooth gradient in the frequency of the sickle cell trait. Starting on a small section of the seacoast between the Casamance River and the Rio Cacheu where the Feloop and Baiote have 1 to 2 percent, the frequency increases going inland to 5 percent among the Mandjak, and then to 15 percent among the Biafada and Mandingo. It thus seems that along the West Atlantic coastal fringe of West Africa the sickle cell gene has spread and is still spreading by mixture and not by large scale migration, while the gene appears to have spread through the tropical rain forest along the Guinea Coast by the migration of the Akan and other Kwa-speaking migrants from the east. The archeology and culture history of West Africa will now be examined in an attempt to provide some explanation for the manner by which the sickle cell gene has spread there.

The Archeology of West Africa
And Origin of the West African Negro

Although there has been less archeological excavation in West Africa than elsewhere in Africa, it is now beginning to appear that West Africa was inhabited during most of man's cultural development, as was most of the continent. Lower Paleolithic hand axes and Middle Paleolithic Levallois flakes have been found in scattered places throughout West Africa (Alimen 1955). However, no rich sites comparable to those in East and South Africa have been excavated for these stages. Nevertheless, the scattered finds indicate the presence of man in West Africa during these periods, which lasted up to the end of the Pleistocene. Following these periods in time, microlithic sites are documented for Ghana (Shaw 1951), French Guinea (Joire 1952), Nigeria (Fagg 1951), and other places in West Africa. Some of these microlithic cultures seem fairly recent and perhaps attributable to the ancestors of the present Negro inhabitants. However, little skeletal material has been found.

The earliest skeletal material which is found close to West Africa is a skull from Singa in the Sudan. This find has been dated by Arkell (1952) as Upper Pleistocene and is associated with a Levallois culture. The skull is stated to be archaic Bushman and related to the Boskop skull from South Africa. From this find it appears that the Bushman was once much more widespread than today and in Upper Pleistocene times Bushman-like peoples were in the Sudan. This statement is supported by the presence of Bushman-like rock paintings and archeological cultures similar to that of the present day Bushman over most of the southern half of the African continent. The presence today in Tanganyika of the Hatsa, who speak a Kahoisan language and still have a predominantly Stone Age culture (Fosbrooke 1956), also supports it.

The first appearance of skeletal material which has Negroid affinities is in this same area of the Sudan, but apparently much later. At Esh Shaheinab, which is on the Nile near Khartoum, several skeletons with Negroid affinities have been found in association with a microlithic hunting and gathering culture, which also had pottery. Around the fringes of the Sahara there are other finds of Negroid skeletal material, all of which seem to belong to this general period. The famous Asselar skull from north of Timbuktu, which is considered to be Negro, is from this general period, and Alimen (1955) also indicates that some of the skeletal material associated with the Capsian culture in Tunisia has Negroid affinities. In addition to this skeletal material, many of the early rock paintings in the Sahara seem to depict Negroid peoples.

The Esh Shaheinab site has been dated by radiocarbon as 5200 years ago, or shortly after the beginnings of agriculture in Egypt. The radiocarbon dates on the Capsian culture are about 7500 years ago. Alimen (1955) indicates that the Neolithic of Capsian tradition is found in French Guinea, but this is probably much later than the Capsian sites which have been dated by radiocarbon. It should also be noted that in this context Neolithic does not mean food-producing, but only that the culture had polished stone artifacts.

The first archeological evidence of the Bantu in South and Central Africa is much later than the evidence from northern West Africa, and appears to be after the beginning of the Christian era. Alimen (1955:304) states: "Iron entered the Congo very late, by means of the Bantu invasion, which later spread to the Rhodesias in only 900 A.D." Further, Alimen states (1955:370) that iron working came to the upper valley of the Orange River in the 13th century A.D. and here too is associated with the arrival of the Bantu. Previous to the expansion of the Bantu, East and South Africa were inhabited by Bushman-like peoples.

The archeological evidence thus seems to indicate that at about the time of the introduction of agriculture into Africa, Negro peoples with a microlithic culture were living around the fringes and even in the middle of the Sahara, while most of South and East Africa was inhabited by Bushman-like peoples. Since the Pygmies would seem to be indigenous to Central Africa, they were perhaps responsible for the microlithic cultures found there. For West Africa there are numerous legends of Pygmies (summary in Schnell 1948), so it is possible that at this time Pygmies also inhabited West Africa. However, Joire (1952) thinks there is no evidence for Pygmies in West Africa and assigns the microlithic sites in French Guinea to the Baga tribe. The diffusion of agriculture through Africa, and its effect on the preceding distribution of peoples will not be considered.

The Introduction of Agriculture and Iron Working into Africa

The first evidence of a farming economy in Africa occurs in Egypt at Fayum, which dates about 4000 B.C. Because of the domesticated plants and animals associated with this culture, it is thought to be derived from Asia Minor (Alimen 1955). Seligman (1939:52) shows instances of Egyptian contact with Negroes in the late predynastic period, which he dates at about 3000 B.C., and Negroes are also known to have been living in the Sudan at Esh Shaheinab at about the same time. The inhabitants of Jebel Moya in the Sudan are also stated to be Negroes, who were forced westward by the Arabs around 700 B.C. (Mukherjee, Rao, and Trevor 1955). Thus, agriculture seems to have spread from Egypt to the Negro peoples who have since been forced south and west by the Arabs and by Berber peoples such as the Tuareg.

Iron working was also introduced into Africa from Asia Minor via Egypt (Forde 1934; Arkell 1955). There was a considerable iron industry flourishing at Meroe in the Sudan in 600 B.C., about which Arkell (1955:147) states: "Indeed there is little doubt that it was through Meroe that knowledge of iron working spread south and west throughout Negro Africa." The next evidence for the spread of iron southwest of the Sudan is in Northern Nigeria where Fagg (1956) has discovered the Nok culture, which is dated in the second half of the first millennium B.C. by geological methods. Assuming that iron working spread here from Meroe, this is about the date which would be expected. This culture contains both iron and stone axes; but since the iron axes have the same shape as the stone ones, this appears to be a transitional culture which had only recently adopted iron working. Since Mukherjee, Rao, and Trevor (1955) found the inhabitants of Jebel Moya to be most similar in physical type to the West African Negro, the westward migration of these people in the first millennium B.C. could very likely have been the method by which iron working was introduced to West Africa. In any case, this appears to be one route by which iron working was introduced into West Africa.

In the western part of West Africa, iron working seems to be somewhat later, and the evidence seems to indicate that it was not introduced via Meroe. Corbeil, Mauny, and Charbonnier (1948) think that iron working was introduced into the Cape Verde region around Dakar by Berbers who arrived there from the north about 300 B.C. Later, Mauny (1952) states that iron working was introduced into this region by the Phoenicians in the first century A.D., since the words for iron in many of the languages of this region seem to be derived from Phoenician. Although it is possible that some peoples along the coast obtained iron from the Phoenicians, it would seem more likely that iron working was brought across the Sahara, since contact with the Phoenician ships would not seem to have been close enough for the transference of all the techniques which iron working requires. Cline (1937) states: "Within the bend of the Niger lies the only large area where iron remains have been found associated with stone-using cultures." However, Nok culture in Northern Nigeria had not been discovered at the time Cline was writing, so that there appear to be two areas with these transitional cultures. In the same area Cline (1937) describes another type of iron working site which has copper and a much richer assemblage altogether. These sites he associates with the Ghana Empire. This empire was founded about 300-400 A.D. (Fage 1955), at about the time the camel was introduced into the western Sahara, and its rise to eminence is associated with increasing trade with Mediterranean civilizations. It thus appears that iron working was introduced into the western part of West Africa shortly before this empire was founded and probably was introduced from the north across the desert.

The preceding evidence indicates that both agriculture and iron working were introduced into West Africa from Asia Minor via Egypt, although both were no doubt diffused along several different routes. Agriculture was present in Egypt centuries before iron working and probably began to spread through Africa before iron working was introduced from Asia Minor. However, this early spread of agriculture seems to have been mostly by stimulus diffusion, since the basic crops of Egypt, wheat and barley, did not spread to the Sudan. Even today, millet and sorghum are the basic crops throughout the Sudan. Both millet and sorghum, or at least some species of them, are considered to have been domesticated in Africa (Miege 1951; Viguier 1945) and to have been cultivated there "since antiquity" (Miege 1951). Viguier (1945:165) states: "Aug. Chevalier considers the western Sudan and its Saharan border as one of the centers of the origin of domesticated sorghum." Since the agricultural methods used for them are similar to those for wheat and barley, and in addition the crops are all grains, it would seem reasonable to postulate that an early spread of agriculture from Egypt involved these crops. The techniques involved in the cultivation of these grains did not entail any considerable technological change from that of a microlithic hunting and gathering culture. The tool assemblage at Fayum in Egypt is not very different from that of the Natufian in Palestine or that of the Capsian. As this early agricultural economy spread, it either drove the hunting cultures before it or perhaps was adopted by these peoples. However, one of the hypotheses of this paper is that this economy could not spread throughout tropical Africa.

Although a Neolithic millet and sorghum economy could spread through the Sudan, it was not until the introduction of iron working and/or better yielding tropical crops that the Negro agriculturalists could exploit the tropical rain forest. Thus, the forest remained the home of primitive hunters until quite recently. In West Africa these hunters appear to have been Negroes whose descendants can be seen today in the low sickling frequency areas of Portuguese Guinea and Eastern Liberia; and in Central Africa they were Pygmies, whose descendants are the low sickling frequency "true" Pygmies, the Babinga of French Equatorial Africa (Hiernaux 1955).

A combination of three factors prevented the spread of this agricultural economy through the tropical rain forest: (1) the poor quality of the soils, which wear out after a few crops; (2) the difficulty of clearing the forest with stone tools; and (3) the low yields of millet and sorghum.

In Northern Ghana and Northern Nigeria, where millet and sorghum are still the basic crops today, in many places the same fields are cultivated year after year (Manoukian 1952; Gourou 1950). On the other hand, in Sierra Leone a new field is cleared every year (McCulloch 1950), and in the forest regions of Nigeria, Gourou (1950) states that it takes 30 years for the soil to recover after one crop, while Forde (1951) indicates that the fields are cultivated for three or four years before being left fallow. Some comparison of the relative yields of the various crops can be obtained from Gourou's (1950:39) figures of yields in the French Sudan, although this is not tropical rain forest. Millet yields 5 cwt. per acre; yams, 15 cwt. per acre; and cassava, 32 cwt. per acre. However, from a nutritional standpoint the important yield is the number of calories per unit of land. Combining data from several African countries, Brock and Autret (1952) give the following figures for the yields of various crops in thousands of calories per hectare: millet yields 1,530; sorghum, 1,854; yams, 3,554; and cassava, 7,090. Thus, when these three factors are considered together, it would seem to be difficult for a Neolithic millet and sorghum economy to exist in a tropical rain forest environment. It should be emphasized, however, that this hypothesis does not mean to imply that there were no agriculturalists in the tropical rain forest prior to the introduction of iron working and tropical root crops. There was undoubtedly some agriculture and "whittling away" at the tropical rain forest in the areas which border on the Sudan. However, these innovations were a necessary prerequisite for the great explosion of the Bantu peoples out of Nigeria, which filled up half a continent in a relatively short time.

Together with iron working, the domestication of two indigenous crops opened the tropical rain forest as a habitat exploitable by the Negro agriculturalists. Chevalier (1952:16) states that the yam, *Dioscorea latifolia*, was domesticated in West Africa. Today the most widespread species of yam in Africa is *D. cayenensis*, which is derived from *D. latifolia* (Chevalier 1946). From its distribution it would seem most probable that these yams were domesticated in Nigeria. With the yam and iron working, the Bantu peoples then spread throughout the Central African tropical rain forest from their original homeland, which Greenberg (1955:116) places in the central Benue River valley in Nigeria. In many places today the Bantu do not have the yam as a staple crop, but this theory only attempts to explain the original rapid spread of the Bantu. This theory is supported by linguistic evidence, by the fact that transitional iron working cultures are known in Northern Nigeria and also by the fact that the spread of iron working in Central and South Africa is associated with the spread of the Bantu. In addition, in several areas where yams are no longer the Bantu staple there is still ritual associated with this crop, which seems to indicate that it was previously more important. For example, among the Kpe in the Cameroons, where cocoyams are now the staple crop, Ardener (1956:46) states: "Although subsidiary in Kpe agriculture, this crop [i.e. yam] is remarkable for the fact that it is the only one to which some degree of ritual is attached. . . . The ritual elements in the cultivation of the yam, the present economic importance of which is quite small, suggests that this crop . . . may have been a staple food in the past history of the Kpe."

Also from Nigeria, some of the Kwa peoples spread in similar fashion through the West African tropical rain forest to the Ivory Coast and forced other Kwa peoples, the Kru and Lagoon speakers, westward into the Ivory Coast and Liberia. The Kru and Lagoon peoples were probably in the tropical rain forest as hunters and gatherers prior to this spread of agriculture. Agriculture has since been introduced to most of the Kru and Lagoon peoples, but it usually has rice as the basic crop, which comes from a different center of dispersal, or manioc, which was introduced into West Africa from the New World. Even today in the Ivory Coast, as several botanists (Miege 1953; Chevalier 1952) have remarked, there is a sharp boundary of yam cultivation on the Bandama River, which is also the border between the Baoule and Kru peoples. In addition, the yam cultivators, such as the Agni, have an elaborate ritual associated with the yam harvest (Rahm 1953; Miege 1953), which indicates great reliance on this crop. Although the Kru peoples have for the most part adopted agriculture, there is still more reliance on hunting in the Kru area (Kerharo and Bouquet 1949), and there are some groups who are still mainly hunters. In Eastern Liberia, Schwab (1947:79) states: ". . . there is one clan or small tribe . . . living to the north of the Tchien near the Nipwe River who have a reputation as elephant hunters, like the pigmies of the southeastern Cameroun."

The cline in the frequency of the sickle cell trait coincides with this spread of yam cultivation. The Kru and Lagoon peoples have almost 0 percent of the sickle cell trait, except where they come in contact with the yam cultivators, while the yam cultivators in the Eastern Ivory Coast, Southern Ghana, and Nigeria all have high frequencies of the trait. Thus, it seems that the sickle cell gene was brought into this part of Africa by the migrations of the yam cultivators westward from Nigeria, and at present both agriculture and the sickle cell gene are spreading to the hunting populations, which were in the forest prior to the spread of yam cultivation.

Perhaps a little later than this spread of yam cultivation, there was another spread of agriculture through the West African tropical rain forest. Porteres (1949) has shown that somewhere around the Middle Niger River Valley, a wild African species of rice, *Oryza glaberrima*, was domesticated. He dates this domestication at about 1500 B.C. (ibid.:560), but the spread of this crop through the tropical forest seems to be much later than the postulated date, and even later than the introduction of iron. There is evidence (Little 1951:26) that the first Mande peoples to enter the tropical rain forest were hunters. Little dates this migration at least 400 years ago. However, the most plausible date seems to be about 1300 A.D., when the Susu appear to have migrated to French Guinea from the Middle Niger region (Joire 1952). Thus, it would seem that the Mande and West Atlantic peoples in the tropical forest were still hunters about 600 years ago, and that rice agriculture has since been introduced to them. Joire (1952) assigns the microlithic archeological sites which are known in French Guinea to the Baga people, who speak a West Atlantic language. These people thus were in the tropical forest prior to the immigration of the Mande peoples and to the later spread of rice agriculture.

The spread of iron working and rice cultivation through this part of the West African tropical rain forest, after the original Mande migration, does not seem to be associated with any large scale migration; it probably occurred by diffusion, since the Mande peoples who have now adopted rice cultivation were in the same location as hunters. Thus, according to the evidence, the spread of rice agriculture by diffusion seems to coincide with the spread of the sickle cell gene by mixture. In addition, the spread of rice cultivation appears to be later than the original Mande migration, as does the spread of the sickle cell gene. Rice cultivation also diffused to the West Atlantic-speaking peoples, as did the sickle cell gene. Thus, the type of gene flow—in one case migration and in the other mixture—which was responsible for the spread of the gene in West Africa seems to be related to the manner of the spread of agriculture. However, agriculture seems to have spread farther than the gene. The Kru peoples in Eastern Liberia, and the West Atlantic peoples in coastal Portuguese Guinea, are today rice cultivators. The reason for this lag in the spread of the sickle cell gene is due first of all to the fact that it takes several generations for the gene to build up to appreciable frequencies, but it also seems to be due to the relationship of the selective advantage of the sickle cell gene to slash and burn agriculture. This relationship is due in turn to the complex epidemiology of malaria in West Africa, which we will now consider.

Man, Malaria, and Mosquito in West Africa

In West Africa the relationship between man, malaria, and mosquito is very highly evolved, due largely to the habits of the major vector of malaria, *Anopheles gambiae*. This mosquito is attracted to human habitations and usually rests in the thatched roofs of an African village. It bites man regularly, and breeds in a variety of places. Wilson (1949) has estimated that 75 percent of the malaria in Africa is due to *A. gambiae*. Its breeding places are so diverse that, when attempting to delimit them, entomologists usually state where it cannot breed. *A. gambiae* cannot breed in (1) very shaded water, (2) water with a strong current, (3) brackish water, (4) very alkaline or polluted water (Holstein 1953).

If we now consider the types of water which would be found in the tropical rain forest, it can be seen that there would be few places for *A. gambiae* to breed in unbroken tropical rain forest. The high emergent shade trees and the trees of the middle "story" of the forest so effectively shade the ground that there would be few, if any, areas that were unshaded. In addition, the layer of humus on the forest floor is very absorbent, so there would be few stagnant pools. It is only when man cuts down the forest that breeding places for *A. gambiae* become almost infinite (De Meillon 1949). First, with continued cutting of the forest, the soil loses all of its humus and becomes laterized. At this stage it is practically impervious to water; puddles are constantly renewed by the frequent tropical rains and so persist indefinitely. Second, man's refuse and his villages provide more abundant breeding places for the mosquito. Third, the swamps become open and hence possible breeding places.

In a hunting population, which does not destroy the forest, malaria would thus not develop this complex relation with man. Malaria could still be present, but not the holoendemic malaria which characterizes most of Africa today. Hunters do not build the type of permanent habitation in which *A. gambiae* lives, and since a hunting population moves frequently the mosquito could not keep up with the human population, so to speak. Also, in the epidemiology of any disease there is a critical size for the population below which the disease cannot persist. Since hunting populations are small, they would be closer to this critical size and perhaps even below it.

The Pygmies provide an example of such a hunting population, but unfortunately no malaria surveys of hunting Pygmies are available. Schwetz, Baumann, Peel, and Droeshant (1933) did examine three groups of Pygmies for malaria and found that they had less than the surrounding Negroes, but these Pygmies were building houses and farming, and so cannot be considered a hunting population. Putnam (1948), who lived with the hunting Pygmies for 20 years, states that they do not suffer from malaria. His account also shows that the Pygmies do not cut down the forest and do not build their rude huts in a clearing but in the middle of the forest. These customs would appear to be the reasons for the absence of malaria among them.

If this complex relationship between parasite, host, and vector which is characteristic of holoendemic malaria could not have developed in hunting populations, then the selective advantage of the sickle cell gene would not be present in these populations. If, as has been postulated, the Feloop and other peoples in Portuguese Guinea and the Kru peoples of Eastern Liberia and the Western Ivory Coast were the last remnants of hunting populations which once were spread through the tropical forest, then the absence of the selective advantage of the sickle cell gene in these populations would have prevented it from becoming established, even if there had been some gene flow from neighboring Sudanic peoples. Although considerable areas of tropical rain forest are shown on any vegetation map of West Africa, these are greatly broken up by agricultural settlements and fields. Nevertheless, the last northern remnants of the forest are located in Portuguese Guinea near one area of low sickling frequencies, and the other area in Eastern Liberia is in the center of the largest remaining block of tropical rain forest.

The frequencies of the sickle cell trait among the Pygmies also support this theory, although the comments of several authorities might seem to contradict it. Regarding the Pygmies and Pygmoids, Hiernaux (1955:463) states: "They generally show a lower frequency of sicklemia than the surrounding populations, as shown in Table 2. In all cases but one, the frequency is lower in the Pygmoids. The most striking difference is between the Bondjo and Babinga, who are true Pygmies." Since most Pygmy groups have formed symbiotic relationships with their Negro neighbors, the frequencies among them can easily be explained by mixture, which is known to be occurring (Putnam 1948).

There is other evidence that A. gambiae has spread rather recently through the West African tropical rain forest. In the area around the Firestone Plantation in Liberia, shortly after the forest had been cut down, Barber, Rice, and Brown (1932) found that A. gambiae accounted for 46 percent of the mosquito population found in the native huts, while A. funestus accounted for 51 percent, and A. nili for 3 percent. However, at the present time in this same area, A. gambiae accounts for almost 100 percent of the mosquito population (Max J. Miller, personal communication). Barber, Rice, and Brown (1932) found holoendemic malaria, which is not present today; however, this change is due to malaria control and not to changes in the mosquito population. These figures thus indicate a significant increase in A. gambiae when the forest is cut down. Even more significant are Barber, Rice, and Brown's comments on the effects of reforestation on the mosquito population. They state (1933:629):

We felt that it would be interesting to know what would be the condition of things when the rubber trees had grown and the unplanted ravines and swamps had become "rejunglized." We surveyed Mt. Barclay Plantation where the stream borders have grown up with brush or long grass. After a long search in the streams we found only two or three larvae, *A. mauritianius* and *A. obscurus*. In a pool near a village *A. costalis* was plentiful.

It can thus be seen that *A. gambiae* (the authors call the species *A. costalis*) was not present in natural water but only near a village. The authors also discuss "rejunglization" as a means of malaria control, but state that it would not be feasible due to the breeding places which would persist around the villages. In the absence of these villages, which are not built by hunting populations, and in the presence of unbroken tropical forest, the intensity of malaria would be much less. This seems to have been the situation in West Africa prior to the spread of slash and burn agriculture. Therefore, the spread of this agriculture is responsible for the spread of the selective advantage of the sickle cell gene, and hence for the spread of the gene itself.

Sickle Cells, Disease, and Human Evolution

The preceding explanation of the distribution of the sickle cell gene and its relation to the culture history of West Africa has broad implications for the role of disease in human evolution. In considering the epidemiology of the sickle cell gene, Neel (1957:167) suggested that either the mutation which resulted in the sickle cell gene was very rare or else the spread of the gene was at present favored by special circumstances of relatively recent origin. The detailed arguments of this paper would seem to show that there are indeed special circumstances of recent origin, while at the same time not excluding the possibility that the mutation is quite rare. The special circumstances are considered to be the conditions necessary to maintain holoendemic malaria due to *Plasmodium falciparum*. This parasite is in fact regarded as evolutionally the most recent species of malaria to parasitize man (Boyd 1949). If, as has been proposed, a mobile hunting population in the tropical rain forest could not develop holoendemic malaria, then this high endemicity would perhaps be even later than the adaptation of the parasite to man as its host. Since the agricultural revolution occurred only about 7000 years ago and spread much later to Africa, it appears that the development of the environmental conditions which are responsible for the spread of the sickle cell gene are relatively recent, as Neel postulated they should be.

The agricultural revolution has always been considered an important event in man's cultural evolution, but it also seems to have been an important event in man's biological evolution. Prior to this revolution, the size of the human population was controlled to a large extent by the size of its food supply, and man's ecological niche was comparable to that of the large carnivores, or more closely perhaps to that of a large omnivore such as the bear. With the advent of the agricultural revolution, the food supply was no longer the major factor controlling the size of human populations. Man broke out of his ecological confinement and there was a tremendous increase in the size of the human population, an increase which was limited only by the available land. Haldane (1949, 1956) has stated that disease became the major factor controlling the size of human populations at this time, and his statement seems to be supported in one case by the spread of holoendemic malaria.

Two results of the agricultural revolution seem to account for this change in the role of disease in human evolution: (1) the great changes in the environment, and (2) the huge increase in the human population. Both of these seem to be involved in the development of holoendemic malaria. First, when man disrupts the vegetation of any area, he severely disrupts the fauna and often causes the extinction of many mammals, particularly the larger ones. When this happens, there are many known instances of the parasites of these animals adapting to man as the new host (Heisch 1956). It is thus possible that the parasitization of man by *P. falciparum* is due to man's blundering on the scene and causing the extinction of the original host. Second, concomitant with the huge increase in the human population, this population became more sedentary and man also became the most widespread large animal. Thus, he became the most available blood meal for mosquitoes and the most available host for parasites. This change resulted in the adaptation of several species of the Anopheline mosquito to human habitations and the adaptation of many parasites to man as their host. Under these conditions, holoendemic malaria and probably many other diseases developed and became important factors determining human evolution. It should be noted, however, that through domestication man has created large populations of other animals and these have influenced the epidemiology of several human diseases including malaria (for malaria examples, see Hackett 1949; Draper and Smith 1957). The sickle cell gene thus seems to be an evolutionary response to this changed disease environment. Hence, this gene is the first known genetic response to a very important event in man's evolution when disease became a major factor determining the direction of that evolution.

REFERENCES

ADAMSON, P. B. 1951 Haematological and biochemical findings in Hausa males. Jour. of Tropical Medicine and Hygiene 54:73-77.

ALIMEN, H. 1955 Préhistoire de l'Afrique. N. Bourbée, Paris.

ALLISON, A. C. 1954a Protection afforded by sickle-cell trait against subtertian malarial infection. British Medical Journal 1:290-294.

——— 1954b The distribution of the sickle-cell trait in East Africa and elsewhere, and its apparent relationship to the incidence of subtertian malaria. Transactions of the Royal Society of Tropical Medicine and Hygiene 48:312-318.

——— 1954c Notes on sickle-cell polymorphism. Annals of Human Genetics 19:39-57.

——— 1956 The sickle-cell and haemoglobin C genes in some African populations. Annals of Human Genetics 21:67-89.

——— 1957 Population genetics of abnormal human haemoglobins. Proceedings of the First International Congress of Human Genetics 430-434. New York, S. Karger.

ARDENER, E. 1956 Coastal Bantu of the Cameroons. London, International African Institute.

ARKELL, A. J. 1952 Egypte et Soudan. Comptes rendus, XIX Congrès Géologique International 5:276-278. Algers.

——— 1955 A history of the Sudan. London, The Athlone Press.

BARBER, M. A., J. B. RICE, and J. Y. BROWN 1932 Malaria studies on the Firestone Rubber Plantation in Liberia, West Africa. American Journal of Hygiene 15:601-633.

BARNICOT, N. A., E. W. IKIN, and A. E. MOURANT 1954 Les groupes sanguins ABO, MNS et Rh des Touareg de l'Air. L'Anthropologie 58:231-240.

BERENGER-FERAND, L. J. B. 1879 Les Peuplades de la Sénégambie. Paris, Ernest Leroux.

BERTHO, J. 1950 La place du dialecte adiukru par rapport aux autres dialectes de la Cote d'Ivoire. Bulletin de l'Institut Francais d'Afrique Noire, Dakar 12:1075-1094.

BEZON, A. 1955 Proportion de sicklémiques observée en pays Kabré (Togo). Médecine Tropicale 15:419-422.

BINSON, J., J. V. NEEL, and W. W. ZUELZER N.D. Unpublished data.

BOYD, M. F. 1949 Historical review. *In*: Malariology: a comprehensive survey of all aspects of this group of diseases from a global standpoint, M. F. Boyd ed. Vol. 1:3-25. Philadelphia, W. B. Saunders.

BRAIN, P. 1953 The sickle-cell trait: a possible mode of introduction into Africa. Man 53:154.

BROCK, J. F., and M. AUTRET 1952 Kwashiorkor in Africa. World Health Organization Monograph Series, No. 8. Geneva.

BRUCE-CHWATT, L. J. N.D. Unpublished data.

CAMBOURNAC, F. J. C. 1959 Rapport sur le paludisme en Afrique Equatoriale. WHO/MAL/58, Afr./Mal/Conf/14.

CHARLES, L. J., and H. M. ARCHIBALD N.D. Unpublished data.

CHEVALIER, A. 1946 Nouvelles recherches sur les ignames cultivées. Revue de Botanique Appliqué et Agriculture Tropicale 26:26-31.

——— 1952 De quelques *Dioscorea* d'Afrique Equatoriale toxiques dont plusieurs variétés sont alimentaires. Revue de Botanique Appliqué et Agriculture Tropicale 32:14-19.

CHOREMIS, C., and L. ZANNOS 1957 Microdrepanocytic disease in Greece. Blood 12:454-460.

CLINE, W. 1937 Mining and metallurgy in Negro Africa. General Series in Anthropology, No. 5. Menasha, George Banta Company.

COLBOURNE, M. J., G. M. EDINGTON 1956 Sickling and malaria in the Gold Coast. British Medical Journal 1:784-786.

COLBOURNE, M. J., G. M. EDINGTON, and M. H. HUGHES 1950 A medical survey in a Gold Coast village. Transactions of the Royal Society of Tropical Medicine and Hygiene 44:271-290.

CORBEIL, R., R. MAUNY, and J. CHARBONNIER 1948 Préhistoire et protohistoire de la presqu'ile du Cap Vert et de l'extrême ouest sénégalais. Bulletin de l'Institut Francais d'Afrique Noire, Dakar 10:378-460.

DE LAVERGNE DE TRESSAN, M. 1954 Inventaire linguistic de l'Afrique Occidentale Français et du Togo. Mémoires de l'Institut Français d'Afrique Noire, No. 30, Dakar.

DE MEILLON, B. 1949 Anophelines of the Ethiopian Region. *In* Malarialogy: a comprehensive survey of all aspects of this group of diseases from the global standpoint, M. F. Boyd ed. Vol. 1:443-482, Philadelphia, W. B. Saunders.

DEMOUGEOT, A. 1944 Notes sur l'organisation politique et administrative du Labe avant et dupuis l'occupation française. Mémoires de l'Institut Français d'Afrique Noire, No. 6, Dakar.

DONNER, E. 1939 Hinterland Liberia. London, Blackie and Son.

DRAPER, C. C., and A. SMITH 1957 Malaria in the Pare area of N. E. Tanganyika. Transactions of the Royal Society of Tropical Medicine and Hygiene 51:137-151.

EDINGTON, G. M., and H. LEHMANN 1954 A case of sickle-cell haemoglobin C disease and a survey of haemoglobin C incidence in West Africa. Transactions of the Royal Society of Tropical Medicine and Hygiene 48:332-335.

——— 1956 The distribution of haemoglobin C in West Africa. Man 56:36.

EVANS, R. W. 1944 The sickling phenomenon in the blood of West African natives. Transactions of the Royal Society of Tropical Medicine and Hygiene 37:281-286.

FAGE, J. D. 1955 An introduction to the history of West Africa. Cambridge, Cambridge University Press.

FAGG, B. 1951 Preliminary report on a microlithic industry at Rap Rock Shelter (Northern Nigeria). Prèmiere Conférence Internationale des Africanistes de l'Ouest 2:439-440, Institut Français d'Afrique Noire, Dakar.

——— 1956 A life-size terra-cotta head from Nok. Man 56:89.

FORDE, C. D. 1934 Habitat, economy, and society. London, Methuen.

——— 1951 The Yoruba-speaking peoples of South-Western Nigeria. London, International African Institute.

——— 1953 The cultural map of West Africa: successive adaptations to tropical forests and grasslands. Transactions of the New York Academy of Science 15:206-219.

FOSBROOKE, H. E. 1956 A stone age tribe in Tanganyika. South African Archeological Bulletin 11:3-8.

GOUROU, P. 1953 The tropical world. New York, Longmans, Green and Co.

GREENBERG, J. H. 1955 Studies in African linguistic classification. New Haven, Compass Publishing Co.

HACKETT, L. W. 1949 Conspectus of malaria incidence in Northern Europe, the Mediterranean Region, and the Near East. In Malariology: a comprehensive survey of all aspects of this group of diseases from a global standpoint, M. F. Boyd ed. Vol. 2:788-799, Philadelphia, W. B. Saunders.

HALDANE, J. B. S. 1949 Disease and evolution. Supplement to La Ricerca Scientifica 19:3-10.

——— 1956 The argument from animals to men, an examination of its validity for anthropology. Journal of the Royal Anthropological Institute 86:1-14.

HEISCH, R. B. 1956 Zoonoses as a study in ecology. British Medical Journal 1:669-673.

HIERNAUX, J. 1955 Physical anthropology and the frequency of genes with a selective value: the sickle cell gene. American Journal of Physical Anthropology 13:455-472.

HOLSTEIN, M. H. 1952 Biologie d'Anopheles gambiae; Recherche en Afrique-Occidentale Française. World Health Organization, Geneva.

HOUIS, M. 1950 Les minorités de la Guinée cotière, situation linguistic. Etudes Guinéennes 4:25-48, Institut Francais d'Afrique Noire, Conakry.

JELLIFFE, D. B., and J. HUMPHREYS 1952 The sickle-cell trait in Western Nigeria. British Medical Journal 1:405.

JELLIFFE, R. S. 1954 The sickle-cell trait in three Northern Nigerian tribes. West African Medical Journal 3:26-28.

JOIRE, J. 1952 La préhistoire de Guinée Française (Inventaire et mise au point de nos connaissances). Conferencia International Africanistas Occidentais 4:295-365, Lisboa.

KERHARO, J., and A. BOUQUET 1949 La chasse en Côte d'Ivoire et en Haute Volta. Acta Tropica 6:193-220.

Lehmann, H. 1954 Distribution of the sickle-cell gene: a new light on the origin of the East Africans. Eugenics Review 46:1-23.

Lehmann, H., and A. B. Raper 1949 Distribution of the sickle-cell trait in Uganda and its ethnological significance. Nature 164:494.

——— 1956 Maintenance of high sickling rate in an African community. British Medical Journal 2:333-336.

Leite, A. S., and L. Re Contribution a l'étude ethnologique des populations africaines. Archives de l'Institut Pasteur d'Algérie 33:344-349.

Linhard, J. 1952 Note complémentaire sur la sicklémie dans la région de Dakar. Revue d'Hematologie 7:561-566.

Little, K. 1951 The Mende of Sierra Leone. London, Routledge and Kegan Paul.

Livingstone, F. B. 1957a Sickling and malaria. British Medical Journal 1:762-763.

——— 1958 The distribution of the sickle cell gene in Liberia. American Journal of Human Genetics 10:33-41.

Manoukian, M. 1952 Tribes of the Northern Territories of the Gold Coast. London, International African Institute.

Mauny, R. 1952 Essai sur l'histoire des métaux en Afrique occidentale. Bulletin de l'Institut François d'Afrique Noire, Dakar 14:545-595.

McCulloch, M. 1950 Peoples of Sierra Leone Protectorate. London, International African Institute.

Miege, E. 1951 Les céréales en Afrique du Nord, le maïs et le sorgho. Revue de Botanique. Appliqué et Agriculture Tropicale 31:137-158.

Miege, J. 1952 L'importance économique des ignames en Côte d'Ivoire. Revue de Botanique Appliqué et Agriculture Tropicale 32:144-155.

Miller, M. N.D. Personal communication.

Mukherjee, R., C. R. Rao, and J. C. Trevor 1955 The ancient inhabitants of Jebel Moya (Sudan). Occasional Publications of the Cambridge University Museum of Archaeology and Ethnology, No. 3, Cambridge.

Neel, J. V. 1951 The population genetics of two inherited blood dyscrasias in man. Cold Spring Harbor Symposiums on Quantitative Biology 15:141-158.

——— 1957 Human hemoglobin types, their epidemiologic implications. New England Journal of Medicine 256:161-171.

Neel, J. V., J. Hiernaux, J. Linhard, A. Robinson, W. W. Zuelzer, and F. B. Livingstone 1956 Data on the occurrence of Hemoglobin C and other abnormal hemoglobins in some African populations. American Journal of Human Genetics 8:138-150.

Pales, L., P. Gallais, J. Bert, and R. Fourquet 1955 Le sicklémie (sickle cell trait) chez certaines populations Nigero-Tchadiennes de l'Afrique Occidentale Française. L'Anthropologie 58:472-479.

Pales, L., and J. Linhard 1951 Sicklémie en A. O. F. Biologie Comparative des Populations de l'A. O. F. Publications Direction Générale de la Santé Publique, Dakar.

Pales, L., and A. Serere 1953 La sicklémie en Afrique Occidentale Française (Haute Volta). L'Anthropologie 57:61-67.

Porteres, R. 1949 Le système de riziculture par franges univariétales et l'occupation des fonds par le riz flottants dans l'Ouest-africain. Revue de Botanique Appliqué et Agriculture Tropicale 29:553-563.

Prost, R. P. A. 1953 Les langues Mandé-sud du groupe Mano-Busa. Mémoires de l'Institut Français d'Afrique Noire, No. 26, Dakar.

Putnam, P. 1948 The Pygmies of the Ituri Forest. In A Reader in General Anthropology, C. S. Coon, ed. New York, Henry Holt.

Rahm, V. 1954 La Côte d'Ivoire, centre de recherches tropicales. Acta Tropica 11:222-295.

RANNEY, H. M.   1954   Observations on the inheritance of sickle-cell hemoglobin and hemoglobin C. Journal of Clinical Investigations 33:1634-1641.

RAOULT, M.   N.D.   Unpublished data.

RAHM, V.   1954   La Côte d'Ivoire, centre de recherches tropicales. Acta Tropica 2:1186-1189.
———   1956   Sickling in relation to morbidity from malaria and other diseases. British Medical Journal 1:965.

REEVE, H. F.   1912   The Gambia. London, Smith, Elder and Co.

ROSE, J. R., and J. K. SULIMAN   1955   The sickle-cell trait in the Mende tribe of Sierra Leone. West African Medical Journal 4:35-37.

SCHNELL, M. R.   1948   A propos de l'hypothèse d'un peuplement Négrille ancien de l'Afrique Occidentale. L'Anthropologie 52:229-242.

SCHWAB, G.   1947   Tribes of the Liberian hinterland. Papers of the Peabody Museum of American Archaeology and Ethnology, Vol. 31, Harvard University, Cambridge.

SCHWETZ, J., H. BAUMANN, PEEL, and DROESHANT   1933   Etude comparative de la malaria chez les pygmées et les indigenes de la forêt de l'Ituri (Congo Belge). Bulletin de la Societé de Pathologie Exotique 26:639-651.

SELIGMAN, C. G. 1939 The races of Africa. T. Butterworth, London.

SHAW, C. T.   1951   Archaeology in the Gold Coast. Première Conférence Internationale des Africanistes de l'Ouest 2:467-499, Institut Français d'Afrique Noire, Dakar.

SINGER, R.   1953   The sickle cell trait in Africa. American Anthropologist 55:634-648.

SOUTHORN, B.   1952   The Gambia. London, George Allen and Unwin.

SUKUMARAN, P. K., L. D. SANGHVI, and G. N. VYAS   1956   Sickle-cell trait in some tribes of Western India. Current Science 25:290-291.

TAUXIER, L.   1924   Nègres Gouro et Gagou. Paris, P. Geuthner.

TRINCAO, C., A. R. PINTO, C. L. ALMEIDA, and E. GOUVEIA   1950   A drepanocitemia entre a tribo papel da Guine Portuguesa. Anais do Instituto de Medicina Tropical, Lisboa 7:125-129.

VANDEPITTE, J. M., W. W. ZUELZER, J. V. NEEL, and J. COLAERT   1955   Evidence concerning the inadequacy of mutation as an explanation of the frequency of the sickle-cell gene in the Belgian Congo. Blood 10:341-350.

VENDEIX, M.   1924   Ethnographie du cercle de Man (Côte d'Ivoire). Revue d'Ethnographie et Traditions Populaires 5:149-169.

VIARD, R.   1934   Les Guerés, Peuple de la Forêt. Paris, Societe de Geographie.

VIGUIER, P.   1945   Les sorghos à grain et leur culture au Soudan Français. Revue de Botanique Appliqué et Agriculture Tropicale 25:163-230.

WALTERS, J. H., and H. LEHMANN   1956   Distribution of the S and C haemoglobin variants in two Nigerian communities. Transactions of the Royal Society of Tropical Medicine and Hygiene 50:204-208.

WESTERMANN, D., and M. A. BRYAN   1952   Languages of West Africa. London, International African Institute.

WILSON, D. B.   1949   Malaria incidence in Central and South Africa. In Malariology: a comprehensive survey of all aspects of this group of diseases from a global standpoint, M. F. Boyd ed. Vol. 2:800-809, W. B. Saunders, Philadelphia.

YENOU, A. D.   1954   Quelques notes historiques sur le pays Alladian (Basse-Côte d'Ivoire). Notes Africaines No. 63:83-88, Institut Français d'Afrique Noire, Dakar.

YOUNG, M. D., and T. H. JOHNSON   1949   A malaria survey of Liberia. Journal of the National Malaria Society 8:247-266.

FOR FURTHER READING

ACCULTURATION

Bohannan, Paul, and Fred Plog (eds.). *Beyond the Frontier*. Natural History Press, Garden City, New York, 1967.
An anthology of readings on the impact of cultures upon one another.

Linton, Ralph (ed.). *Acculturation in Seven American Indian Tribes*. Appleton-Century Co., New York, 1940.
A valuable series of case histories.

Tax, Sol (ed.). *Acculturation in the Americas*. University of Chicago Press, Chicago, Illinois, 1952.
The first book devoted to an anthropological analysis of the problems of the contacts and mixtures of cultures of Europe, Africa, and aboriginal America.

AGGRESSION AND WAR

Alland, Alexander, Jr. *The Human Imperative*. Columbia University Press, New York, 1972.
An excellent critical examination of the views of Lorenz, Ardrey, and Morris on aggression and territoriality.

Bender, Lauretta. *Aggression, Hostility, and Anxiety in Children*. C C Thomas, Springfield, Illinois, 1953.
A clinical study of the sources of aggression in children.

Carthy, J. D., and F. J. Ebling (eds.) *The Natural History of Aggression*. Academic Press, London and New York, 1964.
A stimulating symposium on animal and human aggression.

Clemente, Carmine D., and Donald B. Lindsley (eds.). *Aggression and Defense*. University of California Press, Berkeley & Los Angeles, 1967.
An invaluable symposium dealing especially with neural mechanisms and social patterns.

Dollard, John, et al. Frustration and Aggression. Yale University Press, New Haven, 1939.
   A classic work on the causes of aggressive behavior.

Durbin, E. F. M., and John Bowlby. Personal Aggressiveness and War. Columbia University Press, New York, 1939.
   On the causes of individual aggression and its relation to war.

Eron, Leonard D., Leopold O. Walder, and Monroe M. Lefkowitz. Learning of Aggression in Children. Little Brown & Co., Boston, 1971.
   On unplanned and systematic education for aggressiveness.

Fried, Morton, Marvin Harris, and Robert Murphy (eds.). War: The Anthropology of Armed Conflict and Aggression. Natural History Press, Garden City, New York, 1968.
   A most valuable symposium on the nature, causes, and prevention of war.

Fromm, Erich. The Anatomy of Human Destructiveness. Holt, Rinehart & Winston, New York, 1973.
   A splendid book.

Genovés, Santiago. Is Peace Inevitable? Walker & Co., New York, 1970.
   An admirable discussion of the views of the aggressionists, very constructively done.

Montagu, Ashley (ed.). Man and Aggression. Rev. ed. Oxford University Press, New York, 1973.
   A critical examination, by fourteen authorities, of the claims of some recent writers that man is innately aggressive, claims that are found wanting.

Richter, Derek (ed.). The Challenge of Violence. Ardua Press, Tadworth, Surrey, 1972.
   An uncommonly readable and moving symposium on aggression.

Scott, John Paul. Aggression. University of Chicago Press, Chicago, 1958.
   An excellent account of our knowledge about aggressive behavior in modern society, its causes, control, and consequences.

THE APES

Altmann, Stuart A. (ed.). Social Communication Among Primates. University of Chicago Press, Chicago, 1967.
   Among aspects of primate behavior discussed are dominance, aggression, subordination, social signaling, reproductive behavior, social dynamics, and the neurological and physiological correlates of social behavior.

Buettner-Janusch, John (ed.). Evolutionary and Genetic Biology of Primates. 2 vols. Academic Press, New York, 1963.
   A review of current research on many different aspects of primate biology.

DeVore, Irven (ed.). *Primate Behavior*. Holt, Rinehart & Winston, New York, 1965.
Field studies of monkeys and apes, fascinatingly reported.

Jay, Phyllis C. (ed.). *Primates*. Holt, Rinehart & Winston, New York, 1968.
A fine collection of studies of primate behavior, adaptation, and variability.

Kummer, Hans. *Primate Societies*. Aldine-Atherton, Chicago, 1971.
Patterns of behavioral interaction in primate societies.

Lawick-Goodall, Jane van. *In the Shadow of Man*. Houghton-Mifflin Co., 1971.
The enthralling account of a young Englishwoman's life among chimpanzees in their native habitat.

Morris, Desmond (ed.). *Primate Ethology*. Aldine, Chicago, 1967.
Invaluable studies on the behavior of monkeys and apes.

Morris, Ramona, and Desmond Morris. *Men and Apes*. McGraw-Hill, New York, 1966.
An excellent account of the historical development of our knowledge of the apes.

Napier, John R., and Prue Napier. *A Handbook of Living Primates*. Academic Press, New York, 1967.
A comprehensive catalogue of facts on primate biology and behavior.

Reynolds, Vernon. *The Apes*. Dutton, New York, 1967.
An excellent account of the history and world of the great apes and the gibbon.

Schaller, George B. *The Mountain Gorilla*. University of Chicago Press, Chicago, 1963.
———. *The Year of the Gorilla*. University of Chicago Press, Chicago, 1966.
The two best books on the gorilla in its native habitat.

Schrier, Allan M., Harry F. Harlow, and Fred Stollnitz (eds.). *Behavior of Nonhuman Primates*. 2 vols. Academic Press, New York, 1965.
Modern research trends in the study of primate behavior.

Southwick, Charles H. (ed.). *Primate Social Behavior*. Van Nostrand, Princeton, N.J., 1963.
A helpful volume of readings, mainly on the behavior of monkeys.

Yerkes, Robert M., and Ada W. Yerkes. *The Great Apes*. Yale University Press, New Haven, Conn., 1929.
The classic work, of enduring interest and value, on the behavior of the chimpanzee, orangutan, and gorilla.

APPLIED ANTHROPOLOGY

Arensberg, Conrad M., and Arthur H. Niehoff. *Introducing Social Change*. Aldine Publishing Co., 1964.
  A practical manual on other peoples' cultures, and how to behave in relation to them.

Cochrane, Glynn. *Development Anthropology*. Oxford University Press, New York, 1971.
  A strong and effective coverage of what applied anthropology is, can, and ought to do.

Foster, George M. *Traditional Cultures: And the Impact of Technological Change*. Harper & Row, New York, 1962.
  Applied anthropology in action as exemplified by the approaches made in the field to the fitting of newly developing countries to technological and ideological change.

Gillin, John (ed.). *For a Science of Social Man*. Macmillan, New York, 1955.
  The contributions that psychology, sociology, and anthropology can make towards a social science of man.

Mead, Margaret (ed.). *Cultural Patterns and Technical Change*. Mentor Books, New American Library, New York, 1954.
  Originally published by UNESCO, this volume provides a fascinating series of accounts of different cultures in process of technical change.

Spicer, Edward H. (ed.). *Human Problems in Technological Change*. Russell Sage Foundation, New York, 1952.
  An invaluable compendium on the problems of technological change in nonliterate cultures.

Thompson, Laura. *Toward a Science of Mankind*. McGraw-Hill, New York, 1961.
  A stimulating discussion of anthropology as a unifying science of mankind.

ARCHEOLOGY

Brothwell, Don, and Eric Higgs (eds.). *Science in Archaeology*. Basic Books, New York, 1963.
  On the methods and techniques of archeology, by forty-five authorities.

Caldwell, Joseph R. (ed.). *New Roads to Yesterday*. Basic Books, New York, 1966.
  An illuminating series of studies on Old and New World archeology.

Coles, J. M., and E. S. Higgs. *The Archaeology of Early Man*. Praeger, New York, 1969.
  A comprehensive survey of world paleolithic archeology, designed to provide a perspective in time of the evolution of man's behavior.

Hole, Frank, and Robert F. Heizer. *An Introduction to Prehistoric Archeology*. Second ed. Holt, Rinehart & Winston, New York, 1969.
   The best general introduction to the history, method and theory of archeology.

Oakley, Kenneth. *Frameworks for Dating Fossil Man*. Aldine, Chicago, 1964.
   A fundamental work which correlates the relevant data for both archeological and geological dating of fossil remains, for Middle and Upper Paleolithic sites in Europe, the Near East, and Africa.

Semenov, S. A. *Prehistoric Technology*. Barnes & Noble, New York, 1964.
   A fascinating experimental study of the techniques employed by prehistoric man in the manufacture of his tools.

Willey, Gordon R. *An Introduction to American Archaeology*. Vol. 1. *North and Middle America*. Prentice-Hall, Englewood Cliffs, N.J., 1966.
   The first and most thoroughly informative cultural history of Pre-Columbian America.

Wormington, H. M. *Ancient Man in North America*. Fourth ed. Denver Museum of Natural History, Denver, 1957.
   An excellent and exhaustive account of the archeology of North America.

ART

Adam, Leonhard. *Primitive Art*. Third ed. Penguin Books, Baltimore, 1954.
   A survey of the art of nonliterate peoples from the Paleolithic to modern times.

Bandi, Hans-George, and Johannes Maringer. *Art in the Ice Age*. Frederick A. Praeger, Inc., New York, 1953.
   A beautifully illustrated account of prehistoric art.

Feder, Norman. *American Indian Art*. Harry N. Abrams, Inc., New York, 1967.
   A sumptuous and authoritative volume.

Forge, Anthony (ed.). *Primitive Art and Society*. Oxford University Press, New York, 1972.
   A stimulating symposium volume.

Fraser, Douglas. *Primitive Art*. Doubleday, New York, 1962.
   A beautifully illustrated account of the art of nonliterate peoples.

——— (ed.). *The Many Faces of Primitive Art*. Prentice-Hall, Englewood Cliffs, N.J., 1966.
   A critical anthology, by eleven authorities, on the interpretation of nonliterate art.

Giedion, S. *The Eternal Present: The Beginnings of Art*. Pantheon Books, New York, 1962.
   A magnificently illustrated study of prehistoric art.

Graziosi, Paolo. *Paleolithic Art*. McGraw-Hill, New York, 1960.
The most complete study of the art of the Old Stone Age available.

Laming, Annette. *Lascaux*. Penguin Books, Baltimore, 1959.
A valuable study of the Upper Paleolithic paintings and engravings in the famous Lascaux cave.

Leroi-Gourhan, André. *Treasures of Prehistoric Art*. Harry N. Abrams, Inc., New York, 1967.
Much more than the title implies. A magnificent original study of the meaning of prehistoric art.

Miller, M. D., and F. Rutter. *Child Artists of the Australian Bush*. Harrap & Co., London, 1952.
The story of the discovery of the astonishing artistic ability of Australian aboriginal children, with many supporting illustrations of their work.

Morris, Desmond. *The Biology of Art*. Alfred A. Knopf, Inc., New York, 1962.
A study of the picture-making behavior of the great apes and its relationship to human art.

Otten, Charlotte M. (ed.). *Anthropology and Art*. Natural History Press, Garden City, New York, 1971.
A delightful reader in cross-cultural aesthetics.

Pericot-Garcia, Luis, John Galloway, and Andreas Lommel. *Prehistoric and Primitive Art*. Harry N. Abrams Inc., New York, 1967.
Beautifully illustrative and highly readable.

Roy, Claude. *The Art of the Savages*. Arts Inc., New York, 1961.
A superb little book on the art of nonliterate peoples.

Schmitz, Carl A. *Oceanic Art*. Harry N. Abrams Inc., New York, 1967.
A fine illustrated volume.

Ucko, Peter J., and Andrée Rosenfeld. *Palaeolithic Art*. McGraw-Hill, New York, 1967.
A superlatively good book, presenting a thoroughgoing scientific interpretation of paleolithic art. Excellently illustrated.

Wingert, Paul S. *Primitive Art*. Oxford University Press, New York, 1962.
An excellent study of the styles and traditions of the art of nonliterate peoples.

CULTURE

Benedict, Ruth. *Patterns of Culture*. Mentor Books, New American Library, New York, 1946.

A classic discussion of the meaning of culture as illustrated by four nonliterate cultures.

Bohannan, Paul, and Fred Plog (eds.). *Beyond the Frontier*. Natural History Press, Garden City, New York, 1967.
On the effect of different cultures upon one another.

Childe, V. Gordon. *Man Makes Himself*. Mentor Books, New American Library, New York, 1952.
————. *What Happened in History*. Penguin Books, Baltimore, 1945.
Two books by a great English archeologist which give an authoritative and well-told account of man's progress through the ages.

Honigmann, John J. *Culture and Personality*. Harper & Row, New York, 1954.
————. *Personality in Culture*. Harper & Row, New York, 1967.
Two excellent surveys of the available materials dealing with the interactions between personality and culture.

Hsu, Francis L. K. (ed.). *Aspects of Culture and Personality*. Abelard-Schuman, New York, 1954.
A valuable symposium on the relation between the socialization process and the development of personality.

Kluckhohn, Clyde. *Culture and Behavior*. Free Press, New York, 1962.
A working anthropologist's essays on various aspects of culture.

Kroeber, A. L. *The Nature of Culture*. University of Chicago Press, Chicago, 1952.
An admirable series of studies on the various facets of culture.

————, and Clyde Kluckhohn. *Culture: A Critical Review of Concepts and Definitions*. Papers of the Peabody Museum of Archaeology and Ethnology, Harvard University, Cambridge, Mass., vol. 47, no. 1, 1952.
An invaluable discussion and examination of the concepts of culture held at different times by different writers.

Mead, Margaret. *New Lives for Old: Cultural Transformation—Manus, 1928-1953*. William Morrow & Co., New York, 1956; Mentor Books, New American Library, New York, 1961.
An exciting restudy of the Manus Islanders after they had stepped from the Stone Age into the Air Age, showing, among other things, how speedily such a change can be made.

Schusky, Ernest L., and T. Patrick Culbert. *Introducing Culture*. Prentice-Hall, Englewood Cliffs, N.J., 1967.
A good elementary introduction to the meaning of culture.

White, Leslie A. *The Science of Culture*. Farrar, Straus & Co., New York, 1949.

————. *The Evolution of Culture*. McGraw-Hill, New York, 1959.
Two fundamental and highly original studies.

DOMESTICATION OF PLANTS AND ANIMALS

Curwen, E. Cecil. *Plough and Pasture*. Cobbett Press, London, 1946.
An admirable little book on the acquisition of the arts of agriculture and stock-breeding.

Hafez, E. S. E. (ed.). *The Behaviour of Domestic Animals*. Williams & Wilkins Co., Baltimore, Md., 1962.
A splendid survey of the domestication of animals and the evolution of their behavior.

Struever, Stuart (ed.). *Prehistoric Agriculture*. Natural History Press, Garden City, New York, 1971.
An excellent anthology of readings on the origins of the domestication of plants and animals.

Ucko, Peter J., and G. W. Dimbley. (eds.). *The Domestication and Exploitation of Plants and Animals*. Aldine Publishing Co., Chicago, Illinois, 1969.
A detailed and up-to-date survey by leading authorities.

Zeuner, F. E. *A History of Domesticated Animals*. Harper & Row, New York, 1963.
A masterly work by a great archeologist.

ECONOMICS

Dalton, George (ed.). *Tribal and Peasant Economies*. Natural History Press, Garden City, New York, 1967.
An anthology of studies on economic anthropology.

————. (ed.). *Economic Development and Social Change*. Natural History Press, Garden City, New York, 1971.
A continuation of the above volume, dealing with the modernization and effects thereof on village communities.

Herskovits, Melville J. *Economic Anthropology*. Alfred A. Knopf, Inc., New York, 1952.
On the economics of nonliterate peoples.

LeClair, Edward E. Jr., and Schneider, Harold K. (eds.). *Economic Anthropology*. Holt, Rinehart & Winston, New York, 1968.
Readings in theory and analysis.

Sahlins, Marshall. *Stone Age Economics*. Aldine-Atherton, Inc., Chicago & New York, 1972.

A highly original treatment of tribal economics, together with the correction of many entrenched errors concerning the economic life of gatherer-hunter peoples.

EDUCATION

Gruber, Frederick C. (ed.). *Anthropology and Education*. University of Pennsylvania Press, Philadelphia, 1961.
   Anthropologists discuss education in contemporary pluralistic societies.

Hambly, W. D. *Origins of Education Among Primitive Peoples*. Macmillan, London, 1926.
   The basic book on the subject.

Middleton, John (ed.). *From Child to Adult*. Natural History Press, Garden City, New York, 1970.
   An anthology of readings on education, initiation, and socialization.

Spindler, George D. (ed.). *Education and Culture*. Holt, Rinehart & Winston, New York, 1963.
   A broad and fascinating survey of anthropological approaches to education.

GOVERNMENT AND POLITICS

Bailey, F. G. *Stratagems and Spoils*. Schocken Books, New York, 1969.
   A social anthropology of politics.

Cohen, Ronald, and John Middleton (eds.). *Comparative Political Systems*. Natural History Press, Garden City, New York, 1967.
   Twenty studies in the politics of pre-industrial societies.

Mair, Lucy. *Primitive Government*. Penguin Books, Baltimore, 1966.
   A fine discussion of the law of nonliterate peoples.

Schapera, Isaac. *Government and Politics in Tribal Societies*. Watts & Co., London, 1956.
   An illuminating study based on the native peoples of South Africa.

HISTORY OF ANTHROPOLOGY

Daniel, Glyn E. *A Hundred Years of Archaeology*. Macmillan, New York, 1950.
   The development of archeology from 1840 to 1939.

Haddon, A. C. *History of Anthropology*. Watts & Co., London, 1949.
   An excellent brief introduction to the history of anthropology.

Harris, Marvin. *The Rise of Anthropological Theory*. Thomas Y. Crowell, New York, 1968.
  A splendid history of theories of culture. Highly readable.

Hays, H. R. *From Ape to Angel*. Alfred A. Knopf, Inc., New York, 1958. Paperback: G. P. Putnam's Sons, New York, 1964.
  A very readable informal history of social anthropology.

Hodgen, Margaret T. *Early Anthropology in the Sixteenth and Seventeenth Centuries*. University of Pennsylvania Press, Philadelphia, 1964.
  Very readable.

Kardiner, Abram, and Edward Preble. *They Studied Man*. World Publishing Co., Cleveland and New York, 1961. Paperback: New American Library, New York, 1963.
  The story of ten great innovators in the history of anthropology.

Lowie, Robert H. *The History of Ethnological Theory*. Farrar & Rinehart, New York, 1937.
  The standard work on the subject up to the year 1937.

McCown, Theodore, and Kenneth A. R. Kennedy (eds.). *Climbing Man's Family Tree*. Prentice-Hall, Englewood Cliffs, New Jersey, 1972.
  A collection of major writings on human phylogeny from 1699 to 1971.

Penniman, T. K. *A Hundred Years of Anthropology*. Macmillan, New York, 1952.
  An excellent review of the history of anthropological thought.

Slotkin, J. S. (ed.). *Readings in Early Anthropology*. Aldine, Chicago, 1965.
  Readings in the early writings on anthropology from the earliest times to the end of the eighteenth century.

Stocking, George, Jr. *Race, Culture, and Evolution*. Free Press, New York, 1968.
  Essays in the history of anthropology.

INNOVATION

Barnett, H. G. *Innovation: The Basis of Cultural Change*. McGraw-Hill, New York, 1955.
  An original and stimulating work on the development of novelty in different societies.

Rogers, Everett M. *Diffusion of Innovations*. Free Press, New York, 1962.
  Primarily a sociopsychological approach to diffusion, throwing much light on the processes which lead to the adoption of new ideas.

ON THE INTERRELATIONSHIPS BETWEEN CULTURAL
AND PHYSICAL EVOLUTION

Alland, Alexander Jr. *Evolution and Human Behavior*. Natural History Press, Garden City, New York, 1967.
  An excellent discussion of man's physical and cultural evolution.

Campbell, Bernard (ed.). *Sexual Selection and the Descent of Man 1871-1971*. Aldine Publishing Co., Chicago, 1972.
  A very stimulating discussion by a dozen authorities of the relation of sexual selection to various behavioral and cultural adaptations.

LaBarre, Weston. *The Human Animal*. University of Chicago Press, Chicago, 1954.
  A most interesting discussion of man from the unified standpoint of the cultural and physical anthropologist and depth psychologist.

Montagu, Ashley (ed.). *Culture and the Evolution of Man*. Oxford University Press, New York, 1962.
————. *Culture: Man's Adaptive Dimension*. Oxford University Press, New York, 1968.
  Two books devoted to the reciprocal interaction of genetic constitution and culture in man's evolution.

————. *The Human Revolution*. Bantam Books, New York, 1967.
  Cultural and genetic interaction in the evolution of man.

Roe, Anne, and G. G. Simpson (eds.). *Behavior and Evolution*. Yale University Press, New Haven, 1958.
  The relation between evolutionary pressures and the development of behavior, interestingly discussed by leading authorities.

Spuhler, J. N. (ed.). *The Evolution of Man's Capacity for Culture*. Wayne State University Press, Detroit, 1959.
  Six splendid essays on the interactive effects of man's genetic and cultural history.

Washburn, Sherwood L. (ed.). *Social Life of Early Man*. Aldine Publishing Co., Chicago, 1961.
  An invaluable symposium volume on the evolution of man's behavior.

INTRODUCTORY AND METHODS

Bartlett, F. C. *et al.* (eds.). *The Study of Society: Methods and Problems*. Kegan Paul, London, 1939.
  What the behavioral sciences, and particularly anthropology, have done and can do.

Cohen, Yehudi A. (ed.). *Man in Adaptation*. 3 vols. Aldine, Chicago, 1968.

An excellent introductory reader. The first volume deals with the biosocial background of man's adaptation, the second volume with the cultural present, and the third with the institutional framework.

Epstein, A. L. (ed.). *The Craft of Social Anthropology*. Barnes & Noble, New York, 1967.
An excellent introductory reader. The first volume deals with the biosocial background of man's adaptation, the second volume with the cultural present, and the

Hoebel, E. Adamson. *Anthropology: The Study of Man*. Fourth ed. McGraw-Hill, New York, 1972.
An excellent general introduction to anthropology.

Kluckhohn, Clyde. *Mirror for Man: The Relationship of Anthropology to Modern Life*. McGraw-Hill Paperbacks, New York, 1963.
A fine introduction to what the anthropologist tries to do.

Notes and Queries on Anthropology. Sixth ed. Royal Anthropological Institute, London, 1951.
A useful practical handbook which is informative and helpful to the general reader, and to anyone contemplating fieldwork an indispensable *vade mecum*.

Tax, Sol. (ed.). *Horizons of Anthropology*. Aldine, Chicago, 1964.
A highly readable general overview of anthropology, by anthropologists still in their thirties.

————, *et al*. (eds.). *An Appraisal of Anthropology Today*. University of Chicago Press, Chicago, 1953.
Covering all fields of anthropology.

KINSHIP AND MARRIAGE

Bohannan, Paul, and John Middleton (eds.). *Kinship and Social Organization*. Natural History Press, Garden City, New York, 1968.
An excellent selection of articles, many of them benchmarks, in the study of kinship systems.

———— *Marriage, Family, and Residence*. Natural History Press, Garden City, New York, 1968.
A group of excellent readings on incest and exogamy, marriage, residence, the household, and the family.

Fox, Robin. *Kinship and Marriage*. Penguin Books, Baltimore, 1967.
The best book on the subject.

LANGUAGE

Boas, Franz. *Handbook of American Indian Languages*. Bulletin of the American Bureau of Ethnology, No. 40, Part I, Washington, D.C., 1911.
  Boas' introduction is still one of the best preludes to linguistics available. The body of the work contains some classical examples of linguistic analysis.

Burling, Robbins. *Man's Many Voices: Language in its Cultural Context*. Holt, Rinehart & Winston, Inc., New York, 1970.
  On the way language is affected by culture.

Dineen, Francis P. *An Introduction to General Linguistics*. Holt, Rinehart & Winston, New York, 1967.
  Excellent.

Diringer, David. *Writing*. Frederick A. Praeger, New York, 1962.
  A wide-ranging survey of the subject from its earliest beginnings.

Jensen, Hans. *Sign, Symbol and Script*. G. P. Putnam's Sons, New York, 1969.
  An authoritative account of all the known ways in which man has tried to write.

Landar, Herbert. *Language and Culture*. Oxford University Press, New York, 1966.
  An introduction to the major issues in contemporary linguistics.

Lenneberg, Eric H. *Biological Foundations of Language*. John Wiley & Sons, Inc., New York, 1967.
  A fundamental book.

Moorhouse, A. C. *Writing and the Alphabet*. Cobbett Press, London, 1946.
  Brief and delightful.

Hymes, Dell (ed.). *Language and Culture in Society*.
  A splendid reader in linguistics and anthropology.

Sapir, Edward. *Language*. Harcourt, Brace & Co., New York, 1921.
  The classic anthropological work on the subject.

LAW

Bohannan, Paul (ed.). *Law and Warfare*. Natural History Press, Garden City, New York, 1967.
  Anthropological studies on law, raiding, conflict, and warfare.

Hoebel, E. Adamson. *The Law of Primitive Man*. Harvard University Press, Cambridge, Mass., 1954.
  Describes and analyzes the legal culture of seven selected nonliterate societies, and presents a theory of law and society.

LITERATURE

Astrov, Margot (ed.). *The Winged Serpent*. The John Day Co., New York, 1946.
An anthology of American Indian prose and poetry.

Cushing, Frank H. *Zuñi Folk Tales*. Alfred A. Knopf, Inc., New York, 1931.
Magnificent examples of the literature of a nonliterate people.

Goody, Jack (ed.). *Literacy in Traditional Societies*. Cambridge University Press, New York, 1968.
The importance of writing in the development of cultures.

Greenway, John (ed.). *The Primitive Reader*. Folklore Associates, Hatboro, Pa., 1965.
An anthology of myths, tales, songs, riddles, and proverbs of aboriginal peoples around the world.

————. *Literature Among the Primitives*. Folklore Associates, Hatboro, Pa., 1964.
A stimulating study of the anthropology of literature.

Hamilton, Charles (ed.). *Cry of the Thunderbird*. University of Oklahoma Press, Norman, Oklahoma, 1972.
The American Indian's view of his own life and of the white man.

McLuhan, T. C. (ed.). *Touch The Earth*. Outerbridge & Dienstfrey, New York, 1972.
A self-portrait of Indian existence.

Rothenberg, Jerome (ed.). *Technicians of the Sacred*. Doubleday, New York, 1968.
A range of poetries from Africa, America, Asia, and Oceania.

Trask, Willard R. (ed.). *The Unwritten Song*. 2 vols. Macmillan, New York, 1966/67.
Poetry of the nonliterate and traditional peoples of the world.

MAGIC AND WITCHCRAFT

Middleton, John (ed.). *Magic, Witchcraft, and Curing*. Natural History Press, Garden City, New York, 1967.
Studies on magic, witchcraft, sorcery, divination, and curing.

MAN'S EVOLUTION

Blum, Harold F. "Does the Melanin Pigment of Human Skin Have Adaptive Value?" *Quarterly Review of Biology*, vol. 36, 1961, pp. 50-63.
A stimulating paper questioning current views concerning the adaptive value of skin pigment, and the differences in skin color.

Brace, C. Loring, and Ashley Montagu. *Man's Evolution*. Macmillan, New York, 1968.
An introduction to the study of man's evolution.

Campbell, Bernard. *Human Evolution*. Aldine, Chicago, 1966.
An excellent introduction to the study of man's adaptations.

Day, Michael. *Guide to Fossil Man*. World Publishing Co., Cleveland and New York, 1966.
A most helpful guide and handbook of human paleontology.

Dobzhansky, Theodosius. *Evolution, Genetics and Man*. John Wiley & Sons, Inc., New York, 1955.
An authoritative work on the mechanisms of evolution with especial reference to man.

———. *Mankind Evolving*. Yale University Press, New Haven, Conn., 1962.
On the evolution of man and the genetic basis of culture.

Harrison, G. A., J. S. Weiner, J. M. Tanner, and N. A. Barnicot. *Human Biology*. Oxford University Press, New York, 1964.
An introduction to human biology, evolution, variation, and growth.

Howell, F. Clark. *Early Man*. Time Inc., New York, 1965.
A splendidly illustrated account of the evolution of man.

Howells, William (ed.). *Ideas on Human Evolution*. Harvard University Press, Cambridge, Mass., 1962.
Twenty-eight essays representing recent significant contributions to the unraveling of man's evolution.

———. *Mankind in the Making*. Doubleday, New York, 1967.
A highly readable account of the origin and evolution of man.

Laughlin, W. S., and R. H. Osborne (eds.). *Human Variation and Origins*. W. H. Freeman & Co., San Francisco, 1967.
A collection of twenty-seven articles from *Scientific American* on human biology and evolution.

Montagu, Ashley. *An Introduction to Physical Anthropology*. Third ed. Charles C. Thomas, Springfield, Ill., 1960.
For the layman and beginning student, an introduction to the origin, evolution, and development of man as a physical organism.

———. (ed.). *The Origin and Evolution of Man*. Thomas Y. Crowell Co., New York, 1973.
A reader giving an extensive coverage of the subject.

Pfeiffer, John E. *The Emergence of Man*. Second ed. Harper & Row, New York, 1972.
The unfolding of human evolution.

Washburn, Sherwood L. (ed.). *Classification and Human Evolution*. Aldine, Chicago, 1963.
An invaluable work by leading authorities on the evolution of man and the classification of fossil primates.

————. (ed.). *Social Life of Early Man*. Quadrangle Books, Chicago, 1961.
A valuable symposium on a much-neglected subject.

MUSIC

Bowra, C. M. *Primitive Song*. World Publishing Co., Cleveland and New York, 1962.
An illuminating study of the songs of nonliterate peoples.

Merriam, A. P. *The Anthropology of Music*. Northwestern University Press, Evanston, Illinois, 1964.
A very readable book.

Nettl, Bruno. *Theory and Method in Ethnomusicology*. Free Press, New York, 1964.
A fundamental work on the approach to the study of the music of nonliterate and folk cultures.

MYTHOLOGY

Leach, Edmund (ed.). *The Structural Study of Myth and Totemism*. London, Tavistock Publications, 1967.
A fine symposium on myth and totemism in relation to the theories of Lévi-Strauss.

Marriott, Alice, and Carol K. Rachlin. *American Indian Mythology*. Thomas Y. Crowell, New York, 1968.
The myths and legends of more than twenty American Indian tribes.

Middleton, John (ed.). *Myth and Cosmos*. Natural History Press, Garden City, New York, 1967.
Readings on the relationships between creation myths and folklore, and the human behavior of nonliterate societies.

PHILOSOPHY

Radin, Paul. *Primitive Man as Philosopher*. Appleton-Century, New York, 1927. Reprinted, Dover Publications, New York, 1958.
An extremely interesting and readable discussion of nonliterate man as a thinker.

————. *The World of Primitive Man*. Grove Press, New York, 1960.
The world of primitive man through a synthesis of his philosophies, laws, and governments.

RACE

Allport, Gordon. *The Nature of Prejudice*. Addison-Wesley, Cambridge, Mass., 1953.
One of the best books of its kind.

Asimov, Isaac, and William C. Boyd. *Races and People*. Abelard-Schuman, New York, 1955.
A clear account of the mechanisms of inheritance as they relate to the differentiation of man.

Berghe, Pierre van den. *Race and Racism*. John Wiley & Sons, Inc., 1967.
Very readable.

————. *Race and Ethnicity*. Basic Books, New York, 1970.
A fine analysis of race relations.

Bodmer, W. F., and L. L. Cavalli-Sforza. "Intelligence and Race." *American Scientist*, Vol. 223, 1970, pp. 19-29.
One of the best things ever written on the subject.

Brace, C. L., G. R. Gamble, and J. T. Bond (eds.). *Race and Intelligence*. American Anthropological Association, Washington, D.C., 1971.
A good symposium volume.

Finot, Jean. *Race Prejudice*. E. P. Dutton, New York, 1905.
One of the best and most readable books ever written on the subject of race and race prejudice.

Fredrickson, George H. *The Black Image in the White Mind*. Harper & Row, New York, 1971.
A splendid book.

Gossett, Thomas F. *Race: The History of an Idea*. Southern University Methodist Press, Dallas, Texas, 1963.
An invaluable book.

Jordan, Winthrop D. *White Over Black*. University of North Carolina Press, Chapel Hill, N. C., 1968.
An exemplary study of white attitudes toward blacks.

Haller, John S. Jr. *Outcasts From Evolution*. University of Illinois Press, Urbana, Illinois, 1971.
On scientific attitudes of racial inferiority from 1859 to 1900.

Haller, Mark H. *Eugenics: Hereditarian Attitudes in American Thought*. Rutgers University Press, New Brunswick, N.J., 1963.
  Racism in the guise of eugenics examined.

Huxley, Julian S., and Alfred C. Haddon. *We Europeans*. Harper & Bros., New York, 1936.
  An authoritative demolition of the myth of "race."

King, James C. *The Biology of Race*. Harcourt, Brace, Jovanovich, Inc., 1971.
  An outstanding brief and readable critical examination of the meaning of "race."

Ludmerer, Kenneth M. *Genetics and American Society*. Johns Hopkins University Press, 1972.
  An historical examination of the development of eugenics and its relation to racism in the United States.

Mead, M., T. Dobzhansky, E. Tobach, and R. E. Light (eds.). *Science and the Concept of Race*. Columbia University Press, New York, 1968.
  By far the best book on the subject by twenty contributors drawn from anthropology, biology, ethnology, genetics, physiology, and psychology.

Montagu, Ashley. *Man's Most Dangerous Myth: The Fallacy of Race*. Fourth ed. World Publishing Co., Cleveland and New York, 1964.
  A full discussion of the subject.
——— (ed.). *The Concept of Race*. Free Press, New York, 1964.
  A critical examination of the concept of race by ten authorities.

———. *Statement on Race*. Third ed. Oxford University Press, New York, 1972.
  An annotated examination of the four Statements on Race issued by UNESCO during the last 25 years.

———. *The Idea of Race*. University of Nebraska Press, Lincoln, Nebraska, 1965.
  The origin and development of the idea of race.

Oakesmith, John. *Race and Nationality*. Frederick A. Stokes Co., New York, 1919.
  One of the most scholarly and most readable books ever written on race and its alleged relation to nationality. It contains the most devastating criticism of Houston Stewart Chamberlain's *The Foundations of the Nineteenth Century*.

Pickens, Donald K. *Eugenics and the Progressives*. Vanderbilt University Press, Nashville, Tennessee, 1968.
  The defense of the status quo in the name of eugenics thoroughly anatomized.

Ruchames, Louis (ed.). *Racial Thought in America*. Vol. 1, *From the Puritans to Abraham Lincoln*. University of Massachusetts Press, Amherst, Mass., 1969.
  A most useful work.

Snyder, Louis L. *A History of Modern Ethnic Theories*. Longmans, Green & Co., New York, 1939.
One of the best histories of modern race theories.

UNESCO. *Birthright of Man*. Unipub, New York, 1969.
A beautiful volume of selections relating to the rights of man.

————. *The Race Question in Modern Science*. UNESCO, New York, 1957.
An authoritative and clear discussion of the various aspects of the race question by nine experts.

RELIGION

Cook, S. A. *The Study of Religions*. A. & C. Black, London, 1914.
A good introduction to the study of religion.

Durkheim, Emile. *The Elementary Forms of the Religious Life*. London, Allen & Unwin, 1915.
A great classic, and quite indispensable reading.

Howells, William. *The Heathens: Primitive Man and His Religions*. Doubleday, New York, 1948.
An able and readable account of primitive religion.

La Barre, Weston. *The Ghost Dance*. Doubleday & Co., New York, 1970.
One of the best books ever written on the origins of religion.

Leslie, Charles (ed.). *Anthropology of Folk Religion*. Vintage Books, New York, 1960.
An excellent anthology of anthropological writings on primitive and folk religion.

Middleton, John (ed.). *Gods and Rituals*. Natural History Press, Garden City, New York, 1967.
Readings in religious beliefs and practices.

Norbeck, Edward. *Religion in Primitive Society*. Harper & Bros., New York, 1961.
An excellent discussion of the meaning of religion in nonliterate societies.

Smith, W. Robertson. *The Religion of the Semites*. Third ed. With an introduction and notes by S. A. Cook, New York, The Macmillan Co., 1927.
First published in 1889, this revised and annotated edition of Robertson Smith's book, which became a classic on the day it was published, represents one of the finest studies of the development of religion in the language.

TECHNOLOGY

Singer, Charles, E. J. Holmyard and A. R. Hall (eds.). *A History of Technology*. Vol. 1. Oxford University Press, New York, 1954.
An authoritative account by experts of the technologies of man from the earliest times to the fall of ancient empires.

THEORY

Beattie, John. *Other Cultures*. Free Press, New York, 1964.
A very readable account of the aims, methods, and achievements of social anthropology.

Bidney, David. *Theoretical Anthropology*. Schocken Books, Inc., New York, 1967.
A broad and penetrating survey of the ideas of anthropology.

Harris, Marvin. *The Rise of Anthropological Theory*. Thomas Y. Cromwell Co., New York, 1968.
A fine history of theories of culture.

Manners, Robert O., and David Kaplan (eds.). *Theory in Anthropology*. Aldine, Chicago, 1968.
A fine sourcebook on anthropological theory.

Nadel, S. N. *The Foundations of Social Anthropology*. Cohen & West, London, 1951.
A brilliant book on the methods and ideas of anthropology.

Tax, Sol (ed.). *Horizons of Anthropology*. Aldine Publishing Co., Chicago, 1964.
An excellent survey of twenty contributors of what we know and what we have yet to learn about human nature and behavior.

Tyler, Stephen A. (ed.). *Cognitive Anthropology*. Holt, Rinehart & Winston, New York, 1969.
Dealing with a new theoretical orientation in anthropology, this work focuses on discovering how different peoples organize their cultures.

TRANSITION AND INITIATION

Cohen, Yehudi A. *The Transition from Childhood to Adolescence*. Aldine Publishing Co., 1964.
Cross-cultural studies of initiation ceremonies, legal systems, and incest taboos, and their functions.

Middleton, John (ed.). *From Child to Adult*. Natural History Press, Garden City, New York, 1970.

Readings on education, initiation, and socialization.

Van Gennep, Arnold. *The Rites of Passage*. University of Chicago Press, Chicago, Illinois, 1959.
   The classic work on rites of transition.